Lecture Notes in Computer Science   8792

Commenced Publication in 1973
Founding and Former Series Editors:
Gerhard Goos, Juris Hartmanis, and Jan van Leeuw

T0234264

Editorial Board

Volume Editors

Man Ho Au
Hong Kong Polytechnic University
Department of Computing
Hung Hom, Kowloon, Hong Kong
E-mail: csallen@comp.polyu.edu.hk

Barbara Carminati
University of Insubria
Department of Computer Science
and Communication
Via Mazzini, 5
21100 Varese, Italy
E-mail: barbara.carminati@uninsubria.it

C.-C. Jay Kuo
University of Southern California
Ming Hsieh Department
of Electrical Engineering
3740 McClintock Avenue, EEB 100
Los Angeles, CA 90089-2560, USA
E-mail: cckuo@ee.usc.edu

ISSN 0302-9743   e-ISSN 1611-3349
ISBN 978-3-319-11697-6   e-ISBN 978-3-319-11698-3
DOI 10.1007/978-3-319-11698-3
Springer Cham Heidelberg New York Dordrecht London

Library of Congress Control Number: 2014949205

LNCS Sublibrary: SL 4 – Security and Cryptology

Typesetting: Camera-ready by author, data conversion by Scientific Publishing Services, Chennai, India

Printed on acid-free paper

Springer is part of Springer Science+Business Media (www.springer.com)

Man Ho Au   Barbara Carminati
C.-C. Jay Kuo (Eds.)

Network and System Security

8th International Conference, NSS 2014
Xi'an, China, October 15-17, 2014
Proceedings

 Springer

Preface

The 8th International Conference on Network and System Security, NSS 2014, was held during October 15-17, 2014 in Xi'an, China. The conference was organized and supported by the State Key Laboratory of Integrated Service Networks (ISN), Xidian University, China. The submission and review process was conducted in Easychair system.

There were 155 submissions. Each submission was reviewed by an average of 3 Program Committee members. These papers were evaluated on the basis of their significance, novelty, and technical quality. After a rigorous review process and thorough discussion, the Program Committee selected 35 full papers and 12 short papers respectively for presentation at the conference. These papers covered a wide range of topics within the theme of the conference, including access control, cloud computing, key management and distribution, network and system security, privacy, biometrics, and cryptographic protocols and applications. This Springer volume (LNCS 8792) contain revised versions of the selected papers.

The NSS conference series covers research on all theoretical and practical aspects related to network and system security. NSS aims at providing a leading edge forum to foster interaction between researchers and developers within the network and system security communities, and giving attendees the opportunity to interact with experts in academia, industry, and governments.

In addition to the contributed papers, the conference program comprised two invited keynote talks. The invited speakers were Professor Elisa Bertino (Purdue University, USA) with the topic on "Cloud Security - Research Challenges and Opportunities" and Professor Jiankun Hu (University of New South Wales at the Australian Defence Force Academy, Australia) with the topic on "Bio-Cryptography: Is This Going to Be Big?". We would like to express our sincere thanks to them.

We are very grateful to the people who helped with the conference program and organization. Specifically, we heartily thank the Program Committee and the sub-reviewers for their contributions to the review process. We would also like to express our gratitude to Springer for continuing to support the NSS conference and for the help in the production of the conference proceedings. In addition, we wish to thank the general chairs, Professor Xiaofeng Chen, Professor Dieter Gollmann and Professor Xinyi Huang as well as the Organizing Committee for their excellent contributions to the conference.

Last but not least, our thanks go to all the authors who submitted papers and all attendees. We hope you enjoy the conference!

October 2014

Man Ho Au
Barbara Carminati
C.-C. Jay Kuo

Organization

Honorary Chairs

Xinbo Gao	Xidian University, China
Jianfeng Ma	Xidian University, China
Hui Li	Xidian University, China

General Chairs

Xiaofeng Chen	Xidian University, China
Dieter Gollmann	Hamburg University of Technology, Germany
Xinyi Huang	Fujian Normal University, China

Program Chairs

Man Ho Au	Hong Kong Polytechnic University, China
Barbara Carminati	University of Insubria, Italy
C.-C. Jay Kuo	University of Southern California, USA

Industrial Track Program Chairs

Xiaofeng Chen	Xidian University, China
Xinyi Huang	Fujian Normal University, China

Steering Chair

Yang Xiang	Deakin University, Australia

Steering Committee

Elisa Bertino	Purdue University, USA
Robert H. Deng	Singapore Management University, Singapore
Dieter Gollmann	Hamburg University of Technology, Germany
Xinyi Huang	Fujian Normal University, China
Kui Ren	University at Buffalo, State University of New York, USA
Ravi Sandhu	University of Texas at San Antonio, USA
Wanlei Zhou	Deakin University, Australia

Publicity Chairs

Jin Li	Guangzhou University, China
Muhammad Khurram Khan	King Saud University, Saudi Arabia

Workshop Chairs

Yilei Wang	Ludong University, China

Advisory Committee

Robert H. Deng	Singapore Management University, Singapore
C.-C. Jay Kuo	University of Southern California, USA
Kuan-Ching Li	Providence University, China
Peter Mueller	IBM Zurich Research, Switzerland
Makoto Takizawa	Seikei University, Japan
Yi Mu	University of Wollongong, Australia
Vijay Varadharajan	Macquarie University, Australia

Program Committee

Rafael Accorsi	University of Freiburg, Germany
Gail-Joon Ahn	Arizona State University, USA
Eric Alata	LAAS, France
Joonsang Baek	Khalifa University of Science, Technology and Research, UAE
Carlo Blundo	Università degli Studi di Salerno, Italy
Marco Casassa Mont	Hewlett-Packard Labs, UK
David Chadwick	University of Kent, UK
Aldar C-F. Chan	Institute for Infocomm Research, Singapore
Xiaofeng Chen	Xidian University, China
Mauro Conti	University of Padua, Italy
Frédéric Cuppens	TELECOM Bretagne, France
Wenliang Du	Syracuse University, USA
Jesús Díaz-Verdejo	University of Granada, Spain
Junbin Fang	Jinan University, China
Jordi Forne	Universitat Politecnica de Catalunya, Spain
Steven Furnell	Plymouth University, UK
Alban Gabillon	University of Polynésie Française, French Polynesia
Joaquin Garcia-Alfaro	TELECOM Bretagne, France
Dieter Gollmann	Hamburg University of Technology, Germany
Jinguang Han	Nanjing University of Finance and Economics, China

Lingyu Wang	Concordia University, Canada
Qian Wang	Wuhan University, China
Yu Wang	Deakin University, Australia
Sheng Wen	Deakin University, Australia
Duncan Wong	City University of Hong Kong, China
Wei Wu	Fujian Normal University, China
Qi Xia	University of Electronic Science and Technology of China, China
Shouhuai Xu	University of Texas at San Antonio, USA
Guomin Yang	University of Wollongong, Australia
Wun-She Yap	Universiti Tunku Abdul Rahman, Malaysia
Xun Yi	Victoria University, Australia
Kangbin Yim	Soonchunhyang University, Korea
Yong Yu	University of Electronic Science and Technology of China, China
Tsz Hon Yuen	The University of Hong Kong, China
Jun Zhang	Deakin University, Australia
Cliff Zou	University of Central Florida, USA

Additional Reviewers

Agosta, Giovanni	Fromm, Alexander
Ahlawat, Amit	Fuchs, Ludwig
Al Khalil, Firas	Galdi, Clemente
Ambrosin, Moreno	Gao, Xing
Ambroze, Marcel	Georgiopoulou, Zafeiroula
Autrel, Fabien	Graa, Mariem
Ayed, Samiha	Guo, Xu
Banescu, Sebastian	Holling, Dominik
Blanc, Gregory	Idrees, Sabir
Brumley, Billy	Jiang, Jiaojiao
Büchler, Matthias	Jin, Xing
Cai, Liang	Kumari, Prachi
Camilo Corena Juan	Lalas, Efthymios
Chen, Chao	Li, Chengqing
Chen, Chi	Li, Fudong
Chen, Xiao	Li, Shujun
Chin, Ji-Jian	Liang, Kaitai
Compagno, Alberto	Liu, Daiping
Dargahi, Tooska	Long, Xuelian
Diener, Michael	Lu, Jiqiang
El Samarji, Layal	Ma, Sha
Fereidooni, Hossien	Mannan, Mohammad
Fragkiadakis, Ioannis	Mannes, Elisa

Masoumzadeh, Amirreza
Moataz, Tarik
Mosharraf, Negar
Mykoniati, Maria
Naini, Pooya Monshizadeh
Ni, Jianbing
Ochoa, Martín
Paulino, Alessandra
Pendleton, Marcus
Pitropakis, Nikolaos
Ray, Indrajit
Reisser, Andreas
Rizomiliotis, Panagiotis
Romero-Tris, Cristina
Saleh, Moustafa
Schillinger, Rolf
Sepehrdad, Pouyan

Song, Aiguo
Spolaor, Riccardo
Stengel, Ingo
Sänger, Johannes
Taghavi Zargar, Saman
Tan, Syh-Yuan
Vassilakopoulos, Xenofon
Wu, Di
Wüchner, Tobias
Xu, Zhang
Yan, Fei
Yfantopoulos, Nikos
Zhang, Cong
Zhang, Haichao
Zhang, Yubao
Zhou, Wei
Zhu, Tianqing

Table of Contents

Security Analysis

Public Key Cryptography

System Security

Privacy-Preserving Systems and Bio-metrics

Key Management and Distribution

Short Papers

An Approach for the Automated Analysis
of Network Access Controls
in Cloud Computing Infrastructures

Thibaut Probst[1,2], Eric Alata[1,3], Mohamed Kaâniche[1,4],
and Vincent Nicomette[1,3]

[1] CNRS, LAAS, 7 Avenue du colonel Roche, F-31400 Toulouse, France
[2] Univ de Toulouse, INP de Toulouse, LAAS F-31400 Toulouse, France
[3] Univ de Toulouse, INSA de Toulouse, LAAS F-31400 Toulouse, France
[4] Univ de Toulouse, LAAS, LAAS F-31400 Toulouse, France
{probst,ealata,kaaniche,nicomett}@laas.fr

Abstract. This paper describes an approach for automated security analysis of network access controls in operational Infrastructure as a Service (IaaS) cloud computing environments. Our objective is to provide automated and experimental methods to analyze firewall access control mechanisms aiming at protecting cloud architectures. In order to determine the accessibilities in virtual infrastructure networks and detect unforeseen misconfigurations, we present an approach combining static and dynamic analyses, along with the analysis of discrepancies in the compared results. Our approach is sustained by experiments carried out on a VMware-based cloud platform.

Keywords: security, accessibility analysis, cloud computing, firewall, network.

1 Introduction

Cloud computing is an emerging paradigm which allows the easy hosting and management of infrastructures, platforms and applications, while reducing deployment and operation costs. Providers propose to clients different kinds of resources as services. To satisfy these needs, various technologies like virtualization, new networking concepts, Web services, are mixed in complex architectures. This complexity, along with the presence of many different actors (service providers and consumers, developers, vendors, brokers, etc.) that cannot trust each other, make such environments vulnerable to many security threats [1–3] and raise security concerns for the clients and the providers. To cope with these threats, various security mechanisms can be deployed in the cloud, including firewalls or Identity Access Management (IAM) tools, and Intrusion Detection and Prevention Systems (IDS/IPS). The first category aims to implement network access controls, while the second one aims to detect (and possibly block) attacks in a network or on a host. Cloud environments constantly evolve over time as clients can add or remove instances and users or modify configurations, which could have impacts on the cloud security. Therefore, it is important for

M.H. Au et al. (Eds.): NSS 2014, LNCS 8792, pp. 1–14, 2014.

the client and the provider to monitor and analyze at a regular basis the security level of cloud infrastructures, in order to adapt and improve the configuration of the security tools. In this paper, we focus on analyzing cloud computing firewalls access controls, because they have a direct impact on network accessibility (or reachability) in virtual infrastructures. An accessibility is the first support of attack vectors, hence finding accessibilities is the first step in building attack scenarios and assessing the efficiency of security mechanisms. Various types of firewalls can be deployed in the cloud either in the client's network topology (and thus configured by the client), or at the hypervisor level (and thus configured by the cloud administrator). As a consequence, controls on cloud firewalls are often balanced between the clients and the provider.

The configuration of such firewalls is generally tedious and error prone due to the increasing complexity of virtualized infrastructures. Therefore, efficient methods are needed to analyze network accessibilities in an operational context and identify potential discrepancies with those defined and desired by the clients. Two methods can be used for this purpose: 1) static analysis of devices configuration; 2) dynamic analysis by sending traffic over the network. In traditional network environments, static analysis is generally preferred because dynamic analysis is more intrusive and hardly doable on production environments. However, actual static analysis tools are often not designed to support the analysis of end-to-end accessibilities. Also, such tools may fail to reveal all possible network accessibilities, in particular when hidden and implicit access control rules (not part of firewall specifications) are enforced at different layers of the virtualized infrastructures. We argue that such access control rules could be revealed by dynamic analysis approaches that could complement static analysis. Therefore, our research is aimed at providing automated ways (both static and dynamic) to determine network accessibilities in a client's infrastructure and look for potential discrepancies in the results. We provide the following contributions:

- A static analysis method of cloud components configurations.
- A dynamic analysis method of cloud components.

As an outcome, network accessibilities are provided for both methods, along with an analysis of the discrepancies in firewall access controls by comparing results along with the client's network security policy that we consider provided by the client[1]. Our approach is aimed at taking into account cloud security constraints by protecting the virtual infrastructures during the audits. This is achieved by running the static and dynamic accessibility analysis on a clone of the cloud infrastructure. Moreover, we leverage cloud advantages to perform quicker and deeper audits and we make the process fully automated.

The rest of the paper is organised as follows. Section 2 introduces our approach. Section 3 describes the main phase of our approach about analysis of network access controls. Section 4 presents a VMware-based testbed environment used to validate our approach, along with the experimental results. Section 5 discusses related work. Finally, conclusion and future work are provided.

---

[1] The definition and retrieval of a cloud security policy, along with its implementation as filtering rules, are out of the scope of our contributions.

2 Overview of the Approach: Assumptions and Principles

In this section, we recap the main assumptions we consider in our approach, and then we explain its principles.

Main Assumptions. Our approach focuses on the virtual infrastructure level, that is why the considered cloud service model is IaaS. A virtual infrastructure is defined as a set of virtual datacenters (vDC), where a vDC includes virtual machines (VMs), networks, firewalls and storage. We assume that the firewalls apply stateful packet inspection, and we consider two different types of virtual firewall commonly found in the cloud:

- Edge firewall: gateway for client's networks that routes, filters and translates inbound or outbound traffic. It is generally controlled by the client.
- Hypervisor-based firewall: introspects the traffic sent and received by VMs disregarding the topology. It can act on different scopes, with a set of rules for each scope. A scope is referred to as a client's IP network. This allows the creation of rules inside each client's network and applied to traffic to and from VMs of this network. This kind of firewall is generally managed by the provider, though some cloud portals can give the client access to certain scopes.

The security analysis should not disturb the client's business. It is intended to be fully automated (it does not need human intervention). The security analysis can be performed on demand (audits can be run on the client's will). Provided results correspond to the state of the system at the time when the analysis is run. These reports should be relevant to the actors (clients, provider) that control the analyzed tools. The accessibility analysis operations are run on behalf of the provider, and therefore use administrator rights on the cloud components.

Principles. Our two-phase approach, illustrated in Figure 1, allows the automated analysis of network access controls in a client's virtual infrastructure deployed in a cloud. The first phase prepares the infrastructure to be analyzed by retrieving essential information from the infrastructure and cloning it, so the following steps can be done properly. It can be summarized as follows:

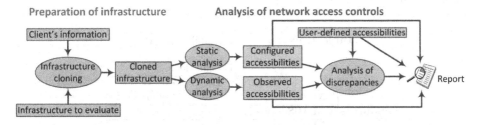

Fig. 1. Overall process

1. Fetch the configuration from the client's vDCs: users' privileges, IP addressing, network connections, etc.
2. Create new vDCs from the configuration information.
3. Copy VMs, networks, firewalls, to the newly created datacenters.
4. Reset cloned VMs administrator password by using single-user mode. This avoids to ask the client any password for further actions on the cloned VMs.

The second phase analyzes access controls statically and dynamically to generate a security analysis report containing the accessibilities found by both methods. These are also compared with the user-defined accessibilities to perform an analysis of discrepancies in the results. This second phase is the core of our contributions and is developed in the next sections. During the audit process, we do not need to know any supplementary information, beyond what is supplied in a traditional cloud subscription process. All the other information we need are automatically retrieved using APIs provided by the cloud infrastructure and without human intervention. We take advantage of cloud computing embedded technologies to run audit operations described later on (cloning infrastructures, deploying and executing programs...).

3   Analysis of Firewall Access Controls

An accessibility is defined as an authorized service from a source to a destination. The set of accessibilities is modeled in an accessibility matrix. The 1st dimension of the matrix references the source VMs (rather than an IP address, because when sending traffic, one does not necessarily know what would be the source address if the machine has several interfaces) or a machine external to the client's networks, and the 2nd dimension references the destination IP addresses. Table 1 gives an example of such a matrix. As mentioned previously, there are two main ways to conduct an accessibility analysis: statically or dynamically. We do it both ways: by extracting and analyzing information from the cloned cloud components configuration (this method falls into the static analysis category); by performing experiments: sending traffic such as network sweeps in order to verify the effective possible communications (this method falls into the dynamic analysis category). We define a discrepancy as an accessibility that has not been noticed in all accessibility matrices: the one of configured accessibilities (generated from static analysis), the one matrix of observed accessibilities (generated from dynamic analysis), and in the user-defined one.

Table 1. Example of accessibility matrix

		Destinations			
		IP A1	IP B1	IP B2	IP C1
	VM A				Service W
Sources	VM B	Service X			Service Y
	VM C	Service Z			

3.1   Static Analysis

To build the accessibility matrix from static analysis, we need to deduce from the cloud configuration all the authorized communications on well-known services from: 1) VMs to IP addresses; 2) VMs to an external location (out of client's infrastructure, and represented as 0.0.0.0); 3) an external location to IP addresses. Deduced accessibilities are modeled as predicates in the form of: $accessibility(X, SPROTO, SPORT, Y, DPROTO, DPORT)$: there is an accessibility from X, on source protocol $SPROTO$ and port $SPORT$, to Y, on destination protocol $DPROTO$ and port $DPORT$.

To generate these end-to-end accessibility predicates, we need to take into account the network topology and the routing/filtering/NAT rules applied to packets. Indeed, we have to care about the interactions of rules within a firewall (for example, a rule can cancel the action of another one) and accross the topology (to memorize the actions done on packets). Furthermore, cloud computing networking and security rules use concepts like grouping (of addresses or objects), as well as service (protocol and port/subprotocol) definitions that need to be taken into account when designing static rule analysis tools. We also modeled two kinds of cloud firewalls: edge and hypervisor-based firewalls (cf. section 2).

The static analysis tool we designed is composed of two main modules: a configuration parser and a logic engine. The configuration parser extracts information from each cloud component configuration and translates them into predicates, and the logic engine uses the latters in logic rules to generate accessibility predicates. That is why we chose the Prolog language to develop a scalable and efficient engine able to quickly and coherently deduce the accessibilities.

Configuration Parser. The configuration parser is used to retrieve the information (in a specific format, which is mostly XML) from components configuration, so it is vendor-specific. Then it transforms this information into Prolog predicates understood by the logic engine. Here are a few examples of Prolog predicates generated by the configuration parser:

- $vm(X)$: X is a VM.
- $edge\_gateway(X)$: X is an edge firewall.
- $introspect\_network(N)$: N is a network scope of a hypervisor-based firewall.
- $network(X, N)$: X is part of network N.
- $route(X, Y, G)$: X has route to Y with G as next hop.
- $snat(W, X, SPROTO, SPORT, T, TPROTO, TPORT)$: W translates X, source protocol $SPROTO$, source port $SPORT$ into $T, TPROTO, TPORT$.
- $allow/block(W, P, X, SPROTO, SPORT, Y, S)$: W has a filtering rule of order N^2 that allows/blocks traffic from source X, on protocol $SPROTO$ and port $SPORT$ to destination Y, on service/service group S.

We developed a configuration parser for VMware vCloud and Linux-based VMs, which corresponds to our targeted environment, as detailed in section 4. It uses a

---

[2] The lower the order, the higher the priority of the rule.

provided REST API and Shell scripts to retrieve XML files from VMs, firewalls, and cloud management modules. Then, we run XSLT processing in conjunction with Python to parse and transform XML into Prolog logic predicates. We designed a XSLT sheet for each configuration we need to parse[3].

Logic Engine. The logic engine runs an internal logic (set of Prolog rules using the previously presented predicates) upon the submission of an accessibility request. Accessibility requests aim to generate the accessibility predicates, as stated earlier. Let us consider the following requests:

- $accessibility(vm\text{-}372, tcp, any, '172.16.2.66', tcp, DPORT)$.
- $accessibility('0.0.0.0', icmp, any, '192.168.1.150', icmp, DPORT)$.

The logic engine is asked to return the accessibility predicates associated to all open TCP ports from vm-372 to 172.16.2.66, and then all the open ICMP subprotocols from 0.0.0.0 (external networks) to 192.168.1.150.

To process such accessibility requests, we designed an algorithm based on a set of Prolog rules, as shown on Figure 2. Starting from the source, the algorithm checks routing, NAT and filtering rules (using the initial parameters) on each edge firewall node of the route from the source to the destination. In our model, an edge firewall can also act as a simple router that allows all the traffic. Then, it checks routing from the destination to the source, but it does not verify filtering there because we consider stateful inspection firewalls. Eventually, it checks filtering at the hypervisor-based firewall, if present, for the appropriate scopes (source and destination network scopes, or the global scope by default).

The algorithm execution tune depends on the number of accessibility requests to execute, because each request may process thousands of Prolog rules. For example, to check whether a traffic is allowed on a firewall, the algorithm first looks for a rule which allows this traffic, where the source and destination can take several values: IP address, address range, group, network, list of IPs, keywords like "any", "internal", "external", etc. The "any" keyword can also be found for destination protocol and port values. Then, we verify that there is no potential denying rule with a higher priority (to take into account the cancellation of an allowing rule) than the previously found accepting rule (the default policy is also assumed as a rule with the lowest priority). All these possible combinations lead to an exponential computational complexity (and can make accessibility requests take too long, which is not acceptable in a cloud audit process). To reduce the execution time, a maximum of rules are precompiled (once and for all) to generate all the associated predicates (for example all the allowed traffic on every firewall, i.e. traffic from/to each VM on every destination protocol and port combinations). Also, the the accessibility requests jobs are multithreaded.

3.2 Dynamic Analysis

In dynamic analysis, real network packets are sent to determine the open ports on some targets. Generally, a port scanner is used from a remote machine controlled

---

[3] We chose not to provide details on XSLT sheets as they are implementation details.

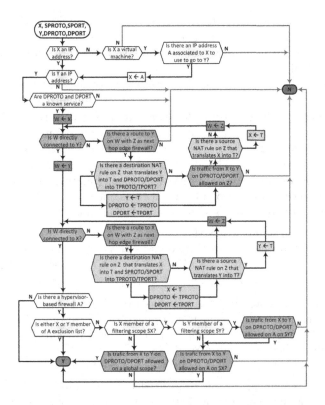

Fig. 2. Accessibility request processing algorithm

by the auditor. Common concerns of this method include the completeness of the results: the remote machine has to be set in all the possible network segments to determine all the possible accessibilities. Furthermore, this one-sided method relies on the ability to interpret network responses in order to determine accessibilities, and this is hard to do in connectionless traffic like UDP.

We are able to address these concerns, because we can easily control all the machines part of the analysis and monitor the traffic effectively received by the destinations. The proposed algorithm (Algorithm 1), is based on the elaboration of pair-to-pair sessions, testing all the possible combinations amongst all the VMs, and from VMs to the external location and vice-versa. A session comprises a server and a client. The client sends TCP, UDP and ICMP packets to the server IP address (if it has several IP addresses, then other sessions will be used) on well-known ports or subprotocols with a specific 4-octet payload we set in the packets. The server listens for all incoming packets and applies two filters: one to detect the specific payload; one to only capture packets addressed to it. Indeed, a server machine could be client of another session. However, it cannot be server twice at a time, which allows at most a total number of concurrent running servers equal to the number of VMs. Note that we set up a sleeping time (t1) between the launch of the server and the client, to make sure that the server is ready to receive packets. The client and server programs were developed using Python sockets and Scapy API. They are automatically deployed on all the VMs prior to the execution of the algorithm. We use a three-dimension session array (1st dimension: clients; 2nd dimension: servers; 3rd dimension: servers IP addresses) to report the done and undone sessions throughout the iterations of the main algorithm. All the values of this array are initialized to false, except when the server and the client are the same (we do not perform local sessions). At the end of each iteration of the algorithm, the clients are monitored to know whether their sending of packets is done so the servers can be interrupted and the results retrieved from them. The algorithm starts by running the VMs to VMs sessions, then the external location to VMs sessions (multithreaded, because the external location can be client of all VMs at the same time), and finally the VMs to the external location sessions sequentially. Let us note:

- NV as the total number of VMs.
- NIP_i as the total number of IP addresses of VM i.
- $NS = \sum_{\substack{0 < i < NV}} (1 + \sum_{\substack{0 < j < NV \\ i \neq j}} NIP_j) + \sum_{\substack{0 < i < NV}} NIP_i$ as the total number of
  sessions. It is composed of the sessions from VMs to other VMs and the external location, and sessions from the external location to VMs.
- $NS_i = NIP_i \times (NV - 1)$ the number of inter-VM sessions for a server i.
- d as the delay between packet sendings.
- NP as the number of packets to be sent in each session.

An iteration is defined as the time needed to execute a session, which is $NP \times d + t1$ (t1 is the sleeping time between the launch of a server and a client). Remember that several sessions can be executed in a single iteration. When VMs have one IP address, $NS_i = NV - 1$, and this is also the number of iterations for inter-VM exchanges (one session as a server per iteration for each VM). However, VMs can have multiple IP addresses (known as multihoming), and a VM cannot be server twice during the same iteration. The number of extra inter-VM sessions related to a server i due to multihoming is noted as $NA_i = NS_i - (NV - 1)$. Multihoming entails $\max\{NA_i\}$ additional iterations (where the extra sessions are executed in parallel according to the algorithm). Therefore, we can deduce the number of iterations for inter-VM exchanges as $NV - 1 + \max\{NA_i\}$. Sessions from the external location to VMs IP address are run in parallel ($\max\{NIP_i\}$ iterations), and sessions from VMs to an external location are run sequentially (NV iterations). Adding the sleeping time (t2) present in the *update_access()* function (ensuring the results of each session are generated on a server before retrieving them), we get an estimation of the execution time:

$T = (2NV - 1 + \max\{NA_i\} + \max\{NIP_i\}) \times (NP \times d + t1) + NS \times t2$

In the formula, we do not take into account the time of code instructions and the time needed to retrieve the accessibilities and write them on disk. Our algorithm has a linear execution time which depends on the number of VMs and IPs per VM. A simple algorithm that would execute each session sequentially would have an exponential execution time depending on the number of sessions (of course the sleeping times we put would be needed and to be considered too).

Algorithm 1. Dynamic analysis algorithm

Require: V: set of VMs and their IP addresses; M: session matrix;
     $this$: external audit machine; $this\_ip$: external audit machine IP address
Ensure: AM: accessibility matrix
 1. $still\_sessions \leftarrow$ True
 2. **while** $still\_sessions$ **do**
 3. $still\_sessions \leftarrow$ False; $S \leftarrow \emptyset$;
 4.   **for** $n \in 1...\mathrm{Card}(V)$ **do**
 5. $session\_found \leftarrow$ False; $vm1 \leftarrow 1$
 6.   **while** $vm1 \leq \mathrm{Card}(V)$ and $!session\_found$ **do**
 7. $vm2 \leftarrow 1$
 8.   **while** $vm2 \leq \mathrm{Card}(V)$ and $!session\_found$ **do**
 9. $ip \leftarrow 1$
10.   **while** $M[vm1][vm2][ip]$ **do** $ip++$ **end while**
11.   **if** $!M[vm1][vm2][ip]$ and $S \cap \{V[vm1],V[vm2],V[vm2][ip]\} == \emptyset$ **then**
12. $still\_sessions \leftarrow$ True
13. $run\_server(\mathrm{V}[vm2]);\ sleep(t1);\ run\_client(\mathrm{V}[vm1])$
14. $S \leftarrow S \cup \{V[vm1],V[vm2],V[vm2][ip]\}$
15. $M[vm1][vm2][ip] \leftarrow$ True; $session\_found \leftarrow$ True
16.   **end if**
17. $vm2++$
18.   **end while**
19. $vm1++$
20.   **end while**
21.   **end for**
22.   **for** $s \in S$ **do** $update\_access(AM,s,t2)$ **end for**
23. **end while**
24. $S \leftarrow \emptyset$;
25. **for** $vm \in 1...\mathrm{Card}(V)$ **do**
26.   **for** $ip \in 1...\mathrm{Card}(vm[ip])$ **do**
27. $run\_server(\mathrm{V}[vm]);sleep(t1);run\_client(this);\ S \leftarrow S \cup \{this,V[vm],V[vm][ip]\}$
28.   **end for**
29. **end for**
30. **for** $s \in S$ **do** $update\_access(AM,s,t2)$ **end for**
31. **for** $vm \in 1...\mathrm{Card}(V)$ **do**
32. $run\_server(this);\ run\_client(\mathrm{V}[vm]);\ update\_access(AM,\{V[vm],this,this\_ip\},t2)$
33. **end for**

---

4   Testbed and Experimental Results

Testbed Environment. To validate the feasibility and efficiency of our algorithms, we run our experiments on a cloud platform based on VMware which is widely used for the deployment of IaaS clouds. This platform includes two physical rack servers (Dell PowerEdge R620 with two Intel Xeon E5-2660 and 64GB of RAM) connected on a network switch (HP 5120-24G EI). The servers run VMware vCloud Suite (VMware top IaaS solution). It includes a hypervisor (VMware ESXi), cloud management software (vCenter, vCloud Director, Microsoft SQL Server) and cloud security management sofware (vShield Manager).

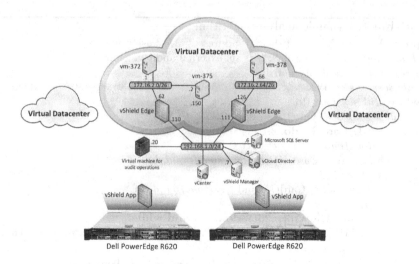

Fig. 3. VMware-based experimental platform: scenario 1

Table 2. User-defined accessibility matrix implemented in scenario 1

		Destinations				
		172.16.2.1	172.16.2.2	192.168.1.150	172.16.2.66	0.0.0.0
Sources	vm-372				echo-request	
	vm-375	MySQL			SSH	
	vm-378	echo-reply				
	0.0.0.0			any		

We deployed two scenarios: one is a small size virtual infrastructure composed of one vDC to illustrate our approach; another one is a large size infrastructure composed of three vDCs to explore the scalability of our approach. Figure 3 illustrates the experimental platform with scenario 1 and its layer 3 topology. VMs run the Debian operating system. VMs and edge firewalls are connected using distributed virtual switches. The audit operations are executed from a VM equipped with 4 CPU cores and 4GB of RAM and running a Debian-based system with the necessary tools and libraries. It is placed in the cloud management network which is external to clients' networks. In scenario 1, there are 3 VMs (one IP address for two of them, two IP addresses for one of them). There are 8 possible inter-VM sessions. Adding the sessions related to the external location (the VM for audit operations), we have a total of 15 sessions. We also implemented a total of 30 routing, filtering and NAT rules on the firewalls in order to implement the accessibility matrix shown in Table 2. In scenario 2, there are 23 VMs (one IP address for 22 of them, two IP addresses for one of them). There are 528 inter-VM possible sessions. Adding the sessions related to the external location, we have a total of 575 sessions. We also implemented a total of 120 routing, filtering and NAT rules on the firewalls. Table 3 summarizes the two scenarios.

Table 3. Examples scenarios

# of	vDCs	VMs	Sessions	Networks	Edge firewalls	Hypervisor-based firewall scopes	Routing, NAT, Filtering Rules
Scenario 1	1	3	15	3	2	3	30
Scenario 2	3	23	575	7	5	7	120

Prior to the execution of the static and dynamic analysis, we used a set of embedded tools provided by VMware to perform the automated cloning phase of the infrastructure. Note that in both scenarios, we consider a total of 587 known TCP, UDP and ICMP services[4], though this can be configured differently.

Static Analysis. In scenario 1, it took 1mn34s to parse the cloud configuration. There are $587 \times 15 = 8805$ accessibility requests executed to build the accessibility matrix, which took 22.61s. Figure 4 is the accessibility graph associated to the generated matrix. In scenario 2, it took 4mn38s to parse the cloud configuration. There are $587 \times 575 = 337525$ accessibility requests to be processed, which took 4mn23s. This shows that our logic engine is scalable, where nearly 38 times more requests are only 12 times slower to execute.

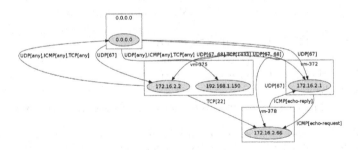

Fig. 4. Accessibility graph generated from static analysis in scenario 1

Dynamic Analysis. In scenario 1, using 2-second sleeping times and a 10ms inter-packet delay, the theoretical execution time of our alorithm would be (cf. section 3.2) $T = (6 - 1 + 2 + 2) \times (587 \times 0.01 + 2) + (15 \times 2) = 1mn41s$. Running the dynamic analysis on our testbed gave a real execution time of 2mn58s. The time overhead is explained by code instructions. Figure 5 is the accessibility graph associated to the generated matrix. In scenario 2, it took 1h16mn08s using the parameters of scenario 1, which is an acceptable result given the size of the infrastructure in this case, and the total number of packets sent (337 525 packets). Note that the inter-packet delay and the sleeping times parameters

---

[4] We used the services from the DARPA Internet network, commonly found under the /etc/services file in Linux-based distributions.

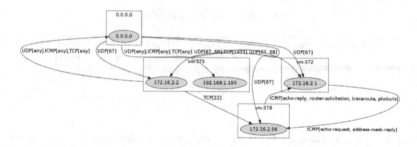

Fig. 5. Accessibility graph generated from dynamic analysis in scenario 1

have to be adjusted according to the capacity of the physical hardware and the size of the infrastructure to analyze. For instance, with a 5ms inter-packet delay and 1-second sleeping times, the duration came down to 56mn47s, and 46mn30s with a 1ms inter-packet delay and 0.5-second sleeping times.

Discrepancy Analysis. Here are the discrepancies reported from scenario 1:

- 0.0.0.0 → 172.16.2.1, 172.16.2.2 (UDP 67): not defined but configured.
- 172.16.2.1 → 172.16.2.2 (UDP 67,68): not defined but configured.
- 172.16.2.2 → 172.16.2.1 (UDP 67,68): not defined but configured.
- 0.0.0.0 → 172.16.2.1, 172.16.2.2 (UDP 67): not defined but observed.
- 172.16.2.1 → 172.16.2.2 (UDP 67,68): not defined but observed.
- 172.16.2.2 → 172.16.2.1 (UDP 67,68): not defined but observed.
- vm-378 → 172.16.2.1 (router-solicitation, traceroute, photuris): not configured but observed.
- vm-372 → 172.16.2.66 (addr-mask-reply): not configured but observed.

The discrepancies noticed in scenario 2 are of the same type. There are not a lot of them, but they can be explained. Implicitly rules (related to UDP ports 67 and 68 traffics) are configured when activating DHCP features, which was omitted in the user-defined accessibility matrix. Furthermore, VMware firewalls let pass more ICMP management traffic (router-solicitation, traceroute, photuris, addr-mask-reply) than configured when allowing echo-request or echo-reply subprotocols.

5   Related Work

Network accessibilities are built by discovering the hosts and analyzing connectivity between them. They could be derived either statically, based on network equipments configuration; or dynamically, by running port scans. In [4], the authors rigorously formulate the problem of reachability in networks. While this is useful as grounding work to understand well this problem, they do not provide methods to collect network information and their model does not handle complex NAT. Furthermore, they do not provide a practical algorithm or experimental results showing the scalability of their approach. The approach presented in [5], about computing accessibility matrices and expressing accessibility queries, is thorough and very relevant. Their data structures, algortihms and query language were a basis to build our static analysis approach, though we kept it simpler and more adapted to cloud networks. We also believe that using an imperative language (Prolog) rather than a declarative one (C++) is more adapted to compute complex accessibility queries. [6, 7] are good examples of analysis of filtering configurations but are restricted to a device scope. They do not compute end-to-end accessibilities, needed in our context.

Considering the general topic of cloud security audits, one can mention the approaches presented in [8, 9], in addition to the publication of recommandations and guidance on security assessments by the Cloud Security Alliance (CSA) [10]. In [8], cloud infrastructures are analyzed using accessibility graphs and vulnerability discovery to build attack graphs and find shortest paths as critical attack scenarios. Although the proposed approach is judicious, their static analysis model includes only one global firewall and thus does not address rules consistency and interactions in complex network topologies. We can also cite the work in [11] on static flow analysis in virtualized infrastructures, where interaction of cloud resources are generated as a graph model. However, they do not take into account filtering rules at the upper levels. Furthermore, both [8] and [11] do not propose a dynamic analysis method to verify network accessibilities. In [9], the authors provide an automated audit system as a service for cloud environments, along with a language to define a cloud security policy. The goal of this system is to allow automatic auditing of VMs following user-defined policies. The policy scenarios are quite thorough and tend to model the security requirements a cloud would have to meet, including network access controls. Although it can audit systems in real time, their solution requires embedding agents within each of the key points of the infrastructure, which is not feasible in proprietary clouds. Our approach is more lightweight as we preserve the original components and execute programs in cloned VMs only for the time of the analysis.

6   Conclusion and Perspectives

In this paper, we have described the basics of our approach to automatically analyze network access controls in cloud computing virtual infrastructures. It aims at identifying accessibilities managed by virtual firewalls, considering a combination of static and dynamic analysis methods to derive accessibilities, along with the analysis of discrepancies in the results. The proposed methodology was designed to take into account the constraints inherent to cloud computing with limited impact on the provider and client's business. Experiments have been carried out on a VMware-based cloud platform to illustrate the feasibility and scalability of our approach. The developed tools shall be integrated in an industrial secured cloud computing framework. Based on our generic approach, we can plan to extend our VMware-based prototype to other IaaS solutions. This would result in the development of adapted configuration parsers and XSLT sheets, and customize the use of provided APIs to manipulate the resources.

Ongoing work includes the extension of the evaluation of cloud security tools to IDS/IPS mechanisms. We are currently exploring the construction and execution of attack scenarios from the accessibilities found, in order to assess the efficiency of deployed IPS/IDS probes. We intend to keep the evaluation process fully automated and without any impact on the client's business.

Acknowledgments. This research is partially funded by the project Secured Virtual Cloud (SVC) of the French program Investissements d'Avenir on Cloud Computing. We are very grateful to the late Yves Deswarte for his support and contributions to this research.

References

1. Jensen, M., Schwenk, J., Gruschka, N., Iacono, L.L.: On technical security issues in cloud computing. In: IEEE International Conference on Cloud Computing, CLOUD 2009, pp. 109–116. IEEE (2009)
2. Studnia, I., Alata, E., Deswarte, Y., Kaâniche, M., Nicomette, V., et al.: Survey of security problems in cloud computing virtual machines. In: Proceedings of Computer and Electronics Security Applications Rendez-vous (C&ESAR 2012), pp. 61–74 (2012)
3. Oktay, Sahingoz: Attack types and intrusion detection systems in cloud computing. In: Proceedings of the 6th International Information Security & Cryptology Conference, pp. 71–76 (2013)
4. Xie, G.G., Zhan, J., Maltz, D.A., Zhang, H., Greenberg, A., Hjalmtysson, G., Rexford, J.: On static reachability analysis of ip networks. In: Proceedings of the IEEE 24th Annual Joint Conference of the IEEE Computer and Communications Societies, INFOCOM 2005, vol. 3, pp. 2170–2183. IEEE (2005)
5. Khakpour, A., Liu, A.X.: Quarnet: A tool for quantifying static network reachability. Michigan State University, East Lansing, Michigan, Tech. Rep. MSU-CSE-09-2 (2009)
6. Marmorstein, R., Kearns, P.: A tool for automated iptables firewall analysis. In: USENIX Association (ed.) ATEC 2005: Proceedings of the Annual Conference on USENIX Annual Technical Conference, p. 44 (2005)
7. Nelson, T., Barratt, C., Dougherty, D.J., Fisler, K., Krishnamurthi, S.: The margrave tool for firewall analysis. In: USENIX Large Installation System Administration Conference (2010)
8. Bleikertz, S.: Automated security analysis of infrastructure clouds. Master's thesis, Norwegian University of Science and Technologys (2010)
9. Doelitzscher, F., Ruebsamen, T., Karbe, T., Knahl, M., Reich, C., Clarke, N.: Sun behind clouds-on automatic cloud security audits and a cloud audit policy language. International Journal on Advances in Networks and Services 6(1 and 2), 1–16 (2013)
10. Alliance, C.S.: Secaas implementation guidance: Security assessments (2012)
11. Bleikertz, S., Groß, T., Schunter, M., Eriksson, K.: Automated information flow analysis of virtualized infrastructures. In: Atluri, V., Diaz, C. (eds.) ESORICS 2011. LNCS, vol. 6879, pp. 392–415. Springer, Heidelberg (2011)

Adopting Provenance-Based Access Control in OpenStack Cloud IaaS

Dang Nguyen, Jaehong Park, and Ravi Sandhu

Institute for Cyber Security, University of Texas at San Antonio
ytc141@my.utsa.edu, {jae.park,ravi.sandhu}@utsa.edu

Abstract. **Provenance-based Access Control** (PBAC) has recently risen as an effective access control approach that can utilize readily provided history information of underlying systems to enhance various aspects of access control in a computing environment. The adoption of PBAC capabilities to the authorization engine of a multi-tenant cloud Infrastructure-as-a-Service (IaaS) such as OpenStack can enhance the access control capabilities of cloud systems. Toward this purpose, we introduce tenant-awareness to the $PBAC_C$ [14] model by capturing tenant as contextual information in the attribute provenance data. Built on this model, we present a cloud service architecture that provides PBAC authorization service and management. We discuss in depth the variations of PBAC authorization deployment architecture within the OpenStack platform and implement a proof-of-concept prototype. We analyze the initial experimental results and discuss approaches for potential improvements.

1 Introduction

Digital provenance data captures history information of system events. The utilization of provenance in computing platforms has demonstrated many benefits in different computing fields [4,6,7,18]. In computer security, the utilization of provenance information facilitates the achievement of many security goals including intrusion detection and insider-threats detection. Harnessing provenance data to provide enhanced access control in different systems and platforms has been the basis of many recent works [2,3,8,17]. The **Provenance-based Access Control** (PBAC) approach, as outlined in [12,14,15], captures application-specific provenance data and uses the information to enable enhanced access control in the underlying application system.

PBAC can effectively be employed in a multi-tenant[1] Infrastructure-as-a-Service (IaaS) cloud environment. Here, users (e.g., Virtual Machine (VM) creators) and data objects (e.g., VM images, VM snapshots, VM instances) are

---

[1] We define a tenant from the perspective of a Cloud Service Provider (CSP), as an independent customer of the CSP responsible for paying for services used by that tenant. Payment is the norm in a public cloud while in a community cloud there often will be other methods for a tenant to obtain services. From the perspective of the tenant, a tenant could be a private individual, an organization big or small, a department within a larger organization, an ad hoc collaboration, and so on. This aspect of a tenant is typically not visible to the CSP in a public cloud.

M.H. Au et al. (Eds.): NSS 2014, LNCS 8792, pp. 15–27, 2014.

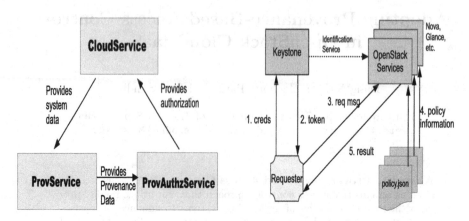

Fig. 1. A provenance-aware cloud architecture overview

Fig. 2. An Overview of OpenStack Authorization

involved in multiple tenants that are being configured with different authorization settings. The utilization of PBAC within a multi-tenant environment under multiple controlling principals can serve to elevate the authorization capabilities of cloud IaaS infrastructures, including but not limited to secure information flow control and prevention of privileges abuse. For example, a VM resource can be created in one tenant, shared and potentially modified in another tenant and then saved as an image for later use. Tenant administrators can specify access control on the shared VM resource based on its provenance data capturing its pedigree in the original tenant. In order to achieve these authorization goals with PBAC, it is essential to enable tenant-awareness in PBAC, a topic we discuss in this paper.

In this work, we focus our study in the IaaS layer of the cloud computing paradigm. Our contributions include a centralized-service architecture that enables provenance-awareness as well as cross-tenant utilization of provenance data for authorization. We proceed to describe the components, and their interactions, of the three service types depicted in Figure 1. We also identify a variety of architecture approaches the services can be deployed in the context of a cloud environment with and without cross-service provenance data sharing. We include several design criteria that can impact the choice of deployment approaches.

2   Preliminaries

Cloud computing paradigm has recently risen as a popular approach that allows efficient utilization of computing resources that can simultaneously minimize related costs and achieve massive scalability at the same time. The concept has real-world practicality and development efforts are heavily invested by both academic and industrial sectors [5]. One of the important properties of cloud computing is multi-tenancy [10], where resources within a physical system are allocated and divided between tenants. The notion of tenants allows organized and secure administration of resources and management of privileged users/consumers of the resources.

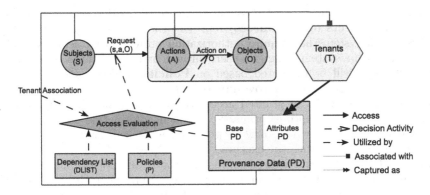

Fig. 3. A Tenant-aware $PBAC_C$ Model

In IaaS platforms, we focus on a multi-tenant single-cloud like a private cloud rather than a multi-cloud environment that is depicted in a hybrid cloud model [10]. In single-cloud environment, all services and associated resources within a cloud are provided by a single provider. Essentially, from the perspective of the tenants, there is a central provenance-aware authorization service that can normalize access control configurations and resolve conflicts across tenants. We adopt this setting in the incorporation of PBAC into cloud IaaS platforms as it naturally allows PBAC to be deployed without much cross-tenant complications.

In multi-cloud environment, individual cloud provider may permit controlled resources movement across cloud boundaries. In this case, it is a little bit more complicated to deploy PBAC as some forms of provenance data sharing are required. In our previous work [13], we proposed several approaches in addressing these concerns through the use of sticky provenance data and cascading sub-queries across tenants. In this paper, we do not explore these issues in depth.

3   Tenant-aware Provenance-Based Access Control

We start with an overview of Provenance-based Access Control (PBAC) models as presented in [12,14,15].

Base PBAC Model ($PBAC_B$): The base PBAC Model ($PBAC_B$) [15] is an access control model which bases the authorization decision on provenance data. In order to effectively utilize provenance information, the $PBAC_B$ model makes use of a specific provenance data model which captures provenance data in directed-acyclic graph format [11]. Such capturing format allows effective ways to extract information through graph traversal queries.

Contextual PBAC Model ($PBAC_C$): The mechanism provided by the $PBAC_B$ model lays a solid foundation for access control that utilizes provenance information. An extended model, $PBAC_C$ [14], further enhances $PBAC_B$. Specifically, the extended model can capture and utilize contextual information associated with the primary entities of system events as attributes and store these as additional provenance data.

As depicted in Figure 3, the primary components of $PBAC_C$ can be briefly described as follows. **Subjects** represent human users interacting with a system.

Actions represent the type of possible interaction a subject can perform in the system. **Objects** (or **Resources**) represent the type of data entities that exist within a system that require authorization protection for security goals. To interact with a system, a human user, through associated subjects, initiates **Requests** that will be evaluated based on **Policies** to determine the access decision (granted or denied). **Provenance Data** contains information on past system events as results of granted access requests and includes two types.[2] *Base* provenance data captures primary component-information of granted and executed access requests while *Attribute* provenance data captures the contextual information associated with the executed access requests.

In order to adopt tenant-awareness, we take the straightforward approach to view tenant as a special type of contextual information that can also be captured as attribute provenance data, as modeled in $PBAC_C$. We then use the relation type "associated with" to capture the semantic relations between tenants and other components such as: *Subjects, Actions, Objects, Dependency Lists, Policies*, and *Provenance Data*. Essentially, a set of atomic, or "base", application-specifically defined causality dependency edges between provenance graph vertices can be expressed with regular-expression based patterns. The graph vertices represent model components that constitute the primary entities of a system such as users or resources. This approach allows more expressive capture of relations between the model components. Meaningful combinations of dependency path expressions can be captured with abstract dependency-name constructs which represent more abstract application-specific semantics of the underlying system. An example is a dependency name "wasOriginallyUploadedBy" which captures any combination of dependency path expressions of actions, which can be multiple instances of modify or copy and ultimately upload, on a particular virtual image. Further application of attribute edges on the upload action instance can reveal the cloud user who originally uploaded the virtual image. These constructs can also be used for PBAC policy specifications. When an access request is generated, the *access evaluation* module extracts the request information to locate the appropriate policies for evaluation. When an access request is granted, the current contextual information is stored as provenance data. This contextual information is uniquely anchored to the action instance of the access transaction in provenance data.

4   Provenance-aware Access Control Cloud Architecture

In this section, we discuss a provenance-aware architecture that can enable PBAC capabilities in cloud environment. Specifically, we describe the main components and their interactions, and how the services can be deployed given various design criteria.

4.1   Architecture Overview

An overview of the architecture of our approach is depicted in Figure 1. We identify the three major types of services within this architecture as follows:

---

[2] While provenance data can capture access requests that are not granted, for simplicity, we assume only granted accesses are stored in provenance data.

Cloud Service (CS) essentially provides a particular IaaS service to client tenants. The types of services include computing (management of virtual resources), authorization, virtual networks, and so on. Examples of the services can be *Amazon Web Services Elastic Compute*, OpenStack *Nova*, etc. These services essentially provide the functionality of the cloud.

Provenance Services (PS) is an IaaS service we propose with the purpose of capturing and managing provenance data that can be generated from any other typical cloud service. The provenance data captures the history information of system events occurring within the cloud services and can be utilized for many purposes. Our focused usage is on PBAC.

PBAC-enabled Authorization Services (PBAS) is an IaaS service we propose with the purpose of providing authorization capabilities to all other cloud services that require authorization. The authorization service is capable of providing PBAC features, but at the same time it can also provide other forms of access control including Role-based Access Control, Attribute-based Access Control, etc. Our focus in this paper is on the provision of PBAC capability for the authorization service.

In summary, the three service types altogether establish an infrastructure that enables PBAC in a IaaS cloud. Specifically, the Cloud Service provides the PS with raw system events that PS selectively stores at provenance storage. The stored provenance data is then used to provide *PBAS* which enhances the security to the Cloud Service. While this work mainly focuses on the scenario where access requests are granted, we also note that it is possible to capture and store the information relating to access requests being denied. This information can allow additional control capability in a system. For example, if the provenance data of an object reflects that there exists three consecutive instances of request denial for a particular action type within certain recent request interval, it may lock the object from any future access or raise a flag indicating a potential threat or vulnerability within the system and request immediate attention with appropriate countermeasures. In this paper, we do not consider denied events as part of provenance data for simplicity and leave it for future study.

4.2   Conceptual Architecture

In this subsection, as shown in Figures 4 and 5 we identify and describe the interaction between the logical architectural components of the three service types. These components establish the fundamental and functional aspects of our architecture approach and can be applied to whichever deployment methods that are discussed later in the paper.

Components Any regular cloud service includes:

- Policy Enforcement Point (PEP): is responsible for receiving and enforcing an access request from a user. The enforcement is based on the evaluation results of that access request generated from the authorization service.
- A User is able to generate a request to the cloud service through any forms of interfaces such as web browsers (e.g., OpenStack Dashboard) or command-line interfaces (e.g., OpenStack Nova pythonclient).

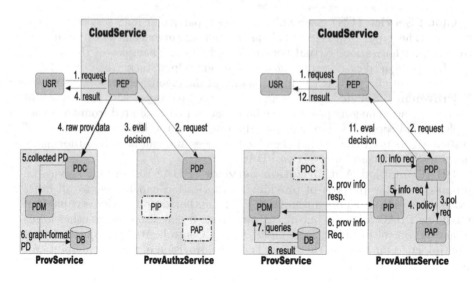

Fig. 4. A Provenance Service for Cloud IaaS

Fig. 5. A PBAC-enabled Authorization Service for Cloud IaaS

The provenance service includes:

- Provenance Data Collector (PDC): is responsible for receiving raw system events data captured from a granted service action request being executed within individual services and potentially performing some filtering to select necessary data only.
- Provenance Data Manager (PDM): is responsible for transforming the collected raw data received from the PDC into provenance graph data format as well as managing the resulting provenance data. The management responsibilities include storing and loading provenance data in and from a database, as well as forming and executing provenance graph queries, and formatting and returning query results thereafter.
- Database (DB): represents persistent storage.

The PBAC-enabled authorization service includes:

- Policy Administration Point (PAP): is responsible for managing access control policies by enabling policies specification, storage and retrieval.
- Policy Information Point (PIP): is responsible for looking up relevant information that is necessary for making an access decision. In regard to PBAC, the PIP is tasked with delivering responses to provenance data requests to the relevant provenance service.
- Policy Decision Point (PDP): serves as the main computing process in deciding how a request should be resolved. In particular, the PDP receives the requests from the PEP, looks up the policy from the PAP, and requests information from the PIP to make decisions, which are then returned to the PEP.

Interactions We proceed to describe how the services perform whenever an access request comes in, as illustrated in Figure 4 and Figure 5. When a request is initiated by a user through any user client interface, the PEP receives the request and proceeds to verify the request with the authorization service by forwarding the request with relevant content to the PDP that resides in the PBAS service. In Figure 4, this interaction is abstracted in steps 2 and 3. It is further elaborated in Figure 5 through steps 2-11. Figure 4 demonstrates what happens after the access request evaluation process is completed. Essentially, if a request is granted, the PEP will enforce the execution of the requested action. The corresponding system event is then captured and sent to the PDC component of the provenance service where certain filtering can be performed to remove unnecessary data. The filtered data is then passed to the PDM for formatting into appropriate provenance data graphs for storage for later use. This completes a functional cycle in the context of an access request being directed at a cloud service.

In Figure 5, upon receiving the request from the PEP (2), the PDP proceeds to perform the evaluation procedure which includes, in sequential order, retrieving the correct policies through the PAP (3,4), searching for information required for policy rules evaluation through the PIP (5,6,9,10), and computing the actual evaluation decisions and returning the final results back to the PEP for enforcement (11). In our architecture, the PIP is responsible for looking up relevant provenance information in the provenance service for carrying out PBAC-related policy rules. The PIP performs this task by communicating with the PDM component of the provenance service by sending query templates. The PDM loads provenance data from its storage, forms appropriate queries and executes them to extract necessary provenance information to return to the PIP.

We proceed to demonstrate the above process with an example. Suppose a user Alice requests to delete a particular virtual machine, "vm1", in a tenant. The policy states that only a user who creates and stops a virtual machine instance can delete it. The PEP receives the request from Alice and delivers necessary information to the PDP. The PDP parses the request information, matches the request to the correct policy through the PAP to extract appropriate rules for the action "delete". The PIP is then sending information including "vm1" and dependency path patterns, e.g "wasVMCreatedBy", that express the semantics of creating and stopping users of a virtual machine instance to the PDM. The PDM forms appropriate queries using the provided information, executes the queries and returns the results back to the PDP. As Alice is shown to be the user who created and stopped "vm1", the PDP sends the approval to the PEP which starts the enforcement of the action. Upon completion, the PEP sends the events information to the PDC. The PDM can then at least generate provenance data which captures the fact that Alice performed "delete" on "vm1".

4.3   Deployment Architecture in OpenStack Systems

Given the above logical architecture discussion, we shift the focus to how the services can be deployed in a cloud IaaS OpenStack system.

Most extant OpenStack cloud services often embed their own authorization service components that can enable authorization mechanisms including RBAC and ABAC.[3] In order to enable PBAC authorization mechanism for the extant OpenStack services, we identify several deployment architectures based on where PS and PBAS are implemented, which presents their own strengths and weaknesses.

First, similar to the current deployment of authorization components, these services can be integrated as structural components of an extant cloud service. In a cloud environment where sharing provenance data in multiple services is not a necessity, this integrated services deployment can significantly reduce the communication decision latency that takes place. Current standalone services, such as Nova and Glance, communicates over HTTP REST interface that can introduce expensive latency. Communication between components within the same service, as either inter-process or intra-process, is much less expensive in comparison. However, the extant cloud service will have more computing load to deal with as it will be required to maintain its own PBAS and PS components. Essentially, the integrated service has to collect, store and manage its own provenance data. This can also reduce the ease of services integration as it becomes more difficult to update changes to any of the embedded services.

Furthermore, in a cloud environment where cross-service provenance data sharing is necessary for purposes such as PBAC, a deployment of integrated PBAC-enabling services is required to employ provenance data sharing mechanisms. As each service stores and manages its own provenance data, PBAC decisions of a service require the provenance data of a different service. The requiring service has to initiate a request to the different service, therefore introduces communication decision latency over HTTP channels. In order to mitigate decision latency, each service can take the approach of maintaining duplicate provenance data of all relevant services. However, this introduces the necessity to synchronize all provenance data storage, and results in synchronization latency over HTTP channels. In scenarios where immediate synchronization is vital to the correctness of a PBAC decision, synchronization latency will affect decision runtime even if the evaluation process is done locally to the extant service. In scenarios where periodic synchronization is acceptable, optimal decision latency can be achieved.

Individual cloud service management of locally maintained provenance data can be complicated. The complications can be alleviated with the standalone deployment method with the cost of communication latency. Essentially, a standalone provenance service enables central provenance data storage and management, which facilitates duplication and synchronization.

In addition, several variety of these two deployment methods, which we term hybrid deployment, can be employed to alleviate some of the issues faced by the above two deployment approach. For example, since not all provenance data is required for PBAC uses, only PBAC-relevant provenance data is necessarily duplicated in individual regular cloud services. Other provenance data, which can be used for auditing, can be stored and managed by standalone provenance service. In this paper, we use the standalone architecture for our OpenStack implementation and experiments.

---

[3] The Swift component utilizes a different form of authorization than most other OpenStack services.

5   An OpenStack Implementation

In this section, we will focus on the application of our approach on the open-source cloud management platform of OpenStack.

5.1   Overview of OpenStack Authorization Architecture

At the IaaS layer, OpenStack comprises several components that provide services to enable a fully functional cloud platform. Each of these components controls access to specific resources through locally maintained JSON policy files. At the IaaS layer, the resources to be protected are composed of API functions and virtual resources such as virtual machine images and instances.

Figure 2 captures a simplified view of the authorization as similarly performed by most OpenStack components. While the solid arrows denote information flow, the fine-dashed arrow indicates the Keystone component is responsible for providing identity service to other OpenStack components. This also provides authorization-required information indirectly using a token. When an access request is made, (1) authentication credentials need to be submitted to Keystone for validation. Once validated, (2) Keystone returns a token which contains necessary authorization information such as roles. (3) The token is then included in the request that is sent to the specific service component. (4) Authorization information is extracted from the token and used in evaluating the rules specified in the policy file native to that service. (5) The final evaluation and/or enforcement result is then returned to the requester.

Policy rules can be specified as individual rules of each criteria or a combination of rules. For Grizzly release, OpenStack authorization engine supports two types of rules: RBAC [16] where decisions are based on role field, ABAC [8] where decisions are either based on the value of a specific field or the comparison of multiple fields' values.

The authorization engine of OpenStack is evolving as additional blue-prints and feature proposals are raised and delivered by the open-source community on a daily basis. Currently, OpenStack does not possess or support any variations of PBAC in its authorization schemes. As our demonstration and discussion of PBAC's usefulness in a multi-tenant cloud IaaS exhibit, it is useful to incorporate PBAC mechanisms into the OpenStack authorization platform for history-based, dynamic and finer-grained access controls.

5.2   Implementation and Evaluation

In this section, we describe and discuss our implementation of a proof-of-concept prototype that realize the above proposed architecture for enabling a PBAC-enabled authorization service within the OpenStack platform. Specifically, we will demonstrate how the OpenStack Computing (Nova) service can utilize the PBAC-enabled authorization for making access control decisions in addition to the current authorization schemes Nova is employing.[4] A similar process can

---

[4] An implementation of the provenance service is also available. However, since the emphasis is more on the PBAC aspect, we do not discuss the details of this component and the associated evaluation. Henceforth, Figure 6 does not depict the PS components.

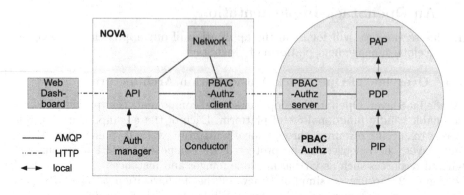

Fig. 6. Nova Implementation Architecture with PBAS Service

be applied on the other services in OpenStack. In this paper, we implement our solution for Nova and Glance components and evaluate the performance runtime for each component under different experiments. Afterward, we provide an analysis of the runtime results.

OpenStack Nova Architecture. First, we describe the current implementation approaches in the OpenStack Nova architecture.[5] As depicted in Figure 6, the Nova components include:[6] *Web Dashboard* is the potential external component that talks to the API, which is the component that receives HTTP requests, converts commands and communicates with other components via the queue or HTTP. *Auth Manager* is a python class component that is responsible for users, projects and roles. It is used by most components in the system for authentication purposes. *Network* is responsible for the virtual networking resources. *Conductor* is responsible for manage database operations.

There are two methods of communication between the service components: intra-service communication is done via AMQP mechanisms while inter-service communication is done via *HTTP REST* mechanisms. These are represented in Figure 6 as continuous lines and dashed lines respectively. Communication between sub-components of the same service can be done locally, such as invocation of the *Auth Manager*.

PBAC-enabled Authorization Implementation. In order to incorporate and enforce PBAC-enabled authorization service, the following components were implemented to extend Nova.

– *PBAC Authorization Client*: a Python class that implements an authorization method that can be invoked whenever an API/ Scheduler/ Network/ Compute method is invoked. The client sends HTTP requests to the PBAC authorization server.

---

[5] Similar architecture applies to Glance, the VM image repository in OpenStack.
[6] This is a partial list of Nova components.

- *PBAC Authorization Server*: a Python class that resides on the PBAC-enabled authorization service. Receives HTTP requests from the PBAC authorization client, forwards the requests to and receives the decisions from the PDP, and returns the decisions to the PBAC authorization client.
- PDP, PIP, and PAP Python implementation for the corresponding architecture components.

Since all access control policies are specified in JSON, we implemented a policy parser class that can interpret policy statements specifying PBAC rules in JSON.

Evaluation and Discussion. In order to evaluate our proof-of-concept prototype, we created and ran the provenance service and the PBAC-enabled authorization service in a Devstack installation of the OpenStack platform.[7] The Devstack is under the OpenStack Grizzly release and is deployed on a virtual machine that has 4GB of memory and runs on Ubuntu 12.04 OS installation. We generated mock provenance data that simulates life cycles of VM images and instances across tenants and is stored in Resource Description Format (RDF)[9] with the Python RDFlib library [1]. We measured the execution performance of the following experiments.

Experiment 1 (e1): The execution time of a Glance command and a Nova command that require checking the associated policy for RBAC requirements (the original DevStack system).

Experiment 2 (e2): The execution time of the commands with the presence of an authorization service which evaluates the RBAC policy the service maintains and additionally PBAC policy where the authorization service also manage provenance service operations.

Experiment 3 (e3): The execution time of the commands with the independent presence of both a provenance service and a PBAC-enabled authorization service. The PBAC-enabled authorization service performs both normal RBAC requirements as well as PBAC requirements, where necessary provenance information is obtained from the provenance service.

Table 1. Evaluation Runtime (secs)

Traversal Distance	Glance(e1)	Glance(e2)	Glance(e3)	Nova(e1)	Nova(e2)	Nova(e3)
No PBAC	0.55	-	-	0.75	-	-
20 Edges	-	0.607	0.642	-	0.902	1.062
1000 Edges	-	0.788	0.852	-	3.620	4.102

For each experiment and each command, we performed 10 runs and took the average run-time. As noted in [14], the size and shape of the underlying provenance graph pose significant impact on query run-time. In this work we evaluated PBAC queries that require depth traversal. Specifically we chose to test the two scenarios

---

[7] We note that in this paper we do not provide experiments for measuring provenance data update processes after granted action request enforced. Having such results can further enrich our insights and belongs in our future line of work.

where graph traversal takes distances of 20 and 1000 edges. These edge parameters were selected to respectively reflect a normal and an extreme use case of a VM image and instance within a cloud IaaS environment. The mock provenance data captures a VM image that is uploaded and modified multiple times and used to create a VM instance, which is suspended, resumed, and taken as a snapshot by multiple cloud users. The policy is specified following the informal grammar provided in [15]. A sample policy rule can specify that a user is only allowed to resume a VM instance if and only if he suspended that instance or a user is only allowed take a snapshot of a VM instance if he uploaded the VM image that instance is created from. The performance results are given in Table 1.

Based on the shown results, we make the following observations. First, compared to the regular execution (e1 approach) of Glance or Nova commands, the incorporation of PBAC services (either e2 or e3 approaches) introduces some overhead for traversal distance of 20 edges, specifically between the 10 to 40 percent range. We also observe that the deployment of separate PBAC and Provenance services also introduces some overhead, specifically between the 5 and 18 percent range due to the additional communication time between provenance service and PBAC service. We observe that for the case of 1000 edges distance, the additional overhead is as expected as depth traversal require recursive implementation. However, the overhead is much more expensive for the Nova command in comparison to the Glance command. The reason for this lies in the authorization implementation of the Nova command. Specifically, the execution of the Nova command generates several authorization calls in contrast to only one from the Glance command. As the number of edges increases, this additional cost increases exponentially.

We propose a potential approach to improve on these performance results. Essentially, it is possible to reduce the performance cost associated with the increase in traversed edges by using meaningful, abstract edges that can equivalently capture the semantics of many base edges. This can help reduce the number of edges and thus produce, for example, a 20 edges run-time for a 1000 edges case.

6 Conclusions and Future Work

In this paper, we identified the potentials of adopting PBAC into the cloud Infrastructure-as-a-Service. To achieve practical deployment of PBAC, we proposed several variations of a centralized provenance and PBAC-enabled authorization services architecture. We demonstrated the architectural implementation in the context of the OpenStack cloud management platform. We implemented, evaluated and analyzed the performance runtime of our proof-of-concept prototype for the Nova and Glance components. From the results and our analysis, our work in this paper constitutes a strong foundation for enhanced authorization in cloud platforms. In order to further consolidate the validity of our approach, we are working on designing and performing more experiments. In addition, our prototype is still in preliminary stage and in need of additional development. We plan to release the prototype as an open source project in the near future.

Acknowledgement. This work is partially supported by NSF CNS-1111925.

References

1. https://code.google.com/p/rdflib/
2. OASIS, Extensible access control markup language (XACML), v2.0 (2005)
3. Bates, A., Mood, B., Valafar, M., Butler, K.: Towards secure provenance-based access control in cloud environments. In: Proceedings of the Third ACM Conference on Data and Application Security and Privacy, CODASPY 2013, pp. 277–284. ACM, New York (2013)
4. Braun, U., Shinnar, A., Seltzer, M.: Securing provenance. In: The 3rd USENIX Workshop on Hot Topics in Security, USENIX HotSec, pp. 1–5. USENIX Association, Berkeley (2008)
5. Creeger, M.: Cloud computing: An overview
6. Hasan, R., Sion, R., Winslett, M.: Introducing secure provenance: problems and challenges. In: Proceedings of the 2007 ACM Workshop on Storage Security and Survivability, StorageSS 2007, pp. 13–18. ACM, New York (2007)
7. Hasan, R., Sion, R., Winslett, M.: Preventing history forgery with secure provenance. Trans. Storage 5(4), 12:1–12:43 (2009)
8. Jin, X., Krishnan, R., Sandhu, R.: A unified attribute-based access control model covering DAC, MAC and RBAC. In: Cuppens-Boulahia, N., Cuppens, F., Garcia-Alfaro, J. (eds.) DBSec 2012. LNCS, vol. 7371, pp. 41–55. Springer, Heidelberg (2012)
9. Klyne, G., Carroll, J.J.: Resource description framework (RDF): Concepts and abstract syntax. World Wide Web Consortium, Recommendation REC-rdf-concepts-20040210 (February 2004)
10. Mell, P., Grance, T.: The NIST definition of cloud computing. Special Publication, 800–145 (2011)
11. Moreau, L., Clifford, B., Freire, J., Futrelle, J., Gil, Y., Groth, P., Kwasnikowska, N., Miles, S., Missier, P., Myers, J., Plale, B., Simmhan, Y., Stephan, E., den Bussche, J.V.: The open provenance model core specification (v1.1), vol. 27, pp. 743–756 (2011)
12. Nguyen, D., Park, J., Sandhu, R.: Dependency path patterns as the foundation of access control in provenance-aware systems. In: 4th USENIX Workshop on the Theory and Practice of Provenance, TaPP 2012. USENIX Association (June 2012)
13. Nguyen, D., Park, J., Sandhu, R.: Integrated provenance data for access control in group-centric collaboration. In: 2012 IEEE 13th International Conference on Information Reuse and Integration (IRI), pp. 255–262 (2012)
14. Nguyen, D., Park, J., Sandhu, R.: A provenance-based access control model for dynamic separation of duties. In: 11th Annual Conference on Privacy, Security and Trust, PST 2013. IEEE (July 2013)
15. Park, J., Nguyen, D., Sandhu, R.: A provenance-based access control model. In: 10th Annual Conference on Privacy, Security and Trust, PST 2012. IEEE (July 2012)
16. Sandhu, R.S., Coyne, E.J., Feinstein, H.L., Youman, C.E.: Role-based access control models. IEEE Computer 29(2), 38–47 (1996)
17. Sun, L., Park, J., Sandhu, R.: Engineering access control policies for provenance-aware systems. In: Proceedings of the Third ACM Conference on Data and Application Security and Privacy, CODASPY 2013, pp. 285–292. ACM, New York (2013)
18. Tan, V., Groth, P.T., Miles, S., Jiang, S., Munroe, S., Tsasakou, S., Moreau, L.: Security issues in a SOA-based provenance system. In: Moreau, L., Foster, I. (eds.) IPAW 2006. LNCS, vol. 4145, pp. 203–211. Springer, Heidelberg (2006)

Identity Privacy-Preserving Public Auditing with Dynamic Group for Secure Mobile Cloud Storage

Yong Yu[1,2], Yi Mu[1], Jianbing Ni[2], Jiang Deng[2], and Ke Huang[2]

[1] Centre for Computer and Information Security Research,
School of Computer Science and Software Engineering,
University of Wollongong, Wollongong, NSW 2522, Australia
{yyong,ymu}@uow.edu.au
[2] School of Computer Science and Engineering,
University of Electronic Science and Technology of China, Chengdu, 611731, China
nimengze@gmail.com, dengjiang@uestc.edu.cn, kevinct12588@163.com

Abstract. With mobile cloud storage, mobile users can enjoy the advantages of both mobile networks and cloud storage. However, a major concern of mobile users is how to guarantee the integrity of the remote data. Taking into account the mobility of mobile devices, in this paper, we propose an identity privacy-preserving public auditing protocol in mobile cloud storage for dynamic groups. In our proposal, a dynamic group key agreement is employed for key sharing among mobile users group and the idea of proxy re-signatures is borrowed to update tags efficiently when users in the group vary. In addition, the third party auditor (TPA) is able to verify the correctness of cloud data without the knowledge of mobile users' identities during the data auditing process. We also analyze the security of the proposed protocol.

1 Introduction

Mobile devices have become convenient terminals to access Internet Service with the adancement of wireless technology. However, because of the computation, energy and storage limitations, mobile devices cannot support complex data mining and large data storage. As a consequence, Mobile Cloud Computing [1–3] is emerged as a new mobile computing paradigm which allows mobile users enjoy the features from both mobile devices, such as mobility, communication and sensing capabilities [4], and cloud computing [5], say, on-demand self-service, ubiquitous network access, rapid resource elasticity, etc.

As one of the dominate services in Mobile Cloud Computing, mobile cloud storage allows mobile users to store data such as contacts, calenders and SMS on clouds to compensate for the low capacity of mobile device storage [6]. In addition, mobile users can access their files via wireless networks at anytime and from anywhere. The risk of data loss is significantly increased, since mobile phones are always vulnerable to eavesdropping, stealing and loss for example. While mobile cloud storage makes these advantages more appealing than

M.H. Au et al. (Eds.): NSS 2014, LNCS 8792, pp. 28–40, 2014.
© Springer International Publishing Switzerland 2014

ever, it also inherits the security threats of conventional cloud computing and causes a group of challenges that are particular to mobile devices offloading jobs through wireless communication channels [7]. Once the files are outsourced to cloud servers to extend the storage capacity, mobile users lose the physical control of their data simultaneously. As a result, the correctness of the files becomes one of the biggest concerns for mobile users in mobile cloud storage scenario. First of all, even though the cloud infrastructures are much more reliable and powerful than mobile devices, they are still facing a multitude of threats from internal and external for data integrity. Gmail's mass email deletion incident [8], Apple's MobileMe's post-launch downtime [9] and T-Mobile Sidekick users' personal data loss incident [10] are all such examples. Secondly, the mobile cloud service providers may not behave faithfully towards the outsourced data for the benefits of their own. For instance, the mobile cloud server may discard the data that have not or rarely been accessed for monetary reasons or even hide the data loss incidents to maintain a good reputation. Therefore, there should be a mechanism to ensure the correctness of the cloud data for mobile users.

Despite some auditing schemes [11–18] have been proposed to guarantee the integrity and availability of users' data in cloud, they are all designed for traditional cloud storage environment without considering the applications for mobile cloud. In the new scenario, public auditing, in which a third party auditor (TPA) is involved to check the integrity of the remote data for mobile users, is highly essential due to low computational capacity of mobile devices. Besides, the data sharing among multiple mobile users is perhaps one of the most beneficial features that motivates the mobile cloud storage, for example, mobile users share contacts and photos among friends and documents for colleagues frequently. Because of the mobility of the devices, the group members change constantly, including members' joining, leaving or revocation. A trivial approach to achieve group dynamic operations is to retrieve the entire outsourced file and re-compute the tags for blocks of this file, and then upload the updated data. This method is inefficient due to a ton of overhead on computation and communication. Therefore, a practical auditing protocol for secure mobile cloud storage is supposed to support public verification as well as group dynamic operation.

Another issue that should be considered in integrity verification for shared data is identity privacy protection against the TPA. Even the TPA follows the execution of an auditing protocol and responds a correct auditing result to a mobile user, TPA is also curious about the identities or other information of mobile users or the relative groups. If the identity information of mobile users are not protected, other confidential information such as the social relationship, circle of friends and family backgrounds will leak to TPA. What's worse, through the auditing process, the TPA will learn extra knowledge such as which mobile user plays a more essential role than others in a particular group or which data block has a higher value than others in shared data. While, the only responsibility for TPA is to check the integrity of the shared data, the mobile users are unwilling to reveal these sensitive information to it. Of cause, all these information might help hackers to find the attack targets or bring disasters to mobile users.

In general cloud storage, several recent works [19–21] help to preserve identity privacy for group users from public auditors. In 2012, Wang et al. proposed the first identity privacy-preserving public auditing mechanism for shared data in untrusted cloud [19] which utilized the ring signature [23] to construct homomorphic authenticators, but this scheme fails to scale well to a large number of users sharing data in a group and does not adapt to dynamic group. In order to address these issues, they used a group signature [24, 25] to design a public auditing scheme [20] which supports group scalability and data sharing among a large number of users in an identity privacy-preserving manner. While this auditing scheme imposes a heavy burden on the storage of block tags because of the large size of the group signature and makes the shared data unloaded by a revoked user be unaccessible for other group members. In 2013, they harnessed a proxy re-signature [26] to construct a public auditing scheme [22] for shared cloud data with efficient user revocation and data sharing without caring about the privacy of the group members. Later, they expanded this scheme to a privacy-preserving public auditing mechanism [21] by applying a dynamic broadcast encryption [27]. In this mechanism, the TPA is able to verify the integrity of shared data without learning identity information of group members and efficiently handle the user joining and revocation simultaneously. Unfortunately, these schemes [21, 22] are vulnerable to the collusion attack launched by a revoked user and the cloud server. In addition, their schemes are impractical to be applied to mobile cloud storage since an original user who acts as a manager to broadcast a group private key for every member in the group is required, but groups in mobile cloud storage are non-center and self-built, so every member has an equal status in the group. In terms of efficiency, every group member has to calculate two bilinear pairing operations to decrypt the ciphertexts to obtain the group private key, which is the most time and energy consumption operation in cryptographical computing and will cause heavy workload for the mobile devices. In 2011, Yang et al. [28] used the tricks due to Shacham et al. [29, 30] and trusted computing technology to design a provable data possession protocol for resource-constrained mobile devices, but their construction only covers limited desirable properties, say stateless verification and public auditing.

Therefore, providing an identity privacy-preserving public auditing protocol supporting efficient group dynamic in mobile cloud storage is the problem we are going to solve in this paper. To the best of our knowledge, our work is among the first few ones to ensure the data integrity in mobile cloud storage. With the prevalence of mobile cloud computing, a foreseeable increase of auditing needs with some particular features for mobile users will be popular in real-world applications. Our contributions can be summarized as the following aspects:

1. We motivate the identity privacy-preserving public auditing with group dynamic for secure mobile cloud storage and discuss the security model and potential security threats.
2. Deriving from the state of art, we propose a concrete public auditing protocol which provides the anonymity to TPA, group dynamic and efficient tag-updating.

3. We prove the security and justify the performance of our protocol through analyzing the computation, communication and storage overhead.
4. In order to be secure against the collusion attack from a revoked mobile user and the cloud server, our protocol offers a solution but with a lose of the efficiency in an acceptable bound.

2   Problem Statement

In this section, we describe mobile cloud storage system model as well as the security model of the data auditing protocol in mobile cloud storage environment.

2.1   The System Model

Mobile cloud storage service involves three entities: mobile users, cloud server and TPA, as illustrated in Fig 1. Mobile users have limited storage space but large amount of data files to be stored. The cloud server has large storage spaces and computation resources and provides cloud storage services to mobile users. The TPA can be a trusted organization that offers the data auditing service. It has expertise and capacities that mobile users do not have and is trusted by the user to check the integrity of the hosted data on behalf of cloud users upon request.

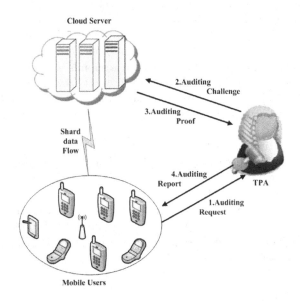

Fig. 1. System model of data auditing in mobile cloud storage

Each entity has his own obligations and benefits. Mobile users enjoy the convenience to store a multitude of files in cloud and share them among group members. Upon a cloud user in the group is corrupted, he can be revoked from the group by other group users. The cloud server will perform the auditing task honestly and will not reveal the content of hosted data to TPA. At the same time, it may be self-interested and has its own benefits, such as to hide data loss accidents to maintain its reputation or discard the files that rarely be accessed to reclaim storage. The TPA contributes to checking the integrity of the cloud data and returns the auditing reports to mobile users.

2.2 System Components

An identity privacy-preserving public auditing protocol consists of eight algorithms, namely KeyGen, GkeyGen, TagGen, Challenge, ProofGen, ProofCheck, Join and Leave as follows.

1. KeyGen: Taking a security parameter κ as inputs, this algorithm generates a public key pk_i and a secret key sk_i for each mobile user U_i in the group $S = \{U_1, \cdots, U_n\}$, where n is the number of mobile users and publishes pk_i.
2. GkeyGen: Taking every (pk_i, sk_i) in S as inputs, this algorithm outputs a group public key Gpk and a group secret key Gsk, and publishes Gpk.
3. TagGen: Taking the group key pair (Gpk, Gsk) and a data block m_j of the file F as inputs, this algorithm generates a tag T_j for each block, which is appended to the block m_j when uploading the file F and will be used for checking the block integrity in auditing phase.
4. Challenge: Taking the request from mobile users as inputs, this algorithm generates a challenge $Chal$ to query the integrity of the data file.
5. ProofGen: Taking as inputs the group public key Gpk, data blocks m_j, tags T_j and the challenge $Chal$, this algorithm responds a proof P for the challenged blocks to the TPA.
6. ProofCheck: Taking the group public key Gpk and the proof P as inputs, the algorithms outputs the verification result of proof P and returns it to mobile users.
7. Join: Taking as inputs each (pk_i, sk_i) in the new group $S' = \{U_1, \cdots, U_n, U_{n+1}, \cdots, U_{n+n'}\}$, where $\{U_{n+1}, \cdots, U_{n+n'}\}$ are the new joined members, this algorithm generates a new group public-secret key pair (Gpk', Gsk'), and updates the block tags.
8. Leave: Taking as inputs every (pk_i, sk_i) in the new group members $S' = \{U_1, \cdots, U_{i-1}, U_{i+1}, \cdots, U_n\}$, where $\{U_i\}$ has departed from the group, this algorithm generates a new group public-secret key pair (Gpk', Gsk'), and updates the block tags.

2.3 Security Model

The security model of data auditing protocols proposed by Ateniese et al. [31,32] ensures that an adversary cannot construct a valid proof without possessing all the challenged blocks, unless it guesses all the missing blocks. We expand this model by considering the GkeyGen, Join and Leave queries to ensure that the adversary will not acquire the capacities of generating the group secret key and forging the valuable tags from GkeyGen, Join and Leave phases. The new security game is shown involving an adversary $\mathcal{A}$ and a challenger $\mathcal{C}$ as follows:

- KeyGen: The challenger $\mathcal{C}$ runs KeyGen algorithm to generate a series of public-secret key pairs (pk_i, sk_i) for mobile users. It offers the public keys pk_i to the adversary $\mathcal{A}$ and keeps sk_i secret.
- Queries 1: $\mathcal{C}$ responses the queries launched by $\mathcal{A}$ and these interactions can be repeated polynomial times.
    1. GkeyGen queries: $\mathcal{A}$ chooses a group $S = \{U_1, \cdots, U_n\}$ to query adaptively. $\mathcal{C}$ generates the group public-secret key pair (Gpk, Gsk) for the group S and responses it to $\mathcal{A}$.
    2. TagGen queries: $\mathcal{A}$ chooses data blocks m_j and a group $S = \{U_1, \cdots, U_n\}$ to query adaptively. $\mathcal{C}$ generates the corresponding tag T_j for each block under the group secret key Gsk and responses them to $\mathcal{A}$.
    3. Join queries: $\mathcal{A}$ chooses the tags T_j under the group S that received from TagGen queries and some new users $S' = \{U'_1, \cdots, U'_{n'}\}$ to query adaptively. $\mathcal{C}$ generates the group public-secret key pair (Gpk, Gsk) for the group $S" = S + S'$ and the updated tags T'_j, and then responses them to $\mathcal{A}$.
    4. Leave queries: $\mathcal{A}$ chooses the tags under the group S that received from TagGen queries and a leaved user U_i to query adaptively. $\mathcal{C}$ generates the group public-secret key pair (Gpk, Gsk) for the group $S' = S \setminus U_i$ and the updated tags T'_j, and then responds with them to $\mathcal{A}$.
- Challenge: $\mathcal{C}$ sends a challenge $Chal$ and a group $S^* = \{U_1^*, \cdots, U_n^*\}$ and requests $\mathcal{A}$ to respond a proof P for the challenged blocks.
- Queries 2: $\mathcal{A}$ can continue to ask for the public-secret key pair (Gpk, Gsk) and updated tags T'_j for any group S as long as $S^* \neq S^* \bigcap S$ and $S \neq S^* \bigcap S$
- Forge: $\mathcal{A}$ generates a proof P for the challenge $chal$ and returns it to $\mathcal{C}$.

If ProofCheck$(Gpk, chal, P) = $ "success", then the adversary has won the data possession game.

Definition 1. *A data auditing protocol is able to guarantee data integrity if for any (probabilistic polynomial-time) adversary $\mathcal{A}$, the probability that $\mathcal{A}$ wins the data possession game on a set of file blocks is negligibly close to the probability that the challenger extracts those file blocks by means of a knowledge extractor.*

2.4   Design Goals

To enable identity privacy-preserving public auditing for mobile cloud data storage, apart from the basic requirements, such as public auditability, stateless verification, blockless verification and batch auditing, our protocol should meet the following desirable security and performance goals:

1. Identity privacy-preserving: to ensure that it is hard for TPA to derive mobile users' identities from the proof during data auditing process.

2. Group dynamic: to adapt to the scenario that the mobile users are dynamic, such as join an existing group or leave a current group.
3. Efficient tag-updating: to enable to re-generate the tags efficiently by the present mobile users in group, when some mobile users leave the group or join an existing group.
4. Security: to ensure that there is no way for a polynomial-time adversary to generate a valid proof, even this adversary behaves as the cloud server colluding with a leaved mobile user.
5. Lightweight: to allow TPA to perform auditing task with minimum overhead of computation and communication and make the computation of generating group key and tags be feasible for mobile devices.

3 Our Construction

Our identity privacy-preserving public auditing protocol derives from compact proofs of retrievability which utilizes a BLS based homomorphic authenticator due to Shacham and Waters [29,30]. For the dynamic of mobile users, we resort to the dynamic asymmetric group key agreement scheme [33], in which a set of users from a temporary group and negotiate to share a public-secret key pair. To achieve the tag-updating, we borrow the idea of proxy re-signature [26], which enables a semi-trusted proxy to transform Alice's signature on a message m into Bob's signature on m. In addition, the message flows of our protocol should be transmitted on a certified channel to avoid the attack proposed by Ni et al. [34]. The details of the protocol are as follows. Let q be a large prime and G and G_T be two multiplicative cyclic groups with the same prime order p, and g be a generator of G. $\hat{e} : G \times G \to G_T$ denotes a bilinear map and $H : \{0,1\}^* \to Z_p^*$, $H_1 : \{0,1\}^* \to G$ represent two cryptographic hash functions. Assume n mobile users form a temporary group $S = \{U_1, \cdots, U_n\}$ to share a file F which is divided into t blocks $\{m_1, \cdots, m_t\}$ after encoded using RS codes.

1. KeyGen: U_i randomly chooses $x_i \in Z_p^*$ and computes g^{x_i}. U_i publishes the public key $pk_i = g^{x_i}$ and keeps the secret key $sk_i = x_i$ privately.
2. GkeyGen: A group of mobile users $S = \{U_1, \cdots, U_n\}$ form a circle structure, with $U_{n+1} = U_1$, $U_0 = U_n$, to negotiate to share a public-secret key pair (Gpk, Gsk). They use the system time N as a timestamp which is the unique identifier for this group. This phase consists of three steps as follows:
   - Step 1: Each U_i calculates his shared key with neighbours $pk_{i,i+1} = pk_{i+1}^{x_i}$ and $pk_{i-1,i} = pk_{i-1}^{x_i}$, and then generates $X_i = H(pk_{i,i+1}) \oplus H(pk_{i-1,i})$ and $M_i = U_i \parallel N \parallel H(S) \parallel X_i$. Finally, U_i published M_i to each mobile user in group S.
   - Step 2: Upon receiving the M_i from all the users, Each mobile user U_i verifies $X_1 \oplus \cdots \oplus X_n \overset{?}{=} 0$. If not, it outputs failure and abort; Otherwise generates a group secret key Gsk as:
     $$Gsk = H(H(pk_{1,2}) \parallel \cdots \parallel H(pk_{i,i+1}) \parallel \cdots \parallel H(pk_{n,1}) \parallel N),$$
     where

$$H(pk_{i-j,i-j+1}) = H(pk_{i,i-1}) \oplus X_{i-1} \oplus \cdots \oplus X_{i-j}.$$

for each $j = \{1, \cdots, n-1\}$.

- Step 3: Each U_i in S computes and publishes the group public key $Gpk = g^{Gsk}$.

3. TagGen: Given the file $F = \{m_1, \cdots, m_t\}$, U_i splits m_j into s sectors $m_j = \{m_{j1}, \cdots, m_{js}\}$, chooses s random values $\{b_1, \cdots, b_s\} \in Z_p$ and computes $u_l = g^{b_l} \in G$ for $l \in [1, s]$. Then, for each block m_j ($j \in [1, t]$), it computes a tag T_j as

$$T_j = (H_1(F_{id} \parallel j) \cdot \prod_{l=1}^{s} u_l^{m_{jl}})^{Gsk}$$

where F_{id} is the unique identifier of the file F and j denotes the block number of m_j. It outputs the set of data tags $T = \{T_j\}_{j \in [1,t]}$ and uploads (F, T) to the cloud server .

4. Challenge: The TPA selects some data blocks to construct a challenge set Q and picks a random $v_j \in Z_p^*$ for each m_j ($j \in Q$), and then sends the challenge $Chal = \{j, v_j\}_{j \in Q}$ to the cloud server.

5. ProofGen: After receiving the challenge $Chal$ from the TPA, the cloud server computes

$$\mu_l = \sum_{j \in Q} v_j m_{jl} \in Z_p \text{ for } 1 \le l \le s,$$

and

$$\sigma = \prod_{j \in Q} T_j^{v_j} \in G.$$

The cloud server responds with the proof $P = \{\mu_1, \cdots, \mu_s, \sigma\}$ to the TPA.

6. ProofCheck: Upon receiving the proof P, the TPA uses the group public key Gpk to check whether

$$\hat{e}(\sigma, g) \stackrel{?}{=} \hat{e}(\prod_{j \in Q} H(F_{id} \parallel j)^{v_j} \cdot \prod_{l=1}^{s} u_l^{\mu_l}, Gpk).$$

If so, return "1" to mobile users; Otherwise, return "0".

7. Join: Suppose a certain outsider $J = \{U_{n+1}, \cdots, U_{n+n'}\}$ wants to join the current group S. They form a new circle structure $S' = \{U_1, \cdots, U_{n+n'}\}$ with $U_{n+n'+1} = U_1$, $U_0 = U_{n+n'}$. A new timestamp N' is chosen based on the system time. The mobile users calculate a new group public-secret key pair (Gpk', Gsk') and update the tags as follows:

   - Step 1: U_1, U_n and $J = \{U_{n+1}, \cdots, U_{n+n'}\}$ follows the step 1 in GkeyGen phase to publish M_i. $pk_{1,2}$ and $pk_{n-1,n}$ are unchanged and the remaining mobile users $\{U_2, \cdots, U_{n-1}\}$ re-publish the previous M_i.
   - Step 2: All the mobile users in S' compute a group secret key Gsk' according to Step 2 in GkeyGen phase and generate the corresponding group public key Gpk'.
   - Step 3: A mobile user in S downloads tags T of file F firstly, and generates a proxy re-signature key $ReGsk = Gsk'/Gsk$. Then it computes $T_j' = T_j^{ReGsk}$ for each T_j in T. Finally, it uploads T' to the cloud and the cloud server updates T to T'.

8. Leave: Assume U_i leaves the group S and the remainders form a new circle structure among users $S' = \{U_1, \cdots, U_{i-1}, U_{i+1}, \cdots, U_n\}$. The neighbourhood changing concerns only U_{n-1} and U_{n+1}. A new timestamp N' is chosen based on system time. The remaining mobile users calculate a new group public-secret key pair (Gpk', Gsk') and update the tags as follows:

- Step 1: U_{i-1} and U_{i+1} follows the step 1 in GkeyGen phase to publish M_i. $pk_{n-2,n-1}$ and $pk_{n+1,n+2}$ are unchanged and the rest users re-publish the previous M_i.
- Step 2: All the mobile users in S' compute the group secret key Gsk' according to Step 2 in GkeyGen algorithm and generate the corresponding group public key Gpk'.
- Step 3: Some mobile user in S' downloads the tags T of the file F firstly, and generates a proxy re-signature key $ReGsk = Gsk'/Gsk$. Then it computes $T'_j = T_j^{ReGsk}$ for each T_j in T. Finally, it uploads T' to the cloud server and the server updates T to T'.

The correctness of the Gsk ensures that every mobile user in group S will generate the same group secret key. The correctness of the data auditing phase is shown as follows:

$$\hat{e}(\sigma, g) = \hat{e}(\prod_{j \in Q} T_j^{v_j}, g)$$

$$= \hat{e}(\prod_{j \in Q}(H_1(F_{id} \| j) \cdot \prod_{l=1}^{s} u_l^{m_{jl}})^{Gsk \cdot v_j}, g)$$

$$= \hat{e}(\prod_{j \in Q}(H_1(F_{id} \| j) \cdot \prod_{l=1}^{s} u_l^{\Sigma_{j \in Q} v_j m_{jl}}), Gpk)$$

$$= \hat{e}(\prod_{j \in Q} H(F_{id} \| j)^{v_j} \cdot \prod_{l=1}^{s} u_l^{\mu_l}, Gpk).$$

Regarding the tag updating, a mobile user generates new tags using the proxy re-signature $ReGsk$. If the user is honest, we have

$$T'_j = T_j^{Gsk'/Gsk}$$

$$= (H_1(F_{id} \| j) \cdot \prod_{l=1}^{s} u_l^{m_{jl}})^{Gsk \cdot Gsk'/Gsk}$$

$$= (H_1(F_{id} \| j) \cdot \prod_{l=1}^{s} u_l^{m_{jl}})^{Gsk'}$$

$$= T_j^{Gsk'},$$

Thus, the verification equation $\hat{e}(\sigma, g) = \hat{e}(\prod_{j \in Q} H(F_{id} \| j)^{v_j} \cdot \prod_{l=1}^{s} u_l^{\mu_l}, Gpk')$ in data integrity checking still holds.

4   Security of the Proposed Protocol

Theorem 1. *The group public-secret key pair is securely generated as long as all the mobile users in group are honest.*

Proof. The security of the group key generation indicates that there is no adversary that can get enough information to generate a valid group secret key. This proof is straight-forward. Our method of generating group public-secret key pair derives from the dynamic asymmetric group key agreement scheme [33]. If the mobile users in group are honest, the correctness of the group key agreement scheme ensures to generate a shared group secret key. According to the security proof in [35], the group public-secret key pair is secure if Diffie-Hellman key agreement scheme is secure, whose security can be reduced to CDH assumption.

Theorem 2. *The data auditing protocol has key privacy with respect to the joining or leaving mobile users as long as s-CDH assumption and s-CDHI assumption hold.*

Proof. In the GkeyGen phase, the Diffie-Hellman key agreement scheme is reused for $n+1$ times to generate secret keys for dynamic groups. Actually, $g^x, g^{x^2}, \cdots,$ $g^{x^{2^v}}$ are immediate values used for computing the group secret keys. We firstly consider the joining case. Suppose a mobile user joins the group in the $(i+1)$th key exchange process, the joining user knows $g^{x^{2^{i+1}}}$ possibly along with some subsequent items. Here we consider the extreme case in which he knows $Q, Q^x, Q^{x+1}, \cdots, Q^{x^w} (Q = g^{x^{2^{i+1}}}, w = v-2^i-1, 0 \le i < v)$ and tries to compute the ith group secret key. If the s-CDHI assumption holds, the joining mobile user is unable to compute $Q^{1/x} = g^{x^{2^i}}$. In addition, since the target group secret key is computed using a hash function, the joining member can not retrieve any information about it. Thus, the data auditing protocol has key privacy with respect to joining members.

Regarding the leaving case, assume a mobile user leaves the group in the ith key exchange process. The leaving mobile user could know $g^{x^{2^{i-1}}}$ along with some foregoing items. Here we consider an extreme case in which he knows $Q, Q^x, Q^{x+1}, \cdots, Q^{x^s} (Q = g^x, w = 2^i - 2, 0 < i \le v)$ and tries to compute the ith group secret key. If the s-CDH assumption holds, the leaving mobile user is unable to compute $Q^{x^{w+1}} = g^{x^{2^i}}$. Besides, since the target group secret key is computed via a hash function, the leaving member can not retrieve any information about it. Thus, data auditing protocol has key privacy with respect to the leaving members.

Theorem 3. *There exists no adversary to generate a corrupted proof that can be accepted by the TPA in the data auditing process within non-negligible probability.*

Proof In the data auditing interactions, the adversary outputs a proof that makes the verification equation hold and is not what would have been computed by the challenger. In the phases of Join and Leave, an honest mobile user acts as a proxy to re-compute the tags using the proxy re-signature key. The capability of the attack that the adversary can get from these two phases is the same as that from the GkeyGen phase, which have been discussed in Theorem 1. Thus, following the proof of the scheme with public verifiability in [30], we are able to reduce the unforgeability of an auditing proof to the CDH assumption.

5   Conclusion

We presented an identity privacy-preserving public auditing protocol in mobile cloud storage for dynamic groups. By exploiting the asymmetric group key agreement scheme, mobile users in group are able to share a group public-secret key pair and generate the tags for the file, so that the TPA enables to audit the integrity of the shared data without knowing the identities of users. Manipulating the proxy re-signature, the mobile user can update the tags in an efficient way.

References

1. Kumar, K., Lu, Y.H.: Cloud computing for mobile users: can offloading computation save energy? IEEE Journal Computer 43(4), 51–56 (2010)
2. Rimal, B.P., Choi, E., Lumb, I.: A taxonomy and survey of cloud computing systems. In: Proceeding of 5th International Joint Conference of INC, IMS and IDC, NCM 2009, Seoul, Korea, pp. 44–51. IEEE Press (2009)
3. Canepa, H., Lee, D.: A virtual cloud computing provider for mobile devices I. In: Proceeding of 1st ACM Workshop on Mobile Cloud Computing and Services Social Networks and Beyond (MCS 2010), vol. 6. ACM Digital Library, San Francisco 2010
4. Huang, D., Xing, T., Wu, H.: Mobile cloud computing service models: a user-centric approach. IEEE Network 27(5), 6–11 (2013)
5. Mell, P., Grance, T.: Draft nist working definition of cloud computing (2009), http://csrc.nist.gov/groups/SNS/cloud-computing/index.html
6. Dinh, H.T., Lee, C., Niyato, D., Wang, P.: A survey of mobile cloud computing: architecture, applications, and approaches. Wireless Communication and Mobile Computing 13(8), 1587–1611 (2013)
7. Fernando, N., Loke, S.W., Rahayu, W.: Mobile cloud computing: a survey. Future Generation Computer Systems 29, 84–106 (2013)
8. Arrington, M.: Gmail disaster: reports of mass email deletions (2006), http://www.techcrunch.com/2006/12/28/gmail-disaster-reports-of-massemail-deletions/index.html
9. Krigsman, M.: Apples mobileme experiences post-launch pain (2008), http://blogs.zdnet.com/projectfailures/?p=908
10. Shiels, M.: Phone sales hit by sidekick loss (2009), http://news.bbc.co.uk/2/hi/technology/8303952.stml
11. Wang, Q., Wang, C., Ren, K., Lou, W., Li, J.: Enabling public auditability and data dynamics for storage security in cloud computing. In: Proceeding of ESORICS 2009, Saint Malo, France, September 21-25, pp. 355–370. IEEE (2009)
12. Wang, Q., Wang, C., Ren, K., Lou, W., Li, J.: Enabling public auditability and data dynamics for storage security in cloud computing. IEEE Transactions on Parallel Distribted Systems 22(5), 847–859 (2012)

13. Wang, C., Ren, K., Lou, W., Li, J.: Toward public auditable secure cloud data storage services. IEEE Network 24(4), 19–24 (2010)
14. Zhu, Y., Hu, H., Ahn, G.J., Stephen, S.: Yau: efficient audit service outsourcing for data integrity in clouds. Journal of Systems and Software 85(5), 1083–1095 (2012)
15. Zhu, Y., Hu, H., Ahn, G.J., Yu, M.: Cooperative provable data possession for integrity verification in multicloud storage. IEEE Transactions on Parallel Distribted Systems 23(12), 2231–2244 (2012)
16. Yang, K., Jia, X.: An efficient and secure dynamic auditing protocol for data storage in cloud computing. IEEE Transactions on Parallel Distribed Systems 24(9), 1717–1726 (2013)
17. Zhu, Y., Wang, S.B., Hu, H., Ahn, G.J., Ma, D.: Secure collaborative integrity verification for hybrid cloud environments. International Journal of Cooperative Information Systems 21(3), 165–198 (2012)
18. Wang, C., Chow, S.S.M., Wang, Q., Ren, K., Lou, W.: Privacy-preserving public auditing for secure cloud storage. IEEE Transactions on Computers 62(2), 362–375 (2013)
19. Wang, B., Li, B., Li, H.: Oruta: privacy-preserving auditing for shared data in the cloud. In: Proceeding of IEEE 5th International Conference on Cloud Computing (IEEE Cloud 2012), Honolulu, HI, USA, June 24-29, pp. 295–302 (2012)
20. Wang, B., Li, B., Li, H.: Knox: Privacy-preserving auditing for shared data with large groups in the cloud. In: Bao, F., Samarati, P., Zhou, J. (eds.) ACNS 2012. LNCS, vol. 7341, pp. 507–525. Springer, Heidelberg (2012)
21. Wang, B., Li, B., Li, H.: Privacy-preserving public auditing for shared cloud data supporting group dynamics. In: Proceeding of IEEE International Conference on Communications (ICC 2013), Budapest, Hungary, June 9-13, pp. 1946–1950 (2013)
22. Wang, B., Li, B., Li, H.: Public auditing for shared data with efficient user revocation in the cloud. In: Proceeding of IEEE Conference on Computer Communications (IEEE INFOCOM 2013), Turin, Italy, April 14-19, pp. 2904–2912 (2013)
23. Boneh, D., Gentry, C., Lynn, B., Shacham, H.: Aggregate and verifiably encrypted signatures from bilinear maps. In: Biham, E. (ed.) EUROCRYPT 2003. LNCS, vol. 2656, pp. 416–432. Springer, Heidelberg (2003)
24. Boneh, D., Boyen, X., Shacham, H.: Short group signatures. In: Franklin, M. (ed.) CRYPTO 2004. LNCS, vol. 3152, pp. 41–55. Springer, Heidelberg (2004)
25. Ferrara, A.L., Green, M., Hohenberger, S., Pedersen, M.Ø.: Practical short signature batch verification. In: Fischlin, M. (ed.) CT-RSA 2009. LNCS, vol. 5473, pp. 309–324. Springer, Heidelberg (2009)
26. Ateniese, G., Hohenberger, S.: Proxy re-signatures: new definitions, algorithms and applications. In: Proceeding of 12th ACM Conference on Computer and Communications Security (ACM CCS 2005), Alexandria, VA, USA, November 07-10, pp. 310–319 (2005)
27. Delerablée, C., Paillier, P., Pointcheval, D.: Fully collusion secure dynamic broadcast encryption with constant-size ciphertexts or decryption keys. In: Takagi, T., Okamoto, T., Okamoto, E., Okamoto, T. (eds.) Pairing 2007. LNCS, vol. 4575, pp. 39–59. Springer, Heidelberg (2007)
28. Yang, J., Wang, H., Wang, J., Tan, C., Yu, D.: Provable Data Possession of Resource-constrained Mobile Devices in Cloud Computing. Journal of Networks 6(7), 1033–1040 (2011)
29. Shacham, H., Waters, B.: Compact proofs of retrievability. In: Pieprzyk, J. (ed.) ASIACRYPT 2008. LNCS, vol. 5350, pp. 90–107. Springer, Heidelberg (2008)
30. Shacham, H., Waters, B.: Compact proofs of retrievability. Journal of Cryptology 26(3), 442–483 (2012)

31. Ateniese, G., Burns, R.C., Curtmola, R., Herring, J., Kissner, L., Peterson, Z.N.J., Song, D.: Provable data possession at untrusted stores. In: Proceeding of ACM CCS 2007, Alexandria, Virginia, USA, October 29-November 2, pp. 598–609 (2007)
32. Ateniese, G., Burns, R.C., Curtmola, R., Herring, J., Kissner, L., Peterson, Z.N.J., Song, D.: Remote data checking using provable data possession. ACM Trans. Inf. Syst. Security 14(1), 12 (2011)
33. Zhao, X., Zhang, F., Tian, H.: Dynamic asymmetric group key agreement for ad hoc networks. Ad Hoc Networks 9, 928–939 (2011)
34. Ni, J., Yu, Y., Mu, Y., Xia, Q.: On the security of an efficient dynamic auditing protocol in cloud storage. IEEE Transactions on Parallel and Distributed Systems (2013), doi:10.1109/TPDS.2013.199
35. Wu, S., Zhu, Y.: Constant-round password-based authenticated key exchange protocol for dynamic groups. In: Tsudik, G. (ed.) FC 2008. LNCS, vol. 5143, pp. 69–82. Springer, Heidelberg (2008)

A Formal Model for Isolation Management in Cloud Infrastructure-as-a-Service

Khalid Zaman Bijon[1], Ram Krishnan[2], and Ravi Sandhu[1]

[1] Institute for Cyber Security & Department of Computer Science
[2] Institute for Cyber Security & Department of Electrical and Computer Engineering
University of Texas at San Antonio

Abstract. Datacenters for cloud infrastructure-as-a-service (IaaS) consist of a large number of heterogeneous virtual resources, such as virtual machines (VMs) and virtual local area networks (VLANs). It takes a complex process to manage and arrange these virtual resources to build particular computing environments. Misconfiguration of this management process increases possibility of security vulnerability in this system. Moreover, multiplexing virtual resources of disjoint customers upon same physical hardware leads to several security concerns, such as cross-channel and denial-of-service attacks. Trusted Virtual Datacenter (TVDc) is a commerical product which informally presents a process to manage strong isolation among these virtual resources in order to mitigate these issues. In this paper, we formally represent this TVDc management model. We also develop an authorization model for the cloud administrative-user privilege management in this system.

Keywords: isolation, virtual resource management, cloud computing.

1 Introduction

Cloud service providers (CSPs) of infrastructure-as-a-service (IaaS) offer a number of heterogeneous virtual resources, e.g. virtual machine (VM), to the cloud customers. Management process of these virtual resources is very complex since the datacenter of a CSP may contain thousands of these resources from different customers and it also increases likelihood of misconfiguration which makes this system vulnerable. On the other hand, multi-tenancy — sharing a hardware resource among different customers' workloads enables cost reductions and economic benefits of the CSPs. However, this situation may also lead to different security vulnerabilities for the customers' workloads such as cross-channel attacks and denial-of-services.

Recently, trusted virtual datacenter (TVDc) [3] proposed an isolation management process in cloud IaaS that addresses these multi-tenancy and management issues. In TVDc virtual machines and their associated resources, such as virtual bridge and virtual local access network (VLAN), are grouped into trusted virtual domains (TVDs). Each TVD, represented as a security clearance (also referred to as color), enforces an isolation policy towards its group members.

M.H. Au et al. (Eds.): NSS 2014, LNCS 8792, pp. 41–53, 2014.

More specifically, resources are only allowed to interact with each other if they are assigned to same color. For instance, VMs with same color can communicate and a VM can run on a hypervisor only if this hypervisor has the same color as that VM. The main goal of this process is to isolate customer workloads from each other. As described in [3], the purpose of this isolation is to reduce the threat of co-locating workloads from different customers by preventing any kind of data flow among these workloads where the data might includes sensitive information of the customers or any virus or malicious code. Again, this simple management process also reduces the incidence of misconfiguration of the virtual-resource management tasks. TVDc [3] also develops a hierarchical administration model based on trusted virtual domains.

In this paper, we develop a formal model for TVDc which we call Formalized-TVDc (also referred as *F-TVDc*). We leverage the attribute based system proposed in [16] in order to represent different properties of the virtual resources, such as color. Then, resources with similar attributes will be arranged together to built a particular computing environment. For instance, a VM can run on a hypervisor (host) if the host has same color of the VM. This formal model consists authorization models for three types of administrative-user operations. We also derive enforcement process for the constraints discussed in [3].

2   Background: Trusted Virtual Datacenter (TVDc)

Trusted virtual datacenter (TVDc) [3] manages isolation by defining a trusted virtual domain (TVD) for a set of VMs and their associated resources that constitute a common administrative unit. The boundary of a TVD is maintained by assigning the TVD identifier to the respective VMs and resources. A TVD identifier represents a security clearance (also referred to as a color to emphasize there is no ordering or structure). For instance, a color can represent the virtual resources of a particular customer or virtual resources running specific workloads of a customer. Hence, basically, a color represents a particular context for the assigned VMs and resources. Figure 1, from [3], shows the TVDc view of the virtual resources running two physical data centers and their resources, such as servers, storage, and network components. The TVDc view separates the association of physical resources for each color. For instance, in figure 1, the red color includes VMs 3, 7, 9, and 11, and associated storages.

In order to manage this isolation process, three different administrative roles are proposed in TVDc: IT datacenter administrator, TVDc administrator , and tenant administrator. Administrative users (also generally referred as admin-users) having IT datacenter administrator role are the superusers in this system. Their main task is to discover the physical and the virtual resources and group the discovered resources into TVDcs. They also define the security labels or colors. IT datacenter admin-users further can assign a TVDc group to both TVDc and tenant admin-users, and assign a set of colors to TVDc admin-users in order to delegate isolation management of resources in that specific TVDc group. The tasks of a TVDc admin-user include assigning colors to the resources, belong

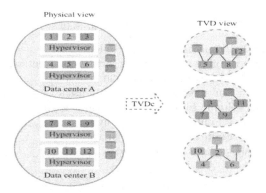

Fig. 1. *TVDc View of the IaaS Cloud Resources [3]*

to the same TVDc group, from her assigned set of colors. She also assigns a color to an admin-user if the admin-user is in the same TVDc group and assigned to the tenant administrator role. The job function of a tenant admin-user is to perform basic cloud administrative operations on the cloud resources, such as boot a VM and connect a VM to a virtual network, if both the resources and the tenant admin-user are in same TVDc group and assigned with same color.

This color-driven isolation management process supports four different types of isolation which are described as follows:

1. **Data Sharing:** In this model, VMs can share data with each other only if they have common colors. In order to constrain this, a VM is allowed to connect to a VLAN only if both the VM and the VLAN have common colors and, therefore, it is restricted to communicate with VMs having same color.
2. **Hyperviosr (host) Authorization:** A host is assigned to a set of colors and is only allowed to run a VM having a color in that set. Therefore, a host's capability to run VMs is isolated to its assigned colors.
3. **Colocation Management:** Two colors can be conflicted with each other if context of operation is mutually exclusive. Colors can be declared to be conflicting and two VMs with conflicted colors are prohibited from running in same host. For instance, VMs A and B with color red and blue respectively which have been declared to be conflicting cannot run on same host.
4. **Management Constraints:** For management isolation, tenant administrative roles are created where each user having this role is restricted to perform administrative operation within a single color.

3 Formal Isolation Management Model (*F-TVDc*)

In this section, we formalize the isolation management process in cloud IaaS which is informally described in TVDc [3]. We call the resulting model as Formalized-TVDc (*F-TVDc*) for ease of reference and continuity. In *F-TVDc*, different properties of the cloud entities are represented as assigned attributes

Table 1. Basic Element-Sets

CLR = Finite set of existing colors
VDc = Finite set of existing virtual data centers
AROLE = {itAdmin, tvdcAdmin, tntAdmin}
AU = Finite set of existing admin-users
VM = Finite set of existing virtual machines
VMM = Finite set of existing hypervisors
BR = Finite set of existing virtual bridges
VLAN = Finite set of existing virtual LANs

to them. For instance, a virtual machine(VM) attribute *color* represents assigned colors to that VM and an administrative user (admin-user) attribute *adminRole* represents assigned role to that user. For this purpose we utilize the attribute based system [16], specifically its attribute representation for the entities in a system. In this attribute based representation of *F-TVDc*, the admin-users can manage the resources in data-center by assigning proper attributes to them. For instance, a TVDc admin-user can assign a set of colors to a host and, consequently, the host is authorized to run a VM if the assigned color of the VM is an element of the set of colors assigned to the host. *F-TVDc* also formally represents an authorization model for these admin-user privileges.

3.1 Basic Components

The sets that contain basic entities of *F-TVDc* are shown in table 1. In *F-TVDc*, CLR contains the existing colors/clearances in the system. We will see later that the colors from CLR will be assigned to the cloud-resources' and admin-users' respective attributes, such as the *admincolor* attribute of an admin-user. The data-center is divided into multiple virtual data-centers. VDc contains the names of these virtual data-centers. There are three administrative roles: IT administrator (itAdmin), TVDc administrator (tvdcAdmin), and tenant administrator (tntAdmin) which are contained in set AROLE. The set AU contains all admin-users in the system. VMM and VM contains the current existing hypervisors (hosts) and the virtual machines(VMs) in the system. Similarly, existing virtual LANs and virtual bridges are contained in set VLAN and BR respectively.

3.2 Attributes

Attributes characterize properties of an entity and are modeled as functions. *F-TVDc* recognize two types of attribute functions for each entity depending on the nature of the functions values: atomic-valued and set-valued. For instance, an admin-user attribute function *adminRole* can only take a single value that indicates the assigned role to that user. On the other hand, the attribute function *admincolor*, representing the assigned colors to an admin-user, can take multiple values. For convenience we understand attribute to mean attribute function for ease of reference. Attributes of an entity, let's say VM attributes, can be formally defined as follows:

Table 2. Attributes Specification

Entity	Attributes	attType	SCOPE
Admin-User	*adminRole*	atomic	AROLE
	adminvdcenter	set	VDc
	admincolor	set	CLR
Virtual Machine	*vmvdcenter*	atomic	VDc
	vmcolor	atomic	CLR
	host	atomic	VMM
	status	atomic	{Running, Stop}
	bridge	set	BR
Hypervisor (**host**)	*vmmvdcenter*	atomic	VDc
	vmmcolor	set	CLR
	vm	set	VM
Virtual Bridge	*brvdcenter*	atomic	VDc
	brcolor	atomic	CLR
	vm	set	VM
	vlan	atomic	BR
Virtual LAN	*vlanvdcenter*	atomic	VDc
	vlancolor	set	CLR
	bridge	set	BR

- ATTR_{VM} is the finite set of VM attributes, where
  attType: ATTR $\rightarrow$ {set, atomic}.

- For each $att \in \text{ATTR}_{\text{VM}}$, SCOPE_{att} is a finite set of atomic values which
  determines the range of att as follows:
  $$\text{Range}(att) = \begin{cases} \text{SCOPE}_{att} \text{ if attType}(att) = \text{atomic} \\ \mathcal{P}(\text{SCOPE}_{att}) \text{ if attType}(att) = \text{set} \end{cases}$$
  where $\mathcal{P}$ denotes the power set of a set.

- An attribute is a function that maps each VM$\in$VM to a value in range, i.e.,

  $$\forall att \in \text{ATTR}_{\text{VM}}. att : \text{VM} \rightarrow \text{Range}(att)$$

Similary, attributes of other entities can be defined. Table 2 shows the necessary attributes for the entities in *F-TVDc* which are described as follows:

- Admin-User (**aUser**) attributes: *adminRole* attribute of an admin-user
  (**aUser**) specifies the assigned administrative role to **aUser**. Note that, an
  aUser can get only one administrative role, hence, *adminRole* is an atomic attribute. Attribute *adminvdcenter* represents the assigned virtual data-center
  of an **aUser**. If the **aUser** is an IT administrator then its *adminvdcenter* contains all the members in **VDc**. Otherwise *adminvdcenter* of an **aUser** contains

only one element from **VDc**. Similarly, *admincolor* specifies the assigned colors to an **aUser**. If an **aUser** is an IT administrator then her *admincolor* contains all the elements of **CLR**. On the other hand, an **aUser** having **tvd-cAdmin** role can get subset of colors from **CLR** and a **tntAdmin** gets only one color. Section 4 represents the operations to assign values of these **aUser** attributes.

- Virtual machine (**VM**) attributes: The **VM** attribute *host* represents the hypervisor (**host**) where a **VM** is running. Attribute *bridge* represents the connected **bridges** of a **VM**. *vmvdcenter* represents the virtual data-center a **VM** belongs to and *vmcolor* specifies the assigned color to that **VM**.
- Hypervisor (**host**) attributes: The *VM* attribute represents the running VMs in a **host**. The *vmmvdcenter* attribute represents its virtual data-centers and *vmcolor* the assigned colors to it.
- Virtual Bridge (**bridge**) attributes: The *VM* attribute of **bridge** specifies the connected **VMs** to a **bridge**. Similarly, *vlan* specifies the **vlan** to which a bridge is connected. Similar to the other entities, *brcolor* and *brvdcenter* represent the virtual data-center and color assigned to a **bridge**. Note these are atomic in this instance.
- Virtual LAN (**vlan**) attributes: The *bridge* attribute of a **vlan** specifies the connected virtual bridges to it. Also, *vlancolor* and *vlanvdcenter* represents the virtual data-center and colors assigned to a **vlan**.

4   Administrative Models

In this section, we discuss administrative operations for the three types of admin-users. Table 3 formally specifies the set of administrative operations for the IT admin-user. The first column specifies the operation name and parameters. The second column specifies the conditions that need to be satisfied to authorize the operation. Attributes and sets that will be updated after an authorized operation are listed in the third column, with the *ɪ* symbol indicating the value after the update. Administrative operations of Table 3 are discussed below.

- **CreateVDC:** First column of table 3 shows that this function takes two parameters: users u and a virtual data-center vdc. Then, in second column, these parameters need to satisfy the given formula which checks if u belongs to **AU**, *adminRole* of u is **itAdmin** and vdc is not present in **VDc**. If the precondition is satisfied, in column 3, vdc is created by adding it to set **VDc**.
- **CreateCl** and **RemoveCl:** Using these two operations, an **itAdmin** can create a new color cl and remove an existing color cl.
- **Add_Cl$_{TVDcAdmin}$:** This function takes three parameters: users u1 and u2, and a color cl. These parameters need to satisfy the given formula in column 2 which checks if u1 has role **itAdmin**, u2 has role **tvdcAdmin** and cl is a valid member in **CLR**. If so, color cl is assigned to **tvdcAdmin** u2 by adding cl to *tvdcAdmincolor* attribute of u2, as shown in column 3.
- **Rem_Cl$_{TVDcAdmin}$:** Using this operation, an **itAdmin** removes a color cl from an admin-user having role **tvdcAdmin**.

Table 3. IT admin-user Operations

Operation	Precondition	Updates
CreateVDC(u, vdc) /*Creates a virtual data-center vdc*/	u∈AU∧vdc∉VDc∧ adminRole(u)=itAdmin	VDc′=VDc∪{vdc}
CreateCl(u,cl) /*Creates a color cl*/	u∈AU∧cl∉CLR∧ adminRole(u)=itAdmin	CLR′=CLR∪{cl}
RemoveCl(u,cl) /*Removes a color cl*/	u∈AU∧cl∈CLR∧ adminRole(u)=itAdmin	CLR′=CLR-{cl}
Add_Cl$_{\text{TVDcAdmin}}$(u1,u2,cl) /*Adds cl to **tvdcAdmin** u2*/	u1∈AU∧adminRole(u1)= itAdmin∧u2∈AU∧cl∈CLR∧ adminRole(u2)=tvdcAdmin∧ cl∉admincolor(u2)	admincolor′(u2)← admincolor(u2)∪{cl}
Rem_Cl$_{\text{TVDcAdmin}}$(u1,u2,cl) /*Removes cl from **tvdcAdmin** u2*/	u1∈AU∧adminRole(u1)= itAdmin∧u2∈AU∧ adminRole(u2)=tvdcAdmin∧ cl∈admincolor(u2)	admincolor′(u2)← admincolor(u2)-{cl}
Assign_VDC$_{\text{Admin}}$(u1,u2,vdc) /*Assigns virtual datacenter vdc to **tvdcAdmin** or **tntAdmin** u2*/	u1∈AU∧adminRole(u1)= itAdmin∧u2∈AU∧vdc∈VDc∧ (adminRole(u2)=tvdcAdmin∨ adminRole(u2)=tntAdmin)	adminvdcenter′(u2)← {vdc}
Assign_VDC$_{\text{VM}}$(u,vm,vdc) /*Assigns virtual datacenter vdc to a virtual machine vm*/	u ∈AU∧vm∈VM∧vdc∈ VDc∧adminRole(u)=itAdmin	vmvdcenter′(vm)← vdc
Assign_VDC$_{\text{VMM}}$(u,vmm,vdc) /*Assigns virtual datacenter vdc to a hypervisor vmm*/	u ∈AU∧vmm∈VMM∧vdc∈ VDc∧adminRole(u)=itAdmin	vmmvdcenter′(vmm)← vdc
Assign_VDC$_{\text{BR}}$(u,br,vdc) /*Assigns virtual datacenter vdc to a bridge br*/	u ∈AU∧br∈BR∧vdc∈ VDc∧adminRole(u)=itAdmin	brvdcenter′(br)← vdc
Assign_VDC$_{\text{VLAN}}$(u,vlan,vdc) /*Assigns virtual datacenter vdc to a virtual lan vlan*/	u ∈AU∧vlan∈VLAN∧vdc∈ VDc∧adminRole(u)=itAdmin	vlanvdcenter′(vlan)← vdc

- **Assign_VDC**$_{\text{Admin}}$: Using this operation an **itAdmin** user assigns a virtual data-center vdc to attribute *adminvdcenter* of a **tvdcAdmin** or **tntAdmin** user.
- **Assign_VDC**$_{\text{VM}}$: A virtual data-center vdc is assigned to the *vmvdcenter* attribute of a virtual machine vm. This value specifies that vm belongs to virtual data-center vdc.
- **Assign_VDC**$_{\text{VMM}}$: Similarly, a virtual data-center vdc is assigned to the *vmmvdcenter* attribute of a hypervisor vmm.

Table 4. TVDc-ADMIN Operations

Operation	Precondition	Updates
Assign_Cl$_{\text{TAdmin}}$(u1, u2,cl) /*Assigns a color cl to a tntAdmin u2*/	u1∈AU∧u2∈AU∧$adminRole$(u1)= tvdcAdmin∧$adminRole$(u2)= tntAdmin∧ $adminvdcenter$(u1)= $adminvdcenter$(u2)∧cl∈ $admincolor$(u1)∧cl∉$admincolor$(u2)	$admincolor'$(u2)← {cl}
Rem_Cl$_{\text{TAdmin}}$(u1, u2,cl) /*Removes the color cl from a tntAdmin u2*/	u1∈AU∧u2∈AU∧$adminRole$(u1)= tvdcAdmin∧$adminRole$(u2)= tntAdmin∧ $adminvdcenter$(u1)= $adminvdcenter$(u2)∧cl∈ $admincolor$(u1)∧cl∈$admincolor$(u2)	$admincolor'$(u2)← ϕ
Add_Cl$_{\text{VMM}}$(u,vmm,cl) /*Adds a color cl to hypervisor vmm*/	u∈AU∧vmm∈VMM∧cl∈ $admincolor$(u)∧$adminRole$(u)= tvdcAdmin∧$adminvdcenter$(u)= $vmmvdcenter$(vmm)	$vmmcolor'$(vmm)← $vmmcolor$(vmm)∪ {cl}
Assign_Cl$_{\text{VM}}$(u,vm,cl) /*Assigns a color cl to virtual machine vm*/	u∈AU∧vm∈VM∧cl∈ $admincolor$(u)∧$adminRole$(u)= tvdcAdmin∧$adminvdcenter$(u)= $vmvdcenter$(vm)	$vmcolor'$(vm)← {cl}
Assign_Cl$_{\text{BR}}$(u,br,cl) /*Assigns a color cl to bridge br*/	u∈AU∧br∈BR∧cl∈ $admincolor$(u)∧$adminRole$(u)= tvdcAdmin∧$adminvdcenter$(u)= $brvdcenter$(br)	$brcolor'$(br)←{cl}
Add_Cl$_{\text{VLAN}}$(u,vlan,cl) /*Adds a color cl to virtual LAN vlan*/	u∈AU∧vlan∈VLAN∧cl∈ $admincolor$(u)∧$adminRole$(u)= tvdcAdmin∧$adminvdcenter$(u)= $vmmvdcenter$(vlan)	$vlancolor'$(vlan)← $vlancolor$(vlan)∪ {cl}

- **Assign_VDC**$_{\text{BR}}$: This operation assigns a virtual data-center named vdc to $brvdcenter$ attribute of a virtual bridge br.
- **Assign_VDC**$_{\text{VLAN}}$: A virtual data-center, vdc, is assigned to the $vlanvdcenter$ attribute of a virtual LAN vlan.

Similarly, table 4 shows the operations for TVDc admin-users. The TVDc admin-users are responsible to assign colors to the tntAdmins and the resources in data-centers where the TVDc admin-users are authorized to exercise their priviledges. The description of these operations are as follows:

- **Assign_Cl**$_{\text{TAdmin}}$: A tvdcAdmin u1 assigns a color cl to a tntAdmin u2. Authorization of this operation needs to satisfy the precondition that u1

Table 5. Tenant-ADMIN Operations

Operation	Precondition	Updates
Boot(u,vm,vmm) /*Boots a virtual machine vm in a **host** vmm*/	$vmcolor(\text{vm})\in admincolor(\text{u})\wedge$ $admincolor(\text{u})\cap vmmcolor(\text{vmm})\neq$ $\emptyset\wedge adminvdcenter(\text{u})=$ $vmvdcenter(\text{vm})\wedge adminvdcenter(\text{u})\in$ $vmmvdcenter(\text{vmm})\wedge vmcolor(\text{vm})\in$ $vmmcolor(\text{vmm})\wedge\text{vm}\in\mathsf{VM}\wedge\text{vmm}\in$ $\mathsf{VMM}\wedge$ Evaluate_CLocConst(vm,vmm)$\wedge$ $\text{u}\in\mathsf{AU}\wedge adminRole(\text{u})=\mathsf{tntAdmin}\wedge$ $status(\text{vm})=\text{Stop}$	$host'(\text{vm})\leftarrow$ vmm $vm'(\text{vmm})\leftarrow$ $vm(\text{vmm})\cup\text{vm}$ $status'(\text{vm})\leftarrow$ Running
ConVmToBr(u,vm,br) /*Connects virtual machine vm to a virtual bridge br*/	$\text{u}\in\mathsf{AU}\wedge vmcolor(\text{vm})\in admincolor(\text{u})\wedge$ $brcolor(\text{br})=vmcolor(\text{vm})\wedge brcolor(\text{br})\in$ $admincolor(\text{u})\wedge\text{br}\in\mathsf{BR}\wedge\text{vm}\in\mathsf{VM}\wedge$ $adminvdcenter(\text{u})=vmvdcenter(\text{vm})\wedge$ $adminvdcenter(\text{u})=brvdcenter(\text{br})\wedge$ $adminRole(\text{u})=\mathsf{tntAdmin}$	$bridge'(\text{vm})\leftarrow$ br $vm'(\text{br})\leftarrow$ $vm(\text{br})\cup$ $\{\text{vm}\}$
ConBrToVLAN(u,br,vlan) /*Connects a virtual bridge br to a virtual LAN vlan*/	$\text{u}\in\mathsf{AU}\wedge brcolor(\text{br})\in admincolor(\text{u})\wedge$ $brcolor(\text{br})\in vlancolor(\text{valn})\wedge$ $vlancolor(\text{vlan})\cap admincolor(\text{u})\neq$ $\emptyset\wedge\text{br}\in\mathsf{BR}\wedge\text{vlan}\in\mathsf{VLAN}\wedge$ $adminvdcenter(\text{u})=vlanvdcenter(\text{vm})\wedge$ $adminvdcenter(\text{u})=vlanvdcenter(\text{br})$ $\wedge adminRole(\text{u})=\mathsf{tntAdmin}$	$bridge'(\text{vlan})\leftarrow$ $bridge(\text{vlan})\cup$ $\{\text{br}\}$ $vlan'(\text{br})\leftarrow$ vlan

and u2 are in the same virtual data-center. Also, the *admincolor* attribute of u2 must contain cl.

- **Rem_Cl$_{\mathsf{TAdmin}}$**: Using this operation a **tvdcAdmin** removes a color from **tntAdmin**.

- **Add_Cl$_{\mathsf{VMM}}$**: This operation adds a color cl to a **host** named vmm if vmm and **tvdcAdmin** are in same virtual data-center. Note that, a **host** can contain multiple colors.

- **Assign_Cl$_{\mathsf{VM}}$, Assign_Cl$_{\mathsf{BR}}$**, and **Add_Cl$_{\mathsf{VLAN}}$**: Using first two operations operations a **tvdcAdmin** u assigns a color cl to a virtual machine vm and a bridge br respectively. Also, using **Add_Cl$_{\mathsf{VLAN}}$** the **tvdcAdmin** adds a color to the *vlancolor* attribute of a virtual LAN. Note that, *vlancolor* attribute can contain multiple colors since a virtual LAN can be connected to multiple virtual bridges.

Now, table 5 shows the administrative operations for tenant admin-users and preconditions to authorize these operations. The operations of the tenant admin-users are to manage cloud resources within their assigned TVD groups, i.e., colors. The operations are described as follows:

- **Boot**: Using this operation a tenant admin-user u boots a VM vm in a hostvmm. Table 5 shows the necessary precondition in order to authorize this operation. The precondition verifies if the u has same color of the vm which is basically an implementation of the management isolation constraint shown in section 2. In addition to that, the precondition also checks if these three entities belong to the same data-center. It also verifies if the host vmm's *vmmcolor* attribute contains the color of the vm's assigned color in *vmcolor* which is an implementation of host authorization isolation which is also shown in section 2. The authorization process of this operation also calls Evaluate_CLocConst function to satisfy the co-location management constraint, also given in section 2, for the vm with other running VMs in vmm. The algorithm 1 shows the evaluation process of Evaluate_CLocConst. Upon successful checking of these conditions the vm is scheduled to the vmm.
- **ConVmToBr**: It connects a VM to a virtual bridge . A VM can only connects to bridge if they have same color and they belongs to the same data-center.
- **ConBrToVLAN**: Using this function a tenant admin-user connects bridge to a VLAN. They can be connected if color of the bridge is present in the *vlancolor* attribute of the VLAN.

Algorithm 1 Colocation Constraints Verification

```
1: procedure EVALUATE_CLOCCONST(reqVm,vmm)
2:     Flag=True
3:     for vm∈VM do
4:         if host(vm)=vmm then
5:             for conele∈ConflictColor do
6:                 if vmcolor(reqVm)≠ vmcolor(vm) then
7:                     if vmcolor(vm)∈conele∧vmcolor(reqVm)∈conele∧status(vm)=Running then
8:                         Flag=False
9:                         return Flag
10:                    end if
11:                end if
12:            end for
13:        end if
14:    end for
15:    return Flag
16: end procedure
```

Algorithm 1 shows the evaluation algorithm of the co-location constraints. It takes two inputs: requested VM (reqVm) and the host (vmm). For each VM running in the vmm, this algorithm verifies if there is any conflict between the assigned color to the *vmmcolor* attribute of VM with the assigned color to the *vmmcolor* of reqVm. Attribute values can have different type of conflicts that can represent various relationships among these such as mutual-exclusion, precondition, etc. A generalized approach to represent the various types of attribute conflict-relations are shown in Bijon et al [4,5]. Here, the conflicting values, i.e. colors, of the attribute *vmmcolor* are stored in a set called ConflictColor where each element in the set contains a set colors that are conflicting with each-other. Formally this set is defined as follows,

ConflictColor = {conele$_1$, conele$_2$, ..., conele$_n$} where conele$_i$ ⊆ **CLR**
If algorithm 1 identifies no conflicts between reqVm and all running VM in vmm, it returns True. Otherwise, it returns a False.

5 Related Work

Presently, cloud providers, such as Amazon Elastic Compute Cloud [1], are highly multiplexed shared resources among different clients for achieving on de-mand scalability and cost effectiveness, although, it raises several issues making security and performance predictability a key concern for the customers [11]. For instance, Ristenpart et al [19] shows that it is possible to initiate a side-channel attacks from a VM to another co-locating VMs in same server. Rocha et al [20] shows different attacking scenarios including stealing cleartext password, private keys, etc. when tenants run their workloads without proper control in cloud. Moreover, complex and limited virtual resource management mechanism in cloud increases the likelihood of the risk of possible misconfiguration. Sea-wall [21] shows that arbitrary sharing of network, in cloud, may cause denial of service attack and performance interferences. Wei et al [23] shows that uncon-trolled snapshots and uses of images cause security risk for both creator and user of it. Sivathanu et al [22] presents an experimental analysis on I/O performance bottleneck when virtual storages are placed arbitrarily in physical storage. Also, several performance and security issues, are basically resulted from unorganized management and multiplexing of resources, are summarized in [12, 14, 15].

In this paper we develop a formal model for isolation management of both admin-users and cloud resources that provides a simple but effective resource management mechanism for cloud. This isolation management is informally ad-dressed in Trusted Virtual Datacenter(TVDc) [2]. TVDc builds upon Trusted Virtual Domains [2,3], which provides strong isolation that significantly enhance the security and management capabilities in cloud IaaS environment. Cabuk et al [8] also utilize Trusted Virtual Domains for the orchestration of various cloud resources. Lohr et al [17] propose isolation management in cloud system which is designed for medical services. This work proposes that the end-user, e.g. a patient, should be able to divide the execution environment for applications into separated domains isolated from each other so that medical data of a patient can only resides within her personal domain. Also, Bleikertz et al [6] develop an assurance language for isolation management in cloud computing environment. Prior literature also contains several processes on users authorization and access control models for cloud IaaS including [7,9] and, also, various processes for vir-tual resource management, e.g., virtual machine placement algorithms [10,13,18] for improving different aspects, e.g. high performance, load balancing.

6 Conclusion

In this paper, we formally represent an isolation management process of virtual resources in cloud IaaS. We utilize attribute-based system [16] in order to repre-sents different properties of cloud resources, such as colors (security clearance), as assigned attributes to them. Then, resources are organized together based on similar attribute values. We also develop a process to enforce co-location constraints for the VMs having conflict with each other which prohibits them to be scheduled in same physical server.

Acknowledgement. This work is partially supported by the NSF (CNS-1111925) and AFOSR MURI grants (FA9550-08-1-0265).

References

1. Aws identity and access management, http://aws.amazon.com/iam/
2. Berger, S., et al.: TVDc: managing security in the trusted virtual datacenter. ACM SIGOPS Operating Systems Review 42(1), 40–47 (2008)
3. Berger, S., et al.: Security for the cloud infrastructure: Trusted virtual data center implementation. IBM Journal of R&D 53(4), 6:1–6:12 (2009)
4. Bijon, K.Z., Krishman, R., Sandhu, R.: Constraints specication in attribute based access control. SCIENCE 2(3), 131 (2013)
5. Bijon, K.Z., Krishnan, R., Sandhu, R.: Towards an attribute based constraints specification language. In: Social Computing, pp. 108–113. IEEE (2013)
6. Bleikertz, S., Groß, T.: A virtualization assurance language for isolation and deployment. In: Policies for Distributed Systems and Networks. IEEE (2011)
7. Bleikertz, S., Kurmus, A., Nagy, Z., Schunter, M.: Secure cloud maintenance - protecting workloads against insider attacks. In: Proc. of the ASIACCS (2012)
8. Cabuk, S., et al.: Towards automated security policy enforcement in multi-tenant virtual data centers. Journal of Computer Security 18(1), 89–121 (2010)
9. Calero, J.M.A., et al.: Toward a multi-tenancy authorization system for cloud services. IEEE Security & Privacy 8(6), 48–55 (2010)
10. Cherkasova, L., et al.: Comparison of the three cpu schedulers in xen. SIGMETRICS Performance Evaluation Review 35(2), 42–51 (2007)
11. Claybrook, B.: Comparing cloud risks and virtualization risks for data center apps, http://searchdatacenter.techtarget.com/tip/0,289483,sid80~gci1380652,00.html
12. Dawoud, W., Takouna, I., Meinel, C.: Infrastructure as a service security: Challenges and solutions. In: IEEE INFOS, pp. 1–8 (2010)
13. Gupta, A., et al.: Hpc-aware vm placement in infrastructure clouds. In: IEEE Intl. Conf. on Cloud Engineering, vol. 13 (2013)
14. Hashizume, K., et al.: An analysis of security issues for cloud computing. Journal of Internet Services and Applications 4(1), 1–13 (2013)
15. Jasti, A., Shah, P., Nagaraj, R., Pendse, R.: Security in multi-tenancy cloud. In: IEEE ICCST, pp. 35–41 (2010)
16. Jin, X., Krishnan, R., Sandhu, R.: A Unified Attribute-Based Access Control Model Covering DAC, MAC and RBAC. In: Cuppens-Boulahia, N., Cuppens, F., Garcia-Alfaro, J. (eds.) DBSec 2012. LNCS, vol. 7371, pp. 41–55. Springer, Heidelberg (2012)

17. Löhr, H., et al.: Securing the e-health cloud. In: Proceedings of the 1st ACM International Health Informatics Symposium, pp. 220–229. ACM (2010)
18. Mills, K., Filliben, J., Dabrowski, C.: Comparing vm-placement algorithms for on-demand clouds. In: IEEE CloudCom, pp. 91–98 (2011)
19. Ristenpart, T., et al.: Hey, you, get off of my cloud: exploring information leakage in third-party compute clouds. In: Proc. of the ACM CCS (2009)
20. Rocha, F., Correia, M.: Lucy in the sky without diamonds: Stealing confidential data in the cloud. In: Proc. of the IEEE DSN-W (2011)
21. Shieh, A., et al.: Sharing the data center network. In: Proceedings of the 8th USENIX Conference on Networked Systems Design and Implementation (2011)
22. Sivathanu, S., Liu, L., Yiduo, M., Pu, X.: Storage management in virtualized cloud environment. In: IEEE CLOUD, pp. 204–211 (2010)
23. Wei, J., et al.: Managing security of virtual machine images in a cloud environment. In: Proc. of the ACM Workshop on Cloud Computing Security (2009)

Extending OpenStack Access Control
with Domain Trust

Bo Tang and Ravi Sandhu

Institute for Cyber Security and Department of Computer Science
University of Texas at San Antonio, One UTSA Circle, San Antonio, TX 78249, US
xyp368@my.utsa.edu, ravi.sandhu@utsa.edu

Abstract. OpenStack has been rapidly established as the most popular open-source platform for cloud Infrastructure-as-a-Service in this fast
moving industry. In response to increasing access control requirements
from its users, the OpenStack identity service Keystone has introduced
several entities, such as domains and projects in addition to roles, resulting in a rather complex and somewhat obscure authorization model.
In this paper, we present a formalized description of the core OpenStack
access control (OSAC). We further propose a domain trust extension
for OSAC to facilitate secure cross-domain authorization. We have implemented a proof-of-concept prototype of this trust extension based on
Keystone. The authorization delay introduced by the domain trusts is
0.7 percent on average in our experiments.

Keywords: Distributed Access Control, Identity Management, Security
in Cloud and Grid Systems, Trust Management.

1 Introduction

Cloud computing is widely anticipated as the next generation computing infrastructure although it is still in its infancy. The concept of cloud computing is attracting attention from both business and technology perspectives. Its
pay-on-the-go business model tremendously minimizes on-premise investment on
IT infrastructures for organizations and individuals. The multi-layered service-
oriented architecture (SOA) design enables cloud service providers (CSPs) to
serve their consumers with centralized software and data centers in a multi-
tenant fashion. However, concerns of security with respect to data location and
control, as well as availability create resistance to cloud adoption. One of the
key issues in this regard is access control.

Multi-tenancy is one of the crucial characteristics of cloud services. We define
a tenant from the perspective of a CSP, as an independent customer of the CSP
responsible for paying for services used by that tenant.[1] A principal responsibility

---

[1] Payment is the norm in a public cloud while in a community cloud there often will
be other methods for a tenant to obtain services. From the perspective of the tenant,
a tenant could be a private individual, an organization big or small, a department
within a larger organization, an ad hoc collaboration, and so on. This aspect of a
tenant is typically not visible to the CSP in a public cloud.

M.H. Au et al. (Eds.): NSS 2014, LNCS 8792, pp. 54–69, 2014.
© Springer International Publishing Switzerland 2014

of the CSP is to maintain isolation across tenants, so that the tenant's users can only access resources within that tenant's scope. Over time it has been recognized that controlled cross-tenant access is desirable and some models for that purpose have been proposed [10,20,21,22]. These models establish cross-tenant trust on a bilateral basis so as to enable appropriate cross-tenant access. Some notion of a trust relationship of this nature has been prevalent in prior work on distributed systems when crossing administrative boundaries. This is exemplified by the well-known mechanisms in Windows Active Directory (AD) [3] and the Grid [6,11].

Our central goal in this paper is to investigate the addition of cross-tenant access in the popular open-source OpenStack [4] platform for cloud infrastructure-as-a-service (IaaS). Specifically, with respect to the Havana release. The general concept of a tenant in a cloud maps to the concept of domain in the Havana release of OpenStack.[2] The identity service in OpenStack, called Keystone, is used to manage users as globally available resources. More specifically, the administrator of a domain can view all the user information and assign any user to roles controlled by that domain. Each user, as created, belongs to a single domain and the domain owner or administrator can only see and manage users within the domain. So far, the use cases of cross-domain access has not been carefully addressed in OpenStack. This lack is the main motivation for this paper.

In this paper, we propose a domain trust model addressing cross-domain access control in OpenStack and provide a proof-of-concept implementation by extending KeyStone. In response to increasing access control requirements from its users, Keystone has introduced several entities, such as domains, projects and groups in addition to roles, resulting in a rather complex and somewhat obscure authorization model. Before we can add cross-domain trust to this model it is necessary to cast the core OpenStack access control (OSAC) model in a formal way which is consistent with familiar terminology from the access control research literature. Development of this formal rigorous statement of OSAC is in itself an important contribution of this paper.

The rest of this paper is organized as follows. Section 2 gives the motivating use case of cross-domain authorization and some of the existing approaches. The formalized OpenStack Access Control (OSAC) model is presented in Section 3, followed by the extended domain trust model in Section 4. To demonstrate the feasibility of the novel domain trust model in OpenStack, we develop a proof-of-concept prototype based on Keystone. This is described in Section 5, along with evaluation results. Related work in the cross-domain trust arena is discussed in Section 6. Finally, we conclude the paper in Section 7.

2   Background and Motivation

In this section, we use a DevOps [1] example to explain why we need cross-domain accesses in the cloud and what potential problems we have in the latest

---

[2] Previous releases of OpenStack employed the term tenant for what has now come to be called project in OpenStack. The term tenant is no longer used in OpenStack. In this paper we use the term tenant as a generic concept in cloud computing, while domain is specific to OpenStack as its realization of a tenant.

OpenStack solution. Also, we discuss the pros and cons of existing cross-domain authorization solutions. The scope and assumptions of our work are given.

Motivation. DevOps is a newly emerged software development methodology that stresses collaboration among software development, quality assurance (QA) and operations. Numerous companies are actively practicing DevOps since it aims to help organizations rapidly produce software products and services [1]. When DevOps for an organization comes into play in an OpenStack cloud, cross-domain accesses become inevitable and requires suitable control. Figure 1 shows the authorization related components in OpenStack giving cross-domain accesses for a DevOps use case. The token information is managed by the centralized identity service. The policy rules are administered and checked against access requests along with user tokens in each distributed cloud service.

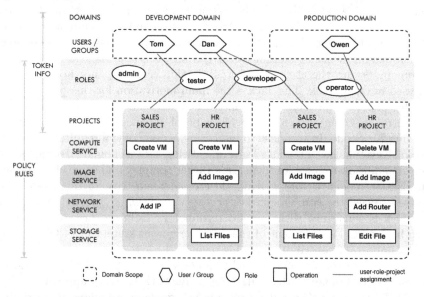

Fig. 1. An DevOps use case of cross-domain accesses

Suppose the organization has two domains in the cloud: *Production* and *Development*. *Production* hosts live applications supporting the organization's daily business requiring strict controls on changes. Meanwhile, *Development* consists of development and testing environments, basically a sandbox, where developers and testers can freely conduct experiments with the cloud resources. The isolation of the two domains is mandatory for best practice and compliance reasons. Each domain contains its own set of users, groups, projects and controlled access to the full-spectrum of cloud services, such as compute, image and network. As shown in Figure 1, Owen is an operator in *Production*. Dan and Tom are a developer and a tester respectively in *Development*. Each domain has two independent projects: *Sales* and *HR*. The users are assigned necessary permissions to access projects in their owning domains to accomplish their daily jobs (each user in OpenStack has a single domain which "owns" the user). In order to process a DevOps case in which a live application in *Sales.Production*[3] needs to be updated by a developer, Dan needs authorization to access the application. The *Production* administrator may prefer not to create another user account for Dan in *Production* but to assign Dan as a developer to *Sales.Production* instead for the following reasons.

- Dan does not have to switch between user accounts in different domains.
- Intra-domain and cross-domain assignments can be distinguished.
- After the DevOps case is completed, *Production* administrator can avoid removing the temporary user and correlated assignments by simply revoking the cross-domain user assignments.

This example is a typical use case for organizations using either public or community clouds. By design, OpenStack supports cross-domain assignments however they are treated much the same as intra-domain assignments. For example, *Production*'s administrator can assign any user from other domains to roles in *Production*'s projects. This approach may cause a series of problems.

a) *Production* administrator should be able to see *Development* users and their assigned roles in all *Development* projects, at least during authorization time, to issue proper cross-domain assignments.
b) *Development* administrator cannot control the cross-domain authorization.
c) Since DevOps jobs are usually temporary, the management of cross-domain authorization should be flexible, convenient and rapid.
d) No option to specify additional controls upon cross-domain accesses.

On the one hand, the visibility of a user's roles inside its owning domain provides crucial information for other domain administrators to authorize access of the user since the users in OpenStack are not global but identifiable inside each domain. On the other hand, the user owner needs to monitor or constrain the roles assigned to its users in other domains in order to prevent violations of security in multi-domain interoperation [7,18]. In this setting, the collaborating domains should both have control over the cross-domain access instead of only one of them.

Letting the cloud administrator take charge of all cross-domain assignments can solve the visibility issue in Problem a) but the administrative overhead may become overwhelming. Moreover, it is inappropriate for the cloud administrator to be so closely involved in the management within individual domains. To address Problem b), mechanisms that involve both domain administrators should be introduced. For Problem c) we need a rapid means to enable or disable cross-domain assignments for better efficiency. As Problem d) refers, collaborative cross-domain accesses rather than intra-domain accesses need more control related to the authorization.

---

[3] We use "." to represent the ownership relation between projects and domains. For example, *Sales.Production* refers to the *Sales* project in *Production* domain.

Existing Approaches. We have found similar problems in Microsoft Windows Active Directory (AD). An AD, comparable with the identity service in Open-Stack, maintains various types of trust relations to allow users in one domain to access resources in another [3]. But they are not directly applicable in the cloud environment since AD is designed to manage identities for a centralized authority but not decentralized ones like in the cloud.

Currently, OpenStack Keystone supports delegation for users. In particular, a user can delegate a part of his or her permissions to another user through a trust relation. The trustee can impersonate the trustor to perform a subset of the permissions that the trustor has been authorized. Issuing a trust relation does not need involvement of the domain administrators so that Problem b) still exists. In addition, it requires a single user to have all the permissions that the requesting user needs in the target project and limits the capability of cross-domain collaborations.

Amazon Web Service (AWS) allows delegating access across accounts (accounts are comparable to OpenStack domains). By creating a trust relation and associating an assumed role with it, the trustor account authorizes the users from the trustee account to access permissions associated with the assumed role in the trustor account. In this way, cross-account accesses are enabled. However, the trust relation cannot support customized control other than the assumed role or be constrained.

Scope and Assumptions. In this paper we assume that cross-domain authorization only happens in a single cloud. Nevertheless, the model we propose may be extended to federated cloud scenarios. We assume the users in our models are properly authenticated as supported by Keystone. Our discussion and implementation are based on the Havana release of OpenStack [4].

3   OpenStack Access Control Model

In this section, we present the core OpenStack Access Control (OSAC) model based on the OpenStack Identity API v3 [5] which is relatively the latest stable version. Since OpenStack is a rapidly changing system solving practical problems, we feel it impossible and unnecessary to model every feature in OpenStack identity service. Instead, we keep only the core components in the model and formally present how they interplay with each other in the authorization and administration processes. Hence, the term core OpenStack Access Control model. For simplicity we will often omit the core prefix.

Core OSAC. Core OSAC extends the traditional RBAC model [12] to support multi-tenancy. The model elements and relations are defined in Figure 2. OSAC contains eight core entity components: Users (U), Groups (G), Projects (P), Domains (D), Roles (R), Services (S), Operations (O) and Tokens (T). Other entities in the OpenStack Identity API are regarded implementation specific such as credentials, regions and endpoints. Each of the entities has a globally unique

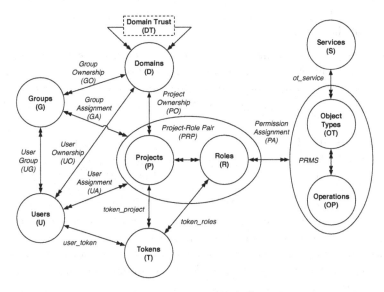

Fig. 2. Core OpenStack Access Control (OSAC) model with domain trust

resource identifier provided by the identity service. The Domain Trust (DT) relationship is shown in dashed lines since it is not currently part of OpenStack but is proposed as an extension in this paper.

Users and Groups. A user represents an individual who can authenticate and access cloud resources. In OpenStack, users are the only consumers of cloud resources. A group is simply a collection of users. Each user or group is owned by one and only one domain. Each group contains only users in its owning domain. Since groups share the nature of users, for convenience reason we understand "users" to mean "users or groups" in the rest of this paper.

Projects. A project is a scope and/or a container of cloud resources. A project manages multiple services and a service segregates its resources into multiple projects. Using a project and a service, we can locate a specific set of resources. For example, the compute service of *Sales.Production* project manages the virtual machine (VM) instances of production applications for the sales department. Each project is owned by one and only one domain.

Domains. A domain is an administrative boundary of users, groups and projects. Domains are mutually exclusive. Each user, group and project belongs to one and only one domain.

Roles. Roles are global names which are used to associate users with any of the projects. A user is assigned a role with respect to a project, in other words to a project-role pair.[4] Users can be authorized permissions only through roles.

---

[4] Users can also be assigned a domain-role pair. This is for administrative usage only and will be discussed in Section 3.

The functions of roles may vary drastically in different services depending on the nature of the service.

Services. A service represents a distributed cloud service. Since OpenStack and most of other cloud systems are designed following service-oriented architecture (SOA) model, cloud applications and resources are delivered to the customers as services. The core service types in OpenStack include compute, image, identity, volume and network.

Object Types and Operations[5]. An object type represents a kind of cloud resources such as VM or image. Each service may provide multiple object types. For example, within the network service, IP and port are different object types. An operation is an access method to the object types. General operations are create, read, update and delete (CRUD) interacting with object types.For example, a typical permission "Delete VM" is a combination of delete operation and VM object type. Note that in cloud environments we cannot specify a particular object in the policy since the objects are created "on-demand". Thus, the finest-grained access control unit is a collection of objects identified by a specific object type and a specific project.

As a role-based authorization model, the central part of OSAC is the assignments related to roles: user assignment (UA), group assignment (GA) and permission assignment (PA) as illustrated in Figure 2. Both groups and users are assigned to project-role pairs but permissions are assigned to roles. As a result, the permissions assigned to a role populates across all the projects. For example, if Dan is assigned a developer role in both *Sales.Development* and *HR.Development*, the permissions available to Dan through the developer role in both projects are identical. This arrangement embodies the multi-tenant nature of cloud resources and provides great flexibility for the assignments as long as the definition of roles is consistent within each service. It is worth noting that user assignments and group assignments are managed centrally in the identity service which permission assignments are distributed into each service.

Tokens. A token represents a subject acting on behalf of a user. A token is issued by the identity service for an authenticated user and then validated by other services whenever the user requests cloud resource accesses. A token may be expired or revoked during its lifetime. The content of a token is encrypted with public key infrastructure (PKI) so that it cannot be altered during transportation. It reveals all the information needed to authorize the access including the accessing user, the target project[6], all the assigned roles in the project[7] and service catalogs. The function *user_tokens* returns the set of tokens that are

---

[5] For clarity, we introduce object types and operations as components of permissions to the OSAC model. There is no specification of these two concepts in the identity service API.

[6] The accessing scope may be project, domain, or even unscoped. For ordinary accesses, a token is scoped to a project

[7] Currently, OpenStack does not support activating an arbitrary subset of roles assigned to a user in the project.

associated with a user, the function *token_project* returns the target project and the function *token_roles* returns the roles assigned to the user in the target project. Typically a user is issued one token for each project. Thus, in a particular project, the permissions available to the user are the permissions assigned to the roles revealed in the correlated token.

We summarize the above in the following definition.

Definition 1. *Core OSAC model has the following components.*

- *U, G, P, D, R, S, OT, OP and T are finite sets of users, groups, projects, domains, roles, services, object types, operations and tokens respectively.*
- *user_owner : $U \to D$, a function mapping a user to its owning domain. Equivalently viewed as a many-to-one relation $UO \subseteq U \times D$.*
- *group_owner : $G \to D$, a function mapping a group to its owning domain. Equivalently viewed as a many-to-one relation $GO \subseteq G \times D$.*
- *project_owner : $P \to D$, a function mapping a project to its owning domain. Equivalently viewed as a many-to-one relation $PO \subseteq P \times D$.*
- *$UG \subseteq U \times G$, a many-to-many relation assigning users to groups where the user and group must be owned by the same domain.*
- *$PRP = P \times R$, the set of project-role pairs.*
- *$PERMS = OT \times OP$, the set of permissions.*
- *ot_service : $OT \to S$, a function mapping an object type to its associated service.*
- *$PA \subseteq PERMS \times R$, a many-to-many permission to role assignment relation.*
- *$UA \subseteq U \times PRP$, a many-to-many user to project-role assignment relation.*
- *$GA \subseteq G \times PRP$, a many-to-many group to project-role assignment relation.*
- *user_tokens : $U \to 2^T$, a function mapping a user to a set of tokens; correspondingly, token_user : $T \to U$, mapping of a token to its owning user.*
- *token_project : $T \to P$, a function mapping a token to its target project.*
- *token_roles : $T \to 2^R$, a function mapping token to its set of roles. Formally, $token\_roles(t) = \{r \in R | (token\_user(t), (token\_project(t), r)) \in UA\} \cup (\bigcup_{g \in user\_groups(token\_user(t))} \{r \in R | (g, (token\_project(t), r)) \in GA\})$.*
- *avail_token_perms : $T \to 2^{PERMS}$, the permissions available to a user through a token, Formally, $avail\_token\_perms(t) = \bigcup_{r \in token\_roles(t)} \{perm \in PERMS | (perms, r) \in PA\}$.*

Role hierarchy (RH) is not supported in OSAC but it could be a reasonable extension for convenience. Depending on operation needs, the hierarchy relation may be added upon roles or to project-role pairs. Both approaches allow specification of role-hierarchy assignments in the centralized identity service while the former also supports distributed assignment since different service may build different structures of role hierarchy as needed. Consideration of these extensions is beyond the scope of this paper.

Administrative OSAC Model. As described previously, the identity information of all the entities including services, domains, users, groups, projects and roles are stored and managed by the Keystone identity service in Open-Stack, as are the assignments associating users and groups with roles in domains or projects. It is worth to note that the permission assignments are separately maintained by each cloud service provider in a policy file. The policy file for the identity service specifies the permissions to manage identities and assignments for administrator roles.

The administrative OSAC (AOSAC) model consists of three levels of administrative roles: *cloud_admin*, *domain_admin* and *project_admin*. As their names indicate, *cloud_admin* refers to top-level administrators with the CSP managing all the information in the identity service; *domain_admin* at the middle-level is able to conduct administrative tasks within the associated domain; and *project_admin* at the bottom-level take the responsibility of managing UA and GA assignments for the associated project. A user can only be assigned to *cloud_admin* role at the installation time of the cloud or by other users with the *cloud_admin* role afterwards. The *domain_admin* and *project_admin* roles are assigned to users by associating the users with the "admin" role in a specific domain or project respectively. Figure 3 illustrates an example administrative role hierarchy in AOSAC.

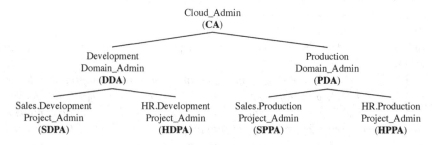

Fig. 3. An example administrative role hierarchy

In the DevOps example described in Section 2, *Development domain_admin* (*DDA*) and *Production domain_admin* (*PDA*) roles are assigned to users owned by each domain respectively. A *PDA* can list and view users, groups and projects in *Production*. He or she can also assign roles, including the "admin" role, in a project of *Production* to a user. A *Sales.Production project_admin* (*SPPA*) can assign roles other than the "admin" role in *Sales.Production* to a user. Note that a *PDA* or a *SPPA* can assign *Dennis@Development* to the "developer" role in *Sales.Production*. As a result, DevOps cross-domain accesses may be authorized. However, the administrative boundary of the two domains are intersected with each other. This may lead to unwanted authorization in cross-domain collaboration, such as the DevOps example.

4   Domain Trust Model

In order to achieve additional control for cross-domain accesses, we propose domain trust models integrating with the OSAC model. From the description in the previous sections, we observe that domains are introduced as administrative boundaries. Bridging domains using trust relations gives a controlled way to allow cross-boundary collaborations. For a user to have roles in a project, a proper trust relation needs to be established between the owning domains of the user and the project.

Domain Trust Relation. The definitions of trust relations vary in different application scenarios. In the field of access control, either explicit or implicit trust relation is essential to decentralized authorization [9]. Thus, in order to properly authorize cross-domain accesses, we have to specify what a trust relation means and how the trust relation interacts with the existing access control model.

Trust is a complicated concept and has been treated in different ways in the context of access control. The following is a list of characteristics related to domain trust relations. Figure 4 depicts the potential combinations.

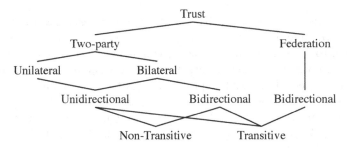

Fig. 4. A tree structure showing characteristics of domain trust relation

Protocol (Two-party vs Federation). Two-party trust is established between two domains. A federation trust exists in an alliance or cooperative association in which a participant that is a domain trusts each other participants and it is also true in return.

Initiation (Bilateral vs Unilateral). When the trustor creates a trust relation, if the trustee is required to confirm, then the trust relation is regarded as bilateral otherwise unilateral. It is worth to note that transferring a unilateral trust relation to a bilateral one is much easier than doing the reverse.

Direction (Bidirectional vs Unidirectional). A bidirectional trust relation requires the actions enabled through the trust relation are equally available for the trustor and the trustee. Conversely, a unidirectional trust, as the name refers, requires availability of the actions only on one side.

Transitivity (Transitive vs Non-transitive). For domain A, B and C, if A trusts B and B trusts C it is implied that A trusts C, then the trust relation is transitive. Otherwise, the trust relation is non-transitive.

In this paper, the domain trust relation is specified as an two-party, unilateral, unidirectional and non-transitive relation. Moreover, it is reflexive meaning each domain trusts itself. It is functionally defined as the following.

Definition 2. *If and only if Domain A trusts Domain B, also written as "A ⊴ B", A or B can perform unidirectional cross-domain authorization.*

The actions enabled through a domain trust relation depend on the trust types defined as follows.

Definition 3. *Based on collaborative access control needs, the domain trust relation described in Definition 2 can be categorized into three useful types.*

- **Type-α**, *requires visibility of the trustee's user information for the trustor to assign trustee's users to roles in trustor's projects, written as "$\unlhd_\alpha$".*
- **Type-β**, *requires the trustor to expose its user information for the trustee to assign trustor's users to roles in trustee's projects, written as "$\unlhd_\beta$".*
- **Type-γ**, *requires the trustor to expose its project information for the trustee to assign trustee's users to roles in trustor's projects, written as "$\unlhd_\gamma$".*

Type-α Trust is used implicitly in current OpenStack since the trustor *domain_admin* and *project_admin* can see the users in all the domains and assign them to roles in the trustor's projects. Type-α Trust is only useful when user related information is not sensitive and available across domains by default. In contrast, Type-β Trust and Type-γ Trust protect user information as sensitive property of each domain. Both of them require dual control. In particular, the trustor manages the trust relation while the trustee manages cross-domain authorization. In this way, cross-domain accesses can be revoked by either end of the trust relation.

OSAC Domain Trust Since we have specifically defined the domain trust relation above, integrating it with OSAC becomes straightforward. The formal definition of the OSAC Domain Trust (OSAC-DT) model follows.

Definition 4. *The OSAC-DT model extends the OSAC model in Definition 1 with the following modifications.*

- *DT $\subseteq$ D $\times$ D, a many-to-many trust relation on D, also written as "$\unlhd$".*
- *UA is modified to require that $(u, (p, r)) \in UA$ only if*
  $project\_owner(p) \equiv user\_owner(u) \lor project\_owner(p) \unlhd_\alpha user\_owner(u) \lor$
  $user\_owner(u) \unlhd_\beta project\_owner(p) \lor project\_owner(p) \unlhd_\gamma user\_owner(u).$
- *GA is modified to require that $(g, (p, r)) \in GA$ only if*
  $project\_owner(p) \equiv group\_owner(g) \lor project\_owner(p) \unlhd_\alpha group\_owner(g)$
  $\lor \quad group\_owner(g) \quad \unlhd_\beta \quad project\_owner(p) \lor project\_owner(p) \quad \unlhd_\gamma$
  $group\_owner(g).$

The modification focuses on the effect of the domain trust relation introduced. Particularly, the project owner has to trust the user owner for *UA* and *GA* to take effect. The trust relation is checked during both authorization time and accessing time so that if it is revoked the correlated cross-domain accesses may be automatically or manually revoked depending upon implementation.

OSAC-DT allows the three types of trust relations to coexist with each other. A specific cross-domain UA or GA is effective as long as the trust relation between the user or group and the project domains satisfy the condition described in Definition 4. In fact, combining Type-α and Type-β trusts we achieve a bilateral trust relation. For example, only if both $Production \trianglelefteq_\alpha Development$ and $Development \trianglelefteq_\beta Production$ exists, then cross-domain authorization by $Production$ is enabled.

By introducing explicit domain trust relation, the following constraints may be enforced over cross-domain authorization.

Separation of Duties (SoD). Some of the collaborations among domains may have conflict of interests which should be addressed by additional constraint policy and lists of mutually exclusive domains.

Minimum Exposure. In collaboration, the over-exposure of user or project information increases security and privacy risks. An effective solution is limiting exposure of information based on each domain or each trust requirements.

Cardinality. A domain may limit the number of domains to be trusted. For example, some domains , such as $Production$, require high-level security and allow only one trusted domain at a time for temporary access if necessary.

The constraints listed above and a lot more are previously not available without domain trust relations.

Domain Trust Administration. The administrative OSAC-DT (AOSAC-DT) model extends the AOSAC model by the administration of domain trust relations and their enabled actions. Since the trust relation is unilateral, only the *cloud_admin* the *domain_admin* of the trustor and have permission to create and revoke a specific domain trust relation. The trust relation enables the *project_admin* and *domain_admin* of the trustor, in case of Type-α trust, or the trustee, in case of Type-β trust or Type-γ trust, to view the user or project information necessary for them to make cross-domain authorization.

5   Prototype and Evaluation in OpenStack

To further explore the feasibility of our OSAC-DT model, we implement a prototype system based on the Havana release of Keystone source code [4]. Furthermore, we conduct experiments on the prototype system in terms of performance and scalability. The results turn out to be convincing that the integrated domain trust introduces minimum authorization overhead.

Implementation Overview. The architecture of our prototype follows the Keystone design. The domain trust verification process intercepts the authentication process. Before Keystone issues the token for a requesting user, the domain trust relations stored in the MySQL database are checked. Only if the requesting user's owning domain is trusted by the target project's owning domain, then the token issuing process can go through. Otherwise, an "unauthorized" response will be returned. For proof of concept purpose, we implement only Type-γ trust in the prototype system. It is straightforward to extend the implementation other types of domain trust relations discussed in Section 4 and similar evaluation results are predicted because the domain trust verification processes are similar.

Evalutation. The implementation and experiments are conducted in experimental Devstack [2] deployments in a private cloud. The core OpenStack services, including Keystone, are running on a single VM. The requesting clients are from the same data center network of the private cloud. Since only Keystone code is modified, the experiments focus on evaluating the token issuing process including sequential processes of authentication, domain trust verification, token composition and network transmission, etc.

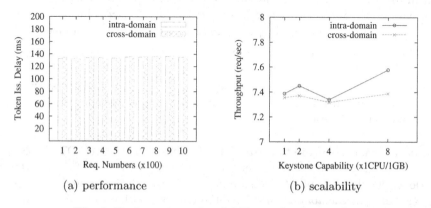

(a) performance   (b) scalability

Fig. 5. Performance and scalability evaluation results

The experiments simulate sequential token requests for one-hundred users and projects owned by ten independent domains. Each user is associated with both intra-domain and cross-domain assignments through ten different roles. As Figure 5a shows, the x-axis represents the requests per user and the y-axis indicates the latency between request time and response time from the client end, also known as the token issuing delay. Comparing the token issuing delay of intra-domain and cross-domain access requests, the domain trust verification process costs 0.96 ms on average or 0.7% performance overhead which is acceptable.

Figure 5b presents the results for scalability tests on our prototype system. The x-axis represents the capability of the VM running Devstack in the unit of "1CPU/1GB RAM". The y-axis is the calculated throughput for the token issuing process. The plotted diagram shows that with ten requests per user, the throughput increase of the prototype system is proportional to the increase of the capability of Keystone servers from 1 unit to 8 units so that the system is scalable and adding the domain trust does not cause scalability problem.

6   Related Work

Role-Based Access Control (RBAC) [12] is a dominant model in single organization scenarios. ROBAC [24], one of the RBAC extensions, is able to manage authorization for multiple organizations, comparable to domains, but collaboration among organizations are not allowed. GB-RBAC [15] supports collaboration among groups. Yet, the group admin can not manage the users inside the group which is different with domains in OpenStack. More importantly, most of RBAC extensions need a centralized authority to administer each collaboration. In the cloud environment, the centralized authority is the cloud service provider (CSP) who is inappropriate and incapable to manage all the collaborations.

Role-based delegation models [8,13,14,23] are designed to solve collaboration problems. However, the chained delegation relations are not flexible enough. Since the entities in the cloud are created on-demand and deleted afterwards, any node of the chain may disappear resulting in void delegation. Comparing to OSAC-DT, the trust relation is always created and maintained by the trustor and non-transitive so that the management of trust relations is simple.

Secure multi-domain interoperation solutions [19,18] leverage role mapping techniques between domains to facilitate interoperation. Role mapping is a form of role hierarchy linking roles across domains. But it cannot be integrated with OpenStack since role hierarchy is not supported. Even if role hierarchy can be established, as we discussed in the OSAC model, role-mapping will not function until the PA becomes project-specific or domain-specific. In OSAC-DT, the trust relations is on domains and only affects UA and GA which are project-specific. Authorization services [6,11,16] in the Grid leverage decentralized trust management [9]. In order to establish collaboration, maintaining credentials between nodes becomes a huge performance overhead which could be avoided in the Cloud by the centralized identity service.

OSAC-DT is closely related to the models like MTAS [10,22], MT-RBAC [20] and CTTM [21]. OSAC-DT differs in its compatibility with the OpenStack Identity API v3. Further, the administrative model also merges with the OpenStack Keystone management. Ray et al [17] propose a formal trust-based delegation model solving similar problems in mobile cloud environment. However, the calculated trust relation is inappropriate and unnecessary between domains in OpenStack since domains have the authority to assign trust relations with each other.

7   Conclusion

In this paper, we present a formalized OpenStack access control model from which we propose a domain-trust extension to better facilitate the decentralized authorization for cross-domain collaborations. There are three useful types of OpenStack-specific domain trust relations, intuitive trust, user-aware trust and project-aware trust, applicable to various collaboration needs. Further, we implement a proof of concept prototype system with project-aware trust based on Keystone Havana release source code. The experiment results show that the integrated domain trust model is acceptable in both performance and scalability.

Acknowledgement. Sincere gratitude is hereby extended to the following. Farhan Patwa, director of ICS, for his patient help on the OpenStack implementation and active connections with the OpenStack community. Dolph Mathews, PTL of Keystone, for his reviews on the preliminary OSAC model and the domain trust blueprint. Dr. Jaehong Park, research associate professor of ICS, for his insights and comments leading to improvement of the OSAC model. This work is partially supported by grants from the National Science Foundation and AFOSR MURI program.

References

1. DevOps, http://en.wikipedia.org/wiki/DevOps
2. Devstack, http://www.devstack.org
3. Microsoft windows active directory,
   http://en.wikipedia.org/wiki/Active_Directory
4. OpenStack Havana Release, http://www.openstack.org/software/havana
5. Openstack identity service api v3 (stable),
   http://developer.openstack.org/api-ref-identity-v3.html
6. Alfieri, R., Cecchini, R., et al.: From gridmap-file to VOMS: managing authorization in a grid environment. Future Generation Computer Systems 21(4), 549–558 (2005)
7. Baracaldo, N., Masoumzadeh, A., Joshi, J.: A secure, constraint-aware role-based access control interoperation framework. In: Proc. of the 5th International Conference on Network and System Security (NSS), pp. 200–207. IEEE (2011)
8. Barka, E., Sandhu, R.: Framework for role-based delegation models. In: Proc. of the Annual Conf. on Comp. Sec. Applications (ACSAC), pp. 168–176. IEEE (2000)
9. Blaze, M., Feigenbaum, J., Lacy, J.: Decentralized trust management. In: Proc. of the 1996 IEEE Symp. on Security and Privacy, pp. 164–173. IEEE (1996)
10. Calero, J.M.A., Edwards, N., et al.: Toward a multi-tenancy authorization system for cloud services. IEEE Security & Privacy, 48–55 (November/December 2010)
11. Chadwick, D.W., Otenko, A.: The PERMIS X. 509 role based privilege management infrastructure, vol. 19, pp. 277–289. Elsevier (2003)
12. Ferraiolo, D.F., Sandhu, R., Gavrila, S., Kuhn, D.R., Chandramouli, R.: Proposed NIST standard for role-based access control. TISSEC 4(3), 224–274 (2001)
13. Freudenthal, E., Pesin, T., et al.: dRBAC: distributed role-based access control for dynamic coalition environments. In: Proc. of ICDCS, pp. 411–420. IEEE (2002)
14. Li, N., Mitchell, J.C., et al.: Design of a role-based trust-management framework. In: Proc. of IEEE Symp. on Sec. and Privacy, pp. 114–130. IEEE (2002)
15. Li, Q., Zhang, X., Xu, M., Wu, J.: Towards secure dynamic collaborations with group-based RBAC model. Computers & Security 28(5), 260–275 (2009)
16. Pearlman, L., Welch, V., Foster, I., et al.: A community authorization service for group collaboration. In: Proc. of Intl. POLICY, pp. 50–59. IEEE (2002)
17. Ray, I., Mulamba, D., Ray, I., Han, K.J.: A model for trust-based access control and delegation in mobile clouds. In: Wang, L., Shafiq, B. (eds.) DBSec 2013. LNCS, vol. 7964, pp. 242–257. Springer, Heidelberg (2013)
18. Shafiq, B., Joshi, J.B., Bertino, E., Ghafoor, A.: Secure interoperation in a multidomain environment employing RBAC policies. IEEE Transactions on Knowledge and Data Engineering 17(11), 1557–1577 (2005)

19. Shehab, M., Bertino, E., Ghafoor, A.: SERAT: SEcure role mApping technique for decentralized secure interoperability. In: Proc. of SACMAT, pp. 159–167 (2005)
20. Tang, B., Li, Q., Sandhu, R.: A multi-tenant RBAC model for collaborative cloud services. In: Proc. of IEEE Conf. on Privacy, Security and Trust, PST (2013)
21. Tang, B., Sandhu, R.: Cross-tenant trust models in cloud computing. In: Proc. of IEEE Conf. on Information Reuse and Integration, IRI (2013)
22. Tang, B., Sandhu, R., Li, Q.: Multi-tenancy authorization models for collaborative cloud services. In: Proc. of Intl. Conf. on Collab. Tech. and Sys., CTS (2013)
23. Zhang, X., Oh, S., Sandhu, R.: PBDM: a flexible delegation model in RBAC. In: Proc. of SACMAT, pp. 149–157. ACM (2003)
24. Zhang, Z., Zhang, X., Sandhu, R.: ROBAC: Scalable role and organization based access control models. In: Proc. of CollaborateCom, pp. 1–9. IEEE (2006)

Hierarchical Solution for Access Control
and Authentication in Software Defined Networks

He Shuangyu, Liu Jianwei, Mao Jian, and Chen Jie

School of Electronics and Information Engineering
Beihang University, Beijing, China, 100191
adgj11005@163.com

Abstract. Software defined network(SDN) one of most popular and influential technique is an emerging network architecture. It has attracted great attention to reform its performance and extend its applications in recent years. Although this new architecture provides all parties with a common programming environment to drive differentiation, almost all studies focus on efficiency and utility. Few efforts have been made to enforce authentications or access control in SDN. In this paper, we propose a hierarchical attribute-based access control scheme by incorporating the hierarchical identity based encryption and cipher-policy attribute based encryption(CP-ABE) system. Combing the hierarchical structure and the characteristic inherited from CP-ABE, the prosed scheme gains not only scalability, but also flexibility and fine-gained access control. Based on this we then present an authentication protocol for this special architecture to enhance the ability of controllers in SDN for managing the users, devices and data flows flexibly.

Keywords: SDN, authentication, access control.

1   Introduction

Software defined network (SDN) is a new network architecture introduced by Nick McKeown [1]   in 2008. Since then, SDN has been one of the most influential paradigms in the IT industry. It has attracted abundant attention from both the academia and industry. SDN inherits the concept of ForCES [2] in which the control plat and the data plat are decoupled. So the design not only benefits network operators from reducing the cast of devices, but also benefits administrators of the whole network domain from increasing the convenience of configuring huge numbers of devices from different equipment manufacturers. Numerous commercial Internet companies take part in the wave of developing SDN, such as Google's B4 [3], Cisco's NFV [4], Huawei's Carrier SDN.

Although SDN has brought the great advantages interesting IT companies, academic researchers, network operators and potential network access users, the security problem of SDN become serious obstacles for its wide development. If no suitable solutions are presented, there is no doubt that the problems will prevent the SDN's wide deployment and usage in future. One of the most significant security

M.H. Au et al. (Eds.): NSS 2014, LNCS 8792, pp. 70–81, 2014.

threats in SDN network is that how to prevent the network statistics traffics data from being stolen by attacker due to its remote management. Compared with traditional architecture, the unique component controller collects and stores the status and traffic data that open APIs can invoke easily. Flow data contain user's information, such as user's habit of surfing Internet, contacts user frequently emailed, place where they stay, which will lead to a victim of spam. Thus, SDN controller should ensure that the sensitive information should be offered only to the ones who are authorized, but in fact open APIs can offer the common information to the public.

In addition to data confidentiality requirement for controller, flexible and fine-grained access control is also important to protect user's information in SDN's overall objectives. However, the access control described in Ethane, which is regard as the prototype of SDN, shows its short for managing access users accurately and efficiently. Traditional authentication technique always needs only one factor, such as password, certificate, fingerprint, and so on. Unfortunately, it can hardly predict the behaviors after the user access in. Once a bug of system is found, a malicious user may have chance to bypass access control policy to gain sensitive information or use network resources illegally.

In this paper, we propose a new authentication with a hierarchical attributed based encryption in order to achieve security and flexible goals for the components in the SDN network. Our scheme enforces the authorization verification during the process of authentication to ensure the user can't obtain the unauthorized information or illegal network resources.

In summary, the contribution of our work is described as follow:

- We propose a hierarchical attribute-based encryption(HABE) for software defined network, incorporating the hierarchical Identity-based encryption and CP-ABE to improve scalability and flexibility of access control for secure SDN. The size of the ciphertext is only growing with the number of attribute in access control policy In our scheme, one can encrypt or decrypt messages with the attributes keys distributed by different domain authority. It is easy to share messages to the members in different domains. Because multiple domain authorities may administrate the attributes in an access control policy, one can form fine-grained control policy and share the messages to the members in different domains easily.
- We demonstrate an authentication protocol based on our HABE scheme for SDN network. The protocol can provide the support of the fine-grained access control and users' information protection. Comparing with the traditional protocols, user in ours' network has the right to choose he prefer to, our scheme also distributes the burden of the access server to deployed controllers.

Paper organization: The rest of the paper is organized as follows. Section II presents the overview of related work. The system model and security assumption are shown in section III. In section IV, we describe our HABE scheme and present how to use it to improve the security in SDN network. In section V, the whole authentication protocol based on the scheme we present before is proposed in detail. Then in section VI, we analysis the security of our protocol and the computation complexity of the scheme and evaluate the performance of the protocol.

2   Related Work

Although this new structure has the advantages of efficient network and flexible reconfiguration, the security problems is still blocking the development of SDN.

Ethane[8], an early form of SDN, provides a model of user access and management, while the user management is so simple that can hardly satisfy the necessary security requirement for large scale deployment. For enhancing the security between controller and applications, IETF in [5]clearly point out the solution to enable multiple organizations to access network resources by using authorization and authentication mechanism. However not all applications need same network privilege and it is no doubt that traditional schemes lead to a complex access control policy and huge waste of storage space of credentials. In current openflow specification [6] security channel established by transport layer security protocol (TLS) provide mutual authentication between controller and switch can reduce the threat that attacker disguises as controller and carry out malicious activities. The authentication with TLS in SDN may provide necessary security in the scenario that single controller administrate the whole network. While unfortunately, multiple controllers will also get into as the same trouble as the solution above in a huge network and this security measure is optional not compulsory. In[7], the author found that the leak of using security mechanism would lead to fraudulent rule insertion and rule modification.

Since Lamport first proposed a password authentication protocol in 1981, there are thousands of the authentication protocol for users' access has been presented based on password [10][11], trusted platform module[12][13], credentials and smart card. With the change of the network structure, controller in SDN possesses partial function of authentication severs and bears the responsibility of access control that raises a question whether the existing protocols can be adopted to this new structure to efficiently verify and manage the entity in network. Until now, in our view, there have been no new security protocols for this novel structure.

ABE scheme is a new encryption system associated with an access control policy. Some ABE schemes [14][15][16][17] can be tracked back to Identity-based encryption. Since Sahai and Waters first introduced the attribute-based encryption [18], several authors have proposed different encryption schemes almost of which can be classify into two categories. One is so-called key-policy attribute based encryption (KP-ABE)[14] and the other is ciphertext-policy attribute based encryption(CP-ABE)[15]. The difference between KP-ABE and CP-ABE is the way that the access control structure associated with private key or cipher text. In other words, in KP-ABE, the user's decryption key is associated with the access structure when key generates and the ciphertext is associated to a set of attributes. Only when the attributes satisfied the access structure the user can decrypt the cipher text. Nevertheless, in CP-ABE the roles of key and ciphertext will be exchange. So comparing with the KP-ABE, CP-ABE is more scalable, because in CP-ABE encryptors can arbitrary decide who has the right to decrypt the messages, while in KP-ABE encryptors can just encrypt messages for some specific ones.

Although ABE schemes provide a fine-grained access control which other encryption system can't support, a single authority may be overload or inefficient and causing the dilemma of the key escrow. In a real world application, considering the attribute key size which is naturally larger than the traditional private key and the security of the authority, distributed system seems to be more suitable. Wang et al [19] proposed hierarchical attribute encryption first for cloud storage that supports fine-grained access control and fully delegation. The scheme uses the disjunctive form policy and demand that the attributes for encrypting should be administrated by the same domain master. Zhi et al [20]. Proposed another HABE scheme called HASBE using the technique of attribute-set which an extended form of CP-ABE manage user's attributes into a recursive set structure. Attributes in a recursive set can be combined easily. However, attributes in different sets need translating from one to another.

3   System Model

As described in Fig.1, the whole system consists of five components: series of SDN controllers, access servers, users and network devices, a trusted authority and a number of domain authorities. The structure that inherits from the Onix [9] is shown in Fig.1.

System structure. The controllers manage users' access requests and network flows and meanwhile dispose sensitive information producing by users, devices, or themselves. The access servers generate the authentication elements to controllers for user access when user finishes its register to servers. A domain authority that is administrated by its parent authority or supervised by trust authority will administrate all parts above in one domain immediately. All these five components are deployed in the hierarchical structure as shown in Fig 1. We assume that no matter root authority or domain authority is trusted and always online. The controller is not completely honest some of which may be apocryphal by malignant for stealing the users' privacy. Moreover, the devices or access users are also untrusted who may want to bypass the access control to achieve honest users' data illegally or use extra network resources without authorization.

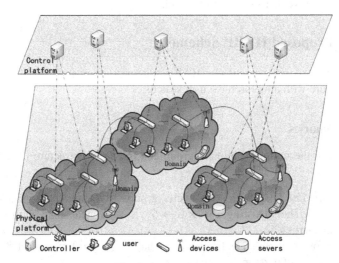

Fig. 1. System Structure

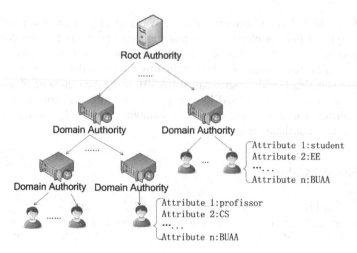

Fig. 2. HABE System model

HABE system model. Simplifying the system model, the HABE model that gets together the advantages of HIBE and ABE is shown in Fig 2. Root authority generates the system params and is charged of managing the lower –layer domain authorities. According to the delegated key delivered from its upper-layer and the system params, the domain authority that acts the role as PKG in HIBE and AA in CP-ABE creates and distributes user attribute key and has responsibility to deliver the delegated key to next domain authority. In our HABE model, the domain can be not only large as a campus network but also small as a single-family network. In the model, the domain authority is marked with a unique ID and a user is represented by a set of attributes that is also named by attribute identity. As HIBE, the domain authority extracts the user's private key and users' ID-tuple consisting of its own identity and the ID-tuple of the domain authority reveals its position in model.

4   The Proposed HABE Scheme

In this section, we first present our HABE scheme, which is suitable to the SDN network structure with a hierarchical user structure.

4.1   Preliminaries

We brief review the notion of bilinear group and the access structure [21] we use in our scheme.

1. Bilinear map: Let G, G1 are two cyclic groups of prime order p, and g be a generator of G.Then existing $e: G \times G \to G_1$ is a bilinear map with these two following properties"
2. Bilinearity: for all $u, v \in G$ and a, b $\in$ Z, we have $e(u^a, v^b) = e(u, v)^{ab}$;
3. Non-degeneracy: $e(g, g) \neq 1$.

We define that G is a bilinear group if the group action in G and a bilinear map e with the existing group G1 can be both computed efficiently.

Linear Secret-Sharing Scheme (LSSS[21]): Secret-sharing scheme Π over a set of parties $\mathcal{P}$ is called linear if:

1. The share for each party form a vector over $\mathbb{Z}_p$;
2. There exists a matrix an M with ℓ rows and n columns called the share-generating matrix for Π. For all i=1,......,ℓ,the i'th row of M we let the function ρ defined the party labeling row i as $\rho(i)$.When we consider the column vector v=(s,r2,...,rn), where $s \in \mathbb{Z}_p$ is the secret to be shared, and $r_2, ..., r_n \in \mathbb{Z}_p$ are random chosen, then Mv is the vector of ℓ shares of the secret s according to Π. The share (Mv)i belong to party $\rho(i)$.

The linear secret sharing-scheme according to the above definition also enjoys linear reconstruction property that is defined as follow: Assuming that Π is an LSSS for an access structure$\mathbb{A}$.S $\in \mathbb{A}$ is any authorized set, and $I \subset \{1,2, ... , \ell\}$ is defined as $I = \{i: \rho(i) \in S\}$. Then, there exist constants $\{w_i \in \mathbb{Z}_p\}_{i \in I}$, such that if$\{\lambda i\}$ are available shares of the secret s, then existing $\sum_{i \in I} w_i \lambda_i = s$. The constants$\{w_i \in \mathbb{Z}_p\}_{i \in I}$ can be found in time polynomial in the size of the matrix M.

4.2   Our Scheme

We now propose our HABE scheme detailly with the operations as follow: System Setup, Create DA, create User.

System Setup. The root authority runs setup algorithm to generate system public parameters PP, and system master key MK_0.The PK may be public later and the MK_0 should be keep secret.

Setup(ℓ) $\to$ (MK_0 , PP). The input parameter ℓ for the setup algorithm is the depth of HABE structure. Then algorithm selects a bilinear group G of prime order p with the generator g and let $e: G \times G \to G_1$ be a bilinear map. Then pick random elements$g_2, g_3, h_1, ..., h_\ell \in G$.Finally compute the system master key$MK_0 = g_2^\alpha \in G$. The algorithm set the public parameters and the master key as follow:

$$PP = \{p, G, G_1, e, g, g_2, g_3, h_1, ..., h_\ell\}$$

$$MK_0 = g_2^\alpha$$

CreateDA: (PP,MK_{k-1})$\to$*(MK_k).*This algorithm is used to generate the master for the domain authority by its parent authority. When a domain authority which is associated with an ID and an attribute set wants to join in the system, its upper authority first check whether it is the legal authority and the attribute set it provided is valid. Then according the public parameters, the upper authority runs createDA algorithm. Assuming that the new domain authority is in the level k with an ID= {I1, I2,...,Ik}, its parent node according its own master key:

$$SK_k= \{g_2^\alpha \cdot (h_1^{ID1} ... h_{k-1}^{ID_{k-1}} \cdot g_3)^r, g^r, h_k^r, ..., h_\ell^r\}=\{a_0, a_1, b_1, ..., b_\ell\};$$

Choose a random number $t \in G_p^*$, and compute :

$$SK_k = \{a_0' = a_0 \cdot b_k^{ID_k} \cdot (h_1^{ID_1} \ldots h_k^{ID_k} \cdot g_3)^t, \; a_1' = a_1 \cdot g^t,$$

$$b_{k+1}' = b_{k+1} \cdot h_{k+1}^t, \ldots, \; b_\ell' = b_\ell \cdot h_\ell^t \};$$

Finally output the SKk to the authority in k'th level.

CreateUser: $(PP, MK_k, \mathbb{A}_u.) \rightarrow (SK_u, a)$. For the attribute A_{DMi} in set $\mathbb{A}_{DM}$ administrated by the domain authority, domain authority choose a random $\beta_{atti} \in \mathbb{z}_p$ as private key for attribute i and compute $PK_{A_{DMi}} = g_i = g^{\beta_{atti}} \in G$ as the attribute's public key. When a new user donated u with an attribute set $\mathbb{A}_u$ wants to join in the system, the domain authority that is supposed to generate the decryption key to him will also firstly check if the user is eligible for the attribute Ai in $\mathbb{A}_u$ and if the Ai is under its administration. For a legal user, the domain authority then runs CreateUser(PP, MK_k, $\mathbb{A}_u$) to generate the user's decryption key. The algorithm chooses a unique random number $r_u \in \mathbb{z}_p$, for each attribute Aui $\in \mathbb{A}_u$, it compute every part of user's decryption key as follow:

$$SK_{u,A_{ui}} = g_2^{\beta_{atti}} g_2^{\alpha} \cdot (h_1^{ID_1} \ldots h_k^{ID_k} \cdot g_3)^{r+r_u}$$

Then the whole decryption for user with the attribute $\mathbb{A}_u$ output as:

$$SK_{u,\mathbb{A}_u} = \{SK_{u,A_{ui}}, g^{r+r_u}\}_{A_{ui} \in \mathbb{A}_u}.$$

Encryption: $(PK_{A_{ui}}, M, ID_{DM}, (A, \rho)) \rightarrow CT$. the encryption algorithm take an LSSS access structure (A, ρ) in which A is an $n \times m$ matrix and $\rho(x)$ is associated the x'th row of M to denote attributes in access structure. Then the domain selects a random $s \in Z_p$, and generates a random vector $\vec{v} = \{s, r_1, \ldots r_n\}$ of which s is the first element. Let $\lambda_x = A_x \cdot \vec{v}$ where A_x denotes the row x of A. In addition, we choose another random vector $\vec{w} = \{0, z_1, \ldots z_n\}$ and let $w_x = A_x \cdot \vec{w}$. For each attribute Aux denoted as $\rho(x)$ in A, encryptor select a random number $Rx \in Z_p$, and finally output the ciphertext C as follow:

$$\{CT = M \cdot e(g, g)^s, \; C_{1,x} = e(g, g)^{\lambda_x}/(e(g_1, g_2)^{R_x} \cdot e(g_{\rho(x)}, g_2)^{R_x}),$$
$$C_{2,x} = (h_1^{ID_1} \ldots h_k^{ID_k} \cdot g_3)^{R_x}, C_{3,x} = g^{R_x} \cdot g^{W_x}) , \; \ldots\ldots, (C_{1,n}, C_{2,n}, C_{3,n})\}$$

Decryption: $(SK_{u,\mathbb{A}_u}, C) \rightarrow M$. Assuming that the received ciphertext C is encrypted with the access structure and the user's private key is satisfied the access structure. For each attribute A_{ux} in user's private keys compute:

$$C_{1,x} \cdot e\left(SK_{u.A_{\rho(x)}}, C_{3,x}\right)/e(C_{2,x}, g^{r+r_u}) = e(g, g)^{\lambda_x} \cdot e(SK_{u.A_{\rho(x)}}, g)^{W_x}$$

Then the decryptor chooses constants $C_x \in Z_p$ which leading to the equation $\sum_x c_x A_x = \{1, 0, \ldots .0\}$; finally, compute:

$$\Pi_x \left(e(g, g)^{\lambda_x} \cdot e\left(SK_{u.A_{\rho(x)}}, g\right)^{W_x}\right)^{C_x} = e(g, g)^s;$$

To receive message M by computing CT/ $e(g, g)^s$.

Observe that: as it has been described above that $\ddot{e}_x = A_x \cdot \vec{v}, W_x = A_x \cdot \vec{W}$ so according to the theory of LSSS the equation:

$$\sum \lambda_x \cdot C_x = \sum A_x \cdot \vec{V} \cdot C_x = s$$

and $\sum W_x \cdot C_x = \sum A_x \cdot \vec{W} \cdot C_x = 0$ are set up.

5   The Proposed Authentication Protocol for SDN with HABE

In this section, we use our scheme to change the traditional way that verifying authorization is always after user's authentication by checking the user's authorization and identity at same time. It is benefited from avoiding unauthorized user to access network resources illegally and providing a fine-grained access control. The protocol is setup in two stages: the first is register and the last one is authentication.

Register

If one who wants to join in a network is a new user for the whole network, he should register first. Firstly the applicant set up its password denoted by pwd; and then select a random $R \in z_p$ cascading after the pwd; and then run hash function H: $\{0,1\}^* \rightarrow \{0,1\}^n$ to compute H(pwd||R).Finally send his request message M={ID_u, H(pwd||R)} to one of access servers by a security channel.

When the access server receives the application, it should check the legality of the qualification of applicant. After that severs also pick up a random number R_u in group z_p compute the messages: $M_u=H(ID_u^{R_u})$, $M_0=g_1^{H(pwd||R)*M_u}$. The M_u is sent back to the application and M_c which is consist of M_0 and H(ID_u) is forwarded to SDN controllers which is authorized to finish authentication with the attribute of authentication for following steps and drop the random Ru. In fact work of the access servers is over; following operation for authentication can be finished by communication between user and authorized controller.

Authentication

(1) After finishing register, when user tries to access the network, the user first choose a random $R_c \in Z_p$, compute $M_{c0}=e(g_1,g_2)^{H(pwd||R)Rc}$, $M_{c1}=g_2^{H(pwd||R)}$, $M_{c2}=g_1^{Mu+Rc}$, $h = H(M_{c0}||M_{c1}||M_{c2}||H(ID))$ .Then user will select the access structure A that he wants the attributes of the controller to be satisfied and utilize HABE encryption we proposed above to encrypted the authentication message C_1: {H(ID),M_{c1}, M_{c2},h}.

(2) The controller will respond the requirement, if it can be able to decrypt the message. Let $q=\frac{e(M_{c2},M_{c1})}{e\ (M_0,g_2)}$ and $h_1 = H(q||M_{c1}||M_{c2}||H(ID))$.Compared h_1 with h_2, if $h_1 \neq h_2$ which means that the applicant provide error messages, controller interrupt the communication. Otherwise, controller then chooses a random $R_r \in Z_p$ and then compute $h_2 = H(H(H(ID)||q||M_{c1}||M_{c2})||M_{r_0})$ and $M_{r_0} = e(g_1,g_2)^{Rr}$.Finally, the controller try to match a suitable access control policy for user and encrypt the responding message C_2: {M_{r_0}, h_2} with the access structure that user's attributes should be satisfied according to that policy.

(3) In the next step, after the user decrypted the response message he will compute the hash value h_3= H(H(H(ID)||M_{c0}||M_{c1}||M_{c2})|M_{r_0}) . And judge whether the

equation: $h3=h_2$ is true. If so, user compute $h_4=H$ (H (ID) $\|h_3$) and encrypt this message by the way we introduced in step (1) which then is delivered to the controller.

(4) The final step: Once the message is decrypted, the controller compare the computed value $h_5=H(H(ID)\|h_2)$ with the received value. When the result of comparing is equal, the whole authentication is finished or it will interrupt by controller. In addition, both of them also can agree the session key between user and controller by computing $H(M_{r_0}^{H(pwd\|R)*Rc}\|C1\|C2)$ for user and $H(M_{c0}^{Rr}\|C1\|C2)$ for controller.

6   Security and Performance Analysis

6.1   security Analysis of the Protocol

Inner attack. In this protocol the password store in severs is hashed combing a random number R which for severs is unknown. In case that the register messages in severs are revealed, adversary can only get the information about H(ID) and M_0 which is used for verify user's identity. Nevertheless, he has no chance to recover the password because only the user knows the random number R and the hash value $H(pwd\|R)$ and random R_u will be dropped once the user has finished register.

Replay attack. After listening to the communication between controller and legal user, the attacker replay the login message to try to pass the authentication process. If the attacker never owns as same attributes as the victim to satisfy the access structure made by the controller, he has no way to encryption the message from controller. In case the attacker's attributes happen to satisfy the controller's access structure leading to encrypting the message, in the case of unknown the secret value Rc, it is scarcely possible that the attacker can compute the value of h4. For controller, it is easy to find a replay attack by comparing the hash value h4 with h5. In the same way, users can also distinguish the replay attack easily by comparing the value h3 with h2.

Man in middle attack. In this type attack, the attacker interrupts the communication between severs and users and try to replace the messages for cheating sever of regarding him as a legal user or acting as sever to user. In our protocol, if the attacker want to hijack session, he should have be able to encrypt the both ciphertext from user and severs which means that he obtains the controller's attributes and user's attributes decryption key at the same time. It is impossibly that this situation will happen, because the domain authority which can be trusted will not provide the user's attribute key to an entity with the attribute 'controller' and vice-versa, only if the private keys are revealed by themselves.

Impersonation attack. In this type attack, the attacker tries to impersonate a legitimate user by forging authentication messages. If he success to access the network, he has to guess the authentication messages about Mu and $H(pwd\|R)$ which is hardly totally accurate in a real polynomial time.

6.2   Performance Analysis

In this part, we analyze the computation efficiency and complexity of each entity system operation of our schemes as follow.

System setup. In the process of the system setup, the trust root's work is selecting series of random numbers and two bilinear groups. The public params and MK_0 will be generated with some exponentiation operations. Therefore, the computation complexity of system setup is O (1).

Create domain authority. In this step, the domain authority generates attributes' public keys, corresponding private keys and transmitting parameters for lower domain authority. Let S be the number of attributes in attribute set A_{DM} that is administrated by the domain authority. The computation complexity consist of an exponentiation with each attribute in attribute set A_{DM}. The computation complexity of the create domain authority operation is O(S).

Create user. The main computation complexity which in this part concentrate on the generation of the user's private key is O(U) in which the U means the attributes number in user's attribute set A_u.

Decryption and Encryption. The computation complexity of the encryption depends on size of the access structure of the data. Let N is the number of the attribute associated to the access structure. So the computation complexity is O(5N) of exponentiation and O(N) of mapping. In same way, the computation complexity of the decryption is O(N) of exponentiation and O(2N) of mapping.

Table 1. Comparison of computation complexity

property	HASBE[20]	Yu's scheme[22]	Wang's scheme[19]	Our scheme
system setup	O(1)	O(A)	O(1)	O(1)
DM create	O(2Q+P)		O(S)	O(S)
user create	O(2Q+P)	O(N)	O(U)	O(U)
user key size	O(2Q+P)	O(N)	O(U)	O(U)
cipher size	O(2N+X)	O(N)	O(CT)	O(3N)
access structure	access tree	access tree	DNF	LSSS
based on	CP-ABE	KP-ABE	CP-ABE	CP-ABE

In Table 1, A is the number of the whole attributes the system administrated and U is the number of attributes associated with a user, N is the number of attributes in an access structure is matched by attributes in a user's private key; C is the number of conjunctive clauses in an access structure. X is the set of translating nodes of the policy tree. Q is the number is attributes in the set of user and P is the number of sets in whole attribute set A in HASBE, T is the depth of the user in the hierarchical system.

Since the authentication process combined with the process of authentication by HABE scheme for flexibility and scalability, the computation complexity will be larger than that in traditional ways. The performance of protocol is shown below excluding the procedure of decryption and encryption for whose performance is proposed above. For the register process the computation is only 2 hash computation;

and for verification, the user need 4 hash computations, 2 exponentiations in group G and 1 exponentiation in group G1 and the controller need 4 hash computation , 2 bilinear pairings Computation and 1 exponentiation in group G1.

7   Conclusion

In this paper, we proposed a HABE scheme for SDN network for achieving flexibility, high scalability, and fine-grained access control. The scheme combines the hierarchical structure and the benefits of the attribute based encryption. Comparing with the other hierarchical schemes, our scheme has the advantages on the store space of the user keys and size of ciphertext. Based on the scheme, we then proposed an authentication protocol associated with the access policy presented by controller and the choice given by user, which provide a security channel and the right of autonomous select communication objects for both user and controller by applying our HABE schemes.

Acknowledgment. This research was supported by the Major State Basic Research Development Program (Grant No. 2012CB315905) and the National Nature Foundation of China (Grant No. 61272501).

References

1. Mckeown, N., Anderson, T., Balakrishnan, H., et al.: OpenFlow: Enabling Innovation in Campus Networks. ACM SIGCOMM Computer Communication Review 38(2), 69074 (2008)
2. Yang, L., Dantu, R., Anderson, T., Gopal, R.: IETF RFC 3746 (April 2004)
3. Jain, S., Kumar, A., Mandal, S., et al.: B4: Experience with a Globally-Deployed Software Defined WAN. In: Proceedings of the ACM SIGCOMM 2013 Conference on SIGCOMM, August 12-16, pp. 3–19 (2013)
4. http://www.sdncentral.com/news/sdn-nfv-technology-trends-watch-2014/2014/01/
5. Hartman, S., Wasserman, M.: Security Requirements in the Software Defined Networking Model (2012), http://tools.ietf.org/html/draft-hartman-sdnsec-requirements-00
6. OpenFlow switch Consortium. OpenFlow Specification V1.0 (2013), http://www.openflow.org/
7. Benton, K.L., Camp, J., Small, C.: OpenFlow Vulnerability Assessment. In: Proceedings of the Second ACM SIGCOMM Workshop on Hot Topics in Software Defined Networking, pp. 151–152. ACM (2013)
8. Casado, M., Freedman, M.J., Pettit, J., Luo, J., Mckeown, N., Ethane, S.S.: Taking control of the enterprise. In: Proceeding of SIGCOMM 2007, Proceedings of the 2007 Conference on Applications,Technologies, Architectures, and Protocols for Computer Communications, pp. 1–12 (2007)
9. Koponen, T., Casado, M., Gude, N., Stribling, J., et al.: Onix: a distributed control platform for large-scale production networks. In: Proceedings of the 9th USENIX Conference on Operating Systems Designing and Implementation (2010)

10. Lamport, L.: Password authentication with insecure communication. Communications of the ACM 22(11), 770–772 (1981)
11. Peyravian, M., Zunic, N.: Methods for protecting password transmission. Computers and Security 19(5), 466–469 (2000)
12. Chen, X., Feng, D.: Direct Anonymous Attestation Based on Bilinear Maps. Journal of Software 21(8), 2070–2078 (2010)
13. Brickell, E., Camenisch, J., Chen, L.: Direct anonymous attestation. In: Proceedings of 11th ACM Conference on Computer and Communications Security, Washington, DC, USA, pp. 132–145 (2004)
14. Goyal, V., Pandey, O., Sahai, A., Waters, B.: Attribute-based encryption for fine-grained access control of encrypted data. In: Proceeding of ACM Conference on Computer and Communications Security, pp. 89–98 (2006)
15. Bethencourt, J., Sahai, A., Waters, B.: Ciphertext-policy attribute-based encryption. In: IEEE Symposium on Security and Privacy, pp. 321–334 (2007)
16. Chase, M.: Multi-authority attribute based encryption. In: Vadhan, S.P. (ed.) TCC 2007. LNCS, vol. 4392, pp. 515–534. Springer, Heidelberg (2007)
17. Goyal, V., Jain, A., Pandey, O., Sahai, A.: Bounded ciphertext policy attribute based encryption. In: Aceto, L., Damgård, I., Goldberg, L.A., Halldórsson, M.M., Ingólfsdóttir, A., Walukiewicz, I. (eds.) ICALP 2008, Part II. LNCS, vol. 5126, pp. 579–591. Springer, Heidelberg (2008)
18. Sahai, A., Waters, B.: Fuzzy identity-based encryption. In: Cramer, R. (ed.) EUROCRYPT 2005. LNCS, vol. 3494, pp. 457–473. Springer, Heidelberg (2005)
19. Wang, G., Liu, Q., Wu, J.: Hierarchical attribute-based encryption and scalable user revocation for sharing data in cloud servers. Computers & security 30(5), 320–331 (2011)
20. Wan, Z., Liu, J., Deng, R.H.: HASBE: A Hierarchical Attribute-Based Solution for Flexible and Scalable Access Control in Cloud Computing. IEEE Transactions on Information Forensics and Security 7(2), 743–754 (2012)
21. Beimel, A.: Secure Schemes for Secret Sharing and Key Distribution. PhD thesis, Israel Institute of Technology, Technion, Haifa, Israel (1996)
22. Yu, S., Wang, C., Ren, K., Lou, W.: Achiving secure, scalable, and fine-grained data access control in cloud computing. In: Proceeding of IEEE INFOCOM 2010, pp. 1–9 (March 2010)

A Limited Proxy Re-encryption
with Keyword Search for Data Access Control
in Cloud Computing

Zhenhua Chen[1,2,*], Shundong Li[1], Yimin Guo[1], Yilei Wang[3], and Yunjie Chu[4]

[1] School of Computer Science, Shaanxi Normal University, Xi'an 710072, China
[2] School of Computer Science and Technology,
Xi'an University of Science and Technology, Xi'an 710054, China
[3] School of Computer Science and Technology, Shandong University,
Jinan 250101, China
[4] Wuhan Bioengineering Institute, Wuhan 431400, China
{chenzhenhua,yiminguo}@snnu.edu.cn, {czh333330,wang_yilei2000}@163.com,
china.yunjiechu@gmail.com

Abstract. In this paper, we introduce a new concept of limited proxy re-encryption with keyword search (LPREKS) for fine-grained data access control in cloud computing, which combines the function of limited proxy re-encryption (LPRE) and that of public key encryption with keyword search (PEKS). However, an LPREKS scheme cannot be obtained by directly combining those two schemes since the resulting scheme is no longer proven secure in our security model. Our scheme is proven semantically secure under the modified Bilinear Diffie-Hellman (mBDH) assumption and the q-Decisional Bilinear Diffie-Hellman inversion (q-DBDHI) assumption in the random oracle model.

Our proposal realizes three desired situations as follows: (1) the proxy cloud server can re-encrypt the delegated data containing some keyword which matches the trapdoor from delegatee, (2) the proxy can only re-encrypt a limited number of delegated data to the delegatee; otherwise, the private key of the proxy will be exposed, and (3) the proxy cloud server learns nothing about the contents of data and keyword.

Keywords: Limited proxy re-encryption, Keyword search, Data access control, Cloud computing.

1 Introduction

1.1 Background and Motivations

Cloud computing is a new computing paradigm wherein the resources are provided as services over the internet. The benefits offered by the public cloud encourage the data owners/organisations to store their data on to the cloud storage

---

* This work was supported in part by the National Natural Science Foundation of China (No. 61272435) and the Fundamental Research Funds for the Central Universities (No. GK261001206).

M.H. Au et al. (Eds.): NSS 2014, LNCS 8792, pp. 82–95, 2014.

provided by the cloud provider, which makes the users reduce maintenance cost and enhance access and availability to data. The data stored in public cloud will not be in the user's control but in cloud storage provider's control whereas the cloud storage server is untrusted. To protect the confidentiality of the outsourced files, the owner encrypts them prior to outsourcing them to an untrusted cloud storage server. For example, user i will have n data $\{d_1, \cdots, d_n\}$ to be stored on to the cloud storage. Each data item can be encrypted with distinct symmetric key and each symmetric key is encrypted with the public key of the data owner i. After this, the encrypted data items and the encrypted symmetric random keys are stored in cloud storage server. User i deletes the data items to save his storage space, and only needs to store a single secret key. When user i wants to give an access to his/her data to another user j, firstly, user i downloads the n encrypted symmetric keys and gets them using his secret key sk_i. Again, user i encrypts the n symmetric random keys of the data items using user j's public key pk_j. This process involves n decryptions and n encryptions. Moreover, user i has to be online to complete the sharing process as he/she is the only one possessing secret key sk_i. These make the data sharing inefficient. An alternative approach is to allow the data owner to delegate most of the computation tasks involved in data access control to untrusted cloud servers, which discloses nothing about the underlying data contents. Furthermore, user i does not need to be online for the data sharing.

To address this problem, Blaze, Bleumer, and Strauss [1] first designed a proxy re-encryption (PRE) scheme, which can be used to provide an access control to outsourced data. The proxy key (re-encryption key) generated by the owner (delegator) to delegate the messages to an authorized user (delegatee) was given to the cloud storage server (which acts as a proxy). By using this scheme, user i should just generate a proxy key and go offline, and the cloud storage server can perform some functions on the ciphertexts such that the authorized user j can access the desired sensitive data. The PRE scheme have many intriguing applications, such as email-forwarding[2], secure file systems [4] and personal health records [3].

Since the proxy is untrusted, many existing proxy re-encryption schemes have the following feature: once receiving the re-encryption key, the proxy is able to re-encrypt all the ciphertexts so that the delegatee can obtain all the plaintexts. This is an intolerable property in many practical applications such as in personal health records (PHR) service transferred to storing data into cloud storage. In this case, it is required a secure protection scheme for the privacy of patient and an accurate access for professional diagnoses and medical care. Consider the following scenario:

Doctor Alice might want PHR encrypted with keywords "vaccination" and "cancer" to be "automatically" converted into the ciphertexts for her assistant Bob via proxy cloud storage server. Furthermore, Alice might want more fine-grained control on the proxy cloud storage server, such that a limited number of PHR encrypted with these keywords can be converted.

Inspired by the scenario above, we are looking for a fine-grained data access control in cloud computing, which allows not only user j to accurately access the data including needed keyword but also the proxy cloud storage server just to re-encrypt a limited number of needed data.

1.2 Contributions

In this paper, we propose a new cryptographic concept, called limited proxy re-encryption with keyword search (LPREKS). LPREKS is the combination of limited proxy re-encryption (LPRE) and public key encryption with keyword search (PEKS), which is appropriate for the above scenario. However, an LPREKS scheme cannot be constructed by directly combining those two schemes. It is because in the PEKS scheme the item in a ciphertext always contains the decryptor's information, while in PRE, the decryptor is changed after re-encryption. In order to use these techniques for PEKS to build an LPREKS scheme, we make a modification on PEKS techniques such that it allows a proxy with a re-encryption key to translate a keyword w encrypted under a public key pk_i into the same keyword encrypted under a different public key pk_j.

We achieve our goals by exploiting an off-the-shelf LPRE [12], and uniquely combing it with the technique for the PRKS [8]. Also, we present a model of LPREKS, and some semantic security notions: privacy for keyword, privacy for message and privacy for secret key of the proxy.

The primary advantages of our scheme is summarized as follows.

1) *Privacy and efficiency.* Our proposed scheme enables the delegator to delegate most of intensive computation tasks to proxy cloud servers without disclosing the contents of data and keywords, which frees the delegator from the heavy computation overhead.
2) *Off-line*: The delegator can be offline in the process of data sharing.
3) *Accuracy*: Our scheme can provide the delegatee with an accurate access to needed data including specific keyword.
4) *Limitation*: The proxy cloud servers can only re-encrypt a limited number of delegated data to the delegatee.

Remark 1. In our scheme, we need the assumption of the proxy to be semi-trusted, i.e., the proxy cloud server does not collude with the delegatees in order to protect the secret key of delegator from collusion attacks.

1.3 Roadmap

The remainder of this paper is organized as follows. In Section 2, we briefly present the related cryptographic assumptions, while in Section 3, we provide the definition and the security model of LPREKS scheme. In Section 4, our protocol is described in detail. Security analysis of the proposed scheme is presented in Section 5. In Section 6, A brief performance analysis of our scheme and a comparison with existing protocols are showed. Finally, conclusions are given in Section 7.

1.4   Related Works

From the seminal paper [1], a new cryptographic primitive, called proxy re-encryption (PRE) is quickly popularized.

Ateniese et al. [4] improved the concept of PRE and employed it to data storage. In order to reduce the trusted requirement of the cloud storage servers, this scheme mainly adopts a method that the delegator can encrypt different level ciphertexts under his own public key, however, the solution cannot completely free the users from the heavy computation overhead of traditional decrypt-and-then-encrypt.

Since the proxy cloud storage server is intrusted, it is desirable to restrict the proxy's ability in PRE. In Indocrypt 2008, Tang [6] proposed the concept of type based proxy re-encryption (TPRE). Shortly afterwards, Weng et al. [7] proposed the concept of conditional proxy re-encryption (CPRE) in AisaCCS 2009. Both primitives aim at a fine-grained delegation. In TPRE or CPRE, every ciphertext is labeled with a type l or a condition t. The proxy is given by the delegator a re-encryption key also labeled with a type l or a condition t. Just the label (or condition) of ciphertext matches that of re-encryption key, the ciphertext can be re-encrypted.

In 2010, the concept of proxy re-encryption with keyword search (PRKS) was introduced by Shao et al. [8], which is based on the techniques for PRE [16] and PEKS [10]. Their scheme achieved two goals: (1) the proxy with a trapdoor including a keyword such as "vaccinations" from a delegatee can test whether the keyword is contained in the delegated data, but learn nothing else about the keyword, and (2) the proxy can re-encrypt the delegated data containing this keyword to the delegatee, but cannot get the content of data. It is seems that the PRKS is suitable for our scenario.

However, in all the schemes above, even with these research results on fine-grained PRE, TPRE, CPRE or PRKS, the proxy can re-encrypt an infinite number of delegated data. The situation is not yet satisfying.

In 2011, Wang et al. [11] constructed a k-times proxy re-encryption, and Purushothama et al. [12] subsequently designed a limited proxy re-encryption (LPRE) for enforcing access control in public cloud in 2013. These two schemes can only re-encrypt a limited number of ciphertexts to outsourced data, and meanwhile, hold good properties such as against collusion attacks, unidirectionality and non-transitivity [4]. They borrow the idea of k-times signature in [14] and in [13], where the proxy should be prevented from re-signing more than k-times message, otherwise the private key of the proxy will be leaked. However, these schemes cannot guarantee the delegatee an accurate access to needed data but restrict the number of re-encrypted ciphertexts.

2   Preliminary

2.1   Bilinear Pairings

Assume that G_1 and G_2 are two groups with the same order q where q is a prime number, and g is a generator of group G_1. A bilinear pairing $\hat{e}$ is a function defined by $\hat{e} : G_1 \times G_1 \to G_2$. For all $a, b \in F_q^*$, $P, Q \in G_1$, we say $\hat{e}$ is an admissible bilinear map if the function $\hat{e}$ satisfies the following three conditions:

1) Bilinear: $\hat{e}(g^a, g^b) = \hat{e}(g, g)^{ab}$.
2) Non-degenerate: $\hat{e}(g, g) \neq \mathbf{1}$.
3) Computable: $\hat{e}(P, Q)$ is efficiently computable.

2.2 Related Complexity Assumptions

For security analysis of our scheme, we summarize some important security problems and assumptions as follows.

- **Modified Bilinear Diffie-Hellman (mBDH) Problem** [9]: Given $g, g^a, g^b, g^c \in G_1$ for some $a, b, c \in Z_q^*$, the mBDH problem is to compute $\hat{e}(g, g)^{ab/c}$.
- **mBDH Assumption** [9]: No PPT algorithm can solve the mBDH problem with a non-negligible advantage.
- **q-Decisional Bilinear Diffie-Hellman Inversion (q-DBDHI) Problem** [18]: Given $g, g^x, g^{x^2}, \cdots, g^{x^q} \in G_1, T \in G_2$ for some $x \in Z_q^*$, the q-DBDHI problem is to determine whether $T = \hat{e}(g, g)^{1/x}$ or not.
- **q-DBDHI Assumption** [18]: No PPT algorithm can solve the q-DBDHI problem with a non-negligible advantage.

3 Definition and Security Model

3.1 Definition

Definition 1. *A limited proxy re-encryption with keyword search (LPREKS) system consists of a 10-tuple of algorithms* $\prod = (Setup, KeyGen, ReKeyGen, Publish, Verify, Enc, ReEnc, Trapdoor, Test, Dec)$ *for message space* M *and keyword space* W:

- *$Setup(1^k) \to PP$. On input security parameter 1^k, the setup algorithm outputs the public parameters PP.*
- *$KeyGen(PP) \to (pk, sk)$. On input public parameters PP, the key generation algorithm outputs a public/private key pair (pk, sk).*
- *$ReKeyGen(PP, sk_i, sk_j) \to rk_{i \to j}$. Given user i's secret key sk_i and user j's secret key sk_j where $i \neq j$, this algorithm outputs a re-encryption key $rk_{i \to j}$. This process is performed by user i, user j and the proxy cloud server.*
- *$Publish(PP, sk_p, n) \to params$. On input a secret key sk_p of the proxy cloud server and a constant value n, the proxy constructs a polynomial f of degree n by randomly choosing n random values $\in Z_q^*$ and setting sk_p as the constant term of f. This algorithm outputs the public parameters corresponding to the coefficients of f.*
- *$Verify(params, pk_p, u, f(u)) \to 1$ or 0. Takes $params, u, pk_p, f(u)$ as input and returns 1 if $f(u)$ is indeed the evaluation point using f at u; otherwise returns 0 where u is randomly chosen by user i.*
  Note: *This process can be executed by knowledge commitment to n.*

– $Enc(PP, pk_i, w, m) \to C_i$. On input a public key pk_i, a keyword w and a message m, the encryption algorithm outputs an original ciphertext C_i for user i.

– $ReEnc(PP, rk_{i \to j}, C_i) \to C_j$. Given a re-encryption key from user i to user j and an original ciphertext C_i for user i, the re-encryption algorithm converts the ciphertext C_i to C_j for user j or an error symbol $\perp$.

– $Trapdoor(PP, w', sk_j) \to T'_{w'}$. Given user j's private key sk_j and a keyword w', this algorithm outputs a trapdoor $T'_{w'}$.

– $Test(PP, C_j, T'_{w'}) \to 1$ or 0. Given a ciphertext C_j and a trapdoor $T'_{w'}$, the test algorithm outputs 1 if $w' = w$, or 0 otherwise.

– $Dec(PP, sk_j, C_j) \to m$. Given a secret key sk_j and a ciphertext C_j for user j, the decryption algorithm outputs a message $m \in M$ or an error symbol $\perp$.

3.2 Security Model

There are three security notions for LPREKS: privacy for keyword, privacy for message and privacy for proxy's secret key. Note that we adopt the assumption to define privacy for keyword, privacy for message and privacy for proxy's secret key: static corruption, i.e., the adversary has to determine the corrupted parties before the computation starts, and it does not allow adaptive corruption of proxy cloud servers between corrupted and uncorrupted parties.

Privacy for Keyword. Under this security notion, the adversary is allowed to get almost all trapdoors except those which are associated to the two specified keywords, however, it cannot decide which keyword corresponds to a given ciphertext. This security notion guarantees that only the one who has the trapdoor can do the test. Formally, we define the security against chosen keyword attack (CKA) using the following game between a challenger and an adversary $\mathcal{A}$ (the security parameter k is given to both players as input).
IND-CKA-LPREKS game

– **Query Phase 1.**
- *KeyGen query*:
1) *Uncorrupted KeyGen query*: The challenger runs KeyGen(PP) and returns a key pair (pk, sk). $\mathcal{A}$ is given pk. Let L_U be the set of honest users indices.
2) *Corrupted KeyGen query*: The challenger runs KeyGen(PP) and returns a key pair (pk, sk). $\mathcal{A}$ is given (pk, sk). Let L_C be the set of dishonest users indices.
- *Trapdoor query*: The adversary can adaptively ask the challenger for the trapdoor $T_w = Trapdoor(sk, w)$ for any keyword $w \in \{0, 1\}^*$ from keyword space of his choice.
- *Re-encryption key query*: The adversary can adaptively ask the challenger for the re-encryption key $rk_{i \to j} = ReKeyGen(sk_i, sk_j)$ for any two public keys pk_i, pk_j. Here, we require that either both pk_i and pk_j

are corrupted, or alternatively both are uncorrupted. As a result, the re-encryption key generation queries between a corrupted key and an uncorrupted key is not allowed.

- **Challenge Phase.** At some point, the adversary $\mathcal{A}$ sends the challenger two keywords w_0, w_1 from the keyword space, a message m from the message space and a public key pk_j on which it wishes to be challenged. The only restriction is that the adversary did not previously ask for the trapdoors T_{w0} or T_{w1}, and the pk_j cannot be corrupted. The challenger picks a random $b \in \{0,1\}$ and gives the adversary $C'_b = ReEnc(PP, ReKeyGen(sk_i, sk_j), Enc(pk_i, w_b, m))$. We refer to C'_b as the challenge ciphertext of LPREKS.
- **Query Phase 2.**
  - *KeyGen query*: Identical to that in Phase 1.
  - *Trapdoor query*: The adversary can continue to ask for trapdoors T_w for any keyword w of his choice as long as $w \neq w_0, w_1$.
  - *Re-encryption key query*: Identical to that in Phase 1.
- **Guess Phase.** Eventually, the adversary $\mathcal{A}$ outputs $b' \in \{0,1\}$ and wins the game if $b' = b$.

We define such adversary $\mathcal{A}$'s advantage in attacking the re-encrypted ciphertext of LPREKS as the following function of the security parameter k:

$$\mathrm{Adv}_{\mathcal{A},w}(k) = |\Pr(b' = b) - \frac{1}{2}|.$$

Definition 2. *We say that an LPREKS is semantically secure against chosen keyword attack if for any polynomial time adversary $\mathcal{A}$ we have that $Adv_{\mathcal{A},w}(k)$ is negligible.*

Remark 2. The CKA security for the ciphertext of LPREKS is almost the same as that for the re-encrypted one except that the challenge ciphertext is of the format $C'_b = Enc(PP, pk, w_b, m)$ not the re-encrypted one.

Privacy for Message. Under this security notion, the adversary is allowed to get all the trapdoors and almost all secret keys except that which is used to encrypt two specified messages, however, it cannot decide which message corresponds to a given ciphertext. This security notion guarantees that only the one who has the private key can decrypt the ciphertexts. Formally, we define the security against chosen plaintext attack (CPA) using the following game between a challenger and an adversary $\mathcal{A}$ (the security parameter k is given to both players as input).

IND-CPA-LPREKS game

- **Query Phase 1.** Identical to that in the security model of privacy for keyword.

- **Challenge Phase.** At some point, the adversary $\mathcal{A}$ sends the challenger two messages m_0, m_1 from the message space, a keyword w from the keyword space and a public key pk_j on which it wishes to be challenged. The only restriction is that the pk_j can be uncorrupted. The challenger picks a random $b \in \{0, 1\}$ and gives the adversary $C'_b = ReEnc(PP, ReKeyGen(sk_i, sk_j),$ $Enc(pk_i, w, m_b))$. We refer to C'_b as the challenge ciphertext of LPREKS.
- **Query Phase 2.**
    - *KeyGen query*: Identical to that in Phase 1.
    - *Trapdoor query*: The adversary can continue to ask for trapdoors T_w for any keyword w of his choice.
    - *Re-encryption key query*: Identical to that in Phase 1.
- **Guess Phase.** Eventually, the adversary $\mathcal{A}$ outputs $b' \in \{0, 1\}$ and wins the game if $b' = b$.

We define such adversary $\mathcal{A}$'s advantage in attacking re-encrypted ciphertext of LPREKS as the following function of the security parameter k:

$$\text{Adv}_{\mathcal{A}, m}(k) = |\Pr(b' = b) - \frac{1}{2}|.$$

Definition 3. *We say that an LPREKS is semantically secure against chosen plaintext attack if for any polynomial time adversary $\mathcal{A}$ we have that $Adv_{\mathcal{A}, m}(k)$ is negligible.*

Remark 3. The CPA security for the ciphertext of LPREKS is almost the same as that for the re-encrypted one except that the challenge ciphertext is of the format $C'_b = Enc(PP, pk, w, m_b)$ not the re-encrypted one.

Privacy for Proxy's Secret Key. This security notion guarantees that the proxy cloud server can only re-encrypt a limited number of ciphertexts corresponding to the keywords. If the proxy re-encrypts more than a specified number of ciphertexts of the delegator, the secret key of the proxy cloud server will be revealed. Formally, we define the security against chosen ciphertext attack (CCA) using the following game between a challenger and an adversary $\mathcal{A}$ where the chosen ciphertext attack (CCA) is different from the traditional one (the security parameter k is given to both players as input).
IND-CCA-LPREKS game

- **Query Phase 1.** Identical to that in the security model of privacy for message.
- **Challenge Phase.** At some point, the adversary $\mathcal{A}$ sends the challenger two messages m_0, m_1 from the message space, a keyword w from the keyword space on which it wishes to be challenged. The challenger picks a random $b \in \{0, 1\}$ and gives the adversary $C'_b = ReEnc(PP, ReKeyGen(pk_p, Enc(pk_i, w, m_b))$ where pk_p is the public key of proxy. We refer to C'_b as the challenge ciphertext of LPREKS.

- **Query Phase 2**. Identical to that in Phase 1.
- **Guess Phase**. Eventually, the adversary $\mathcal{A}$ outputs $b' \in \{0,1\}$ and wins the game if $b' = b$.

We define such adversary $\mathcal{A}$'s advantage in attacking security of LPREKS as the following function of the security parameter k:

$$\text{Adv}_{\mathcal{A},L}(k) = |\Pr(b' = b) - \frac{1}{2}|.$$

Definition 4. *We say that an LPREKS is semantically secure against chosen ciphtertext attack if for any polynomial time adversary $\mathcal{A}$ we have that $Adv_{\mathcal{A},L}(k)$ is negligible.*

4   Proposed Scheme

4.1   Construction

Our scheme $\prod = (Setup, KeyGen, ReKeyGen, Publish, Verify, Enc, ReEnc, Trapdoor, Test, Dec)$ is described as follows:

- *Setup*. This algorithm takes a security parameter 1^k as input, and outputs a bilinear map $\hat{e} : G_1 \times G_1 \to G_2$ defined over two multiplicative groups G_1, G_2 of same prime order q. Choose a random generator $g \in G_1$ and compute $Z = \hat{e}(g,g)$. Furthermore, we need two hash functions $H_1 : \{0,1\}^* \to G_1$ and $H_2 : G_2 \to \{0,1\}^{\log_2 q}$. As a result, we set the public parameters be $(g, Z, \hat{e}, q, G_1, G_2, H_1, H_2)$.
- *KeyGen*. For user i and user j, the key pairs are of the form $(sk_i = a, pk_i = g^a)$ and $(sk_j = b, pk_j = g^b)$, respectively, where a, b are randomly chosen from Z_q^*.
- *ReKeyGen*. The re-encryption key $rk_{i \to j} = b/a (\text{mod } q)$ can be generated as follows:
    1) User i may select a random $r \in Z_q^*$ and send $(sk_i r)(\text{mod } q)$ to user j and r to proxy P.
    2) User j sends $sk_j/(sk_i r)(\text{mod } q)$ to proxy P.
    3) Proxy P computes $sk_j/sk_i(\text{mod } q) = b/a(\text{mod } q)$ as re-encryption key $rk_{i \to j}$.
- *Publish*. For proxy P, the key pair is of the form $sk_p = p, pk_p = g^p$, where p is randomly chosen from Z_q^*. Proxy P chooses randomly and uniformly n values $a_1, \cdots, a_n$ from Z_q^* and constructs a polynomial $f(x)$ of degree n as follow:

$$f(x) = p + a_1 x + a_2 x^2 + \cdots + a_n x^n (\text{mod } q).$$

    Later, he publishes $params = (g^{a_1}, \cdots, g^{a_n})$.
- *Verify*.
    1) User i chooses a random number $u \in Z_q^*$ and sends it to proxy P.

2) Proxy P evaluates $f(x)$ at u and sends $f(u)$ to user i.

3) User i checks whether $Verify(pk_p, params, f(u)) = 1$, namely, $g^{f(u)} = g^p g^{a_1 u} \cdots g^{a_n u^n}$. If it holds, that means proxy P has faithfully committed to n.

- *Enc.* On input $m \in G_2$ and keyword $w \in \{0,1\}^*$, user i randomly chooses $k \in Z_q^*$ and computes $C_1 = mZ^k, C_2 = (g^a)^k, t = \hat{e}(H_1(w), g)^k$ and outputs the ciphertext

$$C_i = (C_1, C_2, t, H_2(t)).$$

- *ReEnc.* Proxy P takes $C_i = (C_1, C_2, t, H_2(t))$ (the ciphertext of user i) as input and outputs the ciphertext C_j for user j using the re-encryption key $rk_{i \to j} = b/a \pmod q$ as follows:

$$C_1' = C_1, \ C_2' = C_2^{b/af(C_1')} = g^{akb/af(C_1')} = g^{bkf(C_1')}, \ C_3' = f(C_1'), \ t' = t$$

Outputs

$$C_j = (C_1', C_2', C_3', t', H_2(t')).$$

Note. $C_3' = f(C_1') = f(C_1)$.

- *Trapdoor.* On input user j' secret key $sk_j = b$ corresponding to the public key $pk_j = g^b$ and a keyword w', outputs a trapdoor $T_{w'}' = H_1(w')^{1/b}$.

- *Test.* Proxy P takes the trapdoor $T_{w'}'$ and the ciphertext $(C_1', C_2', C_3', t', H_2(t'))$ as input, checks whether $H_2(\hat{e}(C_2'^{1/C_3'}, T_{w'}')) = H_2(t')$. If it holds, then outputs 1; otherwise, outputs 0.

- *Dec.* Suppose (C_1', C_2', C_3') be the re-encrypted ciphertext, user j obtains the message m using his secret key $sk_j = b$ by computing the following equation. If

$$Verify(C_1', C_3', g^p, g^{a_1}, \cdots, g^{a^n}) = 1,$$

namely,

$$g^{C_3'} = g^p g^{a_1(C_1')} \cdots g^{a_n(C_1')^n},$$

then

$$m = \frac{C_1'}{\hat{e}(g, C_2')^{1/bC_3'}}.$$

Otherwise, outputs $\perp$.

4.2 Correctness

Decryption Correctness

Correctness(delegator). From ciphertext C_i, user i can compute message m from the following equation using his secret key $sk_i = a$.

$$\frac{C_1}{\hat{e}(g, C_2)^{1/a}} = \frac{mZ^k}{\hat{e}(g, g^{ak})^{1/a}} = \frac{mZ^k}{Z^k} = m$$

Correctness(delegatee). From ciphertext C_j, user j can compute plaintext m from the following equation using his secret key $sk_j = b$.

$$\frac{C_1'}{\hat{e}(g, C_2')^{1/bC_3'}} = \frac{mZ^k}{\hat{e}(g, g^{bf(C_1')k})^{1/bf(C_1')}} = \frac{mZ^k}{Z^k} = m$$

Test Correctness

Correctness(delegator). User i holding the correct trapdoor $T_{w'} = H_1(w')^{1/a}$ under $sk_i = a$ is able to pass the test.

$$H_2(\hat{e}(C_2, T_{w'}))$$
$$= H_2(\hat{e}(g^{ak}, H_1(w')^{1/a}))$$
$$= H_2(\hat{e}(H_1(w'), g)^k)$$
$$= H_2(t) \text{ if } w' = w.$$

Correctness(delegatee). User j holding the correct trapdoor $T_{w'}' = H_1(w')^{1/b}$ under $sk_j = b$ is able to pass the test.

$$H_2(\hat{e}(C_2'^{1/C_3'}, T_{w'}')$$
$$= H_2(\hat{e}(g^{bk}, H_1(w'))^{1/b})$$
$$= H_2(\hat{e}(H_1(w'), g)^k)$$
$$= H_2(t') \text{ if } w' = w.$$

The Number of Re-Encryption Correctness

Suppose that the proxy cloud server re-encrypts more than n ciphertexts corresponding to the keywords $w_1, w_2 \cdots$ to delegatee j. Any adversary (including users i, j) can collect at least $n+1$ re-encrypted ciphertexts $(C_1', C_2', C_3' = f(C_1'))$ and construct a polynomial $f(x)$ of degree n from (C_1', C_3') using Lagrange's interpolation method [17] and then evaluate $f(0) = p$, which will reveal the private key sk_p of proxy cloud server.

5   Security Analysis

Our LPREKS construction relies on the simplified q-DBDHI assumption which was originally proposed in [4]. The simplified q-DBDHI problem is described as follows:

Given (g, g^c, g^b, T), for $g \in G_1$, $c, b \in Z_q^*$ and $T \in G_2$, decide if $T = e(g, g)^{c/b}$ or not .

Lemma 1. *[4] We say that the simplified q-DBDHI is intractable if no polynomial time algorithms have a non-negligible advantage in solving simplified q-DBDHI problem.*

For simplicity, we omit the proof of the following theorems and only give the conclusions.

Theorem 1. *The proposed LPREKS scheme is semantically secure against chosen keyword attack in the random oracle model assuming mBDH is intractable.*

Theorem 2. *The proposed LPREKS scheme is semantically secure against chosen plaintext attack in the random oracle model assuming simplified q-BDHI is intractable.*

Theorem 3. *Let $\mathcal{A}$ be a polynomial time adversary making more than n (n is the constant agreed between delegator and delegatee) re-encryption queries to the proxy in the game described in Section 3.3.3. Then, the $\mathcal{A}$'advantage in breaking the LPREKS scheme is $1/2$.*

6 Performance Analysis and Comparison

In related schemes, the operations for users mainly include encrypting plaintext, generating trapdoor and decrypting ciphertext, while the others are performed by the proxy cloud server. For the computation cost, we only consider the "costly computation". As the computational overhead of modular exponentiations and pairing operation dominate those of other operations, we evaluate the computational overhead of the protocol by counting modular exponentiations and pairing operation. We make a comparison among our protocol with those in [4,8] and [12] in terms of the computation overhead of delegatee and the off-line delegator, the number of re-encrypted ciphertexts, and the accuracy of data access control.

In [4], the protocol can provide an accurate data access control and the proxy can only re-encrypted a limited number of ciphertexts. However, this approach does not completely free the users from the heavy computation overhead of traditional decrypt-and-then-encrypt since the delegator needs to re-encrypt different level ciphertexts under his own public key, which makes the delegator be still on-line for the data access. In encryption phase, the delegator requires 3 modular exponentiations and 1 pairing operation, while in decryption phase, the delegatee requires 1 modular exponentiation and 1 pairing operation.

In [8], the protocol can provide an accurate data access control by means of keyword search. However, this approach cannot prevent the proxy from re-encrypting an infinite number of ciphertexts once obtaining a re-encryption key. In encryption phase, the delegator requires 4 modular exponentiations and 2 pairing operations, while in generating trapdoor phase, it requires 1 modular exponentiation. In decryption phase, the delegatee requires 1 modular exponentiation. and 1 pairing operation.

While in [12], the proxy can only re-encrypt a limited number of ciphertexts whereas the protocol cannot provide an accurate data access control. In encryption phase, the delegator requires 3 modular exponentiations. and 1 pairing operation, while in decryption phase, the delegatee requires 3 modular exponentiations.

The above two schemes in [8,12] are similar to ours where the users only need to perform encryption and decryption operations while re-encryption and test operations using pairing are performed by the proxy cloud server.

In our scheme, we provide not only an accurate data access for delegatee but also a limited number of re-encrypted ciphertexts to restrict the ability of proxy cloud server. Our scheme is very efficient since the number of ciphertexts converted by proxy cloud server do not increase a lot but only one, which does not occupy excess storage space in cloud storage server. Furthermore, the decrypting process of the delegatee is the same as that of the delegator. In encryption phase, the delegator requires 3 modular exponentiation and 2 pairing operations. In generating trapdoor phase, it requires 1 modular exponentiations, while in decryption phase, the delegatee requires 1 modular exponentiation and 1 pairing operation.

The concrete comparison is given in Table 1. We denote modular exponentiations by M_e, denote pairing operation by M_p. The first column is the serial number of four references , the second column is the computation overhead of users (a.k.a., COU), the third column is whether the delegator is off-line (a.k.a., OL), and the fourth and the fifth columns are whether a limited number of re-encrypted ciphertexts (a.k.a., LNREC) and the accuracy of data access control (a.k.a., CDAC) are provided for delegatee, respectively.

Table 1. Comparison of Four Protocols

Protocol	COU	OL	LNREC	CDAC
[4]	$4M_e+2M_p$	no	yes	yes
[8]	$6M_e+3M_p$	yes	no	yes
[12]	$6M_e+1M_p$	yes	yes	no
Ours	$5M_e+3M_p$	yes	yes	yes

From Table 1, it is shown that our scheme achieves better properties and higher efficiency compared with others. To the best of our knowledge, we first provide a limited proxy re-encryption with keyword search for data access control in cloud computing so far.

7   Conclusions

In this paper, we introduced the concept of limited proxy re-encryption with keyword search for data access control in cloud computing, in which an accurate data access control including needed keyword which can match the trapdoor from delegatee was guaranteed. Furthermore, the proxy cloud server was restricted only to re-encrypt a specified number of delegator's ciphertexts. The proxy's private key would be revealed if he re-encrypted more ciphertexts than the number. Our scheme made the delegator not be online for the data sharing process, and the main computation tasks executed by proxy cloud server not disclose the contents of the data and keywords.

References

1. Blaze, M., Bleumer, G., Strauss, M.: Divertible protocols and atomic proxy cryptography. In: Nyberg, K. (ed.) EUROCRYPT 1998. LNCS, vol. 1403, pp. 127–144. Springer, Heidelberg (1998)
2. Khurana, H., Heo, J., Pant, M.: From proxy encryption primitives to a deployable secure-mailing-list solution. In: Ning, P., Qing, S., Li, N. (eds.) ICICS 2006. LNCS, vol. 4307, pp. 260–281. Springer, Heidelberg (2006)
3. Li, M., Yu, S., Ren, K., Lou, W.: Securing personal health records in cloud computing: Patient-centric and fine-grained data access control in multi-owner settings. In: Jajodia, S., Zhou, J. (eds.) SecureComm 2010. LNICST, vol. 50, pp. 89–106. Springer, Heidelberg (2010)
4. Ateniese, G., Fu, K., Green, M., Hohenberger, S.: Improved proxy re-encryption schemes with applications to secure distributed storage. In: Proceedings in NDSS 2005, pp. 1–15 (2005)
5. Ivan, A., Dodis, Y.: Proxy cryptography revisited. In: Proceedings in NDSS 2003, pp. 1–20 (2003)
6. Tang, Q.: Type-based proxy re-encryption and its construction. In: Chowdhury, D.R., Rijmen, V., Das, A. (eds.) INDOCRYPT 2008. LNCS, vol. 5365, pp. 130–144. Springer, Heidelberg (2008)
7. Weng, J., Deng, R.H., Chu, C., Ding, X., Lai, J.: Conditional proxy re-encryption secure against chosen-ciphertext attack. In: Proceeding in ACM ASIACCS 2009, pp. 322–332 (2009)
8. Shao, J., Cao, Z., Liang, X., Lin, H.: Proxy re-encryption with keyword search. Information Sciences 180(13), 2576–2587 (2010)
9. Sahai, A., Waters, B.: Fuzzy identity-based encryption. In: Cramer, R. (ed.) EUROCRYPT 2005. LNCS, vol. 3494, pp. 457–473. Springer, Heidelberg (2005)
10. Boneh, D., Franklin, M.: Identity-based encryption from the weil pairing. In: Kilian, J. (ed.) CRYPTO 2001. LNCS, vol. 2139, pp. 213–229. Springer, Heidelberg (2001)
11. Wang, X.A., Wang, Z., Ding, Y., Bai, S.: k-times proxy re-encryption. In: Proceeding in CIS 2011, pp. 949–953 (2010)
12. Purushothama, B.R., Shrinath, B., Amberker, B.B.: Secure cloud storage service and limited proxy re-encryption for enforcing access control in public cloud. International Journal of Information and Communication Technology 5(2), 167–186 (2013)
13. Hwang, J., Lee, D., Lim, J.: Digital signature scheme with restriction on signing capability. In: Safavi-Naini, R., Seberry, J. (eds.) ACISP 2003. LNCS, vol. 2727, pp. 324–335. Springer, Heidelberg (2003)
14. Choi, C., Kim, Z., Kim, K.: Schnorr signature scheme with restricted signing capability and its application. In: Proceeding in CSS 2003 (2003)
15. Shamir, A.: How to share a secret. Communications of the Association for Computing Machinery 33(3), 612–613 (1979)
16. Canetti, R., Hohenberger, S.: Chosen-ciphertext secure proxy re-encryption. In: ACM CCS 2007, Full version: Cryptology ePrint Archieve: Report 2007/171 (2007)
17. Horowitz, E., Sahani, S., Rajasekaran, S.: Fundamentals of computer algorithms. Universities Press, Hyderabad (2007)
18. Dodis, Y., Yampolskiy, A.: A verifiable random function with short proofs and keys. In: Vaudenay, S. (ed.) PKC 2005. LNCS, vol. 3386, pp. 416–431. Springer, Heidelberg (2005)

psOBJ: Defending against Traffic Analysis with pseudo-Objects

Yi Tang[1,2], Piaoping Lin[1], and Zhaokai Luo[3]

[1] School of Mathematics and Information Science
Guangzhou University, Guangzhou 510006, China
[2] Key Laboratory of Mathematics and Interdisciplinary Sciences of Guangdong
Higher Education Institutes
Guangzhou University, Guangzhou 510006, China
[3] School of Computer Engineering and Science
Shanghai University, Shanghai 200072, China

Abstract. When visiting a web page, a sequence of request-response transactions will be introduced. On one hand, the browser issues requests for objects in order. On the other hand, the server responses with required object contents. This makes the traffic of a specified web page demonstrate pattern features different from other pages. Traffic analysis techniques can extract these features to identify web pages effectively even if the traffic is encrypted. In this paper, we propose a countermeasure method, psOBJ, to defend against traffic analysis by introducing pseudo-objects in browser-server communications. We compose some object fragments into a constructed object, the pseudo-object, and force the object requests and responses on pseudo-objects. By randomly composing pseudo-objects with different number of object fragments with different sizes, the traffic for a given web page could be variable and exhibits different traffic patterns in different visits. We have implemented a proof of concept prototype and validate the psOBJ countermeasure with some state of the art traffic analysis techniques.

Keywords: Encrypted Web Traffic, Web Page Identification, Traffic Analysis, pseudo-Object.

1 Introduction

Web visitors are increasingly concerned with the privacy in their web browsing behaviors. They want to preserve the privacy of the content they have browsed or the web page they have visited. The secure protocol suites, such as SSL, SSH, IPSec, and Tor, etc., are widely used in current web applications to ensure data privacy in flight. These protocols are technically based on the modern encryption methods. The user browsing privacy seems to be preserved when the encryption method is perfect and the encryption key is not broken. However, encryption cannot hide everything in browser-server communications. The encrypted data streams are on web request-response communications, the secure protocols do not change the pattern of the traffic. Some basic traffic features, such as the order,

M.H. Au et al. (Eds.): NSS 2014, LNCS 8792, pp. 96–109, 2014.
© Springer International Publishing Switzerland 2014

number, length, or timing of packets, are closely associated with the original web page and corresponding objects. These explicit and implicit features can be extracted by traffic analysis (TA) and may lead to the disclosure of the web sites and the web pages user visited, or even the user private inputs [2][3][4][6][8][9].

Many proposals against TA attacks are on varying packet features on packet level. Padding extra bytes into transmitting data is the general method. The padding procedure is performed at server side before or after encryption [3][6], and the padded traffic could be similar to a predefined traffic distribution [11]. These efforts are on fine-grained single object analysis and they are not efficient against the coarse-grained aggregated statistics [4]. The BuFLO method intends to cut off the aggregated associations among packet sizes, packet directions, and time costs [4] by sending specified packets in given rates during a given time period. Some other techniques on higher level, such as HTTPOS [7], try to influence the packet generation at server side by customizing specified HTTP requests or TCP headers at client side.

In this paper, we propose psOBJ, a TA defence method on web application level. We try to make a web page with varying traffic features by introducing the notion of pseudo-object. A pseudo-object is an object fragment combination which is composed by a set of fragments of original objects. Our proposed method is on client-server cooperation. We translate a common web page into pseudo-object-enabled (PO-enabled) web page by introducing embedded scripts for pseudo-objects and object identifiers within object tags. When the browser renders the PO-enabled web page, the embedded scripts are triggered and initiate requests for pseudo-objects. We introduce the notion of master object to support the order of browser rendering. Cooperatively, a script running on server will produce object combinations with random sizes and random chosen components, including all the remaining contents of the current master object. This kind of object generating and fetching procedure changes the traffic features of the original web page, and hence may be used to defend against the traffic analysis.

The contribution of this paper can be enumerated as follows.

1. We introduce the notion of pseudo-object to design a new defence method, psOBJ, against traffic analysis.
2. We develop the PO-enabled web page structure to support the requests and responses for pseudo-objects. By composing the pseudo-objects with random number of chosen object fragments with random sizes, the traffic features of PO-enabled web pages can be varied in different visits.
3. We have implemented a proof of concept (POC) prototype with data URI scheme and the AJAX technique, and we demonstrate the effectiveness of psOBJ on defending against some typical TA attacks.

The rest of this paper is structured as follows. In Section 2, we overview some works on traffic analysis. In Section 3, we introduce the notion of pseudo-objects. In Section 4, we discuss the method to construct the pseudo-objects. In Section 5, we conduct some experiments to validate our proposed method. And finally, the conclusion is drawn in Section 6.

2   Traffic Analysis in Encrypted Web Flows

2.1   HTTP Traffic

We view a web page as a set of document resources (objects) that can be accessed through a common web browser. When accessing a web page, the browser first fetches the basic HTML file from a destination server who hosts that file, and then, issues network requests to fetch other objects in sequence according to the order of corresponding objects in retrieved HTML document. This makes the traffic of a certain web page demonstrate distinctive pattern.

Table 1 shows the numbers and sizes of objects related to two typical portal websites, *www.yahoo.com* and *www.sina.com.cn*. Note that many object requests are issued by the browser in order to render the required pages, and hence volumes of object downloading traffic are introduced. As illustrated in Table 1, at least 57 image files are needed to retrieve when visiting *www.yahoo.com* while the number is increased to 158 when visiting *www.sina.com.cn*. Correspondingly, the downloaded volumes of images are reached to $434kB$ and $2,074kB$, respectively. In total, the number and the volume of requests for rendering these two pages are reached to 94, $931kB$ and 321, $2,840kB$, respectively. It implies that these two web pages can easily be distinguished on the number of requests and the volume of downloaded objects.

Table 1. Features of Some Web Pages on Jun. 15, 2014 (source: [12])

Object	*www.yahoo.com*		*www.sina.com.cn*	
	Number	Size (kB)	Number	Size (kB)
HTML	10	108	40	190
Script	19	298	108	277
CSS	3	49	2	6
Image	57	434	158	2,074
Flash	1	39	11	292
Total Requests	94	931	321	2,840

It is well known that HTTP is not a secure protocol which is faced with the leakage of message payloads. As shown in Fig. 1(a), the default HTTP payload is in plain. A simple man-in-the-middle (MITM) attack could easily eavesdrop and intercept the HTTP conversations. HTTPS is designed to resist such MITM attacks by providing bidirectional encrypted transmissions. As shown in Fig. 1(b), the HTTPS payloads are encrypted but the TCP and IP headers are preserved.

We often require tunnel-based transmissions to hide real communicating IP address in some applications. This kind of transmission means that the entire specified IP packet is encapsulated into a new IP packet, i.e., that specified packet is as the payload of that new packet. If the tunnel is encrypted, the encapsulated packet is also encrypted. It implies that both the real IP addresses and port numbers are protected from any MITM attackers. As shown in Fig.

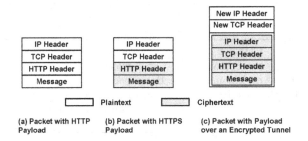

Fig. 1. IP packets without/with encrypted HTTP payloads

1(c), all the IP packet with HTTP payload is encrypted and encapsulated into a new packet with new header. A typical encrypted tunnel is the secure shell (SSH) tunnel. A SSH tunnel can be used to forward a given port on a local machine to HTTP port on a remote web server. It means a user may visit an external web server in private if he can connect to an external SSH server to create an SSH tunnel.

From the viewpoint of confidentiality, it seems that the privacy of the conversations on HTTPS or SSH tunnel is preserved because of the encryption of browsed web pages in flight. However, some traffic features, such as the number of object requests, are consistent in the same way whether or not the traffic is encrypted. A traffic analysis attack can effectively use these features to identify the web page the user visited, or even the data that the user input. For example, when visiting the two portal websites in Table 1, counting the number of object requests can distinguish them easily.

2.2   Traffic Analysis

We abstract a web page *page* as an ordered object set $\{obj_i\}$, i.e., $page = \{obj_i\}$, where each object obj_i is needed to retrieve from some hosted web servers. To render these objects, the src attribute is used to specify the URI for retrieving. With specified URIs, the browser will send a sequence of HTTP requests to servers, and the servers will reply those requests with response packets. It is noted that the order of objects retrieving requests are basically on the order of corresponding objects in *page*.

When the traffic is encrypted and the encryption is perfect, only the encrypted payload size and the packet direction can be sniffed in communication channel. Consider that the popular encryption methods cannot largely enlarge the difference between the length of encrypted message and the length of corresponding plaintext version, we assume that the encryption is approximatively length-preserved. This implies that the size of an encryption object is similar to the size of object in plain. On the other hand, the order of objects in transmitting implies that the aggregated size of packets between two requests is generally related to a certain object size. For example, the traffic vector $\langle (30, \uparrow), (100, \downarrow), (60, \downarrow), (20, \uparrow) \rangle$ denotes four sets of encrypted HTTP traffic,

Table 2. Traffic Analysis Attack Instances

Method	Classifier	Features Considered
LL [6]	naïve Bayes	packet lengths
HWF [5]	multinomial naïve Bayes	packet lengths
DCRS [4]	naïve Bayes	total trace time
		bidirectional total bytes
		bytes in traffic bursts

the first and the last are from client to server with sizes 30, 20, respectively, the others are from server to client with sizes 100, 60, respectively, and we can infer that the client possibly downloads an object with size 160.

We consider three typical TA techniques listed in Table 2.

Liberatore and Levine [6] developed a web page identification algorithm (LL) by using naïve Bayes (NB) classifier. They used the packet direction and the packet length as feature vector. NB classifier is used to predict a label $page$: $page = \arg\max_i P(page_i|F')$ for a given feature vector F' using Bayes rule $P(page_i|F') = \frac{P(F'|page_i)P(page_i)}{P(F')}$, where $i \in \{1, 2, ..., k\}$ and k is the number of web pages. The LL method adopts the kernel density estimation to estimate the probability $P(F'|page_i)$ over the example vector during the training phase, and the $P(page_i)$ is set to k^{-1}. The normalization constant $P(F')$ is computed as $\sum_{i=1}^{k} P(F'|page_i) \cdot P(page_i)$.

Herrmann, Wendolsky, and Federrath [5] proposed a web page identification algorithm (HWF) by using a multinomial naïve Bayes (MNB) classifier. Both LL and HWF methods use the same basic learning method with the same traffic features. The difference is in the computation of $P(F'|page_i)$. The HWF method determines the $P(F'|page_i)$ with normalized numbers of occurrences of features while the LL method determines with corresponding raw numbers.

Most of the works are on single fine-grained packet analysis. In [4], Dyer, Coull, Ristenpart, and Shrimpton proposed an identification method (DCRS) based on three coarse trace attributes. The three coarse features are total transmission time, total per-direction bandwidth, and traffic burstiness (total length of non acknowledgement packets sent in a direction between two packets sent in another direction). They use NB as the underlying machine learning algorithm and build the VNG++ classifier. Their results show that TA methods can reach a high identification accuracy against existed countermeasures without using individual packet lengths. It implies that the chosen feature attributes are more important in identifying web pages.

2.3   The Padding-Based Countermeasures

Visiting a web page means an HTTP session is introduced. This session is composed by a sequence of network request-response communications.

To change the profiles of communicated packets, a simple and effective method is padding extra bytes to packet payloads [9]. Note that the length of packet payload is limited by the length of maximum transmission unit (MTU). When no ambiguity is possible, we also denote the length of MTU as MTU. There exists many padding-based methods [4]. In this paper, we consider the following four padding-based methods.

1. **PadFixed** This method randomly chooses a number $r, r \in \{8, 16, ..., 248\}$, and pads some bytes data to each packet in session. In detail, let len be the original packet length, we pad r bytes data to packet if $r + len \leq$ MTU, otherwise, pad each packet to MTU.
2. **PadMTU** All packet lengths are increased to MTU.
3. **PadRand1** For each packet in session, randomly pick a number $r : r \in \{8, 16, ..., 248\}$ and increase packet length to $\min\{len + r, \text{MTU}\}$ for this packet where len is the original packet length.
4. **PadRand2** For each packet in session, randomly pick a number $r : r \in \{0, 8, ..., \text{MTU} - len\}$ and increase packet length to $len + r$ for this packet where len is the original packet length.

3   The pseudo-Object

Let obj be an object in a web page and $||$ be the concatenation operator.

Definition 1. *A fragmentation of obj with length m is a piece set, $F(obj) = \{obj_1^f, obj_2^f, ..., obj_m^f\}$, such that $obj = ||_{i=1}^m obj_i^f$ where each obj_i^f is not empty.*

For example, let js be a script object whose content is `<script> alert("Hello World!"); </script>`. A fragmentation of this script object with length 3 is the piece set $\{js_1^f, js_2^f, js_3^f\}$, where js_1^f, js_2^f, and js_3^f is `<script> al`, `ert("Hello World!")`, and `; </script>`, respectively. It is obviously that we can reassemble the object js by simply concatenating the fragments in sequence, i.e., $js = js_1^f||js_2^f||js_3^f$.

Another example is for the css object, css, whose content is `hr {color:sienna;}`. A fragmentation of this css object with length 2 is the piece set $\{css_1^f, css_2^f\}$, where css_1^f and css_2^f is `hr` and `{color:sienna;}`, respectively.

Suppose there is an object set S, $S = \{obj_1, obj_2, ..., obj_n\}$, where each obj_i is in a web page with $1 \leq i \leq n$. Let $F(obj_i) = \{obj_{i,1}^f, obj_{i,2}^f, ..., obj_{i,m_i}^f\}$ be a fragmentation of obj_i with length m_i for each obj_i.

Definition 2. *A pseudo-object $psObj$ with length k is $||_{j=1}^k obj_{i_j, n_j}^f$, where each component object $obj_{i_j} \in S$, $obj_{i_j, n_j}^f \in F(obj_{i_j})$, and for any two component object obj_{i_j} and $obj_{i_{j'}}$, $obj_{i_j} \neq obj_{i_{j'}}$ if $i_j \neq i_{j'}$.*

For the two objects, js and css, we discussed before, we can construct some pseudo-objects. For example, the pseudo-object, $psObj_1 = js_1^f||css_1^f$, is concatenated by the first fragment of js and css, while the object $psObj_2 = js_2^f$, is only constructed by the second fragment of js.

Follow the Definition 2, we call the objects associated with a pseudo-object as the component objects, abbreviated as *components*. We also call the fragments associated with a pseudo-object as the component pseudo-fragment. When without causing confusion, we abbreviate the pseudo-fragment as *fragment*. As an example, the components of $psObj_1$ are js and css, and the corresponding fragments are js_1^f and css_1^f.

Definition 3. *The number of bytes contained in a fragment is called the size of the fragment. The sum of the sizes of all fragments in a pseudo-object is called the size of this pseudo-object.*

For example, the size of the fragment js_1^f and css_1^f is 11 and 2, respectively, and hence, the size of the pseudo-object $psObj_1$ is 13.

Note that if we define the third pseudo-object $psObj_3$ as $js_3^f || css_2^f$, we can reassemble the two original objects js and css with the three pseudo-objects $psObj_1$, $psObj_2$, and $psObj_3$. And further, retrieving the three pseudo-objects is basically equivalent to retrieving the two original objects on the view of communicated data. We focus on the the traffic variation. The traffic flows are different not only in the number of retrieved objects but also in the volumes of each retrieved objects. It implies that the traffic feature is different although the accumulative transferred data is invariable. Furthermore, when the traffic is encrypted, it is hard for a traffic analysts to infer the original transferred web page.

In the next section, we will consider to construct the pseudo-objects to change the traffic features dynamically.

4   psOBJ: Varying Web Traffic with pseudo-Objects

In this section, we will discuss psOBJ, the method for changing features of web traffic by introducing pseudo-objects in browser-server communications. We will discuss how to represent pseudo-objects in an HTML document, and how to retrieve those objects from web servers. We will present the structure of pseudo-object-enabled (PO-enabled) HTML document to support retrieving the pseudo-object and assembling the original objects.

4.1   The PO-enabled HTML Document

To render web page, a browser often needs to require different kinds of object from servers. Not all objects are text-based. For the non-text-based objects, such as the image files, describing them directly in fragments is not easy. We consider adopting data URI scheme to handle the non-text-based objects [13].

The data URI scheme allows inclusion of small media type data as immediate data inline. The data URIs are in the form of data:[<mediatype>][;base64],<encoded-data> where the mediatype part specifies the Internet media type and the ;base64 indicates that the data is encoded as base64. For example, the segment <img src="data:image/png;base64,iVBORw0..."> could be used to define an inline image embedded in HTML document. Considering that the base64-code is text-based, the base64-encoded objects can be easily cut into fragments and translated into pseudo-objects.

In order to support retrieving pseudo-objects, it needs to redefine the structure of traditional HTML document. We call the HTML document that can support accessing pseudo-objects as the pseudo-object-enabled (PO-enabled) HTML document. The following demonstrates this kind of PO-enabled HTML document structure with img tags.

```
<html>
    <head> ...... </head>
    <body>
      <script> ......
        function pseudoObject()
          ......
      </script>
          ......
        <img id = objID1>
          ......
        <img id = objID2>
          ......
    </body>
</html>
```

To retrieve the pseudo-objects, the scripts for pseudo-objects must be included in HTML document and the URIs for extern objects are also needed to be changed. Note that the contents within img tags are referred to the object identifier (objID), the browser does not request for the single image file. The script pseudoObject() is initiated to require the pseudo-objects, and assemble them into original objects.

4.2   The Communications for pseudo-Objects

Fig. 2 demonstrates the communications between browser and web server for pseudo-objects in PO-enabled HTML document. When the web browser initiates the request for basic HTML file, the server returns the PO-enabled HTML file. The browser renders this HTML file, and then requires some object features, such as the sizes of the encoded objects, in order to manage the requirements of pseudo-objects. The pseudo-objects are required according to a predefined order and composed at server side with different object fragments. The returned encoded pseudo-objects are then decomposed and dispatched to the browser for rendering. The require-compose-decompose-dispatch procedure will be continue until all objects are downloaded.

In our implementation, a script for the features of objects is initiated at first. This makes the browser issue a request for the number of objects in rendering page and the size of each encoded objects. The server will return a serialized feature vector. This vector can be expressed as the regular expression

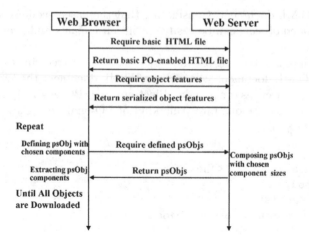

Fig. 2. Communications for pseudo-Objects

`<objID@objlen@<mediatype>(;base64)?,|>{n}`, where `n` is the number of objects in this web page, `objlen` is the size of the object, which is denoted by `objID`, encoded in `text` or `base64`, and each object item is separated by `|`.

With the received encoded object sizes, the browser maintains a buffer to store the downloaded fragment contents for each object. A simple comparing operation could be used to decide whether or not a given object has been downloaded.

The request for pseudo-object is issued on the order of objects in a web page. The required pseudo-object is constituted by the fragments of master object and some slave objects. The master object is the object in current fetching order. It implies that if the current request is for the ith pseudo-object, the ith object is the master object. The number of slave objects and corresponding serial numbers are decided at client side. The pseudo-object request contains the serial numbers of the master object and slave objects. When the server receives the request, it reads all the remaining content of master object, and then reads random size of contents for each slave objects. With the two content parts of objects, the pseudo-object is composed at server side. The format of the pseudo-object is as `<remained-master-object>(|<slave-object-fragment>{sizel, sizeh}){lenl, lenh}`. It implies that besides contains the remained contents of the master object, the number of slave component objects in this pseudo-object is between `lenl` and `lenh`, where each slave fragment sizes are ranged from `sizel` to `sizeh`.

5   Experiments and Discussions

5.1   The Experiment Setup

Our experiments are on artificial web pages with only image objects. We create an image library by picking some image files whose sizes are ranged from $5k$ to

$25k$ from some websites. We then randomly select m image files to construct 200 pseudo-object-enabled web pages, respectively. We also construct 200 traditional web pages with the same number of images for comparison. For each artificial web page, we visit 100 times via HTTPS and SSH tunnel, respectively. We record the traces in each visit, strip packet payloads with TCPurify tool [15], and construct two types of traces set, $\texttt{psDataHTTPS}_m$ and $\texttt{psDataSSH}_m$. For comparing with other TA countermeasures, we also construct 200 traditional web pages with the same number of image and visit them via HTTPS and SSH tunnel. The datasets for comparison tests are $\texttt{TrDataHTTPS}_m$, and $\texttt{TrDataSSH}_m$. In our conducted experiments, we set m as 20, 60, and 100, respectively.

To test the performances against the traffic analysis, we run the code from [14] with classifiers and countermeasures we discussed in Section 2 on our constructed test datasets. The size K of private traces are set to 2^i with $1 \leq i \leq 7$ and 200, respectively. This means that the identifying web page is limited in K web pages. We use the default parameters in original code configuration. For each K with different classifiers and countermeasures, we run the test 10 times and average the accuracy as the ratio of successful identification.

5.2 Visiting Web Pages with psOBJ Method via HTTPS and SSH

We test our proposed psOBJ method against the 3 discussed classifiers on the PO-enabled pages with 60 objects and compare the results with other countermeasures. Fig. 3 and Fig. 4 show the comparison results for the case of HTTPS transmission and SSH transmission, respectively.

For the case of HTTPS transmission, as demonstrated in Fig. 3, the performances of the psOBJ method are different in the 3 classifiers. It is the most effective countermeasure to defend against the DCRS classifier, but for the LL classifier, the effectiveness is neither good nor bad. It is weak in defending against the HWF classifier.

The case for transmission over SSH tunnel is shown in Fig. 4. Comparing with the other four padding-based countermeasures, the psOBJ method minimized the identification accuracy for the DCRS classifier, and for the LL classifier and the HWF classifier, the effectiveness is neither good nor bad.

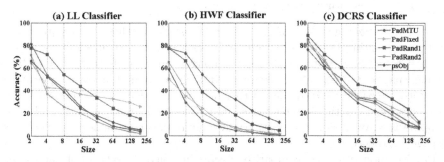

Fig. 3. Accuracy in HTTPS traffic: psOBJ and other countermeasures

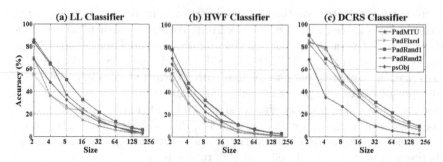

Fig. 4. Accuracy in SSH traffic: psOBJ and other countermeasures

5.3   The psOBJ Method against Different Classifiers

Fig. 5 and Fig. 6 demonstrate the identification accuracy of 3 classifiers on the trace sets for pseudo-object-enabled web pages with different numbers of objects. Fig. 5 shows that the HWF classifier can obtain higher identification accuracy on the HTTPS dataset, while Fig. 6 shows that the LL classifier obtains higher on the SSH dataset.

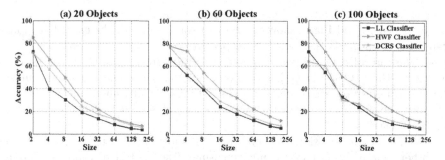

Fig. 5. Accuracy on visiting web pages with psOBJ via HTTPS

5.4   Time Cost for the psOBJ Method

To evaluate the time costs of the proposed psOBJ method, we compare the time costs visiting PO-enabled web pages with visiting traditional web pages. We first construct 10 web pages with m images, and transform them into PO-enabled pages, respectively. Because we intend to evaluate extra computation cost introduced by psOBJ, these pages will be visited in HTTP protocol. We visit each page 10 times, record the total time for loading objects, and then compute the average of time cost. We average the average values for two types of pages, respectively.

Fig. 7 demonstrates the comparison results in visiting two types of web pages, where m is set as 20, 40, 60, 80, and 100. It shows that as the number of

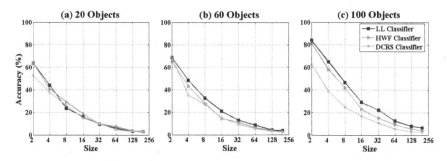

Fig. 6. Accuracy on visiting web pages with psOBJ via SSH tunnel

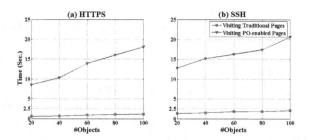

Fig. 7. Loading Time: Traditional Pages and PO-enabled Pages

objects increasing, the extra time cost is also increased. For example, in the case of HTTPS transmission, visiting PO-enabled pages with 20 objects needs 8.53 seconds in average while visiting traditional pages needs 0.53 seconds. For the pages with 100 objects, it averagely needs 18.12 seconds to visit PO-enabled pages while needs 1.12 seconds to visit traditional pages.

5.5   Discussions

Our conducted experiments demonstrate the abilities of the psOBJ method against TA classifiers, especially against the DCRS classifier. The number of object requests in psOBJ is limited in not more than the number of original objects in web page. However, the psOBJ method may introduce extra computation costs in both server side and client side. Since the pseudo-object is composed in base64-encode, it may increase at least 15% of the network traffic volumes.

Our POC implementation is immature. To simplify the implementation, we use the jQuery library and we read the fetching object fragment in byte by byte in server side script implementation. It obviously introduces more computation costs in downloading, reading, and interpreting. Additionally, we do not consider the render order introduced by scripts. And also, we do not consider the case that the objects in page are from different web servers.

5.6   Related Work

Encrypting web traffic is a common strategy to preserve users' privacy while surfing the Web. However, the current encryption suites are focused on transmission content protection and some traffic features cannot be effectively protected. A traffic analysis attack could use these features to infer the users' web browsing habits and their network connections. Identifying web page on encrypted traffic is an important class of traffic analysis attacks.

Sun et al. [9] proposed a classifier based on the Jaccard coefficient similarity metric, and reliably identified a large number of web pages in 100,000 web pages. They also proposed some countermeasures against TA attacks but our proposed method is not addressed. Bissias et al. [2] used cross-correlation to determine web page similarity with features of packet length and timing. Liberatore et al. [6] showed that it is possible to infer web pages with naïve Bayes classifier by observing only the lengths and the directions of packets. Herrmann et al. [5] suggested a multinomial naïve Bayes classifier for page identification that examines normalized packet counts.

Panchenko et al. [8] developed a Support Vector Machine(SVM) based classifier to identify web pages transmitted on onion routing anonymity networks (such as Tor). They used a variety of features, include some totaling data, based on volume, time, and direction of the traffic. Dyer et al. [4] provided a comprehensive analysis of general-purpose TA countermeasures. Their research showed that it is the choosing features, not the analysis tools, that mainly influence the accuracy of web page identification.

Some other attacks are not only depended on network packets. Wang et al. [10] proposed a new web page identifying technique on Tor tunnel. They interpreted the data by using the structure of Tor elements as a unit of data rather than network packets.

Padding extra bytes to packets is a standard countermeasure. Various padding strategies have been proposed to change encrypted web traffic [4]. However, this kind of countermeasures is on a single non-MTU packet, it is vulnerable when using coarse-grain traffic features [4][8]. Traffic morphing [11] tries to make a web page traffic similar to another given web page. This method is also focused on the fine-grain packets and is limited in changing coarse-grain features. Sending specified packets at fixed intervals [4] can reduce the correlation between the observed traffic and the hidden information and demonstrate more capabilities against the coarse-grain feature based analysis. However, it also introduces traffic overhead or delay in communication.

Some countermeasure proposals are on application-level. The browser-based obfuscation method, such as the HTTPOS method [7], takes the existing HTTP and TCP functionalities to generate randomized requests with different object data requirements at client. It changes the number of requests from clients and the distribution of response packet volumes from servers. The HTTPOS method is on splitting the response packets by introducing special HTTP requests or TCP packets. Although it is effective against some of existing classifiers, it increases the number of requests and the number of response packets.

6   Conclusion

We have proposed a countermeasure method, psOBJ, to defend against web page identification based traffic analysis by introducing pseudo-objects. By introducing the pseudo-objects, the traffic for a given web page could exhibit different traffic patterns in different visits. Possible future work may include reducing the computation costs in client side and server side and make it more compatible in current web applications.

Acknowledgments. This paper was partially supported by the Natural Science Foundation of Guangdong Province under grant S2012040007370.

References

1. Backes, M., Doychev, G., Kopf, B.: Preventing Side-Channel Leaks in Web Traffic: A Formal Approach. In: Proceedings of NDSS 2013 (2013)
2. Bissias, G.D., Liberatore, M., Jensen, D., Levine, B.N.: Privacy Vulnerabilities in Encrypted HTTP Streams. In: Danezis, G., Martin, D. (eds.) PET 2005. LNCS, vol. 3856, pp. 1–11. Springer, Heidelberg (2006)
3. Chen, S., Wang, R., Wang, X., Zhang, K.: Side-channel Leaks in Web Applications: a Reality Today, a Challenge Tomorrow. In: Proceedings of IEEE S&P 2010, pp. 191–206 (2010)
4. Dyer, K., Coull, S., Ristenpart, T., Shrimpton, T.: Peek-a-Boo, I still see you: Why Traffic Analysis Countermeasures Fail. In: Proceedings of IEEE S&P 2012, pp.332–346, (2012)
5. Herrmann, D., Wendolsky, R., Federrath, H.: Website Fingerprinting: Attacking Popular Privacy Enhancing Technologies with the Multinomial Naïve-bayes Classifier. In: Proceedings of CCSW 2009, pp. 31–42 (2009)
6. Liberatore, M., Levine, B.: Inferring the Source of Encrypted HTTP Connections. In: Proceedings of ACM CCS 2006, pp. 255–263 (2006)
7. Luo, X., Zhou, P., Chan, E., Lee, W., Chang, R.: HTTPOS: Sealing Information Leaks with Browserside Obfuscation of Encrypted Flows. In: Proceedings of NDSS 2011 (2011)
8. Panchenko, A., Niessen, L., Zinnen, A., Engel, T.: Website Fingerprinting in Onion Routing Based Anonymization Networks. In: Proceedings of ACM WPES 2011, pp. 103–114 (2011)
9. Sun, Q., Simon, D., Wang, Y., Russell, W., Padmanabhan, V., Qiu, L.: Statistical Identification of Encrypted Web Browsing Traffic. In: Proceedings of IEEE S&P 2002, pp. 19–30 (2002)
10. Wang, T., Goldberg, I.: Improved Website Fingerprinting on Tor. In: Proceedings of WPES 2013, pp. 201–212 (2013)
11. Wright, C., Coull, S., Monrose, F.: Traffic Morphing: An Efficient Defense Against Statistical Traffic Analysis. In: Proceedings of NDSS 2009, pp. 237–250 (2009)
12. HTTP Archive, http://httparchive.org
13. Masinter, L.: The "data" URL scheme, http://www.ietf.org/rfc/rfc2397.txt
14. https://github.com/kpdyer/traffic-analysis-framework
15. http://masaka.cs.ohiou.edu/~eblanton/tcpurify/

Universally Composable Secure TNC Protocol Based on IF-T Binding to TLS

Shijun Zhao, Qianying Zhang, Yu Qin, and Dengguo Feng

Institute of Software Chinese Academy of Sciences,
ISCAS, Beijing, China
zqyzsj@gmail.com, {zhangqy,qin_yu,fengdengguo}@tca.iscas.ac.cn

Abstract. Trusted Network Connect (TNC) requires both user authentication and integrity validation of an endpoint before it connects to the internet or accesses some web service. However, as the user authentication and integrity validation are usually done via independent protocols, TNC is vulnerable to the Man-in-the-Middle (MitM) attack. This paper analyzes TNC which uses keys with Subject Key Attestation Evidence (SKAE) extension to perform user authentication and the IF-T protocol binding to TLS to carry integrity measurement messages in the Universally Composable (UC) framework. Our analysis result shows that TNC using keys with SKAE extension can resist the MitM attack. In this paper, we introduce two primitive ideal functionalities for TNC: an ideal dual-authentication certification functionality which binds messages and both the user and platform identities, and an ideal platform attestation functionality which formalizes the integrity verification of a platform. We prove that the SKAE extension protocol and the basic TCG platform attestation protocol, both of which are defined by TCG specifications, UC-realizes the two primitive functionalities respectively. In the end, we introduce a general ideal TNC functionality and prove that the complete TNC protocol, combining the IF-T binding to TLS which uses keys with SKAE extension for client authentication and the basic TCG platform attestation platform protocol, securely realizes the TNC functionality in the hybrid model.

Keywords: Universally Composable security, Trusted Network Connect, SKAE, TLS.

1 Introduction

Many security solutions have been introduced to protect computers from attacks in the network, such as firewalls, virus scan engines and intrusion detection systems. However, as more and more security incidents ascend in numbers, these traditional solutions seem to be not sufficient to counter the current attacks. TNC, an open network access architecture enabling the network operators to authenticate the identity of the platform and perform the integrity verification of the platform before it connects to the network, is promoted and standardized by TCG to build a clean network environment. TNC aims to ensure that the

M.H. Au et al. (Eds.): NSS 2014, LNCS 8792, pp. 110–123, 2014.

integrity status of all the endpoints in the network are safe. The integrity information of an endpoint is collected and stored in a cost-effective, tamper-resistant Trusted Platform Module (TPM).

When an endpoint wants to connect to the network or access some web service, it first calls the IF-T protocol [14,18] to establish a mutually authenticated secure channel with the TNC server, then it runs platform attestation protocol to attest its integrity status to the TNC server. The platform attestation protocol messages are transported in the established secure channel. However, Askan et al. [1] find that running an authentication protocol in a tunneling protocol is vulnerable to Man-in-the-Middle (MitM) attacks, and such attacks can apply to TNC using IF-T protocol. To prevent MitM attacks, TCG promotes the Subject Key Attestation Evidence (SKAE) extension, which enables a cryptographic binding of a platform identity key (which signs integrity information in the platform attestation protocol) with a user certificate. Both the user identity and SKAE extension should be authenticated in the user authentication. The SKAE extension implies that the user authentication and platform attestation happen on the same platform, so MitM attacks won't work.

The UC framework defines the security goal of a protocol by an ideal functionality, which acts as a trusted third party. A good property of UC is the composability: a protocol π communicating with an ideal functionality $\mathcal{F}$ is identical to π calling a subroutine protocol ρ if ρ securely realizes π in the UC framework. This property suits the analysis of layered protocols very well: the high layer protocol invokes the ideal functionality realized by the lower layer protocol without considering the implementation details of the lower layer protocol. TNC is a layered architecture: the bottom layer is IF-T protocol, which establishes a mutual authentication secure channel, and the top layer is platform attestation protocol. So UC suits the analysis of TNC very well, and a proved TNC functionality will benefit the analysis of the protocols above TNC.

1.1 Related Work

To the best of our knowledge, few works on the formal analysis of TNC have been done since the publication of TNC. Zhang et al. [21] provide the first ideal TNC functionality $\mathcal{F}_{\text{TNC}}$, and analyze the EAP-TNC attestation protocol with Diffie-Hellman Pre-Negotiation (D-H PN) [14]. They find a MitM attack on the D-H PN EAP-TNC protocol and patch it by authenticating the Diffie-Hellman keys. However, their analysis is based on the assumption that the tunneled EAP protocol has provided an ideal mutually authenticated secure channel functionality. Some analysis of TNC using the symbolic logic method is proposed recently. Zhang et al. [22] propose a computationally sound symbolic analysis of D-H PN EAP-TNC protocol but not the complete TNC protocol. Xiao et al. [20] analyze the authentication property of the complete TNC protocol based on the IF-T protocol binding to TLS in their extended strand space model. They find that the complete TNC protocol can resist MitM attacks in the case the user is authenticated through a certificate with SKAE extension during the TLS setup phase. This result is in accord with our analysis result in the UC framework.

Until now, most basic ideal cryptography functionalities, such as public key encryption, digital signature, authentication communication, key exchange, and secure channel, have been realized in the UC or similar framework (see, e.g., [3,4,8,11]. Gajek et al. [6] presented the first security analysis of the TLS protocol in the UC framework. They analyzed the key exchange functionality realized by TLS handshake and the secure channel functionality realized by the complete TLS protocol. In our analysis, the functionality provided by IF-T protocol binding to TLS is a variant of secure channel functionality which provides not only user authentication but also platform authentication. Our analysis of IF-T is based on the work of [6].

1.2   Our Contributions

In this paper, we investigate the complete TNC protocol in the UC framework. We adopt the composability of the UC framework in our analysis. We first separate the Complete TNC protocol into IF-T protocol and platform attestation protocol. Then we analyze the two protocols separately. Finally, we analyze the complete TNC protocol in the hybrid model. The following lists our contributions more specifically.

1. We introduce two primitive ideal functionalities for TNC. The first is a dual-authentication certification functionality $\mathcal{F}_{\text{D-Cert}}$ that authenticates both the user and platform identity. This functionality is necessary in the analysis of TNC as authenticating both the user and platform is a basic security policy requirement in TNC. The second is a platform attestation functionality $\mathcal{F}_{\text{P-A}}$ that captures the security requirement of the platform integrity status validation. These two primitive functionalities enable to analyze complex protocols based on SKAE extension and platform attestation in a modular way, and simplify the analysis.

2. We consider the realization of $\mathcal{F}_{\text{D-Cert}}$ and $\mathcal{F}_{\text{P-A}}$. We prove that 1) the SKAE extension creation and processing protocol (which we call SKAE-EX for short), defined in the SKAE specification [13], securely realizes $\mathcal{F}_{\text{D-Cert}}$; and 2) the basic TCG platform attestation protocol realizes $\mathcal{F}_{\text{P-A}}$. On the basis of $\mathcal{F}_{\text{D-Cert}}$, we show that the IF-T protocol binding to TLS which uses keys with SKAE extension for client authentication (which we call IF-TLS-SKAE for short) realizes a dual-authentication secure channel functionality $\mathcal{F}_{\text{D-SC}}$.

3. We introduce a general TNC functionality $\mathcal{F}_{\text{TNC}}$ and show that the complete TNC protocol, combining IF-TLS-SKAE and the basic TCG platform attestation protocol, UC-realizes $\mathcal{F}_{\text{TNC}}$.

1.3   Organization

Section 2 gives a brief overview of the background of this paper, i.e., TNC and the UC framework. Section 3 introduces the dual-authentication certification functionality $\mathcal{F}_{\text{D-Cert}}$, and show that 1) the SKAE-EX protocol securely realizes $\mathcal{F}_{\text{D-Cert}}$, and 2) the IF-TLS-SKAE protocol securely realizes the dual-authentication secure channel functionality $\mathcal{F}_{\text{D-SC}}$. Section 4 introduces the platform attestation functionality $\mathcal{F}_{\text{P-A}}$ and proves that the basic TCG platform attestation protocol realizes $\mathcal{F}_{\text{P-A}}$. Section 5 designs the general TNC functionality $\mathcal{F}_{\text{TNC}}$ and analyzes the complete TNC protocol in hybrid model. Section 6 concludes this work.

2   Background

This section briefly describes the TNC architecture and the UC framework on which our analysis is based.

2.1   TNC in a Nutshell

TNC is an open network architecture that enables network operators to assess the integrity status of endpoints and verify the user and platform identities of endpoints in order to determine endpoints whether to grant access to the network or web services. The integrity information can be collected by the TCG-based integrity measurement architectures [12,9] and stands for the security status of the current system. The integrity information is stored in a TPM, which cannot be compromised by a potentially malicious host system. In order to validate the integrity information of an endpoint, the existence and genuineness of a TPM should be authenticated, i.e., the platform identity authentication.

TCG defines a series of specifications for TNC. The interoperability architecture specification [19] describes how TNC architecture can be implemented and integrated with existing network access control mechanisms such as 802.1X [7]. The IF-T specifications [14,18] define how IF-T can be implemented over other lower layer protocols such as tunneled Extensible Authentication Protocol (EAP) and TLS. The IF-TNCCS messages, carrying the integrity measurement messages, are transported in the IF-T protocol, and its message format is defined in the IF-TNCCS specification [17]. The following gives a brief TNC flow based on the IF-T protocol binding to TLS:

0. Requirement. Before running TNC, the Network Access Requestor (NAR), which represents the endpoint that wants to get access to a TNC protected service, is already on the network thus has an IP address assigned.

1. TLS Setup. NAR establishes a TLS session with the Network Access Authority (NAA), who assesses NAR and decides whether NAR should be granted to access. In this phase, NAR must validate the certificate of NAA, e.g., NAA is authenticated to NAR. The NAR might use a client certificate with SKAE extension for client authentication, and this is the case analyzed in this paper.

2. User Authentication. If NAR isn't authenticated to NAA in the TLS setup phase, user authentication must be performed after TLS setup phase over the established TLS session. The second version of [18] defines that the user

authentication must be performed in the Simple Authentication and Security Layer (SASL) [10] framework, and some standards-based authentication mechanisms are provided in SASL.

3. Platform Attestation. In this phase, the IF-T session is available. NAA assesses the integrity of NAR in the IF-T session established in the above phases. The assessment messages are encapsulated in IF-TNCCS messages. Finally, NAA decides whether to grant NAR to access the protected service.

2.2   The UC Framework

The UC framework [2] is a kind of formal method for the modular design and analysis of multi-party protocols. UC defines an additional entity called the environment $\mathcal{Z}$. It feeds arbitrary inputs to the parties and the adversary, then collects the outputs from the parties and the adversary. $\mathcal{Z}$ interacts with two worlds: the real world and the ideal world. The real world is composed of honest parties running a real protocol and an adversary $\mathcal{A}$ which controls the communication between parties and may corrupt honest parties. The ideal world is composed of dummy parties and a simulator $\mathcal{S}$. The dummy parties simply receive inputs from $\mathcal{Z}$, and forward them to the ideal functionality $\mathcal{F}$, which is a trusted party and performs the ideal cryptographic task. After completing the cryptographic task, $\mathcal{F}$ hands the desired outputs to the dummy parties. The security notion of UC is defined in an indistinguishable way as follows.

Definition 1. *A protocol π UC-realizes (or emulates) an ideal functionality $\mathcal{F}$ if for any adversary $\mathcal{A}$ in the real world, there exists an adversary (simulator) $\mathcal{S}$ in the ideal world such that for any environment $\mathcal{Z}$, the probability that $\mathcal{Z}$ distinguishs whether it is interacting with the real protocol π and $\mathcal{A}$ or with the ideal functionality $\mathcal{F}$ and $\mathcal{S}$ is at most a negligible probability, i.e., $\text{EXEC}_{\pi,\mathcal{A},\mathcal{Z}} \approx \text{EXEC}_{\mathcal{F},\mathcal{S},\mathcal{Z}}$.*

A good feature of UC framework is its composition theorem.

Definition 2 (Composition theorem). *Let π be a protocol that uses subroutine calls to an ideal functionality f. We call π is an f-hybrid protocol. If protocol ρ realizes f, then the composed protocol $\pi^{\rho/f}$, in which each invocation of f is replaced by an invocation of ρ, UC-realizes π. Another way of saying it is, $\pi^{\rho/f}$ UC-realizes π in f-hybrid model, i.e., $\text{EXEC}_{\pi^{\rho/f},\mathcal{A},\mathcal{Z}} \approx \text{EXEC}^{f}_{\pi,\mathcal{S},\mathcal{Z}}$.*

3   SKAE Certification Functionality

This section presents the dual-authentication certification functionality $\mathcal{F}_{\text{D-Cert}}$ authenticating both the user and platform identity. We analyze the SKAE extension creation and processing protocol (SKAE-EX) defined in [13]. SKAE-EX runs in a setting of the existence of 1) an Attestation Identity Key (AIK), which certifies that the user key with SKAE extension is under the protection of the TPM where AIK resides, 2) a trusted certificate authority that registers user

---

Functionality $\mathcal{F}_{\text{D-Cert}}$

Signature Generation: Upon receiving a value (Sign, sid, m) from party S, verify that $sid = (U, P, s)$ for some s (We denote by U the user identity and P the platform identity). If not, then ignore the request. Else send (Sign, sid, m) to the adversary. Upon receiving (Signature, sid, m, σ) from the adversary, verify that no entry $(m, \sigma, 0)$ is recorded. If it is, then output an error message to S and halt. Else, output (Signature, sid, m, σ) to S, and record the entry $(m, \sigma, 1)$.

Signature Verification: Upon receiving a value (Verify, sid, m, σ) from some party S', hand (Verify, sid, m, σ) to the adversary. Upon receiving (Verified, sid, m, ϕ) from the adversary, do:

  1. If $(m, \sigma, 1)$ is recorded then set $f = 1$.
  2. Else, if the signer is not corrupted, and no entry $(m, \sigma', 1)$ for any σ' is recorded, then set $f = 0$ and record the entry $(m, \sigma, 0)$.
  3. Else, if there is an entry (m, σ, f') recorded, then set $f = f'$.
  4. Else, set $f = \phi$, and record the entry (m, σ', ϕ).

Output (Verified, sid, m, f) to S'.

Fig. 1. The Dual-authentication Certification Functionality, $\mathcal{F}_{\text{D-Cert}}$

identities together with public keys. We formalize the global assumptions by utilizing the certification functionality $\mathcal{F}_{\text{Cert}}$ and the certificate authority functionality $\mathcal{F}_{\text{CA}}$ presented in [3]. We assume that the signature of the user key with SKAE extension is secure, so we add the signature functionality $\mathcal{F}_{\text{SIG}}$ presented in [3] to our global assumptions. Our analysis shows that the SKAE extension creation and processing protocol defined in [13] UC-realizes $\mathcal{F}_{\text{D-Cert}}$ in the $(\mathcal{F}_{\text{Cert}}, \mathcal{F}_{\text{CA}}, \mathcal{F}_{\text{SIG}})$-hybrid model. We don't describe $\mathcal{F}_{\text{Cert}}$, $\mathcal{F}_{\text{CA}}$, and $\mathcal{F}_{\text{SIG}}$ in this paper, and for readers who are interested in them please consult [3] for details.

It's reasonable to assume that the AIK certification capability provided by TPM (see [15,16] for details) securely realizes $\mathcal{F}_{\text{Cert}}$, as the AIK certification with the help of a PrivacyCA [5] is the same as the CAS protocol [3] which UC-realizes $\mathcal{F}_{\text{Cert}}$.

3.1 The Dual-Authentication Certification Functionality, $\mathcal{F}_{\text{D-Cert}}$

The ideal dual-authentication certification functionality, $\mathcal{F}_{\text{D-Cert}}$ is presented in Figure 1. It is similar to $\mathcal{F}_{\text{Cert}}$, except that it binds a signature for a message with the user identify and the platform identify, which are encoded in the sid. The dual binding relationship is critical in the complete TNC protocol, and is one of the two essential approaches used in TNC to prevent MitM attacks. This binding relationship shows that the key used in the user authentication is protected by some TPM which is identified by an AIK. If the later platform attestation protocol uses the same AIK, then the user authentication and the platform attestation must operate in the same platform, which prevents MitM attacks.

3.2   Analysis of SKAE-EX

We show that the SKAE-EX protocol UC-realizes $\mathcal{F}_{\text{D-Cert}}$ with the aid of an AIK certified by a trusted PrivacyCA and ideally authenticated communication with a "trusted certification authority". The certified AIK is formalized as $\mathcal{F}_{\text{Cert}}$, and this formalization is reasonable as we have explained that the AIK certification capability is the same as the CAS protocol[3], which UC-realizes $\mathcal{F}_{\text{Cert}}$. The trusted certification authority assumption is formalized as $\mathcal{F}_{\text{CA}}$ which registers user identities with public values. We stress that $\mathcal{F}_{\text{CA}}$ doesn't check the possession of secret key corresponding to the registered public value, which models most practical CAs.

The formal description of SKAE-EX protocol is given in Figure 2.

Theorem 1. *Protocol SKAE-EX securely realizes functionality $\mathcal{F}_{\text{D-Cert}}$ in the $(\mathcal{F}_{\text{Cert}}, \mathcal{F}_{\text{CA}}, \mathcal{F}_{\text{SIG}})$-hybrid model.*

Due to the space limitation, we give the complete proof of above theorem in the full version [23].

3.3   Dual-Authentication Secure Channel Functionality

We describe our dual-authentication secure channel functionality $\mathcal{F}_{\text{D-SC}}$ in Figure 3. $\mathcal{F}_{\text{D-SC}}$ enables the responder of the secure channel to authenticate both the user and the platform identify of the initiator, and guarantees that the adversary gains no more information than some side channel information about the transmitted plaintext m, such as the length of m. The leakage information is expressed by a leakage function $l(m)$.

We argue that the IF-T protocol binding to TLS using keys with SKAE extension for client authentication (IF-TLS-SKAE) securely realizes $\mathcal{F}_{\text{D-SC}}$. Gajek et al. [6] has presented the security analysis of the complete TLS protocol, combining Handshake and Record Layer, in the UC framework. They first showed that the master key generation subroutines in Handshake protocol UC-realize the key exchange functionality $\mathcal{F}_{\text{KE}}$ given the traditional certification functionality $\mathcal{F}_{\text{Cert}}$, then that the complete TLS protocol framework securely realizes secure channel functionality $\mathcal{F}_{\text{SC}}$ in the $\mathcal{F}_{\text{KE}}$-hybrid model. Since 1) we have proved that user keys with SKAE extension UC-realizes the dual-authentication functionality, and 2) the IF-TLS-SKAE protocol is a complete TLS protocol using keys with SKAE extension for client authentication, we directly get theorem 2. The proof can be easily got following the proof of [6].

Theorem 2. *The IF-TLS-SKAE protocol securely realizes functionality $\mathcal{F}_{\text{D-SC}}$.*

---

[3] Readers who are interested in the details of the CAS protocol please consult [3].

Protocol SKAE-EX

Signature Protocol: When activated with input (Sign, sid, m), party S does:

1. S verifies that $sid = (U, P, s)$ for some identifier s; if not then the input is ignored. (That means that S verifies that it's the legitimate user and platform for this sid)

2. If this is the first activation then S does:

   (a) Generates a user key using its TPM. We model the generation by utilizing $\mathcal{F}_{\mathrm{SIG}}$, i.e., sends (KeyGen, (U, s)) to $\mathcal{F}_{\mathrm{SIG}}$.

   (b) Once S obtains a key from the TPM, i.e., receiving (Verification key, $(U, s), v$) from $\mathcal{F}_{\mathrm{SIG}}$, it invokes the AIK of the TPM, which is bound to the platform identity P, to certify that v comes from a genuine TPM identified as P. We model the AIK certification by sending (Sign, $(P, s), v$) to $\mathcal{F}_{\mathrm{Cert}}$.

   (c) After obtaining a certification from AIK, i.e., receiving (Signature, $(P, s), v, \sigma_{\mathrm{AIK}}$) from $\mathcal{F}_{\mathrm{Cert}}$, S sends (Register, $U, v, P, \sigma_{\mathrm{AIK}}$) to $\mathcal{F}_{\mathrm{CA}}$, who doesn't perform any check and just record $(U, v, P, \sigma_{\mathrm{AIK}})$ if this is the first request from S. From then on, the user key is bound to the user identity U.

3. S sends (Sign, $(U, s), m$) to $\mathcal{F}_{\mathrm{SIG}}$. Upon receiving (Signature, $(U, s), m, \sigma$) from $\mathcal{F}_{\mathrm{SIG}}$, S outputs (Signature, sid, m, σ).

Verification Protocol: When activated with input (Verify, sid, m, σ), where $sid = (U, P, s)$, party S' does:

1. S' check whether it has a tuple $(U, v, P, \sigma_{\mathrm{AIK}})$ recorded. If not, then S' sends (Retrieve, U, P) to $\mathcal{F}_{\mathrm{CA}}$, and obtains a response (Retrieve, $U, v, P, \sigma_{\mathrm{AIK}}$). If $v = \perp$ then S' rejects the signature, i.e., it outputs (Verified, $sid, m, 0$). Else it records $(U, v, P, \sigma_{\mathrm{AIK}})$.

2. S' uses its user key to verify σ, i.e., sends (Verify, $(U, s), m, \sigma, v$) to $\mathcal{F}_{\mathrm{SIG}}$, and obtains a response (Verified, $(U, s), m, f$). If $f = 0$, S' outputs (Verified, $sid, m, 0$).

3. S' uses its AIK to verify the SKAE extension, i.e., sends (Verify, $(P, s), v, \sigma_{\mathrm{AIK}}$) to $\mathcal{F}_{\mathrm{Cert}}$, and obtains a response (Verified, $(P, s), v, f$). If $f = 0$, S' outputs (Verified, $sid, m, 0$). Else, S' outputs (Verified, $sid, m, 1$).

Fig. 2. The SKAE-EX protocol for realizing $\mathcal{F}_{\mathrm{D\text{-}Cert}}$

4 Analysis of Platform Attestation

In this section we first introduce the ideal platform attestation functionality $\mathcal{F}_{\mathrm{P\text{-}A}}$ which formalizes the PCR-based platform attestation proposed by TCG, and then show that the TCG platform attestation protocol securely realizes $\mathcal{F}_{\mathrm{P\text{-}A}}$ given an incorruptible $\mathcal{F}_{\mathrm{Cert}}$ functionality. The incorruptibility models the protection capability provided by TPM, a tamper-resistant hardware token.

4.1 Platform Attestation Functionality

We first describe the ideal platform attestation functionality $\mathcal{F}_{\mathrm{P\text{-}A}}$ modeling a prover to attest its PCR information to a verifier informally. See Figure 4 for a precise definition.

Functionality $\mathcal{F}_{\text{D-SC}}$

$\mathcal{F}_{\text{D-SC}}$ proceeds as follows, running with some initiators $(U_1, P_1), \ldots, (U_n, P_n)$ and some responders $S_1, \ldots, S_n$, and parameterized by a leakage function $l : \{0,1\}^* \to \{0,1\}^*$.

1. Upon receiving an input (Establish-session, sid, S_j, initiator) from some initiator (U_i, P_i), send $(sid, (U_i, P_i), S_j)$ to the adversary, and wait to receive an input (Establish-session, sid, (U_i, P_i), responder) from S_j. Once receiving this input, set a boolean variable active. Say that (U_i, P_i) and S_j are the partners of this session.
2. Upon receiving an input (Send, sid, m) from one of the partners of this session, and if active is set, send (Receive, sid, m) to the other partner and (Sent, sid, $l(m)$) to the adversary.

Fig. 3. The Dual-authentication Secure Channel Functionality, $\mathcal{F}_{\text{D-SC}}$

Functionality $\mathcal{F}_{\text{P-A}}$

$\mathcal{F}_{\text{D-SC}}$ proceeds as follows, running with some provers $P_1, \ldots, P_n$ and some verifiers $V_1, \ldots, V_n$, and every prover P_i is initialized with a acceptable PCR status PCR_i.

1. Upon receiving an input (Challenge, sid, P, verifier) from some verifier V, do:
   (a) Send (sid, P, V) to the adversary, and receive an response (Ok, $nonce'$) from the adversary. If V is corrupted, then record $nonce'$, else generate a fresh $nonce$ and record it. Then output (sid, n) to the adversary, V and P (n stands for the recorded nonce).
   (b) Wait to receive an input (Attest, sid, V, prover) from P. Once receiving this input, output (SentPCR, sid, P, V) to the adversary.
2. Upon receiving (SendPCR, sid, V, (n, PCR')) from the adversary, check whether (n, PCR') is recorded. If it's recorded, output (SentPCR, sid, P, (n, PCR')) to V. Else, record the pair (n, PCR), and output (SentPCR, sid, P, (n, PCR)) to V.
3. Upon receiving an input (Corrupt, sid, V, Verifier) from the adversary, mark V as corrupted.
4. Upon receiving an input (Corrupt, sid, P, Prover) from the adversary, change PCR to $\overline{PCR}$.

Fig. 4. The Platform Attestation Functionality, $\mathcal{F}_{\text{P-A}}$

At beginning, each honest prover is initialized with a PCR status which is acceptable for a honest verifier. Through the Challenge interface, a verifier declares that it's willing to verify the PCR status of a prover. This request is forwarded to the prover and the adversary. If the verifier is corrupted, $\mathcal{F}_{\text{P-A}}$ receive a nonce from the adversary and record it. If the verifier is not corrupted, $\mathcal{F}_{\text{P-A}}$ generates a fresh random nonce itself and record it. The nonce is then output to the adversary, the verifier and the prover. Through the Attest interface, the requested prover provides its received nonce and declares that it wants to attest its PCR status to the verifier. After receiving the challenge and attest messages, $\mathcal{F}_{\text{P-A}}$ record the nonce and the current PCR status, then: 1) if the verifier is not corrupted, $\mathcal{F}_{\text{P-A}}$ returns the nonce and the current PCR status to the verifier, and 2) if the verifier is corrupted, and there exists a nonce and a PCR status in the record, $\mathcal{F}_{\text{P-A}}$ asks the adversary whether to return the previous or the current PCR status. Through the corruption interface, the adversary can corrupt any prover or verifier. If the adversary decides to corrupt the prover, the PCR of the prover will be changed to a unacceptable status. $\mathcal{F}_{\text{P-A}}$ captures the intuitive notion of TNC:

1. Once the platform is corrupted, which means that the adversary runs some malicious code on the platform, the PCR will record this code and change to a status which is not acceptable to a honest verifier. This property captures the integrity measurement and storage capability of a platform equipped with a TPM.
2. Against the replay attack for honest parties. $\mathcal{F}_{\text{P-A}}$ sends not only the PCR status but also a fresh nonce aiming to prove that the PCR status is fresh.
3. If the verifier is corrupted, the platform attestation will not be reliable. That is, if the nonce is not fresh, then the adversary can mount a replay attack.

4.2   Analysis of TCG Platform Attestation Protocol

We show that the TCG platform attestation protocol (we call P-Attest for short), depicted in Figure 5, securely realizes $\mathcal{F}_{\text{P-A}}$ given $\mathcal{F}_{\text{Cert}}$ which models an AIK. In order to model the protection capability of TPM, corruption of a prover only changes the PCR status of the prover and the certification party in $\mathcal{F}_{\text{Cert}}$, which means that the AIK is incorruptible.

TCG Platform Attestation Protocol

Each prover is initialized a PCR status which is valid to the verifier.
1. Upon receiving an input (Challenge, sid, P, verifier), verifier V generates a fresh random nonce n, sends (sid, V, n) to P.
2. Upon receiving an input (Attest, sid, V, prover), prover P waits for a nonce n from verifier V. Upon receiving of (sid, V, n), P sets $sid' = (P, sid)$, sets $m = (n, PCR)$, sends (Sign, sid', m) to $\mathcal{F}_{\text{Cert}}$, obtains the response (Signature, sid', m, σ), and sends (sid, P, m, σ) to V.
3. Upon receiving (sid, P, m, σ), V sets $sid' = (P, sid)$, checks whether the nonce in m equals n, sets $m = (n, PCR)$, sends (Verify, sid', m, σ) to $\mathcal{F}_{\text{Cert}}$, and obtains a response (Verified, sid', m, σ, f). If $f = 1$ then V outputs (SentPCR, sid,P,V, (n, PCR)) and halts, else B halts without output.

Fig. 5. The TCG Platform Attestation Protocol

Theorem 3. *The P-Attest protocol securely realizes functionality $\mathcal{F}_{\text{P-A}}$ in the $\mathcal{F}_{\text{Cert}}$-hybrid model.*

Due to the space limitation, we give the complete proof of above theorem in the full version [23].

5 Analysis of Complete TNC

We first introduce our general ideal TNC functionality $\mathcal{F}_{\text{TNC}}$. We then analyze the complete TNC protocol, combining TCG attestation protocol and IF-TLS-SKAE protocol, and show that it realizes the ideal TNC functionality in the $(\mathcal{F}_{\text{D-SC}}, \mathcal{F}_{\text{P-A}})$-hybrid model. To show the usefulness of the dual-authentication feature provided by $\mathcal{F}_{\text{D-SC}}$, we show that the above simulation will not hold if $\mathcal{F}_{\text{D-SC}}$ is replaced with an usual secure channel functionality without dual-authentication feature.

5.1 A General TNC Functionality

Our ideal TNC functionality is depicted in Figure 6. Our functionality $\mathcal{F}_{\text{TNC}}$ is much more general than the TNC functionality presented in [21] as our functionality models the IF-T protocol and the above IF-TNCCS protocol as secure channel and platform authentication functionality respectively, while the TNC functionality in [21] only models the IF-T binding to EAP protocol. Our TNC functionality captures the following TNC features:

1. User Authentication and Platform Authentication. $\mathcal{F}_{\text{D-SC}}$ authenticates both user and platform identities of connecting endpoints.
2. Platform Attestation. $\mathcal{F}_{\text{P-A}}$ abstracts the main goal of the IF-TNCCS protocol carried in the secure channel established by IF-T, that is, the platform integrity attestation.
3. Corrupt Platforms. The $\mathcal{F}_{\text{P-A}}$ models the corruption of a platform in TNC by marking the PCR status as invalid.
4. Corrupt Users. We model a relaxed network policy which mainly validates the integrity status reported by a genuine TPM and the platform identity, that is, "integrity information reported by the platform and by the proof-of-identity supplied by the platform". Even the user of an endpoint is corrupted, the endpoint is able to connect to the network if it has valid PCR status. However, a constrained policy can be easily modeled by changing our functionality.

5.2 Realizing TNC Functionality

Figure 7 shows the complete TNC protocol. We prove it in the following theorem.

Theorem 4. *The complete TNC protocol securely realizes functionality $\mathcal{F}_{\text{TNC}}$ in the $(\mathcal{F}_{\text{D-SC}}, \mathcal{F}_{\text{P-A}})$-hybrid model.*

Due to the space limitation, we give the complete proof of above theorem in the full version [23].

Functionality $\mathcal{F}_{\mathrm{TNC}}$

$\mathcal{F}_{\mathrm{TNC}}$ proceeds as follows, running with some NARs and some NAAs. Each NAR is composed of a user U and a platform P, and is initialized by a valid PCR status PCR.

1. Upon receiving an input (TNC Request, sid, NAR=(U,P), NAA) from some NAR, send $(sid, (U,P),$ NAA) to the adversary, and wait to receive an input (TNC Response, sid, NAR=(U,P), NAA) from NAA. Once receiving this input, set a boolean variable active.
2. Upon receiving (TNC Establish, sid, NAR=(U,P), NAA, f) from the adversary, and if active is set:
   (a) If neither P nor NAA is corrupted, output (TNC Established, sid, NAR=(U,P), NAA, 1) to NAA.
   (b) Else, if NAA is corrupted, output (TNC Established, sid, NAR=(U,P), NAA, f) to NAA.
   (c) Else, if P is corrupted, output (TNC Established, sid, NAR=(U,P), NAA, 0) to NAA.
3. Upon receiving an input (Corrupt Platform, sid, P), change the PCR of P to $\overline{PCR}$ and mark P as corrupted.
4. Upon receiving an input (Corrupt NAA, sid, NAA), mark NAA as corrupted.

Fig. 6. The TNC Functionality, $\mathcal{F}_{\mathrm{TNC}}$

Protocol TNC

1. When activated with input (TNC Request, sid, NAR=(U,P), NAA) by $\mathcal{Z}$, NAR sends an input (Establish-session, sid, (U,P), initiator) to $\mathcal{F}_{\mathrm{D\text{-}SC}}$, then waits for a challenge from NAA.
2. When activated with input (TNC Response, sid, NAR=(U,P), NAA) by $\mathcal{Z}$, NAA do:
   (a) Send an input (Establish-session, sid, (U,P), responder) to $\mathcal{F}_{\mathrm{D\text{-}SC}}$.
   (b) Send an input (Challenge, sid, P, verifier) to $\mathcal{F}_{\mathrm{P\text{-}A}}$, receive (sid, n), and record n.
   (c) Send (Send, sid, n) to $\mathcal{F}_{\mathrm{D\text{-}SC}}$.
3. Upon receiving the challenge n from $\mathcal{F}_{\mathrm{D\text{-}SC}}$, NAR sends (Attest, sid, NAA, prover) to $\mathcal{F}_{\mathrm{P\text{-}A}}$.
4. Upon receiving (SentPCR, sid, P, $m = (n', PCR')$) from $\mathcal{F}_{\mathrm{P\text{-}A}}$, NAA checks whether $n' = n$ and PCR' is valid. If m passes the two checks, NAA sets $f = 1$, else sets $f = 0$. Then NAA outputs(TNC Established, sid, NAR=(U,P), NAA, f).

Fig. 7. The TNC protocol for realizing $\mathcal{F}_{\mathrm{TNC}}$

5.3   Realizing TNC without Dual Authentication

To demonstrate the usefulness of the dual-authentication feature we proposed in this paper, we show that the complete TNC protocol depicted in Figure 7 cannot realize $\mathcal{F}_{TNC}$ if the dual-authentication feature is removed, i.e., replacing $\mathcal{F}_{D\text{-}SC}$ with $\mathcal{F}_{SC}$.

Theorem 5. *The complete TNC protocol doesn't UC-realize functionality* $\mathcal{F}_{TNC}$ *in the* $(\mathcal{F}_{SC}, \mathcal{F}_{P\text{-}A})$*-hybrid model.*

6   Conclusion

We analyze the complete TNC protocol, combining the IF-T binding to TLS and TCG platform attestation protocol, in the UC framework. We show that the SKAE extension introduced by TCG plays an important part in preventing the MitM attack presented in [1]. Our roadmap for the analysis of the complete TNC protocol adopts the modular feature of UC framework. We partition the complete TNC into a secure channel functionality and a platform attestation functionality. Then show that the IF-TLS-SKAE protocol and the basic TCG platform attestation protocol securely realizes the two primitive functionalities respectively. Finally, we use the composition theorem to argue that the complete TNC protocol realizes TNC. Besides, the dual-authentication certification functionality $\mathcal{F}_{D\text{-}Cert}$ and the platform attestation functionality $\mathcal{F}_{P\text{-}A}$ enable us to analyze protocols that use SKAE extension or TCG platform attestation in a modular way.

References

1. Asokan, N., Niemi, V., Nyberg, K.: Man-in-the-middle in tunnelled authentication protocols. In: Christianson, B., Crispo, B., Malcolm, J.A., Roe, M. (eds.) Security Protocols 2003. LNCS, vol. 3364, pp. 28–41. Springer, Heidelberg (2005)
2. Canetti, R.: Universally composable security: A new paradigm for cryptographic protocols. In: Proceedings of the 42nd IEEE Symposium on Foundations of Computer Science, pp. 136–145. IEEE (2001)
3. Canetti, R.: Universally composable signature, certification, and authentication. In: Proceedings of the 17th IEEE Computer Security Foundations Workshop, pp. 219–233. IEEE (2004)
4. Canetti, R., Krawczyk, H.: Universally composable notions of key exchange and secure channels. In: Knudsen, L.R. (ed.) EUROCRYPT 2002. LNCS, vol. 2332, pp. 337–351. Springer, Heidelberg (2002)
5. Chen, L., Warinschi, B.: Security of the TCG Privacy-CA solution. In: 2010 IEEE/IFIP 8th International Conference on Embedded and Ubiquitous Computing (EUC), pp. 609–616. IEEE (2010)
6. Gajek, S., Manulis, M., Pereira, O., Sadeghi, A.-R., Schwenk, J.: Universally composable security analysis of TLS. In: Baek, J., Bao, F., Chen, K., Lai, X. (eds.) ProvSec 2008. LNCS, vol. 5324, pp. 313–327. Springer, Heidelberg (2008)

7. Institute for Electrical and Electronics Engineers (IEEE). IEEE802, Port-Based Network Access Control, IEEE Std 802.1X-2004 (December 2004)
8. Küsters, R., Tuengerthal, M.: Joint state theorems for public-key encryption and digital signature functionalities with local computation. In: IEEE 21st Computer Security Foundations Symposium, CSF 2008, pp. 270–284. IEEE (2008)
9. McCune, J.M., Parno, B.J., Perrig, A., Reiter, M.K., Isozaki, H.: Flicker: An execution infrastructure for tcb minimization. ACM SIGOPS Operating Systems Review 42, 315–328 (2008)
10. Melnikov, A., Zeilenga, K.: Simple Authentication and Security Layer (SASL). Technical report, RFC 4422 (June 2006)
11. Pfitzmann, B., Waidner, M.: A model for asynchronous reactive systems and its application to secure message transmission. In: Proceedings of the 2001 IEEE Symposium on Security and Privacy, S&P 2001, pp. 184–200. IEEE (2001)
12. Sailer, R., Zhang, X., Jaeger, T., Van Doorn, L.: Design and implementation of a tcg-based integrity measurement architecture. In: USENIX Security Symposium, vol. 13, p. 16 (2004)
13. Trusted Computing Group. Subject Key Attestation Evidence Extension Version 1.0, Revision 7 (June 16, 2005)
14. Trusted Computing Group. TNC IF-T: Protocol Bindings for Tunneled EAP Methods Specification Version 1.1, Revision 10 (May 21, 2007)
15. Trusted Computing Group. Trusted Platform Module Library Part 1: Architecture, Family "2.0" Level 00, Revision 00.99 (August 22, 2013)
16. Trusted Computing Group. Trusted Platform Module Library Part 3: Commands, Family "2.0" Level 00, Revision 00.99 (August 22, 2013)
17. Trusted Computing Group. TNC IF-TNCCS: TLV Binding Specification Version 2.0, Revision 16 (January 22, 2010)
18. Trusted Computing Group. TNC IF-T: Binding to TLS Specification Version 2.0, Revision 7 (February 27, 2013)
19. Trusted Computing Group. TNC Architecture for Interoperability Specification Version 1.5, Revision 3 (May 7, 2012)
20. Xiao, Y., Wang, Y., Pang, L.: Security analysis and improvement of TNC IF-T Protocol Binding to TLS. Communications, China 10(7), 85–92 (2013)
21. Zhang, J., Ma, J., Moon, S.: Universally composable secure TNC model and EAP-TNC protocol in IF-T. Science China Information Sciences 53(3), 465–482 (2010)
22. Zhang, Z., Zhu, L., Wang, F., Liao, L., Guo, C., Wang, H.: Computationally sound symbolic analysis of EAP-TNC protocol. In: Chen, L., Yung, M., Zhu, L. (eds.) INTRUST 2011. LNCS, vol. 7222, pp. 113–128. Springer, Heidelberg (2012)
23. Zhao, S., Zhang, Q., Qin, Y., Feng, D.: Universally Composable secure TNC protocol based on IF-T binding to TLS, https://eprint.iacr.org/2014/490.pdf

Revisiting Node Injection of P2P Botnet

Jia Yan[1], Lingyun Ying[1], Yi Yang[1], Purui Su[1], Qi Li[2], Hui Kong[3],
and Dengguo Feng[1]

[1] Trusted Computing and Information Assurance Laboratory, Institute of Software,
Chinese Academy of Sciences
{yangj,yly,yangyi,feng}@tca.iscas.ac.cn, purui@iscas.ac.cn
[2] Institute of Information Security, ETH Zrich
[3] Transwarp Software Inc

Abstract. Botnet armed with P2P protocol is especially robust against various attacks used to be very effective against centralized network. It's especially significant to enhance our understanding of unstructured P2P Botnets which prove to be resilient against various dismantle efforts. Node injection technique is quite effective in enumerating infected hosts from P2P Botnets, but no previous work has investigated the effectiveness of this method in a quantitative manner. In this paper, we propose a peer popularity boosting algorithm to put the popularity of injected peer under control, and a method to tune the node injection rate to achieve better compromise between consumed bandwidth and completeness of node enumeration. Furthermore, we evaluate our methods with varied level of node injections on three live P2P Botnets, the result shows that our method is quite effective in boosting and manipulating injected peer's popularity. In contrast to other methods without manipulation of injected peer's magnitude of dispersion in network, our method not only unlock the full potential of node injections, but also could be adapted to measurements of various needs.

Keywords: P2P Botnet, Node Enumeration, Node injection.

1   Introduction

Botnet is a collection of infected computers remotely controlled by criminals. It poses a critical security challenge to the common good of Internet as its spamming, DDoS activity severely undermine the interests of global Internet users. Among different families of botnet, P2P botnet is probably the most difficult to combat as they do not build upon a central server to disseminate commands and updates, whereas they largely depend on non-centralized P2P network structure which is proved to be highly robust, e.g., Symantec only halved the threat posed by ZeroAccess [9]. To mitigate the damage caused by P2P botnets, anti-virus community needs to enhance their understanding of the working mechanism and runtime information of these networks. Based on the reverse engineering of the P2P protocol the botnet uses, researchers could develop a crawler to gather intelligence and prepare for future attacks. By requesting peer list from other peers

M.H. Au et al. (Eds.): NSS 2014, LNCS 8792, pp. 124–137, 2014.
© Springer International Publishing Switzerland 2014

iteratively, we could retrieve information of peers from botnet, this kind of peer enumeration is called crawling. In crawling P2P network, there are usually two kinds of peers in terms of the accessibility of network a specific peer reside in. If a peer is accessible and routable from any other Internet host, we call it super peer or routable peer (we use super peer and routable peer interchangeably in this paper). Otherwise, we call it normal peer or unroutable peer. Note that, peer and node are also used interchangeably in this paper.

Crawling based approach could not retrieve unroutable peers, unroutable peers would not reply to any requests from other peers. Node injection based approach works by communicating with peers of botnet and tend to inject itself or faked peers into the routing table of other peers. Unroutable peers behind gateways would contact actively with these injected peers. Thus node injection could be of great help to enumerate both routable peers and unroutable peers. The problem of existing work is that they did not evaluate or discuss the level of node injection in depth. It's evident that the result of node enumeration would be vastly different when varied levels of injections are introduced into tracking efforts. However, it's not trivial to analyze the level of node injection as P2P botnet is quite dynamic and seems impossible to exactly measure the distribution of injected peers throughout the P2P network. We propose to make use of actively crawling to measure the injected peer' distribution in routable peers which could reflect to some extent its popularity in the whole network.   Another issue in node injection is that, previous works don't propose any viable methods to manipulate the popularity of injected peers. We bridge the gap and propose a method to boost and manipulate population of specific peer. Note that apart from aggressive node injection based intelligent gathering of P2P Botnet, low-profile node injection is also required as some security researchers would choose to stay under the radar to not be detected by botmasters. Our method provide a glimpse into how to achieve various level of node injection.

In this paper, we model peer popularity through in-degree of the peer in the graph rebuilt upon crawling and present a practical method for boosting and manipulating peer's popularity. Specifically, we make use of real-time measurement of peer in-degree as the basis for tuning of peer injection rates. We evaluate our method through a number of experiments on three live P2P Botnets, our method could effectively boost and manipulate injected peer's popularity which could fits to various needs of botnet tracking. For Sality botnet we also find the optimal peer injection rates where much lower bandwidth is consumed without significant compromise of the node coverage of enumeration.

The remainder of the paper is organized as follows. We present technical background of three live P2P Botnet we would investigate in Section 2. And in Section 3 we propose our popularity boosting method in detail, and discuss various issues involved in manipulating popularity of injected peer. We present related work in Section 5. Section 6 would be our discussion and conclusion of this paper.

2 P2P Botnet Background

P2P botnet is on the rise these days [11]. This paper concentrates on three major live P2P botnets in the wild: ZeroAccess v2 (version 2, four branches of these botnet are named ZA16471, ZA16470, ZA16464 and ZA16465), ZeusGameover (abbreviated as Zeus) and Sality v3.

Table 1. Routing mechanism of P2P Botnets

Botnet	ID	ID available	Routing Mechanism				
			RSize	ESize	OnlySuper	LT	HT
ZeroAccess	T	Y	$16*10^6$	16	N	∞	<1 min
Zeus	P	Y	150	10	N	30min	<30 min
Sality	P	N	1000	1	Y	40min	<40 min

In order to depict the difference in various metrics among these botnets in terms of their P2P protocol design, we outline in Table 1 various properties of these botnets. ZeroAccess and Sality are typical unstructured P2P networks with commands and updates from botmaster gossiped between each other, and ZeusGameover is more like structured network in selecting nearer peers in terms of numeric ID while building peer list replies. RSize in Table 1 is the number of peers that infected bots could contact with in order to update its state, ZeroAccess stores up to 16 million peers which thwart route poison attempt recently initiated by Symantec. ESize is the size of peer list exchanged between two bots in one message. Sality exchanges only 1 peer in each message which is rather inefficient in disseminating updates. ID of these botnets is usually used to distinguish between different infections, as P indicates persistent ID and T indicate temporary ID. The column Available indicates whether ID is available in crawling. We could see that for ZeroAccess, ID is available but of limited use since it would change upon reboot. The ID of Zeus is required in building peer-to-peer messages, therefore could be used to mark unique infection. Whereas for Sality, ID is unique but not available in crawling. There are two parameters of these botnets which are helpful for our research, the time that the injected peer would stay in other peer's routing table which we denote it as LT, and the time that it would stay in other peer's candidate list for building peer list replies where we denote it as HT. Note that for ZeroAccess, once a peer is successfully added to its routing table for real-time routing (also called working routing table), then it will be permanently stored in its backup routing table which could save up to millions of nodes. But with aggressive communication with other peers, its working routing table is highly dynamic and peer entries would get staled very soon.

3 Methodology

In this section, we give out our popularity boosting method, where we leverage the strengths of both active crawling for real-time measurement of in-degree and node injection for attracting large amounts of unroutable peers.

Our method attempts to combine the strength of proactive crawling with reactive node-injection based peer enumeration which is similar to Passive P2P Monitor (PPM) proposed by Kang [7]. However, Kang's approach aims to capture as many peers as possible without much concern of the actual popularity of their injected peers, so it's necessary to devise a efficient method to track or measure the popularity of the peers we have injected which could be of great value for better control of network tracking. Our measurement of the popularity of specific peer in P2P Botnet is based on the observation that peer list responses from many peers are similar to some extent, that significant portions of the peers in these responses are just duplicates. We carefully assumed that the more a peer's duplicates are, the more popular a peer is. The number of duplicates of specific peer could be seen as the in-degree of this peer in the graph rebuilt upon network crawling.

The major objective of node injection is to put the injected peer in as many other peer's routing table as possible. But not every peer could be injected successfully due to different network accessibility. The routable peers could be reached through Internet, thus could be injected directly. Whereas for NATed peers, the only way we could inject a peer is through so-called propagation effect. We assume that the more popular a peer is in routable peers, the more popular a peer is in unroutable peers. Therefore, we confine our node injection to routable peers exclusively. We denote the in-degree of routable peer v as $InDeg(v)$.

Popularity Boosting. Node injection is often accomplished in communicating continuously with other peers in P2P Botnet, but the effect of node injection actually depends on how the network is structured in most cases. Every network has its way of accepting new peers into their internal routing tables, as well as constructing peer list replies to other peers. The node injection pays only when the target peer not only accepts our peers but also helps propagating them to other peers. To our knowledge, although different P2P botnets have vast different design of their P2P protocols, but they would definitely introduce timestamps based peers updating mechanism where recent contacted peers are superior to other peers. From this observation, we could refresh this timestamps as often as possible in order to maximize the possibility of propagating injected peers to other part of the botnet.

There are two time metrics that are essential for the node injection as mentioned in Section 2, LT and HT. Our popularity boosting method works by passively listening and responding to ping checks from remote peers for extending of LT, and actively sending packets to remote peers to refresh injected peer's timestamps regularly in short interval of time for extending of HT. Node injection is carried out through sending packets conforming to the protocols of the P2P Botnet. We call the rate of packets (number of packets sent per time unit) sending to remote peers as node injection rate, and denote it as NIR. By making the NIR high enough, we could extend injected peer's lifetime in other peers' routing tables. We denote the overhead of keeping the connection with a peer as O, then it's evident that O_{LT} is no more than O_{HT}, much less in most cases.

Note that we could not increase NIR arbitrarily, as either ISP network ingress policy does not permit such aggressive activities or P2P Botnets often impose rate-limiting on sending packets and limit the number of contacted IPs per subnet. We call the highest NIR we could achieve as NIR_{max}. We measure popularity of injected peer v through $InDeg(v)$ in the graph we rebuild through crawling. Our *popularity boosting* boosts when $InDeg$ of injected peer is not at least as high as the threshold T (T is a parameter we could customize) by increasing NIR. This is our self-boosting mechanism which could make the injected peer's population indicated by $InDeg$ higher than previous approach. Since previous approach does not measure their injected peer's popularity in real time, and node injection is often reached through maximized flooding of P2P Botnet which is not efficient and effective. therefore we believe our work is the first to shed light on these issues.

If $InDeg$ of injected peer is pretty low, it's straightforward to flood the known peer list for possible node injection. But if the network is quite large, then it's not very efficient to do that. Sending node injection packets to more popular routable peers might be a better choice. Through node enumeration, we could compute the $InDeg$ of all peers which we could reorder the list of peers by ranking of $InDeg$, so one option which could optimize the enumeration is sending packets to those peers with $InDeg$ at least as high as the threshold I (another parameter we should customize). In addition, with $InDeg$ of injected peer being below the threshold I, we ignore this peer temporarily. We inject this peer only if the $InDeg$ of this peer is higher than I in the coming rounds of injections.

In conclusion, our popularity boosting method (denote as PB algorithm) is described in Algorithm 1. It could be configured to make it adapted to specific P2P Botnet or even generic P2P network through parameters *seedpeer* for bootstraping, *injected_peer* for injection, T, I, NIR and W. T and I have been described above. For W, it actually depends on specific botnet as different networks pose different kinds of rate-limiting on communication with other peers, we have to wait for some time to prevent from being banned by remote peers.

Algorithm 1 Node injection with PB ($seedpeer$, $injected\_peer$, T, I, W, NIR)

---

1. set $v = injected\_peer$
2. **repeat**
3. $Crawl_t = \text{crawl\_once(seedpeer)}$
4. $InDeg_{avg} = \sum_{p \in Crawl_t} \frac{InDeg(p)}{|(Crawl_t|}$
5.   **if** injected_peer.indegree $< T$ **then**
6.   **for** p:peer in $Crawl_t$ **do**
7.   **if** $InDeg(p) > InDeg_{avg}$ **then**
8.   inject v into p with NIR
9.   **else**
10.   refresh v in p with NIR
11.   **end if**
12.   **end for**
13.   **end if**
14.   sleep(W)
15. **until** Terminated by user

Note that, we could also optimize our aggressive node injection through customization of our method. For example, if we want to find the optimal node injection rate with less resource consumption without significant compromise of the node coverage. We could concurrently run two trackers, one is optimized tracker (denoted TA), another one is reference tracker (denoted TB). Node coverage is denoted NC here. TB is set up as the reference of NC for TA, and it set NIR to NIR_{max}. For node coverage, the size of all peers enumerated is a good metric which applies to nearly all P2P Botnets. We binary search the best fit for NIR. In other words, TA starts with NIR_{TA} setting to 0, we set higher end of binary search to NIR_{max} and lower end to 0. When NC_{TA} is below a threshold C, then we would increase NIR to the half of the sum of the current value and higher end with lower end set to the computed value of NIR. When NC_{TA} is above the threshold C, then we would decrease NIR to the half of the sum of the current value and lower end with higher end set to the computed value of NIR. Note that the threshold C would not set to 100 percent of NC_{TB} as TA with decreased NIR would definitely not outperform TB. In addition, threshold C is not a single value to match, but a range for the reason of circumventing jitter effects which is beneficial for our search to converge to some fixed value.

4   Evaluation

In this section, we present the results of our experiments when testing our method for boosting and manipulating popularity of injected peer.

4.1   System Design

The architecture of our tracking system (called SPTracker) for enumerating nodes of P2P Botnet is based upon the joint working of two modules: Aggressive Crawler (AC) and Passive Monitor (PM). AC would initiate a crawl periodically at fixed interval of time. PM would passively wait for incoming packets and feed the parsed result back to AC before each round of crawling initiated by AC. The whole process of continuous tracking is outlined in Figure 1. The horizontal line represents the passing time upon which PM starts passive monitoring and AC begins to crawl regularly. We have visualized the data SPTracker collected and made the tracking project available online[1].

Note that before the overall crawling starts, AC would be given a known routable peer list to bootstrap. And in the following crawls AC would take the routable peers collected from both previous crawls and passive monitoring as bootstrap peer list. There are two phases in each round of tracking. In the first phase, upon receiving bootstrap live super peers from PM, AC would send peer list requests to the peers in the list and consume any replies from these peers fed back by the PM. Thus, AC could enumerate peers iteratively until convergence (the overall size of distinct peers stop increasing) or timeout. For the second phase, AC would initiate our PB method, and send many carefully crafted packets to live peers enumerated in the previous phase for node injections.

---

[1] SPTracker Project, Homepage of Project is: http://p2pbotnetracker.net

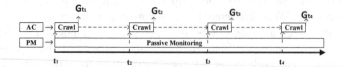

Fig. 1. SPTracker: Continuous Tracking System of P2P Botnet

Note for some botnet with loose admission policy of peers in their routing table, in the first phase of node enumeration, we achieve node injection at the same time, i.e., for P2P botnet ZeroAccess.

4.2 Setup

We begin by reversing and extracting protocol specification of three prominent and live P2P Botnets as mentioned in Section 2. More specifically, we need to empirically set and evaluate several parameters in SPTracker. For the popularity threshold parameter T, it has a upper limit which depends on the NIR_{max} of specific P2P Botnet. Sality and ZeroAccess does not have any rate-limiting mechanism, therefore could be flooded with many packets to maximize our injection efforts. In contrast, ZeusGameover blacklists frequent contacted IPs, all the IPs sending more than 6 packets consecutively with time interval less than 60 seconds would be blocked immediately, and the number of requests from itself are also included. This mechanism strictly limits various kinds of node enumeration and sinkhole efforts. So its NIR_{max} is set to 4 packets per minute conservatively considering additional ping checks a peer would send. Note that although we could send as many packets to Sality nodes as possible, but we could not achieve node injection easily as Sality prioritize live and routable peers with high credits. In our tracking experiments, we would increase NIR of our system to see what popularity of injected peer we could achieve. So, NIR_{max} of Sality and ZeroAccess is only limited by the bandwidth our server could afford. For the threshold parameter I which is equal to the $InDeg$ of qualified peers to be injected, we experiment with different I in node enumeration. For the parameter W, as stated in Table 1, we have to wait 60 seconds before a peer of ZeusGameover botnet clears its IP counter. For ZeroAccess and Sality, we also empirically set it to 60 seconds concerning bandwidth costs.

Our experiments are carried out on a number of dedicated commodity Ubuntu Linux VPS servers with 2GB of memory and 10MB of dedicated network bandwidth. They have different IP addresses but reside in the same ISP with similar configurations to prevent the influence of network heterogeneity. The identification of unique peers is usually skewed by network churn. For tracking of ZeroAccess and Sality, we use IP address to distinguish between different infections. For ZeusGameover, ID is used instead.

4.3   Evaluation Results

First, we give a glimpse of what the in-degrees of routable nodes in P2P Botnet look like. Based on the continuous tracking of routable peers of several live P2P Botnets since October of 2013, we conduct various statistical analysis against the dynamics of P2P Botnet. Based on these analysis, the summary of distribution of in-degree is provided in Table 2. We could see that more than 70% of routable nodes in these botnets have in-degree below 10. Very few of them have in-degree high enough to attract large amounts of unroutable peers. Existing work like [7] injects through low-profile communicating with other peers would fail to achieve high node coverage in unstructured P2P Botnets.

Table 2. average $InDeg$ of routable peers in P2P Botnets

Botnet	InDegree			
	Q1	Median	Q2	Max
ZA16471	3	5	7.15	46.57
ZA16470	4	6	8.79	55
ZA16464	3	4.67	6.83	48
ZA16465	4.25	7.08	10.52	87.31
ZeusGameover	1	1.26	1.7	151.64
Sality	1	3	6.06	121.17

Furthermore, we test our PB algorithm on boosting popularity of injected peers on live P2P Botnets. As many security organization infiltrate ZA16471 branch of ZeroAccess, like Symantec did [9] last year. It's pretty convenient to compare our injection efforts with others, so we target sub branch ZA16471 of ZeroAccess for node injection. In order to unlock the full potential of node injection efforts, we set parameter T to the size of $Crawl_t$, and maximize our injection with NIR setting to NIR_{max}. In addition, every peer with $InDeg$ above 1 would be injected. We also test SPTracker with NIR set to 50% and 25% of NIR_{max} to evaluate the effect of popularity boosting. We call the former test as PT100 and the later two as PT50 and PT25.

The results of three concurrent node enumerations on ZeroAccess Botnet (sub branch ZA16471 specifically) are outlined in Figure 2 and Figure 3. SPTracker captures a snapshot of the whole network every minute, and at the same time record the $InDeg$ of every captured peers and the total size of peers enumerated (including routable peers and unroutable peers), the overall enumeration lasts for 60 minutes. We could see that the $InDeg$ of injected peer has increased dramatically over time for all three tests. Even for injection with much lower NIR (25% of NIR_{max}), the $InDeg$ of injected peer is much more than any other nodes in the ZeroAccess network could achieve (Comparing to the result in Table 2). We know that many security researchers and organizations have been tracking and sinkholing ZeroAccess Botnet for a long time, our method could outperform any other injection efforts. As for the three test we have conducted, the average

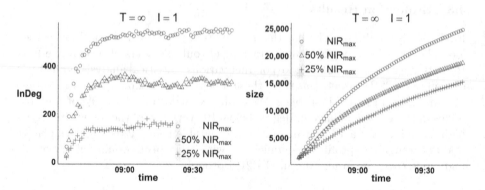

Fig. 2. Indegree of injected peer in ZA16471

Fig. 3. Nodes enumerated in ZA16471

number of injected nodes (indicated by average of $InDeg$) of maximized node injection in PT100 is about 60.6% more than PT50, and 257.2% more than PT25, and the size of nodes enumerated in PT100 is 33.3% more than PT50, and 71.5% more than PT25. We also record the size of routable peers in three tests (refer to Figure 4), they're nearly the same which indicate that the only difference between the results of three tests are size of unroutable peers. For the resource consumption, it's obvious that higher node coverage needs higher bandwidth (refer to Figure 5).

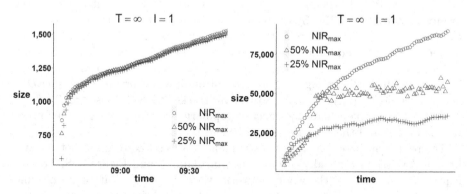

Fig. 4. Routable nodes enumerated

Fig. 5. Packets sent in each round of enumeration

We carried out a number of experiments on popularity boosting using different NIR. The results are presented in Table 3. For ZeroAccess, the $InDeg$ of injected peer could reach up to 683 which accounts for more than half of the size of all routable peers. For ZeusGameover, this botnet poses strict rate-limiting on packets exchanged between peers, so our PB method could not boost popularity of injected peer to the value as high as the most popular nodes had reached in short period of time. But our peer is still one of the most notable peers as we could attract much more nodes than ordinary crawling methods. We find out that if we inject continuously for more than three days, our method could sustainably increase $InDeg$ of injected peers to more than 200, thus our method could also be applied to ZeusGameover botnet without hampered by its strict limitation. Rossow's work makes use of node impersonation to achieve quick node injection [11], but this would conflicts with other nodes and only apply to specific network. For Sality botnet, it's much difficult to achieve node injection as fast as the other two botnets, because we have to build credits gradually.

Table 3. result of node enumeration with different NIR in 24 hours numA/numB, numA is average $InDeg$, and numB is the size of nodes enumerated

Botnet	NIR		
	$0.2*NIR_{max}$	$0.5*NIR_{max}$	NIR_{max}
ZeroAccess	69.3/129031	312.3/161931	683.6/187653
Sality	10.1/58093	15.6/90381	67.4/123871
ZeusGameover	23.4/45903	32.1/89321	45.8/102934

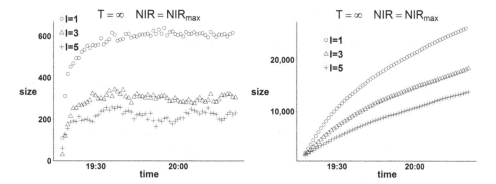

Fig. 6. Indegree of injected peers in ZA16471

Fig. 7. Nodes enumerated in ZA16471

In addition, we investigate on the node enumeration with different threshold I. In this experiment, we also conduct tests on ZA16471 and set NIR to NIR_{max}. I is set to 1, 3 and 5 respectively. From Table 2, we could see that with I setting to 3, about 25% of routable peers are excluded. With I setting to 5, half of routable peers are ignored. The results are outlined in Figure 6 and Figure 7. Increasing of threshold I could significantly downgrade the performance of our enumeration. In this test, we conclude that the more peers we have injected, the more complete view SPTracker could get. Since we prioritize peers with high in-degree which we expect to trade node negligible coverage for reduction on resource consumption. The results demonstrate that for ZeroAccess Botnet with dynamic peer list updating mechanism, aggressive injection is required. Other than ZA16471, we also conduct tests on Sality Botnet, the result is promising as the routable peers in this network is more stable and have a relatively longer lifetime. From the results in Figure 8 and Figure 9, we could find that the *InDeg* of injected peer is roughly the same while setting I to 1 and 2, and the size of nodes enumerated is also roughly the same. Since setting I to 2 could reduce bandwidth costs, we believe careful tuning of I could lead to better enumeration without compromise of node coverage. So for Sality, we find the optimal parameter combination: $I = 2$, $NIR = NIR_{max}$.

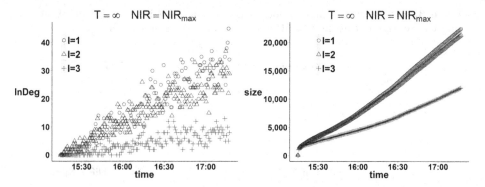

Fig. 8. Indegree of injected peers of Sality   **Fig. 9.** Nodes enumerated of Sality

In order to customize the node enumeration, we have to test against specific botnet with different combinations of parameters like NIR, threshold T and I. T could be used to throttle control the node injection, and has similar effect as the parameter NIR. But we could not know exactly the relationship between varied NIR and the popularity of injected peer, thus T could be well suited to the need of directly control the level of injection. For example, if we want to only covertly infiltrate into P2P Botnet without being noticed by others, then just set corresponding parameter T would work anyway. NIR and I are much volatile options for adjusting node enumeration. This result proves that PB mechanism could stabilize the popularity of injected super peer and make it under control to some extent.

From the experiments above, we managed to demonstrate that our PB method outperforms other methods in boosting and manipulating popularity of injected nodes. Our method could boost in-degree of injected peer to a level which is much more than any other nodes in three live P2P Botnets. For ZeroAccess, the in-degree of injected peer is 14 times larger than maximum in-degree of any nodes in the wild including those nodes set up by other security researchers. Also, through customization of several throttle control parameters, our method could also manipulate popularity of peer with acceptable precision which is handy to be used for various enumerations.

5   Related Work

Previous researches about P2P botnet have different objectives in mind, such as taxonomy [3,15], protocol design [12,14], measurement [6,7,10,13], detection [8], and threat mitigation [4,6]. Measurement of network, or more specifically node enumeration, is a prerequisite for any other in-depth researches of P2P botnet. In this section, we summarize various node enumeration techniques and mechanism adopted by botnet to stay covert from intelligent gathering.

There are two well-known approaches to crawl the P2P botnet, one is sending queries directly to peers from which peer list response is expected, and another approach is setting up peers masquerading as normal peers and makes them filled into other peers' routing table where large numbers of non-responsive peers behind NAT or firewall would phone in. While tracking through native crawling for peer-to-peer network has been extensively used by researchers from academia and industry. It's well known for its weakness of failing to find nodes behind the gateway and the firewall.

The latest systematic node enumeration was done by Rossow which take advantage of node injection techniques [11], they claim to enumerate nodes of various kinds of P2P Botnets and conduct detailed analysis and comparison of resilience of different botnets against information gathering like crawling. They also prove the effectiveness of node injection through a number of experiments. But They did not propose any methods to effectively inject nodes into botnet, also no details (like how many nodes have been injected) about the node injection are provided to further support their hypothesis. Since node enumerations through different level of injection are quite different, we believe it's necessary to investigate node injection in depth to find a better way to achieve node enumeration. Note that Rossow's work makes use of a number of vulnerabilities of P2P Botnet to achieve quick node injections, whereas our method could apply to generic P2P network. Even structured P2P network could be better enumerated through popularity boosting method.

Kang enumerate all the nodes through so called Passive P2P Monitoring (PPM) [7]. Whereas recent P2P botnets favor unstructured protocol with absence of long-lasting ID, e.g., ZeroAccess. In addition, the node coverage achieved by PPM through placing a few nodes in each zone of Overnet-based network does not apply to unstructured network. Kang's work also does not put injected peer's popularity into consideration, thus could not further improve their method both on node coverage and resource consumption.

We have reverse engineered the latest three kinds of live P2P botnets in the wild, further information regarding several P2P botnets this work related with could be found among various technical reports and research papers [1,2,5,9,16].

6   Discussion and Conclusion

As for the applicability and scalability of our method to other P2P Botnets, especially structured botnets like Storm and TDL4, our method could also be helpful as node injection applies to any P2P network with built-in routing tables and mechanism to accept external peers. However, our method does not take scalability into consideration as the total size of all three botnets we have investigated are relatively small comparing to live file-sharing network with millions of nodes, i.e., KAD Network and Mainline Network. But our methods could be trivially adapted to distributed version. Different from trying to inject our peer into every routable nodes, we could take in-degree as a relative measure which could reflect the popularity of injected peers. By splitting whole network space if network is structured or imposing strict limitation on terminating condition, we could distribute enumeration tasks to many independent trackers. And PB method could be applied to single tracker for popularity boosting.

For the anti-measures taken by bot authors, rate-limiting is an effective method to prevent our method from fast boosting and easy manipulation of popularity. But it only slows down our injection efforts, not strictly limit our method from achieving high popularity ultimately. But currently our method relies upon the knowledge of how long our peer would reside in remote peer's two candidate list (LT and HT, defined in Section 3). Further investigation into other methods for manipulation of popularity is needed.

In this paper, we propose to evaluate node injection of P2P botnets quantitatively, which is accomplished through modeling of injected peer's popularity by the in-degree this peer exhibits in the graph rebuilt through active crawling. We propose a method to boost and manipulate popularity of injected peers through real-time measurement of in-degree and tuning of packet injections rate. The result of experiments shows that our method is effective in boosting and manipulating of node injection magnitude which could be suited to various needs of botnet tracking. As a future work, we would look into implementing distributed version of our popularity boosting algorithm to integrate into our tracking system for complete tracking of various live P2P Botnets. Moreover, we would also like to accommodate more P2P botnets, like kelihos.

Acknowledgments. This work has been supported by the National Program on Key Basic Research Project (Grant No. 2012CB315804), the Major Research Plan of the National Natural Science Foundation of China (Grant No. 91118006), and the Beijing Municipal Natural Science Foundation (Grant No. 4122086).

References

1. Zeus-p2p monitoring and analysis. Technical report, CERT POLSKA (2013)
2. Andriesse, D., Rossow, C., Stone-Gross, B., Plohmann, D., Bos, H.: Highly Resilient Peer-to-Peer Botnets Are Here: An Analysis of Gameover Zeus. In: Proceedings of the 8th IEEE International Conference on Malicious and Unwanted Software (MALWARE 2013), Fajardo, Puerto Rico, USA. IEEE Computer Society (October 2013)
3. Dagon, D., Gu, G., Lee, C., Lee, W.: A taxonomy of botnet structures. In: Choi, L., Paek, Y., Cho, S. (eds.) ACSAC 2007. LNCS, vol. 4697, pp. 325–339. Springer, Heidelberg (2007)

4. Davis, C., Fernandez, J., Neville, S., McHugh, J.: Sybil attacks as a mitigation strategy against the storm botnet. In: 3rd International Conference on Malicious and Unwanted Software, MALWARE 2008, pp. 32–40 (2008)
5. Falliere, N.: Sality: Story of a peer to-peer viral network. Technical report, Symantec Labs (2011)
6. Holz, T., Steiner, M., Dahl, F., Biersack, E., Freiling, F.: Measurements and mitigation of peer-to-peer-based botnets: A case study on storm worm. In: Proceedings of the 1st Usenix Workshop on Large-Scale Exploits and Emergent Threats, LEET 2008, pp. 9:1–9:9. USENIX Association, Berkeley (2008)
7. Kang, B.B., Chan-Tin, E., Lee, C.P., Tyra, J., Kang, H.J., Nunnery, C., Wadler, Z., Sinclair, G., Hopper, N., Dagon, D., Kim, Y.: Towards complete node enumeration in a peer-to-peer botnet. In: Proceedings of the 4th International Symposium on Information, Computer, and Communications Security, ASIACCS 2009, pp. 23–34. ACM, New York (2009)
8. Nagaraja, S., Mittal, P., Hong, C.-Y., Caesar, M., Borisov, N.: Botgrep: Finding p2p bots with structured graph analysis. In: Proceedings of the 19th USENIX Conference on Security, USENIX Security 2010, p. 7. USENIX Association, Berkeley (2010)
9. Neville, A., Gibb, R.: Zeroaccess indepth. Technical report, Symantec (2013)
10. Rajab, M.A., Zarfoss, J., Monrose, F., Terzis, A.: My botnet is bigger than yours (maybe, better than yours): Why size estimates remain challenging. In: Proceedings of the First Conference on First Workshop on Hot Topics in Understanding Botnets, HotBots 2007, p. 5. USENIX Association, Berkeley (2007)
11. Rossow, C., Andriesse, D., Werner, T., Stone-Gross, B., Plohmann, D., Dietrich, C., Bos, H.: Sok: P2pwned - modeling and evaluating the resilience of peer-to-peer botnets. In: 2013 IEEE Symposium on Security and Privacy (SP), pp. 97–111 (2013)
12. Sinclair, G., Nunnery, C., Kang, B.-H.: The waledac protocol: The how and why. In: 2009 4th International Conference on Malicious and Unwanted Software (MALWARE), pp. 69–77 (2009)
13. Wang, B., Li, Z., Tu, H., Hu, Z., Hu, J.: Actively measuring bots in peer-to-peer networks. In: International Conference on Networks Security, Wireless Communications and Trusted Computing, NSWCTC 2009, vol. 1, pp. 603–607 (2009)
14. Wang, P., Sparks, S., Zou, C.C.: An advanced hybrid peer-to-peer botnet. In: Proceedings of the First Conference on First Workshop on Hot Topics in Understanding Botnets, HotBots 2007, p. 2. USENIX Association, Berkeley (2007)
15. Wang, P., Wu, L., Aslam, B., Zou, C.: A systematic study on peer-to-peer botnets. In: Proceedings of 18th Internatonal Conference on Computer Communications and Networks, ICCCN 2009, pp. 1–8 (2009)
16. Wyke, J.: The zeroaccess botnet - mining and fraud for massive financial gain. Technical report, SophosLabs (2012)

On Addressing the Imbalance Problem:
A Correlated KNN Approach
for Network Traffic Classification

Di Wu, Xiao Chen, Chao Chen, Jun Zhang, Yang Xiang, and Wanlei Zhou

Deakin University, 221 Burwood Highway, Burwood, Victoria 3125, Australia

Abstract. With the arrival of big data era, the Internet traffic is growing exponentially. A wide variety of applications arise on the Internet and traffic classification is introduced to help people manage the massive applications on the Internet for security monitoring and quality of service purposes. A large number of Machine Learning (ML) algorithms are introduced to deal with traffic classification. A significant challenge to the classification performance comes from imbalanced distribution of data in traffic classification system. In this paper, we proposed an Optimised Distance-based Nearest Neighbor (ODNN), which has the capability of improving the classification performance of imbalanced traffic data. We analyzed the proposed ODNN approach and its performance benefit from both theoretical and empirical perspectives. A large number of experiments were implemented on the real-world traffic dataset. The results show that the performance of "small classes" can be improved significantly even only with small number of training data and the performance of "large classes" remains stable.

1 Introduction

Research community and industry have paid attention to traffic classification during the past few years [17], because it has the potential to solve particular important network security and management issues, such as quality of service (QoS) control, lawful interception and intrusion detection. Traffic classification is useful to detect customers' use of network that conflict with ISPs' terms and policy along with QoS control. Traditional traffic classification approaches include port-based and payload-based methods [14]. However, the traditional methods suffer from a number of practical problems, such as dynamic ports and encrypted applications. To solve these problems, current researches have focused on implementing the ML techniques, which based on analyzing the flow statistical features of traffic flows [17].

However, imbalanced dataset, a problem often found in real world application especially in network traffic, can cause seriously negative effect on classification performance of ML algorithms. This is because some applications are popular and generate a large number of traffic flows (refered as "large class"), while the unpopular applications only generate a small number of traffic flows (refered as "small class").

M.H. Au et al. (Eds.): NSS 2014, LNCS 8792, pp. 138–151, 2014.

In this issue, classifiers always biased in favor of large classes. Large classes can get good classification performance, while small classes get very poor classification performance. Most traditional ML classification algorithms pursue to minimize the error rate which is the percentage of the incorrect predication of the classified labels [10]. This causes the algorithms ignore the difference between types of misclassification errors. In particular, they assume that all these misclassification errors are equal.

Many solutions have been introduced to deal with the imbalance problem of ML algorithms previously both at the data and algorithmic levels. At the data level, researchers proposed different re-sampling mechanisms to solve the imbalance problems such as under-sampling which is a non-heuristic method trying to balance class distributions through the random elimination of large class examples and over-sampling which is a non-heuristic method that aims to balance class distributions through the random replication of small class examples. At the algorithmic level, researchers proposed cost-sensitive learning which focus on incorporating costs in decision-making is another way to improve classifier's performance when learning from imbalanced data sets or manipulating classifiers internally such as weighted distance in kNN [2] and SVM biases algorithm [21]. Some of researchers combine re-sampling mechanisms and algorithmic together as the ensemble learning methods which has established its superiority in ML in recent years, of which Boosting and Bagging are the most successful approaches.

Our work aims to tackle two problems: 1) To identify the imbalance problems in traffic classification when applying ML algorithms, and 2) How to effectively conduct imbalance problems based on ML algorithms such as kNN which can reduce the imbalance problems in traffic classification. The contributions of this paper are listed below:

- We propose a new method to improve the performance of the ML classifier based on kNN approach for small applications. The f-measure and accuracy of the small classes can be improved. In the proposed method, changing decision boundary of kNN algorithm is introduced to increase the performance. The proposed technique can perform much better than the existing ML techniques.
- We develop a system model which can automatically select the best decision boundary to reach the best performance for small classes and keep the performance of large classes stable.

The paper is organized as follows. Section 2 reviews related work in both traffic classification and imbalance classification solutions. A novel classification approach and the theoretical analysis are proposed in Section 3. Section 4 presents a large number of experiments and results which based on a real data set for performance evaluation. Some disscussions related to this work are provided in Section 5. Finally, the paper is concluded in Section 6.

2 Related Work

In ML approaches, a classifier which contains the knowledge structure should be trained with the pre-labelled instances. After that, the output classifier can be used to predict a new incoming instance. It consists of two steps: learning and classifying. Firstly, features of traffic flows will be extracted and formatted as a vector $F = \{f_1, f_2, \ldots, f_n\}$. The class labels (application type) could be get via some approaches (like Deep Payload Inspection). Features and class label will be combined as one instance for training. One training instance can then be represented by a pair containing input, and the expected result $(F, label)$, and the training set is the vector $TS = \{(F_1, label_1), (F_2, label_2), (F_n, label_n)\}$. The training set is the input of ML algorithm, classifier model will be built after training process. In the classifying process, new coming traffic flows $T = \{F_1, F_2, \ldots, F_n\}$ will be labelled by the trained classifier model.

Current research contains supervised methods and unsupervised methods. For the supervised methods, In [15], Moore $et\ al.$ proposed a way using Naive Bayes technique. Original Naive Bayes is not that good to classify traffic, the overall accuracy is 65% approximately. In addition, [1] proposed by Auld in 2007 extends [15] by using Beyesian Neural network approach. It has been approved that overall accuracy is further improved compared to Naive Bayes technique, which can achieve a up to 99% accuracy for data trained and tested on the same day, and 95% accuracy for data trained and tested 8 months apart. In real-time traffic classification, Hullár $et\ al.$ [11] proposed a supervised classification methods using only the first few packets were proposed. Considering the first few packets of flows could be missed or disguised, Nguyen $et\ al.$ [16] studied classifying a sub-flow captured at any given time. For certain popular P2P-TV applications, Bermolen et al. [3] found P2P-TV traffic can simply be identified by the count of packets and bytes exchanged among peers during small time windows. Zhang $et\ al.$ proposed a novel framework called Traffic Classification using Correlation (TCC) [23], which is making use of the side information - flow correlation to improve the performance of the state-of-art NN (Nearest Neighbour) algorithm with only few labelled training instances. Glatz et al. [9] introduced a new scheme to classify one-way traffic into classes such as Malicious Scanning, and Service Unreachable, etc., based on prefixed rules. Thus, no training stage was needed. Jin et al. [12] developed a lightweight traffic classification architecture combining a series of simple linear binary classifiers, and embracing three key innovative mechanisms to achieve scalability and high accuracy. A similar idea of a classifier combination was also applied in Callado et al.s work [5]. Carela-Espanol et al. [6] analyzed the impact of sampling when classifying NetFlow data, and proposed an improvement to the training process in order to reduce the impact of sampling.

Apart from that, some works are using unsupervised methods. Barnaille $et\ al.$ [4] suggest a new approach for early detection of the traffic flows in the Internet by only inspecting the size of first few packets of a TCP flow under the intuition that first few packets can capture the application's negotiation phase which can distinguish the applications effectively. Zander $et\ al.$ proposed a method [22] using AutoClass, which is an unsupervised Bayesian classifier based EM algorithm to cluster Internet traffic in 2005. Wang *et al.* [20] proposed a new Set-Based Constrained K-means (SBCK-means) clustering technique using flow correlation information. Wang et al. [19] proposed integrating statistical feature-based flow clustering with a payload signature matching method to eliminate the requirement of supervised training data. Finamore et al. [8] combined flow statistical feature-based clustering and payload statistical feature-based clustering for mining unidentified traffic. While the both supervised and unsupervised methods reported performance are promising, they did not address the imbalanced data problem in traffic classification

3   Optimised Distance-Based Nearest Neighbor Approach

3.1   System Framework

Fig 1 shows the basic idea of our approach. For a imbalanced dataset, cycles represent the large class which contains more traffic flows, triangles represent the small class with only three traffic flows. After the classification, we found that the supervised ML classifier always bias in favor of big classes in the dataset. On the left side of the decision boundary, all the flows were classified as the cycles class include a triangle flow. One third of the triangle class has been misclassified, this impacts the classification performance of triangle classes seriously. To address this problem, we try to adjust the ML classifier's decision boundary towards the cycle class. However, after we move the decision boundary. two cycles will be classified as the triangle class which effects the classification performance too. Therefore, we apply another approach which is flow correlation [23] to build the information correlation between the same class. This approach can correct the misclassification after we move the decision boundary to ensure the performance of the cycle class.

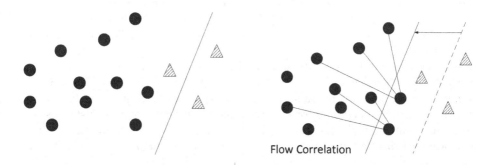

Fig. 1. Problem Statement

Fig 2 shows a new framework of the proposed ODNN. In the 10-fold cross validation, the system use 1% of the whole dataset to test the performance of

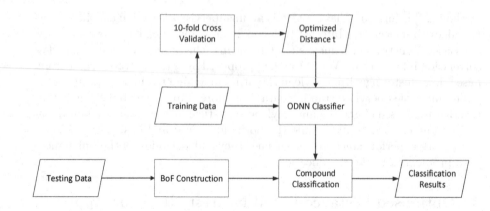

Fig. 2. System Framework

the small classes and get a optimized distance parameter t when the small classes reach the highest performance. After that, the system will use the t and training data to build a ODNN classifier. Flow correlation with BoF Construction analysis is proposed to correlate information in the traffic flows. Finally, the compound classification engine classifies traffic flows into application-based classes by taking all information of statistical features and flow correlation into account.

3.2 Nearest Neighbor Algorithm

Our work is based on KNN algorithm, which is a type of instance-based or lazy learning algorithm. The function is only approximated locally and all computation is deferred until classification. The k-nearest neighbor algorithm is that an object is classified by a majority vote of its neighbors, which the object being labeled to the class most common amongst its k nearest neighbors (k is a positive integer, typically small). If $k = 1$, then the object is simply labeled as the class of the nearest neighbor. Nearest neighbor rules compute the decision boundary which is also possible to compute explicitly and efficiently. Euclidean distance is one of the commonly istance metric for continuous variables. Often, the classification accuracy of kNN can be improved significantly if the distance metric is learned with specialized algorithms such as Large Margin Nearest Neighbor or Neighbourhood components analysis. In our experiment, we just set the $k = 1$ to get the nearest neighbors for classification. Each flow has fixed distances to both large and small classes. We try to adjust the distance to small classes with an optimized distance parameter t if the flow is from small classes, which can improve the classification performance for the small classes.

3.3 Optimised Distance-Based Nearest Neighbor Algorithm

Distance Optimization. The proposed ODNN scheme is based on optimizing the distance parameter of NN alogorithm. For one certain labeled testing flow, if there are only two classes in the data set, the algorithm will calculate two Euclidean distances which are representing the distance from testing flow to large class D_{maj} and small class D_{min}.

$$\begin{cases} D_{maj} = \sqrt{(x_1 - x_2)^2 + (y_1 - y_2)^2} \\ D_{min} = \sqrt{(x_3 - x_4)^2 + (y_3 - y_4)^2} \end{cases}$$

Due to the lack of training samples from the small class, some flows from the small class will be classified as the large class. Thus, the accuracy of small class could drop dramatically. Therefore, we decide to move the decision boundary in the NN algorithm to ensure the accuracy of small class. Firstly, the testing flows are already labeled as different classes. When a testing flow comes in, the system will check the label first. Secondly, if the labeled testing data is from large class we do nothing but if the testing data is from small class the system will compare with the two distances D_{maj} and D_{min}. If $D_{maj} < D_{min}$, they system will introduce a parameter t (t is a positive float, typically increase from 1 to 5.5 with the gap of 0.5). In 10-fold cross validation, the system trying to use D_{min} divided by t to get a new distance D_{nmin} then compare with the D_{maj} again. If the D_{maj} still smaller than D_{nmin}, the t will add 0.5 and do the calculation again.

$$D_{nmin} = \frac{D_{min}}{t}$$

Once the $D_{maj} > D_{nmin}$, the system will take the t which related to the D_{nmin} into the further calculation to get the best performance. Therefore the testing data will be classified as the small class correctly. However, after we move the decision boundary, the system will classify more testing data into the small class which also affects the accuracy of both large class and small class. To deal with this issue, we introduce another method which name is flow correlation.

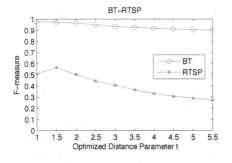 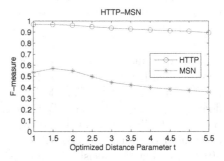

Fig. 3. Optimized Distance Parameter t

Fig 3 shows that how the performance changes with the different Optimized distance parameter t. The dots and stars represent the large class and the small class respectively. In general, the performance of large classes is always higher than the small classes. Importantly, small classes could get the peak of the performance with the t changes and the performance of the large classes stay the same at the peak which proves our assumptions. In BT-RTSP and HTTP-MSN, performance reduce gradually after the peak, however, there is a significant increase between 1 to 1.5 at the beginning which affect by the change of decision boundary. This result shows that our system could increase the performance of the small classes and keep the performance of the large classes.

Flow Correlation. Flow correlation is a new traffic classification method which was proposed by Zhang *et al.* [23]. In that paper, they created a new system model. In the preprocessing step, the system captures IP packets crossing a computer network and constructs traffic flows by IP header inspection. A flow consists of successive IP packets having the same five-tuples which are *src-ip*, *src-port*, *dst-ip*, *dst-port* and *protocol*. After that, a set of statistical features are extracted to represent each flow. Feature selection aims to select a subset of relevant features for building robust classification models. Flow correlation analysis is proposed to correlate information in the traffic flows. Finally, traffic classification engine classifies traffic into application-based classes by taking all information of statistical features and flow correlation into account.

The novelty of their system model is to discover correlation information in the traffic flows and incorporate it into the classification process. Conventional supervised classification methods treat the traffic flows as the individual and independent instances. They do not take the correlation among traffic flows into account. The correlation information can significantly improve the classification performance, especially when the size of training data is very small. In the proposed system model, flow correlation analysis is a new component for traffic classification which takes the role of correlation discovery. Robust classification methods can use the correlation information as input.

We refer to a method bag of flows (BoF) [23] to model correlation information in traffic flows. The rule of constructing a BoF is: if the flows share the same destination IP address, destination port, and transport protocol, in a certain period of time, they are considered as correlated flows. A BoF consists of some correlated traffic flows which are generated by the same application. A BoF can be described by $Q = \{x_1, \ldots \ldots x_n\}$. Where x_i is a feature vector representing the ith flow in the BoF Q. The BoF Q explicitly denotes the correlation among n flows, $\{x_1, \ldots \ldots x_n\}$. Given a BoF as the query, $Q = \{x_1, \ldots \ldots x_n\}$, all flows in the BoF Q will be classified into the predicted class for Q. The BoF model can be combined with kNN algorithm to keep the performance of the large classes after adjusting the decision boundary. We desiged algorithms before we apply the experiments in Algorithm 1.

Algorithm 1. ODNN classifeir

---

input: Training Data, Testing data, The ODNN classifier
output: Classification results
Load Flow correlation algorithm
for *Check the label L of the testing flow* **do**
  if $L = small\ class$ **then**
    for $(i = 1; i < 5; i = i + 0.5)$ **do**
      The new distance D $= d/i$;
      Apply 10-folds cross validation with $D_i\{i = 1, 1.5, ..., 5\}$;
      Compare the f-measure of the different distance $D_i\{i = 1, 1.5, ..., 5\}$;
      if $FMeasure_{D_{i+2}} > FMeasure_{D_{i+1}} > FMeasure_{D_i}$ **then**
        | Replace the $D_i = D_{i+2}$
      end
    end
  else
    | Keep the distance result;
  end
end
Load Traditional kNN algorithm and replace the distance with the fixed
distance D_i

---

4 Performance Evaluation

4.1 Data Set

We use isp trace as our data set. The isp trace was captured by using a passive
probe at a 100Mbps Ethernet edge link of an Internet Service Provider (ISP)
located in Australia. Full packet payloads are preserved in isp trace without
any filtering. The original isp trace is 7-day-long starting from November 27 of
2010. The isp data set consists of 200k flows randomly sampled from 19 major
classes. Table 1. shows the details of the data sets. We disassemble this data set
into different pairs which contains two classes with one large and one small class
respectively. In the experiments, the data set is separated into two parts: 1% for
training and the other one for testing. We report the average performance of 100
random runs for each case.

Table 1. Number of Flows for Each Class

Classes	Number of Flows	Classes	Number of Flows
SSH	99010	BT	98993
HTTP	98990	SMTP	98967
POP3	62545	FTP	10817
EDONKEY	6493	MSN	5569
YAHOOMSG	477	RTSP	366
X11	325	EBUDDY	200

To identify the large and small classes, several previous studies tried to identify elephant flows. Papagiannaki et al. [18] proposed a more sophisticated two-feature classification scheme to identify elephant flows. According to their definition, flows are characterized as elephantbased on both their volume and their persistence in time. Note that the definition of flow in Estan's work they define the large classes as **Prior Definition**: elephant $=$ *flow* $> 1\%$ of link bandwidth.

Based on the consideration above, in Table 1, we can find this data set is a real unbalanced data set. For instance, the BT, HTTP, SSL3, SMTP, SSH etc. these classes occupied the most network flow about 15.73% separately. We consider that kind of classes are large classes in this network flow and others are small like EBUDDY, RSP which only occupy 0.0318% of the whole network.

4.2   Evaluation Measures

Evaluation measures play a crucial role in both assessing the classification performance and guiding the classifier modelling. Traditionally, accuracy is the most commonly used measure for these purposes. However, for classification with the class imbalance problem, accuracy is no longer a proper measure since the rare class has very little impact on accuracy as compared to the prevalent class [7] [13]. For example, in a problem where a rare class is represented by only 1% of the training data, a simple strategy can be to predict the prevalent class label for every example. It can achieve a high accuracy of 99%. However, this measurement is meaningless to some applications where the learning concern is the identification of the rare cases. In order to evaluate the performance of classification approaches, some metrics are widely used by the researchers.

Positives and Negatives. Suppose there is an incoming flow f and a traffic application class C. The output of the classifier is whether one flow belongs to C or not. A common way to evaluate the classifier's performance is to use **True Positives, False Positives, False Positives, False Negatives**. These metrics are defined as following:

- True Positives (TP), flows of class C correctly classified as belonging to class C.
- False Positives (FP), flows not belonging to class C incorrectly classified as belonging to class C.
- True Negatives (TN), flows not belonging to class C correctly classified as not belonging to class C.
- False Negatives (FN), flows of class C incorrectly classified as not belonging to class C.

Precision, Recall and F-measure. Literature also use Precision, Recall, and F-measure to evaluate per-class performance.

- Precision is defined as the ratio of those flows that truly belong class C to those identified as class C, it can be calculated by

$$Precision = \frac{TP}{TP + FP}$$

- Recall is defined as the ratio of those flows correctly classified as belonging to class C to the total number of flows in class C, it can be calculated by

$$Recall = \frac{TP}{TP + FN}$$

- F-measure is a combination of precision and recall, it is a widely adopt metric to evaluate per-class performance, it can be calculated by

$$F - measure = \frac{2 * Precision * Recall}{Precision + Recall}$$

4.3   Experiment and Evaluations

We use the F-measure metric to measure the performance of the both large and small classes on each small data set. We propose the 10-fold cross-validation to find an optimal t. The advantage of the optimization method is: accuracy and speed. This method is applied in the proposed ODNN scheme for performance evaluation. In 10-fold cross-validation, the original training set is randomly partitioned into 10 equal-size subsets. Of the 10 subsets, a single subset is retained as validation data for testing the highest classification performance of small classes with t. The remaining 9 subsets are used as training data. The cross-validation process is then repeated 10 times, with each of the 10 subsets used exactly once as the validation data. The 10 results from the folds are then averaged to produce a single estimation. After that, the system will take the t into the ODNN classifier to get the best performance for small classes. Then, the system will apply the flow correlation to combine the ODNN classifier into the compound classification which can get the optimized classification results.

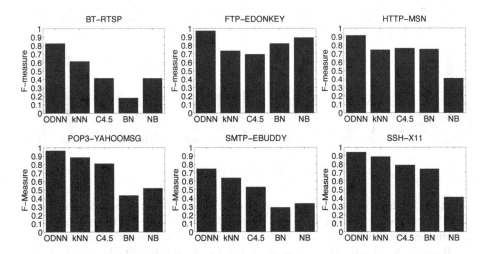

Fig. 4. F-measure Comparision

For performance evaluation, a large number of experiments were conducted on the dataset. We present the average performance of over 100 runs. We compare the proposed ODNN scheme with four state-of-the-art traffic classification methods: kNN, C4.5, BN and NB. Fig 3 shows the F-measure for small classes. In BT-RTSP, the F-measure of our scheme is higher than the second best method NN by about 20%. There are no significant differences among methods of C4.5 and NB, however both are worse than our scheme by about 40%. In FTP-EDONKEY, the improvement of our approach is about 10%, with NB, the second best method is less than our approach about 10%. NB is slightly better than the BN method. In POP3-YAHOOMSG, the F-measure of our scheme achieve 95%, which is higher by about 12% than the second best method kNN. In SSH-X11, the F-measure of our scheme is about 94%. The F-measure of the second best method kNN is about 86%, which is much higher than the other three methods. In HTTP-MSN, the ranking list is our approach, C4.5, BN, kNN and NB. In SMTP-EBUDDY, the F-measure of our scheme is higher than the second best method kNN by over 22%. We observed the superiority of the proposed ODNN scheme was due to its excellent functionality of imbalance data. As described in Section 3, a new two-step optimize distance was applied for imbalance traffic classification. The first step was moving the decision boundary and the second step borrows the idea of the flow correlation method to roughly improve the performance of small classes.

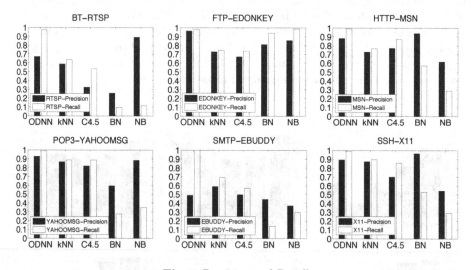

Fig. 5. Precision and Recall

Let us further investigate the reason of why ODNN approach achieved the best F-measure for the small classes. In the 4.2, we can see that the F-measure are affected by the both precision and recall. Fig 5 shows the precision and the recall for each experiment for the small classes. In BT-RTSP, the recall of our scheme is higher than the second best method NN by about 40%. NB has the best precision by 86% which is higher than our scheme by about 23%. However, the recall for NB is only about 15%. Therefore, the F-measure of NB is still lower than our approach. In FTP-EDONKEY, There are no significant differences for recall among our methods and NB by about 97%, however the precision of NB is lower than our scheme by about 20%. In HTTP-MSN, our scheme had the best recall which is 99%, however, the precision is little bit lower than NB by 10%. In POP3-YAHOOMSG, our approach has the best performance for both precision and recall. In SMTP-EBUDDY, the recall of our method reached the top by 1, even the precision is lower than kNN by about 0.1. In SHH-X11, BN has the best precision by about 97%, it is more than our scheme by about 10%. However, our approach still has the best recall by about 99%, while the BN's recall only got 55%. It is significant that, our approach improve both precision and recall, especially when we moving the decision boundary, the recall were improved rapidly compare with the traditional kNN.

5   Conclusion

Network traffic classification is playing a vital role in network management activities, like Quality of Service control, traffic trend analysis and even in intrusion detection system. Early traffic classification techniques are based on port number or payload, recent research has moved to apply ML algorithms with statistical features based classification. Most of the works can successfully tackle the classification of network traffic traces with plenty of training data. However, these methods did not consider the imbalanced problems in traffic classification. In this paper, we proposed a binary classification method to solve the imbalance traffic classification. It will be easy to extent our current into the multivariate classification. This is because a multivariate classification method can divided into different binary classification to solve the problems. We studied the kNN algorithm in traffic classification, and cooperate the pre-process to our data set in order to improve the performance of classifying small classes in traffic classification. Relied on the finding that side flow information, such as flow correlation, can benefit the imbalanced data classification, we propose a new method which not make use of the imbalanced data, but rather flow correlation. Experiments conducted on the real-world traffic data set demonstrate that our proposed framework can significantly improve the classification performance for small classes.

References

1. Auld, T., Moore, A., Gull, S.: Bayesian neural networks for internet traffic classification. IEEE Transactions on Neural Networks 18(1), 223–239 (2007)
2. Barandela, R., Sánchez, J.S., García, V., Rangel, E.: Strategies for learning in class imbalance problems. Pattern Recognition 36(3), 849–851 (2003)

3. Bermolen, P., Mellia, M., Meo, M., Rossi, D., Valenti, S.: Abacus: Accurate behavioral classification of p2p-tv traffic. Computer Networks 55(6), 1394–1411 (2011)
4. Bernaille, L., Teixeira, R., Akodkenou, I., Soule, A., Salamatian, K.: Traffic classification on the fly. SIGCOMM Comput. Commun. Rev. 36(2), 23–26 (2006)
5. Callado, A., Kelner, J., Sadok, D., Alberto Kamienski, C., Fernandes, S.: Better network traffic identification through the independent combination of techniques. Journal of Network and Computer Applications 33(4), 433–446 (2010)
6. Carela-Español, V., Barlet-Ros, P., Cabellos-Aparicio, A., Solé-Pareta, J.: Analysis of the impact of sampling on netflow traffic classification. Computer Networks 55(5), 1083–1099 (2011)
7. Chawla, N.V., Japkowicz, N., Kotcz, A.: Editorial: special issue on learning from imbalanced data sets. ACM Sigkdd Explorations Newsletter 6(1), 1–6 (2004)
8. Finamore, A., Mellia, M., Meo, M.: Mining unclassified traffic using automatic clustering techniques. In: Domingo-Pascual, J., Shavitt, Y., Uhlig, S. (eds.) TMA 2011. LNCS, vol. 6613, pp. 150–163. Springer, Heidelberg (2011)
9. Glatz, E., Dimitropoulos, X.: Classifying internet one-way traffic. In: Proceedings of the 2012 ACM Conference on Internet Measurement Conference, pp. 37–50. ACM (2012)
10. He, H., Garcia, E.A.: Learning from imbalanced data. IEEE Transactions on Knowledge and Data Engineering 21(9), 1263–1284 (2009)
11. Hullár, B., Laki, S., Gyorgy, A.: Early identification of peer-to-peer traffic. In: 2011 IEEE International Conference on Communications (ICC), pp. 1–6. IEEE (2011)
12. Jin, Y., Duffield, N., Erman, J., Haffner, P., Sen, S., Zhang, Z.L.: A modular machine learning system for flow-level traffic classification in large networks. ACM Transactions on Knowledge Discovery from Data (TKDD) 6(1), 4 (2012)
13. Joshi, M.V., Kumar, V., Agarwal, R.C.: Evaluating boosting algorithms to classify rare classes: Comparison and improvements. In: Proceedings of the IEEE International Conference on Data Mining, ICDM 2001, pp. 257–264. IEEE (2001)
14. Karagiannis, T., Papagiannaki, K., Faloutsos, M.: Blinc: multilevel traffic classification in the dark. ACM SIGCOMM Computer Communication Review 35, 229–240 (2005)
15. Moore, A.W., Zuev, D.: Internet traffic classification using bayesian analysis techniques. SIGMETRICS Perform. Eval. Rev. 33(1), 50–60 (2005)
16. Nguyen, T.T., Armitage, G., Branch, P., Zander, S.: Timely and continuous machine-learning-based classification for interactive ip traffic. IEEE/ACM Transactions on Networking (TON) 20(6), 1880–1894 (2012)
17. Nguyen, T.T., Armitage, G.: A survey of techniques for internet traffic classification using machine learning. IEEE Communications Surveys Tutorials 10(4), 56–76 (2008)
18. Papagiannaki, K., Taft, N., Bhattacharyya, S., Thiran, P., Salamatian, K., Diot, C.: A pragmatic definition of elephants in internet backbone traffic. In: Proceedings of the 2nd ACM SIGCOMM Workshop on Internet Measurment, pp. 175–176. ACM (2002)
19. Wang, Y., Xiang, Y., Yu, S.Z.: An automatic application signature construction system for unknown traffic. Concurrency and Computation: Practice and Experience 22(13), 1927–1944 (2010)
20. Wang, Y., Xiang, Y., Zhang, J., Yu, S.: Internet traffic clustering with constraints. In: 2012 8th International Wireless Communications and Mobile Computing Conference (IWCMC), pp. 619–624. IEEE (2012)

21. Wu, G., Chang, E.Y.: Class-boundary alignment for imbalanced dataset learning. In: ICML 2003 Workshop on Learning from Imbalanced Data Sets II, Washington, DC, pp. 49–56 (2003)
22. Zander, S., Nguyen, T., Armitage, G.: Automated traffic classification and application identification using machine learning. In: The IEEE Conference on Local Computer Networks 30th Anniversary, pp. 250–257 (November 2005)
23. Zhang, J., Xiang, Y., Wang, Y., Zhou, W., Xiang, Y., Guan, Y.: Network traffic classification using correlation information. IEEE Transactions on Parallel and Distributed Systems 24(1), 104–117 (2013)

Exploiting the Hard-Wired Vulnerabilities of Newscast via Connectivity-Splitting Attack

Jakub Muszyński[1], Sébastien Varrette[1],
Juan Luis Jiménez Laredo[2], and Pascal Bouvry[1]

[1] Computer Science and Communication (CSC) Research Unit
[2] Interdisciplinary Centre for Security Reliability and Trust (SnT)
University of Luxembourg, 6, rue Richard Coudenhove-Kalergi
L-1359 Luxembourg, Luxembourg

Abstract. Newscast is a model for information dissemination and membership management in large-scale, agent-based distributed systems. It deploys a simple, peer-to-peer data exchange protocol. The Newscast protocol forms an overlay network and keeps it connected by means of an epidemic algorithm, thus featuring a complex, spatially structured, and dynamically changing environment. It has recently become very popular due to its inherent resilience to node volatility as it exhibits strong self-healing properties. In this paper, we analyze the robustness of the Newscast model when executed in a distributed environment subjected to malicious acts. More precisely, we evaluate the resilience of Newscast against *cheating faults* and demonstrate that even a few naive cheaters are able to defeat the protocol by breaking the network connectivity. Concrete experiments are performed using a framework that implements both the protocol and the cheating model considered in this work.

Keywords: Newscast, Fault Tolerance, Peer-to-Peer.

1 Introduction

The popularity of Peer-to-Peer (P2P) systems has increased since their advent in the 2000's. A key issue in these systems is that distribution of data and control across processes is symmetric: tasks or work loads are distributed between peers which are equally privileged, equipotent participants in the distributed application. More precisely, the peers make a portion of their resources, such as processing power, disk storage or network bandwidth, directly available to other network participants, without the need for central coordination by servers or stable hosts. The main advantage of this approach is scalability: a well-designed P2P system can easily scale to millions of processes, each of which can join or leave whenever it pleases without seriously disrupting the system's overall quality of service. One of the facets of classical P2P architecture is the heterogeneity and the extreme volatility of the resources as their owners may reclaim them without warning, leading therefore to what is commonly referred to as *crash faults*. Consequently, a large part of research on P2P systems focuses on routing

M.H. Au et al. (Eds.): NSS 2014, LNCS 8792, pp. 152–165, 2014.

protocols to handle group membership and communications in an automated way that would not require any global management. This approach thus defines a self-managing system. Research in this area mainly intervenes in two directions. On one side, an overlay network is built in the application layer on top of an existing network such as the Internet. Each joining peer has an assigned identifier mapped over a structured topology (for instance like in Chord [10]) which is used to route messages. Another strategy consists in exploiting randomness to disseminate information across a large set of computing resources to maintain a high connectivity within this pool of nodes even in the event of major disasters. Such P2P algorithms fall in the category of epidemic (or gossiping) protocols that do not rely on a predefined structure, but on the emerging overlay network which is used to disseminate information virally. This comes with a bigger overhead in terms of routing performances, counter balanced by a high fault resilience and self-healing properties inherited from the epidemic nature of the protocol. A well-known example based on this paradigm is Newscast [7], a self-organized gossiping protocol for the maintenance of dynamic unstructured P2P overlay networks. Newscast displays a scalable and robust behavior which emerges from the interaction of a simple set of rules: nodes exchange pieces of routing information among randomly selected neighbors. Due to this simplicity, the protocol has been rapidly adopted in academic research: as a platform for distributed optimization [8], as a framework for peer-sampling services [5] or as a way for monitoring the status of large-scale decentralized systems [6].

While the robustness of the Newscast model against *crash faults* has been demonstrated successfully in many previous works [7,11], this paper analyses this protocol under the perspective of a more complex kind of fault often referred to as *cheating fault*. In this case, an attacker falsifies the message of the protocol, if possible in an unnoticeable way *i.e.* conform to the protocol. Depending on the context, the motivation for such a selfish behavior are manifold, ranging from the simple sniffing of traffic information[1], to the will to collapse the infrastructure to disable the associated service. **Therefore, the aim of this paper is to raise an issue on the security of Newscast.** In this article, we demonstrate that even few naive cheaters are able to defeat the protocol by breaking the network connectivity between non-malicious nodes. Concrete experiments are proposed where we demonstrate vulnerability of the protocol.

This paper is organized as follows: Section 2 details the background of this work and reviews related works. Then, the considered fault model and the cheater modelization is reviewed in Section 3. To facilitate the analysis of the cheater impact, we have implemented both the protocol (on top of the GraphStream library [3]) and the cheating model considered in this work. The implementation details are thus provided in Section 4. Then, experimental results are discussed in Section 5 where we demonstrate that the Newscast protocol **is not resilient** against cheating fault. Finally, Section 6 concludes the paper with a summary of our results and provides future directions.

---

[1] Eventually with little or no contribution (*i.e.* computing effort) to the system.

2   Context and Motivations

This section aims at providing general insights into the Newscast protocol and its inherent properties. In particular, the focus is on characterizing the robustness of the protocol when considering different types of failures. In the beginning, we present the protocol as defined in the Newscast seminal paper [7]. Then, some general concepts on fault-tolerance are introduced in order to qualitatively and quantitatively assess the robustness of Newscast. In that sense, we survey the related literature and identify new potential vulnerabilities of the protocol.

2.1   The Newscast Model

Newscast is a gossiping protocol for interconnecting large-scale distributed systems. Without any central services or servers, Newscast differs from other similar approaches [4,10,9] by its simplicity. The membership management follows an extremely simple protocol: in order to join the system, a node only needs to contact a connected node from which it gets a list of neighbors. Additionally, to leave the system, the node only requires to stop communicating for a predefined time. The dynamics of the system follow a probabilistic scheme able to keep a self-organized equilibrium. Such an equilibrium emerges from the loosely-coupled and decentralized run of the protocol within the different and independent nodes. The emerging graph behaves as a small-world [12] allowing a scalable way for disseminating information and, therefore, making the system suitable for distributed computing. Despite the simplicity of the scheme, Newscast is fault-tolerant and exhibits a graceful degradation without requiring an extra mechanism other than its own emergent behavior [11].

Algorithm 1. Newscast protocol in $node_i$

1: Active Thread
2: **while** true **do**
3:      wait t_r
4:      $node_j \Leftarrow$ selected node from $Cache_i$
5:      send $Cache_i$ to $node_j$
6:      receive $Cache_j$ from $node_j$
7:      $Cache_i \Leftarrow$ Aggregate $(Cache_i, Cache_j)$
8: **end while**
9:
10: Passive Thread
11: **while** true **do**
12:     wait until $Cache_k$ is received from $node_k$
13:     send $Cache_i$ to $node_k$
14:     $Cache_i \Leftarrow$ Aggregate $(Cache_i, Cache_k)$
15: **end while**
16:
17: $Cache_{aggregated} \Leftarrow$ Aggregate$(Cache_a, Cache_b)$
18: $Cache_{aggregated} \Leftarrow Cache_a \cup Cache_b$ keeping the
19: Keep the c freshest items in $Cache_{aggregated}$ according with the time-stamp

---

Algorithm 1 shows the pseudo-code of the protocol. Each node keeps its own set of neighbors in a cache that contains $c \in \mathbb{N}$ entries, referring to c other nodes in the network without duplicates. Each entry provides a reference to the node in which it was created and a time-stamp of the entry creation (allowing the replacement of old items).

There are two different tasks that the algorithm carries out within each node. The active thread which pro-actively initiates a cache exchange once every cycle (one cycle takes t_r time units) and the passive thread that waits for data-exchange requests.

Every cycle, each $node_i$ initiates a cache exchange. It selects randomly a neighbor $node_j$ from its $Cache_i$ with uniform probability. Then $node_i$ and $node_j$ exchange their caches and merge them following an aggregation function, consisting of picking the freshest c items from $Cache_i \cup Cache_j$ and merging them into a single cache. Since this function applies in both nodes (the one initiating the request and the one serving the request), the result is that $node_i$ and $node_j$ will have in common the same entries in their respective caches.

2.2 Fault Tolerance and Robustness in Distributed Systems

Fault tolerance can be defined as an ability of a system to behave in a well-defined manner once a failure occurs. A failure is due to an error of the system which is a consequence of a fault. Different kinds of faults are usually distinguished in function of their origin and their temporal duration [1]. They could be intentional or not, software or hardware, *e.g.* modify the processing time of an operation, provide a wrong result or return no result at all. Failures and errors can be classified into the following categories based on their semantics:

- *crash-stop failures*, also called fail-stop: the system stops working and does not execute any operation, nor does it send any signals. This behavior corresponds to what the literature often refers to as *crash faults*;
- *omission* is a communication failure: typically, a message is not transmitted by a communication channel, or not sent by the sending process (send-omission), or not received by the receiving process (receive-omission);
- *duplication* is the opposite from omission: a message is sent or received twice;
- *timing* if the system's behavior deviation concerns only a time criterion (reaction time to a given event for instance);
- *byzantine errors* are arbitrary errors: the system arbitrarily does not have the expected behavior or has an erroneous one;

The detection of failures is outside the scope of this article (the interested reader may refer to [2]). In all cases, Byzantine errors are the hardest to detect, as the behavior of the system is often similar to the expected one. A typical example of a byzantine failure covered in this work comes from volunteer computing where it is called *cheating faults*. In the context of this work, it corresponds to a model where **the attacker (client-side) behaves in a way that does not break the underlying protocol while collapsing the network connectivity**. Again, what makes this kind of fault byzantine and difficult to catch is that the messages exchanged during the protocol, although erroneous and malicious, generally respect the expected format and do not raise an alarm regarding their integrity.

2.3   Fault-Tolerance of the Newscast Protocol

One of the important issues regarding P2P computing is the robustness of the underlying protocols, as they need to provide a coherent view of a large-scale — and potentially — unreliable distributed system. In that sense, the Newscast protocol establishes the dynamics of a changing communication graph which requires to persistently maintain a small-world connectivity. As a first assessment of its robustness, Jelasity and van Steen [7] showed that Newscast maintains such property regardless of the scale or the initial state of the system (*i.e.* the protocol is able to bootstrap from any graph structure and consistently converges to a small-world graph). Nevertheless, two additional issues still need to be considered for characterizing a protocol as robust. The first is related to the spontaneous partitioning of the communication graph, and the second to the resilience of the protocol to failures.

The spontaneous partitioning of the communication graph refers to the probability of a subgraph to become disconnected from the system as a consequence of the protocol dynamics. In Newscast, the probability of a spontaneous partitioning is mainly influenced by the cache size c. Jelasity and van Steen [7] conclude that, while a partition in Newscast may happen if $c < 20$, the probability of spontaneous partitioning is almost negligible for $c \geq 20$ regardless of the size of the network. Previous results, however, do not take into account node failures, which is an inherent feature of large-scale distributed systems. In that sense, Spyros et al. [11] analyse the robustness of Newscast in a failure-prone scenario in which the nodes are removed until none is left. The study leads to the following conclusions: (1) despite failures, the Newscast graph remains connected until a large percentage of nodes are removed, *e.g.* for $c = 40$, almost 90% of the nodes have to be removed to split the graph; (2) when a partition finally takes place, most of the nodes still remain connected in a large cluster. From previous findings, Newscast can be said to be robust: the protocol consistently maintains the desired connectivity, even if considering a high percentage of nodes crashing. However, large-scale distributed systems are also subject to other potential sources of risks. Specifically, malicious users may pose a threat to the system, finding its vulnerabilities and exploiting them to disrupt the connectivity of the graph. This type of failures (*i.e. cheating faults*) also need to be considered for defining a protocol as fully robust. Assessing — and eventually enabling — security in Newscast is, therefore, a necessary step for promoting the uses of the protocol beyond the academic environment.

3   Fault Model and Cheaters Behavior

This study analyses the impact of *cheating faults* on the Newscast paradigm. We now formalize this type of fault, yet some preliminary definitions need to be recalled.

First of all, we consider a directed communication graph $G_t = (\mathcal{V}_t, \mathcal{E}_t)$ at a given time instant t which formally consists of a set of vertices $\mathcal{V}_t$ and a set of edges $\mathcal{E}_t$ between them. $\mathcal{V}_t$ represents the set of connected nodes at the time t. An edge

$e_{i,j} \in \mathcal{E}_t$ connects vertex (or node) n_i with the node n_j. It reflects the fact, that n_j is in the cache of n_i. It follows that the cache-exchange algorithm presented in Section 2.1 leads to a series of graphs G_t, given an initial graph G_0.

For the sake of simplicity, we will assume that the number of non-malicious nodes in the network is constant and equal to n_{honest} $\forall t \geq 0$. In addition, there are n_{cheat} $\forall t \geq t_c$ malicious nodes $i.e.$ cheaters, connecting to the network at time t_c (all of at the same simulation step). Moreover, this corresponds to a partition of the set of vertices in $\mathcal{V}_t$ between non-malicious $i.e.$ honest nodes and cheaters. Thus $\mathcal{V}_t = \mathcal{V}_t^{\text{honest}} \cup \mathcal{V}_t^{\text{cheat}}$, where $|\mathcal{V}_t^{\text{honest}}| = n_{\text{honest}}$ and $|\mathcal{V}_t^{\text{cheat}}| = n_{\text{cheat}}$. Finally, as mentioned before, we assume the cache size of each node remains constant within the graph G_t, $i.e.$ $|Cache_i| = c$ $\forall n_i \in \mathcal{V}_t$.

An important concept to measure the robustness of the Newscast protocol against cheaters is the size of the *connected components* of non-malicious nodes in G_t. A connected component $\hat{\mathcal{C}}_j$ of G_t is a maximal subgraph of G_t such that every vertex $i.e.$ node in $\hat{\mathcal{C}}_j$ is reachable from every other node in $\hat{\mathcal{C}}_j$ following a path in G_t consisting only of honest nodes ($i.e.$ from the set $\mathcal{V}_t^{\text{honest}}$). In the sequel, $\hat{\mathcal{C}}_t^{max}$ will denote the connected component of maximum size for a given time instant t. Obviously, $0 < |\hat{\mathcal{C}}_t^{max}| \leq n_{\text{honest}}$. These notions being defined, we can better formalize cheating faults.

Definition 1 (Cheating fault).
Let $\hat{\mathcal{C}}_t^{max}$ be the connected component of maximum size among the non-malicious nodes $\mathcal{V}_t^{honest}$ for a given time instant t. We say that the G_t has been victim of a cheating fault iff $|\hat{\mathcal{C}}_{t+1}^{max}| < |\hat{\mathcal{C}}_t^{max}|$ in a monotonic way.

3.1   Malicious Nodes

In this work, we consider malicious behavior on the client-side. We assume that cheaters do not cooperate and all of them have full knowledge about the protocol and its implementation.

The neighborhood of a node changes dynamically in Newscast. Each node knows at most $c \in \mathbb{N}$ other peers. This information is refreshed during cache merge — old entries are replaced by freshest ones (as described in Section 2.1). A straightforward approach to deny a given node to make any valid outgoing connection, is to corrupt its cache. Cheaters can achieve this by sending correctly constructed messages containing freshest possible entries, referring to random (and possibly) non-existing peers. After an attack of this kind the only valid address in the cache of the targeted node would be the one of the malicious node itself.

From the protocol design, there is a high chance that a third peer contains an entry pointing to the victim node. Therefore, after some time, the corrupted cache can be restored to a partially valid state by an incoming connection ($i.e.$ self-healing). However, the falsified information will also spread virally into the network. This raises questions which will be answered by the experiments presented in Section 5:

1. How many times does the cheater have to connect to a node to fully disconnect it?
2. Do these connections have to be consecutive?

In addition to the above concerns, we have also explored the option for cheaters to choose more than one target following the round-robin principal. Targets are exchanged after the desired number of connections is reached (*frequency of targets' change*).

Unlike in honest nodes, cheaters do not have to follow the cache size constraint limiting their neighborhood. They could gather all the addresses from received caches, storing them in a set of *discovered addresses*. At the time when a cheater initiates an outgoing connection (active thread), it could select a target from such a set.

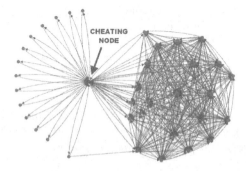

Fig. 1. A visualization of a problem with cheaters accepting addresses from incoming connections. Nodes connected only to the cheater start to flood him with random addresses.

Each cheater inserts cache size c of random addresses into the network at each cache-exchange. Over time, some of the generated entries are returned to them. This problem is most noticeable after significant number of nodes are connected only to the cheater (see Figure 1). Therefore we propose to ignore information received during the incoming connections. This will only slightly affect the process of discovering the network, because information about its members is still obtained through outgoing communication.

Furthermore, malicious nodes do not know about each other and information about which addresses where generated by the other malicious nodes is not shared. Moreover, cheaters could connect to each other. This could lead to a situation when the set of discovered addresses is very big, mainly filled by invalid entries. As a solution, we propose to assign a priority for each discovered address, defined by the number of its occurrences during cache-exchanges. It is motivated by the fact that valid entries should appear more often than the generated ones. After each connection to a given address, the priority is decreased by one, to ensure that a cheater will not be stuck with a single target.

4 Experimental Setup and Implementation Details

In order to assess the impact of cheaters on Newscast, we implemented both the protocol and the cheating model in a framework based on the GRAPHSTREAM [3] (version 1.1.2) Java library for the modeling and analysis of dynamic graphs. This tool allows gathering network statistics (*e.g.* connectivity, biggest cluster size, etc.) and is able to graphically display the dynamics of the system.

The whole simulation is divided into steps (called *simulation steps*). In each simulation step, every node is selected once — in random order — to initiate a cache-exchange according to the protocol's specification [7]. That includes every peer establishing an outgoing connection, sending its cache, receiving a cache from destination and performing the merge (see Section 2.1 for further details).

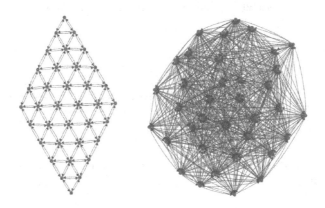

Fig. 2. A sample Newscast network consisting of 36 nodes and cache size equal to 20 after initialization (left) and after bootstrap (right)

At the onset of every experiment (step 0), the network is initialized as a bidirectional grid lattice (see Figure 2). Then we let the protocol run during 50 steps for the network to bootstrap into a stable configuration. After this period cheaters connect according to the protocol.

General parameters of the experiments are gathered in Table 1.

5 Results

We have divided experiments into three groups. In the first place we wanted to check if the network will spontaneously split without cheating faults present. For all the network sizes and both cache size settings, a connection graph was not divided through 100 executions lasting 10000 simulation steps.

The second group of tests was executed with one cheating node attacking a single, fixed, uniformly selected at random target from the network. Its purpose was to determine an estimate on the simulation steps required to completely

Table 1. General parameters of the experiments

Parameters	Values
Network size	$\{100, 200, \ldots, 500\}$
Cache size	$\{20, 40\}$
Number of cheaters	$\{1, 2, \ldots, 5\}$
Number of targets	$\{1, 2, \ldots, 10\}$
Frequency of target changes	$\{1, 2, \ldots, 20\}$
Max. number of simulation steps	10000
Bootstrap time	50
Number of executions	100

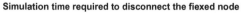

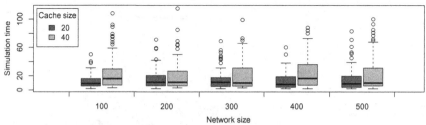

Fig. 3. Time required to disconnect a single, fixed, uniformly selected at random node from the network

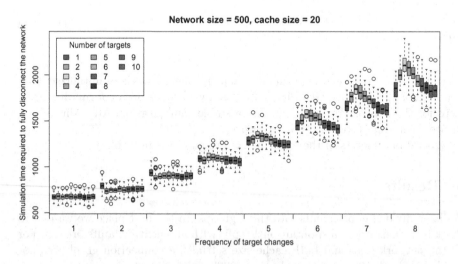

Fig. 4. Influence of frequency of target changes and number of targets on network disconnecting time with one cheater present in the network consisting of 500 nodes and cache size equal to 20

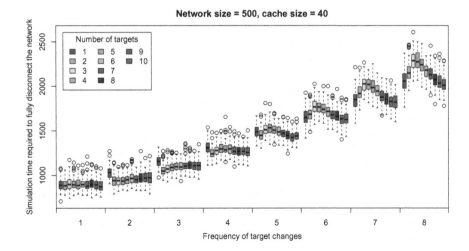

Fig. 5. Influence of frequency of target changes and number of targets on network disconnecting time with one cheater present in the network consisting of 500 nodes and cache size equal to 40

disconnect one peer from the system. Results are presented in Figure 3. As is visible, the average simulation time required to disconnect a single target in most of the cases fits in the range from 1 to 20 (independently from the network or the cache sizes). Basing on these results we have chosen a range for frequency of target changes from 1 to 20 for the next group of tests. It is also worth to note here, that the persistent attack on a single node can take a long time — it is a time required for the network to lose the information about the target. In some cases it took above 100 simulation steps to complete the task by the cheater. This time mainly depends on how well the given address is widespread in the network, as any incoming connection can partially heal the cache of the node. Additionally, obtained results are comparable (within the same cache size settings) independently from the network size.

The last part of the experiments (using all of the parameters from Table 1) was aimed to asses the performance of cheaters fully following the strategy described in Section 3.1. Due to the space constraints, we present only interesting results (see Figures 4–9).

Figures 4 and 5 present influence of frequency of target changes and number of targets on disconnecting time. As is clearly visible, best performance is obtained with one target changed for each outgoing connection. Other combinations of cheaters' parameters are causing degradation of efficiency and stability of the performance. In the optimal configuration, the network is fully disconnected in less than 800 simulation steps (on average) for a cache size equal to 20 and in less than 1000 simulation steps for a cache size equal to 40 (values are better visible on Figure 6). Results for the smaller networks are not presented, as they follow similar trend (only scale is different).

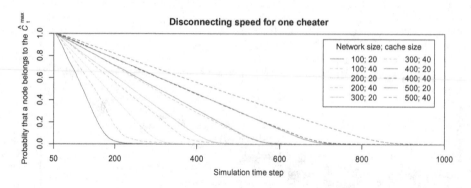

Fig. 6. Disconnecting speed compared between different network sizes and cache sizes values with one cheater only. Probability that a node belongs to the $\hat{\mathcal{C}}_t^{\max}$ is computed by division of the average biggest component size by the network size.

Figure 6 presents the average speed of network degradation for different numbers of nodes and both cache size settings. All the values are scaled to the range of $[0,1]$, by the division of the average biggest cluster size (from 100 executions) by the network size, *i.e.* $|\hat{\mathcal{C}}_t^{\max}|/|\mathcal{V}_t^{\text{honest}}|$ (which yields the probability that a given node $n \in \hat{\mathcal{C}}_t^{\max}$). The speed is almost linear for all the combinations of the relevant parameters, until there is a small cluster left (consisting of less than 20% of the original number of nodes). Nevertheless, the network is fully disconnected in less than 1000 simulation steps for all the cases. Given that the actual Newscast implementation[2] sets the protocol's update phase to 10 seconds, 1000 simulation steps stand for less than three hours of a real execution of a P2P system. This allows us to conclude that even one cheater in the network following the presented model, can have a devastating effect on the functioning of a Newscast network.

So far, we have shown and described results for only one cheater attacking the protocol. Figure 7 presents the influence of the number of cheaters varying from 1 to 5 on the network consisting of 500 nodes with cache sizes set to 20 and 40. It is important to emphasize here again, that cheaters do not know about each other and do not collaborate. Despite the lack of any kind of information sharing between malicious nodes, more of them causes faster loss of the connectivity — for 5 malicious nodes it happens in less than 300 simulation steps, which corresponds to one hour of a real execution time (as mentioned above). Additionally, it is visible that the influence of the bigger cache size loses its value when more cheaters are present in the network (the gap between both settings decreases).

Figures 8 and 9 present scalability of the solution. As visible, if the number of cheaters scales proportionally with the network size — efficiency of the malicious nodes can be maintained. Moreover, the cheating nodes do not interfere with each other, which is the effect of prioritizing the choice of a connection destination according to its frequency of appearance during interaction with the network.

---

[2] *e.g.* http://dr-ea-m.sourceforge.net/

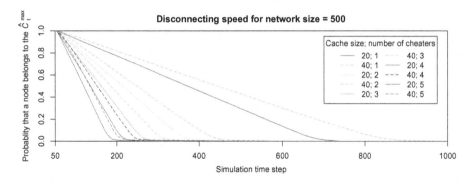

Fig. 7. Disconnecting speed compared between different cache sizes and amount of cheaters working on the network consisting of 500 nodes. Probability that a node belongs to the $\hat{\mathcal{C}}_t^{\max}$ is computed by division of the average biggest component size by the network size.

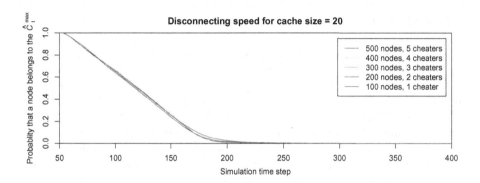

Fig. 8. Scalability of the solution. Disconnection speed is compared between different number of cheaters and network sizes with a constant cache size equal to 20. Probability that a node belongs to the $\hat{\mathcal{C}}_t^{\max}$ is computed by division of the average biggest component size by the network size.

The results presented in this work required considerable computing time such that we used the HPC platform operated at the University of Luxembourg (UL) to run the simulations. For instance, a single run for a network consisting of 500 nodes for a maximum of a 100000 steps, gathering needed network's statistics, required more than three hours.

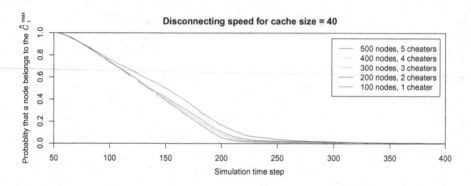

Fig. 9. Scalability of the solution. Disconnection speed is compared between different number of cheaters and network sizes with a constant cache size equal to 40. Probability that a node belongs to the $\hat{C}_t^{max}$ is computed by division of the average biggest component size by the network size.

6 Conclusion

Newscast is a P2P protocol designed to build up connectivity in distributed systems. To that end, nodes exchange routing information and establish an overlay network with the shape of a small-world graph. The emergent graph structure grants scalable access to information and makes the system suitable for distributed applications. In that context, the robustness of the protocol must secure the graph connectivity despite failures or attacks. While in some previous studies Newscast has proved to be resilient to crash faults (*i.e.* when nodes simply fail or stop working), the possibility of the protocol being attacked by malicious users, to the extent of our knowledge, has not been considered yet. Therefore, this paper analyses the resilience of Newscast against cheating faults with a purpose to raise an issue on the security of the protocol. In this context, in order to provide an assessment, we have tried to exploit the potential vulnerabilities of the original design. More precisely, we have modeled a non-cooperative type of cheating node which supplies a list of random non-valid entries to the regular network. Conducted experiments reveal that the protocol is sensitive to such types of attacks, which can lead to the graph being split after a relatively short time from the moment when the malicious nodes have started their activities.

In future work we plan to extend the presented study with a set of countermeasures with the analysis of their influence on the properties of the original solution. Additionally, we are planning to explore more complex *cheating faults*, especially involving coordinated attacks. Furthermore, detection techniques of malicious acts of this kind could be of use to remove cheaters from the network. Finally, having the set of solutions, it is necessary to check how they perform in more realistic environments, *e.g.* when the dynamics of a peer participation (*e.g.* churn) is present.

Acknowledgments. The experiments presented in this paper were carried out using the HPC facility of the University of Luxembourg (UL).

References

1. Avizienis, A., Laprie, J.-C., Randell, B., Landwehr, C.E.: Basic Concepts and Taxonomy of Dependable and Secure Computing. IEEE Transactions on Dependable and Secure Computing 1, 11–33 (2004)
2. Bertholon, B., Cérin, C., Coti, C., Dubacq, J.-C., Varrette, S.: Practical Security in Distributed Systems. In: Distributed Systems; Design and Algorithms, vol. 1, pp. 243–306. Whiley and Son (2011)
3. Dutot, A., Guinand, F., Olivier, D., Pigné, Y.: GraphStream: A Tool for bridging the gap between Complex Systems and Dynamic Graphs. In: Emergent Properties in Natural and Artificial Complex Systems. Satellite Conference within the 4th European Conference on Complex Systems (ECCS 2007), Dresden, Allemagne. ANR SARAH (October 2007)
4. The Gnutella Developer Forum GDF: The annotated gnutella protocol specification v0.4 (2001)
5. Jelasity, M., Guerraoui, R., Kermarrec, A.-M., van Steen, M.: The peer sampling service: Experimental evaluation of unstructured gossip-based implementations. In: Jacobsen, H.-A. (ed.) Middleware 2004. LNCS, vol. 3231, pp. 79–98. Springer, Heidelberg (2004)
6. Jelasity, M., Montresor, A., Babaoglu, O.: Gossip-based aggregation in large dynamic networks. ACM Trans. Comput. Syst. 23(3), 219–252 (2005)
7. Jelasity, M., van Steen, M.: Large-scale newscast computing on the Internet. Technical Report IR-503, Vrije Universiteit Amsterdam, Department of Computer Science, Amsterdam, The Netherlands (October 2002)
8. Laredo, J., Eiben, A., Steen, M., Merelo, J.: Evag: a scalable peer-to-peer evolutionary algorithm. Genetic Programming and Evolvable Machines 11(2), 227–246 (2010)
9. Rowstron, A., Druschel, P.: Pastry: Scalable, decentralized object location, and routing for large-scale peer-to-peer systems. In: Guerraoui, R. (ed.) Middleware 2001. LNCS, vol. 2218, pp. 329–350. Springer, Heidelberg (2001)
10. Stoica, I., Morris, R., Karger, D., Kaashoek, F., Balakrishnan, H.: Chord: A scalable Peer-To-Peer lookup service for internet applications. In: Proceedings of the 2001 ACM SIGCOMM Conference, pp. 149–160 (2001)
11. Voulgaris, S., Jelasity, M., van Steen, M.: A Robust and Scalable Peer-to-Peer Gossiping Protocol. In: Moro, G., Sartori, C., Singh, M.P. (eds.) AP2PC 2003. LNCS (LNAI), vol. 2872, pp. 47–58. Springer, Heidelberg (2004)
12. Watts, D., Strogatz, S.: Collective dynamics of "small-world" networks. Nature 393, 440–442 (1998)

A Meet-in-the-Middle Attack
on Round-Reduced mCrypton
Using the Differential Enumeration Technique

Yonglin Hao[1*], Dongxia Bai[1], and Leibo Li[2]

[1] Department of Computer Science and Technology,
Tsinghua Universtiy, Beijing 100084, China
{haoyl12,baidx10}@mails.tsinghua.edu.cn
[2] Key Laboratory of Cryptologic Technology and Information Security,
Ministry of Education, School of Mathematics,
Shandong University, Jinan, 250100, China
lileibo@mail.sdu.edu.cn

Abstract. This paper describes a meet-in-the-middle (MITM) attack against the round reduced versions of the block cipher mCrypton-64/96/128. We construct a 4-round distinguisher and lower the memory requirement from 2^{100} to 2^{44} using the differential enumeration technique. Based on the distinguisher, we launch a MITM attack on 7-round mCrypton-64/96/128 with complexities of 2^{44} 64-bit blocks and 2^{57} encryptions. Then we extend the basic attack to 8 rounds for mCrypton-128 by adding some key-bridging techniques. The 8-round attack on mCrypton-128 requires a time complexity 2^{100} and a memory complexity 2^{44}. Furthermore, we construct a 5-round distinguisher and propose a MITM attack on 9-round mCrypton-128 with a time complexity of 2^{115} encryptions and a memory complexity of 2^{113} 64-bit blocks.

1 Introduction

mCrypton is a 64-bit block cipher introduced in 2006 by Lim and Korkishko [1]. It is a reduced version of Crypton [2]. It is specifically designed for resource-constrained devices like RFID tags and sensors in wireless sensor networks. According to key length, mCrypton has three versions namely mCrypton-64/96/128.

Quite a few methods of cryptanalysis were applied to attack mCrypton. Under the related-key model, there are two main results. Park [3] launched a related-key rectangle attack on 8-round mCrypton-128 in the year 2009. Then, in 2012, Mala, Dakhilalian and Shakiba [4] gave a related-key impossible differential cryptanalysis on 9-round mCrypton-96/128. These related-key attacks are important basis in estimating the security of a block cipher, but they are not regarded as a real threat to the application of the cipher in practice since they require a powerful assumption that the adversary can ask to modify the unknown key used in the encryption.

---

* Corresponding author.

M.H. Au et al. (Eds.): NSS 2014, LNCS 8792, pp. 166–183, 2014.
© Springer International Publishing Switzerland 2014

For the attacks under the single-key model, there are only two biclique results on mCrypton: [5] managed to attack mCrypton-96/128 and [6] further adapted the methods to all three versions. Like the biclique result on AES [7], the two attacks mount to the full mCrypton but only with a marginal complexity over exhaustive search. In this paper, we try to attack mCrypton under the single-key model using the meet-in-the-middle method.

The meet-in-the-middle (MITM) attack was first introduced by Diffie and Hellman in 1977 [8]. In the past decade, the MITM scenario has become one of the most fruitful cryptanalysis method. It has been used to analyze block ciphers such as DES [9], KASUMI [10], IDEA [11],XTEA [12], KTANTAN [13] and Camellia [14,15]. It also shows good efficiency in the cryptanalysis of hash functions [16,17,18] and is adapted to attack against public key cryptosystem NTRU [19].

Among all the results of MITM attack, the most impressive ones come from the cryptanalysis on AES block cipher in single-key setting [20,21,22,23,24].

Demirci and Selçuk launched the first MITM attack on AES at FSE 2008 [20]. They constructed a 5-round distinguisher and managed to analyze 7-round AES-192 and 8-round AES-256 using data/time/memory tradeoff. Their attack needs a small data complexity of 2^{32}. But its memory complexity reaches 2^{200} since it requires to store a precomputation determined by 25 intermediated variable bytes. The number of parameters can be reduced to 24 by storing the differentials instead of values in the precomputation table. Although modifications was made in [21] and [22], the crisis of memory requirement remained severe.

At ASIACRYPT 2010, Dunkelman, Keller and Shamir [23] introduced the differential enumeration and multiset ideas to MITM attacks and reduced the high memory complexity in the precomputation phase. They proved that if a pair conforms a truncated differential characteristic, the number of desired 24 intermediate variable bytes will descend to 16. Furthermore, at EUROCRYPT 2013, Derbez, Fouque and Jean [24] modified Dunkelman et al.'s attack with the rebound-like idea. They proved that many values in the precomputation talbe are not reached under the constraint of the truncated differential. They further lower the number of desired intermediate variable bytes to 10 and diminish the size of precomputation table by a large scale. Based on the 4-round distinguisher, they gave the most efficient attacks on 7-round AES-128 and 8-round AES-192/256. They also introduced a 5-round distinguisher to analyze 9-round AES-256. In this paper, we apply [24]'s method to mCrypton.

Our Contribution. We construct a 4-round distinguisher of mCrypton and, using the differential enumeration technique, we prove that such a distinguisher can be determined by 11 intermediate variable nibbles. Based on these ideas, we launch a MITM attack on 7 rounds for all three versions of mCrypton, which recovers 36 subkey bits with a low memory complexity of 2^{44} 64-bit blocks. Then, we find some properties of key schedule and extend the basic attack to 8 rounds for mCrypton-128. The 8-round attack recovers 100 subkey bits. Furthermore, we construct a 5-round distinguisher and mount to 9 rounds for mCrypton-128.. This 9-round attack can recover 116 subkey bits with a time complexity of 2^{115}

Table 1. Summary of the Attacks on mCrypton-64/96/128 under the Single-Key Model

Version	Rounds	Data	Time	Memory	Method	Reference
64	7	2^{57}	2^{57}	2^{44}	**MITM**	**Section 4**
	12	2^{48}	$2^{63.38}$	–	Biclique	[6]
96	7	2^{57}	2^{57}	2^{44}	**MITM**	**Section 4**
	12	$2^{27.54}$	$2^{94.09}$	2^{20}	Biclique	[5]
	12	2^{48}	$2^{94.81}$	–	Biclique	[6]
128	7	2^{57}	2^{57}	2^{44}	**MITM**	**Section 4**
	8	2^{57}	2^{100}	2^{44}	**MITM**	**Section 5**
	9	2^{57}	2^{115}	2^{113}	**MITM**	**Section 6**
	12	$2^{20.1}$	$2^{125.84}$	2^{20}	Biclique	[5]
	12	2^{48}	$2^{126.26}$	–	Biclique	[6]

and a memory complexity 2^{113}. Table 1 summarizes our results along with the other previous results of mCrypton-64/96/128 under the single-key model.

Organization of the Paper. Section 2 provides the description of the block cipher mCrypton and some related works. Section 3 describes the 4-round distinguisher of our basic attack and the way in which the differential enumeration method lower the memory complexity. Section 4 describes our basic MITM attack on 7-round mCrypton-64/96/128. In Section 5, we extend the basic attack to 8-round mCrypton-128 using some key bridging techniques. Then, in Section 6 we present a 5-round distinguisher and attack 9-round mCrypton-128. Finally, we summarize our paper in Section 7.

2   Preliminary

This part contains some background information of our attack. It also gives the notations and units used in this article. As is commonly accepted, the plaintexts are denoted by p and ciphertexts by c.

2.1   Description of mCrypton

mCrypton is a 64-bit lightweight block cipher based on SPN design. It consists of 16 4-bit nibbles which are represented by a 4×4 matrix as follows:

$$A = \begin{pmatrix} a_0 & a_1 & a_2 & a_3 \\ a_4 & a_5 & a_6 & a_7 \\ a_8 & a_9 & a_{10} & a_{11} \\ a_{12} & a_{13} & a_{14} & a_{15} \end{pmatrix} \tag{1}$$

It has three versions, categorized by key length, namely mCrypton-64/96/128. All the three versions have 12 rounds and each round consists of 4 transformations as follows.

Nonlinear Substitution γ. This transformation consists of nibble-wise substitutions using four 4-bit S-boxes $S_i(0 \leq i \leq 3)$. The four S-boxes has relationship:

$$S_0 = S_2^{-1}, \quad S_1 = S_3^{-1}.$$

According to our experiments, the S-boxes of mCrypton have the same property with the S-box of AES (Property 1).

Property 1. Given Δ_i and Δ_o two non-zero differences in $\mathbb{F}_{16}$, the equation

$$S_t(x) \oplus S_t(x \oplus \Delta_i) = \Delta_o, \quad \forall t \in [0,3]$$

has one solution on average.

Bit Permutation π.   The bit permutation transformation π has the same function with the MixColumns transformation of AES. It mixes each column of the 4×4 matrix A. For column $i(0 \leq i \leq 3)$, it uses the corresponding column permutations π_i. Suppose

$$A = (A_0, A_1, A_2, A_3)$$

where A is the 4×4 matrix and A_i is its i-th column. Then, we have

$$\pi(A) = (\pi_0(A_0), \pi_1(A_1), \pi_2(A_2), \pi_3(A_3)).$$

According to [1], each π_i is defined for nibble columns $a = (a_0, a_1, a_2, a_3)^t$ and $b = (b_0, b_1, b_2, b_3)^t$ by

$$b = \pi_i(a) \Leftrightarrow b_j = \bigoplus_{k=0}^{3}(m_{(i+j+k)mod4} \bullet a_k).$$

The symbol $\bullet$ means bit-wise AND and the masking nibbles m_i are given by

$$m_0 = 0xe = 1110_2, m_1 = 0xd = 1101_2, m_2 = 0xb = 1011_2, m_2 = 0x7 = 0111_2.$$

π transformation is an involution, which means $\pi = \pi^{-1}$. It has a differential brunch number of 4.

Column-To-Row Transposition τ. This is simply the ordinary matrix transposition. It moves the nibble from the position (i, j) to position (j, i).

Key Addition σ. It is a simple bit-wise XOR operation and resembles the AddRoundKey operation of AES.
The r-th round $(1 \leq r \leq 12)$ of mCrypton applied to a 64-bit state x can be denoted by

$$\rho_{k_r}(x) = \sigma_{k_r} \circ \tau \circ \pi \circ \gamma(x).$$

Like AES, mCrypton also performs an initial key addition transformation (σ_{k_0}) before round 1. In addition, mCrypton adds a linear operation $\phi = \tau \circ \pi \circ \tau$ after round 12. So, the whole process of mCrypton encryption is

$$c = \phi \circ \rho_{k_{12}} \circ ... \circ \rho_{k_1} \circ \sigma_{k_0}(p)$$

Since we use some key bridging skills to analyze mCrypton-128, we briefly introduce the key schedule of mCrypton-128:

Key Schedule of mCrypton-128. The 128-bit internal register

$$U = (U_0, U_1, U_2, U_3, U_4, U_5, U_6, U_7)$$

is first initialized with the 128-bit user key. Each $U_i(0 \leq i \leq 7)$ is a 16-bit (4-nibble) word, occupying a row of the 4×4 matrix. Round keys $k_r(0 \leq r \leq 12)$ are computed consecutively as follows:

$$T \leftarrow S(U_0) \oplus C_r, T_i \leftarrow T \bullet M_i$$

$$k_r = (U_1 \oplus T_0, U_2 \oplus T_1, U_3 \oplus T_2, U_4 \oplus T_3)$$

$$U \leftarrow (U_5, U_6, U_7, U_0^{<<3}, U_1, U_2, U_3, U_4^{<<8}).$$

S is the nibble-wise S-box operation using S-box S_0. C_r is the round constant word for round r. Masking words M_i is to take the i-th nibble of a word:

$$M_0 = 0xf000, M_1 = 0x0f00, M_2 = 0x00f0, M_3 = 0x000f.$$

The symbol $X^{<<n}$ means left rotation of a 16-bit word X by n bits.

2.2   Notations and Units

Here, we summarize the notations that we use through this paper.

State x_r^i: The 64-bit mCrypton state is represented by different small letters. Plaintexts and ciphertexts are represented by p and c. In the r-th round, we denote the internal state after σ_{k_r} transformation by x_r, after γ by y_r, after π by z_r and after τ by w_r. k_r represents the round key while u_r is calculated linearly from k_r with $u_r = \pi \circ \tau(k_r)$. The difference of state x is denoted by Δx. Besides, the superscript represents the position that the state lies in a sequence (or set).

Nibble x[i]: We refer to the i-th nibble of a state x by $x[i]$, and use $x[i, \cdots, j]$ for nibbles at positions from i to j. The nibbles of the state is numbered as the matrix in equation (1).

Bit $x[i]\|_k$: Each nibble has 4 bits numbered 4,3,2,1 from left to right. If we refer to bit k of nibble $x[i]$, we denote it by $x[i]\|_k$.

Bit-wise operators:

   $\|$ concatenate two strings of bits.

   $\oplus$ bit-wise XOR.

   $\bullet$ bit-wise AND.

In this paper, memory complexities of our attacks are measured by the number of 64-bit mCrypton blocks and time complexities by mCrypton encryptions (decryptions).

2.3   The Related Works

From the generic view of meet-in-the-middle attack, the cipher E_K is treated as the combination of three parts $E_K = E_{K_2}^2 \circ E^m \circ E_{K_1}^1$. The E^m part in the middle has some particular property (such as a differential characteristic), according to which we can identify the correct key by finding the appearance of the property under each guess of subkey (K_1, K_2). The following definition will be used in this part.

Definition 1. *(σ-set of AES, [25]) The σ-set is a set of 256 intermediate states of AES that one byte traverses all values (the active byte) and the other bytes are constants (the inactive bytes).*

We denote the σ-set by $(x^0, \cdots, x^{255})$. After we encrypt the σ-set by an encryption function E_K, the i-th byte of the output values will form a 2048-bit ordered sequence $(E_K(x^0)[i], \cdots, E_K(x^{255})[i])$. The sequences with particular properties will be stored in a precompted lookup table for distinguishing the correct key guess during the attack.

In the first MITM attack on AES, Demirci et al. [20] build a distinguisher in E^m associated with σ-set. When a σ-set is encrypted, a certain byte of the 256 output values will form an ordered sequence. Demirci et al. found that such an ordered sequence can be expressed as a function of 25 (or 24 if they only store the differences rather than the values) intermediate byte parameters of E^m. In precomputation phase of their attack, the adversary precomputes the $2^{8 \times 25}$ ordered sequences and stores them in a table. In the online phase, the adversary mounts an attack by guessing the value of K_1, choosing suitable plaintexts to construct a σ-set of E^m, then partially decrypting the ciphertexts by guessing K_2 to get the corresponding ordered sequence, and checking whether the value lies in the precomputed table. If the value is found in the table, the key guess (K_1, K_2) will be kept, otherwise discarded.

We also consider applying the differential enumeration technique proposed by Dunkelman et al. [23] to reduce the memory requirement of the attack. This technique based on the observation that if a message of the σ-set belongs to a pair conforming a spacial truncated differential characteristic, the possible values of the ordered sequence will be restricted to a small subset of the value space. The essence of this technique is fixing some values of intermediate parameters utilizing the truncated differential so that the size of the precomputed table can be diminished by a large scale. On the other hand, additional steps has to be taken in the online phase in order to find a pair satisfying the truncated differential characteristic because the σ-set is constructed only for this kind of pairs. Apparently, the differential enumeration technique reduce the memory requirement but also increase the data and time complexity. It is noticeable that Derbez et al. [24] improved this technique at EUROCRYPT 2013. They further reduced the possible values in the precomputed table by introducing some rebound-like ideas.

3   The 4-Round Distinguisher and the Differential Enumeration Tehcnique

The meet-in-the-middle strategy combined with the differential enumeration technique is the basis of our attack. Imitating those of AES, we define the σ-set of the mCrypton as Definition 2.

Definition 2. (σ-set of mCrypton). *A σ-set is a set of 16 64-bit mCrypton-states that are all different in one nibble (the active nibble) and all equal in the other state nibbles (the inactive nibbles).*

In our basic MITM attack, the middle part E^m starts from x_1 and ends at x_5. So, in the following parts of this paper, we denote the σ-set with an active nibble at position $j (0 \leq j \leq 15)$ by

$$A_j = (x_1^0, ..., x_1^{15}), \qquad (2)$$

and the corresponding ordered sequence constituted by the l-th nibble ($l \in [0, 15]$) of x_5 is denoted by

$$B_j^l = (\Delta^1 x_5[l], \cdots, \Delta^{15} x_5[l]), \qquad (3)$$

where $\Delta^i x_r = x_r^i \oplus x_r^0 (1 \leq i \leq 15, 0 \leq r \leq 12)$.

Proposition 1 shows that 25 intermediate variable nibbles are required to deduce B_j^l from A_j. However, if the x_1^0 of σ-set A_0 belongs to a pair conforming the truncated differential characteristic in Figure 1, we can prove that the corresponding sequence B_0^0 can only have 2^{44} values determined by 11 nibble parameters (Proposition 2). This is the differential enumeration method used in [23] and [24] to lower the memory complexities of their attacks on AES.

Proposition 1. $\forall j \in [0, 15]$ *and* $\forall l \in [0, 15]$. *Let the σ-set be*

$$A_j = (x_1^0, ..., x_1^{15})$$

Then, the corresponding sequence

$$B_j^l = (\Delta^1 x_5[l], \cdots, \Delta^{15} x_5[l])$$

can be fully determined by 25 nibble parameters:

- *1 nibble of x_1^0.*
- *The full 16-nibble state x_3^0;*
- *4 nibbles of x_2^0.*
- *4 nibbles of x_4^0.*

Proof. We just let $j = 0$ and $l = 0$. Then, the 25 nibbles required are:

$$x_1^0[0], x_2^0[0, 1, 2, 3], x_3^0[0, \cdots, 15], x_4^0[0, 4, 8, 12].$$

For the t-th element of B_0^0 ($t \in [1, 15]$), the difference $\Delta^t x_5[0]$ can be deduced from $x_4^0[0, 4, 8, 12]$ and $\Delta^t x_4[0, 4, 8, 12]$.

$\Delta^t x_4[0, 4, 8, 12]$ requires the knowledge of $x_3^0[0, \cdots, 15]$ and $\Delta^t x_3[0, \cdots, 15]$.
$\Delta^t x_3[0, ..., 15]$ is generated linearly from $\Delta^t y_2[0, \cdots, 3]$, which can be deduced
from $x_2^0[0, 1, 2, 3]$ and $\Delta^t x_2[0, 1, 2, 3]$.

$\Delta^t x_2[0, 1, 2, 3]$ is generated linearly from $\Delta^t y_1[0]$, which requires the knowledge
of $x_1^0[0]$ and $\Delta^t x_1[0]$. $\Delta^t x_1[0]$ can be deduced directly from A_0. Hence, all the nibble
parameters required are: $x_1^0[0]$, $x_2^0[0, 1, 2, 3]$, $x_3^0[0, \cdots, 15]$, $x_4^0[0, 4, 8, 12]$.   □

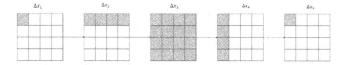

Fig. 1. The 4-round truncated differential characteristic. Dashed nibbles are active.

Proposition 2. *If the x_1^0 of a σ-set A_0 belongs to a pair satisfying the differential characteristic in Figure 1, the corresponding sequence B_0^0 can only take 2^{44} values.*

Proof. According to Proposition 1, B_0^0 is determined by 25 nibbles namely:

$$x_1^0[0], x_2^0[0, 1, 2, 3], x_3^0[0, \cdots, 15], x_4^0[0, 4, 8, 12].$$

But if x_0 of A_0 belongs to one of the pairs conforming the truncated differential characteristic in Figure 1, the corresponding sequence B_0^0 can only take 2^{44} values determined by 11 nibbles namely

$$x_1^0[0], \Delta x_1[0], x_2^0[0, 1, 2, 3], x_4^0[0, 4, 8, 12], \Delta z_4[0],$$

where Δ refers to the difference of the pair conforming the differential characteristic.

The knowledge of $x_1^0[0]$ and $\Delta x_1[0]$ is sufficient to deduce $\Delta x_2[0, 1, 2, 3]$. Combining $x_2^0[0, 1, 2, 3]$ and $\Delta x_2[0, 1, 2, 3]$, we get the 16-nibble difference Δx_3.

Similarly, we can deduce $\Delta y_4[0, 4, 8, 12]$ from $\Delta z_4[0]$. Adding the knowledge of $x_4^0[0, 4, 8, 12]$, the 16-nibble differential Δy_3 is determined.

Since $y_3 = \gamma(x_3)$, according to the property of mCrypton S-boxes (Property 1), we can only get one value on average for each of the 16-nibble state x_3 using super-box matches technique [26].

This is the way we deduce the sequence B_0^0 from the σ-set A_0.   □

The 4-round truncated differential character in Figure 1 is the distinguisher that we use in the following section.

4 The Basic Attack on 7-Round mCrypton-64/96/128

In this part, we describe our basic attack on 7-round mCrypton-64/96/128. This attack can recovery 36 subkey bits. The complete differential path used in this attack can be seen in Figure 4 in Appendix A. This attack is composed of two phases: the precomputation phase and the online phase.

Precomputation Phase: In the precomputation phase, we set up a lookup table containing 2^{44} ordered sequences described as Proposition 2. The procedure is similar to the proof of Proposition 1 and Proposition 2, and is described as follows.

1. For each 44-bit string $x_1^0[0]\|\Delta x_1[0]\|x_2^0[0,\cdots,3]\|x_4^0[0,4,8,12]\|\Delta z_4[0]$, we compute the possible value of the 25 nibbles, namely $x_1^0[0], x_2^0[0,\cdots,3]$, $x_3^0, x_4^0[0,4,8,12]$, only with which can we determine the ordered sequence B_0^0. The procedure is as follows:
   (a) Compute $\Delta x_2[0,\cdots,3]$ with the knowledge of $x_1^0[0]$ and $\Delta x_1[0]$;
   (b) Compute Δx_3 with the knowledge of $x_2^0[0,\cdots,3]$ and $\Delta x_2[0,\cdots,3]$;
   (c) Compute $\Delta y_4[0,4,8,12]$ with the knowledge of $\Delta z_4[0]$;
   (d) Compute Δy_3 with the knowledge of $\Delta y_4[0,4,8,12]$ and $x_4[0,4,8,12]$;
   (e) With the knowledge of Δy_3 and Δx_3 and using the super-box matches, we can determine the possible values of x_3^0 satisfying $\gamma(x_3^0) \oplus \gamma(x_3^0 \oplus \Delta x_3) = \Delta y_3$. According to Property 1, x_3^0 has only one possible value on average.

2. Now that we have obtained the value of the 25 nibbles namely $x_1^0[0], x_2^0[0,\cdots,3], x_3^0, x_4^0[0,4,8,12]$. For all the 15 possible values of $\Delta^t x_1^0[0], t \in [1,15]$, we can compute the t-th element of B_0^0, $\Delta^t x_5[0]$, by executing the following substeps:
   (a) Compute $\Delta^t x_2[0,\cdots,3]$ with the knowledge of $\Delta^t x_0[0]$ and $x_1^0[0]$;
   (b) Compute $\Delta^t x_3$ with the knowledge of $\Delta^t x_2[0,\cdots,3]$ and $x_2^0[0,\cdots,3]$;
   (c) Compute $\Delta^t x_4[0,4,8,12]$ with the knowledge of $\Delta^t x_3$ and x_3^0;
   (d) Compute $\Delta^t x_5[0]$ with the knowledge of $\Delta^t x_4[0,4,8,12]$ and $x_4^0[0,4,8,12]$. And $\Delta^t x_5$ is the t-th element of B_0^0

3. Store all the 2^{44} B_0^0s in a hash table T_s.

Online Phase: In the online phase of this attack, we first find the right pairs satisfying the truncated differential characteristic. Then, for each member of the pairs, we construct its σ-set A_0 and deduce the corresponding ordered sequence B_0^0 through partial encryptions&decryptions. Finally, we check whether the obtained B_0^0 exist in the precomputed lookup table T_s. The detailed procedure is as follows.

1. Encrypt 2^{41} structures of 2^{16} plaintexts such that $p[0,4,8,12]$ takes all values and other nibbles are constants. There are about 2^{31} pairs (p, p') in each structure, so there are 2^{72} pairs in total.
2. Within each structure, select the pairs whose Δc only have difference at positions 0,4,8,12. Since this is a 48-bit filter, approximately 2^{24} of the 2^{72} message pairs will remain after this step.
3. For each remaining pair, assuming that it satisfies the differential path in Figure 4, we do the following substeps.
   (a) Guess the difference value $\Delta x_1[0]$ and linearly deduce $\Delta y_0[0,4,8,12]$.

(b) For each guess, deduce the possible subkey nibbles $k_0[0, 4, 8, 12]$ with the knowledge of $\Delta y_0[0, 4, 8, 12]$ and $\Delta x_0[0, 4, 8, 12] = \Delta p[0, 4, 8, 12]$. According to Property 1, one $k_0[0, 4, 8, 12]$ value can be acquired on average.

(c) Guess the difference value $\Delta y_5[0]$ and deduce $\Delta x_6[0, \cdots, 3]$.

(d) For each guess, deduce the possible $u_7[0, \cdots, 3]$ with the knowledge of $\Delta x_6[0, \cdots, 3]$ and $\Delta y_6[0, 4, 8, 12]$ ($\Delta y_6 = \Delta \tau(c)$). According to Property 1, one $u_7[0, \cdots, 3]$ can be acquired on average.

4. For each deduced subkey $k_0[0, 4, 8, 12] \| u_7[0, \cdots, 3]$, we obtain at least one ordered sequence B_0^0 with the following substeps.

(a) Select one message of the right pair, denoted by p^0, and deduce its $x_1^0[0]$ through partial encryption.

(b) Then, let t traverse through $[1, 15]$ so that we can compute $\Delta^t x_1[0] = x_1^0[0] \oplus t$ and deduce plaintexts p^t with the knowledge of $\Delta^t x_1[0]$ and p^0 through partial decryption. At this point, we have acquired the plaintexts $(p^0, \cdots, p^{15})$ corresponding to the σ-set $(x_1^0, \cdots, x_1^{15})$.

(c) Query the ciphertexts of $(p^0, \cdots, p^{15})$ and deduce the sequence

$$(x_6^0[0, \cdots, 3], \cdots, x_6^{15}[0, \cdots, 3]) \tag{4}$$

through partial decryption with the knowledge of $u_7[0, \cdots, 3]$.

(d) Guess subkey $u_6[0]$ and deduce the ordered sequence $B_0^0 = (\Delta^1 x_5[0], \cdots, \Delta^{15} x_5[0])$ from (4) through partial decryption.

5. Identify the right subkeys $k_0[0, 4, 8, 12] \| u_6[0] \| u_7[0, \cdots, 3]$ by verifying whether the sequence B_0^0 exists in the precomputed lookup table T_s. If $B_0^0 \in T_s$, the key guesses are correct with high probability. The error rate is $2^{44-60} = 2^{-16}$ to be precise.

Complexity Analysis. In the pre-computation phase, T_s contains 2^{44} sequences and each sequence occupies 60 bits of space. So the memory complexity of this attack is dominated by T_s' 2^{44} 64-bit blocks. Since each sequence has 15 nibbles, it requires $2^{44} \times 15 \approx 2^{48}$ encryptions to construct the lookup table. The time complexity of the online phase is dominated by step 1 which involves encrypting $2^{41} \times 2^{16} = 2^{57}$ plaintexts. So the time and data complexity of our attack are both 2^{57}.

5   Extend the Basic Attack to 8 Rounds for mCrypton-128

Using the key bridging technique, we can further attack 8-round mCrypton-128. According to the key schedule of mCrypton-128, the knowledge of k_8 can deduce some bits in k_0 (Proposition 3) with which we can lower the time complexity of the online phase.

Proposition 3. *By the key schedule of mCrypton-128, knowledge of the entire 16-nibble k_8 allows deduce $k_0[6]$, 3 bits of $k_0[2]$ and 1 bit of $k_0[14]$.*

Proof. According to the key schedule of mCrypton-128, the relationship of the 8 bits are:

$$k_0[2]|_{4,3,2} = k_8[3]|_{3,2,1} \tag{5}$$

$$k_0[6]|_{4,3,2} = k_8[7]|_{3,2,1} \tag{6}$$

$$k_0[6]|_1 = k_8[4]|_4 \tag{7}$$

$$k_0[14]|_1 = k_8[12]|_4 \tag{8}$$

The readers may refer to [1] for the detailed key schedule of mCrypton-128. □

In order to make full use of Proposition 3, we deliberately change the form of the truncated differential characteristic of this attack to the one in Figure 2. The σ-set of this attack has an active nibble at position 8 and is denoted by A_8. The corresponding ordered sequence is composed of nibble 0 of x_5 and is denoted by B_8^0. The complete differential characteristic of this attack can be seen in Figure 5 in Appendix A.

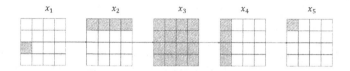

Fig. 2. The differential characteristic for 8-round mCrypton-128

The precomputation phase of this 8-round attack is identical to that of the basic attack. In this phase, we construct a lookup table T_s containing 2^{44} possible values of B_8^0 determined by 11 intermediate variable nibbles namely

$$x_1^0[8], \Delta x_1[12], x_2^0[0,1,2,3], x_4^0[0,4,8,12], \Delta z_4[0].$$

In the online phase, additional subkey has to be deduced so that we can extend the basic 7-round attack to 8 rounds. The procedure of the online phase is as follow.

1. Encrypt 2^{41} structures of 2^{16} plaintexts with active nibbles at positions 2,6,10,14. There are about 2^{31} pairs (p, p') in each structure, so there are 2^{72} pairs in total.
2. For each pair, do the following substeps.
   (a) Guess the difference $\Delta y_6[0, \cdots, 3]$ and compute the subkey k_8 using the super-box matches. Since there are 2^{16} possible values of $\Delta y_6[0, \cdots, 3]$ and each can deduce one k_8 one average (Proposition 1), 2^{16} k_8 values are obtained in this step.
   (b) Deduce $k_0[6]$ from k_8 using Proposition 3 and obtain $\Delta y_0[6]$ through partial encryption. Discard the keys if $\Delta y_0[6]|_4 \neq 0$ because

$$\Delta y_0[6] = m_3 \bullet \Delta z_0[2], \quad m_3 = 0111_2. \tag{9}$$

   This is a one-bit filter so there are 2^{15} subkey guesses left.

(c) Now that we have acquired $z_0[2]\|_{3,2,1}$ from (9), we guess $z_0[2]\|_4$ and compute $\Delta y_0[2,6,10,14]$ with which we can deduce $k_0[2,6,10,14]$. Discard the guesses violating equations (6) and (8) of Proposition 3. This step involves a 1-bit guess and a 4-bit filter, so there are about $2^{15+1-4} = 2^{12}$ subkey guesses remain.

(d) Guess $\Delta y_5[0]$ and deduce the 2^4 possible values of $u_7[0,\cdots,3]$. At this point, we have acquired 2^{16} key guesses of $k_0[2,6,10,14]\|u_7[0,\cdots,3]\|k_8$.

3. For each subkey, select a member of the right pair, guess $u_6[0]$ and construct the sequence B_8^0 through partial encryptions & decryptions.

4. Identify the right guess by checking whether B_8^0 exist in T_s.

Complexity Analysis. Similar to the basic attack, the data complexity of this attack is 2^{57} and the memory complexity is still dominated by the pre-computed lookup table, which is 2^{44} 64-bit blocks to be precise. The time complexity of this attack is dominated by the 3rd step of the online phase which involves a 4-bit guess and 16 encryptions/decryptions to construct B_8^0. Since this step has to be executed on each of the 2^{20} subkey guesses within each of the 2^{72} pairs, the time complexity of this attack is $2^{72} \times 2^{20} \times 2^4 \times 16 = 2^{100}$. The 8-round attack recovers 100 subkey bits namely $k_0[2,6,10,14]\|u_6[0]\|u_7[0,\cdots,3]\|k_8$.

6   9-Round Attack on mCrypton-128

The 15-nibble sequences used in the previous attacks can not provide enough information to identify the correct subkey guesses in the 9-round attack on mCrypton-128. In the 9-round attack, we consider the σ-set with 2 active nibbles containing 256 64-bit blocks and its corresponding ordered sequence consists of 255 nibbles occupying 1020 bits of space. The key bridging technique used in this attack is interpreted as Proposition 4.

Proposition 4. *By the key schedule of mCrypton-128, the knowledge of the entire 16-nibble k_9 allows to deduce $k_0[0,3]$*

Proof. According to the key schedule, we have

$$k_0[3]\|_{4,3,2} = k_9[12]\|_{3,2,1}$$

$$k_0[3]\|_1 = k_9[13]\|_4$$

$$k_0[0] = S_0((k_9[8]\|_{2,1}\|k_9[9]\|_{4,3})) \oplus (k_9[13]\|_{3,2,1}\|k_9[14]\|_4) \oplus 1$$

These relationships can be deduced easily from the key schedule.   □

To fully utilize the key bridging technique, we select the σ-set with active nibbles at positions 0 and 12, denoted by

$$A_{0,12} = \{x_1^0, x_1^1, ..., x_1^{255}\}.$$

As is described in Subsection 2.1, the differential brunch of the π operation in mCrypton is 4. So, we deliberately assign that the x_1^0 of $A_{0,12}$ belongs to a pair

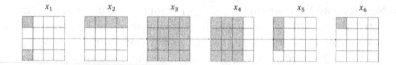

Fig. 3. The 5-round differential characteristic for attacking 9-round mCrypton-128

satisfying the 5-round truncated differential characteristic shown in Figure 3. The ordered sequence corresponding to $A_{0,12}$ consists of $\Delta^t x_6[0](1 \leq t \leq 255)$ and is denoted by

$$B_{0,12}^0 = (\Delta^1 x_6[0], \cdots, \Delta^{255} x_6[0]).$$

Similar to Proposition 1 and 2, the sequence $B_{0,12}^0$ is determined by 42 intermediate variable nibbles namely:

$$x_1^0[0, 12], x_2^0[0, \cdots, 3], x_3^0, x_4^0, x_5^0[0, 4, 8, 12]$$

and the number of desired nibbles can be lowered to 29 with the help of the truncated differential characteristic in Figure 3 by using the differential enumeration method. The 29 decisive nibbles for $B_{0,12}^0$ are namely

$$x_1^0[0, 12], \Delta x_1[0, 12], x_2^0[0, 1, 2, 3], x_3^0, x_5^0[0, 4, 8, 12], \Delta z_5[0]. \tag{10}$$

However, the differential character can only be satisfied when $\Delta z_5[0] = 0x8 = 1000_2$, which means $\Delta z_5[0]$ can only take 1 rather than 2^4 values. Since $\Delta z_5[0]$ can only take 1 value, $\Delta x_5[0, 4, 8]$ can only take $2^{3 \times 3} = 2^9$ values, which is also true for $x_5^0[0, 4, 8]$ according to Property 1. So the total number of the targeted ordered sequence is $2^{4 \times 25 + 9} = 2^{109}$. This 9-round attack is in high accordance with the 8-round one introduced in Section 5, so we only briefly summarize the whole procedure as follow.

Precompuation Phase. Construct the lookup table T_s containing 2^{109} values of $B_{0,12}^0$ determined by 29 nibble parameters listed in (10).

Online Phase

1. Encrypt 2^{25} structures of 2^{32} plaintexts such that $p[\lambda]$, where

$$\lambda = (0, 3, 4, 7, 8, 11, 12, 15),$$

   takes all values and other nibbles are constants. There are 2^{88} pairs in total.
2. For each pair, do the following steps.
   (a) Guess $\Delta y_7[0, \cdots, 3]$ and deduce k_9 using super-box matches. Since there are 2^{16} possible values of $\Delta y_6[0, \cdots, 3]$ and each can deduce averaging one k_9 (Proposition 1), 2^{16} k_9 values are obtained in this step.
   (b) Deduce $k_0[0, 3]$ with the knowledge of k_9 using Proposition 4. Then, compute $\Delta y_0[0, 3]$ and deduce $\Delta y_0[\lambda]$ with the relation between Δy_0 and Δz_0. With the knowledge of $\Delta y_0[\lambda]$, we can further retrieve $k_0[\lambda]$.

(c) Guess $\Delta y_6[0]$ and deduce 2^3 possible values of $u_8[0, \cdots, 3] \| u_7[0]$, where $u_7[0]$ is deduced from the knowledge of $\Delta x_6[0] = 1000_2$.

3. For each subkey, select a member of the right pair and deduce its $B_{0,12}^0$ through partial decryptions.

4. Refer to the T_s and identify the right guess.

Complexity Analysis. The data complexity of the 9-round attack is $2^{25+32} = 2^{57}$. The memory complexity is dominated by the lookup table set up in the precomputation phase, which is $2^{109} \times 1020/64 \approx 2^{113}$ 64-bit blocks to be precise. The time complexity is dominated by the step 3 of the online phase which involves $2^{88} \times 2^{16} \times 2^3 \times 256 = 2^{115}$ encryptions/decryptions. The 9-round attack recovers 116 subkey bits namely $k_0[\lambda] \| u_7[0] \| u_8[0, \cdots, 3] \| k_9$, where $\lambda = (0, 3, 4, 7, 8, 11, 12, 15)$.

7   Conclusion

In this paper, we analyze the lightweight SPN block cipher mCrypton using the meet-in-the-middle (MITM) attack under the single-key model. We use the differential enumeration technique to lower the memory complexity, which used to be the bottleneck of the MITM method. We set up a 4-round distinguisher and manage to launch a basic MITM attack on 7-round mCrypton-64/96/128. Adding some key bridging techniques, we extend the basic attack to 8 rounds for mCrypton-128. We construct a 5-round distinguisher and further mount to 9 rounds for mCrypton-128. The 9-round attack retrieves 116 subkey bits with memory complexity 2^{113} and time complexity 2^{115}.

Acknowledgement. This work has been supported by the National Natural Science Foundation of China (Grant No. 61133013) and by 973 Program (Grant No. 2013CB834205).

References

1. Lim, C.H., Korkishko, T.: mCrypton – A lightweight block cipher for security of low-cost RFID tags and sensors. In: Song, J.-S., Kwon, T., Yung, M. (eds.) WISA 2005. LNCS, vol. 3786, pp. 243–258. Springer, Heidelberg (2006)

2. Lim, C.H.: Crypton: A new 128-bit block cipher. NIsT AEs Proposal (1998)

3. Park, J.H.: Security analysis of mcrypton proper to low-cost ubiquitous computing devices and applications. International Journal of Communication Systems 22(8), 959–969 (2009)

4. Mala, H., Dakhilalian, M., Shakiba, M.: Cryptanalysis of mcryptona lightweight block cipher for security of rfid tags and sensors. International Journal of Communication Systems 25(4), 415–426 (2012)

5. Shakiba, M., Dakhilalian, M., Mala, H.: Non-isomorphic biclique cryptanalysis and its application to full-round mcrypton. IACR Cryptology ePrint Archive 2013, 141 (2013)

6. Jeong, K., Kang, H., Lee, C., Sung, J., Hong, S., Lim, J.I.: Weakness of lightweight block ciphers mcrypton and led against biclique cryptanalysis. Peer-to-Peer Networking and Applications, 1–17 (2013)
7. Bogdanov, A., Khovratovich, D., Rechberger, C.: Biclique cryptanalysis of the full AES. In: Lee, D.H., Wang, X. (eds.) ASIACRYPT 2011. LNCS, vol. 7073, pp. 344–371. Springer, Heidelberg (2011)
8. Diffie, W.: Exhaustive cryptianalysis of the nbs data encryption standard (1977)
9. Dunkelman, O., Sekar, G., Preneel, B.: Improved meet-in-the-middle attacks on reduced-round DES. In: Srinathan, K., Rangan, C.P., Yung, M. (eds.) INDOCRYPT 2007. LNCS, vol. 4859, pp. 86–100. Springer, Heidelberg (2007)
10. Jia, K., Yu, H., Wang, X.: A meet-in-the-middle attack on the full kasumi. IACR Cryptology ePrint Archive 2011, 466 (2011)
11. Demirci, H., Selçuk, A.A., Türe, E.: A new meet-in-the-middle attack on the idea block cipher. In: Matsui, M., Zuccherato, R.J. (eds.) SAC 2003. LNCS, vol. 3006, pp. 117–129. Springer, Heidelberg (2004)
12. Sekar, G., Mouha, N., Velichkov, V., Preneel, B.: Meet-in-the-middle attacks on reduced-round XTEA. In: Kiayias, A. (ed.) CT-RSA 2011. LNCS, vol. 6558, pp. 250–267. Springer, Heidelberg (2011)
13. Bogdanov, A., Rechberger, C.: A 3-subset meet-in-the-middle attack: Cryptanalysis of the lightweight block cipher KTANTAN. In: Biryukov, A., Gong, G., Stinson, D.R. (eds.) SAC 2010. LNCS, vol. 6544, pp. 229–240. Springer, Heidelberg (2011)
14. Lu, J., Wei, Y., Pasalic, E., Fouque, P.-A.: Meet-in-the-middle attack on reduced versions of the camellia block cipher. In: Hanaoka, G., Yamauchi, T. (eds.) IWSEC 2012. LNCS, vol. 7631, pp. 197–215. Springer, Heidelberg (2012)
15. Chen, J., Li, L.: Low data complexity attack on reduced camellia-256. In: Susilo, W., Mu, Y., Seberry, J. (eds.) ACISP 2012. LNCS, vol. 7372, pp. 101–114. Springer, Heidelberg (2012)
16. Aoki, K., Sasaki, Y.: Meet-in-the-middle preimage attacks against reduced SHA-0 and SHA-1. In: Halevi, S. (ed.) CRYPTO 2009. LNCS, vol. 5677, pp. 70–89. Springer, Heidelberg (2009)
17. Sasaki, Y.: Meet-in-the-middle preimage attacks on AES hashing modes and an application to whirlpool. In: Joux, A. (ed.) FSE 2011. LNCS, vol. 6733, pp. 378–396. Springer, Heidelberg (2011)
18. Sasaki, Y., Aoki, K.: Meet-in-the-middle preimage attacks on double-branch hash functions: Application to RIPEMD and others. In: Boyd, C., González Nieto, J. (eds.) ACISP 2009. LNCS, vol. 5594, pp. 214–231. Springer, Heidelberg (2009)
19. Howgrave-Graham, N.: A hybrid lattice-reduction and meet-in-the-middle attack against NTRU. In: Menezes, A. (ed.) CRYPTO 2007. LNCS, vol. 4622, pp. 150–169. Springer, Heidelberg (2007)
20. Demirci, H., Selçuk, A.A.: A meet-in-the-middle attack on 8-round AES. In: Nyberg, K. (ed.) FSE 2008. LNCS, vol. 5086, pp. 116–126. Springer, Heidelberg (2008)
21. Demirci, H., Taşkın, İ., Çoban, M., Baysal, A.: Improved meet-in-the-middle attacks on AES. In: Roy, B., Sendrier, N. (eds.) INDOCRYPT 2009. LNCS, vol. 5922, pp. 144–156. Springer, Heidelberg (2009)
22. Wei, Y., Lu, J., Hu, Y.: Meet-in-the-middle attack on 8 rounds of the AES block cipher under 192 key bits. In: Bao, F., Weng, J. (eds.) ISPEC 2011. LNCS, vol. 6672, pp. 222–232. Springer, Heidelberg (2011)
23. Dunkelman, O., Keller, N., Shamir, A.: Improved single-key attacks on 8-round AES-192 and AES-256. In: Abe, M. (ed.) ASIACRYPT 2010. LNCS, vol. 6477, pp. 158–176. Springer, Heidelberg (2010)

24. Derbez, P., Fouque, P.-A., Jean, J.: Improved key recovery attacks on reduced-round AES in the single-key setting. In: Johansson, T., Nguyen, P.Q. (eds.) EURO-CRYPT 2013. LNCS, vol. 7881, pp. 371–387. Springer, Heidelberg (2013)
25. Daemen, J., Rijmen, V.: AES proposal: Rijndael (1999)
26. Gilbert, H., Peyrin, T.: Super-sbox cryptanalysis: Improved attacks for AES-like permutations. In: Hong, S., Iwata, T. (eds.) FSE 2010. LNCS, vol. 6147, pp. 365–383. Springer, Heidelberg (2010)

Appendix

A   The Complete Differential Characteristics Used in This Article

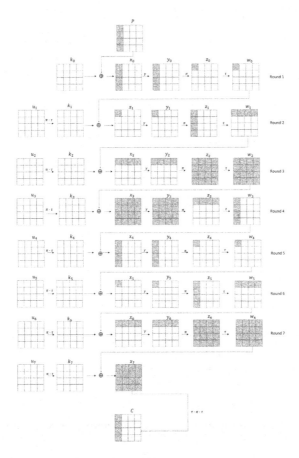

Fig. 4. Complete 7-round differential characteristic used in Section 4

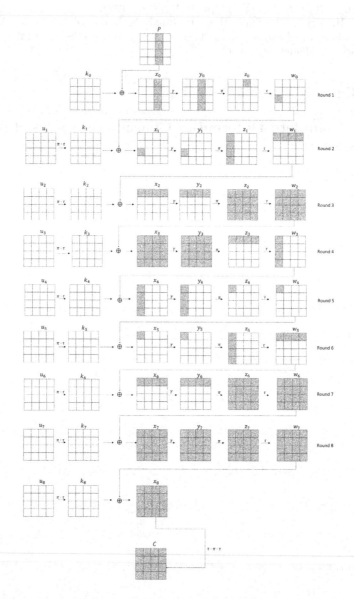

Fig. 5. Complete 8-round differential characteristic used in Section 5

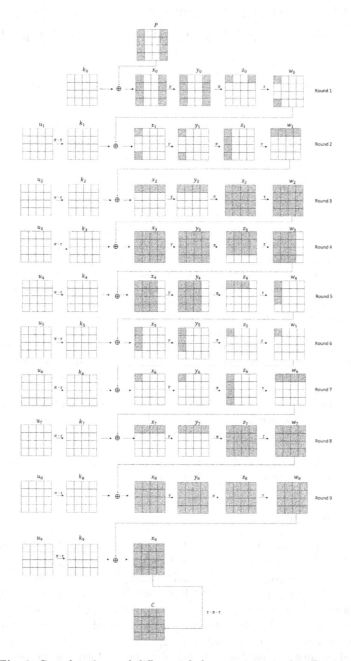

Fig. 6. Complete 9-round differential characteristic used in Section 6

Improving Impossible Differential Cryptanalysis with Concrete Investigation of Key Scheduling Algorithm and Its Application to LBlock

Jiageng Chen, Yuichi Futa, Atsuko Miyaji, and Chunhua Su

School of Information Science,
Japan Advanced Institute of Science and Technology,
1-1 Asahidai, Nomi, Ishikawa 923-1292, Japan
{jg-chen,futa,miyaji,chsu}@jaist.ac.jp

Abstract. Impossible differential cryptanalysis has been proved to be one of the most powerful techniques to attack block ciphers. Based on the impossible differential paths, we can usually add several rounds before or after to launch a key recovery attack. Impossible differential cryptanalysis is powerful not only because the number of rounds it can break is very competitive compared to other attacks, but also unlike differential attacks which are statistical attacks in the essential, impossible differential analysis does not require many statistical assumptions. In this paper, we investigate the key recovery attack part of the impossible differential cryptanalysis. We point out that when taking the (non-linear) key scheduling algorithm into consideration, we can further derive the redundancy among the subkeys, and thus can filter the wrong key at a rather early stage. This can help us control the time complexity and increase the number of rounds we can attack. As an application, we analyze recently proposed lightweight block cipher LBlock, and as a result, we can break 23 rounds with complexity $2^{77.4}$ encryptions without using the whole code block, which is by far the best attack against this cipher.

Keywords: Impossible differential cryptanalysis, key recovery attack, non-linear key scheduling algorithm, LBlock.

1 Introduction

Block ciphers have been investigated for more than three decades, and a lot of powerful methods have been proposed such as differential attack [2], linear attack [14] and so on. Among these techniques, impossible differential cryptanalysis is one of the most powerful attack against block ciphers, especially block cipher with Feistel and General Feistel structures are especially considered to be weak for impossible differential attack as demonstrated in [8] and other works. Since the technique was first published in [1], a lot of ciphers have been carefully investigated against impossible differential attack, which has become a standard default routine when evaluating newly proposed ciphers. Different from differential attack which searches for the right key with the most high probability, impossible differential attack searches the right key by discarding the

M.H. Au et al. (Eds.): NSS 2014, LNCS 8792, pp. 184–197, 2014.

wrong ones, and the process makes sure that the right key remains without being wrongly discarded. Thus compared with the differential attack which has to makes the wrong key randomization hypothesis [3], impossible differential attack provides much more guarantee on the cryptanalysis result we get. Thus if similar results (from the point view of data complexity, computational complexity and the number of rounds) are derived, researchers prefer the result of impossible differential cryptanalysis. We need first to find an impossible differential path, which should not be existed with probability being one. Since there is no probability involved compared with differential attack, good path here means the path that can cover long rounds. There are a lot of researches on how to find such path such as [10]. Generally speaking, finding impossible differential path is a relatively easier job than finding differential path, since the gap between the theory and practice for finding the best differential path is still large. Given the above reasons, impossible differential attack is one of the most trusted methods to measure the strength of the block cipher. In this paper, we would like to focus on the key recovery using impossible differential attack. Different from previous works, we show in this paper that we can further optimize the key recovery step by considering the key scheduling algorithm instead of considering the subkey as independent key bits. By investigating the key scheduling algorithm carefully, we reveal the relationship between the subkey bits guessed in the first rounds and the last rounds, then the redundancy can help us to discard more false key at an early stage efficiently.

Lightweight block ciphers have attracted much of the research attention due to the low computational cost. The security margin they provide is considered to be reasonable given the cost of information being protected. Generally speaking, key size is usually chosen to be 80 bits, while the popular versions of block size are 32, 48 and 64 bits. There are many famous lightweight block ciphers such as PRESENT [4], KATAN/KTANTAN family [6], LBlock [21] and so on. Compared with AES lightweight block ciphers get started only recently, and the lack of enough cryptanalysis will prevent those ciphers from being adopted by the industrial world. In this paper, we target one of the recent proposed cipher LBlock which has not been analyzed thoroughly. In ACNS2011, LBlock [21] was proposed as a lightweight block which targets fast hardware and software implementation. It is designed using 32-round Feistel structure with 64-bit block size and 80-bit key size. In the original paper, the authors gave several attacks against LBlock, among which the impossible differential attack is the best one that can attack 20 rounds. Since, it attracted many analyses using techniques such as differential attack, boomerang attack, integral attack, zero-correlation linear attack, and so on. Among them, impossible differential attack is one of the best attack which can penetrate the largest number of rounds. We summarize the latest analysis results and compare them with our results in Table 1. Another work on impossible differential attack against LBlock [5], done independently by us, can also attack 23 rounds but the balance between data and time complexity are different from each other. Main reason for the differences is how to deal with key scheduling: our work provides a rather specific method to LBlock as well as other ciphers with similar key scheduling structures, regarding how to exploit the weaknesses of the key scheduling algorithm, while they give a general principle to evaluate the complexity of impossible differential attack. Please refer the following table for the comparison.

Table 1. Single key scenario attacks against LBlock

# Round	Methods	Time Complexity	Data Complexity	Source
21	Integral Attack	$2^{62.3}$	$2^{62.3}$	[16]
22	Integral Attack	$2^{2^{70}}$	2^{61}	[17]
22	Zero-Correlation Linear	$2^{71.3}$	$2^{62.1}$	[18]
20	Impossible Differential Attack	$2^{72.7}$	2^{63}	[21]
21	Impossible Differential Attack	$2^{73.7}$	$2^{62.5}$	[11]
22	Impossible Differential Attack	$2^{79.3}$	2^{58}	[9]
23	Impossible Differential Attack	$2^{77.4}$	2^{57}	**Ours**
23	Impossible Differential Attack	$2^{75.36}$	2^{59}	[5]
13	Differential Attack	$2^{42.08}$	Not mentioned	[13]
17	Differential Attack	$2^{67.52}$	$2^{59.75}$	[7]
18	Boomerang Attack	$2^{70.84}$	$2^{63.27}$	[7]
22	Impossible Differential Attack (Related-Key)	2^{70}	2^{58}	[15]
23	Impossible Differential Attack (Related-Key)	$2^{78.3}$	$2^{61.4}$	[19]

This paper is organized as follows. In Section 2, we first give short introduction on impossible differential attack, and then propose an improved version based on the key scheduling algorithm. Section 3 provides main notations and specifications of LBlock. Section 4 gives the concrete attacks against 23 rounds of LBlock and followed by the conclusion in Section 5.

2   Impossible Differential Attack Considering Key Scheduling Algorithm

2.1   Impossible Differential Attack

The basic idea of impossible differential attack is using the impossible differential paths to filter the false key in purpose to reduce the complexity for key recovery. Before the key recovery steps, we will first need a good impossible differential characteristic which covers as many rounds as possible. Usually, this kind of impossible differential characteristic can be built by miss-in-the-middle method. For a truncated input differential α, try to find an output differential γ where $Pr(\alpha \to \gamma) = 1$ in the forward direction. In the same way, find a backward differential path $\beta \to \delta$ with probability 1. If $\gamma \neq \delta$, then $Pr(\alpha \nrightarrow \beta) = 1$. Now based on this impossible differential path, we add some rounds at the beginning and the end of the path to compute the truncated input and output differential

ΔP and ΔC. Suppose the subkeys used during rounds covered by paths $\Delta P \rightarrow \alpha$ and $\Delta C \rightarrow \beta$ are defined to be k_f and k_b, then we try to guess the subkey bits k_f, k_b (or the corresponding extended key bits) to test that given the plaintext and ciphertext pairs following input and output differentials $(\Delta P, \Delta C)$, whether the guessed key bits can be satisfied. If so, then it can be eliminated from the key space. By testing the key space using a large mount of message pairs, the right key is expected to be remained. The general framework is depicted in Figure 1.

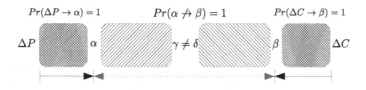

Fig. 1. Impossible Differential Cryptanalysis

To launch a successful impossible differential attack, we wish that both impossible differential characteristic and key recovery rounds can be long so that the total number of rounds we can attack may be increased. There are many previous researches dealing with how to build good impossible differential characteristics such as [10]. Unlike differential path, the space left to be improved seems to be little regarding the impossible differential path. Thus investigating the key recovery in detail may provide us with some further advantages which is only generally studied previously.

2.2 Our Improvement by Investigating Key Scheduling Algorithm

Let's suppose before and after the impossible differential path, we add r_f rounds and r_b rounds. Denote the number of subkey bits involved in the r_f and r_b rounds to be $\#SK_f$ and $\#SK_b$, which are the key bits that are required when computing from difference ΔP (ΔC) to α (β). The traditional way to proceed key recovery phase is to find for each of the $\#SK_f + \#SK_b$ subkey candidate, a set of plaintext and ciphertext pairs that can satisfy the impossible differential path. Let's suppose that for each of the $\#SK_f + \#SK_b$ key candidates, we have N pairs before satisfying the last x-bit condition of the impossible differential path, and denote the probability to be Pr_x. Then the probability for the subkey candidate to remain is $Pr_x = (1-2^{-x})^N$. Thus the number of remaining key candidate is $2^{\#SK_f+\#SK_b} \times (1-2^{-x})^N$, which should be less than the $2^{\#SK_f+\#SK_b}$. Many of the previous researches on impossible differential attack assumes that $\#SK_f + \#SK_b$ is less than the total master key length. In that case, we can filter either SK_f or SK_b to a relatively small amount of number, then brute force the rest of the consecutive key bits related to SK_f or SK_b. The problem here is that SK_f and SK_b are definitely not independent subkeys. Key scheduling algorithm of the block cipher will take a master key as a starting point and generate subkeys for each round from the master key bits. Usually, the subkey generation will go through non-linear operation such S-Box or modular addition, etc. Recent lightweight block ciphers even simplify it by just reusing the master key in different rounds such as TEA(XTEA) [20], or only linear operation such as KATAN family [6]. If we can exploit the relation between SK_f and SK_b, we can reduce the number of total key candidate, and further extend the number of rounds we can attack, since we do not need $2^{\#SK_f + \#SK_b}$ to be less than the total master key bits. The simple reusing or only linear key scheduling algorithm is relatively easy to analyze. Here we focus on the non-linear key scheduling algorithm which is widely deployed, and at the same time it is not as trivial to analyze as the case of linear key scheduling algorithm. Notice that in the previous works such as [12], the authors also exploited the dependent relations between the subkeys. However the attack was somehow more cipher specific one, and is not easy to extend to other applications. Here we propose to proceed the key recovery phase in the following steps:

1. Given the plaintext and ciphertext differences and the first round conditions, make a structure of plaintext and ciphertext pairs which satisfy the input and output difference as well as the first round conditions for each of the first round subkeys that are required to be guessed.
2. Guess the subkey bits for rounds r_f and r_b and discard the wrong plaintext and ciphertext pairs after each condition checking.
3. For each guessed subkey bit, propagate it forwards r_f rounds and r_b rounds backwards respectively to derive subkeys in each of the following rounds until it faces non-linear operation for which more unknown information bits are required to keep going.
4. Resolve the subkey conflicting. If we find that part of input or output of the non-linear function are known, then guess the rest of unknown bits to derive the corresponding input or output. If part of the input or output are already known due to step two, then we get a conflict and the total number of guessed key candidates can be decreased. Then go to step 2 until no more conflicts can be resolved.
5. Finally for each guessed subkey, filter it according to the remaining pairs. After that, we need to map the subkey which are distributed in different rounds to one round, and apply brute force search to recover the rest of the key bits that have not been guessed. Then we know all the consecutive key bits which has the same length as the master key length, and can easily recover the master key.

The biggest difference from the previous researches is step 4. Previously, only plaintext and ciphertext pairs get filtered after each subkey guess. Here if we can also filter the key candidates at an early stage, then we gain an advantage at both computational complexity and the number of rounds we can attack. Just consider the situation where in order to check t-bit condition, we need to guess s-bit subkey where s is much more larger than t. This can be the case for checking the conditions in rounds close to the input or output of the impossible differential path, where many subkeys are involved in computing the internal state. The complexity is computed as the multiplication of the number of guessed key bits and the remaining pairs. It is highly possible that the number of guessed key bits grows so quickly that the total complexity is larger than brute force searching the master key. By reducing the key candidates at the same time as filtering plaintext and ciphertext pairs, we can control and optimize the total complexity.

3   Notations and LBlock

3.1   Notations

We summarize the notations here that will be used in the analysis.

- L_r, R_r: the left and right internal state of round r starting from 0.
- $L_{r,[i]}, R_{r,[i]}$: the i-th nibble of L_r and R_r.
- $\Delta L_{i,[j]}, \Delta R_{i,[j]}$: the difference of i-th nibble of L_r and R_r.
- α_i: differences specified in the rounds before the impossible differential path.
- β_i: differences specified in the rounds after the impossible differential path.
- K_i: The corresponding 80-bit master key used in round i.
- k_i: 32-bit subkey used in round i.
- $k_{r,[i\sim j]}$: i-th bit to j-th bit of subkey k_r. i and j are denoted according to the whole 80-bit index instead of 32-bit index. Assuming $k_0 = [k_{0,79}, k_{0,78}, ..., k_{0,48}]$.

3.2   LBlock

LBlock consists of a 32-round variant Feistel network with 64-bit block size and 80-bit key size. The encryption algorithm works as follows:

1. For $i = 1, 2, ..., 32$, do $L_i = F(L_{i-1}, k_{i-1}) \oplus (R_{i-1} <<< 8)$ and $R_i = L_{i-1}$.
2. Ciphertext is $C = L_{32}||R_{32}$

Here round function F contains a S-Box layer and a diffusion layer which are denoted as S and P.

$$F : \{0,1\}^{32} \times \{0,1\}^{32} \to \{0,1\}^{32}, (L, k_i) \to P(S(L \oplus k_i))$$

There are eight 4-bit S-Boxes for each of the nibbles. Suppose the input and output of the S-box are Y and Z. The S layer can be denoted as

$$Y = Y_7||Y_6||Y_5||Y_4||Y_3||Y_2||Y_1||Y_0 \to Z = Z_7||Z_6||Z_5||Z_4||Z_3||Z_2||Z_1||Z_0$$

$$Z_7 = s_7(Y_7), Z_6 = s_6(Y_6), Z_5 = s_5(Y_5), Z_4 = s_4(Y_4), Z_3 = s_3(Y_3),$$

$$Z_2 = s_2(Y_2), Z_1 = s_1(Y_1), Z_0 = s_0(Y_0)$$

For diffusion layer with the input and output of the layer being Z and U, it can be denoted as:

$$U_7 = Z_6, U_6 = Z_4, U_5 = Z_7, U_4 = Z_5, U_3 = Z_2, U_2 = Z_0, U_1 = Z_3, U_0 = Z_1$$

All the above details are concluded in Figure 2. Since take advantage of key scheduling algorithm, we also give the description here. 80-bit master K is denoted as $K = [k_{79}, k_{78}, ..., k_0]$. Set the first round key to be $k_0 = [k_{79}, ..., k_{48}]$. Then for each of the subkey used in the following round, we do the following updating process before outputting the leftmost 32 bits of K.

1. $K = K <<< 29$
2. $[k_{79}, ..., k_{76}] = S_9[k_{79}, ..., k_{76}]$, $[k_{75}, ..., k_{72}] = S_9[k_{75}, ..., k_{72}]$
3. $[k_{50}, ..., k_{46}] \oplus [i]_2$

Step 2 is the main non-linear operation we will need to consider in detail, and we do not care about step 3.

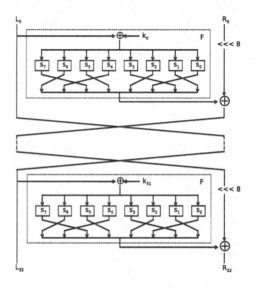

Fig. 2. LBlock

4   Impossible Differential Attack on 23 Rounds of LBlock

We take advantage of the 14 round impossible differential path $(00000000, 000 * 0000) \nrightarrow (000000*0, 00000000)$, which is also used in [9]. We prefix four rounds and suffix five rounds to the 14 round impossible differential path to attack in total 23 rounds of LBlock. Since the differential property is rather symmetric, we could also attack in the five rounds before and four rounds after pattern. Here for the simplicity, we only demonstrate the first one. Figure 3 demonstrates the differential path for the first four and the last five rounds. Our first task is to collect the plaintext and ciphertext pairs that could be used to launch the attack. By propagating the input and output impossible differential in the backward and forward directions, we can get part of the differences of the plaintext and ciphertext pairs. Usually, we first collect pairs that satisfy the plaintext differnece, and then filter the pairs according to the ciphertext difference. However, this approach is time consuming since it first needs to collect a huge amount of data to start with. Here we propose to construct plaintext and ciphertext pairs using conditional impossible differential, which will help to bypass the plaintext and ciphertext difference conditions as well as the first round conditions free of cost.

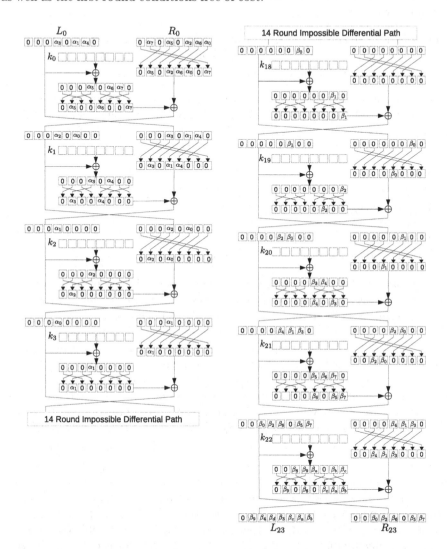

Fig. 3. Differential path for the first four rounds (left side) and last five rounds (right side). α_i and β_i denote some non-zero 4-bit difference.

First let's fix plaintext $L_{0,[0,3,5\sim7]}$ to be some random value in F_2^4. $L_{0,[1,2,4]}$ take all the 16 values and we get 2^{12} plaintexts. Now for each $k_{0,[1,2,4]}$, compute $R_{0,1} = S_2(L_{0,2} \oplus k_{0,2})$, $R_{0,4} = S_4(L_{0,4} \oplus k_{0,4})$ and $R_{0,6} = S_1(L_{0,1} \oplus k_{0,1})$. Take all the 16 values for $R_{0,[0,2]}$, then we have $2^{12} \times 2^8 = 2^{20}$ plaintexts for each of the 12-bit subkey $k_{0,[1,2,4]}$. Any pair taken from them will satisfy the plaintext difference and first round conditions. Now query the corresponding ciphertexts and sort the data according to $L_{23,7}, R_{23,[2,6,7]}$ where there are no output difference. Then we can directly generate $2^{20 \times 2 - 1} \times 2^{-4 \times 4} = 2^{23}$ pairs for each of the 12-bit subkey. Actually, we can further filter the pairs before guessing any key bits. It is based on the following observation.

Theorem 1. *For every S-Box, each input difference leads to average 6.06 possible output differences. And given each possible input and output pair, there are on average $2^{1.4}$ legal key candidates.*

So if both input and output differences to an S-box are known, we know part of them are illegal and can be filtered immediately. By investigating the first four and last five rounds, we conclude the following 12 conditions, and from them we are able to filter part of the plaintext and ciphertext pairs.

- **Round 1:** $\alpha_0 \to \alpha_4$, $\alpha_2 \to \alpha_3$.
- **Round 2:** $\alpha_1 \to \alpha_2$.
- **Round 3:** $\alpha_0 \to \alpha_1$.
- **Round 20:** $\beta_0 \to \beta_3$, $\beta_2 \to \beta_4$.
- **Round 21:** $\beta_3 \to \beta_7$, $\beta_4 \to \beta_5$.
- **Round 22:** $\beta_7 \to \beta_c$, $\beta_5 \to \beta_b$, $\beta_6 \to \beta_a$, $\beta_2 \to \beta_7$.

Note that all the above differences α and β appear in the plaintext and ciphertext difference, and that's why we can use the above condition to further filter the legal pairs by a very quick table lookup. Each of the above condition will allow one pair to pass with probability $\frac{6.06}{16} = 2^{-1.4}$. Thus there remains $2^{23-1.4 \times 12} = 2^{6.2}$ pairs. Let's suppose these $2^{6.2}$ pairs form one structure, and we can build similar structures by taking one of the following procedures. (1), changing the fixed values of $L_{0,[0,3,5\sim7]}, R_{0,[3,5,7]}$. (2), changing the values of $R_{0,[1,4,6]}$ by xoring a constant in F_2^4. We can do (1) since we have not chosen those values yet. For the case of (2), we can explain in this way: in the previous construction, we actually require for example $R_{0,1} = S_2(L_{0,2} \oplus k_{0,2})$ and $R'_{0,1} = S_2(L'_{0,2} \oplus k_{0,2})$. Thus of course $R_{0,1} \oplus R'_{0,1} = S_2(L_{0,2} \oplus k_{0,2}) \oplus S_2(L'_{0,2} \oplus k_{0,2})$. However, this equation still hold if we add a constant C to both $R_{0,1}$ and $R'_{0,1}$. Remember we only need conditions on differences not the exact values. Another point here is that the plaintexts by adding the constant C for one subkey actually has been obtained by another subkey. In other words, the total data complexity will not increase, and many plaintexts can be shared among different subkeys. As a result, we can maximumly build $2^{12+4 \times 8} = 2^{44}$ structures for each of the subkey $k_{0,[1,2,4]}$. Suppose we take n structures, then for each of the subkey $k_{0,[1,2,4]}$, we have $2^{n+6.2}$ legal pairs, and the data complexity is 2^{n+20}.

Key Recovery

The key scheduling algorithm of LBlock is designed in a stream cipher way. At each round, 8-bit subkey go through non-linear S-Box. It is easy to see that as long as the consecutive 80-bit subkey can be recovered, we can easily recover the master key. We start by guessing the subkey bits used in the first four and last five rounds. And by taking advantage of the key scheduling algorithm, we finally map the guessed key bits to the consecutive 80-bit key at round 18. Impossible differential analysis will allow us to reduce the key space, and we brute force search the rest of the space to target the correct key candidate. We investigate round by round as follows.

Round 22

There are 4×4 bit conditions to satisfy at round 22. First let's check the condition $\Delta R_{22,0} = 0$, which involves guessing $k_{22,[50\sim53]}$, the remaining pairs is $2^{n+6.2-2.6} = 2^{n+3.6}$ since we have already filtered $2^{1.4}$ pairs in the data collection phase. We proceed in the similar way for other 4-bit conditions and we will not explain them again. The complexity is around $2 \times 2^{12+4} \times 2^{n+6.2} \times \frac{1}{8 \times 23} \approx 2^{n+15.68}$ 23-round encryptions. Then we do key filtering by using key schedule algorithm. Guess $k_{22,[54\sim57]}$, then by tracing back the key scheduling algorithm, we know $k_{8,[52\sim57]}$ after shifting operation, and $k_{9,[52\sim55]}$. Guess $k_{8,[51,58]}$ so that the 8-bit input to the two S-Boxes are known. Thus we have a 4-bit filtering condition from $k_{9,[52\sim55]}$, which leaves $2^{12+4+2} \times 2^{-4} = 2^{14}$ keys. Guess $k_{19,[59]}$, then we have 2-bit filtering condition between k_{19} and k_{20}. Thus the number of remaining keys become $2^{14+1-2} = 2^{13}$.

For the second 4-bit condition ($\Delta R_{22,6} = 0$), we need to guess $k_{22,[54\sim57]}$, which is already known by computing backward from the known subkey bits. The remaining pairs becomes $2^{n+3.6-2.6} = 2^{n+1}$. It takes $2 \times 2^{13} \times 2^{n+3.6} \times \frac{1}{8 \times 23} = 2^{n+10.10}$ 23 round encryptions.

For the third 4-bit condition ($\Delta R_{22,7} = 0$), we need to guess $k_{22,[62\sim65]}$. The legal number of pairs decreases to $2^{n+1} \times 2^{-2.6} = 2^{n-1.6}$. It takes $2 \times 2^{13+4} \times 2^{n+1} \times \frac{1}{8 \times 23} = 2^{n+11.48}$ 23 round encryptions.

Before the fourth condition, we perform key filtering process. Guess $k_{22,[66\sim69]}$ and $k_{6,[22]}$, by computing backwards, we find $k_{5,64}$ and $k_{2,[65\sim67]}$ have already been guessed, which result in a 4-bit condition. Thus there remains $2^{17} \times 2^5 \times 2^{-4} = 2^{18}$ key candidates. Then proceed the fourth condition checking ($\Delta R_{22,4} = 0$). There remains $2^{n-1.6-2.6} = 2^{n-4.2}$, and it takes $2 \times 2^{18} \times 2^{n-1.6} \times \frac{1}{8 \times 23} = 2^{n+9.88}$ 23 round encryptions. After processing round 23, we can further reduce the key candidates. Guess $k_{17,[60,61]}$, we can compute $k_{16,[62]}$ and $k_{5,[58,59]}$, which are already known. Then the key candidates are reduced to $2^{18+2-3} = 2^{17}$.

Round 21

Round 21 has $4 \times 3 - 1.4 \times 2 = 9.2$ bits conditions to satisfy. For each of the conditions, we only list the key bits that are required to be guessed, while ignore the ones which are already known. For checking condition $\Delta R_{21,6} = 0$, we need to guess $k_{21,[79,0\sim2]}$. The remaining pairs is $2^{n-4.2} \times 2^{-2.6} = 2^{n-6.8}$. It takes $2 \times 2^{17+4} \times 2^{n-4.2} \times \frac{2}{8 \times 23} = 2^{n+11.28}$ 23 round encryptions.

To check condition $\Delta R_{21,1} = 0$, we need to guess $k_{22,[70\sim73]}$, $k_{21,[7\sim10]}$. Notice that this condition is not pre-filtered at the data collection phase, so we have a 4-bit condition here. Thus there remains $2^{n-6.8} \times 2^{-4} = 2^{n-10.8}$ legal pairs. It takes $2 \times 2^{21+8} \times 2^{n-6.8} \times \frac{2}{8 \times 23} = 2^{n+16.68}$ 23 round encryptions.

For the last condition $\Delta R_{21,7} = 0$ in round 21, we guess $k_{21,[78]}$ and $k_{21,[11\sim14]}$. The numnber of pairs get remained is $2^{n-10.8} \times 2^{-2.6} = 2^{n-13.4}$. It takes $2 \times 2^{29+5} \times 2^{n-10.8} \times \frac{2}{8\times23} = 2^{n+17.68}$ 23 round encryptions.

Round 1

After processing Round 21, we go back to the first five rounds to proceed round 1. There are in total two 4-bit conditions in Round 1 and both of them have been pre-filtered and thus only $2 \times 2.6 = 5.2$ bit conditions remained. Let's guess $k_{0,[48\sim50]}$, $k_{1,[27\sim30]}$ and $k_{0,[47]}$, then according to key scheduling algorithm, we can derive $k_{12,[50,51]}$, which are known already. So we first filter the key candidates to leave $2^{34+8-2} = 2^{40}$ key candidates. Then we proceed checking condition $\Delta R_{1,1} = 0$. We have $2^{n-13.4} \times 2^{-2.6} = 2^{n-16}$ pairs remaining, and it takes $2 \times 2^{40} \times 2^{n-13.4} \times \frac{2}{8\times23} = 2^{n+21.10}$ 23 round encryptions.

To check the other condition $\Delta R_{1,4} = 0$, we need to guess $k_{1,[35\sim38]}$. Thus the remaining pairs become $2^{n-16} \times 2^{-2.6} = 2^{n-18.6}$, and it takes $2 \times 2^{40+4} \times 2^{n-16} \times \frac{2}{8\times23} = 2^{n+22.48}$ 23 round encryptions.

Round 20 (Condition 1)

For round 20, there are two 4-bit conditions, and we choose to proceed only one $\Delta R_{20,1} = 0$ first and check the other one after proceeding round 2. By doing so, we can control the computational complexity in a mild way by taking advantage of the key scheduling algorithm. To check $\Delta R_{20,1} = 0$, we will have to guess 12-bit key $k_{20,[36\sim39]}$, $k_{21,[19\sim22]}$ and $k_{22,[74\sim77]}$. After checking 2.6-bit filtering condition, there remains $2^{n-18.6} \times 2^{-2.6} = 2^{n-21.2}$ pairs. It takes $2 \times 2^{44+12} \times 2^{n-18.6} \times \frac{3}{8\times23} = 2^{n+32.46}$ 23 round encryptions.

Round 2

Since the computational complexity is relatively high, by proceeding round 2, we wish to obtain more key bits information than what we actually guessed. First guess $k_{0,[77\sim79]}$ and $k_{10,[0]}$, then we can derive $k_{11,[0,77,79]}$ which leaves $2^{56+4-3} = 2^{57}$ key candidates. Guess $k_{1,[39\sim42]}$ and $k_{14,[40]}$, we can derive $k_{15,[38,39]}$ (known), which leaves $2^{57+5-2} = 2^{60}$ key candidates. Guess $k_{2,[6\sim9]}$, $k_{4,[10]}$ and $k_{15,[11]}$, derive $k_{16,[9\sim11]}$ (known), which result in $2^{60+6-3} = 2^{63}$ key candidates. Now we know all the subkey bits in order to check $\Delta R_{2,4} = 0$. There remains $2^{n-21.2} \times 2^{-2.6} = 2^{n-23.8}$ pairs, and it takes $2 \times 2^{63} \times 2^{n-21.2} \times \frac{3}{8\times23} = 2^{n+36.86}$ 23 round encryptions to test.

Round 20 (Condition 2)

Now let's check the second condition $\Delta R_{20,7} = 0$ of round 20. First guess $k_{20,[41\sim43]}$ and $k_{15,[44]}$, then we derive $k_{3,[40\sim42]}$ which are known. Key candidates becomes $2^{63+4-3} = 2^{64}$. Then guess $k_{21,[27\sim30]}$ and $k_{10,[26]}$, derive $k_{9,[27,28]}$ which are also known. There remains $2^{64+5-2} = 2^{67}$ key candidates. To filter 2.6-bit condition, the remaining pairs become $2^{n-23.8} \times 2^{-2.6} = 2^{n-26.4}$. It takes $2 \times 2^{67} \times 2^{n-23.8} \times \frac{3}{8\times23} = 2^{n+38.26}$ 23 round encryptions to test.

Round 3

Check the condition $\Delta R_{3,4} = 0$ in round 3 which is the last round before the IDC path. We need to guess 8-bit of k_0, 8-bit of k_1, 4-bit of k_2 and 4-bit of

k_3. However, most of the subkey bits are already known, which remains only $k_{2,[11\sim13]}$ to guess. Guess $k_{2,[11\sim13]}$ along with $k_{4,[14]}$, then derive the already known bit $k_{5,[11]}$. Guess $k_{15,[15]}$ and derive the known bits $k_{16,[12\sim14]}$. Then the number of key candidates becomes $2^{67+4+1-1-3} = 2^{68}$. The remaining legal pairs become $2^{n-26.4} \times 2^{-2.6} = 2^{n-29}$, and it takes $2 \times 2^{68} \times 2^{n-26.4} \times \frac{4}{8\times23} = 2^{n+37.08}$ 23 round encryptions to test.

Round 19
One 4-bit condition $\Delta R_{19,0} = 0$ in round 19 requires to guess only $k_{20,[31]}$ while other bits are known at present. Notice that the condition has not been pre-filtered, thus there remains $2^{n-29} \times 2^{-4} = 2^{n-33}$ pairs. The computational complexity is $2 \times 2^{69} \times 2^{n-29} \times \frac{4}{8\times23} = 2^{n+35.48}$ 23 round encryptions.

Round 18
If the guessed key passed the 4-bit condition in round 18, it must be a wrong key and can be discarded from the key candidate list. Guess $k_{21,[23\sim26]}$ which are the only bits needed for checking condition $\Delta R_{18,7} = 0$. We can derive $k_{20,[26]}$ which is known. Thus up to now, we have guessed in total $2^{69+4-1} = 2^{72}$ subkey bits which exists in different rounds. We want to target the 80-bit master key K_{18} at round 18. However, at present we only know 63-bit of K_{18}, which is not yet enough. Before filtering the 72-bit subkey, let's merge the key bits first. Guess $K_{18,[32\sim35]}$, then we can derive $k_{17,[37]}$ and $k_{6,[29,30,35,36]}$, which are known. Now the guessed number of key candidates become $2^{72+4-5} = 2^{71}$. Further guess $K_{19,[3\sim6]}$, derive $k_{18,[8]}$ and $k_{7,[6,7]}$ which are known and the guessed key candidates finally shrink down to $2^{71+4-3} = 2^{72}$, and we have known 74-bit of K_{18}. Finally we can check the last condition to filter these 2^{72} key candidates. There remains $2^{72} \times (1 - 2^{-4})^{2^{n-33}}$ keys. For each of the remaining keys, we brute force search the remaining 6-bit of K_{18}. Thus the complexity of this step can be computed as $2 \times 2^{72} \times (1 + (1 - 2^{-4}) + \cdots + (1 - 2^{-4})^{2^{n-33}-1}) \times \frac{6}{8\times23} + 2^{72} \times (1 - 2^{-4})^{2^{n-33}} \times 2^6$.

Complexity
Since we put the number of structures (data complexity) in the computational complexity as a variable, we can always take the balance between the data complexity and computational complexity. For example let's take $n = 37$, then the data complexity will be 2^{57} which is less than the whole code block. Computational complexity is computed by adding all the cost in each of the steps. As a result, we get $2^{37+15.68} + 2^{37+10.10} + 2^{37+11.48} + 2^{37+9.88} + 2^{37+11.28} + 2^{37+16.68} + 2^{37+17.68} + 2^{37+21.10} + 2^{37+22.48} + 2^{37+32.46} + 2^{37+36.86} + 2^{37+38.26} + 2^{37+37.08} + 2^{37+35.48} + 2^{71.37} + 2^{76.51} \approx 2^{77.4}$ 23 rounds encryptions. We can further reduce the data complexity at the cost of increasing the time complexity. For example, we can also take $n = 33$, in this case, the time complexity will increase to $2^{77.9}$ 23 round encryptions, which is still a legal attack.

5 Conclusion

In this paper, we investigate the impossible differential attack by considering the key scheduling algorithm. Previous works usually treat the subkey used in the first and last rounds to be independent ones. But in fact the subkey bits are not independent and are generated by key scheduling algorithm. It is rather easy to observe the relation when the key scheduling algorithm just simply reuses the master key bits such as XTEA, etc, however, we point out that even the key scheduling algorithm involves non-linear operations such as S-Box, we can still exploit the relation which can be used to reduce the time complexity to improve the number of rounds we can attack. As an application, we investigate LBlock and achieve attacking 23 rounds in single key model without using the whole code block, which is the best single key attack so far.

References

1. Biham, E., Biryukov, A., Shamir, A.: Cryptanalysis of skipjack reduced to 31 rounds using impossible differentials. In: Stern, J. (ed.) EUROCRYPT 1999. LNCS, vol. 1592, pp. 12–23. Springer, Heidelberg (1999)
2. Biham, E., Shamir, A.: Differential cryptanalysis of DES-like cryptosystems. In: Menezes, A., Vanstone, S.A. (eds.) CRYPTO 1990. LNCS, vol. 537, pp. 2–21. Springer, Heidelberg (1991)
3. Blondeau, C., Gérard, B., Nyberg, K.: Multiple differential cryptanalysis using LLR and χ^2 statistics. In: Visconti, I., De Prisco, R. (eds.) SCN 2012. LNCS, vol. 7485, pp. 343–360. Springer, Heidelberg (2012)
4. Bogdanov, A., Knudsen, L.R., Leander, G., Paar, C., Poschmann, A., Robshaw, M.J., Seurin, Y., Vikkelsoe, C.: PRESENT: An ultra-lightweight block cipher. In: Paillier, P., Verbauwhede, I. (eds.) CHES 2007. LNCS, vol. 4727, pp. 450–466. Springer, Heidelberg (2007)
5. Boura, C., Minier, M., Naya-Plasencia, M., Suder, V.: Improved impossible differential attacks against round-reduced lblock. Cryptology ePrint Archive, Report 2014/279 (2014), http://eprint.iacr.org/
6. De Cannière, C., Dunkelman, O., Knežević, M.: KATAN and KTANTAN — A family of small and efficient hardware-oriented block ciphers. In: Clavier, C., Gaj, K. (eds.) CHES 2009. LNCS, vol. 5747, pp. 272–288. Springer, Heidelberg (2009)
7. Chen, J., Miyaji, A.: Differential cryptanalysis and boomerang cryptanalysis of LBlock. In: Cuzzocrea, A., Kittl, C., Simos, D.E., Weippl, E., Xu, L. (eds.) CD-ARES Workshops 2013. LNCS, vol. 8128, pp. 1–15. Springer, Heidelberg (2013)
8. Chen, J., Jia, K., Yu, H., Wang, X.: New impossible differential attacks of reduced-round camellia-192 and camellia-256. In: Parampalli, U., Hawkes, P. (eds.) ACISP 2011. LNCS, vol. 6812, pp. 16–33. Springer, Heidelberg (2011)
9. Karakoç, F., Demirci, H., Emre Harmancı, A.: Impossible differential cryptanalysis of reduced-round LBlock. In: Askoxylakis, I., Pöhls, H.C., Posegga, J. (eds.) WISTP 2012. LNCS, vol. 7322, pp. 179–188. Springer, Heidelberg (2012)
10. Kim, J., Hong, S., Sung, J., Lee, S., Lim, J., Sung, S.: Impossible differential cryptanalysis for block cipher structures. In: Johansson, T., Maitra, S. (eds.) IN-DOCRYPT 2003. LNCS, vol. 2904, pp. 82–96. Springer, Heidelberg (2003)

11. Liu, Y., Gu, D., Liu, Z., Li, W.: Impossible differential attacks on reduced-round LBlock. In: Ryan, M.D., Smyth, B., Wang, G. (eds.) ISPEC 2012. LNCS, vol. 7232, pp. 97–108. Springer, Heidelberg (2012)

12. Lu, J., Dunkelman, O., Keller, N., Kim, J.: New impossible differential attacks on AES. In: Chowdhury, D.R., Rijmen, V., Das, A. (eds.) INDOCRYPT 2008. LNCS, vol. 5365, pp. 279–293. Springer, Heidelberg (2008)

13. Marine, M., Naya-Plasencia, M.: Some preliminary studies on the differential behavior of the lightweight block cipher LBlock. In: ECRYPT Workshop on Lightweight Cryptography, pp. 35–48 (2011)

14. Matsui, M.: Linear cryptanalysis method for DES cipher. In: Helleseth, T. (ed.) EUROCRYPT 1993. LNCS, vol. 765, pp. 386–397. Springer, Heidelberg (1994)

15. Minier, M., Naya-Plasencia, M.: A related key impossible differential attack against 22 rounds of the lightweight block cipher lblock, vol. 112, pp. 624–629. Elsevier North-Holland, Inc., Amsterdam (2012)

16. Sasaki, Y., Wang, L.: Comprehensive study of integral analysis on 22-round LBlock. In: Kwon, T., Lee, M.-K., Kwon, D. (eds.) ICISC 2012. LNCS, vol. 7839, pp. 156–169. Springer, Heidelberg (2013)

17. Sasaki, Y., Wang, L.: Meet-in-the-middle technique for integral attacks against feistel ciphers. In: Knudsen, L.R., Wu, H. (eds.) SAC 2012. LNCS, vol. 7707, pp. 234–251. Springer, Heidelberg (2013)

18. Soleimany, H., Nyberg, K.: Zero-correlation linear cryptanalysis of reduced-round lblock, vol. 2012, p. 570 (2012)

19. Wen, L., Wang, M.-Q., Zhao, J.-Y.: Related-key impossible differential attack on reduced-round lblock. Journal of Computer Science and Technology 29(1), 165–176 (2014)

20. Wheeler, D.J., Needham, R.M.: Tea, a tiny encryption algorithm. In: Preneel, B. (ed.) FSE 1994. LNCS, vol. 1008, pp. 363–366. Springer, Heidelberg (1995)

21. Wu, W., Zhang, L.: LBlock: A lightweight block cipher. In: Lopez, J., Tsudik, G. (eds.) ACNS 2011. LNCS, vol. 6715, pp. 327–344. Springer, Heidelberg (2011)

Cryptanalysis on the Authenticated Cipher Sablier[*]

Xiutao Feng and Fan Zhang

Key Laboratory of Mathematics Mechanization,
Academy of Mathematics and Systems Science, CAS, Beijing, 100190, China

Abstract. Sablier is an authenticated cipher submitted by B. Zhang et al to the CAESAR competition, which is composed of the encryption Sablier v1 and the authentication Au. In this work we first present a state recovery attack against the encryption Sablier v1 with time complexity about 2^{44} operations and data complexity about 24 of 16-bit key words, which is practical in a small workstation. Based on the above attack, we further deduce a key recovery attack and a forgery attack against Sablier. The results show that Sablier is far from the goal of its security design (80-bits security level).

Keywords: CAESAR, authenticated ciphers, Sablier, key recovery attack.

1   Introduction

Authenticated cipher is a cipher combining encryption with authentication, which can provide confidentiality, integrity and authenticity assurances on the data simultaneously and has been widely used in many network session protocols such as SSL/TLS [1,2], IPSec [3], etc. Currently a new competition is calling for submissions of authenticated ciphers, namely CAESAR [4]. This competition follows a long tradition of focused competitions in secret-key cryptography, and is expected to have a tremendous increase in confidence in the security of authenticated ciphers.

Sablier is an authenticated cipher designed by B. Zhang et al and has been submitted to the CAESAR competition [5]. It contains two components: the encryption Sablier v1 and the authentication Au. The former is a 16-bit word oriented stream cipher, and the latter is a message authentication code (MAC) constructed by universal hash based on Toeplitz matrix [6], which is very similar to 128-EIA3 [7] and Grain-128a [8]. Due to simple operations adopted in Sablier v1, including the bitwise XOR, the bitwise logical AND and the bitwise intra-word rotation, Sablier v1 can be efficiently implemented in a resource-constrained environment and the designers expect that its one hardware implementation is 16 times faster than that of Trivium [9]. In this work we evaluate the security of

---

[*] This work was supported by the Natural Science Foundation of China (Grant No. 61121062, 11071285), the 973 Program (Grant No. 2011CB302401).

M.H. Au et al. (Eds.): NSS 2014, LNCS 8792, pp. 198–208, 2014.

Sablier. As a result, we provide a state recovery attack against the encryption Sablier v1 with time complexity about 2^{44} operations and about 24 of 16-bit key words. What is more, it is noticed that the update process of the internal state of Sablier v1 is invertible, the above attack can further induce a key recovery attack and a forgery attack against Sablier. Since these attacks are practical in a small workstation, thus Sablier is insecure.

The rest of this paper is organized as follows: in section 2 we recall Sablier briefly, and in section 3 provide some observations on the encryption Sablier v1. Based on these observations, in section 4 we present a state recovery attack on Sablier v1 and provide the complexity analysis of the attack. In section 5 we further deduce a key recovery attack and a forgery attack against Sablier. Finally section 6 concludes the paper.

2   Description of Sablier

In this section we will recall Sablier briefly, and more details on Sablier can be found in [5].

The structure of Sablier is shown in Fig. 1. It is composed of the encryption Sablier v1 and the authentication Au. The primary recommended parameter set of Sablier is a 10-byte key, a 10-byte nonce and a 4-byte tag. The input of Sablier includes a plaintext P, an optional associated data A and a public message number N, and the output of Sablier is (C, T), where C is an unauthenticated ciphertext and T is an authenticated tag.

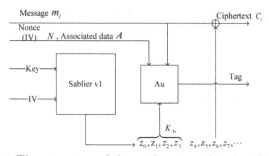

Fig. 1 The structure of the authenticated cipher Sablier

2.1   The Encryption Sablier v1

Sablier v1 is a 16-bit word-based stream cipher, which is shown in Fig. 2. The design of Sablier v1 is inspired by sandglass, and the operation of Sablier can be imaged as the mixing of the sand in a sandglass, or as the shaking of the cocktail in a shaker in the bar. Sablier v1 contains five registers L_i $(i = 1, 2, ..., 5)$, which are used as below:

- L_1 and L_5: the two largest registers, each with four 16-bit words, namely $L_{1,i}, L_{5,i}$ with $1 \le i \le 4$;

- L_2 and L_4: the two second largest registers, each with two 16-bit words, namely $L_{2,i}, L_{4,i}$ with $1 \leq i \leq 2$;
- L_3: the smallest register, consists of one 16-bit word.

For the consistency in the description of Sablier provided by the designers, below we use the same characters to mark both a register and its content, and do not distinguish them strictly. For example, L may be a register, and be also a bit string. Obviously, in the latter case L means the content of the register. According to the specification of Sablier, the running of Sablier v1 is subdivided into two phases: the initialization and the key stream generation.

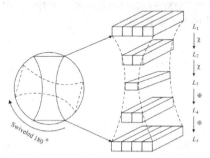

Fig. 2 The structure of the stream cipher Sablier v1

The initialization (KEY/IV setup): The initialization of Sablier v1 is made up of two sub-procedures: loading the key/IV into the registers $L_i (1 \leq i \leq 5)$ and running the cipher 64 rounds without generating any output.

1. Key/IV Loading.

$$
\begin{bmatrix} L_1 \\ L_2 \\ L_3 \\ L_4 \\ L_5 \end{bmatrix} = \begin{bmatrix} L_{1,1}, L_{1,2}, L_{1,3}, L_{1,4} \\ L_{2,1}, L_{2,2}, \\ L_3 \\ L_{4,1}, L_{4,2}, \\ L_{5,1}, L_{5,2}, L_{5,3}, L_{5,4} \end{bmatrix}
$$
$$
= \begin{bmatrix} K_0||IV_0, \ K_1||IV_1, \ K_2||IV_2, \ K_3||IV_3 \\ K_4||IV_4, \ K_5||IV_5 \\ IV_6||K_3 \oplus IV_7 \\ K_6 \oplus IV_0||K_6 \oplus IV_1, \ K_7 \oplus IV_2||K_7 \oplus IV_2 \\ K_8 \oplus IV_4||IV_8, \ K_9 \oplus IV_5||IV_8, \ K_8 \oplus IV_6||IV_9, \ K_9 \oplus IV_7||IV_9 \end{bmatrix},
$$

where "$||$" means the concatenation of two bit strings.

2. State Updating.

1. **For** $0 \leq i \leq 127$ **do**
2. $L_5 \leftarrow (L_{5,1} \oplus L_{5,2} \oplus L_{5,3} \oplus L_{4,2}, \ L_{5,1} \oplus L_{5,2}, \ L_{5,3} \oplus L_{5,4}, \ L_{5,2} \oplus L_{5,3}$
        $\oplus L_{5,4} \oplus L_{4,1})$;

3. $L_4 \leftarrow (L_{4,1} \oplus L_3 \| L_{4,2} \oplus L_3) \ggg 5;$

4. $L_3 \leftarrow L_3 \oplus ((L_{2,1} \oplus 1) \cdot L_{1,2}) \oplus \mathrm{RC}(i);$

5. $L_2 \leftarrow (L_{2,1} \oplus ((L_{1,1} \oplus 1) \cdot L_{1,2}), \ L_{2,2} \oplus ((L_{1,3} \oplus 1) \cdot L_{1,4}));$

6. $(L_1, L_2, L_3, L_4, L_5) \leftarrow (L_5, L_4, L_3, L_2, L_1);$

7. **end for**

where "$\ggg$" means the 32-bit right rotation, and $\mathrm{RC}(i)$ $(0 \le i \le 127)$ are certain constants.

The Keystream Generation: The keystream generation of Sablier v1 mainly consists of two half round operations, namely the lower half round and the upper half round, as shown below:

The keystream generation

$t = 0;$

repeat until enough keystream bits are generated:

{

The lower half round :

$1 : L_5 \leftarrow (L_{5,1} \oplus L_{5,2} \oplus L_{5,3} \oplus L_{4,2}, \ L_{5,1} \oplus L_{5,2}, \ L_{5,3} \oplus L_{5,4},$
$$L_{5,2} \oplus L_{5,3} \oplus L_{5,4} \oplus L_{4,1});$$

$2 : L_4 \leftarrow (L_{4,1} \oplus L_3 \| L_{4,2} \oplus L_3) \ggg 5;$

$3 : L_3 \leftarrow L_3 \oplus ((L_{2,1} \oplus 1) \cdot L_{2,2}) \oplus C_1;$

$4 : L_2 \leftarrow (L_{2,1} \oplus ((L_{1,1} \oplus 1) \cdot L_{1,2}), \ L_{2,2} \oplus ((L_{1,3} \oplus 1) \cdot L_{1,4}));$

$5 : (L_1, L_2, L_3, L_4, L_5) \leftarrow (L_5, L_4, L_3, L_2, L_1);$

The upper half round :

$6 : L_5 \leftarrow (L_{5,1} \oplus L_{5,2} \oplus L_{5,3} \oplus L_{4,2}, \ L_{5,1} \oplus L_{5,2}, \ L_{5,3} \oplus L_{5,4},$
$$L_{5,2} \oplus L_{5,3} \oplus L_{5,4} \oplus L_{4,1}));$$

$7 : L_4 \leftarrow (L_{4,1} \oplus L_3 \| L_{4,2} \oplus L_3) \ggg 5;$

$8 : L_3 \leftarrow L_3 \oplus ((L_{2,1} \oplus 1) \cdot L_{2,2}) \oplus C_2;$

$9 : L_2 \leftarrow (L_{2,1} \oplus ((L_{1,1} \oplus 1) \cdot L_{1,2}), \ L_{2,2} \oplus ((L_{1,3} \oplus 1) \cdot L_{1,4}));$

$10 : (L_1, L_2, L_3, L_4, L_5) \leftarrow (L_5, L_4, L_3, L_2, L_1);$

Output the keystream

$11 : z_t = L_{2,2} \oplus L_3 \oplus L_{5,3};$

$12 : t = t + 1;$

}

end-repeat

where $C_1 = 0x1735$ and $C_2 = 0x9cb6.$

2.2   The Authentication Au

The authentication Au of Sablier is similar to 128-EIA3 [7] and Grain-128a [8] and is constructed by Toeplitz-matrix based universal hash [6] as well.

The input message of Au includes the plaintext P, the initialization vector IV and the associated data A. Let M be the whole message of Au. Then we have $M = A \parallel IV \parallel P \parallel 1$. The output of Au is a 32-bit tag Tag, which is calculated as below:

$$Tag = (z_0 \parallel z_1) \oplus (T \times M), \tag{1}$$

where T is the Toeplitz matrix defined by the sequence $z_3, z_4, L_{4,1}^4, L_{4,1}^5, \cdots$, here $L_{4,1}^t$ denotes the value of the register $L_{4,1}$ at time $t \geq 4$.

3   Some Properties of Sablier v1

In this section we mainly reveal some properties of Sablier v1 during the keystream generation. First we introduce some notations.

Sablier v1 contains 13 of 16-bit word registers. We denote by L these registers, that is,

$$L = (L_{1,1}, L_{1,2}, L_{1,3}, L_{1,4}, L_{2,1}, L_{2,2}, L_3, L_{4,1}, L_{4,2}, L_{5,1}, L_{5,2}, L_{5,3}, L_{5,4}).$$

For $0 \leq i \leq 15$, define

$$L[i] = (L_{1,1}[i], L_{1,2}[i], L_{1,3}[i], L_{1,4}[i], L_{2,1}[i], L_{2,2}[i], L_3[i], L_{4,1}[i], L_{4,2}[i],$$
$$L_{5,1}[i], L_{5,2}[i], L_{5,3}[i], L_{5,4}[i]),$$

and call $L[i]$ the i-th facet register of the registers L, where $x[i]$ means the i-th bit register of x for a 16-bit word register x, $0 \leq i \leq 15$. At time $t \geq 0$, we denoted by L^t and $L^t[i]$ the state of the registers L and the facet register $L[i]$ respectively, where $0 \leq i \leq 15$.

Note that the numbers of bits rotated right at steps 2 and 7 are both 5, for the simplicity, we define the following sequence to describe the information transition among the distinct facet registers:

$$i_0 i_1 \cdots i_{16} = (0, 11, 6, 1, 12, 7, 2, 13, 8, 3, 14, 9, 4, 15, 10, 5, 0).$$

Our attack is mainly due to the following three observations:

Observation 1. *For any $1 \leq j \leq 16$ and $t \geq 0$, the state $L^{t+1}[i_j]$ of the facet register $L[i_j]$ at time $t + 1$ depends only on the states of itself and another facet register $L[i_{j-1}]$ at time t.*

The above observation follows directly from the keystream generation of Sablier v1. Indeed the operations at all steps except steps 2 and 7 in the procedure of the keystream generation are done in the current facet register since both the exclusive or "$\oplus$" and the dot multiplication "$\cdot$" are bitwise. At steps 2 and 7 only the right rotation "$\ggg$" needs the data from other facet registers. For any

$1 \leq j \leq 15$, if the 2-bit values of L_4 after both step 2 and step 7 are known, which are determined by the state of the facet register $L[i_{j-1}]$ at the current time, then the update of the state of the facet register $L[i_j]$ can be done well.

We consider the state $L^t[i_j]$ of the facet register $L[i_j]$ at time t for some integer $1 \leq j \leq 16$, and view them as some unknown variables. Suppose that all extra bit values from the facet register $L[i_{j-1}]$ are known, below we consider how to establish equations on the state variables $L^t[i_j]$ by the output keystream $\{z_t\}_{t \geq 0}$.

By step 11 in the keystream generation we have

$$z_{t+i}[i_j] = L_{2,2}^{t+i}[i_j] \oplus L_3^{t+i}[i_j] \oplus L_{5,3}^{t+i}[i_j], \quad i \geq 0. \tag{2}$$

For any $i \geq 1$, first we get by steps 8, 5 and 3

$$L_3^{t+i}[i_j] = L_3^{t+(i-1)+0.5}[i_j] \oplus (L_{2,1}^{t+(i-1)+0.5}[i_j] \oplus 1) \cdot L_{2,2}^{t+(i-1)+0.5}[i_j] \oplus C_2[i_j]$$

$$= L_3^{t+(i-1)}[i_j] \oplus (L_{2,1}^{t+(i-1)}[i_j] \oplus 1) \cdot L_{2,2}^{t+(i-1)}[i_j]$$

$$\oplus (L_{2,1}^{t+(i-1)+0.5}[i_j] \oplus 1) \cdot L_{2,2}^{t+(i-1)+0.5}[i_j] \oplus C_1[i_j] \oplus C_2[i_j]$$

$$= \cdots$$

$$= L_3^t[i_j] \oplus (L_{2,1}^t[i_j] \oplus 1) \cdot L_{2,2}^t[i_j] \oplus \bigoplus_{k=1}^{i-1}(L_{2,1}^{t+k}[i_j] \oplus 1) \cdot L_{2,2}^{t+k}[i_j]$$

$$\oplus \bigoplus_{k=0}^{i-1}(L_{2,1}^{t+k+0.5}[i_j] \oplus 1) \cdot L_{2,2}^{t+k+0.5}[i_j] \oplus (C_1[i_j] \oplus C_2[i_j]) \cdot (i \bmod 2),$$

where $L_{2,h}^{t+k+0.5}[i_j]$ means the state of $L_{2,h}[i_j]$ after the lower half round at time $t + k$ for $h = 0, 1$ and $0 \leq k \leq i - 1$. Note that all $L_{2,h}^{t+k}[i_j]$ ($h = 0, 1$ and $1 \leq k \leq i - 1$) and $L_{2,h}^{t+k+0.5}[i_j]$ ($h = 0, 1$ and $0 \leq k \leq i - 1$) come from the facet register $L[i_{j-1}]$ and are known, thus at last $L_3^{t+i}[i_j]$ only depends on both $L_3^t[i_j]$ and $(L_{2,1}^t[i_j] \oplus 1) \cdot L_{2,2}^t[i_j]$.

Second, by steps 10, 5 and 1, one can find that the state of the register $L_5[i_j]$ at time $t + i$ is determined by the state of the registers $L_5[i_j]$ and $L_4[i_j]$ at the previous time $t + (i - 1)$. When $i \geq 2$, by steps 10, 9, 5 and 1, the state of the register $L_4[i_j]$ at time $t + (i - 1)$ is further determined by the state of the register $L_4[i_j]$ and $L_5[i_j]$ at time $t + (i - 2)$ and the state of the register $L_2[i_j]$ at time $t + (i - 2) + 0.5$, which comes from the state of the facet register $L[i_{j-1}]$ and is known under the assumption. Thus at last $L_5^{t+i}[i_j]$ is determined only by $L_4^t[i_j]$ and $L_5^t[i_j]$. So we have

Observation 2. *For any given $1 \leq j \leq 16$, we always assume that all extra bit values from the facet register $L[i_{j-1}]$ are known during the update of the state of the facet register $L[i_j]$. If we view the state $L^t[i_j]$ of the facet register $L[i_j]$ at time t as the unknown variables, then $z_{t+i}[i_j]$ can be viewed as an equation on at most six variables $L_{4,1}^t[i_j]$, $L_{4,2}^t[i_j]$, $L_{5,1}^t[i_j]$, $L_{5,2}^t[i_j]$, $L_{5,3}^t[i_j]$, $L_{5,4}^t[i_j]$ and two intermediate variables $L_3^t[i_j] \oplus L_{2,2}^t[i_j]$ and $L_{2,1}^t[i_j] \cdot L_{2,2}^t[i_j]$ for $i \geq 1$.*

By Observation 2 it is known that the 4-bit value of $L_1^t[i_j]$ will never be got no matter how many equations (2) we retrieve. Thus during the execution of the attack we always need to guess these bit variables.

For $i = 0, 1, \cdots, 7$, the exact equations on the state $L^t[i_j]$ of the facet register $L[i_j]$ are established in Appendix A. By these equations it is easy to see that each equation has the form:

$$f_i(X, Y) = z_{t+i}[i_j] \oplus G_i[i_{j-1}], \tag{3}$$

where X means eight unknown variables $L_{2,1}^t[i_j] \cdot L_{2,2}^t[i_j]$, $L_3^t[i_j] \oplus L_{2,2}^t[i_j]$, $L_{4,h}^t[i_j]$ ($h = 0, 1$) and $L_{5,h}^t[i_j]$ ($h = 1, 2, 3, 4$), Y means seven parameter variables $L_{2,1}^{t+k+0.5}[i_{j-1}]$ ($k = 1, 2, 3$) and $L_{2,2}^{t+k+0.5}[i_{j-1}]$ ($k = 0, 1, 2, 3$), f_i is an expression on X and Y, and $G_i[i_{j-1}]$ is a constant only relying on the data from the facet register $L[i_{j-1}]$. So the following conclusion holds:

Observation 3. *Let $g_{i,Y}(X) = f_i(X, Y)$ for $0 \leq i \leq 7$. Define the mapping*

$$G_Y(X) = (g_{0,Y}(X), g_{1,Y}(X), \cdots, g_{7,Y}(X)). \tag{4}$$

Then G_Y is a mapping from 8 bits to 8 bits, and we get at most 2^7 distinct mappings G_Y for an arbitrary facet register $L[i_j]$.

4   A State Recovery Attack

In this section we will present a state recovery attack on Sablier v1 based on the above three observations and provide the complexity analysis of our attack.

4.1   The Pre-computation

For an arbitrary $Y \in F_2^7$, by Observation 3 we can set up a table T_Y to compute X from Z, where $Z = G_Y(X)$. Since Y has totally 128 possible values, thus in practice we need to set up 2^7 tables, and each table contains 2^8 items, each item one byte. The time complexity of the pre-computation is about 2^{15} and the size of the memories used to store those tables is $2^{15}B = 32KB$.

During the execution of the attack, if the state of the facet register $L[i_{j-1}]$ is known for some $1 \leq j \leq 16$, then we can recover the part of the state of the facet register $L[i_j]$ fast by means of these tables. More detailed, when all bit values coming from the facet register $L[i_{j-1}]$ are known, we calculate Y and look up the table T_Y to recover X, which corresponds to the values of six variables $L_{4,1}^t[i_j], L_{4,2}^t[i_j], L_{5,1}^t[i_j], L_{5,2}^t[i_j], L_{5,3}^t[i_j], L_{5,4}^t[i_j]$ and two intermediate variables $L_3^t[i_j] \oplus L_{2,2}^t[i_j]$ and $L_{2,1}^t[i_j] \cdot L_{2,2}^t[i_j]$.

4.2   Online Attack

During the online attack we need to retrieve about 24 of 16-bit key words z_{t+i}, where $0 \leq i \leq 23$. Our attack may start on an arbitrary facet register $L[i_j]$. Without loss of generality, we start at $j = 0$, and the details are shown below:

1. Set $j = 0$;
2. First we guess totally 28-bit values of $L_2^{t+i+0.5}[i_j]$ and $L_2^{t+i+1}[i_j]$ for $i = 0, 1, \cdots, 6$. For each guessed values of $L_2^{t+i+0.5}[i_j]$ and $L_2^{t+i+1}[i_j]$, calculate Y and look up the table T_Y to get $L_4^t[i_j]$, $L_5^t[i_j]$, $L_3^t[i_j] \oplus L_{2,2}^t[i_j]$ and $L_{2,1}^t[i_j]$. $L_{2,2}^t[i_j]$; and then we further guess the 5-bit values of $L_1^t[i_j]$ and $L_3^t[i_j]$, and recover totally 8 states $L^{t+i}[i_j]$ $(i = 0, 1, 2, \cdots, 7)$ of the facet register $L[i_j]$.
3. Consider the next facet register $L[i_{j+1}]$. For each possible states $L^{t+i}[i_j]$ $(0 \le i \le 7+j)$ of the previous facet register $L[i_j]$, we can get $9+j$ equations on the state $L^t[i_{j+1}]$. If these equations have no solution, then we try the next possible states $L^{t+i}[i_j]$ $(0 \le i \le 7+j)$; otherwise, similarly to step 2, we further guess the rest 5-bit values and finally get $9+j$ states of the facet register $L[i_{j+1}]$.
4. Set $j = j + 1$. If $j = 16$, output the state L^t; otherwise, go to step 3.

4.3   The Complexity of the Attack

In step 2 we need to guess totally $4 \times 7 + 5 = 33$ bits and get about 2^{33} possible states $L^{t+i}[i_0]$ $(0 \le i \le 7)$ of the facet register $L[i_0]$ on average. Suppose that there are N_j possible states at the facet register $L[i_j]$. Since we get $9+j$ equations on the state $L^t[i_{j+1}]$ of the facet register $L[i_{j+1}]$ in step 3, eight out of them are used to solve $L^t[i_{j+1}]$ and the rest are used to check whether $L^t[i_{j+1}]$ is correct or not, thus about $N_j \times 2^{-(9+j-8)}$ possible states can be remained on average. So $N_{j+1} \approx N_j \times 2^{-(1+j)} \times 2^5 = N_j \times 2^{4-j}$, and we have

$$N_j \approx 2^{33} \times \prod_{i=0}^{j-1} 2^{4-i} = 2^{33+4j-\frac{1}{2}(j-1)j}.$$

For each possible solutions on the facet register $L[i_j]$ the time of the computation of the state $L^t[i_j]$ by looking up the pre-computation table is very low and we ignore these consumed time. Thus we can get an evaluation of the total time complexity T_c of the above attack, that is,

$$T_c \approx \sum_{j=0}^{15} N_j \approx 2^{44}.$$

5   A Key Recovery Attack and a Forgery Attack against Sablier

In this section we will further deduce a key recovery attack and a forgery attack against Sablier.

5.1   A Key Recovery Attack

Assume that a segment of keystream $\{z_{t+i}\}_{0 \le i \le l}$ have been captured, where $l \ge 24$. By the state recovery attack in section 4 we can recover the state L^t

of Sablier v1 at time t. If we know the exact value of the time t, then we can easily deduce a key recovery attack against Sablier. Indeed, it is noticed that the update processes of the states in both the initialization and the keystream generation are invertible, thus we will recover the key K as soon as we invert the processes of the keystream generation and the initialization step by step.

5.2   A Forgery Attack

If the key K has been known for an attacker, then he can construct a legal pair (C, T) for an arbitrary plaintext P. Below we consider the case that the attacker does not know the key K, that is, he does not know the exact value of the time t. Since the attacker has recover the state L^t of the registers of Sablier v1 at some time t, thus he knows all states L^{t+i} of the registers and the keystream z_{t+i} for any $i \geq 0$. Further he knows the plaintext P_{t+i} corresponding to the ciphertext C_{t+i} after time t. Let $P = \mathcal{P} \parallel p_t p_{t+1} \cdots$ and $P' = \mathcal{P} \parallel p'_t p'_{t+1} \cdots$, where the length of P is identical to that of P', and $\mathcal{P}$ denotes the plaintext before some time t (NOTE: here we do not require that the attacker has the knowledge of $\mathcal{P}$.) Let $\Delta P = P \oplus P' = 0 \parallel \Delta$, where $\Delta = p_t p_{t+1} \cdots \oplus p'_t p'_{t+1} \cdots$, and $T = [\mathcal{T}, T_t]$, where T_t is the Toeplitz matrix defined by the sequence $L^t_{4,1} L^{t+1}_{4+1} \cdots$. Since the attacker knows L^{t+i} for any $i \geq 0$, thus he know T_t as well. Denote by Tag and Tag' of the plaintext P and P' respectively. Then we have

$$Tag = R \oplus (T \times M) = R \oplus (\mathcal{T} \times (\mathcal{A} \parallel \mathcal{IV} \parallel \mathcal{P})) \oplus (T_t \times (p_t p_{t+1} \cdots 1)),$$
$$Tag' = R \oplus (T \times M') = R \oplus (\mathcal{T} \times (\mathcal{A} \parallel \mathcal{IV} \parallel \mathcal{P})) \oplus (T_t \times (p'_t p'_{t+1} \cdots 1)),$$

where R is some unknown constants. So we get

$$Tag \oplus Tag' = T_t \times (\Delta \parallel 0),$$

that is,

$$Tag' = Tag \oplus T_t \times (\Delta \parallel 0).$$

Therefore the attacker can construct a legal tag Tag' for any plaintext P', where P' is just required to have the same length as P and be different from P after time t.

6   Conclusion

In this paper we study the security of the authenticated cipher Sablier. As results, we first give a state key recovery attack on Sablier v1, whose time complexity is about 2^{44} operations and is practical in a small workstation. It is noticed that the update processes of the state of Sablier v1 during the initialization and the key stream generation are invertible, thus we can further deduce a key recovery attack and a forgery attack on the authenticated cipher Sablier. Our results show that Sablier is insecure.

References

1. Frier, A., Karlton, P., Kocher, P.: The SSL 3.0 Protocol, Netscape Communications Corp. (1996), http://home.netscape.com/eng/ssl3/ssl-toc.html
2. Dierks, T., Allen, C.: The TLS Protocol, RFC 2246 (1999)
3. Kent, S., Atkinson, R.: Security Architecture for the Internet Protocol, RFC 2401 (1998)
4. CAESAR, http://competitions.cr.yp.to/index.html
5. Zhang, B., Shi, Z.Q., Xu, C., Yao, Y., Li, Z.Q.: Sablier v1, submission to CAESAR, http://competitions.cr.yp.to/round1/sablierv1.pdf
6. Mansour, Y., Nisan, N., Tiwari, P.: The computational complexity of universal hash functions. Theoretical Computer Science 107(1), 121–133 (1993)
7. 3GPP TS 35.221, Specification of the 3GPP confidentiality and integrity algorithms 128-EEA3 & 128-EIA3. Document 1: 128-EEA3 and 128-EIA3 specification (2010)
8. Agren, M., Hell, M., Johansson, T., Meier, W.: Grain-128a: A New Version of Grain-128 with Optional Authentication, http://lup.lub.lu.se/record/2296437/file/2296485.pdf
9. De Canniere, C., Preneel, B.: Trivium specifications, eSTREAM Project, http://www.ecrypt.eu.org/stream/e2-trivium.html

A Equations on the State $L^t[i_j]$ at Time $t + i$ $(i = 0, 1, \cdots, 7)$

When all bit values from the facet register $L[i_{j-1}]$ are known, we can establish equations on the state $L^t[i_j]$ of the facet register $L[i_j]$, which are shown as below:

$$z_t[i_j] = L_{2,2}^t[i_j] \oplus L_3^t[i_j] \oplus L_{5,3}^t[i_j],$$
$$z_{t+1}[i_j] \oplus G_{t+1} = x[i_j] \oplus L_{5,3}^t[i_j] \oplus L_{5,4}^t[i_j],$$
$$z_{t+2}[i_j] \oplus G_{t+2} = x[i_j] \oplus L_{5,2}^t[i_j] \oplus L_{4,1}^t[i_j],$$
$$z_{t+3}[i_j] \oplus G_{t+3} = x[i_j] \oplus (L_{5,1}^t[i_j] \oplus L_{5,2}^t[i_j])(L_{5,3}^t[i_j] \oplus L_{4,2}^t[i_j] \oplus 1),$$
$$z_{t+4}[i_j] \oplus G_{t+4} = x[i_j] \oplus (L_{5,3}^t[i_j] \oplus L_{4,2}^t[i_j])((L_{5,3}^t[i_j] \oplus L_{5,4}^t[i_j] \oplus 1)(L_{5,2}^t[i_j] \oplus L_{4,1}^t[i_j] \oplus 1) \oplus L_{2,2}^{t+0.5}[i_j]),$$
$$z_{t+5}[i_j] \oplus G_{t+5} = x[i_j] \oplus (L_{5,3}^{t+1}[i_j] \oplus L_{4,2}^{t+1}[i_j])((L_{5,3}^{t+1}[i_j] \oplus L_{5,4}^{t+1}[i_j] \oplus 1)(L_{5,2}^{t+1}[i_j] \oplus L_{4,1}^{t+1}[i_j] \oplus 1) \oplus L_{2,2}^{t+1.5}[i_j]),$$
$$z_{t+6}[i_j] \oplus G_{t+6} = x[i_j] \oplus (L_{5,3}^{t+2}[i_j] \oplus L_{4,2}^{t+2}[i_j])((L_{5,3}^{t+2}[i_j] \oplus L_{5,4}^{t+2}[i_j] \oplus 1)(L_{5,2}^{t+2}[i_j] \oplus L_{4,1}^{t+2}[i_j] \oplus 1) \oplus L_{2,2}^{t+2.5}[i_j]),$$
$$z_{t+7}[i_j] \oplus G_{t+7} = x[i_j] \oplus (L_{5,3}^{t+3}[i_j] \oplus L_{4,2}^{t+3}[i_j])((L_{5,3}^{t+3}[i_j] \oplus L_{5,4}^{t+3}[i_j] \oplus 1)(L_{5,2}^{t+3}[i_j] \oplus L_{4,1}^{t+3}[i_j] \oplus 1) \oplus L_{2,2}^{t+3.5}[i_j]),$$

where G_{t+i} $(1 \leq i \leq 7)$ only depends on the data from the facet register $L[i_{j-1}]$ and

$$x[i_j] = L_3^t[i_j] \oplus L_{2,2}^t[i_j] \oplus L_{2,1}^t[i_j]L_{2,2}^t[i_j],$$
$$L_{5,1}^{t+i+1}[i_j] = L_{5,1}^{t+i}[i_j] \oplus L_{5,2}^{t+i}[i_j] \oplus L_{5,3}^{t+i}[i_j] \oplus L_{4,2}^{t+i}[i_j],$$
$$L_{5,2}^{t+i+1}[i_j] = L_{5,1}^{t+i}[i_j] \oplus L_{5,2}^{t+i}[i_j],$$
$$L_{5,3}^{t+i+1}[i_j] = L_{5,3}^{t+i}[i_j] \oplus L_{5,4}^{t+i}[i_j],$$
$$L_{5,4}^{t+i+1}[i_j] = L_{5,2}^{t+i}[i_j] \oplus L_{5,3}^{t+i}[i_j] \oplus L_{5,4}^{t+i}[i_j] \oplus L_{4,1}^{t+i}[k],$$
$$L_{4,1}^{t+i+1}[i_j] = L_{2,1}^{t+i+0.5}[i_j] \oplus L_{5,1}^{t+i+1}[i_j] \cdot L_{5,2}^{t+i+1}[i_j] \oplus L_{5,2}^{t+i+1}[i_j],$$
$$L_{4,2}^{t+i+1}[i_j] = L_{2,2}^{t+i+0.5}[i_j] \oplus L_{5,3}^{t+i+1}[i_j] \cdot L_{5,4}^{t+i+1}[i_j] \oplus L_{5,4}^{t+i+1}[i_j]$$

for $i = 0, 1, 2$.

It is easy to see that the above equation system only depends on the values of G_{t+i} $(i = 0, 1, \cdots, 7)$, $L_{2,h}^{t+i+0.5}[i_j]$ $(h = 1, 2, i = 0, 1, 2)$ and $L_{2,2}^{t+3.5}[i_j]$. When these values are determined, on average we get one solution

$$(L_{5,1}^t[i_j], L_{5,2}^t[i_j], L_{5,3}^t[i_j], L_{5,4}^t[i_j], L_{4,1}^t[i_j], L_{4,2}^t[i_j], L_3^t[i_j] + L_{2,2}^t[i_j], L_{2,1}^t[i_j] \cdot L_{2,2}^t[i_j]).$$

A Stochastic Cyber-Attack Detection Scheme for Stochastic Control Systems Based on Frequency-Domain Transformation Technique

Yumei Li[1,*], Holger Voos[1], Albert Rosich[1], and Mohamed Darouach[2]

[1] Interdisciplinary Centre for Security Reliability and Trust (SnT),
University of Luxembourg, Luxembourg
[2] Centre de la Recherche en Automatique de Nancy (CRAN),
Universite de Lorraine, France
{yumei.li@uni.lu,Holger.Voos@uni.lu,albert.rosich@uni.lu,
mohamed.darouach@univ-lorraine.fr}

Abstract. Based on frequency-domain transformation technique, this paper proposes an attack detection scheme for stochastic control systems under stochastic cyber-attacks and disturbances. The focus is on designing an anomaly detector for the stochastic control systems. First, we construct a model of stochastic control system with stochastic cyber-attacks which satisfy the Markovian stochastic process. And we also introduced the stochastic attack models that a control system is possibly exposed to. Next, based on the frequency-domain transformation technique and linear algebra theory, we propose an algebraic detection scheme for a possible stochastic cyber-attack. We transform the detector error dynamic equation into an algebraic equation. By analyzing the rank of the stochastic matrix $E\left(Q(z_0)\right)$ in the algebraic equation, residual information is obtained and anomalies in the stochastic system are detected. In addition, sufficient and necessary conditions guaranteeing the detectability of the stochastic cyber-attacks are obtained. The presented detection approach in this paper is simple, straightforward and more ease to implement. Finally, the results are applied to some physical systems that are respectively subject to a stochastic data denial-of-service (DoS) attack and a stochastic data deception attack on the actuator. The simulation results underline that the detection approach is efficient and feasible in practical application.

Keywords: Cyber-attacks detection, Stochastic control system, Stochastic DoS attack, Stochastic data deception attack.

1 Introduction

As networks become ubiquitous and more and more industrial control systems are also connected to open public networks, control systems are increasingly exposed to cyber-attacks [1]-[4]. Some well-known examples are the Nimda attack [2], the SQL Slammer attack [3], the July 2009 cyber-attacks [4]. A control system is vulnerable to these

---

* This work was supported by the Fonds National de la Recherche, Luxembourg, under the project CO11/IS/1206050 (SeSaNet)

M.H. Au et al. (Eds.): NSS 2014, LNCS 8792, pp. 209–222, 2014.

threats and successful attacks on control systems can cause serious consequences which may lead to the loss of vital societal function, financial loss and even loss of life [5]. Therefore, these attacks should be detected as soon as possible in order to prevent serious consequences. In recent years, the problem of cyber-attacks on controlled systems has been realized and it is currently attracting considerable attention (see e.g. [6]-[21]). For example, S. Amin [6] and D. G. Eliades [13] did research on the cyber security of water systems. A.R. Metke [14], S. Sridhar [15], A.H. Mohsenian-Rad [16] and F. Pasqualetti [21] focus on cyber-attacks on smart grid systems. While cyber-attacks in conventional IT systems are only influencing information, cyber-attacks on control systems are changing physical processes and hence the real world [17]. Previous methods and tools used to protect traditional information technology against cyber-attacks might finally not completely prevent successful intrusion of malware in the control system. Therefore, new approaches are needed. Although networked control systems are protected by information technology (IT) security measures, attackers might nevertheless find a way to get unauthorized access and compromise them by means of cyber-attacks. This cyber-attacks should be detected as soon as possible with an acceptable false alarm rate and also be identified and isolated. Therefore, there is an urgent need for an efficient cyber-attack detection system as an integral part of the cyber infrastructure, which can accurately detect cyber-attacks in a timely manner such that countering actions can be taken promptly to ensure the availability, integrity and confidentiality of the systems. These new requirements increase the interest of researchers in the development of cyber-attack detection and isolation techniques [17]-[20]. However, the existing detection approaches [17]-[20] are not yet sufficient to cope with complex cyber-attacks on a control process, which motivates our research in this area.

This paper presents an algebraic detection approach for a stochastic control system under stochastic cyber-attacks and disturbances. The basic idea is to use suitable observers to generate residual information with regard to cyber-attacks, i.e. compromised sensor signals and controller outputs. An anomaly detector for the stochastic system under stochastic cyber-attacks is derived. The main contributions in the paper are as follows. First, we construct a model of stochastic control system with stochastic cyber-attacks which satisfy the Markovian stochastic process. And we also introduced the stochastic attack models that a control system is possibly exposed to. Next, based on the frequency-domain transformation technique and linear algebra theory, we propose an algebraic attack detection scheme for the control system subject to stochastic cyber-attacks and disturbances. F. Hashim [18] also use a frequency domain analysis in the detection of DoS attacks, he proposes the detection algorithm by investigating the frequency spectrum distribution of the network traffic. However, we transform the detector error dynamic equation into an algebraic equation, which make the discussion of the problem simpler and more straightforward. Moreover, we extend the idea in [22] to control systems with stochastic disturbances and apply it to detect a possible stochastic attack. Here, we consider the possible cyber-attacks as the non-zero solutions of the algebraic equation and the residual as its constant vector. By analyzing the rank of stochastic matrix $E\left(Q(z_0)\right)$ in the algebraic equation, the residual information is obtained. Further, based on the rank of $E(Q(z_0))$ and the obtained residual information, we are able to determine the detectability of the possible cyber-attacks. Some sufficient and necessary conditions are obtained, which guarantee that a stochastic cyber-attack is detectable or undetectable. In addition, by using the linear matrix inequation (LMI) algorithm, we also propose an approach for determining the detector gain matrix. Finally, the obtained results are applied to some physical systems that are respectively subject to stochastic data DoS attacks and stochastic data deception attacks on the actuator. Two simulation examples are given to illustrate the effectiveness of the obtained results. In example 1, we discuss a control system that is subjected to a stochastic data deception attack and disturbance. In example 2, we use the laboratory process in [23] that consists of four interconnected water tanks (QTP). Simulation results underline that the proposed attack detection approach is effective and feasible in practical application.

The paper is organized as follows. In section II, the system models and the models of stochastic attacks are introduced. In section III, the main results and proofs are presented. We design an anomaly detector for a control system under stochastic cyber-attacks and disturbances. Some sufficient and necessary conditions guaranteeing the detectability of cyber-attacks are obtained. In section IV, we provide two simulation examples to demonstrate the effectiveness and feasibility of the obtained results. Finally, some conclusions are discussed in Section V.

2   Problem Formulation

Consider the following stochastic control system:

$$
\begin{aligned}
\dot{x}(t) &= Ax(t) + Bu(t) + \alpha(t)F_1 a_k^a(t) + E_1 \omega(t) \\
x(0) &= x_0 \\
y(t) &= Cx(t) + \beta(t)F_2 a_k^s(t) + E_2 v(t)
\end{aligned}
\tag{1}
$$

where $x(t) \in R^n$ is the state vector. x_0 is the initial state, $y(t) \in R^m$ is the measurement output, $u(t) \in R^r$ is the known input vector. $a_k^a(t) \in R^r$ denotes the actuator cyber-attack or the physical attack and $a_k^s(t) \in R^m$ denotes the sensor cyber-attack. $\omega(t)$ and $v(t)$ are systems noise and process noise, respectively. $A, B, F_1, E_1,$ and C, F_2, E_2 are known constant matrices with appropriate dimensions. $\alpha(t)$ and $\beta(t)$ are Markovian stochastic processes taking the values 0 and 1 and satisfy the following probability

$$
\begin{aligned}
E\{\alpha(t)\} &= \mathrm{Prob}\{\alpha(t) = 1\} = \rho \\
E\{\beta(t)\} &= \mathrm{Prob}\{\beta(t) = 1\} = \sigma.
\end{aligned}
\tag{2}
$$

Where event $\alpha(t) = 1$ (or $\beta(t) = 1$) shows the actuator (or the sensor) of the system is subjected to a cyber-attack, so an actuator cyber-attack $a_k^a(t)$ (or a sensor cyber-attack $a_k^s(t)$) occurs; event $\alpha(t) = 0$ (or $\beta(t) = 0$) implies no a cyber-attack on the actuator (or on the sensor). $\rho \in [0, 1]$ (or $\sigma \in [0, 1]$) reflects the occurrence probability of the event that the actuator (or the sensor) of the system is subjected to a cyber-attack. Assuming $\alpha(t)$ and $\beta(t)$ are independent stochastic variables and satisfy

$$
E\{\alpha(t)\beta(t)\} = E\{\alpha(t)\}E\{\beta(t)\}.
\tag{3}
$$

Further, assuming $\alpha(t)$ and $\beta(t)$ are independent of measurement noises $\omega(t), v(t)$ and the initial state x_0. Generally, cyber-attacks targeting control systems mainly include denial-of-service (DoS) attacks and deception attacks. In the sequel of the paper, we introduce these attack models that can be modelled by the stochastic system model (1).

2.1 Modeling Stochastic Data Denial-of-Service Attacks

In stochastic data DoS attacks, the objective of the adversary is to prevent the actuator from receiving control commands or the controller from receiving sensor measurements. Therefore, by jamming the communication channels, compromising devices and preventing them from sending data, attacking the routing protocols, flooding the communication network with random data and so on, the adversary can launch a stochastic data DoS attack that satisfies Markovian stochastic processes. Using the general framework (1), a stochastic DoS attack on the actuator and on the sensors can be respectively modelled as

$$\begin{cases} \alpha(t) \in \{0,1\}, t \geq t_0 \\ F_1 = B \\ a_k^a(t) = -u(t) \end{cases} \quad \text{(I)} \quad \text{and} \quad \begin{cases} \beta(t) \in \{0,1\}, t \geq t_0 \\ F_2 = C \\ a_k^s(t) = -x(t) \end{cases} \quad \text{(II)}$$

2.2 Modeling Stochastic Data Deception Attacks

In stochastic data deception attacks, the adversary attempts to prevent the actuator or the sensor from receiving an integrity data, therefore, he sends false information $\tilde{u}(t) \neq u(t)$ or $\tilde{y}(t) \neq y$ from controllers or sensors. The false information can include: a wrong sender identity, an incorrect sensor measurement or an incorrect control input; an incorrect time when a measurement was observed, or inject a bias data that cannot be detected in the system. The adversary can launch these attacks by obtaining the secret keys or by compromising some controllers or sensors. A stochastic data deception attack on the actuator and on the sensors can be modelled as

$$\begin{cases} \alpha(t) \in \{0,1\}, t \geq t_0 \\ F_1 = B \\ a_k^a(t) = -u(t) + b_k^a(t) \end{cases} \quad \text{(III)} \quad \text{and} \quad \begin{cases} \beta(t) \in \{0,1\}, t \geq t_0 \\ F_2 = C \\ a_k^s(t) = -x(t) + b_k^s(t) \end{cases} \quad \text{(IV)}$$

where $b_k^a(t)$ and $b_k^s(t)$ are deceptive data that the adversary attempts to launch on the actuator and the sensor, respectively.

Especially, when the adversary attempts to launch a detective data $b_k^a(t)$ (or $b_k^s(t)$) that makes the transfer function $G_{b_k^a r}(s)$ (or $G_{b_k^s r}(s)$) is zero, a zero dynamic attack occurs. Where $G_{b_k^a r}(s)$ (or $G_{b_k^s r}(s)$) is the transfer function from the zero attack signal to residual signal. Obviously, a zero dynamic attack is undetectable. A stochastic zero dynamic attack on the actuator and sensor can be respectively modelled as

$$\begin{cases} \alpha(t) \in \{0,1\}, t \geq t_0 \\ F_1 = B \\ a_k^a(t) = b_k^a(t) \\ G_{b_k^a r}(s) = 0 \end{cases} \quad \text{(V)} \quad \text{and} \quad \begin{cases} \beta(t) \in \{0,1\}, t \geq t_0 \\ F_2 = C \\ a_k^s(t) = b_k^s(t) \\ G_{b_k^s r}(s) = 0 \end{cases} \quad \text{(VI)}$$

3   Stochastic Cyber-Attack Detection Scheme Based on Frequency-Domain Description

In this section, our objective is the anomaly detection. We assume the following conditions are satisfied: (1) the pair (A,B) is controllable; (2) (A,C) is observable. For convenience on discussion, we ignore the influence of control inputs in the sequel of the paper because they do not affect to the residual when there are no modeling errors in the system transfer matrix. Therefore, the system can be rewritten (1) as follows

$$
\begin{aligned}
\dot{x}(t) &= Ax(t) + \alpha(t)F_1 a_k^a(t) + E_1 \omega(t) \\
x(0) &= x_0 \\
y(t) &= Cx(t) + \beta(t)F_2 a_k^s(t) + E_2 v(t).
\end{aligned}
\tag{4}
$$

We assume the following anomaly detector

$$
\begin{aligned}
\dot{\widetilde{x}}(t) &= A\widetilde{x}(t) + \widetilde{B}r(t) \\
\widetilde{x}(0) &= 0 \\
r(t) &= y(t) - C\widetilde{x}(t)
\end{aligned}
\tag{5}
$$

where $\widetilde{B}$ is the detector gain matrix, the output $r(t)$ represents the residual.

We consider system (4) and detector (5). Let

$$
e(t) = x(t) - \widetilde{x}(t)
$$

then we obtain the following anomaly detector error dynamic

$$
\begin{aligned}
\dot{e}(t) &= \overline{A}e(t) + \overline{B}a_k(t) + \overline{E}_1 d(t) \\
r(t) &= Ce(t) + \overline{D}a_k(t) + \overline{E}_2 d(t)
\end{aligned}
\tag{6}
$$

with the following matrices

$$
\begin{aligned}
\overline{A} &= (A - \widetilde{B}C),\ \overline{B} = \left[F_1\alpha(t)\ -\beta(t)\widetilde{B}F_2 \right],\ \overline{E}_1 = \left[E_1\ -\widetilde{B}E_2 \right] \\
\overline{D} &= \left[0\ F_2\beta(t) \right],\ \overline{E}_2 = \left[0\ E_2 \right]
\end{aligned}
\tag{7}
$$

and the vectors

$$
a_k(t) = \begin{bmatrix} a_k^a(t) \\ a_k^s(t) \end{bmatrix}, d(t) = \begin{bmatrix} w(t) \\ v(t) \end{bmatrix}, d_1(t) = \begin{bmatrix} a_k(t) \\ d(t) \end{bmatrix}.
\tag{8}
$$

First, we give the definition of an undetectable cyber-attack on control systems which will be used in the sequel of the paper.

Definition 1. For the stochastic control system (4) and the detector (5), if a cyber-attack $a_k(t)$ on the system (4) leads to the residual $r(t)$ of the measurement output equal to zero, then the attack is undetectable.

Before presenting the main results, we first give the following lemmas that can be used to determine the detector gain matrix.

Lemma 1. [8] The error dynamic (6) with $d_1(t) = 0$ is asymptotically stable, if there exists symmetric positive definite matrix $P > 0$ and matrix X such that the following LMI holds

$$\Lambda = A^T P + PA - C^T X^T - XC < 0. \tag{9}$$

When the LMI is solvable, the detector gain matrix is given by $\widetilde{B} = PX$.

Next, based on a frequency-domain description, we transform the error dynamic (6) into the following algebraic equation

$$Q(s)X(s) = B(s) \tag{10}$$

where

$$Q(s) = \begin{bmatrix} \overline{A} - sI & \overline{B}_k & \overline{E}_1 \\ C & \overline{D}_k & \overline{E}_2 \end{bmatrix}, \quad X(s) = \begin{pmatrix} e(s) \\ a_k(s) \\ d(s) \end{pmatrix}, \quad B(s) = \begin{pmatrix} 0 \\ r(s) \end{pmatrix}.$$

Remark 1. Here, due to the cyber-attack $a_k(t)$ is a stochastic signal, matrices $\overline{B}$ and $\overline{D}$ are the resulting stochastic matrices, correspondingly, the system matrix $Q(s)$ is a stochastic matrix. In order to obtain effective results, we introduce $E(Q(s))$ that is a mathematical expectation of the stochastic matrix $Q(s)$ and

$$E\left(Q(s)\right) = E \begin{bmatrix} (A - \widetilde{B}C) - sI & F_1\alpha(t) & -\beta(t)\widetilde{B}F_2 & E_1 & -\widetilde{B}E_2 \\ C & 0 & \beta(t)F_2 & 0 & E_2 \end{bmatrix}$$

$$= \begin{bmatrix} (A - \widetilde{B}C) - sI & \rho F_1 & -\sigma\widetilde{B}F_2 & E_1 & -\widetilde{B}E_2 \\ C & 0 & \sigma F_2 & 0 & E_2 \end{bmatrix}.$$

Further, by discussing the rank of stochastic matrix $E\left(Q(s)\right)$, we obtain some important results.

Theorem 1. For the system (4), assume that the expectation of the stochastic matrix $E(Q(s))$ has full column normal rank. The cyber-attack $a_k(t)$ $(0 \neq a_k(t) \in \overline{G})$ as $t = z_0$ is undetecable, if and only if there exists $z_0 \in \mathbb{C}$, such that

$$E\left(Q(z_0)\right)Y(z_0) = 0. \tag{11}$$

Where

$$E\left(Q(z_0)\right) = \begin{bmatrix} (A - \widetilde{B}C) - z_0I & \rho F_1 & -\sigma\widetilde{B}F_2 & E_1 & -\widetilde{B}E_2 \\ C & 0 & \sigma F_2 & 0 & E_2 \end{bmatrix}$$

$$Y^T(z_0) = \left(e(z_0) \; a_k^a(z_0) \; a_k^s(z_0) \; w(z_0) \; v(z_0) \right)^T$$

$\overline{G}$ is a set of undetectable cyber-attacks and the detector gain matrix $\widetilde{B} = PX$ is given by Lemma 1.

Proof. (if) The proof of the sufficiency is obvious. If there is a $z_0 \in \mathbb{C}$ such that (11) holds for all $a_k(z_0) \in \overline{G}$, it becomes obvious that the equation (10) is homogeneous.

Therefore, the output residual $r(z_0) = 0$ and the cyber-attack $a_k(t)$ as $t = z_0$ is undetectable.

(only if) Assume that the cyber-attack $a_k(t)$ as $t = z_0$ is undetectable and since

$$E(Q(s)) = E \begin{bmatrix} \overline{A} - sI & \overline{B} & \overline{E}_1 \\ \overline{C} & \overline{D} & \overline{E}_2 \end{bmatrix}$$

has full column normal rank, then by the definition 1, there must exist a $z_0 \in \mathbb{C}$ such that the residual $r(z_0) = 0$ and

$$E(Q(z_0))X(z_0) = 0. \tag{12}$$

Substituting (7) into (12), we obtain (11). The proof of Theorem is completed.

From Theorem 1, we can obtain the following corollary:

Corollary 1. For the system (4), assume that the expectation of the stochastic matrix $E(Q(s))$ has full column normal rank. The cyber-attack $a_k(t)$ $(0 \neq a_k(z_0) \in \overline{G})$ as $t = z_0$ is an undetectable zero dynamic attack, if there exists $z_0 \in \mathbb{C}$ and $e_0 \neq 0$, such that

$$\begin{bmatrix} (A - \widetilde{B}C) - z_0I & \rho F_1 & -\sigma \widetilde{B}F_2 \\ C & 0 & \sigma F_2 \end{bmatrix} \begin{pmatrix} e_0 \\ a_0^a \\ a_0^s \end{pmatrix} = 0. \tag{13}$$

Where $e_0 = e(0)$ is an error state zero direction associated with z_0, a_0^a and a_0^s are zero dynamics attack directions on the actuator and the sensor, respectively. Under this condition, we can obtain the zero attack policy as $a_k(t) = \begin{pmatrix} a_0^a \\ a_0^s \end{pmatrix} e^{z_0 t}$ such that the transfer function $G_{a_k^a r}(s) = 0$ and $G_{a_k^s r}(s) = 0$.

Corollary 1 is a consequence of Theorem 1.

Theorem 2. For the system (4), assume that the expectation of the stochastic matrix $E(Q(s))$ has full column normal rank. The cyber-attack $a_k(t)$ $(0 \neq a_k(t) \in \overline{G})$ as $t = z_0$ is undetectable, if and only if there exists $z_0 \in \mathbb{C}$ such that

$$rankE(Q(z_0)) < dim(Y(z_0)). \tag{14}$$

Where $dim(Y(z_0))$ is the dimension of vector $Y(z_0)$.

Proof. (if) Since the expectation of stochastic matrix $E(Q(s))$ has full column normal rank and there is a $z_0 \in \mathbb{C}$ such that

$$rankE(Q(z_0)) < dim(Y(z_0)).$$

It becomes obvious that z_0 is an invariant zero [22] of the detector error dynamic(6). Then by Theorem 1, the cyber-attack $a_k(t)$ as $t = z_0$ is undetectable.

(only if) Assume that the cyber-attack $a_k(t)$ as $t = z_0$ is undetectable, then there must exist a $z_0 \in \mathbb{C}$ such that the residual $r(z_0) = 0$ and the following equation

$$E(Q(z_0))Y(z_0) = B(z_0) \tag{15}$$

is a homogeneous equation, i.e.

$$E(Q(z_0))Y(z_0) = 0. \tag{16}$$

If we assume

$$rankE(Q(z_0)) = dim(Y(z_0))$$

then the homogeneous equation (16) has a zero as its unique solution. However, this is contradictory to the condition that

$$Y\big|_{s=z_0} \neq 0$$

is a solution of (16). Therefore the assumption is false, only

$$rankQ(z_0) < dim(Y(z_0))$$

is true. This finally completes the proof of Theorem 2.

The following theorem shows the condition that the stochastic cyber-attacks are detectable.

Theorem 3. For the system (4), assume that the expectation of stochastic matrix $E(Q(s))$ has full column normal rank. The cyber-attack $a_k(t)$ $(0 \neq a_k(t) \in G)$ is detectable, if and only if the following condition

$$rankE(Q(z_0)) = dim(Y(z_0)) \tag{17}$$

always holds for any $z_0 \in \mathbb{C}$. Where G is a set of detectable cyber-attacks, $dim(Y(z_0))$ is the dimension of vector $Y(z_0)$.

Proof. The proof of the Theorem 3 is similar to that of the Theorem 2, therefore, we omit it.

Actually, the Theorem 3 is equivalent to the following corollary.

Corollary 2. For the system (4), assume that the expectation of stochastic matrix $E(Q(s))$ has full column normal rank. The cyber-attack $a_k(t)$ $(0 \neq a_k(t) \in G)$ is detectable, if and only if no $z_0 \in \mathbb{C}$ exists such that

$$rankE(Q(z_0)) < dim(Y(z_0)) \tag{18}$$

4 Simulation Results

In this section, we provide two simulation examples to illustrate the effectiveness of the obtained results.

Example 1. Consider the following system that is subjected to a stochastic data deception attack (III)

$$
\begin{aligned}
\dot{x}(t) &= Ax(t) + \alpha(t)Ba_k^a(t) + E_1\omega(t) \\
x(0) &= x_0 \\
y(t) &= Cx(t).
\end{aligned}
\tag{19}
$$

and with the following parameters:

$$A = \begin{bmatrix} -0.9 & 0 & 0.1 & 0 \\ 0 & -0.2 & 0 & -0.1 \\ 0 & 0 & -0.4 & 0 \\ 0 & 0 & 0 & -0.3 \end{bmatrix}, B = \begin{bmatrix} 0.03 \\ 0 \\ 0 \\ 0.09 \end{bmatrix}, E_1 = \begin{bmatrix} 0 \\ 0.04545 \\ 0.09090 \\ 0 \end{bmatrix}, C = \begin{bmatrix} 0.5 & 0 & 0 & 0 \\ 0 & 0.5 & 0 & 0 \end{bmatrix}.$$

Applying the Lemma 1, the corresponding detector gain matrix is obtained as follows

$$\widetilde{B} = \begin{bmatrix} 0.58890 & 0 \\ 0 & 3.5714 \\ 0.0981 & 0 \\ 0 & -0.7143 \end{bmatrix}.$$

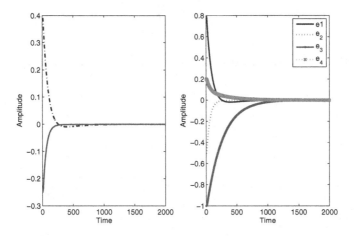

Fig. 1. The time response of residual and error dynamic under $a_k^a(t) = 0$ and $\omega(t) = 0$

Set the initial conditions as $x(0) = [0.8, -0.5, -1, 0.2]^T$ and $\widetilde{x}(0) = [0,0,0,0]^T$. When the stochastic event $\alpha(t) = 0$, the system is not subject to a cyber-attack, i.e. $a_k^a(t) = 0$. The error dynamic without stochastic attacks and noises should be asymptotically stable according to Lemma 1. Fig.1. displays the time response of the residual signal and the error dynamic under $a_k^a(t) = 0$ and $\omega(t) = 0$. Fig.2. displays the time response of the system states and the residual signal under noise $\omega(t) \neq 0$ and attack $a_k^a(t) = 0$. These simulation results show that the system (19) is stable when the attack signal $a_k^a(t) = 0$.

When the stochastic event $\alpha(t) = 1$ and the attacked probability $\rho = 0.8$, the stochastic matrix $rank(E(Q(s))) = 6$, and no z_0 exists such that $rank(E(Q(z_0))) < 6$, that is to say, for any z_0, $rank(E(Q(z_0)))$ has always full column rank. According to Theorem 3, the deception signal $a_k^a(t)$ is detectable. Fig.3. shows the deception signal $a_k^a(t)$ and stochastic noise signal, respectively. Fig.4. shows the time response of the residual and

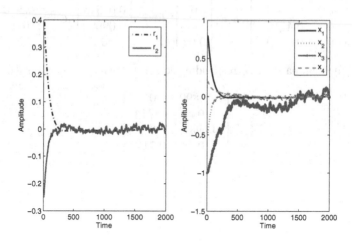

Fig. 2. The time response of residual and system states under $\omega(t) \neq 0$ and $a_k^a(t) = 0$

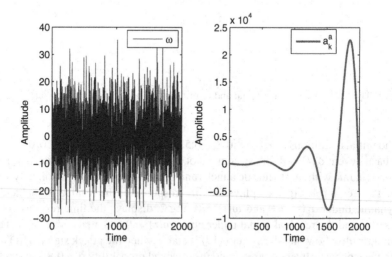

Fig. 3. The noise signal ω (t) and deception attack signal $a_k^a(t)$

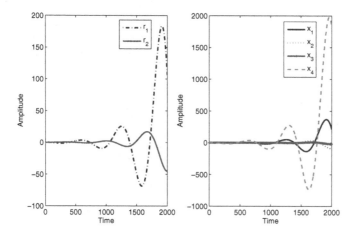

Fig. 4. The time response of residual and plant states under deception signal $a_k^a(t)$

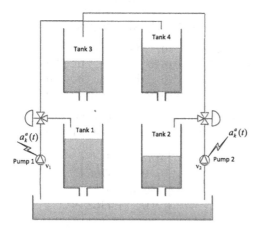

Fig. 5. Quadruple-tank water system

system (19) under the deception signal $a_k^a(t)$. Fig.4. also demonstrates the system can not be work normally under the cyber-attack. Simulation results underline that a cyber-attack can be effectively detected if the condition in the Theorem 3 is satisfied.

Example 2. Consider the model of the QTP (see [23]):

$$\dot{x} = Ax + Bu \qquad (20)$$
$$y = Cx.$$

The QTP controlled through a wireless communication network, which is depicted in Fig.5. In order to detect the attacks on the actuators Pump 1 and Pump 2, we consider

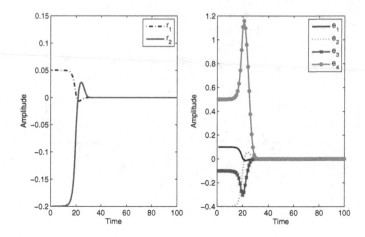

Fig. 6. The time response of residual and error dynamic without attack

the operating points P_+ [23] with the following parameters:

$$A = \begin{bmatrix} -0.0158 & 0 & 0.0256 & 0 \\ 0 & -0.0109 & 0 & 0.0178 \\ 0 & 0 & -0.0256 & 0 \\ 0 & 0 & 0 & -0.0178 \end{bmatrix}, B = \begin{bmatrix} 0.0482 & 0 \\ 0 & 0.0350 \\ 0 & 0.0775 \\ 0.0559 & 0 \end{bmatrix}, C = \begin{bmatrix} 0.5 & 0 & 0 & 0 \\ 0 & 0.5 & 0 & 0 \end{bmatrix}.$$

Assume that the system (20) is subject to a zero dynamic attack (V) on the actuator, the corresponding detector gain matrix can be obtained as follows

$$\tilde{B} = \begin{bmatrix} 0.7852 & 0 \\ 0 & 0.4766 \\ 2.7432 & 0 \\ 0 & 1.4367 \end{bmatrix}.$$

When the stochastic event $\alpha(t) = 0$, i.e. $a_k^a(t) = 0$, Fig.6. displays the error dynamic is asymptotically stable. When the stochastic event $\alpha(t) = 1$ and the attacked probability $\rho = 0.5$, the stochastic matrix $rank(E(Q(s))) = 6$, however, there exists a $z_0 = 0.0127$ such that $rank(E(Q(z_0))) = 5 < 6$. According to Theorem 2, the cyber-attacks signal is undetectable, because it is possible for the adversary to launch a stochastic zero attack signal $a_k^a(t)$ as the following:

$$a_k^a(t) = \begin{bmatrix} -1.074 \\ 1 \end{bmatrix} e^{0.0127t}$$

such that the transfer function $G_{a_k^a r}(s)$ is zero. Fig.7. displays the attack signal $a_k^a(t)$ and the time response of the residual and the QTP under the attack, respectively. It is clear that the QTP can not work normally under the stochastic attack. Simulation results demonstrate that a cyber-attack on the control system is undetectable if the condition in the Theorem 2 is satisfied.

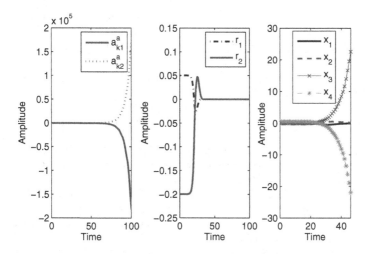

Fig. 7. The attack signal and the time response of residual and plant states under zero dynamic attack $a_k^a(t)$

5   Conclusion

This paper presents an algebraic detection scheme for control systems under stochastic cyber-attacks and disturbances. It is a relatively simple and straightforward detection approach. Based on the frequency-domain transformation technique and linear algebra theory, an effective anomaly detector is derived. Further, some sufficient and necessary conditions are obtained, which guarantee that a stochastic cyber-attack is detectable or undetectable. The main work focuses on stochastic cyber-attacks detection approach on control systems and we mention the stochastic attacks model that control systems are possibly exposed to. The proposed scheme is applied to some physical systems that are subject to the stochastic data DoS attack and data deception attack, respectively. Simulation results underline that the proposed attack detection approach is effective and feasible in practical application. Before the cyber intruders are removed and the security branches are closed, or operators start the repair or exchange of faulty components, the physical process must be kept in a safe state as long as possible. Therefore, next steps that are urgent for us to consider are the cyber-attacks fault-tolerant control and fault estimation on control systems.

References

1. Wolf, M., Daly, P.W.: Security Engineering for Vehicular IT Systems. Vieweg-Teubner (2009)
2. Nimda worm, http://www.cert.org/advisories/CA-2001-26.html
3. Moore, D., Paxson, V., Savage, S., Shannon, C., Staniford, S., Weaver, N.: Inside the Slammer worm. IEEE Security & Privacy 1(4) (2003)
4. New "cyber attacks" hit S Korea, http://news.bbc.co.uk/2/hi/asia-pacific/8142282.stm

5. Slay, J., Miller, M.: Lessons learned from the Maroochy water breach. Critical Infrastructure Protection 253, 73–82 (2007)
6. Amin, S., Galina, A., Schwartz, S., Sastry, S.: Security of Interdependent and Identical Networked Control Systems. Automatica 49(1), 186–192 (2013)
7. Andersson, G., Esfahani, P.M., et al.: Cyber-Security of SCADA Systems. Session: Cyber-Physical System Security in A Smart Grid Enviroment (2011)
8. Li, Y.M., Voos, H., Darouach, M.: Robust H_∞ fault estimation for control systems under stochastic cyber-attacks. In: 33rd China Control Conference, Nanjing, China (accepted, 2014)
9. Rosich, A., Voos, H., Li, Y.M., Darouach, M.: A Model Predictive Approach for Cyber-Attack Detection and Mitigation in Control Systems. In: 52nd IEEE Annual Conference on Decision and Control, Italy, pp. 6621–6626 (2013)
10. Teixeira, A., Pérez, D., Sandberg, H., Johansson, K.H.: Attack Models and Scenarios for Networked Control Systems. In: HiCoNS 2012, Beijing, China, pp. 55–64 (2012)
11. Mo, Y., Sinopoli, B.: False data injection attacks in control systems. In: First Workshop on Secure Control Systems, Stockholm, Sweden (2010)
12. Amin, S., Litrico, X., Sastry, S.S., Bayen, A.M.: Cyber Security of Water SCADA Systems: (I) Analysis and Experimentation of Stealthy Deception Attacks. IEEE Transactions on Control Systems Technology 21(5), 1963–1970 (2013)
13. Eliades, D.G., Polycarpou, M.M.: A fault diagnosis and security framework for water systems. IEEE Transactions on Control Systems Technology 18(6), 1254–1265 (2010)
14. Metke, A.R., Ekl, R.L.: Security technology for smart grid networks. IEEE Transactions on Smart Grid 1(1), 99–107 (2010)
15. Sridhar, S., Hahn, A., Govindarasu, M.: Cyber–physical system security for the electric power grid. Proceedings of the IEEE 99(1), 1–15 (2012)
16. Mohsenian-Rad, A.H., Garcia, A.L.: Distributed internet-based load altering attacks against smart power grids. IEEE Transactions on Smart Grid 2(4), 667–674 (2011)
17. Anjali, S., Ramesh, C.J.: Dual-Level Attack Detection and Characterization for Networks under DDoS. In: International Conference on Availability, Reliability and Security (2010)
18. Hashim, F., Kibria, M.R., Jamalipour, A.: Detection of DoS and DDoS Attacks in NGMN Using Frequency Domain Analysis. In: Proceedings of APCC 2008, copyright(c) 2008 IEICE 08 SB 0083 (2008)
19. Weimer, J., Kar, S., Johansson, K.H.: Distributed Detection and Isolation of Topology Attacks in Power Networks. In: HiCoNS 2012, Beijing, China, pp. 65–71 (2012)
20. Liu, Y., Reiter, M.K., Ning, P.: False data injection attacks against state estimation in electric power grids. In: ACM Conference on Computer and Communications Security, Chicago, USA, pp. 21–32 (2009)
21. Pasqualetti, F.: Secure Control Systems: A Control-Theoretic Approach to Cyber-Physical Security. A Dissertation for the degree of Doctor of Philosophy in Mechanical Engineering (2012)
22. Zhou, K., Doyle, J.C., Glover, K.: Robust and Optimal Control. Prentice-Hall, Inc., Upper Saddle River (1996)
23. Johansson, K.H.: The Quadruple-Tank Process: A Multivariable Laboratory Process with an Adjustable Zero. IEEE Transactions on Control Systems Technology 8(3), 456–465 (2000)

Security Analysis and Improvement
of Femtocell Access Control

Chien-Ming Chen[1], Tsu-Yang Wu[1], Raylin Tso[2], and Mu-En Wu[3]

[1] School of Computer Science and Technology, Harbin Institute of Technology
Shenzhen Graduate School, Shenzhen, China
dr.chien-ming.chen@ieee.org, wutsuyang@gmail.com
[2] Department of Computer Science,
National Chengchi University, Taipei, Taiwan, R.O.C.
raylin@cs.nccu.edu.tw
[3] Department of Mathematics, Soochow University, Taipei, Taiwan, R.O.C.
mnasia1@gmail.com

Abstract. Recently, femtocell solutions have been attracting increasing attention since coverage for broadband radios can effectively eliminate wireless notspots. Typically, a femtocell is designed for use in a home or small business. In 2009, 3GPP (3rd Generation Partnership Program) announced and published the first femtocell standard. In this paper, we first point out that the user equipment (UE) registration procedure, which defined in 3GPP standard, is vulnerable to the denial-of-service (DoS) attack. Then, we propose a mechanism to defend against this attack. For compatibility, the proposed mechanism utilizes the well-defined control message in the 3GPP standard, and modifies the UE registration procedure as little as possible.

Keywords: Femtocell, denial-of-service attack, 3GPP standard, security.

1 Introduction

WiMAX (802.16) [1] and 3G cellular network [2] can provide "last-mile" Internet service for broadband wireless access. However, notspots still occur, for example, in the basement or indoors. For this reason, femtocell technologies have proposed to improve indoor coverage and bandwidth for broadband wireless networks.

The concept of femtocell originates from the success of WiFi access point (AP). Similar to AP, service operators deploy femtocells in notspots. It can provide a more stable bandwidth for subscribers and increase coverage. In general, femtocells are expected to be cheap (<\$200) and widely distributed. Femtocells also provide the following two advantages. First, base stations (also called Macrocells) can shift network loading to the femtocells. Second, femtocells can be easily developed and placed in houses or offices [3].

Recently, 3GPP (3rd Generation Partnership Program) collaborated with Femto Forum and Boradbadn Fourm to create a new femtocells standard. The

M.H. Au et al. (Eds.): NSS 2014, LNCS 8792, pp. 223–232, 2014.

purpose of this standard is to standardize femtocells to be produced in large volumes. In 2009, 3GPP announced and published the first femtocell standard [4]. However, we observed that the user equipment (UE) registration procedure, which defined in the 3GPP standard [4], with closed access mode is vulnerable to the Denial-of-Service (DoS) attack. This is because the femtocells cannot release resources until receiving the verification results from the core network. As a result, a mechanism to overcome this issue is necessary.

In this paper, we first demonstrate that the UE registration procedure is vulnerable to DoS (Denial of Service) attack. We also propose a mechanism to defend against the DoS attack. For compatibility, the proposed mechanism utilizes the well-defined control messages in the 3GPP standard, and modifies the UE registration procedure as little as possible. Performance evaluation and security analysis demonstrate that the proposed mechanism is efficient and can effectively resist to DoS attack.

2　Background

With the rapidly growth of network technology, security issues have been concerned in various network environments [5–14]. In a network environment with femtocells, security issues also receive increasing attention recently.

Closed Subscriber Group (CSG) is introduced in 3G/WiMAX standards [2, 15]. It defines an identity, called Closed Subscriber Group Identity (CSG_id) that femtocells can use to authorize legitimate subscribers [16]. Fig. 1 depicts the access control strategy for subscribers based on CSG identities. Each Subscriber can belong to one or more CSG_id, for example, Bob has two CSG_ids (1 and 2). Contrary to subscribers, each femtocell belongs to one or less CSG_id [17]. Femtocells could restrict accesses for subscribers. They support three access modes: open access mode, hybrid access mode, and closed access mode [16]. Open mode allows any mobile device to access the femtocells without any permission. For instance, John and Alice who's mobile devices are carried with different CSG_ids are allowed to access the femtocell. Customary, open mode is designated for a public environment. The second mode is hybrid mode. Similarly to the open mode, all mobile devices with matched and unmatched CSG_id can access to the hybrid mode. But hybrid mode assign devices that passed CSG_id verification with a higher priority. The last mode is the closed mode. Femtocells only allow restricted devices which hold the same identity as the connected femtocell to access the core network, and reject all others. For a closed mode femtocell, users should register their devices on a list (whitelist).

3　Review of UE Registration Procedure

The 3GPP standard [4] defines two different kinds of UE registration procedure based on the access control mode of femtocell. In our observation, only the UE registration in closed mode suffers from DoS attacks to femtocell, and hence we detail it in the following paragraph.

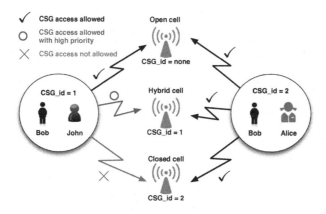

Fig. 1. Access control strategy for subscribers based on CSG identity

Fig. 2 shows each step of the registration procedure when a UE attempts to access a closed mode femtocell. The communication between the femtocell and the security gateway (SeGW) goes through an IPsec tunnel. From steps 1 to 3, RRC connection is established between the UE and the Femtocell. Then, the UE transmits a RRC Initial Direct Transfer message carrying a Location Updating Request message with its identity (e.g., IMSI or TMSI) at step 4. After checking the UE's capabilities (step 5), the Femtocell initiates UE registration towards the Femto-GW (steps 6-8). The Femtocell then sends a RUA Connect message containing the femtocell's access mode to the Femto-GW at step 9. The RUA Connect message triggers the setup of an SCCP connection by the Femto-GW towards the core network (CN) at steps 10-11. The Femto-GW then forwards the femtocell's CSG_id (step 10). Step 12 is an optional mobility management procedures, and the CN may perform Authentication procedure. So far, the access control of the UE is not performed. In other words, the Femtocell has no information to determine if the UE is legal to access the Femtocell or not. Therefore, the Femtocell can not release its resource to the other UEs which also attempt to access the Femtocell. At step 13, the CN performs access control to compare the UE's CSG_id with the Femtocell's CSG_id. The CN then notifies the Femtocell to accept or reject the UE's attempt (step 14). Steps 15-17 complete the rest of work.

As mentioned above, the UE registration is vulnerable to DoS attacks on Femtocells. The messages transmitted between the Femtocell and the SeGW may go through Internet via the IPsec tunnel. Hence, transmission time for messages in the femtocell networks is much longer than one in normal 3G network. It will make DoS attacks more serious.

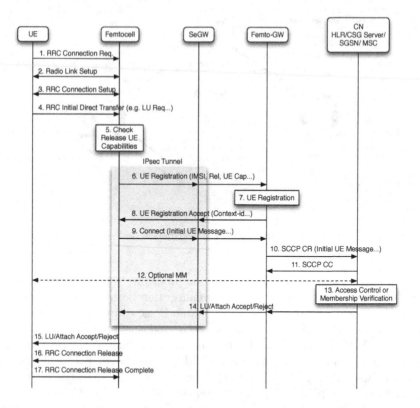

Fig. 2. Procedure of UE registration: in case of closed mode femtocell

4   Mechanism to Defend against DoS Attack

In this section, we define the adversary model and demonstrate that the UE registration procedure is vulnerable to the DoS attack. Then, we design an auto-reject mechanism on the femtocells to prevent this attack. The used notations in this section are listed in Table 1.

4.1   Problem Definition

As mentioned above, the access control verification of the UE registration procedure is executed in the core network. Connecting to a wired network is an essential characteristic of femtocell networks. The transmitted data should pass through an insecure network, e.g., Internet, and enter the core network. Hence, the transmission delay in femtocell networks is greater than in 3G/WiMax network. It means that the malicious subscriber can send a series of connect requests to the femtocell in order to launch a DoS attack. To solve this problem, we attempt to accelerate the access control verification.

Table 1. The Notations

Notation	Description
CN	Core network
M_i	Subscriber i's device
ID_i	Subscriber i's device identity, e.g., IMSI
f_i	Femtocell i
L_i	Femtocell i's blacklist

4.2   Adversary Model

Here we define an adversary model which depends on the capability of the user equipment (UE). In general, the UE will hand over seamlessly from the BS to the femtocell once detecting femtocell signals. In addition to automatic handover, the 3GPP standard provide a manual CSG selection property for the UE [17]. The adversary can request the UE to perform a scan for searching available CSGs. The UE will display the available CSG identities and their femtocell names. Hence, the adversary can manually select a femtocell that she prefers to connect with. The ability of adversary is as follows:

1. An adversary can arbitrarily connect to a femtocell.
2. An adversary can send a series of connect request to a femtocell.

According to the adversary model, the DoS attack [18] is defined as follows.

4.3   Denial-of-Service (DoS) Attack

The purpose of DoS attack is to block legitimate users' system access by reducing system availability. Currently, a residential femtocell can support 2 to 4 mobile devices. This design demonstrates that femtocells easily suffer from DoS attacks. If an adversary sends more than four connect requests to a femtocell simultaneously, the femtocell will be over loaded. This attack works even if the target is a closed mode femtocell, because the femtocell cannot reject illegal users immediately. Based on the UE registration procedure, the femtocell must wait until it receives a response from the core network. The adversary can aim at a femtocell and begin sending a series of request to it. Consequently, the femtocell has no extra resources to serve legitimate users.

4.4   Auto-Reject Mechanism

The auto-reject mechanism is designed on femtocells and consists of creation, blocking, and recovery phases. Each femtocell handles a blacklist to record which client is malicious. When a client attempts to connect with a femtocell and is rejected by access control verification (see step 13 of Fig. 2), the femtocell records the client's identity, IMSI, which is contained in the reject message sent from the core network. The blocked client will be immediately rejected by the femtocell, before its blocking time is expired.

Creation
1. $M_i \rightarrow f_i$: connect request
2. f_i : If $ID_i \in L_i$, go to blocking phase;
    otherwise, execute UE registration procedure.
3. $CN \rightarrow f_i$: Attach Reject message,
4. f_i : Retrieve ID_i from the message, and add ID_i into L_i.
5. $f_i \rightarrow M_i$: Attach Reject message.
Blocking
1. f_i : Check the expiration of blocking time.
    If expired, go to recovery phase; otherwise, reset the expired time of blocking.
2. $f_i \rightarrow M_i$: Attach Reject message.
Recovery
1. f_i : Remove ID_i from L_i, and go to step 2 of creation phase.

Fig. 3. Auto-reject mechanism

Fig. 3 shows the details of auto-reject. In the beginning, f_i checks M_i to see if ID_i exists in the blacklist L_i in the creation phase. If true, f_i checks if M_i's block time is expired or not in the blocking phase. If so, f_i rejects next requests from M_i immediately to reduce the delay time of access control verification. To avoid false positive or other unexpected error, auto-reject mechanism has a recovery mechanism to remove ID_i from L_i. After a period of time, M_i can again attempt to connect to f_i regularly.

5   Performance Evaluation and Security Analysis

In this section, we evaluate the performance of our mechanism through experiments. We also provide a security analysis to show that our design can effectively resist to DoS attack.

5.1   Performance Evaluation

Experiment Setting.   Firstly, we deploy a PicoChip femtocell device [19] under the WiMAX network platform. This femtocell is compatible with 802.16e-2005 specifications on the PHY layer. It connects to a Security Gateway (SeGW) which is implemented on an Intel IXP465 network processor [20]. An IPsec tunnel is also implemented and developed between the SeGW and the femtocell. The backend core network is ran on an emulator. All network services are performed by the emulator. The subscriber's device is a laptop equipped with WiMAX capabilities. displays the interface connected to the laptop, AWB-U210 USB adapter, which is fully compliant with 802.16e (IEEE 802.16e-2005 Wave 2 compliant) [21].

Estimated Results.   In the lab experiment, we measure the overhead of the transmission time between components in the femtocell network. See Fig. 2, the

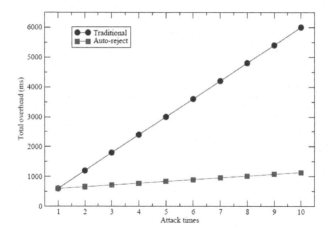

Fig. 4. The estimated results of the auto-reject femtocell and the traditional femtocell

section between the UE and the Femtocell is referred to as A, and its overhead is approximately 10 ms. The section between the Femtocell and the Femto-GW is referred to as B, and its overhead is approximately 110 ms. The section between the Femto-GW and the CN is referred to as C, and its overhead is approximately 30 ms. We use the notation N to represent the number of malicious connection requests. Therefore, the equation to estimate the overhead of the UE registration procedure with the traditional femtocell is derived as follows (optional step 12 is ommitted):

$$(7A + 4B + 3C) * N \ (ms) \tag{1}$$

The femtocell should perform the full procedure to reject every requests. According to Fig. 5, the equation becomes as follows:

$$(7A + 4B + 3C) + (N - 1) * (6A) \ (ms) \tag{2}$$

In order to create the blacklist, the femtocell needs to perform the full procedure once. The rest of the requests only costs $6A$ ms each. For example, if an attacker send 10 requests to the femtocell, the total overhead of the auto-reject femtocell is 1140 ms; the total overhead of the traditional femtocell is 6000 ms. Fig. 4 illustrates that the total overhead of the auto-reject femtocell is much less than the total overhead of the traditional femtocell. Therefore, our proposed approach can prevent femtocell from DoS attack.

5.2   Security Analysis

Here we analyze the security of our auto-reject mechanism.

Secure against Dos Attacks.   As mentioned above, the traditional UE registration is easy suffered from a Dos attack because the access control verification

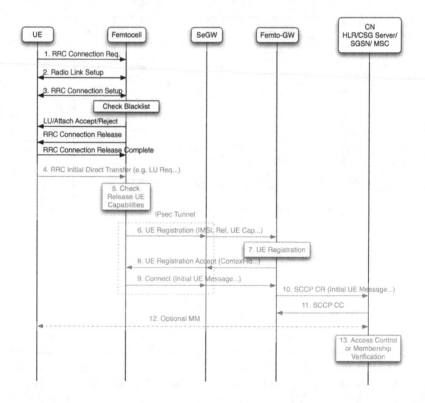

Fig. 5. The benefit of auto-reject mechanism. Gray text signifies omitted steps.

is executed by the core network. In the first step of our mechanism, the femto-cell will check the connection request from subscriber by checking blacklist. If a malicious subscriber wants to send a series of requests to the femtocell, it will be rejected immediately. It is easy to see that our mechanism can efficiently reduce the effects of Dos attacks.

Message Unforgeability.   Since the secure communication between femtocell and core network is relied on IPSec, any malicious subscribers cannot forge attach reject messages to cheat the femtocell.

6   Conclusion

In this paper, we have demonstrated that UE registration procedure defined in 3GPP standard is vulnerable to denial-of-service attack. This attack can block legitimate user's system access; thus, the system availability is reduced. In order to eliminate this security problem, we have proposed a auto-reject mechanism. In fact, our design can utilize the well-defined control message in the 3GPP standard. Finally, performance evaluation and security analysis showed that our design is efficient and can effectively resist to DoS attack.

Acknowledgment. The work of Raylin Tso was supported in part by the National Science Council, Taiwan, R.O.C., under Grant NSC 101-2628-E-004-001-MY2. The work of Mu-En Wu was supported in part by the Ministry of Science and Technology, Taiwan, R.O.C., under Grant MOST 103-2218-E-031-001. The work of Chien-Ming Chen was supported in part by the Project HIT.NSRIF. 2014098 Supported by Natural Scientific Research Innovation Foundation in Harbin Institute of Technology and in part by Shenzhen Peacock Project, China, under Contract KQC201109020055A.

References

1. WiMAX Forum: Femtocells core specification: DRAFT-T33-118-R016v01-B (May 2010)
2. 3GPP: TR-25.820-v8.2.0: 3G Home NodeB Study Item Technical Report (Release 8) (September 2008)
3. Chen, C.M., Chen, Y.H., Lin, Y.H., Sun, H.M.: Eliminating rouge femtocells based on distance bounding protocol and geographic information. Expert Systems with Applications 41(2), 426–433 (2014)
4. 3GPP: TS-25.467-v9.3.0: UTRAN artitechture for 3G Home Node B (HNB) Stage 2 (Release 9) (June 2010)
5. Wu, M.E., Tso, R., Sun, H.M.: On the improvement of fermat factorization using a continued fraction technique. Future Generation Computer Systems 30, 162–168 (2014)
6. Sun, H.M., Wu, M.E., Ting, W.C., Hinek, M.J.: Dual rsa and its security analysis. IEEE Transactions on Information Theory 53(8), 2922–2933 (2007)
7. Wu, T.Y., Tsai, T.T., Tseng, Y.M.: Efficient searchable id-based encryption with a designated server. Annals of Telecommunications-Annales des Télécommunications, 1–12 (2013)
8. Wu, M.E., Chen, C.M., Lin, Y.H., Sun, H.M.: On the improvement of wiener attack on rsa with small private exponent. The Scientific World Journal 2014 (2014)
9. Tso, R.: A new way to generate a ring: Universal ring signature. Computers & Mathematics with Applications 65(9), 1350–1359 (2013)
10. Wang, E.K., Ye, Y., Xu, X.: Location-based distributed group key agreement scheme for vehicular ad hoc network. International Journal of Distributed Sensor Networks 2014 (2014)
11. Tso, R., Huang, X., Susilo, W.: Strongly secure certificateless short signatures. Journal of Systems and Software 85(6), 1409–1417 (2012)
12. Chen, C.M., Wang, K.H., Wu, T.Y., Pan, J.S., Sun, H.M.: A scalable transitive human-verifiable authentication protocol for mobile devices. IEEE Transactions on Information Forensics and Security 8(8), 1318–1330 (2013)
13. Chen, C.M., Lin, Y.H., Chen, Y.H., Sun, H.M.: Sashimi: secure aggregation via successively hierarchical inspecting of message integrity on wsn. Journal of Information Hiding and Multimedia Signal Processing 4(1), 57–72 (2013)
14. Ku, W.C., Chen, C.M., Lee, H.L.: Cryptanalysis of a variant of peyravian-zunic's password authentication scheme. IEICE Transactions on Communications 86(5), 1682–1684 (2003)

15. Kim, R., Kwak, J., Etemad, K.: WiMAX femtocell: requirements, challenges, and solutions. IEEE Communications Magazine 47(9), 84–91 (2009)
16. Golaup, A., Mustapha, M., Patanapongpibul, L.: Femtocell access control strategy in UMTS and LTE. IEEE Communications Magazine 47(9), 117–123 (2009)
17. 3GPP: TS-22.220-v9.3.0: Service requirements for Home NodeBs and Home eN-odeBs (Release 9) (December 2009)
18. Chang, C.C., Wu, C.C., Lin, L.C.: 3gpp sim-based authentication schemes for wireless local area networks. International Journal of Innovative Computing Information and Control (IJICIC) 6(2), 461–474 (2010)
19. picoChip Designs Ltd.: PC203 Femtocell Multi-core DSP (2010), http://www.picochip.com/page/70/Multi-core-PC203
20. Intel Corporation: Intel IXP465 Network Processor, http://www.intel.com/design/network/products/npfamily/ixp465.htm
21. IEEE: Air Interface for Fixed Broadband Wireless Access Systems, Amendment 2: Physical and Medium Access Control Layers for Combined Fixed and Mobile Operation in Licensed Bands (February 2006)

Identity Based Threshold Ring Signature
from Lattices

Baodian Wei[1], Yusong Du[2], Huang Zhang[1], Fangguo Zhang[1],
Haibo Tian[1], and Chongzhi Gao[3]

[1] School of Information Science and Technology,
Guangdong Key Laboratory of Information Security Technology,
Sun Yat-sen University, Guangzhou 510006, P.R. China
weibd@mail.sysu.edu.cn
[2] School of Information Management,
Sun Yat-sen University, Guangzhou 510006, P.R. China
[3] School of Computer Science and Educational Software, Guangzhou University,
Guangzhou 510006, P.R. China

Abstract. In the graded encoding systems that can be used to construct multilinear maps, the graded Computational Deffie-Hellman problem $gGCDHP$ problem is assumed to be hard. We present an equivalent problem, called the variant graded Computational Deffie-Hellman problem $vGCDHP$, and make generalization to get the general graded Computational Deffie-Hellman problem $gGCDHP$. Based on the hardness assumption of $gGCDHP$, we construct the first ID-based threshold ring signature scheme from lattices. The scheme is proved in the random oracle model to be existentially unforgeable and signer anonymous.

Keywords: ID-based, threshold ring signature, multilinear map, ideal lattice.

1 Introduction

Generally speaking, there are two kinds of ways, group signatures [3] and ring signatures[13], to enable any individual of a group to anonymously sign documents on behalf of the entire group. This functionality is desirable in many group-oriented applications such as e-lotteries, e-cash and online games. In group signatures, the group is predefined and there is an entity called group manager that can reveal the identity of the actual signer. In ring signatures, the group is spontaneously created by the signer and no manager exists. Anonymity revocation is not supported. In essence, a ring signature is a publicly verifiable 1-out-of-n signature with an unconditionally anonymous signer. It can be extended as a t-out-of-n version, called threshold ring signature [2] where at least t entities are required to jointly and anonymously sign a given documents. In the public key infrastructure (PKI), threshold ring signatures can not achieve real spontaneity since all group members must pre-enroll the PKI before they can come to generate a valid signature. To solve this problem, an ID-based threshold ring signature scheme was constructed [4].

M.H. Au et al. (Eds.): NSS 2014, LNCS 8792, pp. 233–245, 2014.

The security of [4] is based on the computational Diffie-Hellman problem that is not harder than the discrete logarithm problem. Unfortunately, Shor [15] demonstrated that the factoring and the (elliptic curve) discrete logarithm problems can be efficiently attacked with quantum computers. It is widely believed that it is certainly not sufficient for cryptographic constructions to rely solely on these two problems in the long term. A promising alternative to number-theoretic constructions is lattice-based cryptosystems which offers several concrete advantages. Firstly, the basic lattice operations manipulate relatively small numbers (*e.g.*, in machine-word size) and are inherently parallelizable. The linear operations which require less computational overhead can potentially yield efficient constructions. Secondly, lattice-based cryptosystems are based on the worst-case hard problems whereas factorization-based and discrete logarithm-based cryptosystems are based on the average-case hard problems. In another word, a randomly chosen instance of the lattice-based construction is at least as hard to attack as to solve the worst-case instance of a related lattice problem. Thus, choosing secure keys is easy. Finally, lattice problems are considered currently immune to quantum attacks. The best known algorithms for solving several lattice problems have an exponential complexity in the lattice dimension (in contrast to the sub-exponential algorithm known for factoring). Lattice-based cryptosystems are conjectured to be post-quantum.

Very recently, ideal lattices are used to construct multilinear maps [9]. With this technique as the basic underlying module, we construct the first ID-based threshold ring signature scheme from lattices. It is not a trivial effort to design the scheme by utilizing the multilinearity without any regulation since multilinear maps out of ideal lattices do not perform totally the same as the bilinear maps out of parings. In another word, one can not base the security of the scheme directly on the graded Computational Deffie-Hellman problem($GCDHP$) for the multilinear systems. We introduce the concept of variant graded Computational Deffie-Hellman problem ($vGCDHP$) and we prove that it is equivalent to the problem $GCDHP$. Then we extended $vGCDHP$ to the general graded Computational Deffie-Hellman problem ($gGCDHP$) that we believe is harder than $vGCDHP$ and $GCDHP$. Our ID-based threshold ring signature scheme is based on the corresponding general graded Computational Deffie-Hellman assumption ($gGCDHA$).

1.1   Related Work

Since Bresson *et. al.* extended the ring signatures into threshold ring signatures, many works attempted to construct variant schemes with special properties or construct more efficient schemes by using different techniques.

Separable threshold ring signatures were proposed by Liu *et. al.* in [10] to involve the separability, *i.e.*, the use of various flavours of public keys. Later, individual-linkability was further introduced to form separable linkable threshold ring signatures [16].

In [17],Wang and Han introduced the notion of threshold ring signature into certificateless public key cryptography and proposed a concrete certificateless threshold ring signature scheme that was provably secure in the random oracle model.

Threshold ring signatures from pairings and the ID-based version were proposed in [19] and [4], respectively. Using secret sharing and Lagrange reconstructing techniques, Xu and Lv [21] presented a new ID-based threshold ring signature scheme that needed only two pairings for any ring size and didn't need a trusted party for generating the secret keys. Assuming the hardness of factoring, Xiong *et.al.* [20] proved their ID-based threshold ring signature scheme without pairings secure under the random oracle model.

Based on error-correcting codes, Melchor *et.al.* [11] constructed a constant-size threshold ring signature scheme whose time complexity was linear in ring size and independent of the threshold. Using random linear codes over the field $\mathbb{F}_q$, Cayrel *et.al.* [5] constructed an improved threshold ring signature scheme built on the q-SD identification scheme [7]. It was the first efficient implementation of this type of code-based schemes. Another code-based threshold ring signature scheme was constructed by Dallot and Verganaud [8] who did not derive their construction from any identification.

Petzoldt *et.al.* extended Sakumoto *et.al.*'s multivariate identification scheme [14] to a security-provable threshold ring signature scheme [12] that was the first multivariate scheme of this type. The signatures were at least twice shorter than those in code-based constructions.

The first lattice-based threshold ring signature scheme is proposed by Cayrel *et.al.* [6] who used the short integer solution (SIS) problem as the security assumption. It exhibited a lattice-based cryptosystems with worst-case to average-case reduction in the field of threshold ring signature. Bettaieb and Schrek [1] presented an improvement to their scheme and got a more efficient threshold ring signature. The size of the signature is a significant reduction.

We aim at constructing the ID-based threshold ring signature scheme from lattices. To the best of our knowledge, our work is the first ID-based scheme from lattices. In [18], Wang and Sun proposed a lattice-based ring signature scheme in the random oracle model. The key tool they used was the bonsai tree technique. It didn't seem trivial to extend this scheme into a threshold version.

1.2 Organization

The rest of this paper is divided as follows. In Section 2, we give some preliminaries regarding the formal definition and security model of an ID-based threshold ring signature scheme, graded encoding systems from lattices, the proposed new concepts of variant graded Computational Deffie-Hellman problem ($vGCDHP$) and general graded Computational Deffie-Hellman problem ($gGCDHP$). Subsequently, we describe our ID-based threshold ring signature scheme form lattices in Section 3. Afterwards, we provide the provable security under the random oracle model in Section 4. Lastly, conclusion is drawn and further lines of work is given in Section 5.

2   Preliminaries

2.1   ID-Based Threshold Ring Signature

Generally, an ID-based threshold ring signature scheme is made up of such four algorithms as **Setup, KeyGen, Sign** and **Verify**. Their functionalities are listed as follows.

- **Setup:** On input the security parameter λ, it outputs a master private key s and the corresponding master public key *params* which includes the description of the message space, the signature space, the size N of ring and the threshold $T \leq N$.
- **KeyGen:** On input a signer's identity $ID \in \{0,1\}^*$, the master private key s, it outputs the signer's private key S_{ID}.
- **Sign:** On input a message *msg*, a list that contains N user's identities $\{ID_1, \cdots, ID_N\}$, the private keys $\{S_{ID_{i_1}}, S_{ID_{i_{T'}}}\}$ of $T' \geq T$ members in the list, it outputs an (N, T) ID-based threshold ring signature σ on the message *msg*.
- **Verify:** On input a ring size N, a threshold T, a message *msg*, an alleged (N, T) threshold ring signature σ for this message, a list of N signers' identities $\{ID_1, \cdots, ID_N\}$, it outputs $\top$ as acceptation if σ is a valid signature on the message *msg* that is signed by at least T members in the list, or it outputs $\bot$ as rejection if σ is an invalid signature.

The consistency constraint for the ID-based threshold ring signature scheme should be satisfied by these algorithms. In another word, if $\sigma = \mathbf{Sign}(msg, \{ID_1, \cdots, ID_N\}, \{S_{ID_{i_1}}, \cdots, S_{ID_{i_{T'}}}\})$ where $T' \geq T$, it should hold that **Verify** $(N, T, m, \sigma, \{ID_1, \cdots, ID_N\}) = \top$.

The unforgeability and signer ambiguity for the ID-based threshold ring signature scheme should also be provided. These two security requirements are described by the following definitions.

Definition 1. An (N, T) ID-based threshold ring signature scheme has the existential unforgeability against adaptive chosen-message-and-identity attacks (*EUF-IDTR-CMIA2 secure*) if and only if no adversary has a non-negligible advantage in the following *EUF-IDTR-CMIA2* game played between a challenger $\mathcal{C}$ and a forger $\mathcal{F}$.

EUF-IDTR-CMIA2 game

Setup: Taking the security parameter λ as input, $\mathcal{C}$ runs the **Setup** algorithm to produce the master private key s and the corresponding master public key *params*. He forwards *params* to $\mathcal{F}$.

Queries: $\mathcal{F}$ makes polynomially many queries in an adaptive way. The queries can be types of hash functions, **KeyGen** and **Sign**.

- Hash function queries: $\mathcal{F}$ asks for the values of all hash functions for any input.
- **KeyGen** queries: $\mathcal{F}$ asks $\mathcal{C}$ to compute the private key $S_{ID} = \mathbf{KeyGen}(ID)$ for any chosen identity ID.

- **Sign** queries: $\mathcal{F}$ constructs any list of identities $\{ID_1, \cdots, ID_N\}$ for a threshold $T \le N$, and asks $\mathcal{C}$ to provide an (N, T) ID-based threshold ring signature σ for any chosen message m.

Forgery: $\mathcal{F}$ outputs an (N, T) ID-based threshold ring signature σ that is believed to be signed on message msg by at least T members in the identity list. The restriction is that the pair of msg and identity list has not ever appeared in the set of previous **Sign** queries and less than T private keys in the list has ever been returned by previous **KeyGen** queries.

$\mathcal{F}$ is said to win the game if **Verify**$(N, T, msg, \sigma, \{ID_1, \cdots, ID_N\})$ returns $\top$. The advantage of $\mathcal{F}$ is the probability that he wins the game.

Definition 2. An (N, T) ID-based threshold ring signature scheme has the unconditional signer ambiguity if and only if for any N users with identities $\{ID_1, \cdots, ID_N\}$, any $T' \ge T$ signers $\{ID_{i_1}, \cdots, ID_{i_{T'}}\}$, any message msg, and any signature $\sigma = $ **Sign**$(msg, \{ID_1, \cdots, ID_N\}, \{S_{ID_{i_1}}, \cdots, S_{ID_{i_{T'}}}\})$, any verifier $\mathcal{A}$ that is not one of the T' signers $\{ID_{i_1}, \cdots, ID_{i_{T'}}\}$, and possesses unbounded computing resources, does not have advantage better than $\frac{1}{C_N^T}$ to identify the T participating signers. Equivalently, nobody can catch a member of $\{ID_{i_1}, \cdots, ID_{i_{T'}}\}$ with a probability larger than $\frac{T}{N}$.

2.2   Graded Encoding System from Lattices

Let λ be the security parameter, $\kappa \le poly(\lambda)$ be the multi-linearity level. Define a cyclotomic ring and two quotient rings as follows: $\mathbf{R} = \mathbb{Z}[x]/(x^n + 1)$ where $n = \widetilde{O}(\kappa\lambda^2)$, a power of 2, is large enough to ensure security; $\mathbf{R}_q = \mathbf{R}/q\mathbf{R}$ where the modulus $q = 2^{n/\lambda}$ is large enough to support functionality; $\mathbf{QR} = \mathbf{R}/\mathcal{I}$ where $\mathcal{I}$ is a principal ideal $\mathcal{I} = \langle \mathbf{g} \rangle \subset \mathbf{R}$ generated by a secret short vector $\mathbf{g}$ that is simply drawn from a discrete Gaussian over $\mathbb{Z}^n$, say $\mathbf{g} \leftarrow D_{\mathbb{Z}^n, \sigma}$ with $\sigma = \widetilde{O}(\sqrt{n})$. Set $\mathbf{z}$ be a secret element (not required to be short) chosen at random in $\mathbf{R}_q$.

The GGH's κ-graded encoding system [9] is a system of sets $\mathcal{S} = \{S_i^{(\mathbf{e}+\mathcal{I})} = \{\mathbf{c}/\mathbf{z}^i \in \mathbf{R}_q : \mathbf{c} \in \mathbf{e} + \mathcal{I}, \|\mathbf{c}\| < q^{1/8}\} : \mathbf{e} + \mathcal{I} \in \mathbf{R}/\mathcal{I}, 0 \le i \le \kappa\}$, equipped with eight efficient procedures **Instance generation**, **Ring sampling**, **Encoding**, **Adding**, **Multiplying**, **Zero testing**, **Extraction**.

In the graded system, a level-zero encoding of a coset $\mathbf{e} + \mathcal{I}$ is just a short vector in that coset, a level-i encoding is a vector of the form $\mathbf{c}/\mathbf{z}^i \in \mathbf{R}_q$ with $\mathbf{c} \in \mathbf{e} + \mathcal{I}$ short, and the set of all level-i encodings is $S_i^{(\mathbf{e}+\mathcal{I})}$.

Instance Generation: $(params, \mathbf{p}_{zt}) \leftarrow InstGen(1^\lambda, 1^\kappa)$. Choose a level-one encoding of $1 + \mathcal{I}$, namely an element $\mathbf{y} = [\mathbf{a}/\mathbf{z}]_q$ where $\mathbf{a} \in 1 + \mathcal{I}$ is short and the notation $[\tau]_q$ denotes the reduction of τ modulo q into the interval $[-q/2, q/2)$. Choose $m = O(n^2)$ randomizers $\mathbf{x}_i$ that are just random encodings of zero, namely $\mathbf{x}_i = [\mathbf{b}_i/\mathbf{z}]_q$ where the $\mathbf{b}_i$'s are short elements in $\mathcal{I}$. Denote by $\mathbf{X}$ the matrix with the vectors $\mathbf{x}_i$ as rows, namely $\mathbf{X} = (\mathbf{x}_1|\cdots|\mathbf{x}_m)^T$. Draw a somewhat small ring element $\mathbf{h} \leftarrow D_{\mathbb{Z}^n, \sqrt{q}}$ and set the level-κ zero-testing parameter as

$\mathbf{p}_{zt} = [\mathbf{hz}^{\kappa}/\mathbf{g}]_q$. Choose also a random seed s for a strong randomness extractor. Publish $params = (n, q, \mathbf{y}, \mathbf{X}, s)$ and $\mathbf{p}_{zt}$.

Ring Sampling: $\mathbf{d} \leftarrow samp(params)$. Sample a level-zero encoding of a random coset by drawing a random sort element in $\mathbf{R}$, $\mathbf{d} \leftarrow D_{\mathbb{Z}^n, n\sigma}$.

Encoding: $\mathbf{u}_i \leftarrow enc(params, i, \mathbf{d})$. Draw an m-vector of integer coefficients $\mathbf{r} \leftarrow D_{\mathbb{Z}^m, \sigma^*}$ for large $\sigma^* = 2^{\lambda}\gamma$ with noise-bound γ, and output $\mathbf{u}_i = [\mathbf{dy}^i + \mathbf{rX}]_q$.

Adding: Given the encodings $\mathbf{u}_j = [\mathbf{c}_j/\mathbf{z}^i]_q$ of the cosets $\mathbf{c}_j + \mathcal{I}$'s, output the sum $\sum_j \mathbf{u}_j$ of the form $[\mathbf{c}/\mathbf{z}^i]_q$ where $\mathbf{c} = \Sigma_j \mathbf{c}_j$ is still a short element in the sum $\Sigma_j(\mathbf{c}_j + \mathcal{I})$ of the cosets.

Multiplying: Given the encodings $\mathbf{u}_j = [\mathbf{c}_j/\mathbf{z}^i]_q$ of the cosets $\mathbf{c}_j + \mathcal{I}$'s, output the product $\prod_j \mathbf{u}_j$ of the form $[\mathbf{c}/\mathbf{z}^{\Sigma i}]_q$ where $\mathbf{c} = \Pi_j \mathbf{c}_j$ belongs to the product coset $\Pi_j(\mathbf{c}_j + \mathcal{I})$.

Zero Testing: $isZero(params, \mathbf{p}_{zt}, \mathbf{u}_{\kappa}) \overset{?}{=} 0/1$. To test if a level-$\kappa$ encoding $\mathbf{u}_{\kappa} = [\mathbf{c}/\mathbf{z}^{\kappa}]_q$ is an encoding of zero, just multiply it by $\mathbf{p}_{zt}$ and check whether the resulting element is short, namely $isZero(params, \mathbf{p}_{zt}, \mathbf{u}_{\kappa}) = \begin{cases} 1, \|\mathbf{p}_{zt}\mathbf{u}_{\kappa}\|_{\infty} < q^{3/4} \\ 0, otherwise \end{cases}$.

Extraction: $v \leftarrow ext(params, \mathbf{p}_{zt}, \mathbf{u}_{\kappa})$. To extract a canonical and random representation of a coset from an encoding $\mathbf{u}_{\kappa} = [\mathbf{c}/\mathbf{z}^{\kappa}]_q$, just multiply it by the zero-testing parameter $\mathbf{p}_{zt}$, collect the $(log\ q)/4 - \lambda$ most-significant bits of each of the n coefficients of the result, and apply a strong randomness extractor to the collected bits using the seed from the public parameters, namely $ext(params, \mathbf{p}_{zt}, \mathbf{u}_{\kappa}) = EXTRACT_s(msbs([\mathbf{u}_{\kappa}\mathbf{p}_{zt}]_q))$.

2.3 The *GCDH* Problem and Its Generalization

Definition 3 The graded Computational Deffie-Hellman problem $(GCDHP)$ is, on input $(\mathbf{y}, \mathbf{X}, \mathbf{p}_{zt}) \leftarrow InstGen(1^{\lambda}, 1^{\kappa})$, $\mathbf{u}_0 = [\mathbf{e}_0\mathbf{y} + \mathbf{r}_0\mathbf{X}]_q, \mathbf{u}_1 = [\mathbf{e}_1\mathbf{y} + \mathbf{r}_1\mathbf{X}]_q, \cdots, \mathbf{u}_{\kappa} = [\mathbf{e}_{\kappa}\mathbf{y} + \mathbf{r}_{\kappa}\mathbf{X}]_q$ where $\mathbf{e}_i \leftarrow D_{\mathbb{Z}^n, \sigma}$ and $\mathbf{r}_i \leftarrow D_{\mathbb{Z}^m, \sigma^*}$ for $i = 0, 1, \cdots, \kappa$, to output a level-κ encoding of $\prod_{i=0}^{\kappa} \mathbf{e}_i + \mathcal{I}$, i.e., to generate $\omega \in \mathbf{R}_q$ such that $isZero(params, \mathbf{p}_{zt}, \omega - \mathbf{e}_0 \prod_{i=1}^n \mathbf{u}_i)$ passes. The graded Computational Deffie-Hellman assumption $(GCDHA)$ states that it is computationally intractable to resolve the problem $GCDHP$.

Definition 4 The variant graded Computational Deffie-Hellman problem $(vGCDHP)$ is, on input $(\mathbf{y}, \mathbf{X}, \mathbf{p}_{zt}) \leftarrow InstGen(1^{\lambda}, 1^{\kappa})$, $t \geq 0$, $\mathbf{u}_0 = [\mathbf{e}_0\mathbf{y} + \mathbf{r}_0\mathbf{X}]_q, \mathbf{u}_1 = [\mathbf{e}_1\mathbf{y} + \mathbf{r}_1\mathbf{X}]_q, \cdots, \mathbf{u}_{\kappa} = [\mathbf{e}_{\kappa}\mathbf{y} + \mathbf{r}_{\kappa}\mathbf{X}]_q$ where $\mathbf{e}_i \leftarrow D_{\mathbb{Z}^n, \sigma}$ and $\mathbf{r}_i \leftarrow D_{\mathbb{Z}^m, \sigma^*}$ for $i = 0, 1, \cdots, \kappa$, to output a level-$(\kappa + t)$ encoding of $\mathbf{e}_0^{t+1} \prod_{i=1}^{\kappa+t} \mathbf{e}_i + \mathcal{I}$ for any chosen $\mathbf{e}_{\kappa+1}, \cdots, \mathbf{e}_{\kappa+t} \leftarrow D_{\mathbb{Z}^n, \sigma}$, i.e., to generate $\omega \in \mathbf{R}_q$ such that $isZero(params, \mathbf{p}_{zt}, \omega - \mathbf{e}_0 \prod_{i=1}^{\kappa} \mathbf{u}_i \prod_{i=\kappa+1}^{\kappa+t}(\mathbf{e}_i\mathbf{u}_0))$ passes. The variant graded Computational Deffie-Hellman assumption $(vGCDHPA)$ states that it is computationally intractable to resolve the problem $vGCDHP$.

$GCDHP$ is a special case of $vGCDHP$ when setting $t = 0$. $vGCDHP$ is a special case of $GCDHP$ when adding $\mathbf{u}_{\kappa+1} = \mathbf{e}_{\kappa+1}\mathbf{u}_0, \cdots \mathbf{u}_{\kappa+t} = \mathbf{e}_{\kappa+t}\mathbf{u}_0$. We can understand the relationship between these two problems in another viewpoint as follows. If the task of $GCDHP$ is hard, then it is still hard[1] to compute a level-$(\kappa + t)$ encoding of $\mathbf{e}_0^{t+1} \prod_{i=1}^{\kappa} \mathbf{e}_i \prod_{i=\kappa+1}^{\kappa+t} \mathbf{e}_i + \mathcal{I}$ with the knowledge of $\mathbf{e}_{\kappa+1}, \cdots, \mathbf{e}_{\kappa+t}$. The latter task is that of $vGCDHP$.

Actually, $GCDHP$ and $vGCDHP$ are equivalent, as claimed in the following theorem.

Theorem 1. If there exists a determinant algorithm that can compute $GCDHP$ in polynomial time, then there is also a determinant algorithm to compute $vGCDHP$ in polynomial time, and vice versa.

Proof. If $GCDHP$ is efficiently computable, we can get $\mathbf{v} = \mathbf{e}_0 \prod_{i=1}^{\kappa} \mathbf{u}_i$ and then solve $vGCDHP$ by computing $\mathbf{vu}_0^t \prod_{i=\kappa+1}^{\kappa+t} \mathbf{e}_i$. If $vGCDHP$ is efficiently computable, we can set $t = 0$ and get the solution of $GCDHP$. □

For our scheme, we propose a more general problem and the corresponding assumption based on the problem $vGCDHP$ and the assumption $vGCDHA$.

Definition 5. The general graded Computational Deffie-Hellman problem ($gGCDHP$) is, on input $(\mathbf{y}, \mathbf{X}, \mathbf{p}_{zt}) \leftarrow InstGen(1^\lambda, 1^\kappa), t \geq 0, \mathbf{u}_0 = [\mathbf{e}_0\mathbf{y} + \mathbf{r}_0\mathbf{X}]_q, \mathbf{u}_1 = [\mathbf{e}_1\mathbf{y} + \mathbf{r}_1\mathbf{X}]_q, \cdots, \mathbf{u}_\kappa = [\mathbf{e}_\kappa\mathbf{y} + \mathbf{r}_\kappa\mathbf{X}]_q$ where $\mathbf{e}_i \leftarrow D_{\mathbb{Z}^n,\sigma}$ and $\mathbf{r}_i \leftarrow D_{\mathbb{Z}^m,\sigma^*}$ for $i = 0, 1, \cdots, \kappa$, to output a level-$(\kappa + t)$ encoding of $(\mathbf{x}_1\mathbf{e}_{s_1} + h_1\mathbf{e}_0\mathbf{e}_{s_1}) \prod_{i=2}^{\kappa} \mathbf{x}_i\mathbf{e}_{s_i} \prod_{i=\kappa+1}^{\kappa+t} (\mathbf{x}_i\mathbf{e}_i + h_i\mathbf{e}_0\mathbf{e}_i) + \mathcal{I}$ for any permutation $(s_1, \cdots, s_\kappa)$ of $(1, \cdots, \kappa)$ and any chosen $\mathbf{e}_{\kappa+1}, \cdots, \mathbf{e}_{\kappa+t}, \mathbf{x}_1, \cdots, \mathbf{x}_{\kappa+t} \leftarrow D_{\mathbb{Z}^n,\sigma}, h_1, h_{\kappa+1}, \cdots, h_{\kappa+t} \in_R \mathbb{Z}_q^*$, i.e., to generate $\omega \in \mathbf{R}_q$ such that $isZero(params, \mathbf{p}_{zt}, \omega - (\mathbf{x}_1\mathbf{u}_{s_1} + h_1\mathbf{e}_0\mathbf{u}_{s_1}) \prod_{i=2}^{\kappa} \mathbf{x}_i\mathbf{u}_{s_i} \prod_{i=\kappa+1}^{\kappa+t} (\mathbf{x}_i\mathbf{e}_i\mathbf{y} + h_i\mathbf{e}_i\mathbf{u}_0))$ passes. The general graded Computational Deffie-Hellman assumption ($gGCDHPA$) states that it is computationally intractable to resolve the problem $gGCDHP$.

$vGCDHP$ is a special case of $gGCDHP$ with $\mathbf{x}_1 = \mathbf{x}_{\kappa+1} = \cdots = \mathbf{x}_{\kappa+t} = 0$, $\mathbf{x}_2 = \cdots = \mathbf{x}_\kappa = 1$, and $h_1 = h_{\kappa+1} = \cdots = h_{\kappa+t} = 1$.

3   ID-Based Threshold Ring Signature from Lattices

We construct our ID-based threshold ring signature from lattices with the tool of multilinear maps defined in Section 2.2. The ring size is N and the threshold is T. The zero-testing parameter for the multilinear maps is a level-$2N$ one $\mathbf{p}_{zt} = [\mathbf{h}\mathbf{z}^{2N}/\mathbf{g}]_q$, rather than level-$\kappa$. Moreover, $H(\cdot), H_1(\cdot), H_2(\cdot)$ and $H_3(\cdot)$ are four cryptographic hash functions where $H : \{0,1\}^* \to \mathbf{R}_q, H_1 : \{0,1\}^* \to \mathbb{Z}^n$, $H_2 : \{0,1\}^* \to \mathbb{Z}^m$ and $H_3 : \{0,1\}^* \to \mathbb{Z}_q^*$. $H(ID)$ is constructed out of $H_1(ID)$ and $H_2(ID)$ in such a way as $H_1(ID)\mathbf{y} + H_2(ID)\mathbf{X}$.

Setup: The trusted authority (TA) samples a level-zero encoding of a random coset, *i.e.*, draws a random short element in $\mathbf{R}, d \leftarrow D_{\mathbb{Z}^n,\delta}$ with $\delta = n \cdot \tilde{O}(\sqrt{n})$. d serves as the secret master key. The corresponding public key is the re-randomization of encoding at level one for the master key, *i.e.*, $K = d\mathbf{y} + r\mathbf{X}$,

---

[1] It is easy to get a level-$(\kappa + t)$ encoding of $\mathbf{e}_0^t \prod_{i=1}^{\kappa+t} \mathbf{e}_i + \mathcal{I}$ by computing $\prod_{i=1}^{\kappa} \mathbf{u}_i$ $\prod_{i=\kappa+1}^{\kappa+t}(\mathbf{e}_i\mathbf{u}_0)$. It is also easy to get a level-$(\kappa + t + 1)$ encoding of $\mathbf{e}_0^{t+1} \prod_{i=1}^{\kappa+t} \mathbf{e}_i + \mathcal{I}$ by computing $\mathbf{u}_0 \prod_{i=1}^{\kappa} \mathbf{u}_i \prod_{i=\kappa+1}^{\kappa+t}(\mathbf{e}_i\mathbf{u}_0)$.

where the m-vector of integer coefficients r is drawn from $D_{\mathbb{Z}^m, \delta'}$ for large enough δ'. The system parameters are:

$$params = \{\mathbf{R}, N, T, q, \mathbf{y}, \mathbf{X}, K, H(\cdot), H_1(\cdot), H_2(\cdot), H_3(\cdot), \mathbf{p_{zt}}\}$$

KeyGen: The user P_i with identity ID_i sets his public key $Q_{ID_i} = H(ID_i) = d_i \mathbf{y} + d_i' \mathbf{X}$, where $d_i = H_1(ID_i) \in \mathbb{Z}^n$ and $d_i' = H_2(ID_i) \in \mathbb{Z}^m$. TA produces a private key $S_{ID_i} = dQ_{ID_i}$ for the user P_i.

Sign: Assume the ring being $L = \{P_1, \cdots, P_T, P_{T+1}, \cdots, P_N\}$. Without loss of generality, let $P_1, \cdots, P_T$ be the participating signers and $P_{T+1}, \cdots, P_N$ be the non-participating signers. Anyone P_s with identity ID_s in the group of T participating signers can play the role of a representative in this group and carries out the signing procedures with the help of the other signers. The message to be signed is msg.

- For $i \in \{T+1, \cdots, N\}$, P_s chooses $x_i \in \mathbb{Z}^n, h_i \in \mathbb{Z}_q^*, r_i \leftarrow D_{\mathbb{Z}^m, \delta'}$ and computes $U_i = x_i \mathbf{y} - h_i K + r_i \mathbf{X}$ and $V_i = x_i Q_{ID_i}$.
- For $j \in \{1, \cdots, T\}$, each participating signer P_j with identity ID_j chooses $r_j \in \mathbb{Z}^n, r_j' \leftarrow D_{\mathbb{Z}^m, \delta'}$ and computes $U_j = r_j \mathbf{y} + r_j' \mathbf{X}$.
- P_s computes $h_0 = H_3(L, T, msg, \bigcup_{k=1}^N \{U_k\})$. Then he constructs a polynomial f of degree $N - T$ over $\mathbb{Z}_q$ such that $f(0) = h_0$, and $f(i) = h_i$ for $T+1 \le i \le N$.
- For $j \in \{1, \cdots, T\}$, each participating signer P_j with identity ID_j computes $h_j = f(j)$ and computes $V_j = r_j Q_{ID_j} + h_j S_{ID_j}$.
- P_s computes $V = \prod_{k=1}^N V_k$ and outputs the signature for msg and L as $\sigma = \{\bigcup_{k=1}^N \{U_k\}, V, f\}$.

Verify: Any verifier can check whether a signature $\sigma = \{\bigcup_{k=1}^N \{U_k\}, V, f\}$ for a message msg is generated by at least T signers from the set L of users in such a way:

- Check if the polynomial f has a degree of $N - T$ and a constant term of $H_3(L, T, msg, \bigcup_{k=1}^N \{U_k\})$. Proceed if both conditions are satisfied, reject otherwise.
- For $k \in \{1, \cdots, N\}$ compute $h_k = f(k)$.
- Check whether the zero testing procedure $isZero(params, p_{zt}, \prod_{k=1}^N Q_{ID_k}(U_k + h_k \cdot K) - V \mathbf{y}^N)$ passes. Accept the signature if the test passes, reject it otherwise.

Since rows of $\mathbf{X}$ are all in the coset $\mathbf{0}+\mathbf{I}$, and $\prod_{i=1}^N (\alpha_i + s_i \mathbf{X}) = \prod_{i=1}^N \alpha_i + s' \mathbf{X}$, $\prod_{i=1}^N (\alpha_i + s_i \mathbf{X})$ and $\prod_{i=1}^N \alpha_i$ fall into the same coset $\alpha + \mathbf{I}$ for some $\alpha \in \mathbf{R}$. Consequently, we can verify the consistency of our construction as follows.

$$\prod_{k=1}^N Q_{ID_k}(U_k + h_k K) - V \mathbf{y}^N$$

$$= \prod_{i=T+1}^{N} Q_{ID_i}(U_i + h_i K) \prod_{j=1}^{T} Q_{ID_j}(U_j + h_j K) - \prod_{i=T+1}^{N} V_i \mathbf{y} \prod_{j=1}^{T} V_j \mathbf{y}$$

$$= \prod_{i=T+1}^{N} Q_{ID_i}(x_i \mathbf{y} - h_i K + r_i \mathbf{X} + h_i K) \prod_{j=1}^{T} Q_{ID_j}(r_j \mathbf{y} + r'_j \mathbf{X} + h_j K)$$

$$- \prod_{i=T+1}^{N} x_i Q_{ID_i} \mathbf{y} \prod_{j=1}^{T} (r_j Q_{ID_j} + h_j S_{ID_j}) \mathbf{y}$$

$$= \prod_{i=T+1}^{N} Q_{ID_i}(x_i \mathbf{y} + r_i \mathbf{X}) \prod_{j=1}^{T} Q_{ID_j}(r_j \mathbf{y} + h_j(d\mathbf{y} + r\mathbf{X}) + r'_j \mathbf{X})$$

$$- \prod_{i=T+1}^{N} x_i Q_{ID_i} \mathbf{y} \prod_{j=1}^{T} (r_j Q_{ID_j} + h_j S_{ID_j}) \mathbf{y}$$

$$= \prod_{i=T+1}^{N} Q_{ID_i} x_i \mathbf{y} \prod_{j=1}^{T} (r_j Q_{ID_j} + h_j S_{ID_j}) \mathbf{y} + s_1 \mathbf{X}$$

$$- \prod_{i=T+1}^{N} x_i Q_{ID_i} \mathbf{y} \prod_{j=1}^{T} (r_j Q_{ID_j} + h_j S_{ID_j}) \mathbf{y}$$

$$= s_1 \mathbf{X}$$

This implies that $\prod_{k=1}^{N} Q_{ID_k}(U_k + h_k K) - V\mathbf{y}^N$ lies in the coset of $\mathbf{0} +$ $\mathbf{I}$. Therefore the zero testing procedure $isZero(params, p_{zt}, \prod_{k=1}^{N} Q_{ID_k}(U_k + h_k K) - V\mathbf{y}^N)$ passes.

4   Scheme Analysis

We show in the following theorems that our scheme is existentially unforgeable and signer anonymous.

Theorem 2. If there exists an polynomial-time algorithm $\mathcal{F}$ that can win the *EUF-IDTR-CMIA2* game, then in the random oracle model, the general *gGCDHP* problem can be solved in polynomial time with non-negligible probability.

Proof. Assume that the challenger $\mathcal{C}$ is challenged by a random *gGCDHP* instance $(\mathbf{y}, \mathbf{X}, \mathbf{p}_{zt}), T > 0, \mathbf{u}_0 = [\mathbf{e}_0 \mathbf{y} + \mathbf{r}_0 \mathbf{X}]_q, \mathbf{u}_T = [\mathbf{e}_T \mathbf{y} + \mathbf{r}_T \mathbf{X}]_q, \cdots, \mathbf{u}_N = [\mathbf{e}_N \mathbf{y} + \mathbf{r}_N \mathbf{X}]_q$ where $\mathbf{e}_i \leftarrow D_{\mathbb{Z}^n, \delta/n}$ and $\mathbf{r}_i \leftarrow D_{\mathbb{Z}^m, \delta'}$ for $i = 0, T, \cdots, N$, and output a level-N encoding of $\left(\prod_{i=1}^{T-1} (\mathbf{x}_i \mathbf{e}_i + h_i \mathbf{e}_0 \mathbf{e}_i) \right) (\mathbf{x}_T \mathbf{e}_{s_T} + h_T \mathbf{e}_0 \mathbf{e}_{s_T}) \left(\prod_{i=T+1}^{N} \mathbf{x}_i \mathbf{e}_{s_i} \right) +$ $\mathcal{I}$ for any permutation $(s_T, \cdots, s_N)$ of $(T, \cdots, N)$ and any chosen $\mathbf{e}_1, \cdots, \mathbf{e}_{T-1}$, $\mathbf{x}_1, \cdots, \mathbf{x}_N \leftarrow D_{\mathbb{Z}^n, \sigma}, h_1, \cdots, h_N \in_R \mathbb{Z}_q^*$.

$\mathcal{C}$ will play the role of the challenger for $\mathcal{F}$ in the *EUF-IDTR-CMIA2* game. $\mathcal{F}$ is allowed to make q_H hash queries and q_S signing queries, respectively. It is assumed that $\mathcal{F}$ always queries on the hash $H(\cdot)$ (equally $H_1(\cdot)$ and $H_2(\cdot)$) values of identities before he makes any **KeyGen** query.

$\mathcal{C}$ gives $\mathcal{F}$ the system parameters as $params = \{\mathbf{R}, T, q, \mathbf{y}, \mathbf{X}, K = \mathbf{u}_0, H(\cdot),$ $H_1(\cdot), H_2(\cdot), H_3(\cdot), \mathbf{p}_{zt}\}$. Note that e_0 is unknown to $\mathcal{C}$. This value simulates the master key value for the TA in the game.

Construct a null list L_1 for the hash queries. The tuples of hash queries will appear as $(ID_i, Q_{ID_i}, H_1(ID_i), H_2(ID_i))$. When $\mathcal{F}$ queries on the hash $H(\cdot)$, $H_1(\cdot)$ and $H_2(\cdot)$ values of identities, $\mathcal{C}$ checks the list L_1. If an entry for the query exists, $\mathcal{C}$ sends $\mathcal{F}$ the same answer $H(ID_i) = H_1(ID_i)\mathbf{y} + H_2(ID_i)\mathbf{X}$. Otherwise, with probability of $\frac{q_H - N + T - 1}{q_H}$, $\mathcal{C}$ generates random $\mathbf{e}_i \in \mathbb{Z}^n$ and $\mathbf{e}'_i \in \mathbb{Z}^m$, sets $H_1(ID_i) = \mathbf{e}_i$ and $H_2(ID_i) = \mathbf{e}'_i$, sends $\mathcal{F}$ the answer $Q_{ID_i} = H(ID_i) = \mathbf{e}_i \mathbf{y} + \mathbf{e}'_i \mathbf{X}$, and $(ID_i, Q_{ID_i}, \mathbf{e}_i, \mathbf{e}'_i)$ is appended in the list L_1; with probability of $\frac{N - T + 1}{q_H}$, $\mathcal{C}$ chooses $\mathbf{u}_i$ out of $\mathbf{u}_t, \cdots, \mathbf{u}_n$ without repetition, sends $\mathcal{F}$ the answer $Q_{ID_i} = \mathbf{u}_i$, and $(ID_i, Q_{ID_i}, -, -)$ is appended in the list L_1.

In the **KeyGen** queries, if the Q_{ID_i} is one of the $\mathbf{u}_i$, the game fails; otherwise, $\mathbf{e}_i \mathbf{u}_0$ can serve as the associated private key since $\mathbf{e}_i \mathbf{e}_0 \mathbf{y} + \mathbf{e}_i(r_0 \mathbf{X}))$ and $\mathbf{e}_0 \mathbf{e}_i \mathbf{y} + \mathbf{e}_0(\mathbf{e}'_i \mathbf{X})$ are both encoding of $\mathbf{e}_0 \mathbf{e}_i + \mathcal{I}$.

When $\mathcal{F}$ queries on the H_3 function, $\mathcal{C}$ checks the list L_2. If he finds an entry for the query, $\mathcal{C}$ just sends $\mathcal{F}$ the same answer. Otherwise $\mathcal{C}$ generates a random element in $\mathbb{Z}_q^*$ and uses this value as the answer to $\mathcal{F}$. The query and the answer are stored in list L_2.

Consider that $\mathcal{F}$ queries on **Sign**. $\mathcal{F}$ chooses a group of N users' identities $L = \{ID_1, \cdots, \cdots, ID_N\}$, a threshold value $T \leq N$ and any message msg. $\mathcal{F}$ responds with an (N, T) ID-based threshold ring signature σ as follows.

1. Randomly choose $h_i \in \mathbb{Z}_q^*$ for $i \in \{0, T+1, \cdots, N\}$.
2. Construct over $\mathbb{Z}_q$ a polynomial f with degree of $N - T$ such that $f(i) = h_i$ for $i \in \{0, T+1, \cdots, N\}$.
3. Compute $h_j = f(j)$ for $j \in \{1, \cdots, T\}$.
4. Randomly choose $x_k \in \mathbb{Z}^n$, $r_k \leftarrow D_{\mathbb{Z}^m, \delta'}$ and compute $U_k = x_k \mathbf{y} - h_k K + r_k \mathbf{X}$ for $k \in \{1, \cdots, N\}$.
5. Compute $V = \prod_{k=1}^{N}(x_k Q_{ID_k})$.
6. Assign[2] h_0 as the value of $H_3(L, T, msg, \bigcup_{k=1}^{N}\{U_k\})$; if collision occurs, generate another h_0 and repeat.
7. Output the signature as $\sigma = \{\bigcup_{k=1}^{N}\{U_k\}, V, f\}$.

At the final phase, $\mathcal{F}$ outputs a forged signature $\sigma = \{U, V, f\}$ which is signed by some T members of the group $L = \{ID_1, \cdots, ID_{T-1}, ID_T, ID_{T+1}, \cdots, ID_N\}$. By checking the hash function list, $\mathcal{C}$ can learn the set of $T - 1$ participating signers (w.l.g, $ID_1, \cdots, ID_{T-1}$) who have once queried on their own private keys. When the non-participating signers are exactly those with public keys $Q_{ID_i} = \mathbf{u}_{s_i}$ ($i = T, \cdots, N$), $\mathcal{C}$ solves the challenged general $gGCDHP$ problem by outputting V that should have the form of the encoding of $\left(\prod_{i=1}^{T-1}(x_i \mathbf{e}_i + h_i \mathbf{e}_i \mathbf{e}_0)\right)(x_T \mathbf{e}_{s_T} + h_T \mathbf{e}_0 \mathbf{e}_{s_T})\left(\prod_{i=T+1}^{N} x_i \mathbf{e}_{s_i}\right) + \mathcal{I}$, where $\mathbf{e}_1, \cdots, \mathbf{e}_{T-1}$ are stored

---

[2] Only in the ROM game, can we have such hash assignment since hash is assumed to be controlled by the simulator. In reality, hash functions are public, so this kind of assignment is prohibited and attacks based on the idea in this step can not succeed.

into the hash function list when both queries Q_{ID_i} and S_{ID_i} are made, and $\mathbf{e}_{s_T}, \cdots, \mathbf{e}_{s_N}$ correspond to the permutation of $\mathbf{u}_T, \cdots, \mathbf{u}_N$ that are stored when only queries Q_{ID_i} are made and $\mathbf{u}_i$'s are assigned.

Consider the success probability that $\mathcal{C}$ solves the general $gGCDHP$ problem. The probability that $\mathcal{F}$ does not make the **KeyGen** queries on those $Q_{ID_i} = \mathbf{u}_i$ $(i = T, \cdots, N)$ is $\dfrac{\binom{q_H - N + T - 1}{q_S}}{\binom{q_H}{q_S}}$. For the forged signature, the probability that the T-th unknown participating singer and the $N - T + 1$ non-participating signers are just those who have public keys $Q_{ID_i} = \mathbf{u}_i$ $(i = T, \cdots, N)$ is $\dfrac{\binom{q_H - q_S}{N - T + 1}}{\binom{q_H}{q_S}}$.

Consequently, the success probability for $\mathcal{C}$ is the product $\dfrac{\binom{q_H - N + T - 1}{q_S}}{\binom{q_H}{q_S}} \cdot \dfrac{\binom{q_H - q_S}{N - T + 1}}{\binom{q_H}{q_S}}$. If the gap between q_H and q_S is not too large—this accords with reality, the probability is non-negligible. $\quad\square$

Theorem 3. Our ID-Based threshold ring signature scheme from lattices satisfies the property of unconditional signer ambiguity.

Proof. It can be shown that each item in the threshold ring signature $\{\bigcup_{k=1}^{N}\{U_k\}, V, f\}$ generated according to our construction is uniformly distributed. Considering the polynomial f with degree $N - T$, since it is determined by $h_{T+1}, \cdots, h_N$ randomly chosen and h_0 output by a hash function, its coefficients and the function values $h_1, \cdots, h_T$ appear uniform over $\mathbb{Z}_q^*$. Considering $\bigcup_{k=1}^{N}\{U_k\}$, for $j \in \{1, \cdots, T\}$, $\{U_j\}$ distributes uniformly since $\{r_j\}$ and $\{r_j'\}$ are chosen randomly; for $i \in \{T + 1, \cdots, N\}$, $\{U_i\}$ distributes uniformly since $\{x_i\}$ and $\{r_i\}$ are chosen randomly and h_i are a value derived by the random function f. Similarly, V_i's determined by x_i's are uniformly distributed. And V_j's determined by r_j's and h_j's are distributed uniformly. So does V have the same uniform distribution. For any message m and any identities list L, the distributions of all items of $\{\bigcup_{k=1}^{N}\{U_k\}, V, f\}$ are independent and uniform no matter which T participating signers are.

As has been seen in the construction, the threshold ring signature is produced by at least T participating signers in the ring of L that consists of N users. But the identities of these T participating signers are not explicitly or distinguishably claimed in L, even an adversary with all the private keys corresponding to the set of identities L and unbounded computing resources has only a probability of $\frac{1}{C_N^T}$ to identify the T participating signers. $\quad\square$

5   Conclusion

Ring signatures aim to provide signer anonymity without revocation. They have many kinds of extension. One of those is the threshold ring signature. Threshold ring signatures in the identity based scenarios support the real spontaneity. With the tool of multilinear maps that are constructed from ideal lattices, we propose the first ID-based threshold ring signature scheme from lattices, with purpose to get the resistance against the quantum computer attacks. To achieve that, we introduce a new concept of the problem $vGCDHP$ that is proved to be equivalent to the original problem $GCDHP$ for the graded encoding system. This problem is further generalized as the problem $gGCDHP$, based on which we prove our ID-based threshold ring signature scheme is existentially unforgeable and signer anonymous. The proof is carried out in the random oracle model. The open problem is to construct efficient ID-based threshold ring signatures with provable security in the standard model.

Acknowledgement. The work was supported by 973 Program (No. 2012CB316100) the National Natural Science Foundation of China (No. 61172082, 61309028, 61379154).

References

1. Bettaieb, S., Schrek, J.: Improved Lattice-Based Threshold Ring Signature Scheme. In: Gaborit, P. (ed.) PQCrypto 2013. LNCS, vol. 7932, pp. 34–51. Springer, Heidelberg (2013)
2. Bresson, E., Stern, J., Szydlo, M.: Threshold Ring Signatures and Applications to Ad-hoc Groups. In: Yung, M. (ed.) CRYPTO 2002. LNCS, vol. 2442, pp. 465–480. Springer, Heidelberg (2002)
3. Chaum, D., van Heyst, E.: Group signatures. In: Davies, D.W. (ed.) EUROCRYPT 1991. LNCS, vol. 547, pp. 257–265. Springer, Heidelberg (1991)
4. Chow, S.S.M., Hui, L.C.K., Yiu, S.M.: Identity Based Threshold Ring Signature. In: Park, C.-S., Chee, S. (eds.) ICISC 2004. LNCS, vol. 3506, pp. 218–232. Springer, Heidelberg (2005)
5. Cayrel, P.-L., El Yousfi Alaoui, S.M., Hoffmann, G., Véron, P.: An Improved Threshold Ring Signature Scheme Based on Error Correcting Codes. In: Özbudak, F., Rodríguez-Henríquez, F. (eds.) WAIFI 2012. LNCS, vol. 7369, pp. 45–63. Springer, Heidelberg (2012)
6. Cayrel, P.-L., Lindner, R., Rückert, M., Silva, R.: A Lattice-Based Threshold Ring Signature Scheme. In: Abdalla, M., Barreto, P.S.L.M. (eds.) LATINCRYPT 2010. LNCS, vol. 6212, pp. 255–272. Springer, Heidelberg (2010)
7. Cayrel, P.-L., Véron, P., El Yousfi Alaoui, S.M.: A Zero-Knowledge Identification Scheme Based on the q-ary Syndrome Decoding Problem. In: Biryukov, A., Gong, G., Stinson, D.R. (eds.) SAC 2010. LNCS, vol. 6544, pp. 171–186. Springer, Heidelberg (2011)
8. Dallot, L., Vergnaud, D.: Provably secure code-based threshold ring signatures. In: Parker, M.G. (ed.) Cryptography and Coding 2009. LNCS, vol. 5921, pp. 222–235. Springer, Heidelberg (2009)
9. Garg, S., Gentry, C., Halevi, S.: Candidate multilinear maps from ideal lattices. In: Johansson, T., Nguyen, P.Q. (eds.) EUROCRYPT 2013. LNCS, vol. 7881, pp. 1–17. Springer, Heidelberg (2013)
10. Liu, J.K., Wei, V.K., Wong, D.S.: A Separable Threshold Ring Signature Scheme. In: Lim, J.-I., Lee, D.-H. (eds.) ICISC 2003. LNCS, vol. 2971, pp. 352–369. Springer, Heidelberg (2004)
11. Melchor, C.A., Cayrel, P.L., Gaborit, P., Laguillaumie, F.: A New Efficient Threshold Ring Signature Scheme Based on Coding Theory. IEEE Transactions on Information Theory 57(7), 4833–4842 (2011)

12. Petzoldt, A., Bulygin, S., Buchmann, J.: A multivariate based threshold ring signature scheme. Applicable Algebra in Engineering, Communication and Computing 24(3-4), 255–275 (2013)
13. Rivest, R.L., Shamir, A., Tauman, Y.: How to Leak a Secret. In: Boyd, C. (ed.) ASIACRYPT 2001. LNCS, vol. 2248, pp. 552–565. Springer, Heidelberg (2001)
14. Sakumoto, K., Shirai, T., Hiwatari, H.: Public-key identification schemes based on multivariate quadratic polynomials. In: Rogaway, P. (ed.) CRYPTO 2011. LNCS, vol. 6841, pp. 706–723. Springer, Heidelberg (2011)
15. Shor, P.: Algorithms for quantum computation: discrete logarithms and factoring. In: 35th Annual Symposium on Foundations of Computer Science, pp. 124–134. IEEE Press, New York (1994)
16. Tsang, P.P., Wei, V.K., Chan, T.K., Au, M.H., Liu, J.K., Wong, D.S.: Separable Linkable Threshold Ring Signatures. In: Canteaut, A., Viswanathan, K. (eds.) INDOCRYPT 2004. LNCS, vol. 3348, pp. 384–398. Springer, Heidelberg (2004)
17. Wang, H., Han, S.: A Provably Secure Threshold Ring Signature Scheme in Certificateless Cryptography. In: 2010 International Conference of Information Science and Management Engineering, vol. 1, pp. 105–108. IEEE Press, New York (2010)
18. Wang, J., Sun, B.: Ring Signature Schemes from Lattice Basis Delegation. In: Qing, S., Susilo, W., Wang, G., Liu, D. (eds.) ICICS 2011. LNCS, vol. 7043, pp. 15–28. Springer, Heidelberg (2011)
19. Wei, V.K.: A Bilinear Spontaneous Anonymous Threshold Signature for Ad Hoc Groups. Cryptology ePrint Archive, http://eprint.iacr.org/2004/039
20. Xiong, H., Qin, Z., Li, F., Jin, J.: Identity-based Threshold Ring Signature Without Pairings. In: 6th International Conference on Communications, Circuits and Systems, pp. 478–482. IEEE Press, New York (2008)
21. Xu, F., Lv, X.: A New Identity-Based Threshold Ring Signature Scheme. In: International Conference on Systems, Man, and Cybernetics, pp. 2646–2651. IEEE Press, New York (2011)

Identity-Based Transitive Signcryption

Shuquan Hou, Xinyi Huang*, and Li Xu

Fujian Provincial Key Laboratory of Network Security and Cryptology,
School of Mathematics and Computer Science,
Fujian Normal University, Fuzhou 350007, China
{xyhuang,xuli}@fjnu.edu.cn

Abstract. Transitive signatures allow a signer to authenticate a graph in such a way that given two signatures on adjacent edges (i,j) and (j,k), anyone with public information can compose a signature on edge (i,k). In all existing transitive signature schemes, to prevent signature exposure, a secure channel is required between the signer and the recipient to transfer the signature. To eliminate this need, in this paper we introduce a new notion called Identity-Based Transitive Signcryption (IBTSC) by integrating transitive signatures and identity-based signcryption. We present formal definitions and a concrete construction of IBTSC. In the random oracle model, we prove that the proposed IBTSC scheme is secure in the proposed models of confidentiality and unforgeability for IBTSC. Our design not only preserves all desirable properties of transitive signatures but also prevents signature exposure in an efficient way.

Keywords: Transitive signatures, identity-based signcryption, privacy.

1 Introduction

Let $G = (V, E)$ denote a graph with a finite set V of vertices and a finite set $E \subseteq V \times V$ of edges. To add an edge (i, j) to G, the signer with a public/private key pair (tpk, tsk) can produce a classic signature of edge (i, j). But this approach would be awkward if the graph grows frequently and dynamically. For naturally transitive graphs, where there is an edge from node i to node j whenever there is a path from i to j, an edge can be trivially viewed as valid if there is a chain of signatures that authenticate a sequence of edges forming a path from node i to node j. However, this trivial solution has two inherent shortcomings [24]: (1) signature size grows linearly with the number of nodes on the path; and (2) the loss of privacy as the chain of signatures carries information about the whole path.

Transitive signatures, as introduced by Micali and Rivest [24] in 2002, is an efficient method to dynamically build an authenticated graph edge by edge. Given two signatures on adjacent edges (i, j) and (j, k), anyone with the signer's public key can compute a signature on edge (i, k). With this feature, adding a

---

* Corresponding Author

M.H. Au et al. (Eds.): NSS 2014, LNCS 8792, pp. 246–259, 2014.
© Springer International Publishing Switzerland 2014

new edge (i, k) does not necessarily require the involvement of the original signer, nor the need to demonstrate the whole path from node i to node k. Transitive signatures can be used to authenticate undirected graphs (in which (i, j) and (j, i) represent the same edge) and directed graphs (in which (i, j) and (j, i) represent distinct edges). Possible applications of transitive signatures include administrative domains (where an edge between i and j indicates that i and j are in the same domain), military chains of command (where an edge from i to j indicates that i commands j) [24], and secure routing [2].

The notion of identity-based cryptography was introduced by Shamir [29] in 1984. The essential idea is that the user's public key can be derived from his/her recognized identity information (e.g., e-mail address and ID number), and then the public key would be directly verified without certificate. In 1997, Zheng [34] introduced the concept of signcryption, which achieves both the functions of digital signature and public key encryption in a single logical step, at a cost significantly less than that required by the traditional "signature-then-encryption" method. Malone-Lee [22] then extended the signcryption idea to identity-based cryptography and presented an Identity-Based Signcryption (IBSC) scheme. They gave a model of security for such schemes and sketched the detail of how their scheme can be proved secure in this model. With the functionality of identity-based cryptography in the signcryption scheme, users within the system can use their recognized identity information as their public keys. This greatly reduces the problems with key management that have hampered the mass uptake of public key cryptography on a per individual basis [29].

Motivation. As introduced in [24], transitive signatures for a directed graph can be used to authenticate a military chain of command, where vertices represent personnel and a directed edge (i, j) from i to j means that i commands (or controls) j. In a public network environment, transitive signatures will be readily obtained by the attacker and personnel-relationship in the military chain of command will be leaked. In all existing transitive signature schemes, to prevent signature exposure, a secure channel is required between the signer and the recipient to transfer the signature. In this paper, we introduce the notion of Identity-Based Transitive Signcryption (IBTSC) by integrating the notions of transitive signatures and Identity-Based Signcryption (IBSC). Our design not only preserves all desirable properties of transitive signatures but also eliminates the need of secure channel for signature delivery. As presented in [34], a secure signcryption scheme provides both confidentiality and authentication in a more efficient way than "signature-then-encryption".

1.1 Related Works

Two transitive signature schemes based on discrete logarithm assumption and $\mathcal{RSA}$ assumption were proposed by Micali and Rivest [24]. The discrete logarithm based transitive signatures was proven to be transitively unforgeable under adaptive chosen message attacks, while the natural $\mathcal{RSA}$ based transitive signatures was merely proven transitively unforgeable under non-adaptive chosen message attacks. Shortly afterwards, Bellare and Neven [5,6] proposed a series of transitive signature schemes based on one-more $\mathcal{RSA}$-inversion assumption, factoring assumption, one-more discrete logarithm assumption and one-more gap Diffie-Hellman assumption. All these schemes were proven to be transitively unforgeable under adaptive chosen message attacks. Wang et al. [30] provided the first construction of transitive signature using braid groups. Gong et al. [15] constructed a transitive signature scheme from Linear Feedback Sequence Register (LFSR).

It has been an open problem of building transitive signatures for directed graphs since the seminal work by Micali and Rivest [24]. In fact, Hohenberger [16] even provided evidence that directed transitive signature schemes may be very hard to construct, because they would imply a new mathematical structure called Abelian trapdoor groups with infeasible inversion, which is not known to exist. In 2007, Yi [31] firstly proposed a directed transitive signature scheme for a special case that the directed graph is a directed tree. The security of the scheme is based on a $\mathcal{RSA}$-related assumption and the security of an underlying standard signature scheme [5,14]. Later, Neven [25] presented a conceptually simple and generic construction of a transitive signature scheme for directed trees from any standard signature scheme. This result is more efficient than Yi's [31] scheme and does not rely on any $\mathcal{RSA}$-related assumptions. Recently, Camacho and Hevia [10] proposed a new practical transitive signature scheme for directed trees, which is the most efficient one to the date.

The concept of identity-based cryptography was firstly introduced in 1984 by Shamir [29] whose idea was that the user's public key can be derived from his/her recognized identity information (e.g. e-mail address and PAN number). Several practical identity-based signature schemes have been proposed since 1984 (see [4] for a thorough study of them), but a satisfying identity-based encryption scheme [7] only appeared in 2001. The first Identity-Based Signcryption (IBSC) scheme was proposed by Malone Lee [22] in 2002. They gave a model of security for such schemes and sketched the detail of how their scheme may be proved secure in this model. Since then, many IBSC schemes have been proposed in literature [3,9,12,21,23,26]. Their main objective is to reduce the computational complexity and to design more efficient IBSC schemes. However, most IBSC schemes were proven secure in the random oracle model.

The first IBSC scheme without random oracles was proposed by Yu et al. [32] in 2009. However, Jin et al. [17] and Zhang [33] proved that their scheme is not secure and gave improvement on their scheme. In [19], Li et al. showed that Jin et al.'s scheme [17] does not have the indistinguishability against adaptive chosen ciphertext attacks (IND-$CCA2$) and existential unforgeability against adaptive chosen messages attacks (EUF-CMA). In [20], Li and Takagi showed that Zhang's [33] scheme does not possess IND-$CCA2$ security and proposed an improved IBSC scheme. But the new scheme in [20] does not satisfy either IND-$CCA2$ property or EUF-CMA property as shown by Selvi et al. [27]. Recently, Selvi et al. [28] proposed the first provably secure IBSC scheme in the standard model with both IND-$CCA2$ and EUF-CMA properties. Kushwah and

Lal [18] also proposed a provably secure IBSC scheme without random oracles which has existential signature unforgeability.

1.2 Our Contributions

This paper, for the first time, introduces the notion of Identity-Based Transitive Signcryption (IBTSC) by integrating the notions of transitive signatures and Identity-Based Signcryption (IBSC). We present formal definitions and a concrete construction of IBTSC, with formal security proofs under the random oracle model. Our design not only preserves all desirable properties of transitive signatures but also prevents signature exposure, at a relatively low cost. With the functionality of signcryption, our IBTSC scheme provides both confidentiality and authenticity in a single logical step with significantly less cost than "signature-then-encryption" approach.

We first present some preliminaries required by this paper.

2 Preliminaries

2.1 Notations

Let $\mathbb{N} = \{1, 2, \ldots\}$ denote the set of positive integers. Let ε denote the empty string. If $i_1, \ldots, i_n \in \mathbb{N}$ then $L = i_1 \parallel \ldots \parallel i_n$ is the binary encoding of an ordered list of natural numbers such that $i_1, \ldots, i_n$ are efficiently and uniquely reconstructed from L. Let $x \xleftarrow{R} S$ denote that x is selected randomly from set S. Let $w := v$ denote the assignment of a value v to w.

We say that a function $f : \mathbb{N} \to \mathbb{R}$ is a negligible function if for any polynomial $p(\cdot)$ there exists $k_0 \in \mathbb{N}$ for all $k > k_0 : f(k) < 1/p(k)$. We say that an algorithm is a $\mathcal{PPT}$ algorithm if it is probabilistic and runs in polynomial time. If $\mathcal{A}$ is a $\mathcal{PPT}$ algorithm, then the notation $x \xleftarrow{R} \mathcal{A}(a_1, a_2, \ldots, a_n)$ denotes that x is assigned the outcome of running $\mathcal{A}$ on inputs $a_1, a_2, \ldots, a_n$.

2.2 Graphs

In this paper, we consider a directed graph $G = (V, E)$, whose transitive reduction is a directed tree, and work on its transitive closure. The transitive closure $\widetilde{G} = (\widetilde{V}, \widetilde{E})$ of a graph $G = (V, E)$ is defined to have $\widetilde{V} = V$ and to have an edge (i, j) in $\widetilde{E}$ if and only if there is a path from i to j in G. The transitive reduction $G^* = (V^*, E^*)$ of a graph $G = (V, E)$ is defined to have $V^* = V$ and to have the minimum subset of edges with the same transitive closure as G.

2.3 Bilinear Mapping and Complexity Problems

Let $\mathbb{G}_1$ and $\mathbb{G}_2$ be two cyclic groups of prime order p, and let g be a generator of $\mathbb{G}_1$. We say that a map $e \colon \mathbb{G}_1 \times \mathbb{G}_1 \to \mathbb{G}_2$ is an admissible bilinear mapping if it satisfies the following three properties: 1). Bilinear: $e(g^a, g^b) = e(g, g)^{ab}$ for all $a, b \in \mathbb{Z}_p^*$; 2). Non-degenerate: $e(g, g) \neq 1$; and 3). Computable: there is an efficient algorithm to compute $e(g^a, g^b)$ for all $a, b \in \mathbb{Z}_p^*$. Bilinear mappings, such as modified Weil [8] or Tate [13] pairings, can be obtained from certain elliptic curves. In a specific design, the group $\mathbb{G}_1$ is a subgroup of the group of points of an elliptic curve $\mathbb{E}/\mathbb{F}_p$. The group $\mathbb{G}_2$ is a subgroup of the multiplicative group of a finite field $\mathbb{F}_{p^2}^*$ [7].

- Computational Diffie-Hellman problem (CDH): Given $g, g^a, g^b \in \mathbb{G}_1$, where $a, b \xleftarrow{R} \mathbb{Z}_p$, compute $g^{ab} \in \mathbb{G}_1$.
- Bilinear Diffie-Hellman problem (BDH): Given $g, g^a, g^b\ g^c \in \mathbb{G}_1$, where $a, b, c \xleftarrow{R} \mathbb{Z}_p$, compute $e(g, g)^{abc} \in \mathbb{G}_2$.

3 Identity-Based Transitive Signcryption (IBTSC)

3.1 Formal Definitions of IBTSC

Similar to the schemes in [9,12] that use two-layer designs of signcryption model, our construction also use two-layer designs to replace monolithic signcryption. Two-layer designs of signature followed by encryption is readily adapted to provide multi-recipient encryption of the same message with a shared signature and a single bulk message encryption. In order to extract message/signature pair from any properly formed ciphertext using the recipient's private key, the monolithic unsigncryption is also divided into two-layer designs of decryption followed by verification. As stated in [9,12], the two-layer designs of signcryption model is as efficient as the monolithic signcryption model.

In our Identity-Based Transitive Signcryption (IBTSC) scheme, the signer needs to send encryption of the same edge/signature pair to multi-recipient, and the recipient needs to extract the corresponding edge/signature pair from the ciphertext. Thus, our Identity-Based (directed) Transitive Signcryption (IBTSC) scheme employs the two-layer designs of signcryption model, and consists of the following seven algorithms: IBTSC=(Setup, Extract, TSign, Encrypt, Decrypt, TVf, Comp).

- Setup: The *system parameters generation* algorithm takes as input 1^k where k is the security parameter, and outputs public parameters *params* and a master key *msk* for the system. That is: $(params, msk) \leftarrow \text{Setup}(1^k)$.
- Extract: The *key generation* algorithm takes as input the public parameters *params*, master key *msk* and an identity *ID*, and outputs a private key sk_{ID} corresponding to *ID*. That is: $sk_{ID} \leftarrow \text{Extract}(params, msk, ID)$.
- TSign: The *signing* algorithm takes as input the signer's identity ID_s, the private key sk_{ID_s} and nodes $i, j \in \mathbb{N}$, outputs an original signature σ_{ij} of edge (i, j) and some ephemeral state data r_i, r_j. That is: $(\sigma_{ij}, r_i, r_j) \leftarrow \text{TSign}(sk_{ID_s}, ID_s, i, j)$.

- Encrypt: The *encryption* algorithm takes as input the signer's private key sk_{ID_s}, the user's identity ID_u, nodes $i, j \in \mathbb{N}$, corresponding signature σ_{ij} and the ephemeral state data r_i, r_j, and outputs a ciphertext δ_{ij}. That is: $\delta_{ij} \leftarrow$ Encrypt($sk_{ID_s}, ID_u, i, j, \sigma_{ij}, r_i, r_j$).
- Decrypt: The *decryption* algorithm takes as input the user's private key sk_{ID_u} and ciphertext δ_{ij}, and outputs $(ID_s, i, j, \sigma_{ij})$. That is: $(ID_s, i, j, \sigma_{ij}) \leftarrow$ Decrypt(sk_{ID_u}, δ_{ij}).
- TVf: The *verification* algorithm takes as input the signer's identity ID_s, nodes $i, j \in \mathbb{N}$ and corresponding signature σ_{ij}, and outputs the verification result $d \in \{Acc, Rej\}$. That is: $\{Acc, Rej\} \leftarrow$ TVf(ID_s, i, j, σ_{ij}).
- Comp: The *composition* algorithm takes as input the signer's identity ID_s, nodes $i, j, k \in \mathbb{N}$ and corresponding signatures σ_{ij}, σ_{jk} , and outputs either a composed signature σ_{ik} of edge (i, k) or a symbol $\perp$ to indicate failure. That is: $\{\sigma_{ik}, \perp\} \leftarrow$ Comp($ID_s, \sigma_{ij}, \sigma_{jk}, i, j, k$).

Correctness. The above algorithms require the following correctness properties.

- Correctness of Decrypt: If $(\sigma_{ij}, r_i, r_j) \leftarrow$ TSign(sk_{ID_s}, ID_s, i, j), $\delta_{ij} \leftarrow$ Encrypt($sk_{ID_s}, ID_u, i, j, \sigma_{ij}, r_i, r_j$), and $(\widehat{ID_s}, \hat{i}, \hat{j}, \hat{\sigma}_{ij}) \leftarrow$ Decrypt(sk_{ID_u}, δ_{ij}), then we must have $\widehat{ID_s} = ID_s$, $(\hat{i}, \hat{j}) = (i, j)$ and $\hat{\sigma}_{ij} = \sigma_{ij}$.
- Correctness of TVf: If $(\sigma_{ij}, r_i, r_j) \leftarrow$ TSign(sk_{ID_s}, ID_s, i, j), then we must have TVf(ID_s, i, j, σ_{ij})=Acc.
- Correctness of Comp: Given two legitimate signatures (those obtained from the signer himself or through composition of legitimate signatures [6]) σ_{ij} of edge (i, j) and σ_{jk} of edge (j, k), then we must have TVf(ID_s, i, k, Comp($ID_s, \sigma_{ij}, \sigma_{jk}, i, j, k$))=$Acc$.

3.2   Security Models of IBTSC

Message Confidentiality. The notion of security with respect to confidentiality for public key encryption is indistinguishability of encryptions under adaptive chosen ciphertext attacks (*IND-CCA2*). For IBTSC this notion is defined by the following game played between a challenger $\mathcal{C}$ and an adversary $\mathcal{A}$.

- Setup: $\mathcal{C}$ runs this algorithm to obtain the master key msk and public parameters $params$, and sends $params$ to $\mathcal{A}$.
- Queries(phase 1): The adversary $\mathcal{A}$ makes the following queries adaptively.
  - Extract queries: $\mathcal{A}$ submits an identity ID to $\mathcal{C}$. In response, $\mathcal{C}$ computes the private key sk_{ID} corresponding to ID and returns to $\mathcal{A}$.
  - TSign/Encrypt queries: $\mathcal{A}$ submits a signer's identity ID_s, a user's identity ID_u and an edge (i, j) to $\mathcal{C}$. In response, $\mathcal{C}$ computes the signature σ_{ij} of edge (i, j) under the signer's private key sk_{ID_s}. $\mathcal{C}$ then computes the ciphertext δ_{ij} of edge/signature pair $((i, j), \sigma_{ij})$ under the user's identity ID_u, and returns the ciphertext δ_{ij} to $\mathcal{A}$.

- Decrypt/TVf queries: $\mathcal{A}$ submits a ciphertext δ_{ij}, a recipient's identity ID_u and the signer's identity ID_s to $\mathcal{C}$. In response, $\mathcal{C}$ decrypts the ciphertext δ_{ij} under the user's private key sk_{ID_u}. $\mathcal{C}$ then verifies whether the resulting decryption is a valid edge/signature pair $((i,j), \sigma_{ij})$ under the signer's identity ID_s. If so the challenger $\mathcal{C}$ returns edge/signature pair $((i,j), \sigma_{ij})$ and the signer's identity ID_s to $\mathcal{A}$.
- Challenge: At the end of phase 1, the adversary $\mathcal{A}$ submits two distinct edges (i_0, j_0) and (i_1, j_1), a signer's identity ID_s^* and a user's identity ID_u^* on which $\mathcal{A}$ wishes to be challenged. The adversary $\mathcal{A}$ must not have made an extract query on ID_u^*. The challenge $\mathcal{C}$ randomly chooses a bit $b \in \{0,1\}$. $\mathcal{C}$ signs (i_b, j_b) under the signer's private key $sk_{ID_s^*}$ and encrypts the result under the user's identity ID_u^* to produce the ciphertext δ^*. The challenge $\mathcal{C}$ returns the ciphertext δ^* to $\mathcal{A}$.
- Queries(phase 2): After receiving δ^*, the adversary $\mathcal{A}$ can query adaptively again as in phase 1. But it is not allowed to extract the private key corresponding to ID_u^* or make a Decrypt/TVf query on δ^* under ID_u^*.
- Guess: Eventually, $\mathcal{A}$ outputs a bit b' and wins the game if $b = b'$.

The advantage of an adversary to win the above game is defined as $\mathsf{Adv}_{\mathcal{A}, \mathrm{IBTSC}}^{IND\text{-}CCA2}(k) = |\Pr[b' = b] - 1/2|$.

Definition 1. *We say that a $\mathcal{PPT}$ adversary $\mathcal{A}$ can (t, ϵ)-break the confidentiality of* IBTSC *if $\mathcal{A}$ runs in time at most t, makes at most q_R queries to random oracle (if in the random oracle model), q_e* Extract *queries, q_s* TSign/Encrypt *queries , q_d* Decrypt/TVf *queries and $\mathsf{Adv}_{\mathcal{A}, \mathrm{IBTSC}}^{IND\text{-}CCA2}(k)$ is at least ϵ.*

Signature Unforgeability. The notion of security with respect to authenticity is existential unforgeability against adaptively chosen message attacks (*EUF-CMA*). For IBTSC this notion is defined by the following game played between challenger $\mathcal{C}$ and adversary $\mathcal{A}$.

- Setup: $\mathcal{C}$ runs this algorithm to obtain the master key msk and public parameters $params$, and returns $params$ to $\mathcal{A}$.
- Queries: $\mathcal{A}$ issues a polynomially bounded number of queries just like in the previous game.
- Forge: Finally, $\mathcal{A}$ outputs an edge/signature pair $((i^*, j^*), \sigma_{i^*j^*})$ with identities ID_u^* and ID_s^*. The adversary $\mathcal{A}$ wins the game if:
  1. $ID_s^* \neq ID_u^*$, $\mathsf{TVf}(ID_s^*, i^*, j^*, \sigma_{i^*j^*}) = Acc$.
  2. ID_s^* has never been submitted as one of the Extract queries.
  3. (i^*, j^*) is not on the transitive closure of the graph G formed by all $\mathcal{A}$'s TSign/Encrypt queries.

The success probability of an adversary to win the above game is denoted as $\mathsf{Succ}_{\mathcal{A}, \mathrm{IBTSC}}^{EUF\text{-}CMA}(k)$.

Definition 2. *We say that a $\mathcal{PPT}$ adversary $\mathcal{A}$ can (t, ϵ)-break the unforgeability of* IBTSC *if $\mathcal{A}$ runs in time at most t, makes at most q_R queries to random oracle (if in the random oracle model), q_e* Extract *queries, q_s* TSign/Encrypt *queries, q_d* Decrypt/TVf *queries and $\mathsf{Succ}_{\mathcal{A}, \mathrm{IBTSC}}^{EUF\text{-}CMA}(k)$ is at least ϵ.*

4   The Proposed IBTSC Scheme

In this section, we integrate Neven's [25] directed transitive signature scheme and Chen et al.'s [12] IBSC scheme, and obtain an Identity-Based Transitive Signcryption (IBTSC) scheme. The proposed IBTSC scheme is designed for a directed graph whose transitive reduction is a directed tree.

- Setup: Run this algorithm to obtain the public parameters $params$ and the master key msk.
  1. Choose two groups $\mathbb{G}_1$ and $\mathbb{G}_2$ of prime order p with an admissible pairing $e: \mathbb{G}_1 \times \mathbb{G}_1 \to \mathbb{G}_2$ and pick a generator g of $\mathbb{G}_1$.
  2. Choose the master key $x \xleftarrow{R} \mathbb{Z}_p^*$ and compute the master public key $y = g^x \in \mathbb{G}_1$.
  3. $H_0: \{0,1\}^{k_0} \to \mathbb{G}_1$, $H_1: \{0,1\}^{k_1+n} \to \mathbb{Z}_p^*$, $H_2: \mathbb{G}_2 \to \{0,1\}^{k_0+k_1+n}$ are three one-way and collision-resistant hash functions, where k_0, k_1, n denote the sizes of an identity, an element of $\mathbb{G}_1$ and a message, respectively.
  4. Publish the following public parameters $params :=(\mathbb{G}_1, \mathbb{G}_2, e, p, g, y, H_0, H_1, H_2)$, and keep the master key $msk :=x$ secretly.
- Extract: Run this algorithm to extract the private key for an identity ID. Compute $sk_{ID} = [H_0(ID)]^x \in \mathbb{G}_1$ as the private key of ID and distribute the private key to its owner via a secure channel.
- TSign: The algorithm maintains a state consisting of the root node r, the current tree $G = (V, E)$, and two tables $up[.]$ and $down[.]$. The signer modifies the current state according to the following cases:
  1. $V = \emptyset$: $r \leftarrow i; V \leftarrow V \cup \{i,j\}; E \leftarrow E \cup \{(i,j)\}; up[i] = down[i] = down[j] \leftarrow \varepsilon; up[j] \leftarrow i$.
  2. $i \in V$ and $j \notin V$: $V \leftarrow V \cup \{j\}; E \leftarrow E \cup \{(i,j)\}; up[j] \leftarrow up[i]\|i; down[j] \leftarrow \varepsilon$.
  3. $i \notin V$ and $j = r$: $r \leftarrow i; V \leftarrow V \cup \{i\}; E \leftarrow E \cup \{(i,j)\}; up[i] \leftarrow \varepsilon; down[i] \leftarrow j\|down[j]$.

  In all other cases the signer rejects because the query does not preserve the tree structure of the graph. Then the signer sets $M_i \leftarrow (i, down[i])$ and $M_j \leftarrow (j, up[j])$, and computes as follows:
  1. Choose $r_i, r_j \xleftarrow{R} \mathbb{Z}_p^*$ and compute $R_i \leftarrow [H_0(ID_s)]^{r_i}$, $R_j \leftarrow [H_0(ID_s)]^{r_j}$.
  2. Compute $h_i \leftarrow H_1(R_i\|M_i)$, $\sigma_i \leftarrow sk_{ID_s}^{(r_i+h_i)}$, $h_j \leftarrow H_1(R_j\|M_j)$ and $\sigma_j \leftarrow sk_{ID_s}^{(r_j+h_j)}$.
  3. Return the signature $\sigma_{ij} := (R_i, M_i, \sigma_i, R_j, M_j, \sigma_j)$ of edge (i,j) and send (σ_{ij}, r_i, r_j) to Encrypt.
- Encrypt: For the signer with identity ID_s to encrypt (M_i, M_j) using $(r_i, R_i, \sigma_i, r_j, R_j, \sigma_j)$ output by TSign for a user with identity ID_u.
  1. Compute $w_i \leftarrow e(sk_{ID_s}^{r_i}, H_0(ID_u))$ and $w_j \leftarrow e(sk_{ID_s}^{r_j}, H_0(ID_u))$.
  2. Compute $\delta_i \leftarrow H_2(w_i) \oplus (\sigma_i\|ID_s\|M_i)$, $\delta_j \leftarrow H_2(w_j) \oplus (\sigma_j\|ID_s\|M_j)$ and send the ciphertext $\delta_{ij} :=(R_i, \delta_i, R_j, \delta_j)$ of edge (i,j) to the user.
- Decrypt: For the user with identity ID_u to decrypt the ciphertext δ_{ij} using his private key sk_{ID_u}.

1. Compute $w_i \leftarrow e(R_i, sk_{ID_u})$, $\sigma_i \| ID_s \| M_i \leftarrow \delta_i \oplus H_2(w_i)$, $w_j \leftarrow e(R_j, sk_{ID_u})$ and $\sigma_j \| ID_s \| M_j \leftarrow \delta_j \oplus H_2(w_j)$.
2. Send the signature $\sigma_{ij} := (R_i, M_i, \sigma_i, R_j, M_j, \sigma_j)$ of edge (i, j) to TVf.

- TVf: For the user with identity ID_u to verify the signature σ_{ij} using the signer's identity ID_s.
  1. Compute $h_i \leftarrow H_1(R_i \| M_i)$ and $h_j \leftarrow H_1(R_j \| M_j)$.
  2. If $e(\sigma_i, g) \neq e(y, R_i \cdot [H_0(ID_s)]^{h_i})$ or $e(\sigma_j, g) \neq e(y, R_j \cdot [H_0(ID_s)]^{h_j})$ then return Rej.
  3. If j occurs in $down[i]$, i occurs in $up[j]$, or there exists a node that occurs in both $down[i]$ and $up[j]$, then return Acc; Otherwise, return Rej.

- Comp: Given two signatures σ_{ij} (for the edge (i, j)) and σ_{jk} (for the edge (j, k)), if $\text{TVf}(ID_s, \sigma_{ij}, i, j) = Rej$ or $\text{TVf}(ID_s, \sigma_{jk}, j, k) = Rej$ then return Rej. Otherwise, return $\sigma_{ik} := (R_i, M_i, \sigma_i, R_k, M_k, \sigma_k)$ as the composed signature (for the edge (i, k)).

Correctness. The above algorithms require the following correctness properties.

- Correctness of Decrypt :

$$w_i = e(R_i, sk_{ID_u}) = e([H_0(ID_s)]^{r_i}, [H_0(ID_u)]^x)$$
$$= e([H_0(ID_s)]^{xr_i}, H_0(ID_u))$$
$$= e(sk_{ID_s}^{r_i}, H_0(ID_u)).$$

$$\delta_i \oplus H_2(w_i) = H_2(w_i) \oplus (\sigma_i \| ID_s \| M_i) \oplus H_2(w_i) = \sigma_i \| ID_s \| M_i.$$

$$w_j = e(R_j, sk_{ID_u}) = e([H_0(ID_s)]^{r_j}, [H_0(ID_u)]^x)$$
$$= e([H_0(ID_s)]^{xr_j}, H_0(ID_u))$$
$$= e(sk_{ID_s}^{r_j}, H_0(ID_u)).$$

$$\delta_j \oplus H_2(w_j) = H_2(w_j) \oplus (\sigma_j \| ID_s \| M_j) \oplus H_2(w_j) = \sigma_j \| ID_s \| M_j.$$

- Correctness of TVf :

$$e(\sigma_i, g) = e(sk_{ID_s}^{(r_i + h_i)}, g) = e([H_0(ID_s)]^{x(r_i + h_i)}, g)$$
$$= e([H_0(ID_s)]^{(r_i + h_i)}, g^x)$$
$$= e([H_0(ID_s)]^{r_i} \cdot [H_0(ID_s)]^{h_i}, y)$$
$$= e(y, R_i \cdot [H_0(ID_s)]^{h_i}).$$

$$e(\sigma_j, g) = e(sk_{ID_s}^{(r_j + h_j)}, g) = e([H_0(ID_s)]^{x(r_j + h_j)}, g)$$
$$= e([H_0(ID_s)]^{(r_j + h_j)}, g^x)$$
$$= e([H_0(ID_s)]^{r_j} \cdot [H_0(ID_s)]^{h_j}, y)$$
$$= e(y, R_j \cdot [H_0(ID_s)]^{h_j}).$$

As presented in [25], let (r, t) be the first edge signature issued by the signer. Then one can see from the construction that all descendants j of r have the table entry $up[j]$ describing the path from r to j; all ancestors i of r have the table entry $down[i]$ describing the path from i to r; and all nodes j that are neither descendants nor ancestors of r have the table entry $up[j]$ describing the path from the closest common ancestor of r and j to j. To show the correctness of the TVf algorithm, we distinguish between the following cases. (Figure 1 gives a simple overview of all cases.)

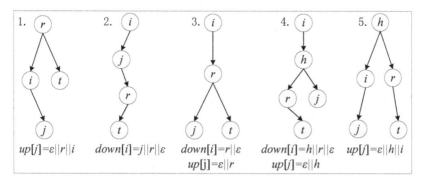

Fig. 1. There exists a path from i to j

1. Both i and j are descendants of r. In this case the node i occurs in $up[j]$ if there exists a path from i to j.
2. Both i and j are ancestors of r. In this case the node j occurs in $down[i]$ if there exists a path from i to j.
3. Node i is an ancestor of r and node j is a descendant of r. In this case the node r occurs in both $down[i]$ and $up[j]$.
4. Node i is an ancestor of r and node j is neither an ancestor nor a descendant of r. Let h be the closest common ancestor of r and j. If there is a path from i to j, then i is also an ancestor of h. In this case node h occurs in both $down[i]$ and $up[j]$.
5. Neither i nor j is an ancestor or a descendant of r. Let h be the closest common ancestor of r and i, and let h' be that of r and j. If there is a path from i to j, then it must hold that $h = h'$. In this case the node i is on the path from h to j, so i occurs in $up[j]$.

- Correctness of Comp : Let (r, t) be the first edge signature issued by the signer. To show the correctness of the Comp algorithm, we distinguish between the following cases (Figure 2 gives a simple overview of all cases). We note that if $\sigma_{ik} := (R_i, M_i, \sigma_i, R_k, M_k, \sigma_k)$, where $M_i = (i, down[i])$ and $M_k = (k, down[k])$, then $\mathsf{TVf}(ID_s,i,k,\mathsf{Comp}(ID_s, \sigma_{ij}, \sigma_{jk}, i, j, k))=Acc$.
  1. i, j and k are descendants of r. In this case the node i occurs in $up[k]$ if there exists a path from i to k.

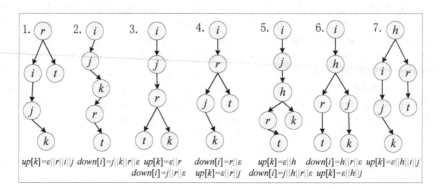

Fig. 2. There exists a path from i to k

2. i, j and k are ancestors of r. In this case the node k occurs in $down[i]$ if there exists a path from i to k.

3. i, j are ancestors of r and k is a descendant of r. In this case the node r occurs in both $down[i]$ and $up[k]$.

4. i is an ancestor of r and j, k are descendants of r. In this case the node r occurs in both $down[i]$ and $up[k]$.

5. i, j are ancestors of r and k is not an ancestor or a descendant of r. Let h be the closest common ancestor of r and k. If there is a path from i to k, then i is also an ancestor of h. In this case node h occurs in both $down[i]$ and $up[k]$.

6. i is an ancestor of r and j, k are not ancestors or descendants of r. Let h be the closest common ancestor of r and k. If there is a path from i to k, then i is also an ancestor of h. In this case node h occurs in both $down[i]$ and $up[k]$.

7. i, j and k are not ancestors or descendants of r. Let h be the closest common ancestor of r and i, and let h' be that of r and k. If there is a path from i to k, then it must hold that $h = h'$. In this case the node i is on the path from h to k, so i occurs in $up[k]$.

Efficiency. Note that the signing algorithm that our scheme uses is similar to the scheme proposed in [11]. Also, the encryption is done in a manner similar to the scheme from [7]. We compare the efficiency of IBTSC with that of the "sign-then-encrypt" method of [1] using the signature scheme of [11], denoted IBS, and the encryption scheme of [7], denoted IBE. In the comparison, the size of ciphertexts does not include the sender identity information.

As one can see from Table 1, IBTSC scheme can save four exponentiation operations in the generation and validation of ciphertexts. IBTSC ciphertexts are more compact than those produced using IBS and IBE.

Table 1. Comparison between IBTSC, IBS and IBE

Scheme	TSign/Encrypt	Decrypt/TVf	Size of ciphertexts
IBTSC	6 exp. in $\mathbb{G}_1$ 2 bp.	2 exp. in $\mathbb{G}_1$ 6 bp.	$(4k_1 + 2n)$ bits
IBS [11] and IBE [7]	6 exp. in $\mathbb{G}_1$ + 2 exp. in $\mathbb{G}_2$ 2 bp.	4 exp. in $\mathbb{G}_1$ 6 bp.	$(6k_1+4n)$ bits

"exp.": one exponentiation computation; "bp.": one bilinear pairing computation; "k_1": the size of an element of $\mathbb{G}_1$; "n": the size of the message.

5   Security Results

In this section, we only present the main security results of the proposed IBTSC scheme, and the detailed proofs are showed in the full version of this paper.

Theorem 1. (Message Confidentiality). *Assume that a $\mathcal{PPT}$ IND-CCA2 adversary $\mathcal{A}$ has an advantage ϵ against the proposed IBTSC scheme when running in time t, asking at most q_i queries to random oracles $H_i(i = 0, 1, 2)$, q_e Extract queries, q_s TSign/Encrypt queries and q_d Decrypt/TVf queries. Then there exists a $\mathcal{PPT}$ adversary $\mathcal{B}$ that can solve the BDH problem in $(\mathbb{G}_1, \mathbb{G}_2)$ with probability at least $\epsilon \cdot (1 - \frac{q_s(q_1+q_s)}{p}) \cdot \frac{1}{q_0 q_2}$.*

Theorem 2. (Signature Unforgeability). *Assume that a $\mathcal{PPT}$ EUF-CMA adversary $\mathcal{A}$ has an advantage ϵ against the proposed IBTSC scheme when running in time t, asking at most q_i queries to random oracles $H_i(i = 0, 1, 2)$, q_e Extract queries, q_s TSign/Encrypt queries and q_d Decrypt/TVf queries. Then there exists a $\mathcal{PPT}$ adversary $\mathcal{B}$ that can solve the CDH problem in $\mathbb{G}_1$ with probability at least $\epsilon \cdot (1 - \frac{q_s(q_1+q_s)}{p})^2 \cdot \frac{1}{4q_0^2(q_1+q_s)^2}$.*

6   Conclusion

In this paper, we introduced a new notion called Identity-Based Transitive Signcryption (IBTSC). The new notion integrates two existing primitives, transitive signatures and identity-based signcryption, in a more efficient way. We defined the security properties–confidentiality and unforgeability–of IBTSC and proposed a concrete design. Security analysis shows that the design satisfies the security requirements in the random oracle model.

Acknowledgement. The authors would like to thank the anonymous reviewers for their constructive comments. This work is supported by National Natural Science Foundation of China (61202450), Fok Ying Tung Education Foundation (141065), Ph.D. Programs Foundation of Ministry of Education of China (20123503120001), Distinguished Young Scholars Fund of Department of Education, Fujian Province, China (JA13062), Fujian Normal University Innovative Research Team (IRTL1207), Natural Science Foundation of Fujian Province

(2013J01222) and Department of Education, Fujian Province, A-Class Project (JA12076).

References

1. An, J.H., Dodis, Y., Rabin, T.: On the security of joint signature and encryption. In: Knudsen, L.R. (ed.) EUROCRYPT 2002. LNCS, vol. 2332, pp. 83–107. Springer, Heidelberg (2002)
2. Ateniese, G., Chou, D.H., de Medeiros, B., Tsudik, G.: Sanitizable signatures. In: De Capitani di Vimercati, S., Syverson, P.F., Gollmann, D. (eds.) ESORICS 2005. LNCS, vol. 3679, pp. 159–177. Springer, Heidelberg (2005)
3. Barreto, P.S.L.M., Libert, B., McCullagh, N., Quisquater, J.-J.: Efficient and provably-secure identity-based signatures and signcryption from bilinear maps. In: Roy, B. (ed.) ASIACRYPT 2005. LNCS, vol. 3788, pp. 515–532. Springer, Heidelberg (2005)
4. Bellare, M., Namprempre, C., Neven, G.: Security proofs for identity-based identification and signature schemes. In: Cachin, C., Camenisch, J. (eds.) EUROCRYPT 2004. LNCS, vol. 3027, pp. 268–286. Springer, Heidelberg (2004)
5. Bellare, M., Neven, G.: Transitive signatures based on factoring and RSA. In: Zheng, Y. (ed.) ASIACRYPT 2002. LNCS, vol. 2501, pp. 397–414. Springer, Heidelberg (2002)
6. Bellare, M., Neven, G.: Transitive signatures: New schemes and proofs. IEEE Transactions on Information Theory 51(6), 2133–2151 (2005)
7. Boneh, D., Franklin, M.: Identity-based encryption from the Weil pairing. In: Kilian, J. (ed.) CRYPTO 2001. LNCS, vol. 2139, pp. 213–229. Springer, Heidelberg (2001)
8. Boneh, D., Lynn, B., Shacham, H.: Short signatures from the Weil pairing. In: Boyd, C. (ed.) ASIACRYPT 2001. LNCS, vol. 2248, pp. 514–532. Springer, Heidelberg (2001)
9. Boyen, X.: Multipurpose identity-based signcryption (a swiss army knife for identity-based cryptography). In: Boneh, D. (ed.) CRYPTO 2003. LNCS, vol. 2729, pp. 383–399. Springer, Heidelberg (2003)
10. Camacho, P., Hevia, A.: Short transitive signatures for directed trees. In: Dunkelman, O. (ed.) CT-RSA 2012. LNCS, vol. 7178, pp. 35–50. Springer, Heidelberg (2012)
11. Cha, J.C., Cheon, J.H.: An identity-based signature from gap diffie-hellman groups. In: Desmedt, Y.G. (ed.) PKC 2003. LNCS, vol. 2567, pp. 18–30. Springer, Heidelberg (2003)
12. Chen, L., Malone-Lee, J.: Improved identity-based signcryption. In: Vaudenay, S. (ed.) PKC 2005. LNCS, vol. 3386, pp. 362–379. Springer, Heidelberg (2005)
13. Frey, G., Müller, M., Rück, H.G.: The Tate pairing and the discrete logarithm applied to elliptic curve cryptosystems. IEEE Transactions on Information Theory 45(5), 1717–1719 (1999)
14. Goldwasser, S., Micali, S., Rivest, R.L.: A digital signature scheme secure against adaptive chosen-message attacks. SIAM J. Comput. 17(2), 281–308 (1988)
15. Gong, Z., Huang, Z., Qiu, W., Chen, K.: Transitive signature scheme from LFSR. JISE. Journal of Information Science and Engineering 26(1), 131–143 (2010)
16. Hohenberger, S.: The cryptographic impact of groups with infeasible inversion. Master's Thesis. MIT (2003)

17. Jin, Z., Wen, Q., Du, H.: An improved semantically-secure identity-based signcryption scheme in the standard model. Computers & Electrical Engineering 36(3), 545–552 (2010)
18. Kushwah, P., Lal, S.: Provable secure identity based signcryption schemes without random oracles. IJNSA. International Journal of Network Security & Its Applications 4(3), 97–110 (2012)
19. Li, F., Liao, Y., Qin, Z.: Analysis of an identity-based signcryption scheme in the standard model. IEICE Transactions 94-A(1), 268–269 (2011)
20. Li, F., Takagi, T.: Secure identity-based signcryption in the standard model. Mathematical and Computer Modelling 57(11-12), 2685–2694 (2013)
21. Libert, B., Quisquater, J.J.: New identity based signcryption schemes from pairings. IACR Cryptology ePrint Archive 2003, 23 (2003)
22. Malone-Lee, J.: Identity-based signcryption. IACR Cryptology ePrint Archive 2002, 98 (2002)
23. McCullagh, N., Barreto, P.S.L.M.: Efficient and forward-secure identity-based signcryption. IACR Cryptology ePrint Archive 2004, 117 (2004)
24. Micali, S., Rivest, R.L.: Transitive signature schemes. In: Preneel, B. (ed.) CT-RSA 2002. LNCS, vol. 2271, pp. 236–243. Springer, Heidelberg (2002)
25. Neven, G.: A simple transitive signature scheme for directed trees. Theor. Comput. Sci. 396(1-3), 277–282 (2008)
26. Selvi, S.S.D., Sree Vivek, S., Pandu Rangan, C.: Identity based public verifiable signcryption scheme. In: Heng, S.-H., Kurosawa, K. (eds.) ProvSec 2010. LNCS, vol. 6402, pp. 244–260. Springer, Heidelberg (2010)
27. Selvi, S.S.D., Vivek, S.S., Vinayagamurthy, D., Rangan, C.P.: On the security of ID based signcryption schemes. IACR Cryptology ePrint Archive 2011, 664 (2011)
28. Selvi, S.S.D., Vivek, S.S., Vinayagamurthy, D., Rangan, C.P.: ID based signcryption scheme in standard model. In: Takagi, T., Wang, G., Qin, Z., Jiang, S., Yu, Y. (eds.) ProvSec 2012. LNCS, vol. 7496, pp. 35–52. Springer, Heidelberg (2012)
29. Shamir, A.: Identity-based cryptosystems and signature schemes. In: Blakely, G.R., Chaum, D. (eds.) CRYPTO 1984. LNCS, vol. 196, pp. 47–53. Springer, Heidelberg (1985)
30. Wang, L., Cao, Z., Zheng, S., Huang, X., Yang, Y.: Transitive signatures from braid groups. In: Srinathan, K., Rangan, C.P., Yung, M. (eds.) INDOCRYPT 2007. LNCS, vol. 4859, pp. 183–196. Springer, Heidelberg (2007)
31. Yi, X.: Directed transitive signature scheme. In: Abe, M. (ed.) CT-RSA 2007. LNCS, vol. 4377, pp. 129–144. Springer, Heidelberg (2007)
32. Yu, Y., Yang, B., Sun, Y., Zhu, S.: Identity based signcryption scheme without random oracles. Computer Standards & Interfaces 31(1), 56–62 (2009)
33. Zhang, B.: Cryptanalysis of an identity based signcryption scheme without random oracles. Journal of Computational Information Systems 6(6), 1923–1931 (2010)
34. Zheng, Y.: Digital signcryption or how to achieve cost (Signature & encryption) << cost(Signature) + cost(encryption). In: Kaliski Jr., B.S. (ed.) CRYPTO 1997. LNCS, vol. 1294, pp. 165–179. Springer, Heidelberg (1997)

GO-ABE:
Group-Oriented Attribute-Based Encryption

Mengting Li[1], Xinyi Huang[1,*], Joseph K. Liu[2], and Li Xu[1]

[1]Fujian Provincial Key Laboratory of Network Security and Cryptology,
School of Mathematics and Computer Science,
Fujian Normal University, Fuzhou 350007, China
{xyhuang,xuli}@fjnu.edu.cn
[2]Infocomm Security Department, Institute for Infocomm Research, Singapore
ksliu@i2r.a-star.edu.sg

Abstract. We introduce a new variant of attribute-based encryption called Group-Oriented Attribute-Based Encryption (GO-ABE for short). In a GO-ABE scheme, each user belongs to a specific group. Users from the same group can pool their attributes and private keys to "match" the decryption policy. That is, if the union of their attributes matches the policy, they can cooperate together to decrypt the ciphertext. But users from different groups cannot make it. We give a security model and an efficient construction of this new notion, with rigorous security and efficiency analysis.

Keywords: Attribute-based, encryption, group-oriented, privacy protection.

1 Introduction

The concept of Attribute-Based Encryption (ABE) was first introduced by Sahai and Waters [18]. In an ABE system, user secret keys and ciphertexts are labeled with sets of descriptive attributes. A user is allowed to decrypt the ciphertext only if there is a match between the attributes of the ciphertext and the secret key. The ABE of Sahai and Waters allows for decryption when at least d attributes overlapped between a ciphertext and a private key. For example, Alice encrypted a document to the attribute set $\{A, B, C\}$. Any user who has attributes that contains two of these attributes could decrypt the document. Therefore, Bob with attributes $\{A, B\}$ can decrypt this document.

One of the very important security requirements of ABE is collusion resistance. If multiple users collude they will not be able to combine their private keys in any useful way for decryption. In other words, if they merge their attributes (and the corresponding private keys), they still cannot decrypt the ciphertext which none of them is able to match the encryption policy individually. In existing designs of ABE, users must decrypt data individually by using their own attributes. Although this is the basic requirement of an ABE, sometimes it may not be preferable in the real life.

---

* Corresponding Author

M.H. Au et al. (Eds.): NSS 2014, LNCS 8792, pp. 260–270, 2014.
© Springer International Publishing Switzerland 2014

1.1   Group-Oriented Attribute-Based Encryption

Consider the following example. In a medical cloud system, the electronic record of patient, called the Personal Health Records (PHR) is stored in a centralized cloud system. This is to ensure different clinics and hospitals can share the same database of the patient. Attribute-based encryption is preferred as the security mechanism to ensure that only a user with a certain set of attributes can access the health information stored in the cloud.

Let us investigate the situation of the sharing of PHR in cloud computing using ABE: the framework proposed by Li et al. in [14] provides break-glass access to PHRs under emergence scenarios. In their framework, the access right of each PHR owner is also delegated to an emergency department (ED) and an emergency attribute is defined for break-glass access. When an emergency happens, the emergency staff needs to contact the ED to verify her identity and the emergency situation. Then the staff obtains temporary read keys for the access. After the emergency is over, the patient can revoke the emergent access via the ED.

Although this can prevent from abuse of break-glass option, the emergency response mechanism of this framework also has some deficiencies. We should consider the situation when we lose contact with the emergency staff or when the emergency staff is unable to contact the ED and cannot get verification of her identity. These situations may lead to a threat to patient safety. We do need a more flexible mechanism to handle with such situations.

Suppose a PHR owner Ashley has problems with her heart and stomach. She requires a cardiologist and a gastroenterologist to jointly diagnose her case in order to get a better treatment since it maybe a very serious disease. The attribute set of her attribute-based access is ("Cardiologist", "Gastroenterologist", 2). In the meanwhile, there is no individual doctor who is specialist in both cardiology and gastroenterology. If normal ABE is used, no one will satisfy this policy. When it is upon emergency, even if we deploy the framework proposed in [14], if no one successfully obtains the emergency key, the safety of patient is threatened. In the real life situation, there are usually two (or more) doctors to jointly diagnose some complicated and serious patients. Therefore it is reasonable to let one cardiologist and one gastroenterologist within the same group "g_1" (e.g. the same hospital) to jointly collaborate to decrypt this patient's health record in the cloud system.

With this in mind, we propose and define a variant of ABE called Group-Oriented Attribute-Based Encryption (GO-ABE). In this new notion, we divide users by groups. Only members from the same group can merge their decryption keys, but users from different groups cannot make it. It means that users from the same group are able to cooperate with each other to decrypt a ciphertext encrypted under a set of attributes α such that a single user may not have enough attributes to match the attribute set α. But users from different groups cannot collude.

1.2 Our Contributions

In this paper, we first propose the concept of GO-ABE. Compared with normal ABE, our solution provides more flexibility that users from the same group can pool their decryption keys together to decrypt a ciphertext encrypted under a set of attributes α which none of them are able to match α individually. We give a concrete construction of our concept. We also prove the security of our scheme under an adapted version of the Selective-Set model proposed in [5]. Moreover, our construction does not use random oracles. We reduce the security of our scheme to the Decisional Modified Bilinear Diffie-Hellman assumption that is similar to the Decisional Bilinear Diffie-Hellman assumption.

1.3 Related Work

Sahai and Waters [18] introduced the concept of Attribute-Based Encryption (ABE), and also presented a particular scheme called Fuzzy Identity-Based Encryption (FIBE). The FIBE scheme builds upon several ideas from Identity-Based Encryption (IBE)[3,6,19].

When a FIBE scheme uses the set-overlap distance, then this scheme is called a Threshold ABE scheme. In Sahai and Waters's original system, they presented a Threshold ABE system in which ciphertexts were associated with a set of attributes α and a user private key was associated with both a threshold parameter d and another set of attributes $\mathcal{A}$. A user would be able to decrypt a ciphertext if and only if at least d attributes overlap between α and $\mathcal{A}$. We also note that other works that dealing with Threshold ABE technique have been conducted[10,15,17,11,8].

In recent years, a number of ABE schemes have been proposed. Goyal, Pandey, Sahai, and Waters [9] clarified the concept of ABE into Key-Policy Attribute-Based Encryption (KP-ABE) and Ciphertext-Policy Attribute-Based Encryption (CP-ABE).

- KP-ABE (such as [1,21,22,14]). In KP-ABE, a ciphertext is associated with a set of attributes and a user private key is associated to a policy for decryption. Recently, key-policy ABE is applied to secure outsourced data in the cloud [21,22,14], where a data owner can encrypt her data and share with multiple authorized users, by distributing keys to them that contain attribute-based access privileges.
- CP-ABE (such as [2,7,12,16,20,13]), to the contrary, is a system where attributes are used to annotate the user private key and the policy over these attributes for decryption is attached to ciphertext. The concept of CP-ABE is closer to the traditional access control methods. The first CP-ABE scheme was given by Bethencourt et al. in 2007 [2]. Since that, CP-ABE is regarded as a promising concept for next-generation access control.

It seems that CP-ABE can be more useful for pratical applications than KP-ABE. The related notion is that of fuzzy identity-based encryption [18], which can be seen as a particular case of both key-policy and ciphertext-policy ABE.

The construction of our scheme is expressed as a CP-ABE scheme.

1.4   Organization

The remainder of this paper is organized as follows. Section 2 is devoted to the preliminaries required by this paper. Section 3 describes the definitions for GO-ABE. Section 4 is the detailed construction. The proof of its security is given in Section 5. In Section 6, we analyze the efficiency of the proposed GO-ABE scheme in terms of time complexity. We conclude this paper in Section 7.

2   Preliminaries

2.1   Group with Bilinear Pairings

We briefly review the facts about groups with efficiently computable bilinear pairings.

Let G_1, G_2 be cyclic (multiplicative) groups of prime order p. g is a generator of G_1. A bilinear pairing $e : G_1 \times G_1 \to G_2$ has the following properties:

- Bilinearity: $e(g^a, g^b) = e(g, g)^{ab}$ for any $a, b \in \mathbb{Z}_p^*$;
- Non-degeneracy: $e(g, g) \neq 1$;
- Computability: There is an efficient algorithm to compute $e(u, v)$ for any u and $v \in G_1$. The bilinear pairings, such as modified Weil or Tate pairings, can be obtained from certain elliptic curves [4].

2.2   Complexity Assumption

Definition 1. (Decisional Bilinear Diffie-Hellman (DBDH) Assumption) *Let a, b, c, $z \in \mathbb{Z}_p^*$ be chosen at random and g be a generator of G. The Decisional BDH assumption is that no polynomial-time adversary is able to distinguish the tuple $(A = g^a, B = g^b, C = g^c, Z = e(g, g)^{abc})$ from the tuple $(A = g^a, B = g^b, C = g^c, Z = e(g, g)^z)$ with more than a negligible advantage.*

Definition 2. (Decisional Modified Bilinear Diffie-Hellman (MBDH) Assumption) *Let $a, b, c, z \in \mathbb{Z}_p^*$ be chosen at random and g be a generator of G. The Decisional MBDH assumption is that no polynomial-time adversary is able to distinguish the tuple $(A = g^a, B = g^b, C = g^c, Z = e(g, g)^{\frac{ab}{c}})$ from the tuple $(A = g^a, B = g^b, C = g^c, Z = e(g, g)^z)$ with more than a negligible advantage.*

3   Formal Definitions of GO-ABE (Group-Oriented Attribute-Based Encryption)

In GO-ABE, we divide users into groups. Only members from the same group can merge their private key components, but users from different groups cannot make it. In other words, users from the same group are able to cooperate with each other to decrypt ciphertexts encrypted under a set of attributes α, but users from different groups cannot collude. The scheme is described as follows. Let $\mathbb{A}$ be the universe of possible attributes. And let $\mathbb{G}$ denote the collection of group identities: $\mathbb{G} = \{g_1, g_2, ..., g_N\}$. The definition given in this section is intended to capture the essence of a basic case of GO-ABE, i.e., GO-ABE with threshold access structures.

Definition 3. (GO-ABE) *A Group-Oriented Attribute-Based Encryption* (GO-ABE) *scheme is parameterized by a universe of possible attributes* $\mathbb{A}$, *a space of group identities* $\mathbb{G}$ *and message space* $\mathbb{M}$, *and consists of the following algorithms.*

1. Setup: This is a randomized algorithm that takes no input other than the implicit security parameter. It outputs the public parameters PK and a master key MK.

2. Encryption: On input a message $m \in \mathbb{M}$, the public parameters PK, and an attribute set α, outputs the ciphertext E.

$$E \leftarrow \mathsf{Encryption}(PK, m, \alpha).$$

3. Key Generation: On input an attribute set $\mathcal{A}$, a group identity $\mathbf{g}$, the master key MK, the public parameters PK and the threshold d, outputs a decryption key $D_{\mathcal{A}}^{\mathbf{g}}$.

$$D_{\mathcal{A}}^{\mathbf{g}} \leftarrow \mathsf{Key\ Generation}(\mathcal{A}, \mathbf{g}, MK, PK, d).$$

4. Decryption: On input the ciphertext E that was encrypted under a set α of attributes, the public parameters PK and a set of users (each with an attribute set $\mathcal{A}_i, i = 1, 2, ..., N$) from the same group $\mathbf{g}$, let $D_{\mathcal{A}_i}^{\mathbf{g}}$ be the private key of each user of attribute set $\mathcal{A}_i$. Note that the private key of each user is only known to its owner. The algorithm outputs the message m if $|\alpha \cap \mathcal{U}| \geq d$ (the threshold), where $\mathcal{U} = \mathcal{A}_1 \cup \mathcal{A}_2 \cup \cdots \cup \mathcal{A}_N$.

$$m \leftarrow \mathsf{Decryption}(E, \alpha, \mathcal{U}, D_{\mathcal{U}}^{\mathbf{g}}, PK).$$

Here, $D_{\mathcal{U}}^{\mathbf{g}} = \{D_{\mathcal{A}_1}^{\mathbf{g}}, D_{\mathcal{A}_2}^{\mathbf{g}}, \cdots, D_{\mathcal{A}_N}^{\mathbf{g}}\}$ is the set of private keys of cooperating users.

3.1   Selective-Set Model for GO-ABE

We define the ciphertext-indistinguishability of GO-ABE under chosen plaintext attacks in the selective-set model. The model is modified from the selective-set model of Fuzzy Identity-based Encryption given in [18].

Init: The adversary $\mathfrak{A}$ declares the set of attributes, α, that he wishes to be challenged upon.

Setup: The challenger runs the Setup algorithm of GO-ABE and sends the adversary the public parameters PK.

Phase 1: $\mathfrak{A}$ is allowed to query the private key $D_{\mathcal{A}}^{\mathbf{g}}$ for $(\mathcal{A}, \mathbf{g})$, i.e., any attribute set $\mathcal{A}$ in any group identifier $\mathbf{g}$.

et $\mathcal{U}_{\mathbf{g}_i} = \mathcal{A}_1^{\mathbf{g}_i} \cup \mathcal{A}_2^{\mathbf{g}_i} \cup \cdots \cup \mathcal{A}_j^{\mathbf{g}_i}$ denote the union of attribute sets with the same group identifier $\mathbf{g}_i$ that appeared in $\mathfrak{A}$'s queries. For any i, the requirement $|\mathcal{U}_{\mathbf{g}_i} \cap \alpha| < d$ must be satisfied.

Chanllenge: $\mathfrak{A}$ submits two equal length messages M_0 and M_1. The challenger flips a fair binary coin, b, and encrypts M_b with α. The ciphertext is passed to the adversary.

Phase 2: Phase 1 is repeated under the same condition as Phase 1.

Guess: $\mathfrak{A}$ outputs a guess b' of b.

The advantage of an adversary $\mathfrak{A}$ in this game is defined as $|\Pr[b' = b] - \frac{1}{2}|$.

Definition 4. *A GO-ABE scheme is secure in the selective-set model if all polynomial time adversaries have at most a negligible advantage in the Selective-Set game.*

4   Construction of GO-ABE Scheme

Recall that we wish to create an ABE scheme in which a ciphertext created using attribute set α can be decrypted only by users from the same group if the union of their attribute sets $\mathcal{U}$ satisfying $|\alpha \cap \mathcal{U}| \geq d$.

In our design, we use a group identity to label users from the same group such that users from the same group can merge their attributes to combine into the secret key, and users from different groups cannot make it.

As described previously, the basic idea of our construction is to add group identities to reflect this feature. Instead of building a new ABE scheme from scratch, we shall enhance an existing construction [18] by extending it with a group identity. When creating private keys, the authority associates a random $d-1$ degree polynomial, $q_{\mathbf{g}}(x)$, for each user from group $\mathbf{g}$, with the restriction that each polynomial has the same valuation at point 0. Below we give a description of our construction.

Let G_1 be a bilinear group of prime order p and g be a generator of G_1. In addition, let $e : G_1 \times G_1 \to G_2$ denote the bilinear pairing. A security parameter, κ, will determine the size of the groups.

We define the Lagrange coefficient $\Delta_{i,S}$ for $i \in \mathbb{Z}_p$ and a set, S, of elements in $\mathbb{Z}_p$:

$$\Delta_{i,S}(x) = \prod_{j \in S, j \neq i} \frac{x-j}{i-j}.$$

Let $\mathbb{A}$ be the universe of attributes. Users' attribute sets will be element subsets of $\mathbb{A}$.

– **Setup**: For simplicity, we can take the first $|\mathbb{A}|$ elements of $\mathbb{Z}_p^*$ to be the universe. Namely, the integers $1, \cdots, |\mathbb{A}| \pmod{p}$.

Then choose random $t_1, \cdots, t_{|\mathbb{A}|}$ uniformly from $\mathbb{Z}_p$. Finally choose random y uniformly from $\mathbb{Z}_p$. The published public parameters are:

$$PK = [T_1 = g^{t_1}, \cdots, T_{|\mathbb{A}|} = g^{t_{|\mathbb{A}|}}, Y = e(g,g)^y].$$

The master key is:

$$MK = [t_1, \cdots, t_{|\mathbb{A}|}, y].$$

- Encryption: We take G_2 to be the message space $\mathbb{M}$. To encrypt a message $m \in G_2$ under a set of attributes α, choose a random value $s \in \mathbb{Z}_p$. Then publish the ciphertext as:

$$E = (\alpha, E' = mY^s, \{E_i = T_i^s\}_{i \in \alpha}).$$

- Key Generation: To generate a private key for attribute set $\mathcal{A}$ from the group $\mathbf{g}$, randomly choose a $d-1$ polynomial $q_\mathbf{g}$, such that $q_\mathbf{g}(0) = y$.
  The private key consists of components, $(D_i)_{i \in \mathcal{A}}$, where $D_i = g^{\frac{q_\mathbf{g}(i)}{t_i}}$ for every $i \in \mathcal{A}$. That is :

$$D_\mathcal{A}^\mathbf{g} = \{D_i = g^{\frac{q_\mathbf{g}(i)}{t_i}} | i \in \mathcal{A}\}.$$

- Decryption: Given a ciphertext, E, encrypted with a key for attribute set α and a set of users (each with an attribute set $\mathcal{A}_i$) from the same group $\mathbf{g}$, where $| \alpha \cap \mathcal{U} | \geq d$, and $\mathcal{U} = \mathcal{A}_1 \cup \mathcal{A}_2 \cup \cdots \cup \mathcal{A}_N$. Let $D_{\mathcal{A}_i}^\mathbf{g}$ be the private key of each user in $\mathcal{U}$. Note that the private key of each user is only known to its owner.
  First, choose an arbitrary d-element subset, S, of $\alpha \cap \mathcal{U}$. Then each user uses his/her private key to compute and publish:

$$\mathbf{d}_i = e(D_i, E_i)^{\Delta_{i,S}(0)} \quad \text{for every } i \in S.$$

Finally, the ciphertext can be decrypted by computing the following:

$$E' / \prod_{i \in S} \mathbf{d}_i$$

$$= E' / \prod_{i \in S} (e(D_i, E_i))^{\Delta_{i,S}(0)}$$

$$= me(g,g)^{sy} / \prod_{i \in S} (e(g^{\frac{q_\mathbf{g}(i)}{t_i}}, g^{st_i}))^{\Delta_{i,S}(0)}$$

$$= me(g,g)^{sy} / \prod_{i \in S} (e(g,g)^{sq_\mathbf{g}(i)})^{\Delta_{i,S}(0)}$$

$$= me(g,g)^{sy} / e(g,g)^{s \sum_{i \in S} q_\mathbf{g}(i) \Delta_{i,S}(0)}$$

$$= me(g,g)^{sy} / e(g,g)^{sq_\mathbf{g}(0)}$$

$$= m.$$

5   Proof of Security

We prove that the security of our scheme in the Selective-Set model of GO-ABE reduces to the hardness of the Decisional MBDH assumption.

Theorem 1. *If an adversary can break our scheme in the Selective-Set model of* GO-ABE, *then a simulator can be constructed to solve the Decisional MBDH problem with a non-negligible advantage.*

Proof. Suppose there exists a polynomial-time adversary $\mathfrak{A}$ that can attack our scheme in the Selective-Set model of GO-ABE with an advantage ϵ. We can build a simulator $\mathcal{B}$ that can solve the Decisional MBDH problem with an advantage at least $\frac{\epsilon}{2}$.

As our scheme is only slightly different from that in [18], we can obtain the proof in a similar way, with the modification that the simulator needs to maintain a list of polynomials when replying private key queries (to ensure that users with the same group identifier will share the same polynomial). Other details of the proof are omitted here.

6   Complexity Analysis

In this section we analyze the efficiency of the proposed GO-ABE scheme in terms of time complexity.

6.1   Simulation Platform

We simulate the performance of GO-ABE to evaluate the running time of various basic operations based on the pairing-based cryptography (PBC) library (version $0.5.12$)[1]. The details of the platform we use are shown in Table 1.

Table 1. Simulation Platform

OS.	Ubuntu 10.10
CPU	Pentium(R) G640
Memory	3.33GB RAM
Hard disk	500G/5400rpm
Programming language	C

---

[1] http://crypto.stanford.edu/pbc/

6.2 Simulation Results

In a simple example with only three attributes $\{A, B, C\}$, the key policy is $(A, B, C, 2)$ in which the threshold $d = 2$. The running time for encrypting the message (random chosen in G_2) is 0.038643s, and the decryption requires 0.017258s. The total running time of the overall algorithms is 0.075061s.

In a more complex case with attribute set $\{A, B, C, D, E\}$ and the policy $(A, B, C, D, E, 4)$, the running time for producing the ciphertext is 0.059703s, and the decryption time is 0.037463s. The running time of other cases is summarized in Table 2 and Table 3.

Table 2. Threshold Policy

No.	Policy
P_1	$(A, B, C, 2)$
P_2	$(A, B, C, D, 3)$
P_3	$(A, B, C, D, E, 4)$
P_4	$(A, B, C, D, E, F, 4)$
P_5	$(A, B, C, D, E, F, G, H, I, 6)$
P_6	$(A, B, C, D, E, F, G, H, I, 8)$

Table 3. Time Cost of Encryption and Decryption

NO.	Encryption	Decryption	Total
P_1	0.038643s	0.017258s	0.075061s
P_2	0.043418s	0.029257s	0.104937s
P_3	0.059703s	0.037463s	0.131487s
P_4	0.061065s	0.038982s	0.137241s
P_5	0.088309s	0.065393s	0.207727s
P_6	0.087002s	0.078800s	0.246870s

The experimental results of "(P_2, P_3)" and "(P_5, P_6)" show that the running time increases with the increase of the threshold d. The threshold d is a more dominating factor than the number of attributes in determining the running time.

7 Conclusion and Future Work

We proposed a new notion called group-oriented attribute-based encryption scheme (GO-ABE), by introducing the concept of "group" to attribute-based encryption (ABE). In GO-ABE, each user belongs to a specific group. Users from the same group can cooperate with each other to decrypt a ciphertext if the union of their attributes satisfies the encryption policy. On the opposite side, users from different groups cannot collude. We also gave an efficient construction with threshold policy by extending Sahai-Waters scheme [18]. We simulated the performance of the proposed scheme and evaluated the running time of various basic operations. We leave the design of GO-ABE with more expressive policies as our future work.

Acknowledgement. The authors would like to thank the anonymous reviewers for their constructive comments. This work is supported by National Natural Science Foundation of China (61202450), Fok Ying Tung Education Foundation (141065), Ph.D. Programs Foundation of Ministry of Education of China (20123503120001), Distinguished Young Scholars Fund of Department of Education, Fujian Province, China (JA13062), Fujian Normal University Innovative Research Team (IRTL1207), Natural Science Foundation of Fujian Province (2013J01222) and Department of Education, Fujian Province, A-Class Project (JA12076).

References

1. Attrapadung, N., Libert, B., de Panafieu, E.: Expressive key-policy attribute-based encryption with constant-size ciphertexts. In: Catalano, D., Fazio, N., Gennaro, R., Nicolosi, A. (eds.) PKC 2011. LNCS, vol. 6571, pp. 90–108. Springer, Heidelberg (2011)
2. Bethencourt, J., Sahai, A., Waters, B.: Ciphertext-policy attribute-based encryption. In: IEEE Symposium on Security and Privacy, SP 2007, pp. 321–334. IEEE (2007)
3. Boneh, D., Franklin, M.: Identity-based encryption from the weil pairing. In: Kilian, J. (ed.) CRYPTO 2001. LNCS, vol. 2139, pp. 213–229. Springer, Heidelberg (2001)
4. Boneh, D., Lynn, B., Shacham, H.: Short signatures from the weil pairing. In: Boyd, C. (ed.) ASIACRYPT 2001. LNCS, vol. 2248, pp. 514–532. Springer, Heidelberg (2001)
5. Canetti, R., Halevi, S., Katz, J.: A forward-secure public-key encryption scheme. In: Biham, E. (ed.) EUROCRYPT 2003. LNCS, vol. 2656, pp. 255–271. Springer, Heidelberg (2003)
6. Cocks, C.: An identity based encryption scheme based on quadratic residues. In: Honary, B. (ed.) Cryptography and Coding 2001. LNCS, vol. 2260, pp. 360–363. Springer, Heidelberg (2001)
7. Emura, K., Miyaji, A., Nomura, A., Omote, K., Soshi, M.: A ciphertext-policy attribute-based encryption scheme with constant ciphertext length. In: Bao, F., Li, H., Wang, G. (eds.) ISPEC 2009. LNCS, vol. 5451, pp. 13–23. Springer, Heidelberg (2009)
8. Ge, A., Zhang, R., Chen, C., Ma, C., Zhang, Z.: Threshold ciphertext policy attribute-based encryption with constant size ciphertexts. In: Susilo, W., Mu, Y., Seberry, J. (eds.) ACISP 2012. LNCS, vol. 7372, pp. 336–349. Springer, Heidelberg (2012)
9. Goyal, V., Pandey, O., Sahai, A., Waters, B.: Attribute-based encryption for fine-grained access control of encrypted data. In: Proceedings of the 13th ACM Conference on Computer and Communications Security, pp. 89–98. ACM (2006)

270 M. Li et al.

10. Herranz, J., Laguillaumie, F., Ràfols, C.: Constant size ciphertexts in threshold attribute-based encryption. In: Nguyen, P.Q., Pointcheval, D. (eds.) PKC 2010. LNCS, vol. 6056, pp. 19–34. Springer, Heidelberg (2010)

11. Ibraimi, L., Petkovic, M., Nikova, S., Hartel, P., Jonker, W.: Ciphertext-policy attribute-based threshold decryption with flexible delegation and revocation of user attributes. Univeristy of Twente, Tech. Rep. (2009)

12. Lewko, A., Okamoto, T., Sahai, A., Takashima, K., Waters, B.: Fully secure functional encryption: Attribute-based encryption and (hierarchical) inner product encryption. In: Gilbert, H. (ed.) EUROCRYPT 2010. LNCS, vol. 6110, pp. 62–91. Springer, Heidelberg (2010)

13. Lewko, A., Waters, B.: Decentralizing attribute-based encryption. In: Paterson, K.G. (ed.) EUROCRYPT 2011. LNCS, vol. 6632, pp. 568–588. Springer, Heidelberg (2011)

14. Li, M., Yu, S., Zheng, Y., Ren, K., Lou, W.: Scalable and secure sharing of personal health records in cloud computing using attribute-based encryption. IEEE Transactions on Parallel and Distributed Systems 24(1), 131–143 (2013)

15. Lin, H., Cao, Z., Liang, X., Shao, J.: Secure threshold multi authority attribute based encryption without a central authority. Information Sciences 180(13), 2618–2632 (2010)

16. Liu, Z., Cao, Z.: On efficiently transferring the linear secret-sharing scheme matrix in ciphertext-policy attribute-based encryption. IACR Cryptology ePrint Archive 2010, 374 (2010)

17. Nali, D., Adams, C.M., Miri, A.: Using threshold attribute-based encryption for practical biometric-based access control. IJ Network Security 1(3), 173–182 (2005)

18. Sahai, A., Waters, B.: Fuzzy identity-based encryption. In: Cramer, R. (ed.) EUROCRYPT 2005. LNCS, vol. 3494, pp. 457–473. Springer, Heidelberg (2005)

19. Shamir, A.: Identity-based cryptosystems and signature schemes. In: Blakely, G.R., Chaum, D. (eds.) CRYPTO 1984. LNCS, vol. 196, pp. 47–53. Springer, Heidelberg (1985)

20. Waters, B.: Ciphertext-policy attribute-based encryption: An expressive, efficient, and provably secure realization. In: Catalano, D., Fazio, N., Gennaro, R., Nicolosi, A. (eds.) PKC 2011. LNCS, vol. 6571, pp. 53–70. Springer, Heidelberg (2011)

21. Yu, S., Wang, C., Ren, K., Lou, W.: Achieving secure, scalable, and fine-grained data access control in cloud computing. In: 2010 Proceedings of the IEEE INFOCOM, pp. 1–9. IEEE (2010)

22. Yu, S., Wang, C., Ren, K., Lou, W.: Attribute based data sharing with attribute revocation. In: Proceedings of the 5th ACM Symposium on Information, Computer and Communications Security, pp. 261–270. ACM (2010)

Jhanwar-Barua's Identity-Based Encryption Revisited

Ibrahim Elashry, Yi Mu, and Willy Susilo

Centre for Computer and Information Security Research,
School of Computer Science and Software Engineering,
University of Wollongong, Wollongong NSW 2522, Australia
ifeae231@uowmail.edu.au, {ymu,wsusilo}@uow.edu.au

Abstract. In FOCS'07, Boneh, Gentry and Hamburg presented an identity-based encryption (IBE) system (BasicIBE) based on the quadratic residuosity (QR) assumption. A BasicIBE encryption of an l-bit message has a short ciphertext of $\log_2 N + 2l$ bits where N is a Blum integer. However, it is not time-efficient due to solving $l+1$ equations in the form $Rx^2 + Sy^2 \equiv 1 \pmod{N}$. Jhanwar and Barua presented a variant of BasicIBE in which the encryptor only solves $2\sqrt{l}$ such equations. The decryptor decrypts the message without solving any such equations. In addition, the decryption key is decreased to only one element in $\mathbb{Z}_N$. However, the ciphertext size increases from a single element to $2\sqrt{l}$ elements in $\mathbb{Z}_N$. In this paper, we revisit the Jhanwar-Barua (JB) system and review its security. We prove that this system is not IND-ID-CPA secure and present a solution to the security flaw of this system. We also point out a flaw in the security proof of the JB system and propose two different security proofs for the fixed system. We prove that it has the same security as the original BasicIBE system.

Keywords: Identity-based Encryption, Quadratic Residuosity Assumption, IND-ID-CPA.

1 Introduction

In 1985, Shamir [1] presented the notion of identity-based encryption (IBE) in which the user's identity represents his public key and consequently, no public key certificate is required. Additionally, the construction of identity-based signature was proposed in the same work, but the construction of identity-based encryption (IBE) was left as an open research problem. The design of a provable secure IBE remained an open problem for sixteen years until Boneh and Franklin [2] proposed a provably secure IBE in the random oracle model based on bilinear maps. Subsequently, there has been a rapid development in IBE based on bilinear maps, such as [3,4,5,6]. The notion of identity-based cryptography is very important in the real world application where the necessity of having to verify the certificates is not a viable solution. In the literature, many such applications have been proposed to date. However, all the previously mentioned IBEs are

M.H. Au et al. (Eds.): NSS 2014, LNCS 8792, pp. 271–284, 2014.
© Springer International Publishing Switzerland 2014

based on pairing operations. According to MIRACL benchmarks, a 512-bit Tate pairing takes 20 ms while a 1024-bit prime modular exponentiation takes 8.80 ms. The pairing computations are expensive compared to normal operations. The costly pairing computation limits it from being used in wide application, specially when time and power consumptions are a major concern such as in limited wireless sensor networks. Hence, the seek for a scheme that does not rely on pairings is desirable. Another approach to design IBEs is based on the quadratic residuosity (QR) assumption. The first IBE based on this approach is due to Cocks [7]. This system is IND-ID-CPA secure in the random oracle model. It is time-efficient compared to pairing-based IBEs, but it produces a long ciphertext of two elements in $\mathbb{Z}_N$ for every bit in the message. The design of efficient IBEs without pairings was an open problem until Boneh, Gentry and Hamburg [8] presented two space-efficient systems (BasicIBE and AnonIBE) in which the ciphertext is reduced from $2l$ elements to only one element in $\mathbb{Z}_N$. As in Cocks' IBE, the security of BasicIBE is based on the QR assumption in the random oracle model. Although the concrete instantiation of BasicIBE is highly space-efficient, this comes at the cost of less time-efficient encryption/decryption algorithms. To encrypt an l-bit message, BasicIBE solves $l + 1$ equations in the form $Rx^2 + Sy^2 \equiv 1 \pmod{N}$ for known values of R, S and N [8]. Solving such an equation requires a 'solubility certificate' and obtaining these certificates requires the generation of primes [7,9,10]. The obtained certificates can be used to solve $Rx^2 + Sy^2 \equiv 1 \pmod{N}$ efficiently using the Cremona-Rusin algorithm [9]. The prime generation is a time-consuming process and it is the bottleneck in the BGH systems. Moreover, the decryption key is l elements in $\mathbb{Z}_N$ because the identity ID is hashed to a different value to encrypt each bit. AnonIBE is based on BasicIBE and it is Anon-IND-ID-CPA secure in the standard model under the interactive quadratic residuosity (IQR) assumption [8]. Moreover, the ciphertext length is reduced to one element in $\mathbb{Z}_N$ plus $l + 1$ bits.

Jhanwar and Barua [11] made some significant observations on the BGH systems (for solving equations in the form $Rx^2 + Sy^2 \equiv 1 \pmod{N}$) and proposed a trade-off system that reduces the private key length but increases the ciphertext length. They found that by knowing the value of $S \pmod{N}$, one can find a random solution to the equation $Rx^2 + Sy^2 \equiv 1 \pmod{N}$ using only one inversion in $\mathbb{Z}_N$. The sender solves only $2\sqrt{l}$ equations in the form $Rx^2 + Sy^2 \equiv 1 \pmod{N}$ using only $2\sqrt{l}$ inversions in $\mathbb{Z}_N$ and thus, no prime generation is required. This increases the encryption/decryption speed dramatically. The private key is only one element in $\mathbb{Z}_N$. However, this system produces a large ciphertext of $2\sqrt{l}$ elements in $\mathbb{Z}_N$. The most interesting part of Jhanwar and Barua [11] is its time- and power-efficiency. It avoids the expensive prime generation operations and replaces it with only one inversion in $\mathbb{Z}_N$. Moreover, there is no expensive-computational operations such as pairing or even modular exponentiation. We compare between the (JB) system and some other efficient IBE systems such as Boneh-Boyen IBE [5] and IBE systems with more powerful adversary such as Boneh, Raghunathan, Segev (BRS) IBE [12]. We also compare it to other pairing-free IBE such as Cock's IBE [7] and BGH IBEs [8]. In the table, the symbol m represents prime modular exponentiation while e and p represents pairing operation and prime generation respectively. l represents the message length. The simple x in the table represents a parameter in BRS IBE which is function of the security parameter, the length of the identity and a prime p [12]. The symbols G and G_T represents an element in two groups G and G_T such that $e : G \times G \to G_T$.

Table 1. Comparison between Various IBEs and the JB IBE

	Expensive Mathematical Operations	Ciphertext Length
Cock's	0	$2l(\log N)$
The BasicIBE	$(l+1)p$	$\log N + 2l$
The AnonIBE	$(2l+1)p$	$\log N + l + 1$
Jhanwar-Barua	0	$2\sqrt{l}\log N + 2l$
Boneh-Boyen	$e+3m$	G_T+2G
BRS	$m+(x)e$	$G+(x)G_T$

Our Contributions. We revisit the JB system, and identify some security issues with the system. We prove that an IND-ID-CPA adversary can attack this system and hence it is not IND-ID-CPA secure. The attack comes from mistakenly reusing the same y to encrypt multiple bits and hence, these bits are encrypted using the same key. We also present a solution to the security flaw of this system. We also point to a flaw of the security proof of the JB system and present two security proofs for the fixed system. We prove that it is as secure as the BasicIBE system. We note here that the fixed JB system is as efficient as the original system.

2 Definitions

2.1 IND-ID-CPA

The IND-ID-CPA security model of an IBE system is described as a game between an adversary $\mathcal{A}$ and a challenger $\mathcal{C}$ [1,2]. This game is as follows:

- Setup(λ): $\mathcal{C}$ generates the public parameters (PP) and sends them to $\mathcal{A}$ and keeps the master secret (MSK) to himself.
- Query Phase: In this phase, $\mathcal{A}$ sends private key queries to $\mathcal{C}$ for identities ID_s of his choice. These queries are adaptive based on previous queries.
- Challenge: Satisfied with private key queries, $\mathcal{A}$ sends to $\mathcal{C}$ two messages m_1 and m_2 for an identity ID^*. $\mathcal{C}$ tosses a coin $b \in [0,1]$ randomly and encrypts m_b using ID^*. Note that ID^* must not be queried in the query phase.
- Guess: $\mathcal{A}$ outputs $\bar{b} \in [0,1]$. $\mathcal{A}$ wins the game if $b = \bar{b}$.

The advantage of $\mathcal{A}$ to attack a system ξ and win this game is:

$$IBEAdv_{A,\xi}(\lambda) = |pr[\bar{b} = b] - \tfrac{1}{2}|.$$

If $\mathcal{A}$ submits two pairs of (ID_0, m_0) and (ID_1, m_1) in the challenge phase, then this game is called the ANON-IND-ID-CPA security model. The advantage of the adversary winning this game is the same as above.

2.2   QR Assumption and Jacobi Symbols

For a positive integer N, define the following set [8]:

$$J(N) = [a \in \mathbb{Z}_N : \left(\tfrac{a}{N}\right) = 1],$$

where $\left(\tfrac{a}{N}\right)$ is the Jacobi symbol of a w.r.t N. The Quadratic Residue set $QR(N)$ is defined as follows.

$$QR(N) = [a \in \mathbb{Z}_N : gcd(a, N) = 1 \wedge x^2 \equiv a \pmod{N} \text{ has a solution}].$$

Definition 1. *Quadratic Residuosity Assumption: Let RSAgen(λ) be a probabilistic polynomial time (PPT) algorithm. This algorithm generates two equal size primes p, q. The QR assumption holds for RSAgen if it cannot distinguish between the following two distributions for all PPT algorithms $\mathcal{A}$ [8].*

$$P_{QR}(\lambda) : (N, V)(p, q) \leftarrow RSAgen(\lambda), N = pq, V \in_R QR(N),$$
$$P_{NQR}(\lambda) : (N, V)(p, q) \leftarrow RSAgen(\lambda), N = pq, V \in_R J(N) \setminus QR(N).$$

In other words, the advantage of $\mathcal{A}$ against QR assumption $QRAdv_{A, RSAgen}(\lambda) =$

$$|\Pr[(N, V) \leftarrow P_{QR}(\lambda) : \mathcal{A}(N, V) = 1]| - |\Pr[(N, V) \leftarrow P_{NQR}(\lambda) : \mathcal{A}(N, V) = 1]|.$$

is negligible. i.e. $\mathcal{A}$ cannot distinguish between elements in $J(N) \setminus QR(N)$ and elements in $QR(N)$.

3   BasicIBE [8]

BasicIBE encrypts an l-bit message m using a square $S \equiv s^2 \pmod{N}$ where $s \in_R \mathbb{Z}_N$, the user's identity ID and a pair of Jacobi symbols for each bit. It first hashes ID to different values $H(ID, i) = u^a R_i = r_i^2$ where $a \in \{0, 1\}$, $u \in J(N) \setminus QR(N)$ and i is the bit index. Then it solves the equations $R_i x_i^2 + S y_i^2 \equiv 1 \pmod{N}$ and $u R_i \bar{x}_i^2 + S \bar{y}_i^2 \equiv 1 \pmod{N}$ to get $(x_i, y_i, \bar{x}_i, \bar{y}_i)$. The ciphertext is $(S, c, \bar{c})$ where $c \leftarrow [c_1, c_2, c_3, ..., c_l]$, $c_i = m \cdot \left(\frac{2 + 2y_i s}{N}\right)$ and $\bar{c} \leftarrow [\bar{c}_1, \bar{c}_2, \bar{c}_3, ..., \bar{c}_l]$, $\bar{c}_i = m \cdot \left(\frac{2 + 2\bar{y}_i s}{N}\right)$. To decrypt, one needs to know the square-root of R_i or $u R_i$. If $R_i = r_i^2$, the message is $m_i = c_i \cdot \left(\frac{1 + x_i r_i}{N}\right)$ and if $u R_i = r_i^2$, the message is $m_i = \bar{c}_i \cdot \left(\frac{1 + \bar{x}_i r_i}{N}\right)$.

3.1 BGH Product Formula

BasicIBE [8] has to solve $2l$ equations in the form $Rx^2 + Sy^2 \equiv 1 \pmod{N}$ to encrypt/decrypt a message m of length l by computing pairs (x_i, y_i), $(\bar{x}_i, \bar{y}_i) \in \mathbb{Z}_N^2$ such that:

$$R_i x_i^2 + S y_i^2 \equiv 1 \pmod{N} \quad and \quad u R_i \bar{x}_i^2 + S \bar{y}_i^2 \equiv 1 \pmod{N}. \tag{1}$$

Boneh, Gentry and Hamburg presented a product formula which only solves $l + 1$ equations to encrypt/decrypt a message [8].

Lemma 1. *For $i = 1, 2$ let (x_i, y_i) be a solution to $R_i x^2 + S y^2 \equiv 1 \pmod{N}$. Then (x_3, y_3) is a solution to*

$$R_1 R_2 x^2 + S y^2 \equiv 1 \pmod{N}, \tag{2}$$

where $x_3 = \frac{x_1 x_2}{S y_1 y_2 + 1}$ and $y_3 = \frac{y_1 + y_2}{S y_1 y_2 + 1}$.

During encryption/decryption, BasicIBE solves the following equations:

$$R_i x_i^2 + S y_i^2 \equiv 1 \pmod{N} \quad and \quad u x^2 + S y^2 \equiv 1 \pmod{N} \tag{3}$$

and then uses Lemma 1 to find solutions to $u R_i \bar{x}_i^2 + S \bar{y}_i^2 \equiv 1 \pmod{N}$.

4 The JB System [11]

4.1 JB Product Formula

Jhanwar and Barua [11] presented a variant of BasicIBE (the JB System). They used a variant of Lemma 1 to implement their system. This lemma states that:

Lemma 2. *For $i = 1, 2$ let (x_i, y_i) be a solution to $Rx^2 + S_i y^2 \equiv 1 \pmod{N}$. Then (x_3, y_3) is a solution to*

$$Rx^2 + S_1 S_2 y^2 \equiv 1 \pmod{N}, \tag{4}$$

where $x_3 = \frac{x_1 + x_2}{R x_1 x_2 + 1}$ and $y_3 = \frac{y_1 y_2}{R x_1 x_2 + 1}$.

4.2 The System Structure

The JB system is explained as follows.

- Setup(λ): Using RSAgen(λ), generate (p, q). Calculate the modulus $N \leftarrow pq$. Choose a random $u \in J(N) \setminus QR(N)$ and choose a hash function $H : ID \rightarrow J(N)$. The public parameters PP are $[N, u, H]$. The master secret MSK parameters are p, q and a secret key K for a pseudorandom function $F_K : ID \rightarrow \{0, 1, 2, 3\}$.
- KeyGen(MSK, ID): Calculate $R \leftarrow H(ID) \in J(N)$ and $w \leftarrow F_K(ID) \in \{0, 1, 2, 3\}$. Choose $a \in \{0, 1\}$ such that $u^a R \in QR(N)$. Let $[z_0, z_1, z_2, z_3]$ be the four square roots of $u^a R \in \mathbb{Z}_N$, then $r \leftarrow z_w$.

– Encryption(PP, ID, m): To encrypt a message $m \in \{-1, 1\}^l$ execute the following algorithm:

> $k \leftarrow \sqrt{l}$, $R \leftarrow H(ID) \in J(N)$
> **foreach** $i \in [1, l]$ **do**
>> **if** $i \leq k$ **then**
>>> $s_i \in_R \mathbb{Z}_N$, $s_i^2 \equiv S_i \pmod{N}$, $[x_i, y_i] \leftarrow Rx_i^2 + S_i y_i^2 \equiv 1 \pmod{N}$
>>> $[\overline{x}_i, \overline{y}_i] \leftarrow uR\overline{x}_i^2 + S_i \overline{y}_i^2 \equiv 1 \pmod{N}$
>>> $c_i \leftarrow m_i \cdot \left(\frac{2y_i s_i + 2}{N} \right)$, $\overline{c}_i \leftarrow m_i \cdot \left(\frac{2\overline{y}_i s_i + 2}{N} \right)$
>>
>> **else**
>>> $(j_1, j_2) \leftarrow i = k \cdot j_1 + j_2$, $y_{j_1, j_2} \leftarrow \frac{y_{j_1} y_{j_2}}{Rx_{j_1} x_{j_2} + 1}$, $\overline{y}_{j_1, j_2} \leftarrow \frac{\overline{y}_{j_1} \overline{y}_{j_2}}{uR\overline{x}_{j_1} \overline{x}_{j_2} + 1}$
>>> $c_i \leftarrow m_i \cdot \left(\frac{2y_{j_1, j_2} s_{j_1} s_{j_2} + 2}{N} \right)$, $\overline{c}_i \leftarrow m_i \cdot \left(\frac{2\overline{y}_{j_1, j_2} s_{j_1} s_{j_2} + 2}{N} \right)$
>>
>> **end**
>> $c \leftarrow [c_1, ..., c_l], \overline{c} \leftarrow [\overline{c}_1, ..., \overline{c}_l], x \leftarrow [x_1, ..., x_k]$ and $\overline{x} \leftarrow [\overline{x}_1, ..., \overline{x}_k]$
> **end**

The ciphertext is $C \leftarrow (c, \overline{c}, x, \overline{x})$

– Decrypt(C, r): To decrypt $C \leftarrow (c, \overline{c}, x, \overline{x})$, execute the following algorithm:

> **foreach** $i \in [1, l]$ **do**
>> **if** $r^2 = R$ **then**
>>> **if** $i > k$ **then**
>>>> $(j_1, j_2) \leftarrow i = k \cdot j_1 + j_2$, $x_i \leftarrow \frac{x_{j_1} + x_{j_2}}{Rx_{j_1} x_{j_2} + 1}$
>>>
>>> **end**
>>> $m_i \leftarrow c_i \cdot \left(\frac{x_i r + 1}{N} \right)$
>>
>> **end**
>> **if** $r_i^2 = uR$ **then**
>>> **if** $i > k$ **then**
>>>> $(j_1, j_2) \leftarrow i = k \cdot j_1 + j_2$, $\overline{x}_i \leftarrow \frac{\overline{x}_{j_1} + \overline{x}_{j_2}}{uR\overline{x}_{j_1} \overline{x}_{j_2} + 1}$
>>>
>>> **end**
>>> $m_i \leftarrow \overline{c}_i \cdot \left(\frac{\overline{x}_i r + 1}{N} \right)$
>>
>> **end**
> **end**

5   The Security Flaw of the JB System

The idea behind the JB system is based on a time-space trade-off of BasicIBE [8]. To decrease the number of $y, \overline{y}$ elements, the system solves only two sets of $k = \sqrt{l}$ equations. Each set is used to generate c and $\overline{c}$ respectively. A bit $m_{i < k}$ is encrypted with $y_i, \overline{y}_i$ while a bit $m_{i > k}$ is encrypted with $y_{j_1, j_2} \leftarrow (y_{j_1}, y_{j_2})$ where $i = k \cdot j_1 + j_2$. Assume that there are two bits $m_{i_1 > k}, m_{i_2 > k}$ where $i_1 = k \cdot j_1 + j_2$ and $i_2 = k \cdot j_2 + j_1$, then $x_{j_1, j_2} = x_{j_2, j_1} = \frac{x_{j_1} + x_{j_2}}{Rx_{j_1} x_{j_2} + 1}$ and $y_{j_1, j_2} = y_{j_2, j_1} = \frac{y_{j_1} y_{j_2}}{Rx_{j_1} x_{j_2} + 1}$. Consequently, bits i_1, i_2 are encrypted/decrypted using the same key. The same idea goes for $\overline{x}_{j_1, j_2}, \overline{y}_{j_1, j_2}$. Based on this security flaw, an IND-ID-CPA adversary can win an IND-ID-CPA game against this system as follows:

- An adversary $\mathcal{A}$ chooses $i_1, i_2 > k$ such that $i_1 = k \cdot j_1 + j_2$ and $i_2 = k \cdot j_2 + j_1$.
- In the challenge phase, $\mathcal{A}$ sends to the challenger $\mathcal{C}$ two messages $m, \overline{m}$. These messages are chosen at random with $m_{i_1} = m_{i_2}$ and $\overline{m}_{i_1} \neq \overline{m}_{i_2}$.
- In the guess phase, the adversary $\mathcal{A}$ checks the bits c_{i_1}, c_{i_2}. If $c_{i_1} = c_{i_2}$ then $b = 0$ and if $c_{i_1} \neq c_{i_2}$ then $b = 1$.

To overcome this security flaw, j_1 must not be equal to j_2 for all values of j_1 and j_2. i.e., $j_1 \neq j_2$ for all $[j_1, j_2] \in [1, k]$. This means that the number of k equations (i.e. the number of y elements) required for encrypting a message with length l is more than $\sqrt{l}$. Next, we deduce the relation between k and l in order to make the JB system IND-ID-CPA secure. Fig. 1 represents a message m as a table.

1	2	....	k	k (Total Bits)
(1,1)	(1,2)	....	(1, k)	k
~~(2,1)~~	(2,2)	....	(2, k)	k-1
~~(3,1)~~	~~(3,2)~~	....	(3, k)	k-2
.	.	.	.	.
.	.	.	.	.
~~(k,1)~~	~~(k,2)~~	~~.....~~	(k, k)	1

Fig. 1. The maximum number of l-bit encrypted by k elements of y_{j_1, j_2}

Each row is encrypted using k elements of y_i. The first row is encrypted by the first k elements of y_i. The second row is encrypted by the combination of y_1 and all values of $y_1, ..., y_k$. The third row is encrypted by the combination of y_2 and all values of $y_1, ..., y_k$ and so on. In the third row, the value $y_{2,1}$ is eliminated because it is equal to $y_{1,2}$. In the fourth row, the values of $y_{3,1}$ and $y_{3,2}$ are eliminated because they are equal to $y_{1,3}$ and $y_{2,3}$ respectively. Symmetrically, one can find the number of eliminated bits in each row until the last row, where only $y_{k,k}$ is used. The maximum number of bits that can be encrypted using k values of y is:

$$l \leq k + k + k - 1 + k - 2 + ... + 1 \leq \frac{k^2 + 3k}{2}. \tag{5}$$

For example, if the message length is 100 bits, then the minimum number of solved equations must be $200 \leq k^2 + 3k$, $k \geq 13$, which is larger than $\sqrt{l} = \sqrt{100} = 10$.

6 The JB System Security Proof

In this section, we first point out a flaw in the security proof presented in [11] for the JB system, then we present two rigorous security proofs for the fixed system. In the JB system security proof, the authors assumed that, if an adversary $\mathcal{A}$ guessed the first k Jacobi symbols on the form $\left(\frac{2y_{j_1}s_{j_1}+2}{N}\right)$ and $\left(\frac{2y_{j_2}s_{j_2}+2}{N}\right)$, he will be able to guess the distribution of the rest $l-k$ Jacobi symbols $\left(\frac{2y_{j_1,j_2}s_{j_1}s_{j_2}+2}{N}\right)$. That is obviously because $y_{j_1,j_2}s_{j_1}s_{j_2}$ depends on $y_{j_1}s_{j_1}$ and $y_{j_2}s_{j_2}$ and consequently, the JB security is reduced by a factor of $\frac{1}{2^k}$. We prove that this claim needs revision. In fact, we prove that guessing the Jacobi symbols $\left(\frac{2y_{j_1,j_2}s_{j_1}s_{j_2}+2}{N}\right)$ from $\left(\frac{2y_{j_1}s_{j_1}+2}{N}\right)$ and $\left(\frac{2y_{j_2}s_{j_2}+2}{N}\right)$ is as hard as guessing them from other independent Jacobi symbols $\left(\frac{2y_js_j+2}{N}\right)$ and $\left(\frac{2y_is_i+2}{N}\right)$. That is because Damgard [14] showed that the distribution of Jacobi symbols sequences is random. If an adversary knows $\left(\frac{a}{N}\right)$, it is a hard problem for him to find $\left(\frac{a+1}{N}\right)$ for an unknown value a. Although a and $a+1$ are highly related, the Jacobi symbols $\left(\frac{a}{N}\right)$ and $\left(\frac{a+1}{N}\right)$ look random and indistinguishable from the adversary point of view. Based on the above, we present the following Lemma.

Lemma 3. *The distribution of the last $l-k$ bits of the JB system encryption key in the form of $\left(\frac{2y_{j_1,j_2}s_{j_1}s_{j_2}+2}{N}\right)$ does not depend on the distribution of the first k bits in the form $\left(\frac{2y_{j_1}s_{j_1}+2}{N}\right)$ and $\left(\frac{2y_{j_2}s_{j_2}+2}{N}\right)$.*

Proof. Damgard proved that the following is a hard problem [14].

Theorem 1. *Let J be the Jacobi sequence modulo N with a starting point a and length $P(k)$, for a security parameter k and polynomial P. Given J, find $\left(\frac{a+P(k)+1}{N}\right)$.*

This means that, knowing $\left(\frac{a}{N}\right),\left(\frac{a+1}{N}\right),\left(\frac{a+2}{N}\right),....,\left(\frac{a+a_1}{N}\right),....,\left(\frac{a+a_2}{N}\right),....,$ $\left(\frac{a+P}{N}\right)$, it is a hard problem to find $\left(\frac{a+P+1}{N}\right)$.

We first choose a and P such that $a+P+1 = 2y_{j_1,j_2}s_{j_1}s_{j_2}+2$, then we can write the above sequence in two different forms:

$$\left(\frac{a}{N}\right),\left(\frac{a+1}{N}\right),\left(\frac{a+2}{N}\right),....,\left(\frac{2y_{j_1}s_{j_1}+2}{N}\right),....,\left(\frac{2y_{j_2}s_{j_2}+2}{N}\right),....,\left(\frac{a+P}{N}\right)$$

where $a_1 = 2y_{j_1}s_{j_1}+2-a$, $a_2 = 2y_{j_2}s_{j_2}+2-a$.

$$\left(\frac{a}{N}\right),\left(\frac{a+1}{N}\right),\left(\frac{a+2}{N}\right),....,\left(\frac{2y_js_j+2}{N}\right),....,\left(\frac{2y_is_i+2}{N}\right),....,\left(\frac{a+P}{N}\right)$$

where $a_1 = 2y_js_j+2-a$, $a_2 = 2y_is_i+2-a$.

Since $\mathbb{Z}_N$ is an additive group, the values of a_1, a_2 and P exist in both sequences for any value y or s. From the above equations, guessing the Jacobi symbol $\left(\frac{2y_i s_{j_1} s_{j_2} + 2}{N}\right)$ from $\left(\frac{2y_{j_1} s_{j_1} + 2}{N}\right)$ and $\left(\frac{2y_{j_2} s_{j_2} + 2}{N}\right)$ is as hard as guessing them from independent Jacobi symbols.   □

We note here that in the JB system, it is much harder to guess the Jacobi symbols $\left(\frac{2y_{j_1, j_2} s_{j_1} s_{j_2} + 2}{N}\right)$ than the Damgard problem because the only available Jacobi symbols in the whole sequence are $\left(\frac{2y_{j_1} s_{j_1} + 2}{N}\right)$ and $\left(\frac{2y_{j_2} s_{j_2} + 2}{N}\right)$.

We now present two different security proofs for the fixed JB system.

Theorem 2. *Suppose the QR assumption holds for RSAgen and F is a secure PRF. Then the proposed JB system is IND-ID-CPA secure based on the QR assumption when H is modelled as a random oracle. In particular, suppose $\mathcal{A}$ is an efficient IND-ID-CPA adversary, then there exist efficient algorithms B_1, B_2 whose running time is the same as that of $\mathcal{A}$ such that:*

$$IBEAdv_{\mathcal{A}, JB}(\lambda) \leq 2QRAdv_{B_2, RSAgen}(\lambda) + PRFAdv_{B_1, F}(\lambda).$$

To prove this theorem, we first introduce Lemma 4.

Lemma 4. *Let $N = pq$ be an RSA modulus, $S, R \in J(N)$. Then*

- *1-When $R \in J(N) \setminus QR(N)$, $S \in QR(N)$, the Jacobi symbols $\left(\frac{g(s)}{N}\right)$ for any function g are uniformly distributed in $\{\pm 1\}$, where s is a random variable uniformly chosen among the four square roots of S modulo N and $g(s)g(-s)R \in QR(N)$ for all the four values of s.*
- *2-When $S \in J(N) \setminus QR(N)$, $R \in QR(N)$, the Jacobi symbols $\left(\frac{f(r)}{N}\right)$ for any function f are uniformly distributed in $\{\pm 1\}$, where r is a random variable uniformly chosen among the four square roots of R modulo N and $f(r)f(-r)S \in QR(N)$ for all the four values of r.*
- *3-When $S, R \in QR(N)$, the Jacobi symbols $\left(\frac{g(s)}{N}\right)$ and $\left(\frac{f(r)}{N}\right)$ are constant, i.e. the same for all four values of r and s .*

Proof. Let $s, \bar{s}$ be the four square roots of $S \in QR(N)$ such that $\bar{s} = s \pmod{p}$ and $\bar{s} = -s \pmod{q}$, then the four square roots of S are $\{\pm\bar{s}, \pm s\}$. We can assume the same for $R \in QR(N)$ and the four square roots are $\{\pm\bar{r}, \pm r\}$, where $\bar{r} = r \pmod{p}$ and $\bar{r} = -r \pmod{q}$.

Case 1

$$\left(\frac{g(s)g(-s)R}{N}\right) = \left(\frac{g(s)g(-s)R}{p}\right) = \left(\frac{g(s)g(-s)R}{q}\right) = 1.$$

$$\left(\frac{R}{p}\right) = \left(\frac{R}{q}\right) = -1,$$

$$\left(\frac{g(s)g(-s)}{p}\right) = \left(\frac{g(s)g(-s)}{q}\right) = -1,$$

$$\left(\frac{g(s)}{p}\right) = -\left(\frac{g(-s)}{p}\right) \quad and \quad \left(\frac{g(s)}{q}\right) = -\left(\frac{g(-s)}{q}\right),$$

$$\left(\frac{g(s)}{N}\right) = \left(\frac{g(-s)}{N}\right).$$

$$\left(\frac{g(\bar{s})}{p}\right) = \left(\frac{g(s)}{p}\right).$$

$$\left(\frac{g(\bar{s})}{q}\right) = \left(\frac{g(-s)}{q}\right) = -\left(\frac{g(s)}{q}\right),$$

$$\left(\frac{g(\bar{s})}{p}\right)\left(\frac{g(\bar{s})}{q}\right) = -\left(\frac{g(s)}{p}\right)\left(\frac{g(s)}{q}\right),$$

$$\left(\frac{g(\bar{s})}{N}\right) = -\left(\frac{g(s)}{N}\right),$$

$$\left(\frac{g(\bar{s})}{N}\right) = \left(\frac{g(-\bar{s})}{N}\right) = -\left(\frac{g(s)}{N}\right) = -\left(\frac{g(-s)}{N}\right).$$

That means that among the four Jacobi symbols $\left(\frac{g(\bar{a})}{N}\right)$, $\left(\frac{g(-\bar{a})}{N}\right)$, $\left(\frac{g(a)}{N}\right)$, $\left(\frac{g(-a)}{N}\right)$ two are $+1$ and two are -1. Case 2 and Case 3 can be proven similarly to Case 1.

(*High Level Idea of the Proof*). Before presenting the formal proof, we first illustrate the idea of the proof as follows. The security proof is based on successfully proving that the distribution of the Jacobi symbols $\left(\frac{2y_i s_i+2}{N}\right)$, $\left(\frac{2\bar{y}_i s_i+2}{N}\right)$, $\left(\frac{x_i r+1}{N}\right)$ and $\left(\frac{\bar{x}_i r+1}{N}\right)$ are random in $\{\pm 1\}$ and thus, the ciphertext is indistinguishable from random. This is achieved by replacing the variables u, R, S in the equation $uRx_i^2 + Sy_i^2 = 1 \pmod{N}$ with other variables based on the QR problem such that one of Case 1 or Case 2 in Lemma 4 holds.

We define two sequences of games and let W_i represents the winning of the i_{th} game and $\overline{W}_i$ represents the winning of the $\bar{i}_{th}$ game by the adversary $\mathcal{A}$. Any of these sequences proves the security of the JB system. These games are defined as follows.

- **Game-0**. This game is the usual adversarial game.
- **Game-1**. This game replaces the PRF F with a truly random function.
- **Game-2**. This game explains how to simulate the hash function H.

- **Game-3**. This game sets $u \in QR(N)$.
- **Game-4**. This game explains how to respond to an encryption query from $\mathcal{A}$.
- **Game-$\overline{4}$**. This game explains how to respond to an encryption query using the *Decrypt* algorithm.
- **Game-5**. This game sets $R \in J(N) \setminus QR(N)$.
- **Game-$\overline{5}$**. This game sets $S_i \in J(N) \setminus QR(N)$.
- **Game-6** and **Game-$\overline{6}$** replace the message m with a random number z.

The detail of the proof is as follows.

- Game-0. This is the usual adversarial game for defining the IND-ID-CPA security of IBE protocols. The challenger picks the random oracle $H : ID \to J(N)$ at random from the set of all such functions in the *Setup* algorithm and allows $\mathcal{A}$ to query H at arbitrary points. Thus, we have

$$|\Pr[W_0] - \frac{1}{2}| = IBEAdv_{\mathcal{A},JB}(\lambda).$$

- Game-1. This is the same as Game-0, with the following change. In *Setup* algorithm, instead of using a PRF F to respond to $\mathcal{A}$'s private key queries, we use a truly random function $f : ID \to \{0,1,2,3\}$. If F is a secure PRF, $\mathcal{A}$ will not notice the difference between Game-0 and Game-1. In particular, there exists an algorithm B_1 (whose running time is about the same as that of $\mathcal{A}$) such that

$$|\Pr[W_1] - \Pr[W_0]| = PRFAdv_{B_1,F}(\lambda).$$

- Game-2. (N, u, H) are the public parameters PP given to $\mathcal{A}$ in the previous game where u is uniform in $J(N) \setminus QR(N)$ and the random oracle H is a random function $H : ID \to J(N)$. We make the following change in the random oracle H in this game. The challenger responds to a query to $H(ID)$ by picking $a \in_R \{0,1\}$ and $v \in_R \mathbb{Z}_N$ and setting $H(ID) = u^a v^2$. Thus the challenger implements a random function $H : ID \to J(N)$ as in the previous game. The challenger responds to a private key query as follows.
Suppose $R = H(ID) = u^a v^2$ for some $a \in_R \{0,1\}$ and $v \in_R \mathbb{Z}_N$. The challenger responds to a private key query for ID by setting either $R^{\frac{1}{2}} = v$ (when $a = 0$) or $uR^{\frac{1}{2}} = uv$ (when $a = 1$). Since v is uniform in $\mathbb{Z}_N$ this will produce a square root of R or uR which is also uniform among the four square roots, as in the previous game. Thus, $\mathcal{A}$'s views in Game-1 and Game-2 are identical and therefore,

$$|\Pr[W_1] = \Pr[W_2]|.$$

- Game-3. In this game, the challenger chooses u uniformly in $QR(N)$ instead of $J(N) \setminus QR(N)$. Since this is the only change between Game-2 and Game-3, $\mathcal{A}$ will not notice the difference assuming that the QR assumption holds for RSAgen. In particular, there exists an algorithm B_2 (whose running time is about the same as that of $\mathcal{A}$) such that:

$$|\Pr[W_3] - \Pr[W_2]| = QRAdv_{B_2,RSAgen}(\lambda).$$

- Game-4. We describe below in detail how, in this game, the challenger responds to an encryption query from $\mathcal{A}$.
  - He chooses $R \in QR(N)$ and sets $H(ID) = R$. (*)
  - He chooses $s \in_R \mathbb{Z}_N$ and computes $S_i = s_i^2$.
  - He sets $c \leftarrow Encrypt(PP, ID, m)$.
  - He sends (S, c) to $\mathcal{A}$.

  Since this game is the same as Game-3, thus:

  $$|\Pr[W_4] = \Pr[W_3]|.$$

- Game-$\overline{4}$. This game is the same as Game-3 except that the challenger handles encryption queries from $\mathcal{A}$ differently. To encrypt a message m for an identity ID the challenger does the following.
  - He chooses $R \in QR(N)$ and sets $H(ID) = R$.
  - He chooses $s \in_R \mathbb{Z}_N$ and computes $S_i = s_i^2$. (*)
  - He sets $c \leftarrow Decrypt(r, PP, (S, m))$.
  - He sends (S, c) to $\mathcal{A}$.

  It is easy to see that $c_i = m_i \cdot \left(\frac{1 + x_i r}{N}\right)$ is a unique encryption of m. Since this game is the same as Game-3, thus:

  $$|\Pr[\overline{W}_4] = \Pr[W_3]|.$$

- Game-5. In this game, we make a change in the challenge phase. We replace the line (*) in Game-4 with the following:
  - He chooses $R \in J(N) \setminus QR(N)$ and sets $H(ID) = R$.

  Since the only difference between Game-5 and Game-4 is that $R \in J(N) \setminus QR(N)$ in Game-5 instead of $R \in QR(N)$ in Game-4, $\mathcal{A}$ will not notice the difference assuming that the QR assumption holds for RSAgen. In particular, there exists an algorithm B_2 (whose running time is about the same as that of $\mathcal{A}$) such that:

  $$|\Pr[W_5] - \Pr[W_4]| = QRAdv_{B_2, RSAgen}(\lambda).$$

- Game-$\overline{5}$. This game is similar to Game-5. We replace the line (*) in Game-$\overline{4}$ with the following:
  - He chooses $s \in_R \mathbb{Z}_N$ and computes $S_i = -s_i^2$ for the first k bits and sets $S_i = -S_{j_1} S_{j_1} = -s_i^2 = -(s_{j_1} s_{j_1})^2, i = k \cdot j_1 + j_2$ for the last $l - k$ bits.

  Since $S_i = -s_i^2$, $S_i \in J(N) \setminus QR(N)$. The only difference between Game-$\overline{5}$ and Game-$\overline{4}$ is that $S_i \in J(N) \setminus QR(N)$ in Game-$\overline{5}$ instead of $S_i \in QR(N)$ in Game-$\overline{4}$ so $\mathcal{A}$ will not notice the difference assuming that the QR assumption holds for RSAgen. In particular, there exists an algorithm B_2 (whose running time is about the same as that of $\mathcal{A}$) such that:

  $$|\Pr[\overline{W}_5] - \Pr[\overline{W}_4]| = QRAdv_{B_2, RSAgen}(\lambda).$$

- Game-6: In this game, we replace the message $m^{(b)}$ by a random string $z \in_R \{-1, 1\}^l$ i.e., $c_i = z_i \cdot \left(\frac{2y_i s_i + 2}{N}\right)$ and $\overline{c}_i = z_i \cdot \left(\frac{2\overline{y}_i s_i + 2}{N}\right)$ where $y_i = y_{j_1, j_2}$ and $s_i = s_{j_1} s_{j_2}$, $i = k \cdot j_1 + j_2$ for the last $l - k$ bits. We first prove that $(2y_i s_i + 2)(-2y_i s_i + 2)R \in QR(N)$.

Proof. Let $g(s_i) = (2y_is_i + 2)$, then we have

$$g(s_i)g(-s_i)R = 4(y_is_i + 1)(-y_is_i + 1)R,$$
$$g(s_i)g(-s_i)R = 4(1 - (y_is_i)^2),$$
$$g(s_i)g(-s_i)R = 4(Rx_i^2)R = (2Rx_i)^2 \in QR(N).$$

Similarly, we can prove that $(2\overline{y}_is_i + 2)(-2\overline{y}_is_i + 2)uR \in QR(N)$.
Since $S_i \in QR(N)$, $R \in J(N) \setminus QR(N)$, $(2y_is_i + 2)(-2y_is_i + 2)R \in QR(N)$ and $(2\overline{y}_is_i + 2)(-2\overline{y}_is_i + 2)uR \in QR(N)$ and based on Lemma 3, Case 1 in lemma 4 can be applied and the distribution of the Jacobi symbols $\left(\frac{2y_is_i+2}{N}\right)$ and $\left(\frac{2\overline{y}_is_i+2}{N}\right)$ are random in $\{\pm 1\}$. Thus, $\mathcal{A}$ will not be able to distinguish between Game-5 and Game-6. i.e.

$$|\Pr[W_6] = \Pr[W_5]|.$$

- Game-$\overline{6}$: In this game, we replace the message $m^{(b)}$ by a random string $z \in_R \{-1,1\}^l$ i.e., $c_i = z_i \cdot \left(\frac{x_ir+1}{N}\right)$ and $\overline{c}_i = z_i \cdot \left(\frac{\overline{x}_ir+1}{N}\right)$. We first prove that $(xr + 1)(-xr + 1)S_i \in QR(N)$.

Proof. Let $f(r) = (xr + 1)$, then we have

$$f(r)f(-r)S_i = (x_ir + 1)(-x_ir + 1)S_i,$$
$$f(r)f(-r)S_i = (1 - (x_ir)^2) = 1 - x_i^2R,$$
$$f(r)f(-r)S_i = (S_iy_i^2)S_i = (S_iy_i)^2 \in QR(N).$$

Similarly, we can prove that $(\overline{x}_ir + 1)(-\overline{x}_ir + 1)S_i \in QR(N)$.
Since $R \in QR(N)$, $S_i \in J(N) \setminus QR(N)$, $(xr + 1)(-xr + 1)S_i \in QR(N)$ and $(\overline{x}_ir + 1)(-\overline{x}_ir + 1)S_i \in QR(N)$ and based on Lemma 3, Case 2 in lemma 4 can be applied and the distribution of the Jacobi symbols $\left(\frac{x_ir+1}{N}\right)$ and $\left(\frac{\overline{x}_ir+1}{N}\right)$ are random in $\{\pm 1\}$. Thus, $\mathcal{A}$ will not be able to distinguish between Game-$\overline{5}$ and Game-$\overline{6}$. i.e.

$$|\Pr[\overline{W}_6] = \Pr[\overline{W}_5]|.$$

- Clearly in Game-6 and Game-$\overline{6}$ we have

$$|\Pr[W_6] = \Pr[\overline{W}_6] = \frac{1}{2}|.$$

Combining all the previous equations proves theorem.

7   Conclusion

In this paper, we reviewed the security of the JB system. We showed that this system is not IND-ID-CPA secure. We also presented a solution to overcome this security flaw. We also pointed out a flaw of the security proof of the JB system and presented two security proofs that show that the fixed JB system is as secure as the original BasicIBE system.

References

1. Shamir, A.: Identity-based cryptosystems and signature schemes. In: Blakely, G.R., Chaum, D. (eds.) CRYPTO 1984. LNCS, vol. 196, pp. 47–53. Springer, Heidelberg (1985)
2. Boneh, D., Franklin, M.: Identity-based encryption from the Weil Pairing. In: Kilian, J. (ed.) CRYPTO 2001. LNCS, vol. 2139, pp. 213–229. Springer, Heidelberg (2001)
3. Gentry, C.: Practical Identity-Based Encryption Without Random Oracles. In: Vaudenay, S. (ed.) EUROCRYPT 2006. LNCS, vol. 4004, pp. 445–464. Springer, Heidelberg (2006)
4. Waters, B.: Efficient identity-based encryption without random oracles. In: Cramer, R. (ed.) EUROCRYPT 2005. LNCS, vol. 3494, pp. 114–127. Springer, Heidelberg (2005)
5. Boneh, D., Boyen, X.: Efficient Selective-ID Secure Identity-Based Encryption Without Random Oracles. In: Cachin, C., Camenisch, J. (eds.) EUROCRYPT 2004. LNCS, vol. 3027, pp. 223–238. Springer, Heidelberg (2004)
6. Boneh, D., Boyen, X.: Secure Identity Based Encryption Without Random Oracles. In: Franklin, M. (ed.) CRYPTO 2004. LNCS, vol. 3152, pp. 443–459. Springer, Heidelberg (2004)
7. Cocks, C.: An identity based encryption scheme based on quadratic residues. In: Honary, B. (ed.) Cryptography and Coding 2001. LNCS, vol. 2260, pp. 360–363. Springer, Heidelberg (2001)
8. Boneh, D., Gentry, C., Hamburg, M.: Space-Efficient Identity Based Encryption Without Pairings. In: Proceedings of the 48th Annual IEEE Symposium on Foundations of Computer Science, FOCS 2007, pp. 647–657. IEEE Computer Society (2007)
9. Cremona, J.E., Rusin, D.: Efficient solution of rational conics. Math. Comput. 72, 1417–1441 (2003)
10. Cohen, H.: A course in computational algebraic number theory. Springer-Verlag New York, Inc., New York (1993)
11. Jhanwar, M., Barua, R.: A Variant of Boneh-Gentry-Hamburg's Pairing-Free Identity Based Encryption Scheme. In: Yung, M., Liu, P., Lin, D. (eds.) Inscrypt 2008. LNCS, vol. 5487, pp. 314–331. Springer, Heidelberg (2009)
12. Boneh, D., Raghunathan, A., Segev, G.: Function-private identity-based encryption: Hiding the function in functional encryption. In: Canetti, R., Garay, J.A. (eds.) CRYPTO 2013, Part II. LNCS, vol. 8043, pp. 461–478. Springer, Heidelberg (2013)
13. Barua, R., Jhanwar, M.: On the number of solutions of the equation $Rx^2 + Sy^2 = 1 \bmod N$. Sankhya A - Mathematical Statistics and Probability 72, 226–236 (2010), 10.1007/s13171-010-0010-9
14. Damgård, I.B.: On the Randomness of Legendre and Jacobi Sequences. In: Goldwasser, S. (ed.) CRYPTO 1988. LNCS, vol. 403, pp. 163–172. Springer, Heidelberg (1990)

Lightweight Universally Composable Adaptive Oblivious Transfer

Vandana Guleria and Ratna Dutta

Department of Mathematics
Indian Institute of Technology Kharagpur
Kharagpur-721302, India
vandana.math@gmail.com, ratna@maths.iitkgp.ernet.in

Abstract. We propose an efficient universally composable (UC) adaptive k-out-of-N oblivious transfer ($\mathsf{OT}^N_{k\times 1}$) protocol over composite order bilinear group employing Groth-Sahai proofs, Boneh-Boyen signature and Bresson, Catalano and Pointcheval (BCP) encryption. Our scheme is proven to be UC secure in the presence of malicious adversary in static corruption model under decision Diffie-Hellman (DDH), subgroup decision (SD) and l-strong Diffie-Hellman (SDH) assumption. The proposed protocol is lightweight in the sense that it is storage-efficient with low communication and computation overheads as compared to the existing UC secure similar schemes.

Keywords: Oblivious transfer, universally composable security, Groth-Sahai proofs.

1 Introduction

Adaptive oblivious transfer (OT) protocol is an extensively used primitive in oblivious search of large database where a sender S does not want to reveal the entire database to a receiver R. For instance, it has been extensively used in many cryptographic applications including fair exchange in e-commerce and secure multi-party computation. In *1-out-of-2 oblivious transfer* (OT^2_1) protocol, a sender S having 2 messages m_0, m_1 interacts with a receiver R holding input $\sigma \in \{0, 1\}$ in such a way that the receiver R learns m_σ and remains oblivious to other message $m_{1-\sigma}$ while σ does not get revealed to the sender S. The OT^2_1 has been generalized to *1-out-of-N oblivious transfer* (OT^N_1) [19] which enables the receiver R to learn 1-out-of-N messages $m_1, m_2, \ldots, m_N$, hold by the sender S and remains oblivious to the other $N - 1$ messages. The OT^N_1 is further extended to *non-adaptive k-out-of-N oblivious transfer* (OT^N_k) [15] and *adaptive k-out-of-N oblivious transfer* ($\mathsf{OT}^N_{k\times 1}$) [9], [16]. In OT^N_k, the receiver R learns simultaneously all the k messages $m_{\sigma_1}, m_{\sigma_2}, \ldots, m_{\sigma_k}, \sigma_j \in \{1, 2, \ldots, N\}, j = 1, 2, \ldots, k$, whereas in $\mathsf{OT}^N_{k\times 1}$ protocol, the receiver R may learn $m_{\sigma_{i-1}}$ before deciding on σ_i. The $\mathsf{OT}^N_{k\times 1}$ consists of one *initialization phase* in which the sender S encrypts the messages $m_1, m_2, \ldots, m_N$, and k *transfer phases* in each

M.H. Au et al. (Eds.): NSS 2014, LNCS 8792, pp. 285–298, 2014.

of which the receiver R interacts with the sender S and recovers one of the k messages $m_{\sigma_1}, m_{\sigma_2}, \ldots, m_{\sigma_k}, \sigma_j \in \{1, 2, \ldots, N\}, j = 1, 2, \ldots, k$, of its choice.

Rabin [21] introduced the oblivious transfer protocol following which a wide variety of OT protocols [9], [19] have been designed. The security of the OT protocols [9], [19], [21] are in simulation-based-model where the simulator uses adversarial rewinding that allows the simulator to rewind the adversary's state to previous computation state and start the computation from there. Although the aforementioned OT protocols satisfy both the sender's security and the receiver's security, they become insecure under concurrent execution when composed with arbitrary protocols. To address this, Canetti and Fischlin [12] introduced ideal functionality for OT protocol in *universal composable* (UC) framework [11]. The UC secure [12] OT protocols can be securely composed with arbitrary protocols even under concurrent execution without employing adversarial rewinding. The first efficient, UC secure OT_1^2 protocols have been proposed by Peikert *et al.* [20]. Green and Hohenberger [16] introduced the adaptive UC secure $OT_{k \times 1}^N$ proto-col. Later, Rial *et al.* [22] designed an efficient UC secure priced $OT_{k \times 1}^N$ protocol. Zhang *et al.* [24] constructed an identity based $OT_{k \times 1}^N$ protocol in composite or-der bilinear group. However, the security analysis is not in UC framework and uses random oracles in semi honest corruption model where parties can not de-viate from the protocol specification. Composite order bilinear pairing has been shown to be very useful in many cryptographic protocols and has several advan-tages over prime order. Recently, Seo [23] pointed that projection property could not be defined in bilinear pairing of prime order. Projecting bilinear pairings are used for designing cryptosystems. Initially, finding composite order bilinear pair-ing has become the bottleneck, but with the construction proposed by Zhang [25], Freeman [14] and Boneh *et al.* [6] computing bilinear pairing of composite order is comparable to that of prime order. Designing efficient, UC secure $OT_{k \times 1}^N$ protocol is not a trivial task. In this paper, we construct a UC secure $OT_{k \times 1}^N$ protocol in composite order bilinear groups inspired by the work of [16], [22] and [24]. We employ Boneh and Boyen (BB) [3] signature together with a particular case of Bresson, Catalano and Pointcheval (BCP) [7] encryption. Besides, we use subgroup decision (SD) based Groth-Sahai proofs [17] to withstand attacks against malicious adversaries.

In initialization phase, the sender encrypts each message using BCP encryp-tion and BB signature to generate ciphertext database, whereas in each of k transfer phases, the receiver recovers a message of its choice. The BB signature checks malicious behavior of the receiver. Transfer phase occurs when the re-ceiver convinces the sender by non-interactive zero knowledge (NIZK) proof [17] that the ciphertext the receiver has blinded corresponds to an actual ciphertext database published by the sender in initialization phase. To control the mali-cious behavior of the sender, the sender provides the receiver non-interactive witness indistinguishability (NIWI) [17] proof that the secret used by the sender in transfer phase for the blinded ciphertext is the same as the secret used in generating ciphertext database.

We provide a concrete security analysis of our OT protocol in UC framework assuming the hardness of DDH over composite order group, SD and l-Strong Diffie-Hellman (l-SDH) problems. Our security model addresses the malicious adversary which can deviate from its protocol specification. The corruption model is static in which adversary pre-decides the corrupted parties before the execution of the protocol. Throughout the protocol execution, corrupted parties remain corrupted and honest parties remain honest in static corruption model.

We emphasize that our protocol is more efficient in terms of computation cost and communication overheads as compared to [16], [22] which are, to the best of our knowledge, the only existing UC secure adaptive oblivious transfer protocols with the same security levels as ours. As pairing and exponentiation operations are the most expensive operations as compared to addition and multiplication operations, the proposed protocol uses less number of pairing and exponentiation operations than [16] and [22].

2   Background

Notations: Throughout, we use ρ as the security parameter, $x \xleftarrow{\$} A$ means sample an element x uniformly at random from the set A, $y \leftarrow B$ indicates y is the output of algorithm B, $\mathbb{N}$ denotes the set of natural numbers and $X \stackrel{c}{\approx} Y$ indicates X is computationally indistinguishable from Y. A function $f(n)$ is *negligible* if $f = o(n^{-c})$ for every fixed positive constant c.

2.1   Bilinear Pairing and Complexity Assumptions

Definition 1. *(Bilinear Pairing) Let $\mathbb{G}_1, \mathbb{G}_2$ and $\mathbb{G}_T$ be three multiplicative cyclic groups of composite order $n = pq$ which is a product of two primes. The map $e : \mathbb{G}_1 \times \mathbb{G}_2 \to \mathbb{G}_T$ is bilinear if it satisfies the following conditions:*
(i) Bilinear $- e(x^a, y^b) = e(x,y)^{ab} \ \forall \ x \in \mathbb{G}_1, y \in \mathbb{G}_2, a, b \in \mathbb{Z}_n^*$.
(ii) Non-Degenerate $- e(x, y)$ generates $\mathbb{G}_T, \ \forall \ x \in \mathbb{G}_1, y \in \mathbb{G}_2, x \neq 1, y \neq 1$.
(iii) Computable $-$ The pairing $e(x, y)$ is computable efficiently $\forall \ x \in \mathbb{G}_1, y \in \mathbb{G}_2$.

If $\mathbb{G}_1 = \mathbb{G}_2$, then e is *symmetric* bilinear pairing. Otherwise, e is *asymmetric* bilinear pairing. Throughout the paper, we use symmetric bilinear pairing.

Definition 2. *(Decisional Diffie-Hellman (DDH) assumption [7] over a group of composite order) Let $\mathbb{G}$ be a multiplicative cyclic group of composite order $n = pq$ with a generator g. The DDH assumption in $\mathbb{G}$ states that given $g^x, g^y, z_0 = g^{xy}$ and $z_1 = g^t$, $x, y, t \xleftarrow{\$} \mathbb{Z}_n$, it is hard to distinguish z_0 from z_1.*

Definition 3. *(l-Strong Diffie-Hellman (SDH) assumption in $\mathbb{G}_p$ [3], [13]) Let $\mathbb{G}$ be a group of order $n = pq$ with a generator g and $\mathbb{G}_p$ be its subgroup of prime order p. The l-SDH assumption in $\mathbb{G}_p$ states that given $(l+1)$-tuple $(g, g^q, g^{qx^2}, \ldots, g^{qx^l})$, $x \in \mathbb{Z}_p^*$ as input it is hard to output a pair $(c, g^{\frac{q}{x+c}}), c \in \mathbb{Z}_p$.*

The l-SDH assumption is proven to be true in generic group model [3].

Definition 4. *(Subgroup Decision (SD) assumption [5]) Let $\mathbb{G}$ be a group of order $n = pq$ with a generator g and $\mathbb{G}_q$ be its subgroup of prime order q. The subgroup decision assumption states that given $h \in \mathbb{G}$ as input, it is hard to decide whether h is random generator of $\mathbb{G}$ or $\mathbb{G}_q$.*

2.2 Groth-Sahai Proofs [17]

Groth and Sahai [17] show how to construct non-interactive zero-knowledge (NIZK) proofs and non-interactive witness indistinguishable (NIWI) proofs under the SD assumption which are used in our protocol construction. Let us first briefly explore Groth-Sahai commitments. We use algorithm BilinearSetup to generate bilinear pairing.

BilinearSetup is an algorithm which on input security parameter ρ generates two large primes p, q of length ϱ. It generates a cyclic group $\mathbb{G}$ of order $n = pq$ with a generator μ and bilinear mapping $e : \mathbb{G} \times \mathbb{G} \to \mathbb{G}_T$. The groups $\mathbb{G}_p$ and $\mathbb{G}_q$ represent unique subgroups of group $\mathbb{G}$ of order p and q respectively. The public parameters are params $= (n, \mathbb{G}, \mathbb{G}_T, e, \mu)$ and secret trapdoor is $t = (p, q)$, i.e, (params, t) $\leftarrow$ BilinearSetup(1^ρ).

Depending on the public parameters, there are two types of settings in Groth-Sahai proofs - *perfectly sound* setting in subgroup $\mathbb{G}_p$ of $\mathbb{G}$ and *witness indistinguishability* setting. We describe below how to commit a group element $X \in \mathbb{G}$ in both the settings for Groth-Sahai proofs.

Commitment in Perfectly Sound Setting in $\mathbb{G}_p$: Generate public parameters params $= (n, \mathbb{G}, \mathbb{G}_T, e, \mu)$ $\leftarrow$ BilinearSetup(1^ρ). In this setting, the common reference string is GS $=$ (params, u), where u is generator of order q subgroup $\mathbb{G}_q$ of $\mathbb{G}$. To commit $X \in \mathbb{G}$, one picks $r \xleftarrow{\$} \mathbb{Z}_n$ and sets Com(X) $= Xu^r$. As order of u is q, (Com(X))^q maps X uniquely in the order p subgroup $\mathbb{G}_p$ of $\mathbb{G}$.

Commitment in Witness Indistinguishability Setting: Generate public parameters params $= (n, \mathbb{G}, \mathbb{G}_T, e, \mu)$ $\leftarrow$ BilinearSetup(1^ρ). In this setting, the common reference string is GS $=$ (params, u), where u is generator of $\mathbb{G}$. To commit $X \in \mathbb{G}$, one picks $r \xleftarrow{\$} \mathbb{Z}_n$ and sets Com(X) $= Xu^r$. One can note that Com(X) perfectly hides the message X.

Let Commit be an algorithm which on input $X \in \mathbb{G}$ and GS, generates Com(X), i.e, Com(X) $\leftarrow$ Commit(GS, X).

Theorem 1. *[17] The common reference string in perfectly sound setting and witness indistinguishability setting is computationally indistinguishable under the SD assumption.*

2.3 Non-Interactive Verification of Pairing Product Equation [17]

The Groth-Sahai proofs are two party protocols with the prover and the verifier and consist of three PPT algorithms AGSSetup, AGSProve and AGSVerify described in Algorithms 1-3 respectively. Groth-Sahai proofs show how to verify the general pairing product equation

$$\prod_{i=1}^{n} e(\mathcal{A}_i, \mathcal{Y}_i) \prod_{i=1}^{m} e(\mathcal{X}_i, \mathcal{B}_i) \prod_{i=1}^{m} \prod_{j=1}^{n} e(\mathcal{X}_i, \mathcal{Y}_i)^{a_{i,j}} = t_T, \tag{1}$$

in a non-interactive way, where $e : \mathbb{G}_1 \times \mathbb{G}_2 \to \mathbb{G}_T$ is a bilinear pairing, $\mathcal{X}_{i=1,2,...,m} \in \mathbb{G}_1, \mathcal{Y}_{j=1,2,...,n} \in \mathbb{G}_2$ are variables, $\mathcal{A}_{i=1,2,...,n} \in \mathbb{G}_1, \mathcal{B}_{j=1,2,...,m} \in \mathbb{G}_2, a_{i,j} \in \mathbb{Z}_n$ are constants and $t_T \in \mathbb{G}_T$. In our construction, we use following types of pairing product equations for a symmetric bilinear pairing e which are particular cases of equation 1. In symmetric bilinear pairing $\mathbb{G}_1 = \mathbb{G}_2 = \mathbb{G}$.

$$e(x, g_3)e(y, w) = e(g_3, g_3), \tag{2}$$
$$e(x, y) = e(g_3, g_3), \tag{3}$$

where, $x, y \in \mathbb{G}$ being secret values and $g_3, w \in \mathbb{G}, e(g_3, g_3) \in \mathbb{G}_T$ being public. Let us illustrate how the prover and the verifier use Algorithms 1-3 to verify the pairing product equations 2 and 3. The equation 2 is linear while equation 3 is non-linear. The prover wants to convince the verifier in a non-interactive way that he knows the solution x, y to equations 2 and 3 without revealing anything about x and y to the verifier. Let $\mathcal{E}$ be the set of all equations which the prover wishes to prove in non-interactive way to the verifier and $\mathcal{W}$ be the set of all secret values in $\mathcal{E}$. The set $\mathcal{W}$ is referred as witnesses of statement $\mathcal{E}$. We follow the notation of [10] for writing equations in statement. In reference to equations 2 and 3, $\mathcal{E} = \{e(x, g_3)e(y, w) = e(g_3, g_3) \wedge e(x, y) = e(g_3, g_3)\}$ and $\mathcal{W} = (x, y)$. Let $(\mathsf{params}, \mathsf{t}) \leftarrow \mathsf{BilinearSetup}(1^\rho), \mathsf{params} = (n, \mathbb{G}, \mathbb{G}_T, e, \mu)$ and $\mathsf{t} = (p, q)$.

Algorithm 1. AGSSetup
Input: μ and $\mathsf{t} = (p, q)$.
Output: GS $= u$.
1: $u = \mu^p$ is a generator of $\mathbb{G}_q$.
2: GS $= u$;

Algorithm 2. AGSProve
Input: GS $= u, \mathcal{E} = (\mathsf{eq}_1, \mathsf{eq}_2, \dots, \mathsf{eq}_m)$,
  $\mathcal{W} = (h_1, h_2, \dots, h_l)$.
Output: π.
1: for $(i = 1, 2, \dots, l)$
2:   $\mathsf{Com}(h_i) \leftarrow \mathsf{Commit}(\mathsf{GS}, h_i)$;
3: for $(i = 1, 2, \dots, m)$
4:   Generate P_i for equation $\mathsf{eq}_i \in \mathcal{E}$;
5:   $\pi = (\mathsf{Com}(h_1), \mathsf{Com}(h_2), \dots, \mathsf{Com}(h_l), \mathsf{P}_1, \mathsf{P}_2, \dots, \mathsf{P}_m)$;

The algorithm AGSSetup is run by a trusted party which on input a generator μ of group $\mathbb{G}$ and trapdoor $\mathsf{t} = (p, q)$ generates the common reference string GS in perfectly sound setting in the subgroup $\mathbb{G}_p$ of group $\mathbb{G}$ so that u is a generator of the order q subgroup $\mathbb{G}_q$ of $\mathbb{G}$. The trusted party makes GS public.

The prover runs the algorithm AGSProve and generates commitments to x and y in perfectly sound setting using algorithm Commit. The prover uses $\mathsf{GS} = u$ generated by AGSSetup described in algorithm 1 and sets $\mathsf{Com}(x) = xu^r, r \xleftarrow{\$} \mathbb{Z}_n$, $\mathsf{Com}(y) = yu^s, s \xleftarrow{\$} \mathbb{Z}_n$. The prover also generates the proof components P_1 for equation 2 and P_2 for equation 3, where $\mathsf{P}_1 = g_3^r w^s, \mathsf{P}_2 = x^s(yu^s)^r$. The prover sets the proof $\pi = (\mathsf{Com}(x), \mathsf{Com}(y), \mathsf{P}_1, \mathsf{P}_2) \leftarrow \mathsf{AGSProve}(\mathsf{GS}, \mathcal{E}, \mathcal{W})$ and gives π to the verifier (see [18] for the generation of proof components).

Algorithm 3. AGSVerify

Input: GS = u, π.
Output: Either ACCEPT or REJECT.
1: for $(i = 1, 2, \ldots, m)$
2:      Replace the variables in eq_i by their commitments;
3:      Use proof components P_i of eq_i to check the validity of eq_i;
4: if (All eq_i, $i = 1, 2, \ldots, m$ are valid)
5:      return ACCEPT;
6: else
7:      return REJECT;

The algorithm AGSVerify is run by the verifier. The verifier checks whether Com(x), Com(y), and proof components P_1, P_2 satisfy

$$e(\mathsf{Com}(x), g_3)e(\mathsf{Com}(y), w) = e(g_3, g_3)e(u, \mathsf{P}_1) \tag{4}$$

$$e(\mathsf{Com}(x), \mathsf{Com}(y)) = e(g_3, g_3)e(u, \mathsf{P}_2). \tag{5}$$

Note that the verifier knows all the components in equations 4 and 5 as it receives Com(x), Com(y), P_1, P_2 from the prover and g_3, w, u are public. If equations 4 and 5 hold, the verifier outputs ACCEPT, otherwise, REJECT. Note that the equations 4 and 5 hold iff the equations 2 and 3 are valid. In the above example, the proof π consists of 4 group elements and the verification of π requires 7 pairing computation of which 2 pairing can be precomputed. For more details, we refer to [18].

2.4 Security Model

Universally Composable (UC) Framework [12]: The security of the proposed protocol is analyzed in UC framework. The security is defined by comparing the execution of the protocol in the *real world* to the *ideal world*. The real world consists of parties $P_1, P_2, \ldots, P_M$ running the protocol Π and adversary $\mathcal{A}$ who has the ability of corrupting the parties and blocking the message exchange between the parties. The ideal world consists of dummy parties $\widetilde{P_1}, \widetilde{P_2}, \ldots, \widetilde{P_M}$, the ideal world adversary $\mathcal{A}'$ and trusted party called ideal functionality $\mathcal{F}$. Dummy parties give their inputs to $\mathcal{F}$ and get back their respective outputs from $\mathcal{F}$. An interactive distinguisher called *environment machine* $\mathcal{Z}$ is introduced. It interacts freely with $\mathcal{A}$ throughout the execution of the protocol Π in the real world and with $\mathcal{A}'$ throughout the execution of $\mathcal{F}$ in the ideal world. The task of the environment machine $\mathcal{Z}$ is to distinguish with non-negligible probability between the execution of Π in the real world and the execution of $\mathcal{F}$ in the ideal world.

$\mathcal{F}_{\mathsf{CRS}}^{\mathcal{D}}$ **Hybrid Model:** As OT protocol can be UC-realized only in the presence of common reference string (CRS) model, let us describe the $\mathcal{F}_{\mathsf{CRS}}^{\mathcal{D}}$-hybrid model [12] that UC realizes a protocol parameterized by some specific distribution $\mathcal{D}$. Upon receiving a message (sid, P_i), $i = 1, 2, \ldots, M$, from the party P_i, where sid is session identity, $\mathcal{F}_{\mathsf{CRS}}^{\mathcal{D}}$ first checks if there is a recorded value crs. If not, $\mathcal{F}_{\mathsf{CRS}}^{\mathcal{D}}$ generates crs $\xleftarrow{\$} \mathcal{D}(1^\rho)$ and records it. Finally, $\mathcal{F}_{\mathsf{CRS}}^{\mathcal{D}}$ sends (sid, crs) to the party P_i and the adversary. The sid is given by $\mathcal{Z}$. No two copies of $\mathcal{F}$ can have the same sid. Two parties are said to have the same sid if and only if they are participants of the same instance of a protocol. The sid is used to distinguish between different instances of the same protocol.

Functionality of Oblivious Transfer: The OT protocol is a two party protocol between the sender S and the receiver R. In the ideal world, the parties give their inputs to the ideal functionality $\mathcal{F}_{\mathsf{OT}}^{N \times 1}$ and get back their respective outputs. These requirements are shown in Figure 1 by the oblivious transfer functionality $\mathcal{F}_{\mathsf{OT}}^{N \times 1}$ following [12].

The functionality $\mathcal{F}_{\mathsf{OT}}^{N \times 1}$ interacts with the sender S and the receiver R as follows:
1. Upon receiving a message $(\mathsf{sid}, \mathsf{S}, \langle m_1, m_2, \dots, m_N \rangle)$ from S, $\mathcal{F}_{\mathsf{OT}}^{N \times 1}$ stores $\langle m_1, m_2, \dots, m_N \rangle$, where $m_i \in \{0,1\}^\eta$, $i = 1, 2, \dots, N$, and η is the length of m_i which is fixed and is known to both the parties.
2. Upon receiving a message $(\mathsf{sid}, \mathsf{R}, \sigma \in \{1, 2, \dots, N\})$ from R, $\mathcal{F}_{\mathsf{OT}}^{N \times 1}$ checks if a message $(\mathsf{sid}, \mathsf{S}, \langle m_1, m_2, \dots, m_N \rangle)$ was previously recorded.
- If no, $\mathcal{F}_{\mathsf{OT}}^{N \times 1}$ sends nothing to R.
- Otherwise, $\mathcal{F}_{\mathsf{OT}}^{N \times 1}$ sends $(\mathsf{sid}, \mathsf{request})$ to S. The sender S returns $(\mathsf{sid}, \mathsf{S}, b)$, in response to the request by $\mathcal{F}_{\mathsf{OT}}^{N \times 1}$ and the adversary. If $b = 0$, then $\mathcal{F}_{\mathsf{OT}}^{N \times 1}$ sends $(\mathsf{sid}, \bot)$ to R, else $\mathcal{F}_{\mathsf{OT}}^{N \times 1}$ returns (sid, m_σ) to R.

Fig. 1. Functionality for adaptive oblivious transfer

Definition 5. *Let $\mathcal{F}_{\mathsf{OT}}^{N \times 1}$ be the oblivious transfer functionality described in Figure 1. A protocol Π securely realizes the ideal functionality $\mathcal{F}_{\mathsf{OT}}^{N \times 1}$ if for any real world adversary $\mathcal{A}$, there exists an ideal world adversary $\mathcal{A}'$ such that for any environment machine $\mathcal{Z}$, $\mathsf{IDEAL}_{\mathcal{F}_{\mathsf{OT}}^{N \times 1}, \mathcal{A}', \mathcal{Z}} \overset{c}{\approx} \mathsf{REAL}_{\Pi, \mathcal{A}, \mathcal{Z}}$, where $\mathsf{IDEAL}_{\mathcal{F}_{\mathsf{OT}}^{N \times 1}, \mathcal{A}', \mathcal{Z}}$ is the output of $\mathcal{Z}$ after interacting with $\mathcal{A}'$ and dummy parties interacting with $\mathcal{F}_{\mathsf{OT}}^{N \times 1}$ in the ideal world and $\mathsf{REAL}_{\Pi, \mathcal{A}, \mathcal{Z}}$ is the output of $\mathcal{Z}$ after interacting with $\mathcal{A}$ and the parties running the protocol Π in the real world.*

2.5 Symmetric Encryption

Symmetric encryption consists of three PPT algorithms. The randomized algorithm $\mathsf{KeyGen_{SYM}}$ produces uniformly distributed key ke for security parameter ρ. The algorithm $\mathsf{Enc_{SYM}}$ encrypts the message m under the key ke, i.e, $C \leftarrow \mathsf{Enc_{SYM}}(\mathsf{ke}, m)$. The algorithm $\mathsf{Dec_{SYM}}$ decrypts the ciphertext C using secret key ke. The same key ke is used for encryption and decryption purposes.

3   Protocol

Our adaptive $\mathsf{OT}_{k \times 1}^N$ protocol completes in two phases– (i) initialization phase to generate ciphertext database cDB and (ii) transfer phase to recover a designated message obliviously. Initialization phase is done offline and executes once while transfer phase is carried out online and executed k times adaptively.

On a high level, our approach is as follows. We employ a particular case of Bresson, Catalano and Pointcheval (BCP) [7] encryption, Boneh and Boyen (BB) [3] signature and subgroup decision (SD) based Groth-Sahai proofs [17]. The BB [3] signature adapted to a group of composite order by Chandran et al. in [13]. The sender S has database $\mathsf{DB} = (m_1, m_2, \ldots, m_N)$. It signs the index i of each message m_i with BB signature in initialization phase, where $i = 1, 2, \ldots, N$. The BB signature is used to keep a check on the malicious behavior of the receiver R. The message m_i is encrypted with BCP encryption. The generated ciphertext database $\mathsf{cDB} = (\Phi_1, \Phi_2, \ldots, \Phi_N)$ is published by S. The receiver R verifies the ciphertext database cDB by verifying a pairing product equation for each $\Phi_i, i = 1, 2, \ldots, N$. If the verification holds, transfer phase is performed. Otherwise, R aborts the execution. In each transfer phase, R randomizes the ciphertext Φ_{σ_j} which it wants to decrypt, where $j = 1, 2, \ldots, k$. To make sure that R randomizes the ciphertext that was previously published through cDB by S, R proves non-interactively knowledge of a valid signature for its randomized ciphertext without revealing anything. For this, R gives non-interactive zero knowledge (NIZK) proof for its randomized ciphertext Φ_{σ_j}. In order to recover the message m_{σ_j}, R interacts with S. The sender S raises its secret value to the randomized value provided by R. The sender S also gives non-interactive witness indistinguishable (NIWI) proof that it uses the same secret values those were used in generating the ciphertext database cDB in initialization phase.

Our OT protocol invokes five randomized algorithms, namely, ADOTCrsGen, ADOTInitialize, ADOTInitializeVerify, ADOTRequest, ADOTRespond and a deterministic algorithm ADOTComplete as described below in Algorithms 4-9 respectively. We will use algorithms AGSSetup, AGSProve and AGSVerify discussed in section 2.2. A pictorial view of high-level description of our OT protocol is given in Figure 2.

Algorithm 4. ADOTCrsGen

Input: Security parameter ρ.
Output: $\mathsf{crs} = (\mathsf{params}, g, \psi(g), \mathsf{GS_S}, \mathsf{GS_R})$.
1: Generate $(\mathsf{params}, t) \leftarrow \mathsf{BilinearSetup}(1^\rho)$;
2: Generate $g = (\mu)^q$ which is element of order p in $\mathbb{G}$;
3: Pick $\xi_1, \xi_2 \xleftarrow{\$} \mathbb{Z}_n^*$, set $g_1 = \mu^{\xi_1}, g_2 = \mu^{\xi_2}$;
4: Compute $\psi(g) = (1+n)^{\lambda(n) \cdot \mathsf{DLog}_\mu(g)} = (1+n)^{\lambda(n) \cdot q}$;
5: $\mathsf{GS_R} \leftarrow \mathsf{AGSSetup}(g_1, t)$;
6: $\mathsf{GS_S} \leftarrow \mathsf{AGSSetup}(g_2, t)$;

The algorithm ADOTCrsGen given above on input a security parameter ρ by the trusted party $\mathcal{F}_{\mathsf{CRS}}^{\mathcal{D}}$ generates the common reference string $\mathsf{crs} = (\mathsf{params}, g, \psi(g),$ $\mathsf{GS_S}, \mathsf{GS_R})$. The public parameter $\mathsf{params} = (n, \mathbb{G}, \mathbb{G}_T, e, \mu) \leftarrow \mathsf{BilinearSetup}(1^\rho)$ consists of a symmetric bilinear mapping $e : \mathbb{G} \times \mathbb{G} \to \mathbb{G}_T$, a generater μ of group $\mathbb{G}$ and the order n of groups $\mathbb{G}$ and $\mathbb{G}_T$ which is the product of two primes p and q. The primes p and q are of length ϱ. The algorithm $\mathsf{BilinearSetup}$ has been discussed in section 2.2. The map $\psi : \mathbb{G} \to \mathbb{G}' \subseteq \mathbb{Z}_{n^2}^*$ is a homomorphism from $\mathbb{G}$ to $\mathbb{G}'$ which is contained in $\mathbb{Z}_{n^2}^*$, where $\mathbb{G}'$ is a cyclic group of order n

$$\text{crs} = (\text{params}, g, \psi(g), \text{GS}_S, \text{GS}_R)$$
$$\text{params} = (n, \mathbb{G}, \mathbb{G}_T, e, \mu)$$

Sender S (DB)   Receiver R

$(\text{PK}, \text{SSK}, \text{SK}, \text{cDB}) \leftarrow \text{ADOTInitialize}$
$\text{PK} = (h, y)$
$\text{SK} = z$
$\text{SSK} = x$
$\text{cDB} = (\varPhi_1, \varPhi_2, \dots, \varPhi_N)$

$\xrightarrow{(\text{sid}, S, \text{PK}, \text{cDB})}$

$\qquad\qquad\qquad\qquad\qquad\qquad\qquad\qquad\qquad$ $\text{ACCEPT} \leftarrow \text{ADOTInitilaizeVerify}$

$\qquad\qquad\qquad\qquad$ Transfer Phase

$\qquad\qquad\qquad\qquad\qquad\qquad\qquad\qquad\qquad$ $\sigma_j \in \{1, 2, \dots, N\}, j = 1, 2, \dots, k$
$\qquad\qquad\qquad\qquad\qquad\qquad\qquad\qquad\qquad$ $(\mathsf{Q}_{\text{request}_j}, \mathsf{Q}_{\text{private}_j}) \leftarrow \text{ADOTRequest}$
$\qquad\qquad\qquad\qquad\qquad\qquad\qquad\qquad\qquad$ $\mathsf{Q}_{\text{request}_j} = (d_j, \pi_j)$
$\qquad\qquad\qquad\qquad\qquad\qquad\qquad\qquad\qquad$ $\mathsf{Q}_{\text{private}_j} = (\sigma_j, v_j)$
$\qquad\qquad\qquad\qquad\qquad\qquad\qquad\qquad\qquad$ $\pi_j \leftarrow \text{AGSProve}$

$\xleftarrow{(\text{sid}, R, \mathsf{Q}_{\text{request}_j})}$

$(s_j, \delta_j) \leftarrow \text{ADOTRespond}$
$s_j = d_j^z$
$\delta_j \leftarrow \text{AGSProve}$

$\xrightarrow{(\text{sid}, S, s_j, \delta_j)}$

$\qquad\qquad\qquad\qquad\qquad\qquad\qquad\qquad\qquad$ $m_{\sigma_j} \leftarrow \text{ADOTComplete}$

Fig. 2. Initialization phase and jth transfer phase of our $\text{OT}^N_{k\times 1}$ protocol, $j = 1, 2, \dots, k$

generated by $(1 + n)$. The map ψ is a private function and defined as $\psi(\alpha) = (1 + n)^{\lambda(n)\text{Dlog}_\mu(\alpha)}$, where $\text{Dlog}_\mu(\alpha)$ represents discrete logarithmic of α with respect to μ, i.e, if $\alpha = \mu^x$, then $\text{Dlog}_\mu(\alpha) = x$ and $\lambda(n)$ is the Carmichael function, $\lambda(n) = l.c.m(\phi(p), \phi(q))$ and $g.c.d\ (\lambda(n), n) = 1$, where $\phi(\cdot)$ is Euler's totient function. One who knows the factorization of n can only compute $\lambda(n)$. Only the value $\psi(g)$ is made public. The sender S generates non-interactive zero-knowledge (NIZK) proof using Groth-Sahai common reference string GS_S and R creates non-interactive witness indistinguishable (NIWI) proof using Groth-Sahai common reference string GS_R. The common reference string crs is made public and trapdoor t is kept hidden.

Algorithm 5. ADOTInitialize

Input: crs, $\text{DB} = (m_1, m_2, \dots, m_N)$, $m_i \in \mathbb{Z}_n$, $i = 1, 2, \dots, N$.
Output: (PK, SSK, SK, cDB).

1: Choose $z \xleftarrow{\$} [0, \frac{n}{2^\ell}], x \xleftarrow{\$} \mathbb{Z}_n^*$;
2: Set $h = g^z$, $y = g^x$ and $\psi(h) = \psi(g)^z$;
3: Set $\text{PK} = (h, y)$, $\text{SSK} = x$ and $\text{SK} = z$;
4: for $(i = 1, 2, \dots, N)$ do
5: $\quad r_i \xleftarrow{\$} [0, \frac{n}{2^\ell}]$;
6: $\quad$ Generate BB signature on r_i as $\mu^{\frac{1}{x+r_i}}$;
7: $\quad$ Generate ciphertext of m_i as $(g^{r_i}, \psi(h^{r_i}) \cdot (1 + n)^{m_i})$, where $\psi(h^{r_i}) = \psi(h)^{r_i}$;
8: $\quad$ Encrypt $\psi(h^{r_i})$ with key h^{r_i} using symmetric encryption as $\text{Enc}_{\text{SYM}}(h^{r_i}, \psi(h^{r_i}))$;
9: $\quad$ Set ciphertext $\varPhi_i = \left(g^{r_i}, \psi(h^{r_i}) \cdot (1 + n)^{m_i}, \mu^{\frac{1}{x+r_i}}, \text{Enc}_{\text{SYM}}(h^{r_i}, \psi(h^{r_i}))\right)$;
10: Set ciphertext database $\text{cDB} = (\varPhi_1, \varPhi_2, \dots, \varPhi_N)$;

The algorithm ADOTInitialize, on input crs, N messages $(m_1, m_2, \dots, m_N)$ by S, generates public key PK, signature secret key SSK, secret key SK and encrypted database cDB of N messages for S as in algorithm 5. The sender S sends $(\mathsf{PK}, \mathsf{cDB})$ to R and keeps $(\mathsf{SSK}, \mathsf{SK})$ secret to itself. In each ciphertext $\Phi_i = (c_i^{(1)}, c_i^{(2)}, c_i^{(3)}, c_i^{(4)})$, $i = 1, 2, \ldots, N$, the tuple $(\psi(c_i^{(1)}), c_i^{(2)}) = (\psi(g^{r_i}), \psi(h^{r_i}) \cdot (1 + n)^{m_i})$ is a BCP encryption of message m_i, $c_i^{(3)} = \mu^{\frac{1}{x + r_i}}$ is a BB signature on r_i and $c_i^{(4)}$ is the encryption of $\psi(h^{r_i}) \in \mathbb{Z}_{n^2}^*$ using secret $h^{r_i} \in \mathbb{G}$. As the map $\psi(\alpha)$ is a private function, one can not compute it even if he knows α but does not know $\mathsf{Dlog}_\mu(\alpha)$. Also the Carmichael function $\lambda(n)$ is not public. Computing $\psi(\alpha)$ is as hard as discrete logarithmic problem and factoring problem. In line 2 of algorithm ADOTInitialize, S is able to compute $\psi(h)$ because of the homomorphic property of ψ and publicly available value $\psi(g)$, where $h = g^z$, $\psi(h) = \psi(g^z) = \psi(g)^z = (1 + n)^{\lambda(n)qz}$. One who knows h^{r_i} is still unable to recover $\psi(h^{r_i})$ because of the hardness of discrete logarithmic problem and factoring problem. Therefore, symmetric encryption is used to encrypt $\psi(h^{r_i})$ under the key h^{r_i} which is secret. Now one who has the key h^{r_i} can only decrypt $c_i^{(4)} = \mathsf{Dec}_{\mathsf{SYM}}(h^{r_i}, \psi(h^{r_i}))$ to recover $\psi(h^{r_i})$. The key space of symmetric encryption is the group generated by g which is a subgroup of $\mathbb{G}$ and message space is $\mathbb{Z}_{n^2}^*$. Anyone can check the correctness of the ciphertext Φ_i by verifying $e(c_i^{(3)}, y \cdot c_i^{(1)}) = e(\mu, g)$, for $i = 1, 2, \ldots, N$.

Algorithm 6. ADOTInitializeVerify
Input: $\mathsf{PK} = (h, y), \mathsf{cDB} = (\Phi_1, \Phi_2, \ldots, \Phi_N)$.
Output: (Either ACCEPT or REJECT).
1: for $(i = 1, 2, \ldots, N)$ do
2:    Parse Φ_i as $(c_i^{(1)}, c_i^{(2)}, c_i^{(3)}, c_i^{(4)})$;
3:    if $(e(c_i^{(3)}, y \cdot c_i^{(1)}) = e(\mu, g))$;
4:      Φ_i is correct;
5:    else
6:      return REJECT;
7:      break;
8: return ACCEPT;

Algorithm 7. ADOTRequest
Input: $\mathsf{crs}, \mathsf{PK} = (h, y), \mathsf{cDB} = (\Phi_1, \Phi_2, \ldots, \Phi_N), \sigma_j$.
Output: $(\mathsf{Q}_{\mathsf{request}_j}, \mathsf{Q}_{\mathsf{private}_j})$.
1: Parse Φ_{σ_j} as $(c_{\sigma_j}^{(1)}, c_{\sigma_j}^{(2)}, c_{\sigma_j}^{(3)}, c_{\sigma_j}^{(4)})$;
2: $v_j \xleftarrow{\$} [0, \frac{n}{2^\ell}]$;
3: $d_j = c_{\sigma_j}^{(1)} \cdot g^{v_j}, t_j = h^{v_j}$;
4: $\mathcal{E}_{1,j} = \{e(c_{\sigma_j}^{(1)}, h)e(t_j, g) = e(d_j, h) \wedge e(c_{\sigma_j}^{(3)}, y \cdot c_{\sigma_j}^{(1)}) = e(\mu, g))\}$;
5: $\mathcal{W}_{1,j} = (c_{\sigma_j}^{(1)}, t_j, c_{\sigma_j}^{(3)})$;
6: $\pi_j \leftarrow \mathsf{AGSProve}(\mathsf{GS}_R, \mathcal{E}_{1,j}, \mathcal{W}_{1,j})$;
7: $\mathsf{Q}_{\mathsf{request}_j} = (d_j, \pi_j), \mathsf{Q}_{\mathsf{private}_j} = (\sigma_j, v_j)$;

The receiver R checks the validity of the ciphertext Φ_i by invoking the algorithm ADOTInitializeVerify given above in initialization phase by verifying equation $e(c_i^{(3)}, y \cdot c_i^{(1)}) = e(\mu, g)$, for $i = 1, 2, \ldots, N$. If ciphertext database cDB is valid, transfer phase will take place. Otherwise the execution will be aborted by R.

The algorithm ADOTRequest, on input crs, cDB and R's choice of $\sigma_j \in \{1, 2, \ldots, N\}, j = 1, 2, \ldots, k$, generates $(\mathsf{Q}_{\mathsf{request}_j}, \mathsf{Q}_{\mathsf{private}_j})$ for S using GS_R as given above in algorithm 7. The receiver R gives $\mathsf{Q}_{\mathsf{request}_j}$ to S and keeps $\mathsf{Q}_{\mathsf{private}_j}$ secret to itself. In $\mathsf{Q}_{\mathsf{request}_j} = (d_j, \pi_j)$, the value $d_j = c_{\sigma_j}^{(1)} \cdot g^{v_j}$ guarantees the masked versions of $c_{\sigma_j}^{(1)}$ and NIWI proof π_j consists of commitments to witnesses in $\mathcal{W}_{1,j}$ generated by AGSProve in Algorithm 2 and proof components for non-interactive verification of equations in statement $\mathcal{E}_{1,j}$ in line 4 of algorithm 7. The proof generation for 1st equation in statement $\mathcal{E}_{1,j}$ is similar to equation 2 and that for 2nd equation in statement $\mathcal{E}_{1,j}$ is similar to equation 3 of section 2.3.

Following the notation of [10] for writing equations in statement $\mathcal{E}_{1,j}$, the first equation corresponds to the masked version of $c_{\sigma_j}^{(1)}$ and 2nd equation guarantees valid signature held by R. These checks enable one to detect whether R deviates from the protocol execution. Thus $\mathcal{E}_{1,j}$ in line 4 of Algorithm 7 is a statement set by R to convince S that $\mathsf{Q}_{\mathsf{request}_j}$ is framed correctly.

Algorithm 8. ADOTRespond

Input: $\mathsf{crs}, \mathsf{PK} = (h, y), \mathsf{SK} = z, \mathsf{Q}_{\mathsf{request}_j} = (d_j, \pi_j)$.
Output: (s_j, δ_j).
1: **if** $(\mathsf{AGSVerify}(\mathsf{GS}_R, \pi_j) = \mathsf{ACCEPT})$
2:     Extract h from PK;
3:     Compute $s_j = d_j^z$;
4:     Set $\mathcal{E}_{2,j} = \{e(s_j, g)e(d_j^{-1}, a_1) = 1 \wedge$
         $e(g, a_1) = e(g, h)\}$;
5:     Set $\mathcal{W}_{2,j} = (s_j, a_1)$;
6:         $\delta_j \leftarrow \mathsf{AGSProve}(\mathsf{GS}_S, \mathcal{E}_{2,j}, \mathcal{W}_{2,j})$;
7: **else**
8:     abort the execution;

Algorithm 9. ADOTComplete

Input: $\mathsf{crs}, \mathsf{GS}_S, \mathsf{cDB}, s_j, \delta_j, \mathsf{Q}_{\mathsf{private}_j} = (\sigma_j, v_j)$,
         $\mathsf{PK} = (h, y)$.
Output: m_{σ_j}.
1: **if** $(\mathsf{AGSVerify}(\mathsf{GS}_S, \delta_j) = \mathsf{ACCEPT})$
2:     Extract h from PK;
3:     Extract (σ_j, v_j) from $\mathsf{Q}_{\mathsf{private}_j}$;
4:     Parse Φ_{σ_j} as $(c_{\sigma_j}^{(1)}, c_{\sigma_j}^{(2)}, c_{\sigma_j}^{(3)}, c_{\sigma_j}^{(4)})$;
5:     Recover $h^{r\sigma_j}$ by computing $\frac{s_j}{h^{v_j}}$;
6:     Decrypt $\mathsf{Dec}_{\mathsf{SYM}}(h^{r\sigma_j}, c_{\sigma_j}^{(4)}) = \psi(h^{r\sigma_j})$;
7:     Compute $B = \frac{c_{\sigma_j}^{(2)}}{\psi(h^{r\sigma_j})} \pmod{n^2}$;
8:     Set $m_{\sigma_j} = \frac{B-1}{n}$;
9: **else**
10:     abort the execution;

The algorithm ADOTRespond given above, on input crs, PK, SK and $\mathsf{Q}_{\mathsf{request}_j}$ by S, first invokes algorithm AGSVerify to verifiy the NIWI proof π_j using GS_R. If the proof π_j is valid, ADOTRespond generates s_j using secret key SK and construct NIZK proof δ_j by AGSProve in algorithm 2 using GS_S. The proof δ_j consists of commitments to elements in $\mathcal{W}_{2,j}$ and proof components for equations in statement $\mathcal{E}_{2,j}$ in line 4 of algorithm 8. The proof generations for 1st and 2nd equation in statement $\mathcal{E}_{2,j}$ are similar to equation 2 in section 2.3. The first equation in statement $\mathcal{E}_{2,j}$ guarantees that s_j is generated using SK. The second equation indicates that a_1 is equal to h. Thus $\mathcal{E}_{2,j}$ in line 4 of Algorithm 8 is a statement set by S in order to convince R that the response s_j is correctly framed. To allow the simulation of the proof δ_j, we add a second variable $a_1 = h$ in line 4 of algorithm ADOTRespond. For more details see [16].

The algorithm ADOTComplete given above, on input crs, DB, s_j, δ_j and $\mathsf{Q}_{\mathsf{private}_j}$ by R, first checks the validity of NIZK proof δ_j using GS_S following AGSVerify in Algorithm 3. If the proof δ_j is valid, ADOTComplete in line 5 recovers $h^{r\sigma_j} = \frac{s_j}{h^{v_j}} = \frac{(d_j)^z}{h^{v_j}} = \frac{(c_{\sigma_j}^{(1)} g^{v_j})^z}{h^{v_j}} = \frac{(g^{r\sigma_j} g^{v_j})^z}{h^{v_j}} = \frac{h^{r\sigma_j} h^{v_j}}{h^{v_j}}$ as $h = g^z$. The value B in line 7 is computed as $B = \frac{c_{\sigma_j}^{(2)}}{\psi(h^{r\sigma_j})} = \frac{\psi(h^{r\sigma_j}) \cdot (1+n)^{m\sigma_j}}{\psi(h^{r\sigma_j})} = (1+n)^{m\sigma_j} \pmod{n^2} = 1 + nm_{\sigma_j}$. Using B in line 8, m_{σ_j} is recovered as $\frac{(B-1)}{n}$.

4   Security Analysis

Theorem 2. *The adaptive oblivious transfer protocol Π presented in section 3 securely realizes the ideal functionality $\mathcal{F}_{OT}^{N \times 1}$ in the $\mathcal{F}_{CRS}^{D}$-hybrid model described in section 2.4 under the SD, DDH over composite order and l-SDH assumption.*

Proof. Because of lack of space, proof will be given in full version.

5   Comparison

In this section, we compare our proposed protocol with some existing protocols. Note that our protocol belongs to the family of Green and Hohenberger' [16] UC secure $OT_{k\times 1}^{N}$ protocol. Green and Hohenberger [16] introduced the first adaptive UC secure $OT_{k\times 1}^{N}$ protocol by using semantically secure Boneh, Boyen and Shacham (BBS) [4] encryption under the hardness of Decision Linear (DLIN) problem together with Camenisch-Lysyanskaya (CL) signature [8] secure under Lysyanskaya, Rivest, Sahai and Wolf (LRSW) assumption and Boneh-Boyen signature built from Boneh-Boyen [2] selective-id identity based encryption scheme. Later, Rial *et al.* [22] proposed an efficient UC secure priced $OT_{k\times 1}^{N}$ protocol, where authors used BBS [4] encryption and P-signatures [1] unforgeable under hidden strong Diffie-Hellman (HSDH) and triple Diffie-Hellman (TDH) assumption. Zhang *et al.* [24] proposed the first identity based adaptive oblivious transfer protocol in composite order bilinear group with security analysis in random oracle model in semi honest corruption model where parties follow the protocol specification. In contrast to [16], [22] and [24], our scheme is proven to be UC secure in composite order bilinear group using BCP encryption, BB signature and SD based Groth-Sahai proofs in the presence of malicious adversaries.

Table 1. Comparison Summary (IP stands for initialization phase, TP for transfer phase, CRSG for crs generation, $\alpha X + \beta Y$ for α elements from the group X and β elements from the group Y)

$OT_{k\times 1}^{N}$	Pairing PO		Exponentiation EXP			Communication		Storage	
	TP	IP	TP	IP	CRSG	Request	Response	crs-Size	(cDB + PK)Size
[16]	$\geq 207k$	$24N+1$	$249k$	$20N+13$	18	$(68G_1 + 38G_2)k$	$(20G_1 + 18G_2)k$	$7G_1 + 7G_2$	$(15N+5)G_1 + (3N+6)G_2$
[22]	$> 450k$	$15N+1$	$223k$	$12N+9$	15	$(65G)k$	$(28G)k$	$23G$	$(12N+7)G$
[24]	$2k$	–	$2k$	N	–	$(1G)k$	$(1G)k$	–	$(N)\mathbb{Z}_n$
Ours	$11k+2$	$N+1$	$15k$	$(3N+2)G + (2N+1)\mathbb{Z}_{n^2}^{*}$	$5G + 1\mathbb{Z}_{n^2}^{*}$	$(6G)k$	$(5G)k$	$4G + 1\mathbb{Z}_{n^2}^{*}$	$(2N+2)G + N\mathbb{Z}_{n^2}^{*}$

Our protocol has the same security level as in [16] and [22]. We also compare the complexity of the proposed protocol with [16] and [22] which are only existing UC secure adaptive oblivious transfer protocols with similar security levels as illustrated in Table 1. The scheme of [16] and [22] uses prime order bilinear pairing whereas that of [24] and ours uses composite order. The complexity is given by computational and communication overhead in initialization phase and k transfer phases of $OT_{k\times 1}^{N}$ protocol. We count the number of pairings and exponentiations in our proposed protocol to determine computation overhead. In addition, some computation cost is also involved because of symmetric encryption in initialization phase and symmetric decryption in each transfer phase. Let PO stands for the number of pairing operations and EXP for the number of exponentiation operations. Then $PO = 6 + 5 = 11$ together with 2 pre-computed pairings and $EXP = 9 + 6 = 15$ for each transfer phase. Also, $PO = N + 1$ and $EXP = (3N + 2)\mathbb{G} + (2N + 1)\mathbb{Z}_{n^2}^*$ for initialization phase and $EXP = 5\mathbb{G} + 1\mathbb{Z}_{n^2}^*$ for crs generation. The communication complexity in the proposed protocol is measured by the number of group elements transferred from S to R and from R to S, with other values ignored. In addition to storage cost $(2N + 2)\mathbb{G} + N\mathbb{Z}_{n^2}^*$, it also consists of N symmetric encrypted elements. As illustrated in Table 1, our protocol performs less number of PO and EXP operations as compared to [16], [22] but more in comparison to [24]. The scheme proposed in [24] does not take into account the malicious activities of the parties. Also, security analysis in [24] has been done using random oracles.

6 Conclusion

We have proposed a UC secure adaptive k-out-of-N ($\mathsf{OT}_{k \times 1}^N$) oblivious transfer protocol. In the proposed scheme, the sender published encrypted messages. The receiver recovers the message without revealing its choice of message to sender. The protocol is secure in the presence of malicious adversary under the decisional Diffie-Hellman, subgroup decision (SD) and l-Strong Diffie-Hellman (SDH) assumptions in the common reference string model. Our scheme uses Bresson, Catalano and Pointcheval (BCP) encryption and BB signature together with Groth -Sahai non-interactive zero knowledge proofs and non-interactive witness indistinguishability proofs. Our scheme is computationally efficient and has low communication overhead. The protocol can be composed with other protocols securely for concurrent executions.

References

1. Belenkiy, M., Chase, M., Kohlweiss, M., Lysyanskaya, A.: P-signatures and noninteractive anonymous credentials. In: Canetti, R. (ed.) TCC 2008. LNCS, vol. 4948, pp. 356–374. Springer, Heidelberg (2008)
2. Boneh, D., Boyen, X.: Efficient selective-id secure identity-based encryption without random oracles. In: Cachin, C., Camenisch, J.L. (eds.) EUROCRYPT 2004. LNCS, vol. 3027, pp. 223–238. Springer, Heidelberg (2004)
3. Boneh, D., Boyen, X.: Short signatures without random oracles. In: Cachin, C., Camenisch, J.L. (eds.) EUROCRYPT 2004. LNCS, vol. 3027, pp. 56–73. Springer, Heidelberg (2004)
4. Boneh, D., Boyen, X., Shacham, H.: Short group signatures. In: Franklin, M. (ed.) CRYPTO 2004. LNCS, vol. 3152, pp. 41–55. Springer, Heidelberg (2004)
5. Boneh, D., Goh, E.J., Nissim, K.: Evaluating 2-dnf formulas on ciphertexts. In: Kilian, J. (ed.) TCC 2005. LNCS, vol. 3378, pp. 325–341. Springer, Heidelberg (2005)
6. Boneh, D., Rubin, K., Silverberg, A.: Finding composite order ordinary elliptic curves using the cocks–pinch method. Journal of Number Theory 131(5), 832–841 (2011)

7. Bresson, E., Catalano, D., Pointcheval, D.: A simple public-key cryptosystem with a double trapdoor decryption mechanism and its applications. In: Laih, C.-S. (ed.) ASIACRYPT 2003. LNCS, vol. 2894, pp. 37–54. Springer, Heidelberg (2003)

8. Camenisch, J., Lysyanskaya, A.: Signature schemes and anonymous credentials from bilinear maps. In: Franklin, M. (ed.) CRYPTO 2004. LNCS, vol. 3152, pp. 56–72. Springer, Heidelberg (2004)

9. Camenisch, J., Neven, G., Shelat, A.: Simulatable adaptive oblivious transfer. In: Naor, M. (ed.) EUROCRYPT 2007. LNCS, vol. 4515, pp. 573–590. Springer, Heidelberg (2007)

10. Camenisch, J., Stadler, M.: Efficient group signature schemes for large groups. In: Kaliski Jr., B.S. (ed.) CRYPTO 1997. LNCS, vol. 1294, pp. 410–424. Springer, Heidelberg (1997)

11. Canetti, R.: Universally composable security: A new paradigm for cryptographic protocols. In: FOCS 2001, pp. 136–145. IEEE (2001)

12. Canetti, R., Lindell, Y., Ostrovsky, R., Sahai, A.: Universally composable two-party and multi-party secure computation. In: ACM 2002, pp. 494–503. ACM (2002)

13. Chandran, N., Groth, J., Sahai, A.: Ring signatures of sub-linear size without random oracles. In: Arge, L., Cachin, C., Jurdziński, T., Tarlecki, A. (eds.) ICALP 2007. LNCS, vol. 4596, pp. 423–434. Springer, Heidelberg (2007)

14. Freeman, D., Scott, M., Teske, E.: A taxonomy of pairing-friendly elliptic curves. Journal of Cryptology 23(2), 224–280 (2010)

15. Garay, J., Wichs, D., Zhou, H.S.: Somewhat non-committing encryption and efficient adaptively secure oblivious transfer. In: Halevi, S. (ed.) CRYPTO 2009. LNCS, vol. 5677, pp. 505–523. Springer, Heidelberg (2009)

16. Green, M., Hohenberger, S.: Universally composable adaptive oblivious transfer. In: Pieprzyk, J. (ed.) ASIACRYPT 2008. LNCS, vol. 5350, pp. 179–197. Springer, Heidelberg (2008)

17. Groth, J., Sahai, A.: Efficient non-interactive proof systems for bilinear groups. In: Smart, N.P. (ed.) EUROCRYPT 2008. LNCS, vol. 4965, pp. 415–432. Springer, Heidelberg (2008)

18. Haralambiev, K.: Efficient cryptographic primitives for noninteractive zero-knowledge proofs and applications. Ph.D. thesis, New York University (2011)

19. Naor, M., Pinkas, B.: Oblivious transfer with adaptive queries. In: Wiener, M. (ed.) CRYPTO 1999. LNCS, vol. 1666, pp. 573–590. Springer, Heidelberg (1999)

20. Peikert, C., Vaikuntanathan, V., Waters, B.: A framework for efficient and composable oblivious transfer. In: Wagner, D. (ed.) CRYPTO 2008. LNCS, vol. 5157, pp. 554–571. Springer, Heidelberg (2008)

21. Rabin, M.O.: How to exchange secrets by oblivious transfer. Technical Report TR-81, Harvard Aiken Computation Laboratory (1981)

22. Rial, A., Kohlweiss, M., Preneel, B.: Universally composable adaptive priced oblivious transfer. In: Shacham, H., Waters, B. (eds.) Pairing 2009. LNCS, vol. 5671, pp. 231–247. Springer, Heidelberg (2009)

23. Seo, J.H.: On the (im)possibility of projecting property in prime-order setting. In: Wang, X., Sako, K. (eds.) ASIACRYPT 2012. LNCS, vol. 7658, pp. 61–79. Springer, Heidelberg (2012)

24. Zhang, F., Zhao, X., Chen, X.: Id-based adaptive oblivious transfer. In: Youm, H.Y., Yung, M. (eds.) WISA 2009. LNCS, vol. 5932, pp. 133–147. Springer, Heidelberg (2009)

25. Zhang, Y., Xue, C.J., Wong, D.S., Mamoulis, N., Yiu, S.M.: Acceleration of composite order bilinear pairing on graphics hardware. In: Chim, T.W., Yuen, T.H. (eds.) ICICS 2012. LNCS, vol. 7618, pp. 341–348. Springer, Heidelberg (2012)

Certificate-Based Conditional Proxy Re-Encryption

Jiguo Li[*], Xuexia Zhao, and Yichen Zhang

College of Computer and Information Engineering, Hohai University,
Nanjing 210098, China

Abstract. A proxy re-encryption scheme (PRE) allows a semi-trusted proxy to convert a ciphertext encrypted under one key into an encryption of the same plaintext under another key. In the process of the arithmetic processing, proxy should be able to learn as little information about the plaintext as possible. Conditional proxy re-encryption (CPRE) is a primitive which only those ciphertexts satisfying one condition set by the delegator can be re-encrypted correctly by the proxy. In this paper, we combine the conditional proxy re-encryption with certificate-based encryption and propose a certificate-based conditional proxy re-encryption scheme. The proposed scheme is proved secure against chosen-ciphertext security (CCA) in the random oracle model.

Keywords: certificated-based encryption, proxy re-encryption, CCA security, random oracle model.

1   1   Introduction

With the rapid development of information technology, the importance of information security has been greatly improved. Imagine such an example: Alice uploads the files, which allow specified users to access, encrypted under Alice's public key to an untrusted server (such as the public cloud storage). When users need to access the data, first Alice should decrypt the encrypted file, and then re-encrypt it with a new key, but Alice might not be able to transform the files in time.

In order to effectively solve these issues, Blaze, Bleumer and Strauss [1] proposed the concept of proxy re-encryption (PRE) in Eurocrypt 1998. In the scheme, Alice (delegator) entrusts the right of decryption to Bob (delegatee) via a proxy (an untrusted server). However, a formal definition of PRE was not given in this paper. Ateniese et al. [2] solved this problem. They showed how to construct unidirectional schemes using bilinear maps, even if the proxy and delegatee collude, they can not learn anything about the delegator's private key. Many PRE schemes [3-6] with different security properties have been proposed. To extend the above notion to the

---

[*] This work is supported by the National Natural Science Foundation of China [60842002, 61272542, 61103183, 61103184]; the Fundamental Research Funds for the Central Universities [B13020070, 2010B07114]; China Postdoctoral Science Foundation Funded Project [20100471373]; the "Six Talent Peaks Program" of Jiangsu Province of China [2009182] and Program for New Century Excellent Talents in Hohai University.

M.H. Au et al. (Eds.): NSS 2014, LNCS 8792, pp. 299–310, 2014.

identity-based cryptographic setting, Green and Ateniese [7] proposed the first identity-based proxy re-encryption (IB-PRE). Later, Chu and Tzeng [8] proposed an identity-based proxy re-encryption without random oracles. However traditional PRE could not adapt to the application of all actual situations, for example, Alice does not want to delegate the decryption rights of all the files, but only a subset of the files to a particular user. Conditional proxy re-encryption (CPRE) [9-11] were proposed, in the scheme Alice flexibly authorizes the decryption rights based on the conditions attached to the messages to Bob via proxy. Ateniese, Benson and Hohenberger [12] presented a key-private proxy re-encryption scheme. In the case of key privacy, even if the attacker owns proxy re-encryption key, he can not distinguish the delegatee. In other words, the attacker can not distinguish between a proxy key and a random value, which makes the identity of the recipient confidential. Shao, Liu and Zhou [13] achieved key privacy without losing CCA security in proxy re-encryption, which can resist adaptive chosen ciphertext attack. PRE has been widely applied to many occasions, such as distributed file system, encryption of spam filtering, public cloud storage so on.

However, in the traditional public key infrastructure (PKI) setting, it is limited to the certificate management problems and the drawback of third-party queries; in the identity-based setting, there are also two disadvantages: the inherent key escrow problem and the difficult of the key distribution. To fill this gap, in Eurocrypt 2003, Gentry [14] proposed a new paradigm: the certificate-based cryptography, which enjoys the best parts of the traditional PKI and identity-based schemes. Certificate-based cryptography solves the key escrow problem and key distribution problems as in the identity-based setting, and eliminates the third-party queries as in the PKI. Therefore it is much more safety and efficient to implement the PRE into the certificate-based cryptography. Lu, Li and Xiao [15] proposed a forward-secure certificate-based encryption scheme. Furthermore, Lu and Li [16] proposed a generic construction about forward-secure certificate-based encryption. Sur et al. [17] combined the concept of the certificate-based encryption and proxy re-encryption, and proposed a new notion: the certificate-based proxy re-encryption (CB-PRE). The scheme is secure against chosen ciphertext attack in the random oracle model.

Our Contribution

In order to control the power of the proxy, we introduce conditional proxy re-encryption idea into the certificate-based encryption so that only a certain subset of the ciphertexts can be re-encrypted to the designate delegatee, and formalize the definition and the security model of certificate-based conditional proxy re-encryption (CB-CPRE). Furthermore, we propose a certificate-based conditional proxy re-encryption scheme, so that only those ciphertexts which meet the condition could be re-encrypted correctly by the proxy. Our scheme is proved secure against chosen-ciphertext security (CCA) in the random oracle model under the bilinear Diffie-Hellman assumption.

2   Formal Definition and Security Models

In this section, we introduce some related mathematical knowledge: the complexity assumption required in the scheme. We present the formal definition of the certificate-based conditional proxy re-encryption scheme and refine its security models.

Definition 1 Bilinear Pairing

We briefly show the notion of the bilinear maps. The detailed knowledge is showed in the literature [18-19].

Let G_1 and G_2 be multiplicative cyclic groups with prime order p, and g be a generator of G_1. We say $e : G_1 \times G_1 \to G_2$ is an admissible bilinear map with the following properties:

— Bilinear: $e(g^a, g^b) = e(g, g)^{ab}$ for all $a, b \in Z_p^*$ and $g \in G_1$.
— Non-degenerate: $e(g, g) \neq 1$, where 1 is the unit of G_2.
— Computable: e can be efficiently computed.

Notice that the bilinear maps are defined in the symmetric setting, since we have $e(g^a, g^b) = e(g, g)^{ab} = e(g^b, g^a)$.

Definition 2 The Bilinear Diffie-Hellman (BDH) Assumption

Our scheme is based on the intractability of the Bilinear Diffie-Hellman problem [18-19] in G_1, G_2. The BDH problem is defined as follows:

Let $e : G_1 \times G_1 \to G_2$ be a bilinear map, and g be a random generator of G_1 and ε is a negligible value. Given a tuple of values $(g, g^a, g^b, g^c) \in G_1^4$ as input, compute $e(g, g)^{abc} \in G_2$. We say that the BDH assumption holds in (G_1, G_2) if for all probabilistic polynomial time algorithms B, the following condition holds.

$$\left| \Pr[B(g, g^a, g^b, g^c)] = e(g, g)^{abc} \right| \leq \varepsilon.$$

where $a, b, c \in Z_p^*$ are randomly selected.

2.1   The Formal Definition of Certificate-Based Conditional Proxy Re-Encryption

Certificate-based conditional proxy re-encryption (CB-CPRE) is an extended certificate-based encryption scheme. Inspired by [6], the scheme involves three participants: a delegator, a proxy and a delegatee. Only the condition c is included in the ciphertext, the proxy owning the conditional re-encryption key $rk_{i,c,j}$ could convert the ciphertext encrypted by the sender using both the user U_i's public key and condition c into the user U_j's ciphertext, so the user U_j could use his own secret key sk_j to decrypt the ciphertext. By conditional re-encryption, user U_i could have a flexible control to the delegation.

A CB-CPRE scheme includes the following algorithms:

— **Setup** $\left(1^\lambda\right)$: Run by the CA. This algorithm takes a security parameter 1^λ as input, it generates the global parameters *params* and CA's master key *msk* .

— **KeyGen** $\left(params\right)$: Run by user U_i . This algorithm takes the global parameters *params* as input, it generate user's public key pk_i and corresponding secret key sk_i .

— **Certify** $\left(params,msk,\tau,id_i,pk_i\right)$: Run by the CA. This algorithm takes the global parameters *params* , master key *msk* , time period τ , user's identity id_i and public key pk_i as input, it generates user id_i's certificate $Cert_{\tau,i}$.

— **Enc** $\left(params,\tau,id_i,pk_i,c,m\right)$: Run by sender. This algorithm takes the global parameters *params* , time period τ , user's identity id_i , user's public key pk_i , condition c and message m as input, it generates ciphertext C_i . Both C_i and c should be sent to the message receiver.

— **ReKeyGen** $\left(params,Cert_{\tau,i},sk_i,c,id_j,pk_j\right)$: Run by user U_i . This algorithm takes the global parameters *params* , user U_i's certificate $Cert_{\tau,i}$ and secret key sk_i , user U_j's identity id_j and public key pk_j and condition c as input, it generates re-encryption key $rk_{i,c,j}$.

— **ReEnc** $\left(params,C_i,rk_{i,c,j}\right)$: Run by the proxy. This algorithm takes the global parameters *params* , user U_i's ciphertext C_i and re-encryption key $rk_{i,c,j}$ as input, it generates ciphertext C_j or the error symbol $\perp$.

— **Dec1** $\left(params,C_i,Cert_{\tau,i},sk_i,c\right)$: Run by the user U_i . This algorithm takes the global parameters *params* , user U_i's certificate $Cert_{\tau,i}$ and secret key sk_i , ciphertext C_i and condition c as input, it generates message m or the error symbol $\perp$.

— **Dec2** $\left(params,C_j,Cert_{\tau,j},sk_j\right)$: Run by the user U_j . This algorithm takes the global parameters *params* , user U_j's certificate $Cert_{\tau,j}$ and secret key sk_j , ciphertext C_j as input, it generates message m or the error symbol $\perp$.

Correctness: Intuitively, a CB-CPRE scheme is correct if Dec1 algorithm and Dec2 algorithm always output the expected decryption of a properly generated ciphertext. The following propositions hold:

— $Dec1(params, sk_i, Cert_{\tau,i}, C_i) = m$

— $Dec2(params, sk_j, Cert_j, \mathrm{Re}\,Enc(params, C_i, rk_{i,c,j})) = m$

2.2   The Security Model of Certificate-Based Conditional Proxy Re-Encryption

Refer to the security model of Gentry [14, 20-24], certificate-based proxy re-encryption [17] and type-based proxy re-encryption [6], it is defined using two different games: In Game 1, the Type I adversary models an uncertified entity; in Game 2, the Type II adversary models the honest-but-curious certifier who knows the master key msk.

The security of Game 1 is defined according to the following game:

Setup: The challenger C takes as input a security parameter 1^λ, and runs the Setup algorithm. It gives $params$ to adversary A, and keeps msk to itself.

Phase 1: A makes the queries adaptively, the challenger C handles as follows:

— **Public key queries** (id_i): The challenger C runs KeyGen $(params)$ to obtain a key pair (pk_i, sk_i) and adds (id_i, pk_i, sk_i) to the table T_s, it gives pk_i to A.

— **Private key queries** (pk_i): The challenger C searches whether pk_i has been created in the table T_s. If it exists in the table T_s, C responds A with sk_i. Otherwise, C runs KeyGen $(params)$ to obtain a key pair (pk_i, sk_i) and adds (id_i, pk_i, sk_i) to the table T_s, it returns sk_i to A.

— **Certificate queries** (τ, id_i, pk_i) : The challenger C runs Certify $(params, msk, \tau, id_i, pk_i)$, and responds certificate $Cert_{\tau,i}$ to A.

— **Re-encryption key queries** (pk_i, c, pk_j): The challenger C runs Private key queries (pk_i) to get sk_i, and Certificate queries (τ, id_i, pk_i) to get $Cert_{\tau,i}$, then runs ReKeyGen $(params, Cert_{\tau,i}, sk_i, c, id_j, pk_j)$ to get $rk_{i,c,j}$, C responds A with $rk_{i,c,j}$.

— **Re-encryption queries** (pk_i, pk_j, c, C_i): The challenger C runs Re-encryption key queries (pk_i, c, pk_j) to get $rk_{i,c,j}$ and runs ReEnc $(params, C_i, rk_{i,c,j})$ to get C_j, and responds A with C_j.

— **Decryption1 queries** (pk_i, C_i, c): The challenger C runs Private key queries (pk_i) to get sk_i, and Certificate queries (τ, id_i, pk_i) to get $Cert_{\tau, i}$, then runs Dec1 algorithm to get m or the error symbol $\perp$. C responds A with the result.

— **Decryption2 queries** (pk_j, C_j): The challenger C runs Private key queries (pk_j) to get sk_j, and Certificate queries (τ, id_j, pk_j) to get $Cert_{\tau, j}$, then runs Dec2 algorithm to get m or the error symbol $\perp$. C responds A with the result.

Challenge: Once A decides that Phase 1 is over, it outputs challenge condition c^* and challenge identity id_{i^*} which has not been queried $Cert_{\tau, i^*}$, selects two equal length plaintexts (m_0, m_1). The challenger C picks a random bit $b \in \{0,1\}$, then computes the challenge ciphertext $C^* = Enc(\tau, id_{i^*}, pk_{i^*}, c^*, m_b)$, and sends it to A.

Phase 2: A continues making the queries as in the Phase 1, but it is subject to the following restrictions:

— A is not permitted to issue the Certificate queries $(\tau, id_{i^*}, pk_{i^*})$ to get the target Certificate $Cert_{\tau, i^*}$.

— A is not permitted to issue the Re-encryption queries $(pk_{i^*}, pk_j, c^*, C_{i^*})$ if $Cert_{\tau, j}$ is known.

— A is not permitted to issue the Re-encryption key queries (pk_{i^*}, c^*, pk_j) if A has queried $Cert_{\tau, j}$.

— A is not permitted to issue either the Decryption1 queries on (pk_{i^*}, c^*, C_{i^*}) or Decryption2 queries on (pk_j, C_j), where (pk_j, C_j) is the derivative of the challenge pair (pk_{i^*}, c^*, C_{i^*}):

  a) If C_j is the result of Re-encryption queries $(pk_{i^*}, pk_j, c^*, C_{i^*})$;

  b) If C_j is the result of ReEnc $(C_{i^*}, rk_{i^*, c^*, j})$.

Guess: Finally, A outputs the guess b'. The adversary wins if $b = b'$.

We define the advantage of the above adversary as:

$$Success A (1^\lambda) = |\Pr[b' = b] - 1/2|$$

Definition 3   CB-CPRE security against Type I adversary
We say that the CB-CPRE is secure against chosen-ciphertext attack for Type I
adversary if the probability of A_I winning in the Game 1 is negligible in polynomial
time. In other words, $SuccessA_I\left(1^\lambda\right) \le \varepsilon$.

The security of Game 2 is defined according to the following game:

Setup: The challenger C takes as input a security parameter 1^λ, and runs the
Setup algorithm. It gives *params* and *msk* to adversary A_{II}.

Phase 1: A_{II} makes the queries adaptively, the challenger C handles as follows:

— **Public key queries** $\left(id_i\right)$: The challenger C runs KeyGen $\left(params\right)$ to
obtain a key pair $\left(pk_i, sk_i\right)$ and adds $\left(id_i, pk_i, sk_i\right)$ to the table T_s, it gives
pk_i to A_{II}.

— **Private key queries** $\left(pk_i\right)$: The challenger C searches whether pk_i has been
created in the table T_s. If it exists in the table T_s, then C responds A_{II} with
sk_i. Otherwise, C runs KeyGen$\left(params\right)$ to obtain a key pair $\left(pk_i, sk_i\right)$ and
adds $\left(id_i, pk_i, sk_i\right)$ to the table T_s, it returns sk_i to A_{II}.

— **Re-encryption key queries** $\left(pk_i, c, pk_j\right)$: The challenger C runs Private key
queries $\left(pk_i\right)$ to get sk_i, and runs ReKeyGen
$\left(params, Cert_{\tau,i}, sk_i, c, id_j, pk_j\right)$ to get $rk_{i,c,j}$, responds A_{II} with $rk_{i,c,j}$.

— **Re-encryption queries** $\left(pk_i, pk_j, c, C_i\right)$: The challenger C runs Re-encryption
key queries $\left(pk_i, c, pk_j\right)$ to get $rk_{i,c,j}$ and runs ReEnc $\left(params, C_i, rk_{i,c,j}\right)$ to
get C_j, and responds A_{II} with C_j.

— **Decryption1 queries** $\left(pk_i, C_i, c\right)$: The challenger C runs Private key
queries $\left(pk_i\right)$ to get sk_i, and Certify $\left(params, msk, \tau, id_i, pk_i\right)$ to get $Cert_{\tau,i}$,
then runs Dec1 algorithm to get m or the error symbol $\perp$. C responds A_{II}
with the result.

— **Decryption2 queries** $\left(pk_j, C_j\right)$: The challenger C runs Private key
queries $\left(pk_j\right)$ to get sk_j, and Certify $\left(params, msk, \tau, id_j, pk_j\right)$ to get $Cert_{\tau,j}$,
then runs Dec2 algorithm to get m or the error symbol $\perp$. C responds A_{II}
with the result.

Challenge: Once A_{II} decides that Phase 1 is over, it outputs challenge condition c^*
and challenge identity id_{i^*} which has not been queried sk_{i^*}, selects two equal length

plaintexts (m_0, m_1). The challenger C picks a random bit $b \in \{0,1\}$, then computes the challenge ciphertext $C^* = Enc(\tau, id_{i^*}, pk_{i^*}, c^*, m_b)$, and sends it to $A_{||}$.

Phase 2: $A_{||}$ continues making the queries as in the Phase 1, but it is subject to the following restrictions:

— $A_{||}$ is not permitted to issue the Private key queries (pk_{i^*}) to get the target private key sk_{i^*}.

— $A_{||}$ is not permitted to issue the Re-encryption queries $(pk_{i^*}, pk_j, c^*, C_{i^*})$ if sk_j is known.

— $A_{||}$ is not permitted to issue the Re-encryption key queries (pk_{i^*}, c^*, pk_j) if sk_j is known.

— $A_{||}$ is not permitted to issue either the Decryption1 queries on (pk_{i^*}, c^*, C_{i^*}) or Decryption2 queries on (pk_j, C_j), where (pk_j, C_j) is the derivative of the challenge pair (pk_{i^*}, c^*, C_{i^*}):

    a)   If C_j is the result of Re-encryption queries $(pk_{i^*}, pk_j, c^*, C_{i^*})$;

    b)   If C_j is the result of ReEnc $(C_{i^*}, rk_{i^*, c^*, j})$.

Guess: Finally, $A_{||}$ outputs the guess b'. The adversary wins if $b = b'$.

    We define the advantage of the above adversary as:

$$SuccessA_{||}(1^\lambda) = \left| \Pr[b' = b] - 1/2 \right|$$

Definition 4   CB-CPRE Security against Type II Adversary
We say that the CB-CPRE is secure against chosen-ciphertext security for Type II adversary if the probability of $A_{||}$ winning in the Game 2 is negligible in polynomial time. In other words, $SuccessA_{||}(1^\lambda) \leq \varepsilon$.

3   Certificated-Based Conditional Proxy Re-Encryption

Our construction is based on Gentry [14] CBE scheme with small modification. We use its ciphertext as the first ciphertext and add an extra element to make the re-encryption feasible. This scheme is constructed as follows:

Setup (1^λ): Let G_1 and G_2 be the groups of prime order p, where $p \geq 2^\lambda$, and g be the generator of G_1. Let $e: G_1 \times G_1 \to G_2$ be a bilinear map. The CA picks a random number $\alpha \in Z_p^*$ as master key and computes $g_1 = g^\alpha$. $H_1: \{0,1\}^* \to G_1$, $H_2: \{0,1\}^n \times G_2 \to Z_p^*$, $H_3: G_1 \times Z_p^* \to G_1$, $H_4: G_2 \to \{0,1\}^n$, $H_5: \{0,1\}^* \to G_1$, $H_6: \{0,1\}^* \to G_1$ are hash functions. $params = \{G_1, G_2, g, g_1, e, H_1, H_2, H_3, H_4, H_5, H_6\}$ is published as the global parameters and the master key $msk = \alpha$ keeps secret.

KeyGen: The user U_i takes the global parameters $params$ as input, then picks a random value $x_i \in Z_p^*$ as his private key sk_i, and computes a corresponding public key $pk_i = g^{x_i}$.

Certify: The CA takes period time τ, identity id_i, public key pk_i, the master key α as input, computes $s_i = H_1(\tau, id_i, pk_i)$ and $Cert_{\tau,i} = s_i^\alpha$. The CA sends $Cert_{\tau,i}$ to the user U_i.

Enc: To encrypt a message $m \in \{0,1\}^n$, a user performs as follows:
— Compute $s_i = H_1(\tau, id_i, pk_i)$, $h_i = H_3(pk_i, c)$, where $c \in Z_p^*$ is a condition.
— Pick a random value $\delta \in G_2$, compute $r = H_2(m, \delta)$.
— Compute the ciphertext $C_i = (C_1, C_2, C_3, C_4, C_5)$ as:

$C_1 = g^r$, $C_2 = \delta \cdot \left(e(pk_i, h_i) \cdot e(s_i, g_1) \right)^r$, $C_3 = m \oplus H_4(\delta)$, $C_4 = e\left(s_i^c, pk_i \cdot g_1 \right)^r$,
$C_5 = H_5(C_1, C_2, C_3, C_4)^r$.

ReKeyGen: On input $\langle Cert_{\tau,i}, x_i, c, id_j, pk_j \rangle$, user U_i does the following steps:
— Pick a random value $y \in Z_p^*$, compute $rk_1 = g^{y \cdot x_i}$.
— Set $h_i = H_3(pk_i, c)$, then compute $rk_2 = \left(h_i \cdot pk_j^y \right)^{-x_i}$.
— Set $s_j = H_1(\tau, id_j, pk_j)$, $k = e(Cert_{\tau,i}, s_j)$, pick a random value $R \in G_2$, then compute $rk_3 = Cert_{\tau,i} \cdot H_6(k, id_j, pk_j, R)$.
— Set $s_i = H_1(\tau, id_i, pk_i)$, compute $rk_4 = R \cdot e(g_1, s_j)^{y \cdot x_i}$, $rk_5 = \left(Cert_{\tau,i} \cdot s_i^{x_i} \right)^c$.
— Set $rk_{i,c,j} = (rk_1, rk_2, rk_3, rk_4, rk_5)$.

ReEnc: On input $\langle C_i, rk_{i,c,j}, \rangle$, the proxy performs as following steps:

- If $e(C_1, H_5(C_1, C_2, C_3, C_4)) = e(g, C_5)$ holds, then continues; otherwise, it outputs $\perp$.

- If $e(rk_5, C_1) = C_4$ holds, then continues; otherwise, it outputs $\perp$.

- Compute $\omega_1 = e(C_1, rk_2)$, $\omega_2 = 1/e(C_1, rk_3)$ and $C_2' = C_2 \cdot \omega_1 \cdot \omega_2$.

- Set $C_1' = C_1$, $C_3' = C_3$, $C_4' = rk_1$, $C_5' = rk_4$ and output a new ciphertext $C_j = (C_1', C_2', C_3', C_4', C_5')$.

Dec1: On input $\langle C_i, x_i, Cert_{\tau,i}, c \rangle$, user U_i does the following steps:

- If $e(C_1, H_5(C_1, C_2, C_3, C_4)) = e(g, C_5)$ holds, then continues; otherwise, it outputs $\perp$.

- Set $h_i = H_3(pk_i, c)$, then compute $\delta = C_2 / (e(C_1, h_i^{x_i}) \cdot e(C_1, Cert_{\tau,i}))$.

- Compute $m = C_3 \oplus H_4(\delta)$ and $r = H_2(m, \delta)$.

- If $g^r = C_1$ holds, then outputs m, otherwise outputs $\perp$.

Dec2: On input $\langle C_j, x_j, Cert_{\tau,j} \rangle$, user U_j does the following steps:

- Compute $s_i = H_1(\tau, id_i, pk_i)$, and $R = C_5' / e(C_4', Cert_{\tau,j})$.

- Compute $k = e(s_i, Cert_{\tau,j})$, $\delta = C_2' \cdot e(C_1', C_4')^{x_j} \cdot e(C_1', H_6(k, id_j, pk_j, R))$.

- Compute $m = C_3' \oplus H_4(\delta)$ and $r = H_2(m, \delta)$.

- If $g^r = C_1$ holds, then outputs m, otherwise outputs $\perp$.

4   Security Analysis

According to the definition and security model of CB-CPRE provided in section 2, we prove our scheme is secure against chosen-ciphertext attack. Due to the space limitation, we delete the proof of theorems. The reader refers to our full version.

Theorem 1: Suppose that a Type I adversary A has advantage ε against our CB-CPRE scheme which makes at most q_{H_i} $(i = 2, 4)$ oracle queries, q_{re} Re-encryption queries, q_{d_1} Decryption1 queries and q_{d_2} Decryption2 queries during the polynomial time t. Then there exists an challenger C that can solve a random instance of BDH problem in (G_1, G_2) with success probability

$$\varepsilon' \geq \frac{1}{q_{H_4}} \left(2\varepsilon - \frac{q_{re} + q_{d_1} + q_{d_2}}{p} - \frac{q_{H_2}\left(1 + q_{d_1} + q_{d_2}\right)}{2^n} \right).$$

Theorem 2: Suppose that a Type II adversary A_{II} has advantage ε against our CB-CPRE scheme which makes at most $q_{H_i} (i = 2,4)$ oracle queries, q_{re} Re-encryption queries, q_{d_1} Decryption1 queries and q_{d_2} Decryption2 queries during the polynomial time t. Then there exists an challenger C that can solve a random instance of BDH problem in (G_1, G_2) with success probability

$$\varepsilon' \geq \frac{1}{q_{H_4}} \left(2\varepsilon - \frac{q_{re} + q_{d_1} + q_{d_2}}{p} - \frac{q_{H_2}\left(1 + q_{d_1} + q_{d_2}\right)}{2^n} \right).$$

5   Conclusion

In this paper, we formalize the definition and the security model of certificate-based conditional proxy re-encryption and propose a certificate-based conditional proxy re-encryption scheme. Based on BDH assumption, the proposed scheme is proved secure against chosen-ciphertext security in the random oracle model. Our scheme enables the delegator to implement fine-grained policy with one key pair, where only those ciphertexts satisfying one condition set by the delegator can be re-encrypted correctly by the proxy. The proposed scheme has potential application in cloud computing.

Acknowledgments. We would like to thank anonymous referees for their helpful comments and suggestions.

References

1. Blaze, M., Bleumer, G., Strauss, M.: Divertible Protocols and Atomic Proxy Cryptography. In: Nyberg, K. (ed.) EUROCRYPT 1998. LNCS, vol. 1403, pp. 127–144. Springer, Heidelberg (1998)
2. Ateniese, G., Fu, K., Green, M., Hohenberger, S.: Improved Proxy Re-Encryption Schemes with Applications to Secure Distributed Storage. ACM Transaction on Information and System Security 9(1), 1–30 (2006)
3. Canetti, R., Hohenberqer, S.: Chosen-Ciphertext Secure Proxy Re-Encryption. In: Proceedings of the 14th ACM Conference on Computer and Communications Security, pp. 185–194 (2007)
4. Libert, B., Vergnaud, D.: Unidirectional Chosen-Ciphertext Secure Proxy Re-Encryption. In: Cramer, R. (ed.) PKC 2008. LNCS, vol. 4939, pp. 360–379. Springer, Heidelberg (2008)
5. Shao, J., Cao, Z.: CCA-Secure Proxy Re-encryption without Pairings. In: Jarecki, S., Tsudik, G. (eds.) PKC 2009. LNCS, vol. 5443, pp. 357–376. Springer, Heidelberg (2009)

6. Tang, Q.: Type-Based Proxy Re-Encryption and Its Construction. In: Chowdhury, D.R., Rijmen, V., Das, A. (eds.) INDOCRYPT 2008. LNCS, vol. 5365, pp. 130–144. Springer, Heidelberg (2008)

7. Green, M., Ateniese, G.: Identity-Based Proxy Re-Encryption. In: Katz, J., Yung, M. (eds.) ACNS 2007. LNCS, vol. 4521, pp. 288–306. Springer, Heidelberg (2007)

8. Chu, C.K., Tzeng, W.G.: Identity-Based Proxy Re-Encryption without Random Oracles. In: Garay, J.A., Lenstra, A.K., Mambo, M., Peralta, R. (eds.) ISC 2007. LNCS, vol. 4779, pp. 189–202. Springer, Heidelberg (2007)

9. Fang, L., Susilo, W., Wang, J.: Anonymous Conditional Proxy Re-Encryption without Random Oracle. In: Pieprzyk, J., Zhang, F. (eds.) ProvSec 2009. LNCS, vol. 5848, pp. 47–60. Springer, Heidelberg (2009)

10. Weng, J., Deng, R.H., Ding, X., Chu, C.K., Lai, J.: Conditional Proxy Re-Encryption Secure Against Chosen-Ciphertext Attack. In: Proceedings of the 2009 ACM Symposium on Information, Computer and Communications, pp. 322–332. ACM (2009)

11. Vivek, S.S., Selvi, S.S.D., Radhakishan, V., Pandu Rangan, C.: Conditional Proxy Re-Encryption - A More Efficient Construction. In: Wyld, D.C., Wozniak, M., Chaki, N., Meghanathan, N., Nagamalai, D. (eds.) CNSA 2011. CCIS, vol. 196, pp. 502–512. Springer, Heidelberg (2011)

12. Ateniese, G., Benson, K., Hohenberger, S.: Key-Private Proxy Re-Encryption. In: Fischlin, M. (ed.) CT-RSA 2009. LNCS, vol. 5473, pp. 279–294. Springer, Heidelberg (2009)

13. Shao, J., Liu, P., Zhou, Y.: Achieving Key Privacy without Losing CCA Security in Proxy Re-Encryption. Journal of Systems and Software 2012(85), 655–665 (2012)

14. Gentry, C.: Certificate-Based Encryption and the Certificate Revocation Problem. In: Biham, E. (ed.) EUROCRYPT 2003. LNCS, vol. 2656, pp. 272–293. Springer, Heidelberg (2003)

15. Lu, Y., Li, J.G., Xiao, J.M.: Forward-Secure Certificate-Based Encryption. In: Proceedings of the Fifth International Conference on Information Assurance and Security, pp. 57–60 (2009)

16. Lu, Y., Li, J.G.: Forward-Secure Certificate-Based Encryption and Its Generic Construction. Journal of Networks 5(5), 527–534 (2010)

17. Sur, C., Park, Y., Shin, S., Phee, K.: Certificate-Based Proxy Re-Encryption for Public Cloud Storage. In: Seventh International Conference on Innovative Mobile and Internet Services in Ubiquitous, pp. 159–166 (2013)

18. Boneh, D., Franklin, M.: Identity-Based Encryption from the Weil Pairing. In: Kilian, J. (ed.) CRYPTO 2001. LNCS, vol. 2139, pp. 213–229. Springer, Heidelberg (2001)

19. Boneh, D., Boyen, X.: Efficient Selective-ID Secure Identity-Based Encryption without Random Oracles. In: Cachin, C., Camenisch, J.L. (eds.) EUROCRYPT 2004. LNCS, vol. 3027, pp. 223–238. Springer, Heidelberg (2004)

20. Li, J.G., Huang, X.Y., Mu, Y., Susilo, W., Wu, Q.H.: Certificate-Based Signature: Security Model and Efficient Construction. In: López, J., Samarati, P., Ferrer, J.L. (eds.) EuroPKI 2007. LNCS, vol. 4582, pp. 110–125. Springer, Heidelberg (2007)

21. Li, J.G., Huang, X.Y., Mu, Y., Susilo, W., Wu, Q.H.: Constructions of Certificate-Based Signature Secure against Key Replacement Attacks. Journal of Computer Security 18(3), 421–449 (2010)

22. Li, J.G., Wang, Z.W., Zhang, Y.C.: Provably Secure Certificate-Based Signature Scheme without Pairings. Information Sciences 233(6), 313–320 (2013)

23. Li, J.G., Huang, X.Y., Hong, M.X., Zhang, Y.C.: Certificate-based Signcryption with Enhanced Security Features. Computers and Mathematics with Applications 64(6), 1587–1601 (2012)

24. Li, J.G., Huang, X.Y., Zhang, Y.C., Xu, L.Z.: An Efficient Short Certificate-Based Signature Scheme. Journal of Systems and Software 85(2), 314–322 (2012)

A Secure Obfuscator for Encrypted Blind Signature Functionality*

Xiao Feng[1,2] and Zheng Yuan[1,2,**]

[1] Beijing Electronic Science & Technology Institute, Beijing 100070, P.R. China
zyuan@tsinghua.edu.cn, sxzyfx@163.com
[2] School of Telecommunications Engineering, Xidian University, Shaanxi 710071, P.R. China

Abstract. This paper introduces a new obfuscation called obfuscation of encrypted blind signature. Informally, Alice is Signer and Bob is Recipient. Bob needs Alice to sign a message, but he does not want Alice to know what the message is. Furthermore, Bob doesn't want anyone to know the interactive process. So we present a secure obfuscator for encrypted blind signature which makes the interactions process unintelligible for any third party, while still keeps the original functionality of encrypted blind signature. We use schnorr's blind signature scheme and linear encryption scheme as blocks to construct a new obfuscator. Moreover, we propose two new security definitions: blindness w.r.t encrypted blind signature (EBS) obfuscator and one-more unforgeability(OMU) w.r.t EBS obfuscator, and prove them under Decisional Linear (DL) assumption and the hardness of discrete logarithm, respectively. We also demonstrate that our obfuscator satisfies the Average-Case Virtual Black-Box Property(ACVBP) w.r.t dependent oracle, it is indistinguishable secure. Our paper expands a new direction for the application of obfuscation.

Keywords: Obfuscation, Blind signature, Indistinguishable security.

1 Introduction

Obfuscation in cryptography has been formally proposed by Barak, Goldreich et al.[1] at the first time. Although it is a theoretical hot spot, there hasn't been much progress in recent years. The implementation of obfuscation mainly depends on how to construct a secure obfuscator. Informally, obfuscator is an algorithm program which can transform a program into a new unintelligible program while its original functionality holds. Barak et al. suggested that an obfuscator should satisfy the following three properties:

1. Functionality: the obfuscated program has the same functionality as the original program.

* This work is supported by the National Natural Science Foundation of China (No.61070250), and Beijing Natural Science Foundation (N0.4132066), and the 12th Five-year Cryptography Development Foundation of China (No.MMJJ201101026), and Scientific Research and Post-graduate Training Cooperation Project-Scientific Research Base-New Theory of Block Cipher and Obfuscation and their Application Research.
** To whom correspondence should be addressed.

M.H. Au et al. (Eds.): NSS 2014, LNCS 8792, pp. 311–322, 2014.
© Springer International Publishing Switzerland 2014

2. Polynomial Slowdown: the description length and running time of the obfuscated program are at most polynomially larger than the original program's.
3. Virtual Black-Box Property(VBP): Anything that can be efficiently computed from obfuscated program can be efficiently computed given oracle access to the original program.

Obfuscation has profound effects on both theory and application, such as software protection, homomorphic encryption, removing random oracles and transforming private-key encryption into public-key encryption. Despite all that, Barak et al. proved the impossibility of obfuscation even under a very weak definition. Later, more impossible obfuscation results of natural functionalities were shown in [2][3][4][5]. Even so, some cryptologists have been dedicating to conduct a series of explorations, and they found that there still exist simple classes of functions such as point functions[6][7][8][2][3][9] with the possibility of obfuscation.

Before 2007, several positive results of obfuscation were mainly about simple functions. The obfuscation of complicated cryptographic functionality was firstly proposed by Hohenberger et al.[10] in TCC'07. They obfuscated re-encryption functionality and proved the security of obfuscator in the standard model. In brief, the re-encryption functionality is the one that takes a ciphertext for a message encrypted under Alice's public key and transforms it into a ciphertext for the same message under Bob's public key. Hohenberger et al. presented an improved security property called ACVBP. Following the definition of ACVBP[10], Hada [11] showed a secure obfuscation for encrypted signature, which generated a signature on a given message under Alice's secret signing key and then encrypted the signature under Bob's public encryption key. Later, on the basis of Honhenberger's results, Nishanth Chandran et al. [12] refined the delegation of access of re-encryption functionality, and demonstrated the security of collusion-resistant obfuscation. Other obfuscations of complicated cryptographic functionality are based on above schemes so far.

Blind signature has a wide range of applications in e-cash and electronic election. A blind signature is a protocol introduced by Chaum [13] for protecting the anonymity of signer, which was based on the RSA digital signature scheme. Unlike general digital signature scheme, blind signature requires that the signer signs the message without knowing the message or the resulting signatures while the user can verify it publicly. It's an interactive protocol between the signer and recipient. A blind signature must satisfy the following properties:

1. Unforgeability: Adversary can not produce a legal blind signature on message after interacting with signer.
2. Blindness: The signatures of two given messages are computationally indistinguishable even under a set of known message-signature pairs.

Afterwards, on the basis of Schnorr's signature scheme, Okamoto[14] put forward a blind signature scheme named Schnorr's blind signature whose security was based on discrete logarithm problem, Schnorr then proved its security in [15].

Our Contributions. In this paper, we firstly use Schnorr's blind signature scheme and linear encryption scheme[16] as blocks to construct a new functionality of a special blind signature inspired by Hada's Encrypted Signature (ES) functionality in [11], we called it encrypted blind signature (EBS) functionality. Then, we construct a secure obfuscator for this functionality. In order to prove the security of the obfuscator , we present two new security definitions, blindness and one-more unforgeability (EBS) w.r.t encrypted blind signature(EBS) obfuscator. The main method is constructing different adversaries to break the hardness assumption under security definition of ACVBP w.r.t dependent oracle, the scheme is insecure if any adversary succeeds. The specific progress refers to section 5. We also prove that the OMU w.r.t EBS functionality implies OMU w.r.t EBS obfuscator under the assumption that EBS obfuscator satisfies ACVBP w.r.t dependent oracle set. Obviously, we have OMU w.r.t EBS obfuscator. At last, we present the security proof of EBS obfuscator. i.e., the EBS obfuscator satisfies ACVBP w.r.t dependent oracle. Thus, we illustrate that under the ACVBP w.r.t dependent oracle, generating a blind signature on a message and then encrypting the signature are functionally equivalent to encrypt the signing key and then generate a blind signature on the message.

The paper is organized as follows: Section 2 gives preliminaries which contain three parts; Section 3 constructs the secure obfuscator for special EBS functionality; Then section 4 proposes new security definitions with respect to the basis of theorem's proof and section 5 gives the proof .

2 Preliminaries

In this section, we present the basic security definition and the hardness assumption that our proofs rely on.

2.1 Bilinear Maps

Set $BM setup$ be an initialization algorithm: on input security parameter 1^k, outputs the bilinear map parameters as $(q, g, \mathbb{G}, \mathbb{G}_T, e)$, where $\mathbb{G}, \mathbb{G}_T$ are groups of prime order $q \in \Theta(2^k)$, g is a generator of $\mathbb{G}$ and e is an efficient bilinear mapping from $\mathbb{G} \times \mathbb{G}$ to $\mathbb{G}_T$. The mapping e satisfies the following two properties:

- Bilinear: For all $g \in \mathbb{G}$ and $a, b \in \mathbb{Z}_q$, $e(g^a, g^b) = e(g, g)^{ab}$.
- Non-degenrate: If g generates $\mathbb{G}$, then $e(g^a, g^b) \neq 1$.

2.2 Complexity Assumptions

Definition 1. *(DL Assumption) For every PPT machine D, every polynomial $p(\cdot)$, all sufficiently large $n \in \mathbb{N}$, and every $z \in \{0, 1\}^{ploy(n)}$,*

$$\left| Pr \left[\begin{array}{l} p = (q, \mathbb{G}, \mathbb{G}_T, e, g) \leftarrow Setup(1^n); \\ a \leftarrow \mathbb{Z}_q; b \leftarrow \mathbb{Z}_q; r \leftarrow \mathbb{Z}_q; s \leftarrow \mathbb{Z}_q; \\ decision \leftarrow D(p, (g^a, g^b), (g^{r+s}, (g^a)^r, (g^b)^s), z). \end{array} : decision = 1 \right] - \right.$$
$$\left. Pr \left[\begin{array}{l} p = (q, \mathbb{G}, \mathbb{G}_T, e, g) \leftarrow Setup(1^n); \\ a \leftarrow \mathbb{Z}_q; b \leftarrow \mathbb{Z}_q; r \leftarrow \mathbb{Z}_q; s \leftarrow \mathbb{Z}_q; t \leftarrow \mathbb{Z}_q; \\ decision \leftarrow D(p, (g^a, g^b), (g^t, (g^a)^r, (g^b)^s), z). \end{array} : decision = 1 \right] \right| \leq \frac{1}{p(n)}$$

2.3   The Definition of General Security

In this subsection we represent the structure of public-key encryption (PKE) scheme and digital blind signature (DBS) scheme firstly. Then we review the security definition of public-key encryption (PKE) scheme and digital blind signature (DBS) scheme.

$Setup$ is an algorithm that generates a parameter, on security parameter 1^n, which is used commonly by multiple users in a pair of PKE and DBS schemes.

A probabilistic public key cryptosystem PKE is a probabilistic polynomial time Turing machine Π that contains three algorithm:

(1)EKG: on inputs p generates a pair of pubic-secret key (pk, sk) and outputs the description of two algorithms, E and D such that

(2)E is a probabilistic encryption algorithm: for some constants p , public key pk and a plaintext m, returns the ciphertext c, let $MS(p, pk)$ be the message space defined by (p, pk).

(3)D is a deterministic decryption algorithm: for some constants p, secret key sk and ciphertext c, returns the plaintext m.

The security of a public-key encryption scheme is indistinguishability of Encryptions against CPAs. The details as follow.

Definition 2. *(Indistinguishability of Encryptions against CPAs) A PKE scheme (EKG, E, D) satisfies the indistinguishability if the following condition holds: For every PPT machine pair (A_1, A_2)(adversary), every polynomial $p(\cdot)$, all sufficiently large $n \in \mathbb{N}$, and every $z \in \{0, 1\}^{poly(n)}$,*

$$2 \cdot Pr \begin{bmatrix} p \leftarrow Setup(1^n); (pk, sk) \leftarrow EKG(p); \\ (m_1, m_2, h) \leftarrow A_1(p, pk, z); b \leftarrow \{0, 1\}; c \leftarrow E(p, pk, m_b); \\ d \leftarrow A_2(p, pk, (m_1, m_2, h), c, z); \\ b = d. \end{bmatrix} - 1 \leqslant \frac{1}{p(n)}$$

where we assume that A_1 produces a valid message pair m_1 and $m_2 \in MS(p, pk)$ and a hint h.

A digital blind signature DBS also contains three algorithms:

(1)SKG: generates a pair of pubic-secret key (pk, sk) on input p.

(2)(S, U) is a probabilistic interactive signing algorithm: for some constants p , secret key sk and l-bit plaintext $m = m_1 m_2 \cdots m_l \in MS(p, pk)$, the execution of algorithm $S(sk)$ (by signer), and algorithm $U(pk, m)$ (by user) for message m generates the signature σ, where $MS(p, pk)$ is the message space defined by (p, pk).

(3)V is a deterministic verification algorithm: for some constants p, public key pk, message m and signature σ, if σ is the valid signature of m, it accepts; Otherwise returns $\perp$.

The security of a blind signature scheme includes one-more unforgeability and blindness.

Definition 3. *(Blindness) A blind signature scheme $DBS = (SKG, (S, U), V)$ is called blind if for any efficient algorithm A_3, all sufficiently large $n \in \mathbb{N}$, and every $z \in \{0, 1\}^{poly(n)}$, there exists*

$$2 \cdot Pr \left[\begin{array}{l} p \leftarrow Setup(1^n); (pk, sk) \leftarrow SKG(p); \\ b \leftarrow \{0, 1\}; (\sigma_0, \sigma_1) \leftarrow A_3^{<\cdot, U(pk,m_b)>^1, <\cdot, U(pk,m_{1-b})>^1}(p, pk, z); \\ b^* \leftarrow A_3(\sigma_0, \sigma_1); \\ b = b^*. \end{array} \right] - 1 \leqslant \frac{1}{p(n)}$$

where A_3 is the malicious Signer and U is the honest user. If $\sigma_0 = \perp$ or $\sigma_1 = \perp$, then the Signer is not informed about the other signature.

Note that we use $X^{<\cdot, Y(y_0)>^1, <\cdot, Y(y_1)>^1}$ to define the process that X invokes arbitrarily ordered executions with $Y(y_0)$ and $Y(y_1)$, but interacts with each algorithm only once.

Definition 4. *(One-more Unforgeability) A DBS scheme $(SKG, (S, U), V)$ is unforgetable if for any efficient algorithm A_4(the malicious user), every polynomial $p(\cdot)$, all sufficiently large $n \in \mathbb{N}$, and every $z \in \{0, 1\}^{poly(n)}$, there exist*

$$Pr \left[\begin{array}{l} p \leftarrow Setup(1^n); (pk, sk) \leftarrow SKG(p); \\ ((m_1^*, \sigma_1^*), \ldots, (m_{k+1}^*, \sigma_{k+1}^*)) \leftarrow A_4^{\ll S_{p,sk} \gg^k}(p, pk, z); \\ if\ m_i^* \neq m_j^*\ for\ i \neq j; \\ V(p, pk, m_i^*, \sigma_i^*) = Accept\ for\ all\ i; then\ return\ 1. \end{array} \right] \leqslant \frac{1}{p(n)}$$

where $S_{p,sk}$ is the signing oracle (circuit) .

Note that we use $X^{\ll Y \gg^k}$ to define the process that X samples access to Y for at most k times.

3   Construct the Secure Obfuscator for Special EBS Functionality

In this section we construct a secure obfuscator for the blind signature and prove the security based on the generalized ACVBP definition.

3.1   Schnorr's Blind Signature

We use Schnorr's blind signature scheme[14] as a block to build the EBS functionality. The specific process is as follows:

$SKG(p)$

1. Parses $p = (q, \mathbb{G}, \mathbb{G}_T, \mathbf{e}, g)$.
2. Selects $g_1 \in \mathbb{G}$ and $x \in \mathbb{Z}_q$ randomly.
3. Outputs the secret key $sk = g_1^x$ and public key $pk = (g_1, g^{g_1^x})$, where $y = g^{g_1^x}$.

$Sign(p, sk, m)$

1. Parses $p = (q, \mathbb{G}, \mathbb{G}_T, \mathbf{e}, g)$.
2. Signer selects $k \in \mathbb{Z}_q$ randomly and computes $t = g^k \mod p$, then sends t to Recipient.
3. Recipient selects $\alpha, \beta \in \mathbb{Z}_q$ randomly and computers $\omega = tg^\alpha y^\beta \mod p$, then computes $c = H(m||\omega)$ and $c' = c - \beta \mod q$, sends c' to Signer.

4. Signer computes $u = k - c' \cdot sk \bmod q$, and sends u to Recipient.
5. Recipient computes $v = u + \alpha \bmod q$.
6. Recipient outputs signature $\sigma = (c, v)$.

$Verify(p, pk, m, \sigma)$

1. Parses $p = (q, \mathbb{G}, \mathbb{G}_T, \mathbf{e}, g)$, $pk = (g_1, g_1^{g_1^x})$, $m = m_1, m_2, \ldots, m_n$, and $\sigma = (c, v)$.
2. Computes $g^v y^c = \omega$.
3. Accepts if $H(m||\omega) = c$; otherwise outputs $\perp$.

3.2   Linear Encryption Scheme

Boneh's linear encryption scheme[16] is another block to build the EBS functionality. The detail is as follows:

$EKG(p)$:

1. Parses $p = (q, \mathbb{G}, \mathbb{G}_T, \mathbf{e}, g)$.
2. Selects $a \in \mathbb{Z}_q$ and $b \in \mathbb{Z}_q$ randomly.
3. Outputs the secret key $sk_e = (a, b)$ and public key $pk_e = (g^a, g^b)$.

$Enc(p, pk_e, m)$

1. Parses $p = (q, \mathbb{G}, \mathbb{G}_T, \mathbf{e}, g)$.
2. Selects $r \in \mathbb{Z}_q$, $s \in \mathbb{Z}_q$ randomly.
3. Computes $(c_1, c_2, c_3) = ((g^a)^r, (g^b)^s, g^{r+s}m)$.
4. Outputs $c = (c_1, c_2, c_3)$.

$Verify(p, sk_e, c)$

1. Parses $p = (q, \mathbb{G}, \mathbb{G}_T, \mathbf{e}, g)$, $sk_e = (a, b)$, and $c = (c_1, c_2, c_3)$.
2. Outputs $m = c_3/(c_1^{1/a}/c_2^{1/b})$.

Theorem 1. *[16] Under DL assumption, the linear encryption scheme satisfies the indistinguishability.*

3.3   Functionality of EBS

EBS functionality consists of the blind signature scheme and encryption scheme above.

– $EBS_{p,sk,pk_e}(m)$
  1. Run $(\sigma_1, \sigma_2) \leftarrow BlindSign(p, sk, m)$.
  2. Run $C_1 \leftarrow Enc(p, pk_e, \sigma_1)$.
  3. Run $C_2 \leftarrow Enc(p, pk_e, \sigma_2)$.
  4. Output (C_1, C_2).
– $Keys_{p,sk,pk_e}(keys)$:
  1. Output (p, pk, pk_e), where pk is the public key corresponding to sk.

Let $C_{EBS} = \{C_n\}$ denote a class of circuit for EBS functionality which we want to obfuscate.

3.4   The Obfuscator for the EBS Functionality

We construct a circuit C_{p,sk,pk_e} which contains a common parameter p, the signing secret key sk and the public encryption key pk_e. Note that the important point of obfuscation is how to Rerandomize the Enc to make the two results scalar homomorphic. Here, we use the $ReRand$ algorithm, given a cipertext (c_1, c_2, c_3) and public key $pk_e = (g^a, g^b)$, to Rerandomize the ciphertext (c_1, c_2, c_3) as following: $(c_1(g^a)^{r'}, c_2(g^b)^{s'}, c_3 g^{r'+s'}) \leftarrow ReRand(p, pk_e, (c_1, c_2, c_3))$, where $r', s' \in \mathbb{Z}_q$ are random parameters.

Given a circuit C_{p,sk,pk_e}, the detail of our obfuscator for the EBS Functionality Obf_{EBS} is as below:

1. Extracts (p, sk, pk, pk_e), where $sk = g_1^x$, $pk = g^{g_1^x}$ and $pk_e = (g^a, g^b)$.
2. Parses $p = (q, \mathbb{G}, \mathbb{G}_T, \mathbf{e}, g)$.
3. *Signer* runs $Enc(p, pk_e, sk) \rightarrow (c_1, c_2, sk') = ((g^a)^r, (g^b)^s, g^{r+s} g_1^x)$ to obtain a new signing secret key $sk' = g^{r+s} g_1^x$, computes the corresponding public signing key $pk' = (g_1, g^{g^{r+s} g_1^x})$, where $y' = g^{g^{r+s} g_1^x}$, and sends (c_1, c_2) to *Recipient*.
4. *Signer* selects a random parameter $k \in \mathbb{Z}_q$, then sends $t = g^k$ to *Recipient*.
5. Randomly chooses $\alpha, \beta \in \mathbb{Z}_q$, *Recipient* counts $\omega' = t g^\alpha (y')^\beta$, $c' = H(m||\omega')$, and $c'' = c' - \beta$, then transmits c'' to *Signer*.
6. *Signer* gives *Recipient* u', where $u' = k - c'' \cdot sk'$.
7. *Recipient* gets $(c', v') = (H(m||\omega'), u' + \alpha)$.
8. *Recipient* computes $c_3 = c_1^{1/a} c_2^{1/b} c'$, rerandomizes the ciphertext (c_1, c_2, c_3) as $C_1 = (c_1', c_2', c_3') \leftarrow ReRand(p, pk_e, (c_1, c_2, c_3))$
   (Note: $(c_1', c_2', c_3') = ((g^a)^{r+r'}, (g^b)^{s+s'}, c' g^{r+r'+s+s'})$.
9. *Recipient* computes $C_2 \leftarrow Enc(p, pk, v')$. (We define $C_2 = (c_1'', c_2'', c_3'')$).
10. *Recipient* outputs the encrypted blind signature $\sigma = (C_1, C_2)$.

The output signature $\sigma = (C_1, C_2)$ is blind to the *Signer*, as *Signer* couldn't recognize either (c', v') or (α, β). But *Recipient* can verify the signature σ by following verification algorithm $V(p, pk, m, \sigma)$:

1. Computes $c' = c_3'/((c_1')^{1/a}(c_2')^{1/b})$, $v' = c_3''/((c_1'')^{1/a}(c_2'')^{1/b})$, $g^{v'} y'^{c'} = \hat{\omega}$, and $H(m||\hat{\omega}) = \hat{c}$.
2. If $\hat{c} = c'$, accepts $\sigma = (C_1, C_2)$; otherwise outputs $\perp$.

Obviously, the obfuscation can be executed in polynomial time and has the same functionality compared with the original blind signature. So we omit the two proofs about functionality and polynomial slowdown.

4   The New Security Definition of the Blind Signature in the Context of EBS

We modify the above **definition 3, 4** to adapt to our proposals in the context of EBS. As we need to prove the security of blind signature in the presence of the obfuscator we proposed. In this section, we allow any Signer to access the obfuscation circuit which still satisfied the security properties as follow:

Definition 5. *(Blindness w.r.t. EBS Obfuscator) An encrypted signature scheme EBS = $(SKG, EKG, (S, U), V)$ w.r.t obfuscator is called blind if for any efficient algorithm A_3, all sufficiently large $n \in \mathbb{N}$, and every $z \in \{0, 1\}^{poly(n)}$, there exists*

$$2 \cdot Pr \left[\begin{array}{l} p \leftarrow Setup(1^n); (pk, sk) \leftarrow SKG(p); (pk_e, sk_e) \leftarrow EKG(p); \\ C' \leftarrow Obf(C_{p,sk,pk_e}); \\ b \leftarrow \{0,1\}; (\sigma_0, \sigma_1) \leftarrow A_3^{<\cdot, U(pk,m_b)>^1, <\cdot, U(pk,m_1-b)>^1}(p, pk, pk_e, C', z); \\ b^* \leftarrow A_3(\sigma_0, \sigma_1); \\ b = b^*. \end{array} \right] - 1 \leqslant \frac{1}{p(n)}$$

where A_3 is the malicious Signer and U is the honest user. If $\sigma_0 = \perp$ or $\sigma_1 = \perp$, then the Signer is not informed about the other signature.

Definition 6. *(One-more Unforgeability w.r.t. EBS Obfuscator) An EBS scheme $(SKG, EKG, (S, U), V)$ is unforgetable if for any efficient algorithm A_4(the malicious user), every polynomial $p(\cdot)$, all sufficiently large $n \in \mathbb{N}$, and every $z \in \{0, 1\}^{poly(n)}$, there exists*

$$Pr \left[\begin{array}{l} p \leftarrow Setup(1^n); (pk, sk) \leftarrow SKG(p); (pk_e, sk_e) \leftarrow EKG(p); \\ C' \leftarrow Obf(C_{p,sk,pk_e}); \\ ((m_1^*, \sigma_1^*), \ldots, (m_{k+1}^*, \sigma_{k+1}^*)) \leftarrow A_4^{\ll S_{p,sk} \gg^k}(p, pk, pk_e, C', z); \\ if\ m_i^* \neq m_j^*\ for\ i \neq j; \\ V(p, pk, m_i^*, \sigma_i^*) = Accept\ for\ all\ i;\ then\ return\ 1. \end{array} \right] \leqslant \frac{1}{p(n)}$$

where $S_{p,sk}$ is the signing oracle (circuit) .

Definition 7. *(ACVBP w.r.t Dependent Oracles) Let $T(C)$ be a set of oracles dependent on the circuit C. A circuit obfuscator Obf for C satisfies the ACVBP w.r.t dependent oracle set T if the following condition holds: There exists a PPT oracle machine S (simulator) such that, for every PPT oracle machine D (distinguisher), every polynomial $p(\cdot)$, all sufficiently large $n \in \mathbb{N}$, and every $z \in \{0, 1\}^{poly(n)}$,*

$$\left| Pr \left[\begin{array}{l} C \leftarrow C_n; \\ C' \leftarrow Obf(C); \\ b \leftarrow D^{\ll C, T(C) \gg}(C', z). \end{array} : b = 1 \right] - Pr \left[\begin{array}{l} C \leftarrow C_n; \\ C'' \leftarrow S^{\ll C \gg}(1^n, z); \\ b \leftarrow D^{\ll C, T(C) \gg}(C'', z). \end{array} : b = 1 \right] \right| \leqslant \frac{1}{p(n)}$$

where $D^{\ll C, T(C) \gg}$ means that D has sampling access to all oracles contained in $T(C)$ in addition to C.

5   The Security of Special EBS Obfuscator

In this section, we attribute the security of special EBS obfuscator to DL assumption and the random oracle model. Although our obfuscation can remove the random oracle in theory, there still have no effective methods to do it. The reason why we prove it in random oracle model is that the signature scheme we choose is secure in random model, which is a inherent property of the original signature scheme.

At first, we will prove the completeness property of our special EBS obfuscator. Informally, the signature is complete if for any message m, verification algorithm $V(p, pk, m, \sigma)$ always set up, i.e., the probability: $Pr_{V(p,pk,m,\sigma)} = 1$.

Lemma 1. *The EBS obfuscation is complete.*

Proof. Once the user receives the signature $\sigma = (C_1, C_2)$, he finishes the following proceeds in a polynomial reduction:

1. Computes $c' = c_3'/((c_1')^{1/a}(c_2')^{1/b})$.
2. Computes $v' = c_3''/((c_1'')^{1/a}(c_2'')^{1/b})$.

According to the verification algorithm, he has $g^{v'}(y')^{c'} = g^{u'+\alpha}g_1^{s x'c'} = g^{u'+\alpha+g_1^x c'}$. As $u' = k - c'' \cdot sk'$ and $c'' = c' - \beta$, he obtains the equation $u' + \alpha + g_1^x c' = k + \alpha + \beta sk'$. Thus, $g^{v'}y'^{c'} = g^k g^\alpha g^{\beta sk'}$. Since $t = g^k$ and $y' = g^{sk'}$, he gets $g^{v'}y'^{c'} = tg^\alpha g^\beta = \omega'$. Then, the equation $H(m||\omega') = c'$ must be established. We outcome the completeness of EBS obfuscation.

Theorem 2. *Under DL assumption, for the EBS obfuscator and two messages m_0, m_1 selected by the malicious Signer A_3, the distributions of σ_0 and σ_1 are computationally indistinguishable.*

Proof. The blindness of EBS obfuscator follows directly from the hardness of DL assumption in the group $\mathbb{G}$. More formally, we show that if an adversary A_3 can distinguish the signatures (σ_0, σ_1) of two message m_0 and m_1 under sk with non-negligible probability, then we construct an adversary A' that will break the DL assumption with advantage ϵ as well.

At first, we analyze the result of EBS obfuscator: we get $\sigma = (C_1, C_2) = ((g^a)^{r+r'}, (g^b)^{s+s'}, c'g^{r+r'+s+s'}, (g^a)^{r''}, (g^b)^{s''}, v'g^{r''+s''})$, where r, s, r', s', r'', s'' are all random parameters. As the process of obfuscation above, we have $c' = H(m||\omega'), v' = k - c' \cdot sk' + \beta \cdot sk' + \alpha$, where k, α, β are random and $\omega' = g^k g^\alpha (y')^\beta$. So when the secret key sk' is fixed, v' depends on the value of c' (i.e, v' and c' are linearly dependent). Thus the value of C_2 relies on c'. Since C_1 and C_2 have the same form, we can only consider C_1 in the following work(C_2 also has the same result, we omit it here). Let $\hat{s} = s + s'$, $\hat{r} = r + r'$, so we have $C_1 = (g^{\hat{r}}, g^{\hat{s}}, g^{\hat{r}+\hat{s}})$.

A' works as follows:

- A' receives as input a tuple $(g, (a, b), B = g^{\hat{r}}, K = g^{\hat{s}}, W)$ where g is a random generator of the group $\mathbb{G}$ and r, s are random exponents. The goal of A' is to determine whether $W = g^{\hat{r}+\hat{s}}$.
- A' picks a random generator g of group $\mathbb{G}$.
- On receiving two messages m_0 and m_1 from A_3, A' flips a bit b randomly and sends the signature $\sigma_b := ((g^a)^{\hat{r}}, (g^b)^{\hat{s}}, c_b W)$ as the signature of m_b to A_3.
- A_3 replies with a bit b^*. A' simply outputs 1 if $b = b^*$ (i.e., guessing that $W = g^{\hat{r}+\hat{s}}$); otherwise outputs a random bit(i.e., W is a random parameter).

It is easy to see that when W is random, the signature σ_b is independent of b and hence the success probability of A_3 is exactly $\frac{1}{2}$ in this case. When $W = g^{\hat{r}+\hat{s}}$, the signature σ_b has the same distribution as the result of EBS obfuscator. According to the assumption, the adversary A_3 has advantage at least ϵ. That is, A' succeeds in determining whether $W = g^{\hat{r}+\hat{s}}$ with non-negligible advantage, A' breaks the DL assumption.

Theorem 3. *[15] The blind signature is one-more unforgeable if discrete logarithm is hard.*

Theorem 4. *Let $T(C_{p,sk,pk_e})$ be $S_{p,sk}$. If the EBS obfuscator satisfies ACVBP w.r.t dependent oracle set T, then the one-more unforgeability(OMU) w.r.t the EBS functionality implies the one-more unforgeability w.r.t EBS obfuscator.*

Proof. We show that, if there exists an adversary A_4 to break the OMU w.r.t Obf when the OMU w.r.t EBS is satisfied, then it will contradict the ACVBP w.r.t dependent oracle set T of EBS obfuscator. Let the distinguisher D has sample access to $T(C_{p,sk,pk_e})$ to check whether A_4 succeeds in breaking OMU w.r.t Obf.

1. Inputs a circuit C(either an obfuscated circuit or a simulated circuit) and an auxiliary-input z.
2. Extracts (p, pk, pk_e) through sampling access to C_{p,pk,pk_e}.
3. Samples access to $S_{p,sk}$ at most k times $((m_1^*, \sigma_1^*), \ldots, (m_k^*, \sigma_k^*)) \leftarrow A_4^{\ll S_{p,sk} \gg^k}$ (p, pk, pk_e, C, z) to simulate $(m_{k+1}^*, \sigma_{k+1}^*)$.
4. $V(p, pk, m_{k+1}^*, \sigma_{k+1}^*) = Accept$ for $m_{k+1} \neq m_i$ where $i \in \{1, k\}$.

If C is an obfuscated circuit, then the probability D outputs 1 which is equal to the probability that A_4 breaks OMU w.r.t Obf, which is non-negligible by the assumption. And if C is a simulated circuit, then the probability that D outputs 1 is negligible, otherwise, A_4 can break the OMU w.r.t EBS functionality. So the probability which ACVBP established is non-negligible. Hence it will contradict the ACVBP w.r.t dependent oracle set T of EBS obfuscator. Theorem is established.

Theorem 5. *Let $T(C_{p,sk,pk_e})$ be $S_{p,sk}$. The EBS obfuscator satisfies ACVBP w.r.t dependent oracle set T under DL assumption.*

Proof. According to the EBS obfuscator we proposed, the security proof of obfuscator containing an interactive process between Signer and Recipient is a little different from the previous work. We use the variant of Hada's proof method. At first, we construct a simulator S to simulate the behaves of the obfuscated circuit; the execution process is as follows(Note that the value (p, pk, pk_e) is easy to get through sampling access to C_{p,pk,pk_e}. So we mainly focus on $(sk', (c_1, c_2))$.):

1. Inputs the security parameter 1^n and an auxiliary-input z.
2. Extracts (p, pk, pk_e) through sampling access to C_{p,pk,pk_e}.
3. Parses $p = (q, \mathbb{G}, \mathbb{G}_T, \mathbf{e}, g)$ and $pk = (g_1, g^{g_1^\tau})$.
4. Randomly selects $Junk \leftarrow \mathbb{G}$.
5. Computes $c_1, c_2, c_3 \leftarrow Enc(p, pk_e, Junk)$ and sets $sk' = c_3$.
6. Outputs $(sk', (c_1, c_2))$.

And then we consider the worst case that the interactive values are captured by adversary already, i.e., the value of $k, t, c'', u', v', \omega'$ are known(ω' can get by computing $g^{v'} y'^{c'}$), we proved the output distribution of S is indistinguishable from the real distribution (C_1, C_2) for any PPT distinguisher. In particular, when the distinguisher is permitted to sampling access to $CS = \{C_{p,sk,pk_e}, S_{p,sk}\}$, assume the probability that a distinguisher $D^{\ll C,S \gg}$ distinguishes the two output distributions above is non-negligible. In other word, the probability of the following formula is non-negligible. And let $z = (k, t, c'', u', v', \omega')$ be the auxiliary-input, we have:

Real one:

$$
Pr \begin{bmatrix}
p \leftarrow Setup(1^n); (pk_e, sk_e) \leftarrow EKG(p); \\
(pk, sk) = (g^{g_1^x}, g_1^x) \leftarrow SKG(p); \\
(c_1, c_2, sk') \leftarrow Enc(p, pk_e, sk); \\
pk' = (g_1, g^{g^{r+s}g_1^x}); \\
b \leftarrow D^{\ll C,S \gg}((p, pk_e, pk', sk', (c_1, c_2)), (k, t, c'', u', v', \omega')); \\
b = 1.
\end{bmatrix}
$$

Junk one:

$$
Pr \begin{bmatrix}
p \leftarrow Setup(1^n); (pk_e, sk_e) \leftarrow EKG(p); \\
(pk, sk) = (g^{g_1^x}, g_1^x) \leftarrow SKG(p); \\
Junk \leftarrow \mathbb{G}; \\
(c_1, c_2, sk') \leftarrow Enc(p, pk_e, Junk); \\
pk' = (g_1, g^{g^{r+s}g_1^x}); \\
b \leftarrow D^{\ll C,S \gg}((p, pk_e, pk', sk', (c_1, c_2)), (k, t, c'', u', v', \omega')); \\
b = 1.
\end{bmatrix}
$$

Third we construct an adversary (A_1, A_2) to break the indistinguishability of the linear encryption scheme. A_1 produces a message pair $(m_1, m_2) = (sk, Junk)$ and an associated hint $h = pk$. Given a ciphertext c(of either m_1 or m_2), A_2 distinguishes the results of m_1 and m_2 by distinguisher D as follows:

1. Parses $p = (q, \mathbb{G}, \mathbb{G}_T, e, g)$ and pk_e, cipertext c and auxiliary $z = (k, t, c'', u', v', \omega')$.
2. Get the output m_1, m_2 of A_1, $h = pk = g^{g_1^x}$ and $c = (c_1, c_2, sk')$, let $pk' = g^{c_3}$.
3. Simulates $D^{\ll C,S \gg}((p, pk_e, pk', sk', (c_1, c_2)), (k, t, c'', u', v', \omega'))$.
4. Outputs the result of D.

If c is a ciphertext of m_1, then the probability A_2 outputs 1 which is equal to the first probability, otherwise, it is equal to the later probability. According to the Theorem 1, the difference of the two probability above is negligible which contradicts to the assumption. Theorem is established.

6   Conclusion

A new functionality for obfuscation has been proposed in this paper under DL assumption and the hardness of discrete logarithm. Following Hohenberger and Hada's steps, we present two new security definitions, even more our scheme is a further application which not only protects the Signer's secret key from revealing, but also keeps the signature blinding from the Signer. This functionality is very useful in E-Cash and E-Vote. At the same time, our scheme resists different PPT adversaries and satisfies ACVBP w.r.t dependent oracle property. Furthermore, we will continue to focusing the research and application of obfuscation.

References

1. Barak, B., Goldreich, O., Impagliazzo, R., Rudich, S., Sahai, A., Vadhan, S., Yang, K.: On the (im)possibility of obfuscating programs. In: Kilian, J. (ed.) CRYPTO 2001. LNCS, vol. 2139, pp. 1–18. Springer, Heidelberg (2001)
2. Goldwasser, S., Kalai, Y.T.: On the impossibility of obfuscation with auxiliary input. In: Proceedings of the 46th Annual IEEE Symposium on Foundations of Computer Science, FOCS 2005, Pittsburgh, PA, USA, October 23-25, pp. 553–562 (2005)
3. Wee, H.: On obfuscating point functions. In: Proceedings of the 37th Annual ACM Symposium on Theory of Computing, STOC, Baltimore, MD, USA, May 22-24, pp. 523–532 (2005)
4. Hofheinz, D., Malone-Lee, J., Stam, M.: Obfuscation for cryptographic purposes. In: Vadhan, S.P. (ed.) TCC 2007. LNCS, vol. 4392, pp. 214–232. Springer, Heidelberg (2007)
5. Bitansky, N., Canetti, R.: On strong simulation and composable point obfuscation. In: Rabin, T. (ed.) CRYPTO 2010. LNCS, vol. 6223, pp. 520–537. Springer, Heidelberg (2010)
6. Canetti, R.: Towards realizing random oracles: Hash functions that hide all partial information. In: Kaliski Jr., B.S. (ed.) CRYPTO 1997. LNCS, vol. 1294, pp. 455–469. Springer, Heidelberg (1997)
7. Canetti, R., Miccianico, D., Reingold, O.: Perfectly one-way probabilistic hash functions. In: STOC, pp. 72–89 (2010)
8. Lynn, B., Prabhakaran, M., Sahai, A.: Positive results and techniques for obfuscation. In: Cachin, C., Camenisch, J.L. (eds.) EUROCRYPT 2004. LNCS, vol. 3027, pp. 20–39. Springer, Heidelberg (2004)
9. Canetti, R., Dakdouk, R.R.: Obfuscating point functions with multibit output. In: Smart, N.P. (ed.) EUROCRYPT 2008. LNCS, vol. 4965, pp. 489–508. Springer, Heidelberg (2008)
10. Hohenberger, S., Rothblum, G.N., Shelat, A., Vaikuntanathan, V.: Securely Obfuscating re-encryption. In: Vadhan, S.P. (ed.) TCC 2007. LNCS, vol. 4392, pp. 233–252. Springer, Heidelberg (2007)
11. Hada, S.: Secure obfuscation for encrypted signatures. In: Gilbert, H. (ed.) EUROCRYPT 2010. LNCS, vol. 6110, pp. 92–112. Springer, Heidelberg (2010)
12. Chandran, N., Chase, M., Vaikuntanathan, V.: Functional Re-encryption and Collusion-Resistant Obfuscation. In: Cramer, R. (ed.) TCC 2012. LNCS, vol. 7194, pp. 404–421. Springer, Heidelberg (2012)
13. Chaum, D.: Blind Signatures for Untraceable Payments. In: Rivest, R.L., Sherman, A., Chaum, D. (eds.) Preceedings of CRYPTO 1982, New York, pp. 199–203 (1983)
14. Okamoto, T.: Provably Secure and Practical Identification Schemes and Corresponding Signature Schemes. In: Brickell, E.F. (ed.) CRYPTO 1992. LNCS, vol. 740, pp. 31–53. Springer, Heidelberg (1993)
15. Schnorr, C.P.: Enhancing the Security of Perfect Blind DL-Signatures. Information Sciences 176(10), 1305–1320 (2006)
16. Boneh, D., Boyen, X., Shacham, H.: Short Group Signatures. In: Franklin, M. (ed.) CRYPTO 2004. LNCS, vol. 3152, pp. 41–55. Springer, Heidelberg (2004)

Attribute-Based Signing Right Delegation

Weiwei Liu, Yi Mu, and Guomin Yang

School of Computer Science and Software Engineering,
University of Wollongong, Wollongong, NSW 2522, Australia
wl265@uowmail.edu.au, {ymu,gyang}@uow.edu.au

Abstract. Attribute-based signature and proxy signature are both very useful in many real-world applications. In this paper, we combine the special features of both signatures and propose an attribute-based proxy signature scheme, where the original signer, who possesses a set of attributes, can delegate his/her signing right to a designated proxy signer. By verifying the signature, a verifier can be convinced that the signature is generated by the proxy signer who has obtained the delegation from a legitimate signer whose attributes satisfy a predicate. However, the verifier cannot tell from the signature who is the original signer. We provide the formal definition and adversarial models for attribute-based proxy signature, and an efficient scheme that supports threshold predicates.

Keywords: proxy signature, attribute-based signature, threshold predicate.

1 Introduction

Proxy signature is a special type of digital signature and has been found useful in many real-world applications, for example, distributed computing [9] and grid computing [1]. Proxy signature allows an original signer to delegate his/her signing rights to a proxy signer who then can issue signatures on behalf of the original signer. The first proxy signature scheme was proposed by Mambo, Usuda and Okamoto in 1996 [8]. They discussed three different types of proxy signature, namely full delegation, partial delegation and delegation by warrant. Later, Kim et al. [2] proposed a new type of proxy signature combing partial delegation and warrant, and demonstrated that schemes combining partial delegation and warrant can provide a higher level of security than schemes based on partial delegation and warrant separately. Since then many proxy signature schemes based on partial delegation and warrant have been proposed (e.g.,[3,13,11,12,14,5]).

Attribute-based signature (ABS) is another special type of digital signature that has been proposed recently. It can be treated as an extension of identity-based signature (IBS) but has better fine-grained control over the signer's identification information. In an ABS, a signer with attribute set $\mathcal{A}$ will first obtain a secret key from the central authority (or key generation center), and then can use the obtained secret key to sign any messages. The signature can be verified with regards to an attribute predicate Υ and the verification will be successful if and

M.H. Au et al. (Eds.): NSS 2014, LNCS 8792, pp. 323–334, 2014.
© Springer International Publishing Switzerland 2014

only if the signer's attribute set $\mathcal{A}$ satisfies Υ. However, the verifier cannot gain any information about the signer's attributes except the fact that they satisfy the pre-claimed predicate. Several ABS schemes have been proposed recently to support different types of predicates. Li et al. [4] proposed two ABS constructions supporting flexible threshold predicates. In their schemes, the predicate is a set of n attributes, and the signer must possess at least k ($k \leq n$) of them in order to generate a valid signature. The verifier can be convinced that the signer is really holding k out of n attributes, but cannot find out which k attributes are possessed by the signer. Later, Maji et al. [7] proposed another ABS scheme where the attribute predicates can be expressed as monotone-span programs. Then in [10], Okamoto and Takashima proposed the first ABS scheme that can support more general non-monotone predicates. We noticed the paper regarding attribute-based signature has recently been proposed in [6]; However, the adversarial models in [6] are not properly defined. In addition, the application scenario is different from our work.

In this paper, we are interested in signing right delegation under the attribute-based setting environment. The proposed scheme can be regarded as a variant of attribute-based proxy signature schemes(ABPS). ABPS has many potential applications, for example, attribute-based authentication [7]. Consider a database whose access control is described in a policy such that only users who hold authorised attribute keys can access it. An authorised user can delegate his/her signing rights to another user so that the latter can also access the database and collect information when the former is not available. The delegated signer is called a proxy of the original authorised signer. In our proposed scheme, the verifier can be convinced that a valid proxy signer holds the right delegation from an original signer and therefore can access the database. The attributed based proxy signature can be regarded as a certificate for accessing the database.

The rest of the paper is organized as follows. We introduce some preliminaries in Section 2. The formal definition and security model of ABPS is presented in Section 3. We then present our ABPS scheme in Section 4 and prove its security in Section 5. The paper is concluded in Section 6.

2   Preliminaries

2.1   Bilinear Map

Let $\mathbb{G}_1$, $\mathbb{G}_2$ be two cyclic groups of prime order p and g a generator of $\mathbb{G}_1$. The $e : \mathbb{G}_1 \times \mathbb{G}_1 \to \mathbb{G}_2$ is said to be an admissible bilinear map if the following conditions hold:

- Bilinearity: $e(g_1^a, g_2^b) = e(g_1, g_2)^{ab}$ for all $g_1, g_2 \in \mathbb{G}_1$ and $a, b \in_R \mathbb{Z}_p$.
- Non-degeneracy: There exists $g_1, g_2 \in \mathbb{G}_1$ such that $e(g_1, g_2) \neq 1_{\mathbb{G}_2}$.
- Computability: There is an efficient algorithm to compute $e(g_1, g_2)$ for all $g_1, g_2 \in \mathbb{G}_1$.

2.2 Complexity Assumption

Definition 1 *Computational Diffie-Hellman (CDH) Problem*: *Given* g, $g^a, g^b \in \mathbb{G}_1$ *for some random* $a, b \in \mathbb{Z}_p$, *compute* $g^{ab} \in \mathbb{G}_1$. *Define the success probability of a polynomial algorithm* $\mathcal{A}$ *in solving the CDH problem as*:

$$Succ_{\mathcal{A},\mathbb{G}_1}^{CDH}(\kappa) = \Pr[\mathcal{A}(g, g^a, g^b) = g^{ab} : a, b \in_R \mathbb{Z}_p]$$

where $\kappa = \log(p)$ *is the security parameter.*

Definition 2 *Computational Diffie-Hellman (CDH) Assumption*: $Succ_{\mathcal{A},\mathbb{G}_1}^{CDH}(\kappa)$ *is negligible in* κ.

2.3 Lagrange Interpolation

Given t points $q(1), q(2), ..., q(t)$ on a $t-1$ polynomial q, one could use Lagrange interpolation to compute $q(i)$ for any $i \in \mathbb{Z}_p$ through

$$q(i) = \sum_{j=1}^{t} q(j)\Delta_{j,s}(i).$$

The Lagrange coefficient $\Delta_{j,S}(i)$ of $q(j)$ in the computation of $q(i)$ can be computed as

$$\Delta_{j,S}(i) = \prod_{1 \leq \pi \leq t, \pi \neq j} \frac{i - \pi}{j - \pi}.$$

3 Attribute-Based Proxy Signature Definition and Security Model

3.1 Definition

An attribute-based proxy signature scheme is parameterized by a universe of possible attributes $\mathbb{A}$, a warrant space $\mathbb{M}_w$, and a message space $\mathbb{M}$. It consists of the following algorithms.

- **ABPS.Setup**: takes a security parameter 1^κ as input and outputs the public parameters *params* and a master secret key *MSK* for the central authority.
- **ABPS.KeyGen**: takes *params* as input and outputs a proxy key pair (pk, sk).
- **ABPS.AttrKeyGen**: takes $(MSK, params, \omega)$ as input where $\omega \subseteq \mathbb{A}$ is the attribute set of a user and outputs an attribute key sk_ω.
- **ABPS.DskGen**: takes $(sk_\omega, m_w \in \mathbb{M}_w, \Upsilon)$ as input, where m_w is a warrant specified by the original signer, Υ is a predicate such that there exists $\omega' \subseteq \omega$ which satisfies $\Upsilon(\omega') = 1$, and outputs a delegation key dsk.
- **ABPS.ProSig**: takes $(dsk, sk, m \in \mathbb{M})$ as input, and outputs a proxy signature σ.

– **ABPS.ProVer**: takes $(\Upsilon, pk, m_w, m, \sigma)$ as input, and outputs 1 ('accept') or 0 ('reject').

Correctness: We require that for any warrant and message spaces $\mathbb{M}_w, \mathbb{M} \subseteq \{0,1\}^*$ and any security parameter $\kappa \in \mathbb{N}$, if

$$(params, MSK) \leftarrow \textbf{ABPS.Setup}(1^\kappa),$$

$$(pk, sk) \leftarrow \textbf{ABPS.KeyGen}(params),$$

$$sk_\omega \leftarrow \textbf{ABPS.AttrenKenGen}(MSK, params, \omega),$$

$$dsk \leftarrow \textbf{ABPS.DskGen}(sk_\omega, m_w, \Upsilon),$$

then

$$\textbf{ABPS.ProVer}(\Upsilon, pk, m_w, m, \textbf{ABPS.ProSig}(dsk, sk, m)) = 1.$$

3.2   Security Model for ABPS

In an attribute-based proxy signature scheme, the security consideration is different from that for a traditional proxy signature or attribute-based signature. According to the definition of attribute-based proxy signature, we consider three different types of adversaries:

1. $\mathcal{A}_I$: an outsider attacker who only has the universe of attributes $\mathbb{A}$ and the public key pk_p of the proxy signer and tries to forge a valid proxy signature σ.
2. $\mathcal{A}_{II}$: a malicious proxy signer that possesses the private key sk_p and a valid warrant m_w from the original signer, and tries to forge a valid proxy signature σ for another warrant m_w^*.
3. $\mathcal{A}_{III}$: a malicious original signer that possesses the attribute key sk_ω and the public key pk_p of the proxy signer, and tries to forge a valid proxy signature σ without knowing the private key sk_p of the proxy signer.

It is obvious that if an attribute-based proxy signature scheme is secure under $\mathcal{A}_{II}$ or $\mathcal{A}_{III}$, it is also secure against $\mathcal{A}_I$. Thus we will only focus on the adversarial models with regards to $\mathcal{A}_{II}$ and $\mathcal{A}_{III}$ in the rest of this paper. Before we formally define each adversarial model, we first introduce three types of oracle queries that will appear in the models:

– **Attribute Key Generation Query**: $\mathcal{A}$ can query the attribute key for an attribute set $\omega \subseteq \mathbb{A}$ of his choice to the attribute key generation oracle $\mathcal{O}_{AKG}(\cdot)$. The corresponding attribute key sk_ω is then generated and returned to $\mathcal{A}$.
– **Delegation Query**: $\mathcal{A}$ can query the delegation oracle $\mathcal{O}_{DKG}(sk_\omega, \cdot, \cdot)$ with any warrant m_w and access structure Υ of his choice. The corresponding delegation key dsk is generated and returned to $\mathcal{A}$.
– **Proxy Signing Query**: $\mathcal{A}$ can query the proxy signing oracle $\mathcal{O}_{PS}(dsk, sk_p, \cdot)$ with any message m of his choice. A valid proxy signature on m is generated and returned to $\mathcal{A}$.

We define the selective adversarial game between a malicious proxy signer $\mathcal{A}_{II}$ and a simulator $\mathcal{S}$ as follows:

- **Initial Phase:** $\mathcal{A}_{II}$ chooses and outputs a challenge predicate Υ^* that will be used in forging a proxy signature.
- **ABPS.Setup Phase:** The simulator $\mathcal{S}$ runs **ABPS.Setup** to generate the $params$ and MSK, and sends $params$ to $\mathcal{A}_{II}$.
- **ABPS.KeyGen Phase:** The simulator $\mathcal{S}$ also runs the **ABPS.KeyGen** to generate the key pairs (pk_p, sk_p) of the proxy signer, and sends (pk_p, sk_p) to $\mathcal{A}_{II}$.
- **Attribute Key Generation Queries:** $\mathcal{A}_{II}$ selects an attribute set $\omega \in \mathbb{A}$, the simulator $\mathcal{S}$ runs $sk_\omega \leftarrow$ **ABPS.AttrKeyGen**$(MSK, params, \omega)$ and returns sk_ω to $\mathcal{A}_{II}$.
- **Delegation Queries Phase:** $\mathcal{A}_{II}$ chooses any predicate Υ such that $\Upsilon \neq \Upsilon^*$ and any warrant m_w of his choice and queries the delegation oracle $\mathcal{O}_{DKG}$. $\mathcal{S}$ generates the delegation key $dsk \leftarrow$ **ABPS.DskGen**$(sk_\omega, \Upsilon, m_w)$ and sends dsk to $\mathcal{A}$.
- **Proxy Signing Queries Phase:** $\mathcal{A}_{II}$ chooses a warrant $m_w \in \mathbb{M}_W$ and a message $m \in \mathbb{M}$ and queries the proxy signing oracle $\mathcal{O}_{PS}$. If m_w has appeared in a Delegation Query, a special symbol '$\perp$' is returned to $\mathcal{A}_{II}$. Otherwise, $\mathcal{S}$ generates

$$dsk \leftarrow \textbf{ABPS.DskGen}(sk_\omega, \Upsilon, m_w),$$

$$\sigma \leftarrow \textbf{ABPS.ProSign}(dsk, sk_p, m_w, m)$$

and returns σ to $\mathcal{A}_{II}$.
- **Forgery Phase:** Finally, $\mathcal{A}$ outputs a proxy signature σ^* on message m^* for a warrant m_w^* and the predicate Υ^*.

We say $\mathcal{A}_{II}$ wins the game if

- **ABPS.ProVer**$(\Upsilon^*, pk_p, m_w^*, m^*, \sigma^*) = 1$;
- (m_w^*, Υ^*) has not been queried to $\mathcal{O}_{DSK}$;
- Attribute sets ω^* satisfying $\Upsilon^*(\omega^*) = 1$ have not been submitted to the attribute key generation oracle $\mathcal{O}_{AKG}$.

Define the advantage of a malicious adversary $\mathcal{A}_{II}$ in winning the game as

$$Adv_{\mathcal{A}_{II}}^{spcwcma}(\kappa) = \Pr[\mathcal{A}_{II} \text{ Wins the game}].$$

Definition 1. *We say an attribute-based proxy signature scheme is secure against the $\mathcal{A}_{II}$ under the selective-predicate and chosen warrant and message attacks if for any probabilistic polynomial time $\mathcal{A}_{II}$, $Adv_{\mathcal{A}_{II}}^{spcwcma}(\kappa)$ is negligible in κ.*

The adversarial game between a malicious original signer $\mathcal{A}_{III}$ and a simulator $\mathcal{S}$ is defined as follows:

- **ABPS.Setup Phase**: The simulator $\mathcal{S}$ runs the **ABPS.Setup** to generate the *params* and MSK, and sends *params* and MSK to $\mathcal{A}_{III}$.
- **ABPS.KeyGen Phase**: The simulator generates

$$(pk_p, sk_p) \leftarrow \textbf{ABPS.KeyGen}$$

and sends pk_p to $\mathcal{A}_{III}$.
- **Proxy Signing Queries Phase**: $\mathcal{A}_{III}$ queries the proxy signing oracle $\mathcal{O}_{PS}$ by providing a warrant m_w, a valid delegation key dsk for m_w, and a message m of his choice. The simulator $\mathcal{S}$ generates the proxy signature $\sigma \leftarrow \textbf{ABPS.ProSign}(dsk, sk_p, m_w, m)$ and returns σ to $\mathcal{A}_{III}$.
- **Forgery Phase**: Finally, $\mathcal{A}_{III}$ outputs a proxy signature σ^* on message m^* for a warrant m_w^* and predicate Υ^*.

We say $\mathcal{A}_{III}$ wins the game if

- $\textbf{ABPS.PorVer}(\Upsilon^*, pk_p, m_w^*, m^*, \sigma^*) = 1$;
- (m_w^*, m^*) has not been queried to $\mathcal{O}_{PS}$;

Define the advantage of a malicious adversary $\mathcal{A}_{III}$ in winning the game as

$$Adv_{\mathcal{A}_{III}}^{cma}(\kappa) = \Pr[\mathcal{A}_{III} \text{ Wins the game}].$$

Definition 2. *We say an attribute-based proxy signature scheme is secure against the $\mathcal{A}_{III}$ under chosen message attacks if for any probabilistic polynomial time $\mathcal{A}_{III}$, $Adv_{\mathcal{A}_{III}}^{cma}(\kappa)$ is negligible in κ.*

4   Attribute-Based Proxy Signature Scheme

In our system, the original signer holds a set of attributes and delegates his signing rights to a proxy signer with a normal public/private key pair.

1. **ABPS.Setup**: First, define the universe of attributes U as elements in $\mathbb{Z}_p$. Let the $d-1$ default set of attributes from $\mathbb{Z}_p$ which has no intersection with U be $\Omega = \{\Omega_1, \Omega_2, \ldots, \Omega_{d-1}\}$ and let ω^* be another default attribute set with $\omega^* \subseteq U$. Select a random generator $g \in_R \mathbb{G}_1$ and a random number $x \in \mathbb{Z}_p^*$, set $g_1 = g^x$. Pick random elements g_2 and compute $Z = e(g_1, g_2)$. Select a collision resistant hash function $H : \{0, 1\}^* \to \mathbb{G}_1$. The public parameters are $params = (g, g_1, g_2, Z, H)$. The master secret key is $MSK = x$.
2. **ABPS.KeyGen**: The user selects one random number $x_p \in_R \mathbb{Z}_p^*$ and set the private and public key pair as $(sk_p, pk_p) = (x_p, g^{x_p})$.
3. **ABPS.AttrKeyGen**: To generate a private key for an attribute set ω, proceed as follows:
   - Choose a $d-1$ polynomial q such that $q(0) = x$;
   - Generate a new set of attribute $\hat{\omega} = \omega \cup \Omega$. For each $i \in \hat{\omega}$, choose $r_i \in_R \mathbb{Z}_p$ and compute $d_{i0} = g_2^{q(i)} \cdot H(attr_i)^{r_i}$ and $d_{i1} = g^{r_i}$;
   - The private key $D_i = \{(d_{i0}, d_{i1})\}, i \in \hat{\omega}$.

4. **ABPS.DskGen**: Given a warrant m_w, the original signer selects a k-element subset $\omega' \subseteq \omega \cap \omega^*$ and the delegation signing key is generated as follows:
   - The original signer selects a default attribute subset $\Omega' \subseteq \Omega$ with $|\Omega'| = d - k$, chooses $n + d - k$ random values $r_i' \in \mathbb{Z}_p$, where $i \in \omega^* \cup \Omega'$;
   - The original signer chooses a random value $s \in \mathbb{Z}_p$ and computes $\sigma_0 = \prod_{i \in \omega' \cup \Omega'} d_{i0}^{\Delta_{i,S}(0)} \prod_{i \in \omega^* \cup \Omega'} H(attr_i)^{r_i'} H(m_w)^s$,
   $\{\sigma_i = d_{i1}^{\Delta_{i,S}(0)} g^{r_i'}\}_{i \in \omega' \cup \Omega'}$, $\{\sigma_i = g^{r_i'}\}_{\omega^*/\omega'}$, $\sigma_0' = g^s$;
   - The delegation signing key is $dsk = (\sigma_0, \{\sigma_i\}_{i \in \omega^* \cup \Omega'}, \sigma_0')$.

5. **ABPS.ProSign**: Given dsk, sk_p and a message $m \in \{0,1\}^*$. The proxy signature $\sigma_M = (\sigma_{M_1}, \sigma_{M_2}, \sigma_{M_3}, \sigma_{M_4})$ is generated as follows:
   - Compute $\sigma_{M_1} = \sigma_0 \cdot H(m)^{sk_p}$, $\sigma_{M_2} = \{\sigma_i\}_{i \in \omega^* \cup \Omega'}$, $\sigma_{M_3} = \sigma_0'$.

6. **ABPS.Verification**: Given $\sigma_M = (\sigma_{M_1}, \sigma_{M_2}, \sigma_{M_3}, \sigma_{M_4})$, m_w and Υ_{k,ω^*}, the verifier first check whether the proxy signer follow the rules specified in the warrant. If no, output reject, otherwise, the verifier checks the following equation:

$$\frac{e(g, \sigma_{M_1})}{\prod_{i \in \omega^* \cup \Omega'} e(H(attr_i), \sigma_i) e(H(m_w), \sigma_{M_3}) e(pk_p, H(m))} \stackrel{?}{=} Z.$$

If the equation holds, output accept, where it can be assured that the signature is generated form some user possessing k attributes among ω^*, otherwise, output reject.

- **Correctness:** The correctness of the verification is justified by the following equations:

$$\frac{e(g, \sigma_{M_1})}{\prod_{i \in \omega^* \cup \Omega'} e(H(attr_i), \sigma_i) e(H(m_w), \sigma_{M_3}) e(pk_p, H(m))}$$

$$= \frac{e(g, \sigma_0 \cdot H(m)^{sk_p})}{\prod_{i \in \omega^* \cup \Omega'} e(H(attr_i), \sigma_i) e(H(m_w), \sigma_{M_3}) e(pk_p, H(m))}$$

$$= \frac{e(g, \prod_{i \in \omega' \cup \Omega'} d_{i0}^{\Delta_{i,S}(0)} \prod_{i \in \omega^* \cup \Omega'} H(attr_i)^{r_i'} H(m_w)^s \cdot H(m)^{sk_p})}{\prod_{i \in \omega^* \cup \Omega'} e(H(attr_i), \sigma_i) e(H(m_w), \sigma_{M_3}) e(pk_p, H(m))}$$

$$= \frac{e(g, \prod_{i \in \omega' \cup \Omega'} d_{i0}^{\Delta_{i,S}(0)}) e(g, \prod_{i \in \omega^* \cup \Omega'} H(attr_i)^{r_i'}) e(H(m_w), g^s) e(pk_p, H(m))}{\prod_{i \in \omega^* \cup \Omega'} e(H(attr_i), \sigma_i) e(H(m_w), \sigma_{M_3}) e(pk_p, H(m))}$$

$$= \frac{e(g, \prod_{i \in \omega' \cup \Omega'} d_{i0}^{\Delta_{i,S}(0)}) e(g, \prod_{i \in \omega^* \cup \Omega'} H(attr_i)^{r_i'})}{\prod_{i \in \omega^* \cup \Omega'} e(H(attr_i), \sigma_i)}$$

$$= \frac{e(g, \prod_{i \in \omega' \cup \Omega'} g_2^{q(i) \cdot \Delta_{i,S}(0)}) e(g, \prod_{i \in \omega' \cup \Omega'} H(attr_i)^{r_i \cdot \Delta_{i,S}(0) + r_i'}) e(g, \prod_{i \in \omega^*/\omega'} H(attr_i)^{r_i'})}{e(g, \prod_{i \in \omega' \cup \Omega'} H(attr_i)^{r_i \cdot \Delta_{i,S}(0) + r_i'}) e(g, \prod_{i \in \omega^*/\omega'} H(attr_i)^{r_i'})}$$

$$= e(g, g_2^{q(0)})$$
$$= e(g, g_2^x)$$
$$= e(g^x, g_2)$$
$$= Z.$$

5   Security Analysis

In this section we analyse the security of the above attribute-based proxy signature scheme against $\mathcal{A}_{II}$ and $\mathcal{A}_{III}$ adversaries.

Theorem 1. *Our attribute-based proxy signature scheme is secure against the $\mathcal{A}_{II}$ chosen warrant and chosen message attacks if the CDH Problem is hard.*

Proof. The proof is by contradiction in the selective predicate security model. Suppose that an adversary $\mathcal{A}_{II}$ has an advantage ϵ in attacking the proposed scheme, then we can build an algorithm $\mathcal{B}$ that use $\mathcal{A}_{II}$ to solve the CDH problem. Let $\mathbb{G}_1$ be a bilinear pairing group of prime order p, $\mathcal{B}$ is given $g, g^\alpha, g^\beta \in \mathbb{G}_1$ which is a random instance of the CDH problem. Its goal is to compute $g^{\alpha\beta}$. Algorithm $\mathcal{B}$ will simulate the challenger and interact with the forger $\mathcal{A}_{II}$ as described below, let's recall the definition of $\mathcal{A}_{II}$, $\mathcal{A}_{II}$ is a malicious proxy signer possessing the private key of the proxy signer. With this in mind, the simulation is as follows:

1. **Initial Phase:** $\mathcal{A}_{II}$ chooses a predicate Υ^*_{k,ω^*} as the challenge predicate.
2. **Setup:** Let the default attribute set Ω be $\{\Omega_1, \ldots, \Omega_{d-1}\}$. $\mathcal{B}$ sets $g_1 = g^\alpha, g_2 = g^\beta$, where g^α, g^β are inputs of the CDH problem. $\mathcal{B}$ sets the public parameters as:
   - $\mathcal{B}$ chooses random $x_p \in_R \mathbb{Z}_p^*$ and sets $sk_p = x_p, pk_p = g^{x_p}$.
   - $\mathcal{B}$ sends $(\mathbb{G}_1, \mathbb{G}_2, e, p, g, g_1, g_2, H)$ and (sk_p, pk_p) to $\mathcal{A}_{II}$.
3. **Hash queries:** In order to make the simulation easy to follow, we regard the attribute, warrant and message queries as H_1, H_2 and H_3 queries respectively. Assume $\mathcal{B}$ keeps hash tables T_1, T_2 and T_3 for the queries.
   (a) H_1 **Query:** Assume $\mathcal{A}_{II}$ makes q_{H1} attribute queries, for each query on attribute $attr_i$, $\mathcal{B}$ simulates as follows:
       - If $attr_i$ have existed in T_1, a same value $H(attr_i)$ is returned to $\mathcal{A}_{II}$.
       - Otherwise,
         • If $attr_i \in \omega^* \cup \Omega^*$, $\mathcal{B}$ chooses random $a_i \in \mathbb{Z}_p$ and returns $H(attr_i) = g^{a_i}$ to $\mathcal{A}_{II}$. $\mathcal{B}$ adds $(attr_i, H(attr_i))$ to T_1.
         • If $attr_i \notin \omega^* \cup \Omega^*$, $\mathcal{B}$ chooses random $a_i, b_i \in \mathbb{Z}_p$ and returns $H(attr_i) = g^{-a_i} g^{b_i}$ to $\mathcal{A}_{II}$. $\mathcal{B}$ adds $(attr_i, H(attr_i))$ to T_1.
   (b) H_2 **Query:** Assume $\mathcal{A}_{II}$ makes q_{H2} warrant queries, $\mathcal{B}$ selects a random number $\delta \in (0, q_{H2})$, for each query on warrant m_{w_i}, $\mathcal{B}$ simulates as follows:
       - If m_{wi} have existed in T_2, a same value $H(m_{w_i})$ is returned to $\mathcal{A}_{II}$.
       - Otherwise,
         • If $i \neq \delta$, $\mathcal{B}$ chooses random $a'_i, b'_i \in_r \mathbb{Z}_p$ and returns $H(m_{w_i}) = g_1^{b'_i} g^{a'_i}$. $\mathcal{B}$ adds $(m_{w_i}, H(m_{w_i}))$ to T_2.
         • If $i = \delta$, $\mathcal{B}$ chooses random b'_i and returns $H(w_i) = g^{a'_i}$. $\mathcal{B}$ adds $(m_{w_i}, H(m_{w_i}))$ to T_2
   (c) H_3 **Query:** Assume $\mathcal{A}_{II}$ makes q_{H3} message queries, for each query on message m_i, $\mathcal{B}$ simulates as follows:
       - If m_i has existed in T_3, a same value $H(m_i)$ is returned to $\mathcal{A}_{II}$.
       - Otherwise, $\mathcal{B}$ chooses random $r_i \in_R \mathbb{Z}_p$ and returns $H(m_i) = g^{r_i}$. $\mathcal{B}$ adds $(m_i, H(m_i))$ to T_3.

4. **Attribute key extraction queries**: Assume $\mathcal{A}_{II}$ issues an attribute key extraction query on an attribute set ω such that $|\omega^* \cap \omega| < k$. Following the analysis in [4], we first define three sets Γ, Γ', S in the following manner: $\Gamma = (\omega \cap \omega^*) \cup \Omega^*$ and $\Gamma \subseteq \Gamma' \subseteq S$ with $|\Gamma'| = d - 1$. Let $S = \Gamma' \cup \{0\}$. The simulation on the attribute key D_i is as follows:

 - For $i \in \Gamma'$: $D_i = (g_2^{\tau_i} H(attr_i)^{r_i}, g^{r_i})$, where $\tau_i, r_i \in_R \mathbb{Z}_p$.
 - For $i \notin \Gamma'$, D_i could be simulated as:

$$D_i = (g_2^{\frac{\Delta_{0,S}(i)b_i}{a_i} + \sum_{j \in \Gamma'} \Delta_{j,S}(i)q(j)} (g_1^{-a_i} g^{b_i})^{r_i'}, g_2^{\frac{\Delta_{0,S}(i)}{a_i}} g^{r_i'}),$$

where $r_i' \in_R \mathbb{Z}_p$. It is a correct key because it implicitly sets

$$r_i = \frac{\Delta_{j,S}(i)q(j)}{a_i}\beta + r_i'.$$

As we know,

$$q(i) = \sum_{j \in \Gamma'} \Delta_{j,S}(i)q(j) + \Delta_{0,S}(i)q(0),$$

thus we have,

$$g_2^{q(i)} H(attr_i)^{r_i} = g_2^{\frac{\Delta_{0,S}(i)b_i}{a_i} + \sum_{j \in \Gamma'} \Delta_{j,S}(i)q(j)} H(attr_i)^{r_i'}$$

and

$$g^{r_i} = g_2^{\frac{\Delta_{0,S}(i)}{a_i}} g^{r_i'}.$$

5. **Delegation signing key queries**: $\mathcal{A}_{II}$ can also issue a query for a warrant W for an attribute set ω with k' values out of an n'-value attribute set ω. The delegation signing key query could be simulated as follows:

 - If $|\omega \cup \omega^*| < k$, $\mathcal{B}$ can generate a simulated private key for ω as in the attribute key simulation and get a signature for ω on W normally.
 - If $|\omega \cap \omega^*| > k$, $\mathcal{B}$ selects a random $(d - k')$-element subset Ω' from Ω. If $H(W) \neq g^{a_i}$, in order to simulate $(g_2^x \prod_{i \in \omega \cup \Omega'} H(attr_i)^{r_i} H(w)^{r_a}, \{g^{r_i}\}_{i \in \omega \cup \Omega'}, g^{r_a})$
   - Choose $r_a' \in \mathbb{Z}_p$ and set $r_a' = \frac{1}{c}\beta + r_a$. Then

$$g_2^x \prod_{i \in \omega \cup \Omega'} H(attr_i)^{r_i} H(w)^{r_a} = (g_1^c g^{a_i})^{r_a'} \prod_{i \in \omega \cup \Omega'} H(attr_i)^{r_i} g_2^{-\frac{a_i}{c}},$$

$$g^{r_a} = g_2^{\frac{-1}{c}} g^{r_a'}$$

   when $H(W) = g_1^c g^{a_i}$.

6. **Proxy signing queries**: Assume $\mathcal{A}_{II}$ makes q_{ps} proxy signing queries. If $\mathcal{A}_{II}$ issues a proxy signature queries for a message $m \in \{0,1\}^*$ under a warrant W for a predicate Υ, in order to simulate $\sigma = \sigma_0 \cdot H(m)^{sk_p}$, $\mathcal{B}$ generates the delegation signing key σ_0 as in the **delegation signing queries** and answers the proxy signing queries as follows:

- If m_i has existed in T_3, then return $\sigma = \sigma_0 \cdot pk_p^{r_i}$ as the proxy signature to $\mathcal{A}_{II}$, where $H(m_i) = g^{r_i}$ exists in T_3.
- If m_i does not appear in T_3, then choose random $r_i \in \mathbb{Z}_p$ and return $\sigma = \sigma_0 \cdot pk_p^{r_i}$ as the proxy signature to $\mathcal{A}_{II}$. $\mathcal{B}$ adds $(m_i, H(m_i))$ to T_3.

7. **Forgery**: Assume $\mathcal{A}_{II}$ outputs a valid proxy signature

$$\sigma^* = (\sigma_0^*, \{\sigma_i^*\}_{i \in \omega^* \cup \Omega^*}, \sigma_0')$$

for predicate Υ_{k,ω^*}^*. If $H(m_w) \neq g^{a_\delta'}$ or $\overline{\Omega^*} \neq \Omega^*$ where $\overline{\Omega^*}$ are the dummy attributes, $\mathcal{B}$ will abort. Therefore

$$\sigma^* = (\sigma_0^*, \{\sigma_i^*\}_{i \in \omega^* \cup \Omega^*}, \sigma_0')$$

$$= (g_2^\alpha \prod_{i \in \omega^* \cup \Omega^*} H(attr_i)^{r_i} H(m_w)^{r_a} H(m)^{sk_p}, \{g^{r_i}\}_{i \in \omega^* \cup \Omega^*}, g^{r_a}).$$

Thus $\mathcal{B}$ can compute

$$g^{\alpha\beta} = \frac{\sigma_0^*}{\prod_{i \in \omega^* \cup \Omega^*} (\sigma_i^*)^{a_i} (\sigma_0')^{a_\delta'} (pk_p)^{r_i}}$$

because $H(attr_i) = g^{a_i}$, $H(m_w) = g^{a_\delta'}$.

Next, we analysis the success probability of $\mathcal{B}$, $\mathcal{B}$ will not abort if the following conditions holds:

- $H(m_w) = g^{a_\delta}$.
- Correct guess of $d - k$ elements Ω^* from Ω.

Therefore the success probability of $\mathcal{B}$ in solving CDH problem is:

$$Succ_{\mathcal{B}}^{CDH} = \frac{\epsilon}{q_{H2} C_{d-1}^{d-k}}.$$

Theorem 2. *Our attribute-based proxy signature scheme is secure against the $\mathcal{A}_{III}$ chosen message attacks if the CDH Problem is hard.*

Proof. Let $\mathbb{G}_1$ be a bilinear pairing group of prime order p. Algorithm $\mathcal{B}$ is given $g, g^\alpha, g^\beta \in \mathbb{G}_1$ which is a random instance of the CDH problem. Its goal is to compute $g^{\alpha\beta}$. Algorithm $\mathcal{B}$ will simulate the challenger and interact with the adversary $\mathcal{A}_{III}$ as described below.

Let's recall the definition of the adversary $\mathcal{A}_{III}$. $\mathcal{A}_{III}$ has the attribute key of the original signer as well as the public of the proxy signer, thus the attribute key extraction and delegation queries are not needed here. The simulation is performed as follows:

1. **Setup:** $\mathcal{B}$ sets the public keys of the users and the common parameter as :
   - $\mathcal{B}$ selects a random generator $g \in_R \mathbb{G}_1$ and two random number $x, g_2 \in_R \mathbb{Z}_p^*$, then $\mathcal{B}$ chooses a $d-1$ degree polynomial q with $q(0) = x$ and computes $g_1 = g^x$. $\mathcal{B}$ sets $sk_p = \alpha, pk_p = g^\alpha$, where g^α, g^β are inputs of the CDH problem.
   - $\mathcal{B}$ then sends $(\mathbb{G}_1, \mathbb{G}_2, e, p, g, x, g_1, g_2, H)$ and pk_p to $\mathcal{A}_{III}$.
2. **Hash queries:** Assume $\mathcal{A}_{III}$ makes q_{H1}, q_{H2}, q_{H3} times for attribute, warrant and message queries, respectively. $\mathcal{B}$ maintains hash tables T_1, T_2, T_3 for attribute, warrant and message queries. For the hash queries for the attribute and warrant, $\mathcal{B}$ performs the same as in Theorem 1. For the message query on any m of $\mathcal{A}_{III}$'s choice, $\mathcal{B}$ chooses a random number $I \in (1, q_{H3})$, for each query on message m_i, if $(m_i, H(m_i))$ exits in hash table, $\mathcal{B}$ just returns $H(m_i)$ to $\mathcal{A}_{III}$, otherwise, the simulation is performed as follows:
   - If $m_i \neq m_I$, $\mathcal{B}$ chooses random $r_i \in_R \mathbb{Z}_p$, returns $H(m_i) = g^{r_i}$ and adds $(m_i, H(m_i))$ to T.
   - If $m_i = m_I$, $\mathcal{B}$ chooses random $r_I \in_R \mathbb{Z}_p$, return $H(m_I) = (g^\beta)^{r_I}$.
3. **Proxy Signing Queries:** Suppose $\mathcal{A}_{III}$ issues a proxy signing query for a message $M \in \{0,1\}^*$ under a warrant W with predicate Υ_{k,w^*}. $\mathcal{B}$ first generates the attribute key sk_ω using the same method as the **attribute key extraction queries** in Theorem 1. Then $\mathcal{B}$ generates the delegation key $dsk = (\sigma_0, \{\sigma_i\}_{i \in \omega^* \cup \Omega'}, \sigma_0')$ using the method same as **Delegation signing key queries** in Theorem 1. Then $\mathcal{B}$ simulates the proxy signature queries as follows:
   - If $M \in T_3$, assume $H(M) = g^{r_M}$, $\mathcal{B}$ simulates the proxy signature $\sigma = (\sigma_1, \sigma_2, \sigma_3)$ where $\sigma_1 = \sigma_0 \cdot pk_p^{r_M}$, $\sigma_2 = \{\sigma_i\}_{i \in \omega^* \cup \Omega'}$ and $\sigma_3 = \sigma_0'$.
   - If $M \notin T_3$, $\mathcal{B}$ chooses random $r^* \in_R \mathbb{Z}_p$ and simulates the proxy signature as $\sigma_1 = \sigma_0 \cdot pk_p^{r^*}$, $\sigma_2 = \{\sigma_i\}_{i \in \omega^* \cup \Omega'}$ and $\sigma_3 = \sigma_0'$. $\mathcal{B}$ adds $(M, H(M))$ to hash table T.
4. **Forgery:** Assume that the adversary $\mathcal{A}_{III}$ can output a proxy signature $\sigma^* = (\sigma_1^*, \sigma_2^*, \sigma_3^*,)$ of the message M^* under the warrant W^* for predicate Υ^* such that:
   - (M^*, W^*) has not been submitted as one of the proxy signing queries.
   - $\sigma^* = (\sigma_1^*, \sigma_2^*, \sigma_3^*)$ is a valid proxy signature.
   In this case, if $M^* = m_I$, $\mathcal{B}$ can compute:

$$g^{\alpha\beta} = \left(\frac{\sigma_1^*}{g_2^x \prod_{i \in \omega \cup \Omega^*} (\sigma_2^*)^{a_i} (\sigma_3^*)^{a_\delta'}} \right)^{\frac{1}{r_I}}$$

Next, we analyse the success probability of $\mathcal{B}$. $\mathcal{B}$ will not abort if the following conditions hold:

- $H(m_w) = g^{a_\delta}$.
- $H(M) = (g^\beta)^{r_I}$.
- Correct guess of $d-k$ elements Ω^* from Ω.

Therefore,

$$Succ_{\mathcal{B}}^{CDH} = \frac{\epsilon}{q_{H2}(q_{H3} + q_{ps})C_{d-1}^{d-k}}.$$

6   Conclusion

In this paper, we studied attribute-based proxy signature (ABPS) for threshold predicates. We presented a formal security model and a concrete construction of ABPS scheme. Our model has considered different types of potential adversaries against an ABPS scheme. An interesting feature of our scheme is that it offers original signer privacy, that is even the proxy signer cannot find out who is the original signer except that the original signer's attributes satisfy a pre-claimed predicate. We leave the problem of building ABPS for other types of predicates as our future work.

References

1. Foster, I., Kesselman, C., Tsudik, G., Tuecke, S.: A security architecture for computational grids. In: Proceedings of the 5th ACM Conference on Computer and Communications Security, pp. 83–92. ACM (1998)
2. Kim, S., Park, S., Won, D.: Proxy signatures, revisited. In: Han, Y., Quing, S. (eds.) ICICS 1997. LNCS, vol. 1334, pp. 223–232. Springer, Heidelberg (1997)
3. Lee, B., Kim, H., Kim, K.: Strong proxy signature and its applications. In: Proc of SCIS, vol. 1, pp. 603–608 (2001)
4. Li, J., Au, M.H., Susilo, W., Xie, D., Ren, K.: Attribute-based signature and its applications. In: ASIACCS, pp. 60–69 (2010)
5. Liu, W., Yang, G., Mu, Y., Wei, J.: k-time proxy signature: Formal definition and efficient construction. In: Susilo, W., Reyhanitabar, R. (eds.) ProvSec 2013. LNCS, vol. 8209, pp. 154–164. Springer, Heidelberg (2013)
6. Liu, X., Ma, J., Xiong, J., Zhang, T., Li, Q.: Personal health records integrity verification using attribute based proxy signature in cloud computing. In: Pathan, M., Wei, G., Fortino, G. (eds.) IDCS 2013. LNCS, vol. 8223, pp. 238–251. Springer, Heidelberg (2013)
7. Maji, H.K., Prabhakaran, M., Rosulek, M.: Attribute-based signatures. In: Kiayias, A. (ed.) CT-RSA 2011. LNCS, vol. 6558, pp. 376–392. Springer, Heidelberg (2011)
8. Mambo, M., Usuda, K., Okamoto, E.: Proxy signatures for delegating signing operation. In: ACM Conference on Computer and Communications Security, pp. 48–57 (1996)
9. Clifford Neuman, B.: Proxy-based authorization and accounting for distributed systems. In: Proceedings of the13th International Conference on Distributed Computing Systems, pp. 283–291. IEEE (1993)
10. Okamoto, T., Takashima, K.: Efficient attribute-based signatures for non-monotone predicates in the standard model. IACR Cryptology ePrint Archive, 2011, 700 (2011)
11. Wang, G.: Designated-verifier proxy signature schemes. In: Sasaki, R., Qing, S., Okamoto, E., Yoshiura, H. (eds.) Security and Privacy in the Age of Ubiquitous Computing. IFIP, vol. 181, pp. 409–424. Springer, Boston (2005)
12. Wu, W., Mu, Y., Susilo, W., Seberry, J., Huang, X.: Identity-based proxy signature from pairings. In: Xiao, B., Yang, L.T., Ma, J., Muller-Schloer, C., Hua, Y. (eds.) ATC 2007. LNCS, vol. 4610, pp. 22–31. Springer, Heidelberg (2007)
13. Xu, J., Zhang, Z., Feng, D.: ID-based proxy signature using bilinear pairings. In: Chen, G., Pan, Y., Guo, M., Lu, J. (eds.) ISPA-WS 2005. LNCS, vol. 3759, pp. 359–367. Springer, Heidelberg (2005)
14. Yu, Y., Mu, Y., Susilo, W., Sun, Y., Ji, Y.: Provably secure proxy signature scheme from factorization. Mathematical and Computer Modelling 55(3-4), 1160–1168 (2012)

Countering Ballot Stuffing and Incorporating Eligibility Verifiability in Helios

Sriramkrishnan Srinivasan, Chris Culnane[1], James Heather[2], Steve Schneider[1], and Zhe Xia[3,*]

[1] Department of Computing, University of Surrey, Guildford GU2 7XH, U.K.
{c.culnane,s.schneider}@surrey.ac.uk
[2] Chiastic Security Ltd
james@chiastic-security.co.uk
[3] Department of Computing, Wuhan University of Technology, 430063, China
xiazhe@whut.edu.cn

Abstract. Helios is a web-based end-to-end verifiable electronic voting system which has been said to be suitable for low-coercion environments. Although many Internet voting schemes have been proposed in the literature, Helios stands out for its real world relevance. It has been used in a number of elections in university campuses around the world and it has also been used recently by the IACR to elect its board members. It was noted that a dishonest server in Helios can stuff ballots and this seems to limit the claims of end-to-end verifiability of the system. In this work, we investigate how the issue of ballot stuffing can be addressed with minimum change to the current vote casting experience in Helios and we argue formally about the security of our techniques. Our ideas are intuitive and general enough to be applied in the context of other Internet voting scheme and they also address recent attacks exploiting the malleability of ballots in Helios.

Keywords: End-to-End Verifiable Voting, Helios, Token-Controlled Encryption.

1 Introduction

A number of end-to-end (e2e) verifiable voting schemes have been proposed in the literature. It is argued that these schemes provide a number of verifiability properties.

- **Individual Verifiability:** the property whereby a voter can check that his vote has been correctly included in the tally by checking that it has been published on the election's bulletin board (BB).
- **Universal Verifiability:** the property whereby anyone can check that the outcome of the election corresponds to the list of published ballots.

---

* Corresponding author.

M.H. Au et al. (Eds.): NSS 2014, LNCS 8792, pp. 335–348, 2014.
© Springer International Publishing Switzerland 2014

Eligibility Verifiability is a less talked about property of e2e voting systems. This is the property whereby anyone can check that the published ballots have been cast by eligible voters and that only one ballot is tallied for each eligible voter. We argue this is of primary importance as eligibility verifiability (EV) ensures that ballot stuffing attacks are thwarted. Another property of end-to-end verifiable voting schemes is *ballot independence* whereby observing a voter's interaction with an election system should not allow an adversary to cast a vote that is somehow related.

To our knowledge, only a few Internet voting schemes have explicitly incorporated EV and provided defenses against ballot stuffing, e.g. JCJ/Civitas [10,5] and Cobra [7]. These schemes are also coercion-resistant i.e. a voter can appear to conform to the orders of an adversary while voting as desired. In JCJ/Civitas, these properties are achieved with the use of asymmetric key pairs for every voter, individual voter credentials and a framework for managing real and fake credentials. It can be argued, that although theoretically the gold standards, schemes like JCJ/Civitas put too much stress on intricate voter knowledge of the system and for most voters in the real world, the schemes are unusable.

Helios [1,2] takes the approach of catering to elections in low-coercion environments and aims to achieve usability. Helios stands out for its real world relevance and it has been used in a number of elections in university campuses around the world (see for example [2]) and it has also been used in the IACR presidential elections since 2010 [9]. Our work aims to address what we perceive to be some shortcomings in the Helios protocol, in particular the lack of eligibility verifiability. A dishonest Helios server can subvert the system by stuffing ballots i.e. submitting votes for voters who have not done so themselves [12]. A number of recent attacks [6,11] have also highlighted the fragility of the complex ballot structure in Helios and our work also addresses these attacks that exploit the malleability of the ballots in Helios. Our work incorporates eligibility verifiability in Helios, without the need for asymmetric keys-pairs for voters and ensures that the complexity of the scheme, in particular the voter experience, remains as close to the current experience as possible and the techniques are general enough to be applied to other internet voting schemes.

1.1 Structure of This Paper

The rest of the paper is structured as follows. In Section 2, we describe a number of possible methods to incorporate eligibility verifiability in Helios. Our main solution in Section 3 makes novel use of a primitive known as Token Controlled Encryption (TCE) [3] and in Section 4 we describe TCE and security models for TCE with the goal of arguing formally about the security of our proposed construction. We conclude with some comments in Section 5.

2 Incorporating Eligibility Verifiability in Helios

The basic functionality we would like to achieve, to ensure EV is that ballots are somehow tied uniquely to voters and we want to ensure that the various parties running the election are not able to stuff ballots. Anyone can then verify that ballots are not only tied to legitimate voters but also that they were cast by legitimate voters themselves and no one else.

To ensure this functionality, it seems necessary to assume some kind of private voter credential. However, we would like the use of this credential to be as less onerous on the voter as far as possible. In particular, we do not want voters to be able to manage and manipulate asymmetric keys. We would like to adhere to Benaloh's Ballot Casting Assurance principle [4]. In particular, we would like to ensure that although we use a private voter credential, no voter specific information is signaled to or used by the ballot creation device which can be used to influence its behavior. These requirements rule out the "obvious" solution of voters signing their existing Helios ballots before posting to the WBB. If a PKI for voter keys can be assumed to exist and if we assume that voters are able to use and manipulate these keys, it is unclear what benefits a protocol like Helios offers over a much more involved protocol like JCJ/Civitas.

We will assume for the remainder of the discussion that the party initiating the election supplies individual voters with a private one-time voter credential prior to the voting day. As an example, in the case of the IACR election, this is the IACR election management committee rather than the Helios server itself. In addition, voter authentication to the Helios server is leveraged using some existing system. We will call the one-time credential a token for reasons that will be described shortly and we will also assume that the party generating the one-time tokens is not the same party that manages user-authentication to the Helios server, or the Helios server itself. We note that such natural separation between the various entities already exists in the existing Helios use case scenarios. Thus, there are three distinct entities performing distinct functions and we assume that they do not collude.

We want to ensure that the Helios server and the service providing user authentication to the Helios server are both unable to stuff ballots. In addition, we also want security against the party generating the voter credentials and we want to ensure that this party is not able to violate the privacy of voters or stuff ballots itself.

In the remainder of this section, we will take a brief detour to describe the features of a novel primitive called Token Controlled Encryption that we will employ. Subsequently, we will describe a modified Helios work flow that will highlight the new setup process as well as the voter's view of the system.

Token-controlled public key encryption (TCE), introduced by Baek, Safavi-Naini and Susilo [3] is a cryptographic primitive in which senders encrypt messages with the public keys of receivers and a secret *token*. The token is delegated to a third-party, who is entrusted with releasing the token to the receiver when some conditions elaborated by the sender are satisfied. Receivers cannot decrypt encrypted messages until they obtain the corresponding token and the third-party who is entrusted with the token is unable to obtain any information about the original message. In addition, the communication and computational overheads for releasing the token are small.

2.1   Token Controlled Encryption

A TCE scheme is defined in terms of four probabilistic polynomial time (PPT) algorithms:

- TCE.KeyGen: A randomized key generation algorithm that on input a security parameter 1^k, outputs a public key pk and a matching private key sk. Associated to each public/private key pair are a message space MsgSp, a ciphertext space CtSp and a token space TokSp.
- TCE.TokenGen: A randomized token generation algorithm that on input a security parameter 1^k, outputs a random token $tok \in$ TokSp.
- TCE.Enc: A randomized encryption algorithm that on input pk, $tok \in$ TokSp and message $m \in$ MsgSp returns a ciphertext $c \in$ CtSp.
- TCE.Dec: A decryption algorithm that on input a secret key sk, a token $tok \in$ TokSp and a ciphertext $c \in$ CtSp, returns either a message $m \in$ MsgSp or a failure symbol $\perp$.

These algorithms must satisfy the consistency requirement that decryption with the appropriate token undoes encryption: i.e. $\forall (pk, sk) \leftarrow$ TCE.KeyGen(1^k), $\forall tok \in$ TokSp, $\forall m \in$ MsgSp, $\forall c = $ Enc(pk, tok, m), Dec$(sk, tok, c) = m$.

Note in particular that the token generation algorithm does not require any inputs other than the security parameter.

To motivate the use of Token Controlled Encryption we describe briefly an application known as the Millionaire's will problem. A Millionaire wishes to write his will and entrust it to his sons, but he does not want them to be able to read the will till his demise. In the traditional setting, the will is entrusted to a lawyer, but our millionaire does not wish to reveal the contents of the will to his lawyer. A solution to this problem is proposed that uses a TCE scheme. The sons generate key pairs for a TCE scheme and publish the public key. The millionaire writes a will for his sons, encrypts it using the public key of the TCE scheme and gives the encrypted will to his sons. He entrusts the token to his lawyer and trusts that the lawyer will only reveal the token at a pre-appointed time. The lawyer does not have access to the private keys used to create the encrypted will and therefore is unable to obtain any information about the contents of the will. The sons do not have the token till the appointed time and therefore cannot decrypt the encrypted will. We will use TCE along the lines of the example above, with some tweaks, to achieve EV in Helios.

2.2   The Modified Helios Workflow to Incorporate Eligibility Verifiability

In the following section we describe a modified Helios workflow to incorporate EV in Helios. Key differences in the Setup and Voting process from the regular workflow are highlighted in **bold**. The Tallying phase now needs a few additional steps at the start.

Setup

- An election officer and a set of trustees are selected. The election officer is in charge of running the election server and bulletin board. We will refer to the election officer as the Helios server in subsequent discussions. The election officer publishes a set of common system parameters on the BB and the trustees jointly generate an asymmetric key pair i.e. the joint public key is generated by combining each trustee's public key share. The share of the private key of each trustee is kept secret.
- Each trustee's public key is published on a BB along with a proof that the respective trustees know the corresponding private key share. The joint public key is also published with a proof of correct construction.
- **The Helios server also generates an election specific key pair for a TCE scheme and publishes the public key for the TCE scheme, and a proof of knowledge of the private key on the BB. The Helios server keeps the private key for the TCE scheme secret.**
- The election officer publishes a candidate list.
- A hash that includes all the above information, called the election fingerprint is published on the BB.
- The election officer also publishes a list of eligible voters. We note that there is an implicit assumption here that the list of eligible voters is somehow made available to the election officer.
- **The party in charge of generating the list of eligible candidates also sends to the individual voters a one-time election specific token. It commits to a list of tokens against names of eligible voters; it can do so by supplying a cryptographic hash of a file in which the voter names and tokens are stored and the Helios server can publish this on the BB. The token list is kept secret.**

Voting Process

- The voter launches a browser script which downloads the global parameters published by the election officer. The script recomputes the election fingerprint and the voter should check that the fingerprint corresponds to the value published on the BB.
- The voter inputs his vote to the browser script. The script encrypts the vote with the joint public key and also generates a proof that the encrypted vote is constructed correctly i.e. only permitted values are encrypted. In the discussions that follow, we will call this the regular Helios ballot.
- **The voter inputs a token. This may either be the "real" token that is sent to the voter or a "fake" token.**
- **The regular Helios ballot is now encrypted using the public key of the TCE scheme.**
- The encrypted ballot is displayed to the voter.
- The voter may choose to either audit the ballot or cast it.

- If the voter decides to audit the encrypted ballot then the script provides her with the random data used to create the ballot. The voter should then take this random data and re-create the ballot independently (ideally on another platform) to verify that it was indeed well formed. Audited votes cannot be cast and the browser script will prompt the voter to re-create an encrypted vote.
- If the voter decides to cast the ballot, she submits her login credentials to the script which submits the ballot to the election officer. The election officer authenticates the voter, and posts the ballot to the election BB next to the voter's identity. The script deletes the randomness used to create the ballot.
- Voters can check the BB to be assured that their ballots appear on the bulletin board unchanged.

Tallying. Some extra steps are introduced in the tallying phase and these are outlined below.

- When the voting phase is over, the token list is revealed. The cryptographic hash can be recomputed and compared to the hash committed to on the BB and this ensures that the token list is the same committed to at the start of the election.
- The Helios server publicly reveals the election specific TCE private key.
- Every ballot against a voter's name is decrypted with the token revealed for that voter and the TCE private key. All ballots created with "fake" tokens will be automatically rejected as the decryption will fail. Where multiple ballots are created with a "real" token, a policy such as "consider last vote cast" can be used to select one voter per voter. Decryption reveals the regular Helios ballot.

All other aspects of tallying remain the same. In particular, proofs of all the ballots revealed from the process above are checked to ensure they are allowed encryptions. They are then tallied as normal.

2.3   Comments on the New Workflow

- The significant change in the Setup phase is that the Helios server now generates an election specific key-pair for a TCE scheme. This key-pair can be thresholded if greater assurance is required in its generation and perhaps to ensure that a key from an earlier election is not reused. Otherwise a regular key-pair suffices. The private key is revealed publicly during the tallying phase, so this TCE key-pair is truly election specific.
- The voting process in this new proposal still adheres to the principle of Ballot Casting Assurance. Although a voter token is used in the ballot construction phase, it is not tied to a voter's identity.
  Note that in the spirit of TCE, the token is small, so we can safely assume that the token can be represented in human understandable form and that the

voter is able to generate "fake" tokens in his head and input them easily to the ballot creation device. It is possible to envisage that the "real" token is sent as a QR code to the voter by mail or on a mobile handset, and that a separate application can generate "fake" tokens etc. It is also possible to have multiple tokens generated by more than one authority and these can be combined by the script during cote creation. This ensures that not too much trust is placed in one authority generating the tokens. We do not discuss these enhancements except to mention they are possible to keep the discussion simple.

– The voter is able to submit multiple ballots. This may include multiple ballots with "fake" tokens, but also multiple ballots with the "real" one. Ballots created with "fake" tokens will be automatically rejected, while a policy such as consider last vote submitted with "real" token" can be used to choose one vote per voter. The general spirit of this approach is in the lines of JCJ/Civitas. Our contribution lies in incorporating the ideas into the existing Helios workflow and ensuring a significantly simpler workflow for the voter without voter asymmetric keys.

– Encrypting the regular Helios ballot with the TCE public key ensures that individual ballot components of the regular Helios ballot are no longer available to those observing the BB during the election phase, rendering ballot malleability attacks infeasible. Replay attacks will also not work as ballots are bound to private user tokens. The only possibility of exploiting the individual ballot components is to somehow re-use them in a subsequent election after they are revealed in the tallying phase. This is clearly a more remote threat and one that can be easily mitigated by generating one time election specific keys as well. It is also possible to incorporating the tokens in the signature proofs of knowledge. This will enable public checkability of the proofs once the TCE decryption is completed, as tokens as publicly revealed while also ensuring that ballots are tied uniquely to election specific voter tokens.

– The audit process is unchanged and is still designed to assure the voter that the encrypted vote does in fact correspond to the choices made by the voter and cannot check attacks due to malware.

– In keeping with the spirit of Helios, we assume that some existing infrastructure is used to manage login of voters to the Helios server. Our only requirement is that this should not be same infrastructure that supplies the one-time tokens to the voters. In our construction, the Helios server itself can send out username and passwords to the voters by email and this does not enable it to stuff ballots. In the existing setup, the Helios server is able to stuff ballots whether it manages logins of voters to the system or not.

– If the infrastructure that generates the tokens also manages logins to the Helios server, then this infrastructure may be able to stuff ballots. It can be argued that this is a lesser threat than the possibility of the Helios server itself stuffing ballots and one that it is easily mitigated by leveraging login by an arbitrary existing infrastructure. On the other hand, in the existing Helios workflow, even when arbitrary infrastructure is leverages to supply login for voters, the Helios server itself may stuff ballots and it is not clear how this can be checked.

3   Security of Our Proposed Construction

We will introduce the security notions for TCE scheme more formally in the next section. Informally, we have the following types of adversaries and the following security requirements.

- Adversaries without knowledge of the private key and token. In our setting these correspond to general external adversaries i.e. other than the party generating the tokens, or the Helios server itself. In the context of TCE schemes, these are called Type-1 outside adversaries. We will require that ciphertexts are indistinguishable to these adversaries. This is captured in the security game TCE.1 in Section 4.1.
- Adversaries without knowledge of the private key, but with access to the token. In our setting this corresponds to the party generating the tokens. In the context of TCE schemes these are called Type-2 outside adversaries. We will require that ciphertexts are indistinguishable to these adversaries. This is captured in the security game TCE.2 in Section 4.2.

  As discussed earlier, this type of adversary is not able to stuff ballots, under the assumption that they do not control the infrastructure that supplies login credentials. This is because, with knowledge of the token and public key, this adversary can create valid ballots for a particular voter. As briefly discussed earlier, it is also possible to have the tokens generated by more than one party and delivered to the voter who will supply all tokens to the browser script. This prevents a single token generating entity from being able to stuff ballots. In this second scenario, a token generating party may also supply the authentication infrastructure.
- Adversaries with knowledge of the private key, but without access to the token. In our setting, this corresponds to the Helios server itself. In the context of TCE schemes, these are called inside adversaries. We require that ciphertexts are indistinguishable to these adversaries. This is captured in the security game TCE.3 in Section 4.3.
- Finally, to prevent ballot stuffing by the Helios sever itself, we require the much stronger security property that the the inside adversary against the TCE scheme is not able to make ciphertexts created under one token decrypt successfully under another token. This is captured in the security game TCE.4 in Section 4.4.

To summarize, assuming that the system is instantiated with a concrete TCE scheme meeting the appropriate security notions outlined above our construction satisfies the following properties.

- The Helios server, despite possessing the private key that corresponds to the public key used to encrypt the regular Helios ballot, is unable gain any information till the token is made available. Although the regular Helios ballot is already encrypted, the new procedure ensures that the individual ciphertext components of the regular Helios ballot are not available to anyone before the tallying phase, including the Helios server.

- The Helios server is also unable to generate valid ciphertexts without knowledge of the voter tokens and this ensures that ballot stuffing attacks are rendered infeasible as all ballots generated without the legitimate voter token are automatically rejected.
- Even when the private key for the TCE scheme and voter tokens are made public, the public decryption only reveals the regular Helios ballots, ensuring the same privacy and integrity guarantees as in regular Helios.

4   Security Notions for Token Controlled Encryption

Baek, Safavi-Naini and Susilo [3] first proposed security models for TCE schemes. Galindo and Herranz [8] identified the security models considered in [3] as being inadequate as the issue of a single ciphertext decrypting to different messages under different tokens is not addressed. They introduced an improved security model termed the *strong existential token unforgeability* model and proposed a generic construction starting from any trapdoor partial one-way function and secure in the ROM. Below we give the various security notions for TCE schemes and in Section 4.5 we talk briefly about concrete instantiations, but leave the details to the original sources.

As mentioned earlier, two types of adversaries can be considered against TCE schemes. "Outside" adversaries who do not have access to the private key and "Inside" adversaries, who possess the receiver's private key (i.e. the receiver's themselves). In addition, Outside adversaries are further categorized as Type 1 Outside adversaries, who do not possess the token and Type 2 Outside adversaries who have access to the token (the semi-trusted third party) respectively.

We will capture security against these different types of adversaries in terms of various security games that the adversary plays against a challenger $\mathcal{C}$. The adversary will be given access to one or more of the following oracles with suitable restrictions on their use.

- A token embedded encryption oracle: The adversary can query the token embedded encryption oracle with a message m and receives the ciphertext c created with the target token tok^* and the public key of the receiver i.e. $c = \text{Enc}(pk, tok^*, m)$.
- A decryption oracle: The adversary can query the decryption oracle with a ciphertext/token pair and receives back the decryption of the ciphertext under the specified token and secret key of the receiver. i.e $m = \text{Dec}(sk, tok, c)$. Here m is either a valid plaintext or $\bot$ to indicate failure of decryption.

4.1   TCE.1: Security Against Type-1 Outside Adversaries

We consider the following game between the adversary $\mathcal{A}$ and a challenger $\mathcal{C}$, which captures security against an outside adversary $\mathcal{A}$ whose goal is to break the confidentiality of the TCE ciphertext created with a fixed token. The adversary $\mathcal{A}$ does not have access to the private key or to the token used to encrypt the message.

The challenger C takes as input the security parameter 1^k and runs algorithm TCE.KeyGen of the TCE scheme to obtain (pk, sk) i.e. $(pk, sk) \leftarrow$ TCE.KeyGen(1^k). The challenger C also runs algorithm TCE.TokenGen to obtain a target token tok^* i.e. $tok^* \leftarrow$ TCE.TokenGen(1^k).

The adversary is given the public keys pk but not the corresponding secret key sk or the target token tok^*. The game proceeds as follows.

- **Phase 1:** A issues a series of adaptively selected encryption queries on messages m to the token embedded encryption oracle. A also issues a series of adaptively selected decryption queries on ciphertext/token pairs (c, tok) to the decryption oracle.
- **Challenge:** After A decides to end Phase 1, it outputs two equal length messages m_0 and m_1. C selects $b \xleftarrow{\$} \{0,1\}$, sets $c^* = \text{Enc}(pk, tok^*, m_b)$ and gives c^* to A.
- **Phase 2:** This phase proceeds as in Phase 1.
- **Guess:** A outputs a bit b' and wins the game if $b' = b$.

The advantage of A against the TCE scheme in the above TCE.1 security game is defined to be:

$$\mathbf{Adv}_A^{\text{TCE.1}}(k) = |\Pr[b' = b] - 1/2|$$

where the probability is measured over the random choices of coins of A and C.

A scheme is said to be TCE.1 secure if the advantage of all PPT adversaries is negligible as a function of the security parameter k.

No restriction is placed on the decryption queries in Phase 1. This is because the token is not known to the adversary and it is argued that the query on (c^*, tok^*) must occur with negligible probability, implying that the token must be chosen from an exponentially large space.

4.2   TCE.2: Security Against Type-2 Outside Adversaries

This is very similar to security against Type-1 outside adversaries except that now the adversary also has access to the target token. Thus, the adversary can be thought to be the semi-trusted third party entrusted with the token, who attempts to break the confidentiality of TCE ciphertexts. Security against Type-2 adversaries is captured in terms of a game very similar to the security game stated above with the restriction that the adversary cannot query the decryption oracle with the challenge ciphertext and target token.

The challenger C takes as input the security parameter 1^k and runs algorithm TCE.KeyGen of the TCE scheme to obtain (pk, sk) i.e. $(pk, sk) \leftarrow$ TCE.KeyGen(1^k). The challenger C also runs algorithm TCE.TokenGen to obtain a target token tok^* i.e. $tok^* \leftarrow$ TCE.TokenGen(1^k).

The adversary is given the target token tok^* and the public key pk but not the corresponding secret key sk. The game proceeds as follows.

- **Phase 1:** $\mathcal{A}$ issues a series of adaptively selected encryption queries on messages m to the token-embedded encryption oracle . $\mathcal{A}$ also issues a series of adaptively selected decryption queries on ciphertext-token pairs (c, tok) to the decryption oracle.
- **Challenge:** After $\mathcal{A}$ decides to end Phase 1, it outputs two equal-length messages m_0 and m_1. $\mathcal{C}$ selects $b \xleftarrow{\$} \{0, 1\}$, sets $c^* = \texttt{Enc}(pk, tok^*, m_b)$ and gives c^* to $\mathcal{A}$.
- **Phase 2:** This phase proceeds as in Phase 1 with the restriction that the adversary may not query the decryption oracle with (c^*, tok^*).
- **Guess:** $\mathcal{A}$ outputs a bit b' and wins the game if $b' = b$.

The advantage of $\mathcal{A}$ against the TCE scheme in the TCE.2 security game is defined to be:

$$\mathbf{Adv}_{\mathcal{A}}^{\text{TCE.2}}(k) = |\Pr[b' = b] - 1/2|$$

where the probability is measured over the random choices of coins of $\mathcal{A}$ and $\mathcal{C}$.

A scheme is said to be TCE.2 secure if the advantage of all PPT adversaries is negligible as a function of the security parameter k.

4.3 TCE.3: Security against Inside Adversaries

Insider adversaries are those who possess the appropriate private keys but not the target token and attempt to break the confidentiality of TCE ciphertexts i.e. they are receivers of TCE ciphertexts to whom the token has not yet been released by the semi-trusted third party.

The challenger $\mathcal{C}$ takes as input the security parameter 1^k and runs algorithm TCE.KeyGen of the TCE scheme to obtain (pk, sk) i.e. $(pk, sk) \leftarrow \texttt{TCE.KeyGen}(1^k)$. The challenger $\mathcal{C}$ also runs algorithm TCE.TokenGen to obtain a target token tok^* i.e. $tok^* \leftarrow \texttt{TCE.TokenGen}(1^k)$.

The adversary is given the public key pk and corresponding secret key sk but not the target token tok^*. The game proceeds as follows.

- **Phase 1:** $\mathcal{A}$ issues a series of adaptively selected encryption queries on messages m to the token embedded encryption oracle.
- **Challenge:** After $\mathcal{A}$ decides to end Phase 1, it outputs two equal length messages m_0 and m_1. $\mathcal{C}$ selects $b \xleftarrow{\$} \{0, 1\}$, sets $c^* = \texttt{Enc}(pk, tok^*, m_b)$ and gives c^* to $\mathcal{A}$.
- **Phase 2:** This phase proceeds as in Phase 1.
- **Guess:** $\mathcal{A}$ outputs a bit b' and wins the game if $b' = b$.

The advantage of $\mathcal{A}$ against the TCE scheme in the above TCE.3 security game is defined to be:

$$\mathbf{Adv}_{\mathcal{A}}^{\text{TCE.3}}(k) = |\Pr[b' = b] - 1/2|$$

where the probability is measured over the random choices of coins of $\mathcal{A}$ and $\mathcal{C}$.

A scheme is said to be TCE.3 secure if the advantage of all PPT adversaries is negligible as a function of the security parameter k.

4.4   TCE.4: Strong Existential Token Unforgeability

In the original works by [3], the issue of a ciphertext created with one token decrypting correctly with another token was not considered. A new security notion termed the "Strong Existential Token Unforgeability" capturing this requirement was first introduced in [8].

The challenger C takes as input the security parameter 1^k and runs algorithm TCE.KeyGen of the TCE scheme to obtain (pk, sk) i.e. $(pk, sk) \leftarrow$ TCE.KeyGen(1^k).

The adversary is given the public key pk but not the corresponding secret key sk. The game proceeds as follows.

- 1: $\mathcal{A}$ issues a series of decryption queries on adaptively selected ciphertext/token pairs (c, tok) to the decryption oracle.
- 2: $\mathcal{A}$ outputs two different tokens tok_1 and tok_2 and a ciphertext c. The adversary wins the game if $\mathsf{Dec}(sk, tok_1, c) = m_1$ and $\mathsf{Dec}(sk, tok_2, c) = m_2$ with $m_1 \neq m_2 \neq \perp$.

The advantage of $\mathcal{A}$ against the TCE scheme in the above TCE.4 security game is defined to be:

$$\mathbf{Adv}_{\mathcal{A}}^{\mathrm{TCE.4}}(k) = |\Pr[\mathsf{Dec}(sk, tok_1^*, c) = m_1 \wedge m_2 = \mathsf{Dec}(sk, tok_2^*, c) \wedge m_1 \neq m_2 \neq \perp]|$$

where the probability is measured over the random choices of coins of $\mathcal{A}$ and C.

A scheme is said to be TCE.4 secure if the advantage of all PPT adversaries is negligible as a function of the security parameter k.

This is a very strong but necessary security requirement. Here we ask that it should be infeasible for an adversary to make up a new token after the challenge ciphertext is received, and that this should be the case even if the challenge ciphertext is created by the adversary.

4.5   Constructions of TCE Schemes

As observed in [3] a somewhat intuitive construction for TCE scheme may proceed as follows. Let (pk, sk) be the keys of a PKE scheme with encryption algorithm E. Let E' be the encryption algorithm of a symmetric key scheme. Then, to encrypt a message m to a receiver with public key pk, choose a key k for the symmetric scheme at random and send ciphertext $\mathsf{Enc}(pk, \mathsf{Enc}'(k, m))$. The receiver is able to decrypt the ciphertext with his secret key sk but cannot obtain the message till he obtains the symmetric key k.

Intuitively, this basic approach achieves the functionality we desire to achieve EV in Helios. However, the authors in [3] observe that for this scheme to be proven secure the symmetric encryption scheme must be IND-CCA secure and it is not straightforward to analyze the security of the construction.

Two specific instantiations for TCE schemes are proposed in [3] which are TCE.1, TCE.2 and TCE.3 secure in the Random Oracle Model. However, it is shown in [8] that these schemes are not TCE.4 secure. A generic construction for a TCE scheme starting from any trapdoor partial one-way function and secure in the ROM is proposed in [8].

5   Conclusion

We have discussed the lack of Eligibility Verifiability in Helios which leads to ballot stuffing attacks and proposed a solution to incorporate EV and counter ballot stuffing without significantly affecting the existing voter experience. Furthermore, the additional cryptography does not in any way impact the existing protocol and implementation and can be seamlessly incorporated to the existing code base. The proposed solution does not introduce any onerous asymmetric key management for voters as in schemes such as JCJ/Civitas which are the only schemes that incorporate EV but with much greater usability challenges for voters. We argue formally about the security of our new ideas which make novel use of a primitive known as Token Controlled Encryption. Our ideas make minimal change to the existing voter experience in Helios and in particular, the principle of Ballot Casting Assurance is retained and in addition, attacks exploiting the knowledge and malleability of individual ciphertext components in Helios are thwarted.

Acknowledgement. Dr. Sriramkrishnan Srinivasan was at the University of Surrey when this work was carried out. This work was funded by the UK Engineering and Physical Sciences Research Council (EPSRC) under grant EP/G025797/1, and we are grateful to the anonymous reviewers for their valuable comments on the paper.

References

1. Adida, B.: Helios Web-based open-audit voting. In: van Oorschot, P.C. (ed.) USENIX Security Symposium, pp. 335–348. USENIX Association (2008)
2. Adida, B., De Marneffe, O., Pereira, O., Quisquater, J.: Electing a university president using open-audit voting: analysis of real-world use of helios. In: Proceedings of the 2009 Conference on Electronic Voting Technology/Workshop on Trustworthy Elections, p. 10. USENIX Association (2009)
3. Baek, J., Safavi-Naini, R., Susilo, W.: Token-controlled public key encryption. In: Deng, R.H., Bao, F., Pang, H., Zhou, J. (eds.) ISPEC 2005. LNCS, vol. 3439, pp. 386–397. Springer, Heidelberg (2005)
4. Benaloh, J.: Simple verifiable elections. In: Proceedings of the USENIX/Accurate Electronic Voting Technology Workshop 2006 on Electronic Voting Technology Workshop, p. 5. USENIX Association (2006)
5. Clarkson, M.E., Chong, S., Myers, A.C.: Civitas: A secure remote voting system. In: Chaum, D., Kutylowski, M., Rivest, R.L., Ryan, P.Y.A. (eds.) Frontiers of Electronic Voting. Dagstuhl Seminar Proceedings, vol. 07311, Internationales Begegnungs- und Forschungszentrum fuer Informatik (IBFI), Schloss Dagstuhl, Germany (2007)

6. Cortier, V., Smyth, B.: Attacking and fixing helios: An analysis of ballot secrecy. In: CSF, pp. 297–311. IEEE Computer Society (2011)
7. Essex, A., Clark, J., Hengartner, U.: Cobra: toward concurrent ballot authorization for Internet voting. In: EVT 2012 (2012)
8. Galindo, D., Herranz, J.: A generic construction for token-controlled public key encryption. In: Di Crescenzo, G., Rubin, A. (eds.) FC 2006. LNCS, vol. 4107, pp. 177–190. Springer, Heidelberg (2006)
9. Haber, S., Benaloh, J., Halevi, S.: The helios e-voting demo for the iacr. International Association for Cryptologic Research (2010),
   http://www.iacr.org/elections/eVoting/heliosDemo.pdf
10. Juels, A., Catalano, D., Jakobsson, M.: Coercion-resistant electronic elections. In: Atluri, V., di Vimercati, S.D.C., Dingledine, R. (eds.) WPES, pp. 61–70. ACM (2005)
11. Smyth, B.: Replay attacks that violate ballot secrecy in helios. Cryptology ePrint Archive, Report 2012/185 (2012), http://eprint.iacr.org/
12. Smyth, B., Ryan, M., Kremer, S., Kourjieh, M.: Towards automatic analysis of election verifiability properties. In: Armando, A., Lowe, G. (eds.) ARSPA-WITS 2010. LNCS, vol. 6186, pp. 146–163. Springer, Heidelberg (2010)

iCryptoTracer: Dynamic Analysis on Misuse of Cryptography Functions in iOS Applications

Yong Li, Yuanyuan Zhang, Juanru Li, and Dawu Gu

Dept. of Computer Science and Engineering
Shanghai Jiao Tong University
Shanghai, China
yyjess@sjtu.edu.cn

Abstract. Cryptography is the common means to achieve strong data protection in mobile applications. However, cryptographic misuse is becoming one of the most common issues in development. Attackers usually make use of those flaws in implementation such as non-random key/IV to forge exploits and recover the valuable secrets. For the application developers who may lack knowledge of cryptography, it is urgent to provide an efficient and effective approach to assess whether the application can fulfill the security goal by the use of cryptographic functions. In this work, we design a cryptography diagnosis system *iCryptoTracer*. Combined with static and dynamic analyses, it traces the iOS application's usage of cryptographic APIs, extracts the trace log and judges whether the application complies with the generic cryptographic rules along with real-world implementation concerns. We test *iCryptoTracer* using real devices with various version of iOS. We diagnose 98 applications from Apple App Store and find that 64 of which contain various degrees of security flaws caused by cryptographic misuse. To provide the proof-of-concept, we launch ethical attacks on two applications respectively. The encrypted secret information can be easily revealed and the encryption keys can also be restored.

1 Introduction

Mobile devices such as smartphones and tablet computers are becoming the vessel of personal information such as contact list, physical location, social information and even banking service, online payment. As the popularity of such devices grows, the malicious software have the increasing impact on personal privacy. Current mobile OSes(mainly Android and iOS) use layered security strategies to endow the dominance to the end-users to control the access of the sensitive data. Aiming at providing high security assurance, iOS is designed with various security features. At system level, full-disk encryption, ASLR [1], sandboxing profile and privilege assignment are adopted to fulfil access control policy [2]. At applications level, the Apple App Store scrutinizing on the applications also reduces the risk of malicious behaviors in the apps as a beneficial supplement. Besides for those built-in security features, third-party iOS developers resort

M.H. Au et al. (Eds.): NSS 2014, LNCS 8792, pp. 349–362, 2014.

to modern cryptographic algorithms to provide stronger protection on sensitive data.

It is possible that the emphasis on cryptographic techniques for protecting information mitigates the attention to the issue of cryptographic usage. The security of the primitives are provided by intellectual properties or industrial standards. There is a tendency to focus on problems that are mathematically interesting to the exclusion of implementing problems which must be solved in order to actually increase operational security. We've seen lots of security applications contradicting to some basic cryptography applying rules caused by developer's ignorance of general cryptographic usage guidelines, or sometimes the ambiguous documentation misleading to defective implementations. Both facts could result in software vulnerability or privacy leaks.

The well-known *Citibank* iOS application [3] and *Starbucks* application [4], for instance, storing the customer's privacy information such as payment passcode, bank account number, etc. The Verge has reported that Starbucks' iPhone application stores user passwords in plaintext. By connecting iOS device through iTunes, an attacker can easily retrieve the password and payment records. Therefore, it's crucial to evaluate the correctness of cryptographic usage inside the emerging third-party iOS applications.

As a contrast to the open-source Android system, iOS is a proprietary operating system and is relatively close. Developing a third-party security analysis extension for iOS system requires essential work and is difficult for lacking details of the operating system. Recent studies on iOS application mainly apply static analysis to detect security vulnerability such as privacy leak. Egele et al. proposed PiOS [7] based on static analysis using a control-flow graph to identify from where the sensitive data leaks. However, static analysis tends to be less accurate due to the dynamic messaging mechanism of iOS applications, which are primarily developed with Objective-C. Most iOS applications are heavily based on event-driven schemes. Simply analyzing an application with static analysis is not feasible because the dynamic events can not be predicted, the inputs can not be constructed either, parameters may be generated while executing, and the return value is unforeseeable. Such dynamic characteristic determines that many information can only be monitored accurately at runtime and in this situation dynamic analysis would be a better choice.

Dynamic analysis of iOS applications is facing lots of challenges. One challenge is that encryption is input-related, so that some data should be provided. iOS Applications are GUI-rich, and most of input areas are of *UITextField* component, and sometimes files should be provided as input, so manual work is inevitable during test. To study iOS kernel and Objective-C runtime to dynamically observe the application running in iOS, we have to resort to instrumentation and API hooking techniques. To the best of our knowledge, no previous dynamic analysis on cryptographic usage has been proposed on mobile system so far.

An approach to diagnose the implementation code to assure the proper validity of cryptographic usage is in demand. We present *iCryptoTracer* to fulfill such purpose. As a cryptographic usage vetting system (we use *crypto-vetting* to indicate the whole diagnosis process in the following) based on static and dynamic analysis techniques, *iCryptoTracer* situates at Core OS layer gathering crucial information (we call it *crypto-trace* in this work) at iOS runtime that cannot be observed by static analysis, such as the sequence of API calls, arguments and return values. Afterwards, *iCryptoTracer* conducts analysis on the *crypto-trace* files according to some generic rules to diagnose the vulnerability of usage. We diagnose 98 typical security-oriented iOS applications and find out 64 of them contain various degrees of security flaw in cryptographic misuse aspect. We validate the effectiveness of *iCryptoTracer* diagnosis by successfully launching ethical attacks on two iOS applications as proof-of-concept, including a banking application and a password managing application.

The rest of the paper is organized as follows: Section 2 presents the preliminaries on the techniques we adopt to implement *iCryptoTracer*. Section 3 describes the design philosophy of our work. The implementation of *iCryptoTracer* is presented in Section 4. As well as the evaluation of our work in section 5, we also present typical ethical attacks against two applications that have been judged as weak implementation of cryptography by *iCryptoTracer*. Section 6 lists related work, Section 7 is about the limitation, and Section 8 concludes the paper.

2   Messaging in iOS

In this section, the basics of Objective-C runtime, *message swizzling* and *Common Crypto* libSystem will be briefly introduced.

2.1   Messaging

Objective-C is a strict superset of the C programming language that adds object-oriented features to the basic language. An innegligible characteristic of Objective-C is *messaging*, i.e. objc_msgSend. The invoking of object method in Objective-C is not direct but through virtual method tables(*vtables*), i.e., a *message* is sent to a receiver and these messages are handled by the dynamic dispatch function objc_msgSend. A message consists of the receiver of the message(object in Figure 1), method name(method), parameter names(para name$_i$) and their argument value(arg$_j$). The method name and parameter names are called *selector*. There is a one-one mapping between selectors and the code region of the method(see Figure 2), i.e. *selector$_A$* mapping on *IMP$_a$*, *selector$_B$* on *IMP$_b$*, and so on. Then, objc_msgSend will forward the *message* to the receiver to execute the code region.

2.2   *Method Swizzling*

As we discussed above, there exsits mapping between selector and its implementation. Objective-C provides a mechanism to allow developers to exchange or modify the mapping, which allows a selector to be redirected at runtime. This is

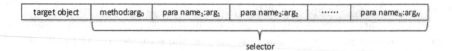

| target object | method:arg$_0$ | para name$_1$:arg$_1$ | para name$_2$:arg$_2$ | ⋯⋯ | para name$_N$:arg$_N$ |

selector

Fig. 1. A syntax of a *message*

called *method swizzling*. Consider *selector$_A$* mapping *IMP$_a$* and *selector$_B$* mapping *IMP$_b$*, we can exchange their mapping and the result is *selector$_A$* mapping *IMP$_b$* and *selector$_B$* mapping *IMP$_a$*(see Figure 3). Also, for a selector, we can modify its function by redirecting it to another implementation developed by ourselves(Figure 4). By utilizing modification, **API hook** is enabled, which is essential in *iCryptoTracer*'s tracing module(see Figure 5).

Fig. 2. Method Swizzling - Original mapping   **Fig. 3.** Method Swizzling - Exchange

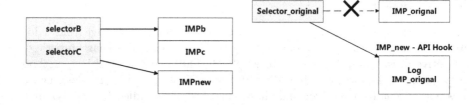

Fig. 4. Method Swizzling - Modification   **Fig. 5.** Method Swizzling - Modification

2.3 *Common Crypto* Library in iOS Security Framework

Apple provides open source *Common Crypto* library for cryptographic usage. Being a part of *Security Framework* in iOS, the library consists of various kinds of cryptography APIs, such as symmetric encryption, HMAC and digests, etc. By calling API from the lib, developers can encrypt target data with some algorithm. However, documentation going with the lib is not very specific, and explanation of cryptography is not provided. As a result, simply calling API from *Common Crypto library* does not necessarily mean data is well protected by encryption.

3   System Design

In this section, we elaborate the design of *iCryptoTracer*.

3.1   Overview of *iCryptoTracer*

iCryptoTracer diagnoses the cryptographic usage adopting static-dynamic combined analysis on a target security application. The structure of *iCryptoTracer*, as depicted in Figure 6, is designed to meet the requirement that the diagnosis of *iCryptoTracer* should be intelligible. *iCryptoTracer* monitors overall cryptographic functions in the application, meanwhile, it is vigilant against the threats to sensitive data, which is the purpose we design the system. The intuition behind is that a complete sensitive information protection scheme must be based on a series of proper cryptographic functions. In other word, as long as the sensitive information is not confined inside a closure area, i.e., encrypted packet or file using cryptographic functions, it is of insecure status and may be illegally acquired. Hence, it is able to reveal potential insecure data protection or sensitive data leakage through checking the improper using of cryptographic functions in an application.

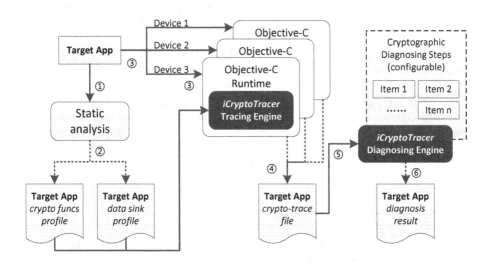

Fig. 6. Overview of *iCryptoTracer* architecture

To accurately evaluate the improper using of cryptographic functions, we mainly take account of the sensitive data when it is at stake such as sending through network or writing to a file and make the following assumptions: First, the security of the cryptographic primitives, which are the basic blocks in cryptography(e.g., AES block cipher, SHA-512 hash functions, etc.), are guaranteed by industrial standards and have been verified widely. Application should only use standard cryptographic primitives to protect the data. Second, the sensitive data of interests usually involves in cryptographic operations under specified cryptographic usage strategy(i.e., cryptographic protocols). Cryptographic usage strategy is the operating parameters or operating orders of cryptographic primitives on sensitive data. Even the primitives are solid, a proper usage strategy is also crucial for building a solid protection scheme.

Based on these assumptions, *iCryptoTracer* tries to locate two typical flaws: 1) the sensitive data, when sending through network or writing to a file, is not protected with any cryptographic functions. Sensitive information is the critical protege and should be under the protection of cryptographic operations. If there exists no cryptographic operation related to sensitive information, the protection must be insecure. 2) the sensitive data, when sending through network or writing to a file, is protected with cryptographic functions but with improper usage strategy.

Among various factors to concern in security context, *iCryptoTracer* takes the following three types of contents into account: 1) sensitive information to be protected, 2) cryptographic primitives, and 3) cryptographic usage strategy. However, for the dynamic analysis of iOS application, it is very difficult to deploy advanced information flow tracking techniques such as taint analysis. The approach adopted by *iCryptoTracer* is therefore a synthetic one. That is to say, our approach synthesizes information collected from separated spots during the runtime and diagnoses the problems. It first scans the target application to spot and put surveillance on all the possible *data sinks*. *Data sinks* are spots that are tightly related to several specific system APIs, such as network I/O and file I/O APIs. The information of data sink is gathered by static analysis on applications. Then, *iCryptoTracer* scans and records the cryptographic function APIs locations in the application, especially those that wraps those I/O as the diagnosis objectives for further use. After these two steps, *iCryptoTracer* generates the *cryptographic functions profile* and the *data sink profile*(step 1-2 in Figure 6). With the guide from *cryptographic functions profile* and *data sink profile*, *iCryptoTracer* monitors those API calls at runtime adopting *message swizzling* technique. Those related function calls are redirected to the *tracing engine* of *iCryptoTracer*, and all useful information including sequence of API calls, arguments, return values, etc. are logged as the *crypto-trace* file (step 3-4 in Figure 6). Finally, *iCryptoTracer* synthesizes information recorded in the *crypto-trace* file with its *diagnosis engine* and judges whether a cryptographic function usage flaw exists in the application.

3.2   Static Analysis

The iOS applications(in the form of *ipa* file) are downloaded from Apple Store, which are encrypted with device-dependent key. We first extract the binary of the applications by means of reverse engineering on the *ipa* file. To identify the crucial API invoking points, we filter the API calls concerning data operation, transmission and encryption and resolve the location into two files *crypto funcs profile* and *data sink profile*.

Static analysis helps us to locate the position of the APIs, which aids the system to narrow down the APIs to observe during the dynamic analysis phase. As we described in the previous section, static analysis is not capable of collecting sufficient runtime information, so more precise information on the target APIs in the *profiles* will be collected during runtime.

3.3   Log Tracing

The *messaging* realizes the redirection of the system calls to cryptographic APIs. As indicated in two *profiles* we acquired from static analysis, those specific calls are wrapped and extended with a logging function. It takes record of the relevant API information, such as method names, arguments, return values, etc. and stores them into a log file. A typical log entry is as below:

```
1    func : CCCrypt
2    algorithm : kCCAlgorithmAES128
3    dataIn : tN/m8LhVi5xRsjKWnvFvXPz6y5qPN0HZknNQHqiLs0Q=
4    dataOut:2088002061679122
5    dataOutAvailable:48
6    iv :! zmcbbmmyyana...
7    key : cxlbylvyfrever !!
8    op : kCCDecrypt
9    options : kCCOptionPKCS7Padding
10   returnValue :0
```

In this entry, *CCCrypt* is the name of the method the application called. The *algorithm* field reveals the information of the *kCCAlgorithmAES128* cryptographic algorithm invoked inside method *CCCrypt*. In this case, it is an *AES* encryption with 128-bit block. The fields of *iv* and *key* indicate the IV and encryption key in use, and the *options* field reveals the data padding method.

3.4   Trace Log Diagnosis

After the log tracing phase, the collected log is delivered to the *diagnosis engine*(Figure 6). In order to ensure a comprehensive analysis, we introduce cross-reference diagnosis to analyze the trace logs from different security context. We collect cryptographic logs for the same iOS application executed on various devices with different versions of operating system. The diversity we introduced tends to bring multiple trace logs. Then the diagnosis engine could detect possible invariance from the synthesis of several logs, which usually indicates the non-randomness *iCryptoTracer* is designed to have a configurable *diagnosis engine*, the successive diagnosis exam items should be defined carefully. There are quite many generic cryptographic rules in security application developing [8] [9], such as the choice of encryption mode, randomness of IV and encryption keys, etc. Based on those rules and a full study of *Common Crypto* library, diagnosis will be conducted on the log following the exams as below:

Item 1: Using constant encryption keys. The randomness of the encryption keys is mandatory. Intuitively, a constant key hard-coded can be easily observed, thus the resulting secrecy of encryption is not guaranted.

Item 2: Using a non-random IV for CBC encryption. As elaborated in [9], the CBC-mode construction should always use a random IV. However, a common error is to use fixed (usually all zero) IV in real-world implementations.

Item 3: Using stateless encryption. There are mainly two kinds of encryption interfaces in *Common Crypto* library: the stateless encryption APIs and the stateful ones. The stateless encryption is deterministic, that is, if the same message is encrypted twice with the same key, the identical ciphertext is returned. A deterministic encryption is not secure, because a distinguisher which distinguishes message streams with repeated messages can be created by detecting repeats in the encrypted message blocks [8].

4   Implementation

We implement the design of *iCryptoTracer* (see Figure 6) in a prototype that supports iOS version from 6.1.3 to 7.0.6. *iCryptoTracer* requires a jailbroken device as its runtime environment to inject a hooking dynamic library into the application during the execution, which redirects and logs target APIs. In the following, we present selected implementation details of *iCryptoTracer*.

4.1   Static Analysis

Common ipa files downloaded from App Store are encrypted so that they should be decrypted before the analysis stage. To decrypt the analyzed app, *iCryptoTracer* resorts to **Clutch** [10] to dump the code segment of an ipa file in memory and fix the encrypted ipa file as a workable executable on a jailbroken device. Then iCryptoTracer implements a script of IDA to statically analyze the binary code to find out the imported APIs that are concerned.

4.2   Tracing Engine

As the major part of dynamic analysis at Objective-C runtime, *tracing engine*(Figure 6) locates in between Core OS and Core Service layers. It is mainly based on *message swizzling* introduced in Section 2.

The main idea of *tracing engine* is to redirect the API calls and dynamically log information such as parameters based on the *profiles* at runtime. We realize this by utilizing *method swizzling* (Section 2.2), that is, replacing $Selector_{orignal}$'s original mapping implementation, $IMP_{original}$ to a new one, IMP_{new}, and the latter including log functions (added) and $IMP_{original}$, which enables hooking and logging, and makes sure the original method be executed (see Figure 5). Through this way, both hooking and logging are achieved at the same time.

Table 1. Applying the diagnosis based on the items

	Pass all the item exams	Happen at data sink
Healthy	YES	-
Weak	NO	NO
Critical	NO	YES

Tracing engine has been implemented to monitor three types of APIs: 1) cryptographic functions, 2) file I/O APIs, and 3) network I/O APIs. The cryptographic functions are provided by *Common Crypto* library of the iOS. Any invoking of cryptographic functions in this library are completely recorded as part of the trace. The tracing of the data flow is obtained by hooking the file I/O and network communication related APIs. When the target application is running, and if any of those APIs are invoked, the related information such as parameters will be recorded as part of the trace.

4.3   Diagnosis Engine

Diagnosing engine is responsible for three tasks: 1) comprehending the *crypto-trace* logs, 2) detecting invariance in the synthesis of the logs, and 3) applying the exam rules and output diagnosis result.

Notice that the log obtained from *tracing engine* is actually incomprehensible byte stream from memory, so parsing on the trace file is required. *Diagnosis engine* contains a parsing module to resolve data according to API specifications, and data is encoded with base64 and saved in a SQLite database, which can be decoded and analyzed later in the following diagnosis steps. Then, entries in multiple cryptographic logs are synthesized and *Diagnosis engine* will extract each field of the same cryptographic operation in multiple logs. Finally, given the synthesized information, *Diagnosis engine* exams the security weakness according to the three exam items we proposed in Section 3. The *Diagnosing engine* is perceptible to determine which exam item the function breaks, so the target application that passes through all the exams will get a higher evaluation value. We define three security degree for diagnosed iOS applications, *critical*, *weak*, and *healthy*, see Table 1.

Critical. We define that if any of the cryptography uses in this application does not pass one or more item exams, and this encryption operation is happening at one or more *data sinks* to be *critical*.

Weak. We define that cryptography use which does not pass all item exams, but the encryption operation is not at any *data sink* to be *weak*.

Healthy. We define the cryptography which pass all item exams to be *healthy*.

After the evaluation of the cryptographic use of a target iOS application, *iCryptoTracer* outputs a file called *diagnosis result* at the end of the diagnosis procedure. The overall evaluation result (*Critical, Weak*, or *Healthy*) is given, and the locations of suspicious encryption functions and their relevant *data sink* are included as well. Given the diagnosis result, not only the application users, but also the program developers can benefit from the detail introspection for next stage improvement on their works.

5   Evaluation

In this section, we analyze the effectiveness of *iCryptoTracer* by applying on the selected security-oriented applications downloaded from Apple's App Store. The results are carefully analyzed to measure the security of the target application. Finally, we give two specific cases on misuse of crypto-functions. An ethical attack is launched against the applications to prove the effectiveness of *iCryptoTracer* in locating the weakness of a security-oriented application.

5.1   Selection of Test Apps

To demonstrate the effectiveness of *iCryptoTracer*, 98 typical security-oriented applications from the official Apple App Store are chosen as the target applications, see Table 2. These applications contain privacy related information, such as online payment password, bank account number, SMS, confidential files, etc. These applications are relative to online bank and online payment, or personal passwords management, such as *Alipay* and *1password*. The former is the most popular online payment application and it has been downloaded for more than 10 million times from China, and the latter is a popular application that stores and manages nearly all the personal passwords and files in a centralized way.

5.2   Testing on Selected Apps

iCryptoTracer has been implemented on several testbeds that supports from iOS 6.1.3 to iOS 7.0.6 on various models of iPhone and iPad. 98 selected security applications are diagnosed through *iCryptoTracer*. The diagnosis procedure only requires manually installation of those target applications on testbed devices. The running of the diagnosis is fully automatic and silent at backstage. Each of the application receives 10 different forged inputs, e.g., 10 forged bank account numbers for online banking application, or 10 different files for file protection applications, in order to extend the analysis results.

According to the outputs, we have in Table 2 the number of the applications with defective implementations we have found during the diagnosis. The results show that 64 out of 98 target applications have various security flaws. Moreover, 8 of 64 unhealthy applications are diagnosed as *critical*. As to *critical* applications, it require little effort to recover the secret message sent via *data sinks*. We give two ethical attacks in the following section. The overall diagnosis results are listed in Table 2.

Table 2. Diagnosis results of 98 applications

Category	Total	Healthy	Weak	Critical
online bank	28	8	20	0
mobile payment	22	6	16	0
account protection	16	8	5	3
file protection	32	12	15	5

Table 3. Case Study

Encryption	Key	IV	Option	Key Repetition
AES 128	njwftwr,xjtxrft.		No Padding	YES
3DES	1234567890def13579ace	init vec	PKCS7Padding	YES

5.3 Case Studies

As we can see from the evaluation section, there exist a lot of applications breaking encryption rules, and some of them can be easily attacked. We select two typical applications for further study.

Ethical Attack on a Banking Application. We use *iCryptoTracer* to evaluate a banking application (for security issue we hide the actual name of the application) that is used for querying user's account activities and performing e-trading. This application is diagnosed as *critical*, which means there exists a misuse of cryptographic function related to *data sink*. In detail, this application does not pass the examines on Exam item 2 and 3. It employs non-random key and an empty IV, see the first record in Table 3.

The misused function is an AES encryption with an empty IV and a fixed key, i.e. the same key is repeatedly used in different cryptographic contexts. We run the same banking application on a non-jail-break iOS device, and provide username and password as input. In a configured WLAN with a sniffer, we are able to eavesdrop the encrypted communication data between the app and server. By applying the encryption algorithm, fixed key and empty IV obtained from *iCryptoTracer*, we can decrypt the encrypted communication data, including username and password, which should be well protected by the app. Furthermore, we successfully use the decrypted username and password to log into the on-line bank.

Ethical Attack on a Password Management Application. We perform the diagnosis on a password management application, which claims to be able to protect user's privacy through encryption and the encryption algorithm applied is of open standard. In order to use the application, users have to enter a password, which proves to be irrelevant to encryption but only for authorization. The application can automatically encrypt user's privacy data, such as passwords and files, and save on the device. For the sake of convenience, the encrypted data can be exported for backup through iTunes. It's true that the application utilizes *3DES* for encryption, but from its tracing log obtained from *iCryptoTracer*, we find out that the application's encryption is of serious flaw, i.e. a simple constant key and a fixed IV are used in different encryption contexts. First, we encrypted test files with the application on a non-jailbreak iOS device, and then exported encrypted data to a computer with the help of iTunes. By applying the constant key and fixed IV (see 3) logged by crypto-trace file in *iCryptoTracer*, all test files are instantly decrypted.

6   Related Work

With the development of mobile system, it gains more and more popularity and attention from researchers, especially on Android and iOS. MoCFI [11] and CFR [12] are both designed to defend iOS applications from control flow attacks. They are of system's security, but have nothing to do with encryption analysis. Egele et al. presented an approach - PiOS [7], which is able to automatically create control flow graphs (CFG) from decrypted iOS binaries and then perform reachability analysis on CFGs to identify possible leaks of user's privacy data from device to third parties. The test results of PiOS demonstrate that a majority of iOS applications leak the device ID. Han et. al [13] also presented a way by massively examining security-sensitive APIs to detect potential access to sensitive resources that may cause privacy breach or security risks. Static analysis is a kind of reference and more proof is needed from dynamic analysis.

Due to the dynamic characteristic of Objective-C, runtime attack aimed at iOS system is invented [14] [15]. The attack results show that by dynamically loading methods, static analysis can be easily bypassed. As a complement for static analysis, dynamic analysis for mobile system has already been presented, such as *TaintDroid* [16]. However, Android and iOS are totally different mobile systems and the technique on Android can never be implemented on iOS due to its close-source. Szydlowski et al. presented a dynamic way to analyze iOS applications [17], whose method is to analyze iOS applications in a static way at first, and then set breakpoints at objc_msgSend methods while running. The most obvious limitation is there will be a lot of breakpoints during running process, which may crash the running application. Also, by setting breakpoints at every objc_msgSend methods, the specific method is unknown, and there will be too much data obtained from registers and memory.

Bhargavan et al. [5] illustrate tools that can be used to verify the security of cryptographic protocol implementations, and Mitchell et al. present Murφ [6] which is able to detect vulnerabilities in cryptography and security protocols. Both of their work are achieved on PC platform. For cryptographic misuse analysis on mobile system, Egele et al. developed a light-weight static analysis approach to check for common flaws of encryption use for Android apps, CRYPTOLINT [9]. Its main idea is to use static program slicing to identify flows between cryptographic keys, initialization vectors and similar cryptographic material and the cryptographic operations. Anyway, it is inevitable that static analysis misses the data generated during runtime and sometimes error-prone, especially when the binary program can load function or methods in a dynamic way. Our work is similar to CRYPTOLINT, but we apply the analysis in a dynamic way on iOS and can be a better complement to static analysis. Though *iCryptoTracer*'s efficiency may not as good as CRYPTOLINT, it's more specific and accurate.

7   Limitation

iCryptoTracer diagnoses limited types of APIs and its information at the specific surveillance location such as *data sinks*, so it can not be categorized as a full-grained information flow analysis system. Moreover, for some developers, they may resort to a third-party cryptography library instead of Apple's *Common Crypto* libSystem, *iCryptoTracer* is not yet capable of analysing third-party security libraries. To achieve this, *iCryptoTracer* has to be equipped with cryptographic primitive identification and other advanced dynamic analysis techniques, which will be presented in our other works soon.

While *iCryptoTracer* can automatically analyze and verify the cryptography use of iOS applications, it still can not verify the security of protocol. During tracing process, in order to provide input data for GUI-rich applications, human interaction or manual work for input is required, which lead to lower efficiency than static analysis.

8   Conclusion

In this paper, we proposed a diagnosis system *iCryptoTracer* for security iOS applications to assess whether the fashion of cryptographic usage leads to a proper notion of security. The diagnosis process is a staged procedure combining static and dynamic analysis techniques. For static analysis, we can efficiently locate the methods to observe later on during iOS runtime. Dynamic analysis helps to collect method call information that cannot deduce at static analysis stage.

Designed as an automatic diagnosis system, *iCryptoTracer* works silently at backstage monitoring the running of the target applications. In the end, *iCryptoTracer* outputs the diagnosis result by given rules and steps. A target application can be considered as *healthy* only when it passes all the item exams. Any *weak* or *critical* application will be diagnosed with a detail result including the defectively implemented APIs and their corresponding *data sinks* locations.

We have diagnosed 98 security iOS applications and found 65.3% of which are suffering from various degree of vulnerability from defective implementation of misuse. Further study on the misuse leads to two ethical attacks on two chosen applications, a banking application and a password management application. We successfully recovered the personal information encrypted and sent via network.

References

1. Esser, S.: Antid0te 2.0 - aslr in ios. In: Hack In the Box (HITB) (2011)
2. Apple: ios security guide (2014)
3. Staff, P.: Citibank admits security flaw in its iphone app, http://nypost.com/2010/07/26/citibank-admits-security-flaw-in-its-iphone-app/
4. Hollister, S.: Starbucks admits its iphone app stores unencrypted user passwords, http://www.theverge.com/2014/1/15/5313648/starbucks-admits-ios-app-stored-passwords-in-plain-text
5. Bhargavan, K., Fournet, C., Corin, R., Zalinescu, E.: Cryptographically verified implementations for tls. In: Proceedings of the 15th ACM Conference on Computer and Communications Security, pp. 459–468. ACM (2008)
6. Mitchell, J.C., Mitchell, M., Stern, U.: Automated analysis of cryptographic protocols using murphi, pp. 141–151. IEEE Computer Society Press (1997)
7. Egele, M., Kruegel, C., Kirda, E., Vigna, G.: Pios: Detecting privacy leaks in ios applications. In: Proceedings of the Network and Distributed System Security Symposium, NDSS (February 2011)
8. Bellare, M., Rogaway, P.: Introduction to modern cryptography, http://cseweb.ucsd.edu/~mihir/cse207/classnotes.html
9. Egele, M., Brumley, D., Fratantonio, Y., Kruegel, C.: An empirical study of cryptographic misuse in android applications. In: Proceedings of the 2013 ACM SIGSAC Conference on Computer and Communications Security, CCS 2013, pp. 73–84. ACM, New York (2013)
10. Cracks, K.J.: Fast ios executable dumper, https://github.com/KJCracks/Clutch
11. Davi, L., Dmitrienko, A., Egele, M., Fischer, T., Holz, T., Hund, R., Stefan: Mocfi: A framework to mitigate control-flow attacks on smartphones. In: Symposium on Network and Distributed System Security, NDSS (February 2012)
12. Pewny, J., Holz, T.: Control-flow restrictor: Compiler-based cfi for ios. In: Proceedings of the 29th Annual Computer Security Applications Conference, ACSAC 2013, pp. 309–318. ACM, New York (2013)
13. Han, J., Yan, Q., Gao, D., Zhou, J., Deng, R.H.: Comparing mobile privacy protection through cross-platform applications. In: Proceedings of the Network and Distributed System Security Symposium (NDSS), San Diego, CA (February 2013)
14. Han, J., Kywe, S.M., Yan, Q., Bao, F., Deng, R., Gao, D., Li, Y., Zhou, J.: Launching generic attacks on iOS with approved third-party applications. In: Jacobson, M., Locasto, M., Mohassel, P., Safavi-Naini, R. (eds.) ACNS 2013. LNCS, vol. 7954, pp. 272–289. Springer, Heidelberg (2013)
15. Wang, T., Lu, K., Lu, L., Chung, S., Lee, W.: Jekyll on ios: When benign apps become evil (2013)
16. Enck, W., Gilbert, P., Chun, B.G., Cox, L.P., Jung, J., McDaniel, P., Sheth, A.N.: Taintdroid: An information-flow tracking system for realtime privacy monitoring on smartphones. In: Proceedings of the 9th USENIX Conference on Operating Systems Design and Implementation, OSDI 2010, pp. 1–6. USENIX Association, Berkeley (2010)
17. Szydlowski, M., Egele, M., Kruegel, C., Vigna, G.: Challenges for dynamic analysis of iOS applications. In: Camenisch, J., Kesdogan, D. (eds.) iNetSec 2011. LNCS, vol. 7039, pp. 65–77. Springer, Heidelberg (2012)

Formal Verification
of Finite State Transactional Security Policy

N. Rajamanickam[1], R. Nadarajan[1], and Atilla Elçi[2]

[1] PSG College of Technology, Coimbatore, India
[2] Aksaray University, Aksaray, Turkey
nrm@mca.psgtech.ac.in

Abstract. Security policy helps to ensure that system always takes the desired input action sequence and works in a proper manner. Formal verification of finite state transactional security policy is necessary to check whether the given policy conforms to the specification. One way to specify finite state transactional security policy is by using a filter automaton. A filter automaton is an action sequence transformer that maps an input action sequence into another, so that the output action sequence obeys the specified policy. A method for verification of finite state transactional security policy enforced by filter automata is being proposed. The observable actions finite security automaton and the observable actions finite truncation automaton are used to verify a finite state transactional security policy.

Keywords: transaction isolation, security policy, finite edit automata, formal verification.

1 Introduction

Any computer system can be regarded as a state transition system. A computer security policy partition the states of this state transition system into authorized states and unauthorized states. A secure system is a system that starts in one of the authorized states, and cannot enter into an unauthorized state [5, 6]. General purpose security policies are important for securing a system from general threats. Application dependent security policies are important for securing the system from threats specific to that system. The first automata based solution for defining an application dependent security policy was proposed by Fred B.Schneider and Bowen Alpern [2, 14]. They defined security automaton as a non deterministic automaton for enforcement of safety policies. Security automaton moves from one state to another according to input actions, and halts the system when it finds violation of security policy. Jay Ligatti, Lujo Bauer and David Walker [10–12] introduced the deterministic version of security automata named truncation automata. There are certain systems which should not be stopped for any reason (even for violation of security policy) for it needs to run 24×7 to provide service. For such systems Jay Ligatti, Lujo Bauer and David Walker [10–12] introduced edit automata, which is a program transformer. This

M.H. Au et al. (Eds.): NSS 2014, LNCS 8792, pp. 363–376, 2014.

edit automaton accepts input actions sequence and produces output action sequence. Danièle Beauquier, Joëlle Cohen and Ruggero Lanotte [3] introduced finite edit automata and characterized the security properties which are enforceable by finite edit automata. In this paper we introduce the filter automaton. Filter automaton is useful for verification of a policy in the perspective of a particular entity. We create a safe transfer policy using filter automaton. We verified whether this policy produces acceptable sequences of actions to the underlying system.

We proceed as follows. In section 2, we discuss current developments happening in automata based solution for security policy. The automata used for specification of safety policies are discussed in section 3. Section 4 discusses the techniques used for enforcement of transactional security policies. Safe transfer policy for bank transaction is described in section 5. Verification of finite state transactional security policy is the subject of Section 6. Section 7 discuss possibilities of formal verification in various automata based solutions. Section 8 is for conclusion and future work.

2   Related Work

Edit automata is now a popular framework in computer security. Several authors have contributed towards this concept. Zhenrong Yang, Aiman Hanna, Mourad Debbabi [16] developed team edit automata for studying the correlation among security properties. Chamseddine Talhi, Nadia Tawbi and Mourad Debbabi [15] have done characterization of security policies that are enforceable by execution monitors constrained by memory limitations using bounded history automata. In [4] Danièle Beauquier, Joëlle Cohen and Ruggero Lanotte developed pushdown edit automata to enforce context free policies. Richard Gay, Heiko Mantel and Barbara Sprick [8] proposed a framework for reliably enforcing security in distributed systems named service automata. In service automata security is enforeced in a decentralized fashion. Service automata enables security monitoring in distributed systems such as service oriented architectures. Gabriele Costa and Ilaria Matteucci [7] proposed gate automata as a formalism for the specification of both security and trust policies. Rajamanickam and Nadarajan [13] developed timed edit automata for implementing real-time transactional security properties. Even though several authors have contributed towards specification of security policy, so far none of them has contributed towards verification. In this paper we describe a technique for verification of finite state transactional security policy from the perspective of an entity.

3   Safety Policy

A safety policy ensures that "bad thing" does not happen during execution [1]. Formally safety policy can be defined as follows: P is a safety policy if and only if

$$(\forall s : s \in Q^\omega : s \not\models P \Rightarrow (\exists i : 0 \leq i : (\forall \beta : \beta \in Q^\omega : s_i \beta \not\models P)))$$

Here Q is the set of program states, Q^ω is the set of infinite sequences of program states, $s \models P$ denotes execution s is in property P and s_i denotes the partial execution consisting of first i states in s. Safety policy can be modeled using various automata techniques. A class of Büchi automata was introduced in [2, 14] named the security automata for enforcing safety policy. A security automaton S is a four tuple (A, Q, Q_0, δ) where

A - countable set of actions
Q - countable set of states
Q_0 - countable set of start states
$\delta : Q \times A \to 2^Q$ is a non deterministic transition function

The truncation automaton is a deterministic version of non deterministic security automaton. A truncation automaton T is a four tuple (A, Q, q_0, δ) where

A - set of actions
Q - countable set of states
q_0 - start state
$\delta : Q \times A \to Q$ is deterministic Turing machine computable partial transition function

Finite state safety policy is a safety policy which could be enforced by a finite state machine. A finite security automaton FS is a four tuple (A, Q, Q_0, δ) where

A - finite set of actions
Q - finite set of states
Q_0 - finite set of start states
$\delta : Q \times A \to 2^Q$ is non deterministic transition function

A class of deterministic muller automata, is called finite truncation automata. A finite truncation automaton FT is a four tuple (A, Q, q_0, δ) where

A - finite set of actions
Q - finite set of states
q_0 - start state
$\delta : Q \times A \to Q$ is deterministic partial transition function

4   Transactional Security Policy

A transactional security policy is a combination of a security policy (safety policy, liveness policy) and a transactional property(atomicity, consistency, isolation and durability). Edit automaton is an abstract machine that checks the sequence of actions and transforms the input action sequence when it deviates from the specified policy. Edit automaton is capable of

- suppressing the input action
- inserting a sequence of actions

Accepting the input action is possible by suppressing it, and inserting it again into the output sequence. By using these powers edit automaton can change the input actions so that output actions obey the given policy. An edit automaton E is a four tuple (A, Q, q_0, δ) where

A - set of actions
Q - countable set of states
q_0 - start state
$\delta : Q \times A \to Q \times (A \cup null)$ is deterministic Turing machine computable total transition function

Edit automaton is capable of enforcing a special kind of policy called infinite renewal property. An infinite renewal property is one in which every valid infinite-length action sequence has infinitely many valid prefixes. All transactional properties (atomicity, consistency, isolation and durability) are infinite renewal properties. Finite state transactional security policy is a transactional security policy which could be enforced by a finite state machine. A finite edit automaton is an edit automaton with a finite set of states. A finite edit automaton effectively enforces regular security policy. A finite edit automaton FE is a four tuple (A, Q, q_0, δ) where

A - finite set of actions
Q - finite set of states
q_0 - start state
$\delta : Q \times A \to Q \times (A \cup null)$ is deterministic total transition function

A filter automaton is a finite edit automaton with multiple input tapes and multiple output tapes. A filter automaton F is a six tuple $(I, O, A, Q, q_0, \delta)$ where

I - finite set of input tapes
O - finite set of output tapes
A - finite set of actions
Q - finite set of states
q_0 - start state
$\delta : Q \times \{I, A\} \to Q \times (O \times \{A \cup null\})$ is deterministic total transition function

A filter automaton is useful in verifying the security policy from the perspective of a particular entity.

5   Safe Transfer Policy Using Filter Automata

The safe transfer policy is for transfer of money from one bank account to another safely. This policy ensures that only one amount transfer transaction should take place for a particular bank account at a particular time(transaction isolation). The customer can change his/her address details during the amount transfer transaction. The customer can give command to change his/her phone number while the amount transfer transaction is ongoing, but the change will be effective only after completion of the amount transfer transaction. The customer should not change his/her email id during the transaction. The safe transfer policy is enforced using a filter automata with two input tapes and two output tapes. The two input tapes are IC(input from customer) and IS(input from service). The two output tapes are OS(output to service) and OC(output to customer). This filter automaton takes(or produces) the following input(or output) actions.

AC - Address Change
AT - Amount Transfer
EC - Email Change
PNC - Phone Number Change
TD - Transfer Done
error - Error Message

Figure 1 shows the safe transfer policy. Here the actions shown above the transition lines are input actions and those shown below the transition lines are output actions.

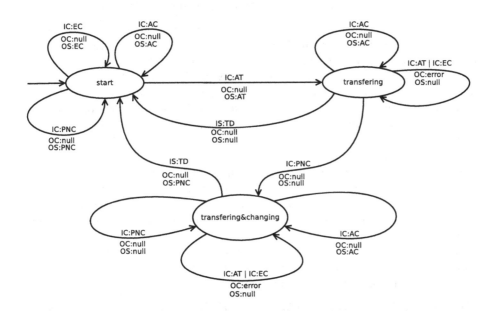

Fig. 1. The Safe Transfer Policy

6 Verification of the Safe Transfer Policy

Formal verification of finite state transactional security policy is necessary to ensure that the customer transaction will be efficient and safe. In order to verify a finite state transactional security policy we need observable actions finite security automaton and observable actions finite truncation automaton.

6.1 Observable Actions Finite Security Automata

For the given filter automaton the set of all possible action sequences for an entity (and observable by the entity) can be identified by creating an observable actions finite security automaton.

Definition 1. *The observable actions finite security automaton of a given filter automaton for an entity is a finite security automaton, which accepts only the possible action sequences for (and observable by) the entity and rejects all other action sequences.*

For the given filter automaton, the observable actions finite security automaton can be created by OAFSA (Observable Actions Finite Security Automata) creation algorithm. This algorithm has two phases. The phase I (Algorithm 1) takes filter automaton and entity e as inputs and produces an observable actions finite security automaton with sequence of input actions per transition as output. An observable actions finite security automation with sequence of input actions per transition is a finite security automaton with the following transition function:

$$\delta : Q \times A^* \to 2^Q \text{ is non deterministic transition function.}$$

Here A^* is the set of finite sequences of input actions. If an entity observes more than one output tapes and if a transition provides output actions in those tapes, these actions will be taken in alphabetical order of names of the output tapes. So the filter automaton should be designed accordingly. For a simpler policy design, we can assume that each entity should observe only one input tape and one output tape. The phase II (Algorithm 2) is for conversion from the observable actions finite security automaton with sequence of input action per transition to the observable actions finite security automaton with single input action per transition.

In the filter automaton from a particular state q_x there may be more than one out going transitions, which are producing same output action b. So in the observable actions finite security automaton from the corresponding state q_x there may be more than one outgoing transitions which take the same input action b. And also in the given filter automaton the output action may be *null*. So in the observable actions finite security automaton the corresponding transition input is *null* (ϵ transition). So the resultant observable actions finite security automaton is a non deterministic automaton.

Theorem 1. *The observable actions finite security automaton with sequence of input actions per transition, created by the OAFSA creation algorithm phase I for the given filter automaton and entity e, accepts only the possible sequences of actions for (and observable by) the entity e, of the given filter automaton and rejects all other sequences of actions.*

Lemma 1. *The observable actions finite security automaton with sequence of input actions per transition, created by the OAFSA creation algorithm phase I for an entity e, accepts only the possible sequences of actions for (and observable by) the entity e, of the given filter automaton.*

Algorithm 1: OAFSA creation algorithm Phase I
Input: Filter Automaton, entity e
Output: Observable Actions Finite Security Automaton with sequence of input actions per transition

1. From the filter automaton create a finite security automaton (sequence of input actions per transition) with the following
   A - the same set of actions available in the filter automaton
   Q - the same set of states available in the filter automaton
   q_0 - the same start state of the filter automaton
   δ' - transition table : for each transition δ_j from q_x to q_y which takes a_{δ_j} as input action from the tape I_{δ_j} and produces
   $b_{\delta_{j1}}$ as output action on the tape $O_{\delta_{j1}}$,
   $b_{\delta_{j2}}$ as output action on the tape $O_{\delta_{j2}}$,
   $b_{\delta_{j3}}$ as output action on the tape $O_{\delta_{j3}}$,
   ...
   in the filter automaton do
   begin
   (a) create a transition δ'_j from q_x to q_y with empty input action sequence
   (b) if tape I_{δ_j} is observable for entity e insert the input action a_{δ_j} in the input action sequence
   (c) for each $O_{\delta_{ji}}$ in $\{\ O_{\delta_{j1}}, O_{\delta_{j2}}, O_{\delta_{j3}}, \dots\}$ do
   if tape $O_{\delta_{ji}}$ is observable for entity e insert the action $b_{\delta_{ji}}$ in the input action sequence
   end
2. The resultant (non deterministic) finite security automaton is the observable actions finite security automaton with sequence of input actions per transition

Algorithm 1: OAFSA Creation Algorithm Phase I

Proof. For each transition of the given filter automaton there is a transition in observable actions finite security automation (with sequence of input action per transition). If the input tape and/or some of the output tapes in the transition of filter automaton are observable by the entity e, then the corresponding input action and/or the corresponding list of output actions are included in the input action sequence of transition of observable actions finite security automaton. If all tapes of actions in that transition of filter automaton, are unobservable then the corresponding transition in observable actions finite security automaton has empty input action sequence (*null* transition or ϵ transition). So if we run both automaton parallely, atleast one run of the observable actions finite security automaton moves states in lockstep with filter automaton. So observable actions finite security automaton accepts all sequences of actions for (observable by) the entity e, of filter automaton.

Lemma 2. *If the observable actions finite security automaton with sequence of input actions per transition, created by the OAFSA creation algorithm phase I for an entity e, accepts an action sequence x_1, x_2, x_3, ... then atleast for any one of the input action sequence, the given filter automaton provides $T'_1 : x_1$,*

Algorithm 2: OAFSA creation algorithm Phase II
Input: Observable Actions Finite Security Automaton with sequence of input actions per transition
Output: Observable Actions Finite Security Automaton with single input action per transition

1. From the observable actions finite security automaton with sequence of input actions per transition create a finite security automaton with the following

   A - the same set of actions available in the observable actions finite security automaton with sequence of input actions per transition

   Q - include all states available in the observable actions finite security automaton with sequence of input actions per transition

   q_0 - the same start state of the observable actions finite security automaton with sequence of input actions per transition

   δ' - transition table : for each transition δ_j from q_x to q_y which takes $a_1, a_2, a_3, \ldots, a_n$ as input action sequence with n input actions do
   begin
      if input action sequence has only single input action a_1 then include
        transition δ_j in δ'
      else
        begin
          (a) create $n-1$ new states named $q_{\delta_{j1}}, q_{\delta_{j2}}, q_{\delta_{j3}}, \ldots, q_{\delta_{j(n-1)}}$ and
             include them in Q.
          (b) create following n transitions and include them in δ'
             transition from q_x to $q_{\delta_{j1}}$ which takes a_1 as input action
             transition from $q_{\delta_{j1}}$ to $q_{\delta_{j2}}$ which takes a_2 as input action
             transition from $q_{\delta_{j2}}$ to $q_{\delta_{j3}}$ which takes a_3 as input action
             . . .
             transition from $q_{\delta_{j(n-1)}}$ to q_y which takes a_n as input action
        end
      end

2. The resultant (non deterministic) finite security automaton is the observable actions finite security automaton with single input action per transition.

Algorithm 2: OAFSA Creation Algorithm Phase II

$T_2' : x_2$, $T_3' : x_3$, ... the sequences of actions for (and observable by) the entity e (where T_1', T_2', T_3', ... are input/output tapes observable by the entity e).

Proof. Assume the observable actions finite security automaton (with sequence of input actions per transition) accepts the input action sequence x_1, x_2, x_3, ... then one or more runs of the observable actions finite security automaton accepts this action sequence. Consider any one of the runs of observable actions finite security automaton which accepts the input action sequence x_1, x_2, x_3, ... and assume that this run goes through the states s_1, s_2, s_3, ... Now consider the corresponding states s_1, s_2, s_3, ... in the filter automaton, the run which goes through these states and the input action sequence of this run. Assume that this input action sequence is $T_1 : a_1$, $T_2 : a_2$, $T_3 : a_3$, ... If we give the input action sequence $T_1 : a_1$, $T_2 : a_2$, $T_3 : a_3$, ... to the filter automaton, it will go through the states s_1, s_2, s_3, ... and will produce observable action sequence $T'_1 : x_1$, $T'_2 : x_2$, $T'_3 : x_3$, ... where T'_1, T'_2, T'_3, ... are input/output tapes observable by the entity e. So if the observable actions finite security automaton accepts an action sequence x_1, x_2, x_3, ... then atleast for any one of the input action sequence, the given filter automaton provides $T'_1 : x_1$, $T'_2 : x_2$, $T'_3 : x_3$, ... the sequences of actions for (and observable by) the entity e.

Proof. Proof's of Lemma 1 and Lemma 2 show that observable actions finite security automaton with sequence of input actions per transition created by OAFSA creation algorithm phase I accepts only the possible sequences of actions for (and observable by) the entity e, of the given filter automaton.

We have two entities for the safe transfer policy - customer and service. For the service entity the observable tapes are IS (input from service) and OS(output to service). Figure 2 shows the observable actions finite security automaton with the sequence of input actions per transition for the safe transfer policy from the perspective of service. Figure 3 shows the same with single input action per transition for the safe transfer policy from the perspective of service.

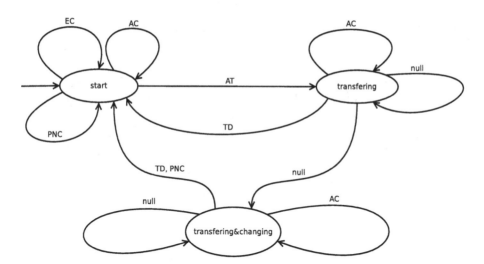

Fig. 2. Observable Actions Finite Security Automaton with sequence of input actions per transition

6.2   Observable Actions Finite Truncation Automata

Definition 2. *The observable actions finite truncation automaton of a given filter automaton for an entity is a finite truncation automaton which accepts only the possible action sequences for (and observable by) the entity and rejects all other action sequences.*

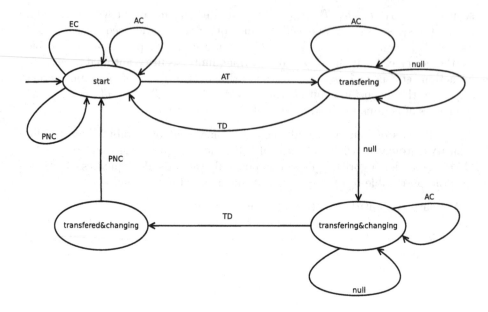

Fig. 3. Observable Actions Finite Security Automaton with single input action per transition

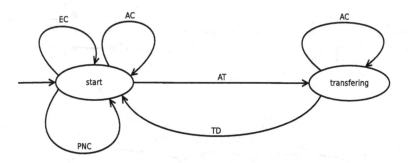

Fig. 4. Observable Actions Finite Truncation Automaton

A non deterministic finite security automata can be converted into a deterministic one, by using McNaughton Theorem [9]. Observable actions finite truncation automaton can be created by converting the non deterministic observable actions finite security automaton into a deterministic automaton. Figure 4 shows the observable actions finite truncation automaton for the safe transfer policy. The transition table for observable actions finite truncation automaton is shown in Table 1.

Table 1. Transition Table for Observable Actions Finite Truncation Automaton

Actions	Observable Actions Finite Truncation Automaton states	
	start	transfering
AC	start	transfering
AT	transfering	reject
EC	start	reject
PNC	start	reject
TD	reject	start

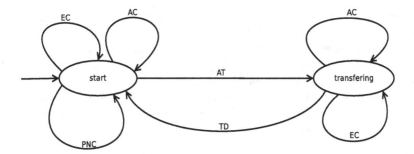

Fig. 5. Finite Truncation Automaton for Acceptable Action Sequences of the Underlying System

Table 2. Transition Table for Finite Truncation Automaton

Actions	Finite Truncation Automaton States	
	start	transferring
AC	start	transferring
AT	transferring	reject
EC	start	transferring
PNC	start	reject
TD	reject	start

6.3 Verification

The underlying system takes specific set of action sequences. It does not accept overlap in amount transfer transaction. Also it accepts phone number change operation outside of an amount transfer transaction. So the PNC action should not come in between AT and TD. It accepts email change action at any time. Following are examples for acceptable action sequences:

1. $AC, AT, TD, PNC, AT, TD, EC, AT, TD, \ldots$
2. $PNC, AT, TD, AC, AT, TD, EC, \ldots$
3. $AC, EC, AT, TD, AT, TD, PNC, \ldots$

In the above example action sequences PNC action comes before amount transfer transaction or after completion of amount transfer transaction. Also note that there is no overlap in the amount transfer transaction. Following are example action sequences which are not acceptable by the underlying system:

1. $AT, AC, PNC, TD, EC \ldots$
2. $AT, AC, AT, TD, TD, EC \ldots$

In the first action sequence the PNC action comes within amount transfer transaction (in between AT and TD). In the second action sequence two amount transfer transactions overlap. Figure 5 shows the finite truncation automaton for the acceptable action sequences of the underlying system. The transition table for the finite truncation automaton is shown in Table 2. If the unacceptable action sequences are given to the safe transfer policy it converts them into acceptable action sequences. Table 3 shows these input action sequences and their respective output action sequences.

Table 3. Observable Action Sequence from Safe Transfer Policy

S.No	Input Action Sequence	Output Action Sequence
1	$AT, AC, PNC, TD, EC \ldots$	$AT, AC, TD, PNC, EC \ldots$
2	$AT, AC, AT, TD, TD, EC \ldots$	$AT, AC, TD, EC \ldots$

Formal verification of safe transfer policy could be done by creating the Cartesian product of the observable actions finite truncation automaton and the finite truncation automaton. The Cartesian product is shown in Table 4. This table consists of only the reachable states from the start state (here the start state is (start, start)). This transition table shows that the finite truncation automaton accepts all possible input action sequences accepted by the observable actions finite truncation automaton. So all action sequences produced by given filter automaton is acceptable for the underlying system.

Table 4. Transition Table for Cartesian Product of Observable Actions Finite Truncation Automaton and Finite Truncation Automaton

Actions	Cartesian Product Automaton States	
	(start,start)	(transferring,transferring)
AC	$start_{(OAFTA)}, start_{(FTA)}$	$transferring_{(OAFTA)}, transferring_{(FTA)}$
AT	$transferring_{(OAFTA)}, transfering_{(FTA)}$	$reject_{(OAFTA)}, reject_{(FTA)}$
EC	$start_{(OAFTA)}, start_{(FTA)}$	$reject_{(OAFTA)}, transferring_{(FTA)}$
PNC	$start_{(OAFTA)}, start_{(FTA)}$	$reject_{(OAFTA)}, reject_{(FTA)}$
TD	$reject_{(OAFTA)}, reject_{(FTA)}$	$start_{(OAFTA)}, start_{(FTA)}$

7   Discussion

Formal verification of edit automaton is impossible. Because edit automaton is equivalent in computational power to Turing machines. So it is in general undecidable to verify a given edit automaton. Formal verification of a finite edit automaton could be done by using the OAFSA creation algorithm, if we assume finite edit automaton is a special case of filter automaton with only two tapes(input tape and output tape).

8   Conclusion

Formal verification of a security policy is necessary, if it is complex and have large number of states. Transactional security policy enforced by filter automaton can be verified, whether it produces acceptable input action sequences to the underlying system. The observable actions finite truncation automaton identifies the set of all possible observable action sequences of a given filter automaton. By comparing this set of action sequences with the allowed action sequences one can verify whether the given filter automaton produces acceptable action sequences to the underlying system. In order to check whether the given filter automaton is the most suitable for the underlying system, we need to verify, how effectively the given filter automaton implements the soundness and transparency properties [11]. For these two properties are abstract, we are trying to find out ways to render them concrete and verify that the given filter automaton is sufficiently suitable for the underlying system. An extension of this work may help to verify security policies using service automata [8] in distributed systems. We are also trying to find a method for verification of real-time transactional security policy enforced by timed edit automaton [13].

Acknowlegement. We would like to thank Dr.N.Geetha for her valuable comments and suggestions. We also thank our anonymous reviewers for their comments and suggestions.

References

1. Alpern, B., Schneider, F.B.: Defining liveness. Information Processing Letters 21, 181–185 (1985)
2. Alpern, B., Schneider, F.B.: Recognizing safety and liveness. Distributed Computing 3, 117–126 (1987)
3. Beauquier, D., Cohen, J., Lanotte, R.: Security policies enforcement using finite edit automata. Electronic Notes in Theoretical Computer Science 229, 19–35 (2009)
4. Beauquier, D., Cohen, J., Lanotte, R.: Security policies enforcement using finite and pushdown edit automata. International Journal of Information Security 12, 319–336 (2013)
5. Bishop, M.: Computer Security: Art and Science. Addison-Wesly (2002)
6. Bishop, M., Venkatramanayya, S.S.: Introduction to Computer Security. Pearson Education (2006)
7. Costa, G., Matteucci, I.: Gate automata-driven run-time enforcement. Computers and Mathematics with Applications 63, 518–524 (2012)
8. Gay, R., Mantel, H., Sprick, B.: Service automata. In: Barthe, G., Datta, A., Etalle, S. (eds.) FAST 2011. LNCS, vol. 7140, pp. 148–163. Springer, Heidelberg (2012)
9. Khoussainov, B., Nerode, A.: Automata Theory and its applications. Birkhäuser (2001)
10. Ligatti, J., Bauer, L., Walker, D.: More enforceable security policies. In: Foundations of Computer Security Workshop (2002)
11. Ligatti, J., Bauer, L., Walker, D.: Edit automata: enforcement mechanism for run-time security policies. International Journal of Information Security 4, 2–16 (2005)
12. Ligatti, J., Bauer, L., Walker, D.: Run-time enforcement of nonsafety policies. ACM Transactions on Information and System Security 12, 19:1–19:41 (2009)
13. Rajamanickam, N., Nadarajan, R.: Implementing real-time transactional security property using timed edit automata. In: Proceedings of the Sixth International Conference on Security of Information and Networks, Aksaray, Turkey, pp. 429–432 (November 2013)
14. Schneider, F.B.: Enforceable security policies. ACM Transactions on Information and System Security 3, 30–50 (2000)
15. Talhi, C., Tawbi, N., Debbabi, M.: Execution monitoring enforcement under memory-limitation constraints. Information and Computation 206, 158–184 (2008)
16. Yang, Z., Hanna, A., Debbabi, M.: Team edit automata for testing security property. In: Third International Symposium on Information Assurance and Security, pp. 235–240 (2007)

Fingerprint Indexing Based on Combination of Novel Minutiae Triplet Features

Wei Zhou[1], Jiankun Hu[1,*], Song Wang[2], Ian Petersen[1],
and Mohammed Bennamoun[3]

[1] School of Engineering and Information Technology,
The University of New South Wales,
Canberra, Australia ACT 2600
wei.zhou@student.adfa.edu.au,
{J.Hu,i.petersen}@adfa.edu.au
[2] School of Engineering and Mathematical Sciences,
LaTrobe University,
Melbourne, Australia VIC 3086
song.wang@latrobe.edu.au
[3] School of Computer Science and Software Engineering,
The University of Western Australia,
Perth, Australia WA 6009
m.bennamoun@csse.uwa.edu.au

Abstract. Fingerprint indexing is a process of pre-filtering the template database before matching. The most common features used for fingerprint indexing are based on minutiae triplets. In this paper, we investigated the indexing performance based on some commonly used features of minutiae triplets and proposed to combine these features with some novel features of minutiae triplets for fingerprint indexing. Experiments on FVC 2000 DB2a and 2002 DB1a show that the proposed indexing method can perform better than state-of-the-art schemes for full fingerprint indexing, meanwhile, experimental results on NIST SD 14 show that the performance is improved significantly after the new features are added to the feature space, and is fairly good even for partial fingerprint indexing.

1 Introduction

Biometrics such as fingerprint, face, iris, keystroke dynamics and ECG have been widely used for authentication [1] [2] [3] [4] [5], of which fingerprint is an ideal biometric trait for many applications in modern security systems, ranging from access control, criminal identification, to the emerging bio-cryptography [6] [7] [8] [9] [10] [11] [12] [13]. Among these applications, access control is a fingerprint verification (or fingerprint authentication) process, which is used to verify whether the fingerprint of a claimed identity matches the corresponding fingerprint enrolled and stored in a database; criminal identification is a process of

---

* Corresponding author.

M.H. Au et al. (Eds.): NSS 2014, LNCS 8792, pp. 377–388, 2014.

fingerprint identification (or fingerprint retrieval), which is used to identify an unknown person by searching a template fingerprint database. Fingerprint identification is a process of one-to-many comparisons and is usually time-consuming if the template database is large. Conventional solutions are based on exclusive classification techniques whereby fingerprints are first classified into several classes to reduce the search space, such as Arch, Loop and Whorl. Such exclusive classification based schemes are not effective enough because more than 90% of fingerprints belong to only three super classes (left loops, right loops and whorls).

To address these problems, fingerprint indexing (or continuous fingerprint classification) was developed, whereby instead of classifying fingerprints into limited and predefined classes, fingerprint indexing techniques use feature vectors to describe fingerprints. Through similarity preserving transformations, these feature vectors form a multidimensional feature space, where similar fingerprints characterized by similar features are arranged as neighbors in the feature space. For identification, the query fingerprint is mapped into a point in the same feature space, and the neighboring fingerprints are compared one by one until a match is found or a certain number of the neighbors have been compared. The penetration rate, defined as the percentage of database searched until a match is found, and the hit rate, defined as the probability of retrieving the correct identity, are commonly used to measure the performance of an indexing scheme. Higher hit rate together with lower penetration rate means better indexing performance.

Among various fingerprint features, level 1 features (Orientation Field, Singular Points, Ridge Frequency) and level 2 features (minutiae) are often used for fingerprint indexing, wherein features extracted from minutiae triplets formed by minutia points are most popular. In this paper, we investigated the performance of fingerprint indexing based on some common features of minutiae triplets and proposed an indexing scheme by combining these features with some novel features which are easily obtainable from minutiae information. We carried out a series of experiments on both full and partial fingerprint databases to evaluate the proposed approach. Experimental results on FVC 2000 DB2a and 2002 DB1a show that the proposed indexing approach can achieve better performance than state-of-the-art methods for full fingerprint indexing. Meanwhile, the experimental results of the indexing scheme on partial fingerprints, which were generated from NIST SD 14, by adding new features incrementally to the common feature set, show that the performance is much better after new features are considered, and can even be comparable to that on full fingerprint indexing if the parameters are chosen properly.

The rest of this paper is organized as follows. Section 2 is a brief introduction to the related work on fingerprint indexing. Section 3 elaborates on the generation of the minutiae triplets features including both common features and the newly proposed features, and the indexing scheme based on these features. Experimental evaluations on several public fingerprint databases are demonstrated in Section 4 and Section 5 concludes the whole work.

2 Related Work

2.1 Full Fingerprint Indexing Techniques

A number of fingerprint indexing schemes based on level one features have been proposed since 1990s. Lumini et al. [14] were the first to propose the idea of indexing for fingerprint identification and used orientation field as feature vectors. Cappelli et al. [15] used fingerprint prototype masks to generate feature vectors and studied several different strategies. In addition to these level one features which are primarily used for fingerprint indexing, some other features have also been investigated. Bhanu and Tan [16] proposed to index fingerprints using minutiae triplets. Boer et al. [17] investigated the use of the orientation field, FingerCode and minutiae triplets as the input feature vectors and concluded that the orientation field performs the best if only a single type of feature were to be used. Wang et al. [18] proposed to use FOMFE (Fingerprint Orientation Model based on 2D Fourier Expansion) coefficients as feature vectors for fingerprint indexing, which has achieved the fastest feature generation speed. All of these indexing techniques are reported to be able to achieve a high hit rate at a low penetration rate when applied on full fingerprint images [16].

2.2 Partial Fingerprint Indexing Techniques

Different from full fingerprint images, the missing part of a partial fingerprint may contain significant information which is hardly feasible, therefore, researchers attempted to make full use of all levels of features that can be extracted from the existing segments. Feng and Jain [19] [20] developed a multi-staged filtering system to reduce the search space while retrieving the potential candidates for large-scale latent fingerprint matching. Yuan et al. [21] used the number of matched minutiae polygons derived from matching information of minutiae triplets as well as minutiae triplets themselves to speed up the indexing. Alessandra et al. [22] proposed to index latent fingerprint by fusion of level 1 and level 2 features. These filtering or indexing schemes either depend on the singular points which are hardly found in the partial fingerprint segment, or involve excessive computation on the minutiae information. Wang and Hu [23] applied FOMFE model [18] to address partial fingerprint identification from another angle. They developed algorithms to extend the partial ridge flows smoothly into the unknown segment and used the reconstructed features to form the indexing space. This approach has shown very promising results in reducing the size of candidate lists for matching when applied in fingerprint indexing, and the feature set does not include singular points.

3 The Proposed Indexing Scheme

In this paper, we employ the local features derived from each noncollinear minutiae triplet for fingerprint indexing.

3.1   Fingerprint Representation

The features of a minutia extracted from a fingerprint image usually include its coordinates (x, y), local ridge orientation θ and minutia type (ridge bifurcation or ending denoted by 1 or 0). In our approach, a commercial fingerprint verification software VeriFinger SDK [24] was adopted to extract minutiae information for both full fingerprint images and partial fingerprint images. After extraction, the resulting minutiae are sorted according to their y coordinates in an ascending order, which will benefit the choose of minutiae points to form minutiae triplets.

Common Features of Minutiae Triplets

- **Triangle handedness [16]:** Suppose P_1, P_2, P_3 are the three minutiae to form a triangle and their y coordinates are in an ascending order. We choose P_1 as the first vertex and use (x_i, y_i) to denote the coordinates of minutiae $P_i, i = 1, 2, 3$. Define $\phi = (x_2 - x_1) \times (y_3 - y_1) - (y_2 - y_1) \times (x_3 - x_1)$. If $\phi > 0$, P_1, P_2, P_3 are in counter-clockwise order, then we set the vertices as $\{P_1, P_2, P_3\}$; otherwise, we order the vertices as $\{P_1, P_3, P_2\}$. By this means, we make sure that the vertices of all triangles are arranged in the counter-clockwise direction. Before the extraction of other features, we suppose P_1, P_2, P_3 are already in counter-clockwise order.
- **Lengths of each side [25]:** Let $Z_i = x_i + jy_i$ be the complex number $(j = \sqrt{-1})$ corresponding to the coordinate (x_i, y_i) of $P_i, i = 1, 2, 3$. Define $Z_{21} = Z_2 - Z_1$, $Z_{32} = Z_3 - Z_2$, and $Z_{13} = Z_1 - Z_3$. The length of each side is defined as $\{L_1, L_2, L_3\}$, wherein $L_1 = |Z_{21}|$, $L_2 = |Z_{32}|$, and $L_3 = |Z_{13}|$.
- **Triangle type [16]:** Let $\gamma = 4\gamma_1 + 2\gamma_2 + \gamma_3$, where γ_i is the type of minutiae $P_i, i = 1, 2, 3$. If P_i is a bifurcation point, $\gamma_i = 1$, or else $\gamma_i = 0$. We have $\gamma \in \{0, 1, 2, 3, 4, 5, 6, 7\}$.

New Features of Minutiae Triplets. According to our investigation, when the above features are used for fingerprint indexing, a triangle in the top left of a query sample may map to another triangle in the bottom right of a template fingerprint image, which will introduce errors. Enlightened by the feature of triangle type, we define a type of new feature, namely triangle position. Besides, to make full use of the local ridge orientation θ, we introduce another feature, namely orientation differences.

- **Triangle position:** Suppose the fingerprint image is aligned roughly. We divide the segment into 4 equal-sized blocks. Similar to quadrant partition, we let 1 denote the upper right block, 2 denote the upper left block, 3 denote the lower left block and 4 denote the lower right block. Let $\rho_i, i = 1, 2, 3$ be the block type of minutiae $P_i, i = 1, 2, 3$, $\rho_i \in \{1, 2, 3, 4\}$. Define $\varrho = 100\rho_1 + 10\rho_2 + \rho_3$ as the triangle position, then the number of triangle positions is 4^3.
- **Orientation differences:** Let θ_i be the local orientation of minutiae $P_i, i = 1, 2, 3$. We represent orientation difference between each pair of adjacent vertices as $\alpha_i, i = 1, 2, 3$, wherein $\alpha_1 = \theta_2 - \theta_1$, $\alpha_2 = \theta_3 - \theta_2$, and $\alpha_3 = \theta_1 - \theta_3$.

The final feature set of a minutiae triplet is in the form of an eight tuple $\{L_1, L_2, L_3, \gamma, \varrho, \alpha_1, \alpha_2, \alpha_3\}$. Among these features, L_1, L_2, L_3 and γ are the commonly used features of minutiae triplets for indexing [16] [21], and $\alpha_1, \alpha_2, \alpha_3$ and ϱ are the newly designed ones since they are simple, discriminative and easy to obtain even with the singular areas missing (see Section 4).

3.2   Indexing Scheme

Parameters. To reduce the number of false correspondences obtained from querying the indexing space, some parameters on length and orientation difference are introduced.

- **Relative length difference:** Assume the length of each side of a triangle formed by minutiae triplet does not change much in different impressions of the same finger. Let L and L' be L_1, L_2, or L_3 in a query image and a template image, respectively. We constrain $|L - L'| < \delta_L$.
- **Relative rotation:** Assume the orientation difference does not change much in different impressions of the same finger. Let α and α' be α_1, α_2, or α_3 in a query image and a template image, respectively. We constrain $|\alpha - \alpha'| < \delta_O$.

Therefore, δ_L and δ_O are the main parameters for the indexing process.

Registration Process. Since certain distortion in the sides of triangles should be allowed, we adopt quantization to implement feature space clustering. During the registration process, each triangle in a template image is characterized by an eight-tuple vector, which means each fingerprint is viewed as a collection of points distributed in the index space with each point characterizing an eight-dimensional feature vector. Then, we quantize the triangles by the lengths of their three sides. Suppose the maximum side of all the triangles in the database is L_{max}, then the indexing space is partitioned into $(L_{max}/\delta_L)^3$ clusters. Each of the points is assigned to one of the pre-defined clusters based on the quantization rule. This process is repeated for every template fingerprint in the database. Thus, a cluster in the index space will have a list of fingerprint indices that have at least one point assigned to that cluster. Besides, the cluster also stores the remaining features ($\{\gamma, \varrho, \alpha_1, \alpha_2, \alpha_3\}$) in the eight-tuple vector for further processing except for the lengths of each side.

Query Process. During the query process, when a query sample fingerprint q is presented, it is first represented as a set of points with eight-dimensional feature vectors. Next, these points are mapped to individual clusters in the index space. A set of possible matching indices corresponding to a small number of clusters are then determined. After that, each point of the query fingerprint is further compared with the possible matching points in the clusters, and those points that satisfy the following requirements will be chosen:

Table 1. Performance Evaluation on FVC 2000 DB2a – Hit Rate

δ_L	δ_O	HR (%)						
		$PR = 1\%$	$PR = 2\%$	$PR = 3\%$	$PR = 4\%$	$PR = 5\%$	$PR = 10\%$	$PR = 20\%$
4	15	85	87	88	89	89	90	92
	30	84	86	87	87	88	90	92
	60	81	85	86	87	87	89	92
5	15	86	88	89	90	**91**	**92**	**94**
	30	85	86	88	89	89	91	**94**
	60	82	84	86	87	88	91	93
6	15	**88**	**90**	**90**	**91**	**91**	**92**	**94**
	30	86	88	89	89	90	**92**	**94**
	60	82	86	88	88	89	91	93

Table 2. Performance Evaluation on FVC 2002 DB1a – Hit Rate

δ_L	δ_O	HR (%)						
		$PR = 1\%$	$PR = 2\%$	$PR = 3\%$	$PR = 4\%$	$PR = 5\%$	$PR = 10\%$	$PR = 20\%$
4	15	89	91	92	92	92	93	95
	30	88	90	91	91	92	93	94
	60	84	87	87	88	89	92	93
5	15	90	**93**	**94**	**94**	**94**	**95**	**96**
	30	89	91	91	92	93	**95**	**96**
	60	85	88	88	89	91	92	94
6	15	**91**	92	93	93	**94**	**95**	95
	30	88	90	91	92	92	93	95
	60	84	86	87	88	89	91	94

- The triangle types γ and γ' are the same.
- The triangle positions ϱ and ϱ' are the same.
- $|\alpha - \alpha'| < \delta_O$.

Finally, the qualified indices are sorted in the candidate list by their occurring frequency in descending order.

4   Experimental Results

To evaluate the proposed fingerprint indexing approach, statistical experiments have been carried out on several popular public databases. Section 4.1 illustrates the performance of the proposed scheme on full fingerprint databases including both FVC 2000 DB2a and 2002 DB1a. Section 4.2 demonstrates the performance on partial fingerprint database generated from NIST SD 14. The whole experiment was implemented in Matlab on a workstation PC with the following configurations: Intel(R) Core(TM)i7 3.4GHz, 16GB memory, 64-bit Operating System.

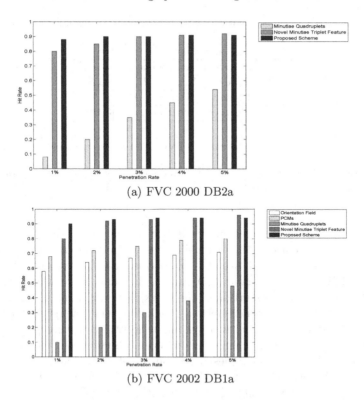

(a) FVC 2000 DB2a

(b) FVC 2002 DB1a

Fig. 1. Performance comparison of different indexing schemes on FVC databases

4.1 Performance on Full Fingerprint Databases

Most of the published techniques for full fingerprint indexing have been evaluated on FVC 2000 DB2a and FVC 2002 DB1a. FVC 2000 DB2a contains 800 fingerprints from 100 subjects (8 impressions per subject) captured using a capacitive fingerprint scanner. FVC 2002 DB1a also contains 800 fingerprints from 100 fingers (8 impressions per finger), but it was captured using a optical fingerprint scanner. In our experiment, we chose the first impression of each subject (100 in total) to form the template database and the rest as the query samples (700 in total) for both FVC 2000 DB2a and FVC 2002 DB1a.

The performance of the fingerprint indexing scheme is evaluated by reporting the hit rate (HR) at certain penetration rates (PR). We tested the proposed indexing scheme using different parameter settings, wherein distortion scale of the triangle sides δ_L is set to be 3, 4, or 5, distortion scale of the orientation difference δ_O is set to be 15, 30, or 60, and the maximum number of candidates to be considered is 20.

Table 1 and Table 2 show the performance of the proposed indexing approach on FVC 2000 DB2a and FVC 2002 DB1a, respectively, wherein the best performance at a certain penetration rate is highlighted in bold. We can see from these

Table 3. Average penetration rate on FVC 2002 DB1a when hit rate is 100%

Minutiae Triplets [16]	38.1%
Low-order Delaunay Triangle [26]	18.1%
Minutiae Quadruplets [27]	11.8%
Novel Minutiae Triplets [21]	9.9%
Proposed Scheme	**3.51%**

Table 4. Average penetration rate on FVC 2000 DB2a when hit rate is 100%

SIFT Features [28]	Minutiae Quadruplets [27]	Novel Minutiae Triplets [21]	Proposed Scheme
91%	26%	22%	**5.24%**

tables that even if the penetration rate is very low (e.g. 1%), the hit rate is high (above 80%). Different choice of δ_L and δ_O results in different performance. For FVC 2000 DB2a, the best choice of δ_L and δ_O is 6 and 15, respectively, and for FVC 2002 DB1a, the best choice of δ_L and δ_O is 5 and 15, respectively.

Fig. 1(a) shows the comparison of the indexing performance of our approach on FVC 2000 DB2a with other methods, including minutiae quadruplets based indexing [27] and indexing with novel minutiae triplet feature [21]. Fig. 1(b) shows the comparison of indexing performance of the proposed method on FVC 2002 DB1a with other techniques based on orientation field [29], PCMs [30], minutiae quadruplets [27] and novel minutiae triplet feature [21]. We can see that the proposed scheme outperforms other state-of-the-art methods, especially when the penetration is very low (1% and 2%).

Table 3 and Table 4 show the results on FVC 2002 DB1a and FVC 2000 DB2a for comparisons with other methods using another measurement, respectively, that is the average penetration rate when the hit rate is 100%. We can see from both tables that the proposed indexing scheme can achieve much better performance than other method evaluated using the same measurement.

4.2   Performance on Partial Fingerprint Database

Related works on partial fingerprint indexing have used NIST special database 27 (SD 27) as the query image set, however, feature extraction in NIST SD 27 is manually done [20] [22] [21] and cannot be operated automatically. Since the objective of this experiment is fingerprint indexing on partial fingerprints, we use another public database NIST special database 14 (SD 14) [31] in this test.

NIST SD 14 consists of 54000 ink-rolled prints scanned from fingerprint cards. There are two impressions recorded for each finger, namely, the F (First) prints ranging from F00001 to F27000 and the S (Second) prints ranging from S00001 to S27000. In our experiments, we chose the last 2000 F prints to constitute the template database and the last 2000 S images as the query samples. Before indexing, we segmented both the template and sample images to remove peripheral regions and make the remainder frame lie in a north-south direction as much as possible. The image size after segmentation is 480×512 pixels.

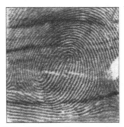

(a) Full   fingerprint image

(b) Partial fingerprint image

Fig. 2. A typical partial fingerprint image in our experiment and its corresponding full image

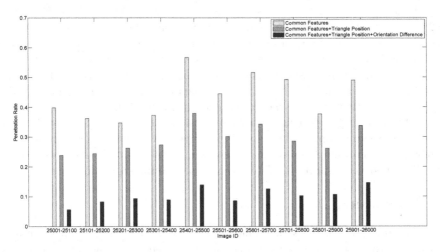

Fig. 3. Performance improvement of using new features incrementally on NIST SD 14

For each sample image, we used a routine of NIST Biometric Image Software [32], namely Mindtct, to obtain a quality map marking reliability of local fingerprint image areas at different levels. Then, we extracted an image foreground with the highest quality level and produced a partial fingerprint segment by keeping only the high quality areas. Figure 2 shows a typical example of such partial fingerprint images generated in the test and its corresponding full fingerprint. Therefore, partial fingerprints generated in our experiment do not contain any singularity, and even singularity regions are usually removed. In this way, we can generate a sample image set composed of partial fingerprints.

Fig. 3 illustrates the performance improvement of fingerprint indexing on NIST SD 14 when the new features are used incrementally. In this experiment, the last 2000 F prints ($F25001 \sim F27000$) constitute the template database and 1000 S prints ($S25001 \sim S26000$) are divided into 10 groups as the query samples. Parameters δ_L and δ_O were set to be 4 and 15, respectively. As is

Table 5. Performance Evaluation on NIST SD 14 – Penetration Rate

δ_L	Penetration Rate (%)		
	$\delta_O = 15$	$\delta_O = 30$	$\delta_O = 60$
4	15	13.28	14.63
5	12.25	11.48	13.29
6	10.25	10.12	10.27

shown in Fig. 3, the penetration rate decreased by at least 1/3 when the triangle position was used as an extended feature, and the the penetration rate further decreased by at least 1/2 when the orientation difference was used as another extended feature.

Table 5 is the performance of the indexing approach on NIST SD 14 with different choice of δ_L and δ_O. In this experiment, the last 2000 F prints ($F25001 \sim F27000$) form the template database and the last 2000 S prints ($S25001 \sim S27000$) are used as the query samples. We can see that when δ_L and δ_O are 6 and 30 respectively, the performance is the best (nearly 10%) in this test.

As mentioned before, existing techniques on partial fingerprint indexing approaches were evaluated on NIST SD 27, which need human involvement to extract features. However, the partial sample images used in our experiments are generated from full fingerprint images by erosion and are not used elsewhere, so there is no related comparable work. According to the indexing performance of other methods on full fingerprint databases in Table 3 and Table 4, we can see that 10% penetration rate is fairly good for partial fingerprint indexing.

5   Conclusion

In this paper, we proposed an indexing scheme by combining some common features with some novel features of minutiae triplets for fingerprint indexing. Experimental evaluation on full fingerprint databases FVC 2000 DB2a and 2002 DB1a show that the proposed indexing approach can achieve better performance than state-of-the-art methods. We also investigated the performance improvement on partial fingerprint database generated from NIST SD 14 when these new features were added to the feature space incrementally. The experimental results show that the performance is improved significantly after new features are considered, and can be comparable to that on full fingerprint indexing under certain parameter settings.

Acknowledgment. The work in this paper was supported by Australian Research Council (ARC) Linkage Project LP120100595.

References

1. Xi, K., Hu, J., Han, F.: Mobile device access control: an improved correlation based face authentication scheme and its java me application. Concurrency and Computation: Practice and Experience 24(10), 1066–1085 (2012)

2. Xi, K., Tang, Y., Hu, J.: Correlation keystroke verification scheme for user access control in cloud computing environment. Comput. J. 54(10), 1632–1644 (2011)
3. Sufi, F., Khalil, I.: Faster person identification using compressed ecg in time critical wireless telecardiology applications. J. Network and Computer Applications 34(1), 282–293 (2011)
4. Sufi, F., Khalil, I.: An automated patient authentication system for remote telecardiology. In: International Conference on Intelligent Sensors, Sensor Networks and Information Processing, ISSNIP 2008, pp. 279–284 (December 2008)
5. Sufi, F., Khalil, I., Hu, J.: Ecg-based authentication. In: Stavroulakis, P., Stamp, M. (eds.) Handbook of Information and Communication Security, pp. 309–331. Springer, Heidelberg (2010)
6. Ahmad, T., Hu, J., Wang, S.: Pair-polar coordinate-based cancelable fingerprint templates. Pattern Recogn. 44(10-11), 2555–2564 (2011)
7. Wang, S., Hu, J.: Alignment-free cancelable fingerprint template design: A densely infinite-to-one mapping (ditom) approach. Pattern Recogn. 45(12), 4129–4137 (2012)
8. Xi, K., Ahmad, T., Han, F., Hu, J.: A fingerprint based bio-cryptographic security protocol designed for client/server authentication in mobile computing environment. Journal of Security and Communication Networks 4(5), 487–499 (2011)
9. Xi, K., Hu, J.: Introduction to Bio-cryptography. In: Handbook of Information and Communication Security. Springer (2010)
10. Yang, W., Hu, J., Wang, S., Stojmenovic, M.: An alignment-free fingerprint bio-cryptosystem based on modified voronoi neighbor structures. Pattern Recognition 47(3), 1309–1320 (2014)
11. Wang, S., Hu, J.: Design of alignment-free cancelable fingerprint templates via curtailed circular convolution. Pattern Recognition 47(3), 1321–1329 (2014)
12. Yang, W., Hu, J., Wang, S., Yang, J.: Cancelable fingerprint templates with delaunay triangle-based local structures. In: Wang, G., Ray, I., Feng, D., Rajarajan, M. (eds.) CSS 2013. LNCS, vol. 8300, pp. 81–91. Springer, Heidelberg (2013)
13. Yang, W., Hu, J., Wang, S.: A finger-vein based cancellable bio-cryptosystem. In: Lopez, J., Huang, X., Sandhu, R. (eds.) NSS 2013. LNCS, vol. 7873, pp. 784–790. Springer, Heidelberg (2013)
14. Lumini, A., Maio, D., Maltoni, D.: Continuous versus exclusive classification for fingerprint retrieval. Pattern Recogn. Lett. 18(10), 1027–1034 (1997)
15. Cappelli, R., Lumini, A., Maio, D., Maltoni, D.: Fingerprint classification by directional image partitioning. IEEE Trans. Pattern Anal. Mach. Intell. 21(5), 402–421 (1999)
16. Bhanu, B., Tan, X.: Fingerprint indexing based on novel features of minutiae triplets. IEEE Trans. Pattern Anal. Mach. Intell. 25(5), 616–622 (2003)
17. de, J.B., Bazen, A.M., Gerez, S.H.: Indexing fingerprint databases based on multiple features. In: Proceedings SAFE, ProRISC, SeSens 2001, Utrecht, The Netherlands, STW, pp. 300–306 (November 2001)
18. Wang, Y., Hu, J., Phillips, D.: A fingerprint orientation model based on 2D fourier expansion (fomfe) and its application to singular-point detection and fingerprint indexing. IEEE Trans. Pattern Anal. Mach. Intell. 29(4), 573–585 (2007)
19. Feng, J., Jain, A.K.: Filtering large fingerprint database for latent matching. In: Proc. Int. Conf. on Pattern Recognition (ICPR 2008), pp. 1–4 (2008)
20. Jain, A.K., Feng, J.: Latent fingerprint matching. IEEE Transactions on Pattern Analysis and Machine Intelligence 33(1), 88–100 (2011)

21. Yuan, B., Su, F., Cai, A.: Fingerprint retrieval approach based on novel minutiae triplet features. In: 2012 IEEE Fifth International Conference on Biometrics: Theory, Applications and Systems (BTAS), pp. 170–175 (2012)
22. Paulino, A.A., Liu, E., Cao, K., Jain, A.K.: Latent fingerprint indexing: Fusion of level 1 and level 2 features. In: Biometrics: Theory, Applications and Systems, Washington, D.C. (2013)
23. Wang, Y., Hu, J.: Global ridge orientation modeling for partial fingerprint identification. IEEE Trans. Pattern Anal. Mach. Intell. 33(1), 72–87 (2011)
24. VeriFinger: Verifinger sdk (2013), http://www.neurotechnology.com/verifinger.html
25. Germain, R., Califano, A., Colville, S.: Fingerprint matching using transformation parameter clustering. IEEE Computational Science Engineering 4(4), 42–49 (1997)
26. Liang, X., Bishnu, A., Asano, T.: A robust fingerprint indexing scheme using minutia neighborhood structure and low-order delaunay triangles. IEEE Transactions on Information Forensics and Security 2(4), 721–733 (2007)
27. Iloanusi, O., Gyaourova, A., Ross, A.: Indexing fingerprints using minutiae quadruplets. In: 2011 IEEE Computer Society Conference on Computer Vision and Pattern Recognition Workshops (CVPRW), pp. 127–133 (2011)
28. Shuai, X., Zhang, C., Hao, P.: Fingerprint indexing based on composite set of reduced sift features. In: 19th International Conference on Pattern Recognition, ICPR 2008, pp. 1–4 (2008)
29. Jiang, X., Liu, M., Kot, A.: Fingerprint retrieval for identification. IEEE Transactions on Information Forensics and Security 1(4), 532–542 (2006)
30. Liu, M., Yap, P.T.: Invariant representation of orientation fields for fingerprint indexing. Pattern Recogn. 45(7), 2532–2542 (2012)
31. SD14: Nist special database 14 (2013), http://www.nist.gov/srd/nistsd14.cfm
32. NBIS: Nist biometric image software (2013), http://www.nist.gov/itl/iad/ig/nbis.cfm

Privacy Preserving Biometrics-Based and User Centric Authentication Protocol

Hasini Gunasinghe and Elisa Bertino

Purdue University,
West Lafayette, IN, United States
{huralali,bertino}@purdue.edu

Abstract. We propose a privacy preserving biometrics-based authentication protocol by which users can authenticate to different service providers from their own devices without involving identity providers in the transactions. Authentication is performed through a zero-knowledge proof of knowledge protocol which is based on a cryptographic identity token created using the unique, repeatable and revocable biometric identifier of the user and a secret provided by the user which enables two-factor authentication as well. Our approach for generating biometric identifiers from the user's biometric image is based on the support vector machine classification technique in conjunction with a mechanism for feature extraction from the biometric image. The paper includes experimental results on a dataset of iris images and a security and privacy analysis of the protocol.

Keywords: Privacy, Security, Biometrics, Authentication.

1 Introduction

The safe and secure use of web-based services requires strong authentication mechanisms able to provide assurance about the identity of the service users while, at the same time, protecting the privacy of these users. Biometrics represents a relevant technology for authentication, especially today that mobile devices include biometric sensors allowing users to conveniently provide biometrics for authentication. However, whereas biometrics has many advantages such as uniqueness, its use raises privacy concerns. Upon user enrollment, a biometrics-based authentication system typically stores information extracted from biometrics, referred to as biometric template, into some database. This template is then matched with the template generated when the user needs to authenticate. Security of the biometric template database is thus critical to assure the privacy of biometrics. If the biometric template database is compromised, users may lose their biometric identity permanently due to the lack of revocability. To address such problem, approaches have been proposed to create revocable biometric identifiers (BIDs) [3] and biometric keys (BKs)[1]. With respect to these approaches, it is crucial that BIDs and BKs do not leak sensitive

---

[1] A BID is a repeatable binary string derived from biometrics whereas a BK is a cryptographic key generated from biometrics.

M.H. Au et al. (Eds.): NSS 2014, LNCS 8792, pp. 389–408, 2014.

information about the original biometric image. At the same time, they should preserve the uniqueness nature of the biometrics, that is, no two individuals should be assigned the same BID or BK. Also, as two readings of the same biometric such as face, iris and fingerprints of the same individual are usually not identical, it is crucial that the generated BID or BK is repeatable, in the sense that each time the BID or BK is generated from a user's biometric template, we should get a BID or BK which is equal to the one generated at enrollment time.

In a typical biometrics-based identity management architecture, a user initially enrolls his/her biometrics at a trusted authority usually referred to as identity provider (IDP). When the user needs to authenticate to a third party service provider, the service provider contacts the IDP for the biometrics-based authentication of the user. The service provider thus relies on the IDP for authenticating the user so that the user does not to have to register his/her biometrics at the third party service provider, thereby better protecting his/her biometrics-based identity. However, this type of architecture, referred to as IDP-centric identity management, raises other types of privacy concerns. Because the IDP is involved in each transaction, it can infer sensitive information such as users' transaction behavior with different service providers.

User-centric identity management architectures address such issues as they do not require the involvement of the IDP in the transactions the users carry out with the service providers. Under such architectures, after the initial enrollment with the IDP, the user can authenticate to the service provider in a secure manner, without involving the IDP. In the VeryIDX system, for example, upon enrollment at the IDP, the user is given some cryptographic authentication token using which the user can authenticate directly to the service provider without having to disclose passwords or other authentication information to the service provider [9]. The design of this kind of identity management solution is however challenging when dealing with biometrics-based authentication through users' mobile phones. The use of mobile phones requires digital identity management solutions able to prevent identity theft in cases in which the phone is stolen, lost or compromised. Today there are commercial products [1] which support biometrics-based user authentication through mobile devices. However, they do not address the above privacy concerns.

The goal of this paper is to propose a privacy preserving and secure protocol for authenticating users from mobile devices to service providers based on their biometrics that addresses the above challenges. The main contributions of this paper can be summarized as follows:

1. We introduce the usage of perceptual hash of biometric images to improve the accuracy of BID generation from a support vector machine (SVM) classifier model.
2. We propose a privacy preserving protocol for user authentication to service providers through mobile devices using BIDs and the techniques to ensure the security of the proposed protocol.
3. An experimental evaluation of the BID generation technique on a dataset of iris biometric images [12], [11].

There is both ongoing and past research that investigates reliable biometrics-based authentication mechanisms. Out of previous research work, the one which is closest to the biometrics-based authentication mechanism that we propose, is by Bhargav-Spantzel et al. [3]. Such previous approach has some major drawbacks which make it not suitable for authentication in mobile devices. It assumes a centralized IDP which is involved in both the enrollment and verification of the biometric identity of the users. In particular, such previous protocol requires that the user connects at the IDP when having to authenticate, as the IDP stores the SVM classifier which is required to generate the BID[2]. Such previous approach is thus an IDP-centric identity management approach, and therefore it makes it possible for the IDP to learn information about transactions executed by the users. Even if such previous protocol [3] were extended for use in mobile devices by storing the SVM classifier on the mobile device to allow the user to authenticate without connecting to the IDP, leakage of the internals of the SVM classifier by a malicious user of the system or an attacker who steals the user's mobile phone, could compromise the BIDs of all the other users of the system, as the SVM classifier is the same for all the users of the system. By contrast, in our approach, each user has a different customized SVM classifier. The image hashing mechanism used in [3] also does not perform with good accuracy when used to classify biometric images that are not present when training the SVM classifier, which is the main reason why we use the perceptual hashing mechanism which improves the accuracy in classifying newly captured biometric images. Furthermore, based on our experiments, the approach for generating BIDs proposed by Bharghava-Spantzel et al. [3] does not assure repeatability in practice (although it seems theoretically achievable), because it depends on the repeatability of the probability estimates provided as classification output by the SVM classifier with respect to multiple classes. Therefore, we make use of a single class prediction output provided by the SVM classifier when generating the BID. We also define an extension to the core protocol which supports the application of error correction codes on the feature vector extracted from the biometric image, in order to improve the repeatability of the biometric identity without compromising the uniqueness.

The rest of the paper is organized as follows. Section 2 introduces the main concepts used in our solutions. Section 3 explains our approach. Details and results of the experiments are presented in Section 4. We analyze the security of our approach in Section 5. We discuss related work in Section 6 and outline conclusions and future work in Section 7.

2   Background

In what follows we introduce the main concepts and techniques which are used as building blocks in our solution.

---

[2] We describe the SVM classifier in details in sections 2.2 and 3.1.

2.1   Perceptual Hash

A perceptual hash (P-Hash) is a signature of an underlying media source file's perceptual content [7]. While perceptual hashing applies to all multimedia types such as audio, video and images, we will only consider images as the media type of interest in our discussion. Perceptual hashes are intended to establish the perceptual equality in different images that look similar. In order to serve this purpose, perceptual image hashing functions extract features from the image and calculate a hash value based on these features. In general, there are four properties that need to be satisfied by a P-Hash function [14] which can be summarized as: equal distribution (unpredictability) of hash values, pairwise independence for perceptually different images, invariance for perceptually similar images, and distinction of perceptually different images. We leverage those properties to identify the similarity in the biometric images of the same user, captured at different times.

Many different perceptual image hashing functions have been proposed in the literature and one should select the relevant P-Hash function based on the application scenario. The Discrete Cosine Transformation (DCT) based hash is the mostly used one with several implementations available such as the publicly available pHash library by Zauner [14], [7]. The DCT is a linear and invertible function. The most common variation of the DCT is the type-II DCT which is the one used in our solution, which we simply refer to as DCT.

Algorithm 1 lists the P-Hash algorithm based on the DCT. The conversion to greyscale using luminance (line 2) is common to all P-Hash functions since the essential information resides in the luminance component of the image [14]. Resizing (line 4) is done to simplify computing the DCT of the image. 64 low frequency DCT coefficients are extracted for computing the hash, which constitutes a square matrix of size 8×8 (line 8). The low frequency coefficients are considered to be perceptually most significant because most of the image information tends to be concentrated in a few low frequency components of the DCT. The elements of one dimensional array created from the DCT coefficient matrix are normalized based on the median, to compute the final hash as listed in lines 17-19. Accordingly, the final hash output of the P-Hash function does not reveal the actual low frequencies; it just represents a very rough relative scale of the frequencies to the median.

2.2   Support Vector Machine

Given a set of training examples composed of pairs of the form $\{x_i, y_j\}$, the SVM classification technique finds a function $f(x)$ that maps each attribute vector x_i to its associated class y_j, $j = 1, 2, 3 \ldots n$ where n is the total number of classes represented by training data. The SVM is a discriminative classifier defined by separating hyper planes, that is, given the labeled training data, the algorithm outputs optimal hyper planes (i.e. maximum separating hyper planes) which categorize new samples which are also known as testing data. The SVM algorithm includes a kernel function which maps training data to improve its

Algorithm 1. Biometric Image Hashing Algorithm

1: $I \leftarrow$ input image.
// Preprocessing: (lines 2-4)
2: $I_1 \leftarrow$ convert I to greyscale using its luminance.
// apply mean filter on I_1:
3: $I_2 \leftarrow$ convolution of I_1 with a 7×7 kernel.
4: $I_3 \leftarrow$ resize I_2 to 32×32.
// generate DCT matrix: C of size 32×32
5: $C[n,m] = \sqrt{\frac{2}{N}} . \cos(\frac{(2m+1).n\pi}{2N})$, where $m, n = 0, \ldots, N-1$ & $N = 32$
6: $C' \leftarrow$ transpose of C.
// generate DCT coefficient matrix of I_3: (lines 7-8)
7: $I_4 \leftarrow C. I_3. C'$
8: $V \leftarrow$ extract 8×8 DCT coefficient matrix from I_4:
$v(i,j) = I_4(i,j)$ where $i = 1, \ldots, 8; j = 1, \ldots, 8$
// Rows of matrix V are concatenated to form one dimensional array Z
9: **for** each i where $0 < i < 9$ **do**
10:    **for** each j where $0 < j < 9$ **do**
11:       $z[8 * (i-1) + j] = v(i,j)$
12:       $j++$
13:    **end for**
14:    $i++$
15: **end for**
16: $m \leftarrow$ median of all $z[k]$ where $0 < k < 65$.
// calculate P-Hash H
17: **for** each k where $0 < k < 64$ **do**
18:
$$H(k) = \begin{cases} 0 & \text{if } z[k] < m \\ 1 & \text{if } z[k] \geq m \end{cases}$$

19: **end for**
20: **return** hash H.

---

resemblance to a linearly separable set of data. This increases the dimensionality of data. We incorporate the Radial Basis Function (RBF) kernel with optimal values for C and γ parameters [3] selected based on k-fold cross validation accuracy in grid search, as we discuss in Section 4. We use the prediction output of the trained SVM classifier to generate the BID of the user, during enrollment as well as during authentication.

2.3   Pedersen Commitment

The Pedersen commitment [10] is a secure commitment scheme whose security is based on the hardness of solving discrete logarithms. The operation of this

---

[3] C trades off misclassification of training samples against simplicity of the decision surface in the SVM. A low value of C makes the decision surface smooth, while a high value of C aims at classifying all training examples correctly. γ is a kernel specific parameter which determines the RBF width.

commitment scheme, which involves a committer and a verifier, can be described by following three steps.

Setup: Let p and q be large primes, such that q divides $p - 1$. Typically p is of 1024 bits and q is of 160 bits. G_q is a unique, order-q sub group of Z_p^* -which is the multiplicative group of order p. A trusted party chooses g -a generator of G_q and h $(= g^a \bmod p$ where 'a' is secret) -an element of G_q such that it is computationally hard to find $log_g h$, and publishes (p, q, g, h).

Commit: The committer creates the commitment of $x \in Z_q$ by choosing $r \in Z_q$ at random and computing: $C(x, r) = g^x h^r \bmod p \in G_q$.

Open: To open the commitment, the committer reveals x and r and the verifier checks if $C = g^x h^r$ to verify the authenticity of the commitment.

The Pedersen commitment has two properties: it is unconditionally hiding - every possible value of x is equally likely to be committed in C, and it is computationally binding - one cannot open the commitment with any $x' \neq x$, unless he can compute $log_g h$. We leverage these properties to hide the BID of the user in an identity token.

2.4 Zero Knowledge Proof of Knowledge Protocol

A zero knowledge proof of knowledge (ZKPK) protocol is a protocol by which the owner of a secret can prove to a verifier his/her knowledge about the secret without making it any easier for the verifier to obtain the actual secret. In our work, we use the protocol listed in Protocol 1 to prove the knowledge of the two secret values x and r hidden in the Pedersen commitment, without revealing the actual values of x and r to the verifier. This protocol has three properties: completeness - if the committer and verifier are honest, the protocol succeeds with overwhelming probability; soundness - the protocol does not allow the committer to prove a false statement; and zero knowledge - the proof does not leak any information about the secrets. We leverage these properties in our solution for the user to prove that he/she is the actual owner of the BID and the secret hidden in the identity token.

Let U denote the committer and V denote the verifier.

Protocol 1. Zero Knowledge Proof of Knowledge

1: $U \rightarrow V$: U randomly picks $y, s \in Z_q$ and sends $d = g^y h^s \in G_q$ to V.
2: $V \rightarrow U$: V sends random challenge $e \in Z_q$ to U.
3: $U \rightarrow V$: U sends $u = y + ex$ and $v = s + er$ to V.
4: V: accepts if $g^u h^v = dC^e$.

2.5 Hadamard Error Correction Code

There are two main types of error correction code (ECC): convolutional codes - which are processed on a bit-by-bit basis, and block codes - which are processed on a block-by-block basis. The Hadamard ECC (HECC) [4] falls into the second category, in which a large stream of data is broken into fixed size blocks called 'message' and each message is encoded to a codeword in the HECC, before being sent over a noisy channel. At the receiver end, the received n-bit long block is decoded in order to recover the original message. Codewords in the HECC are derived from a Hadamard matrix which is a square orthogonal matrix consisting of elements 1, -1. The Hadamard codewords matrix is obtained from the Hadamard matrix and the Hadamard negative matrix by replacing -1 with 0:

$$HC_{nx2n} = \begin{bmatrix} H_{nxn} \\ -H_{nxn} \end{bmatrix}$$

In general, an instance of the HECC, represented as $\{n, k, d\}_q$, encodes messages of size k with codewords of size n which are generated from the Hadamard matrix of size n where n $= 2^{k-1}$. It applies on an alphabet of size q and can correct errors up to $\lfloor (d-1)/2 \rfloor$ number of bit errors where d $(= 2^{k-2})$ represents the distance or the number of bit positions in which any two distinct codewords differ. Therefore, the size of the codeword matrix, the error correction capability and also the overhead due to encoding (which is denoted by $1 - (k/n)$) differ based on the parameters of the particular instance of the block code. We make use of this technique to correct errors occurring in the features extracted from different biometric images of the same user. To enhance security, we incorporate a pair of encoding and decoding algorithms that involve a secret key, as introduced by Kande et al. [6], instead of directly encoding the feature vector obtained at the enrollment time, as described in Section 3.

2.6 Key Derivation from a Password

In our proposed scheme, three secrets $(S_i : i \in \{1, 2, 3\})$ are used in different steps of the protocol: S_1 - is combined with the class label output by the SVM to generate the BID of the user (size: 128 bits); S_2 - is used as the secret r in the Pedersen Commitment (size: 160 bits); S_3 - is the key used in error correction encoding/decoding algorithm (size: 104 bits). In order to address usability concerns, such as the user having to enter three passwords during the execution of the protocol, and security concerns, such as having to store the secrets somewhere and the secrets not being uniformly randomly distributed in the key space, we make use of the password based key derivation function 2 (PBKD2) for deriving the three secrets from a single password provided by the user, which involves PKCS#5 as the pseudo random function (PRF) and a salt value to make dictionary attacks harder. The key derivation algorithm is thus as follows. We first generate a secret S as:
S = PBKDF2 (PKCS#5, Password, Salt, derived key length (=392 bits)).
We then partition S into three parts of which the first is S_1 with 128 bits, the second is S_2 with 160 bits, and the third is S_3 is 104 bits.

3 Our Approach

In what follows we first present an overview of our methodology for training and customizing the SVM classifier, generating unique and repeatable BIDs from biometric images, and using the BIDs for generating cryptographic identity tokens in order to perform multi-factor authentication with ZKPK protocol. Then we present our proposed protocol for privacy preserving biometrics-based authentication of users in a user-centric identity management system.

3.1 Methodology

As biometric images of the same individual captured at different times are not identical, we rely on the output of SVM classification to generate a repeatable BID. We selected the P-Hash as the feature extraction mechanism after comparing it with the singular vector decomposition (SVD) based image hashing mechanism used in [3] in order to improve the accuracy of the SVM classification (see Section 4 for experimental results).

3.1.1 Training and Customizing the SVM Classifier

The IDP trains a SVM classifier using the P-hash vectors computed from biometric images of a population of different individuals including several biometric images from each individual. We refer to such classifier as the base SVM model. How the set of biometric images is selected to train the base SVM model is based on the organizational context of the IDP. For example, in the case of an organization under one administrative domain, the IDP can collect biometric images of the existing employees and train the base SVM model. In contrast, in the case of a public authority which is going to manage users' biometrics-based identity enrollment, the IDP can train the initial base SVM model using the biometric images obtained from a sample population of citizens or even from publicly available biometric datasets. A customized SVM model is then created for each user in the system, from the trained base SVM model during the enrollment of the user in the system. The customization is done by replacing each class label in the original model with a new class label, which is a randomly generated integer. The customized SVM model generated for a particular user is different from the customized SVM models of all other users in the system since each customized model uses different sets of random integers as class labels. When a user enrolls his/her biometric at the IDP, the user is given the customized SVM model to be stored in the user's device along with the authentication client application, as described in Section 3.2. The SVM model is customized for each user in order to prevent an attacker, who by some means gains access to the trained SVM model in a user's device, from learning all possible class labels that are used to construct the BIDs of all the users in the system. The trained and customized SVM model which is saved as a structured file can later be loaded in order to obtain the classification output when the user performs biometrics-based authentication. The authentication process uses the customized SVM model and it is thus independent from the base SVM model (see Figure 2).

It is important to note that both types of IDP mentioned above can periodically build a new base SVM model with the biometric images of the new users added to the system, thus introducing more classes to the SVM model. Because the users who already enrolled have a customized SVM model obtained at the enrollment time, they can continue using such customized model independent from the updates made to the base SVM model at the IDP. Experimental details concerning the training of the SVM model using the biometric hash vectors obtained from the biometric images are discussed in Section 4.

3.1.2   Generating the BID

The BID generation takes place in two main phases of the protocol that we propose, namely enrollment and authentication. As shown in Figure 1, there are two main phases in the BID generation process. During phase 1, the biometric image is captured, preprocessed, and the P-Hash of the image is computed by extracting the features from the image. The output of this phase is the biometric hash vector which is a binary array of 64 bits. This hash vector is then given as input to the trained and customized SVM model in order to obtain the classification output which is the class label that represents the class that the hash vector belongs to. This class label concatenated with the secret S_1, which is derived from user's password, is the BID of the user. The class label is an integer represented by 32-bits and S_1 is 128-bits as mentioned in Section 2.6. Therefore, the generated BID (which is 160-bits) is an element of Z_q defined in Section 2.3. This BID is then used to create the cryptographic identity token as described in the following section.

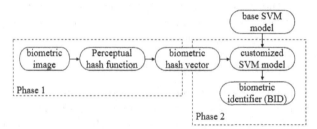

Fig. 1. BID generation during enrollment

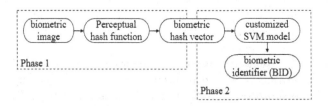

Fig. 2. BID generation during authentication

3.1.3   Creating Cryptographic Identity Token from the BID

The cryptographic identity commitment to be included in the identity token (IDT) is computed using the Pedersen commitment scheme with the BID and a random secret as input as described in Section 2.3. This random secret is the S_2 derived from user's password as described in Section 2.6, which is 160-bits

---

Algorithm 2. Creating Biometrics-based Identity Token

1: $x \leftarrow \text{BID} \mid S_1$ (| represents concatenation)
2: $r \leftarrow S_2$
3: $c \leftarrow g^x h^r$
4: $IDT \leftarrow$ Create identity token with following fields:
   Commitment (c):
   Expiration Timestamp:
   From:
   To:
5: **return** IDT digitally signed by the IDP.

---

long and hence is an element of Z_q. The public parameters (p, q, g, h) required for the commitment scheme are initialized and published by the IDP. As listed in Algorithm 2, in addition to the 'Commitment' and 'Expiration timestamp' fields, we also explicitly add 'From' and 'To' fields in the IDT in order to avoid certain types of attacks on the ZKPK identity verification protocols referred to as Mafia fraud attacks which is further discussed in Section 5. In the 'From' field, the user can request the IDP to include a pseudonym of the user in order to prevent identity linkability. In the 'To' field, user can request the IDP to include a commitment on the name of the service provider to whom the IDT will be provided, in order to prevent a malicious service provider from impersonating the user to another service provider.

3.2   Biometrics-Identity Management Protocol

There are three main parties involved in our protocol: users, the IDP, and the service provider (also called relying party). The protocol consists of two main phases: Enrollment - by which the user obtains his/her biometrics-based cryptographic identity token digitally signed by the IDP; Authentication - by which the user proves his/her biometrics-based identity at the third party service providers. While the enrollment phase involves all three parties mentioned above, the authentication phase involves only the user and the service provider.

Let IDP denote the identity provider, U denote the user, SP denote the service provider and IDT denote the cryptographic identity token based on the user's biometric. Please note that when we refer each of these entities, both human and software aspects related to them are implied. For example, when we refer to U in the protocol, we refer to the actions taken by both the human user and the software installed in user's device such as the software provided by the IDP as well as by the SP. Protocol 2a lists the steps executed during the enrollment phase. The secure channel mentioned in the step 1 of protocol 2a refers to a channel with message level security. In order to prevent a malicious user from providing a fake biometric image instead of the actual biometric image in step 1, the enrollment of the user's biometric should be executed at the IDP following the necessary legal processes such as requiring the user to visit the authority in person and proving his/her identity using a legal identifier that he/she possesses, such as SSN or passport, which is outside the technical scope of our

Protocol 2a. Enrollment Phase

1: $U \rightarrow IDP$:

  - Provides the biometric image and password over a secure channel.
  - Sends details for 'From' and 'To' fields of the IDT (optional).

2: IDP:

  - Customizes the base SVM for the user.
  - Computes the P-Hash of the user's biometric image.
  - Obtains SVM prediction output for the computed P-Hash vector.
  - Derives three secrets from user's password by choosing a salt value (t). (see section 2.6)
  - Creates the BID. (see section 3.1.2)
  - Creates the cryptographic identity commitment. (see sections 2.3 and 3.1.3)
  - Creates the IDT (see section 3.1.3).

3: $IDP \rightarrow U$: provides the authentication client application along with the trained and customized SVM model, the IDT, and the salt value (t).

current work. In order to enable a user to perform biometrics-based authentication from his/her mobile device(s) without involvement of the IDP, the BID generation software which is a part of the authentication client application listed in the step 3 of protocol 2a, the trained and customized SVM model, and the salt value (t) used in deriving the secrets based on the user's password are provided to the user by the IDP at the end of the enrollment phase. Those artifacts can be saved and installed securely on the user's mobile device(s) through the provisioning mechanisms of the Trusted Execution Environment (TEE) enabled in the modern mobile devices. Today there are commercial mobile devices that facilitate application developers in making use of hardware based TEE such as the onboard credential (ObC) architecture [8]. We assume the use of such techniques to securely store these sensitive meta-data related to the proposed protocol in order to prevent identity theft in cases in which the user's device is stolen by a computationally powerful attacker as discussed under different adversary models in Section 5. We utilize the standard PKI based digital signature for digitally signing the IDT in our protocols. The user can provide the IDT obtained at the end of the execution of protocol 2a, when signing up with the service provider, by executing the Protocol 2b.

Protocol 2b. User signs up at SP

1: $U \rightarrow SP$: U signs up at SP and provides the IDT to SP as a strong identifier.
2: SP: verifies the signature and the expiration date on the IDT.
3: SP: stores the IDT linked to user's identity.

As shown in Protocol 2b, the service provider verifies the digital signature of the IDP and the expiration time stamp on the IDT and stores the IDT linked to the user's identity to be used in multi-factor authentication during subsequent authentication attempts. Note however that it also possible for the service provider not to store the IDT as the authentication client application can send the token to the service provider whenever the user needs to authenticate. Web services APIs exposed by the service providers are usually accessed from the user's device(s) through web based or native client applications provided by the service provider. However, making each service provider's client able to handle biometrics-based authentication of the user is neither secure nor efficient. Therefore, service providers' clients can delegate the authentication step to the authentication client application installed in the user's device which is provided by the IDP during the enrollment phase.

During authentication, as shown in Protocol 2c, the cryptographic identity commitment is created following the same steps as in Protocol 2a after which the authentication client application sends it to the corresponding service provider along with the IDT that was obtained during enrollment. Upon receiving the authentication request, the service provider verifies the signature of the IDP on the IDT. If the signature verification is successful, the service provider and the user execute the ZKPK protocol, described in Section 2.4, in order for the user to prove his/her ownership of the biometrics and knowledge of the secrets involved in the IDT. If the ZKPK protocol succeeds, the service provider creates a session for the user and provides the session details to the authentication client application. After the authentication application hands over the control back to the service provider's client along with the session information, the service provider's client can perform the transactions requested by the user with the corresponding service provider.

Protocol 2c. Authentication Phase

1: U:

      − Captures the biometric image and inputs the password.
      − Computes the P-Hash of the biometric image.
      − Obtains the SVM prediction output for the computed P-Hash.
      − Derives three secrets from the password and the stored salt value (t). (see section 2.6)
      − Creates the BID. (see section 3.1.2)
      − Creates the cryptographic identity commitment (C'). (see sections 2.3 and 3.1.3)

2: $U \rightarrow SP$: Sends the IDT and the commitment (C') along with the authentication request.
3: SP: verifies signature of the IDP on the IDT.
4: **if** signature verification is successful **then**
5:     $U \leftrightarrow SP$: executes ZKPK protocol for two-factor authentication.
6:     SP: accepts U as authenticated if ZKPK protocol succeeds.
7: **end if**

3.3   Extended Protocol with Support for Error Correction Code

We extend the core protocol presented in the previous section to improve the repeatability of the biometric identity of the user by performing error correction on the biometric feature vector obtained from the feature extraction mechanism, which is the P-Hash. The reason why the commitment created during authentication may not match the commitment included in the IDT is that the SVM classification output obtained during authentication is not the same as the output obtained during enrollment, assuming that the user has provided the correct password. In such cases, the authentication client application installed in the user's device performs error correction on the biometric feature vector, using some meta-data provided by the IDP during enrollment. We use HECC [4] for error correction encoding and decoding. However, for security, we do not directly encode the biometric hash vector obtained during the enrollment and store it in the user's device. The reason is that if an attacker gets hold of it, the attacker can easily decode it to obtain the actual hash vector which is highly sensitive data. Therefore we adopt the secure error correction encoding and decoding mechanism introduced by Kande et al. [6] in which a secret key is encoded using HECC and then XORED with the biometric hash vector in order to create the error correction meta-data to be used in the decoding phase during authentication.

3.3.1   Error Correction Encoding Algorithm

The equation (1) given below is used to encode the error correction meta-data during enrollment time, which is to be used during authentication time. X is the biometric feature vector obtained during enrollment time, 'key' is the secret, Z is the error correction meta data provided to the user and HE stands for Hadamard Encoding.

$$Z = HE(key) \oplus X \qquad (1)$$

In the use of this algorithm in [6], X is a biometric feature vector of size 1188 bits (obtained using a feature extraction mechanism called Iris Code), and they have used HECC instance of $(32, 6, 16)_2$ which results in a key length of 222 bits ($= 6 \times 37$: message size $\times$ number of blocks), which is large enough to resist brute force attacks. In our case, since the feature vector, which is the P-Hash, is of only 64 bits length, and since we utilize the HECC instance of $(16, 5, 8)_2$ based on our experimental evaluation (see Section 4), the required key size happened to be only 20 bits (5×4) which is not long enough to be resistant against brute force attacks. In order to make the secret key large enough, we repeatedly concatenate the biometric hash vector to itself 5 times. Therefore, in the use of equation (1) in our extended protocol, $X = X_1 \mid X_2 \mid X_3 \mid X_4 \mid X_5$ where X_i is $x_{i1}, x_{i2}, ..., x_{i64}$ which is the 64 bits long biometric hash vector computed using the P-Hash and 'key' is S_3 (the first 100 bits of S_3 derived from the user's password). Z is stored in the TEE of user's mobile device which is used to store the SVM classifier as well. X and S_3 protect each other as one time pads and are secure as long as both Z and the password are not stolen.

3.3.2   Error Correction Decoding Algorithm

During authentication, the error correction decoding algorithm performs block-wise decoding (block size is 16 bits) as listed in Algorithm 3. Like in the encoding algorithm, Y is the biometric feature vector extracted from the biometric image of the user, repeatedly concatenated with itself for 5 times, and similarly Y' is the error corrected feature vector concatenated to itself 5 times and HD stands for Hadamard Decoding. After we obtain Y', we extract the first 64 bits of it

---

Algorithm 3. Error Correction Decoding Algorithm

1: In blocks of 16 bits:
　　Do: $S = Y \oplus Z = Y \oplus [HE(S_3) \oplus X]$
2: **if** $S_3 = $ HD(S): **then**
3:　　Y' = HE(S_3)$\oplus Z$ (=X)
4: **else**
5:　　Y' = Y
6: **end if**

---

which is the error corrected feature vector of the user's biometric image captured during authentication. This error corrected feature vector is then given as input to the SVM classifier to obtain the classification output which is used to build the BID of the user. This error correcting decoding process needs to be performed only if the commitment created during the authentication does not match the commitment created during enrollment which is included in the IDT.

4 Experiments

We have conducted experiments to evaluate the proposed protocol for biometrics-based authentication, using both the SVD based hash [3] and the P-Hash as the feature extraction mechanisms and using iris images as biometrics. The SVM model was trained by finding the optimal parameters for the SVM algorithm as described in Section 4.1.1. We measured the accuracy in classifying the biometric images during authentication (which were not present during training of the SVM classifier), along with other measurements. We also present the results of the experiments carried out with the extended protocol using error correction code.

4.1 Data Set and Experimental Setup

The experiments were conducted on a laptop machine with the Ubuntu 13.4 OS, Intel Core i7-3537U CPU, and 5 GB memory. The experiments were conducted in two rounds with iris images from the two UBIRIS V.1 [12] and UBIRIS V.2 [11] databases.

Iris is considered as the most accurate biometric trait in the context of biometrics, and is being used in different domains such as airport check-in and refugee control [2]. Since the accuracy of current systems depends on the accuracy of the iris image capturing process which requires the cooperation from the user such as requiring the user to stand close to the camera and look for a period of about three seconds, the UBIRIS databases have been built with the purpose of analyzing the methodologies to recognize users with minimum cooperation. The iris images in UBIRIS V.1 were captured in environments with some minimal constraints, whereas the UBIRIS V.2 images were captured in non-constrained environments such as at-a-distance and on-the-move, with more realistic noise factors [11]. However, the quality of the images in UBIRIS V.2 seems better than those in UBIRIS V.1.

4.1.1 Experiments on the Core Protocol

500 iris images were selected from each of the above databases including 5 images from each of the 100 individuals. The training data set was constructed with the first four images from each individual and the testing data set was constructed with the fifth image from each individual. Feature extraction and computation of the P-Hash of the iris images were executed using the DCT based P-Hash function implemented in the publicly available pHash library [14]. The SVM model was built using the LIBSVM library [5]. The SVM type used was C-SVC which is intended for multi-class classification and the type of kernel function used was Radial Basis Function. The P-Hash output was formatted and prepared as input for the SVM classifier such that each bit is marked as a feature in an input vector of 64 elements. Given the training data, a range of values for the optimal pair of C and γ parameters of the SVM model was selected by evaluating 10-fold cross validation accuracy (CV accuracy) of each combination of values within the range of: $C - \{2^{-10}, 2^{15}\}$ and $\gamma - \{2^{-10}, 2^{15}\}$ using grid search. Finally the SVM classifier was trained using the C and γ values selected by evaluating the aforementioned range of C and γ values for the best CV accuracy in grid search, as listed in Table 1.

4.1.2 Experiments on the Extended Protocol

We tried to further improve the classification accuracy by correcting errors occurring in the P-Hash vector of the biometric image captured during authentication time when compared to the P-Hash vector of the biometric image of the same user captured at enrollment time, using the encoding and decoding algorithms described in Section 3.3, which are based on Hadamard Error Correction Code. We applied this to the data set on which SVM showed better classification accuracy which is UBIRIS V.2. Experiments were carried out with Hadamard Codes of increasing length to find the optimal length in terms of improved accuracy and low overhead.

4.2 Results

The results summarized in the Table 1 demonstrate the accuracy of classifying a biometric image captured at authentication time which was thus not known to the classifier at the training time, false rejection rate (FRR), and false acceptance rate (FAR). With P-Hash as the feature extraction mechanism, the accuracy of classifying previously unknown biometric samples is 88% for the UBIRIS.v2 dataset and 79% for the UBIRIS.v1 dataset. In contrast, the SVD based hashing mechanism results in accuracy below 62% for both data sets. It is important to emphasize that the proposed protocol is flexible enough to adapt to any other feature extraction mechanism as well, if it contributes to even better accuracy in SVM classification of the biometric images of the users.

Another criterion to evaluate the classification performance is on the basis of falsely classified images. The FAR and the FRR are two commonly used metrics to quantify the probability of falsely classified images. FRR is the probability that perceptually similar images are identified as different while FAR is the probability that perceptually different images are identified as similar. The latter is the crucial factor in a biometrics-based authentication system. According to Table 1, both FRR and FAR for the P-Hash are comparatively low for both datasets. Table 2 summarizes the SVM classification performance when the error correction was applied to P-Hash vectors of the biometric images of UBIRIS V.2 dataset, by varying the length of the Hadamard Codes. An Hadamard Code length of 0 means that no error correction was applied. As we can observe, with the increasing length of Hadamard Codes, the accuracy of the SVM classification increases due to the increase of error correction capability. However, the overhead resulting from the error correction also increases because the ratio of message size(k) to the Hadamard Code size(n) decreases. Therefore, considering the trade off between improvement of accuracy and the overhead, using 16-bit Hadamard codes seems the best trade-off in order to correct errors occurring in the P-Hash vector of the user's biometric image at authentication time, if the commitment created during authentication time does not match the commitment in the IDT

Table 1. Summary of the Experimental Results w/o Error Correction

Data Set	Measurement	P-Hash based SVM	SVD-Hash based SVM
(a)	Best CV accuracy in grid search	85.75%	52.5%
	Optimal values for C & γ	$C=16$, $\gamma=0.0078125$	$C=8$, $\gamma=1024$
	Accuracy of classification during authentication	88%	61%
	FRR	0.12	0.39
	FAR	0.0012	0.0039
(b)	Best CV accuracy in grid search	75.75%	43.5%
	Optimal values for C & γ	$C=128$, $\gamma=0.00097656$	$C=32$, $\gamma=512$
	Accuracy of classification during authentication	79%	49%
	FRR	0.21	0.51
	FAR	0.0021	0.0051

(a) UBIRIS V.2 (b) UBIRIS V.1

Table 2. Summary of the Experimental Results with Error Correction

Hadamard Code Length	0	8	16	32	64
Accuracy of classification during authentication	88	89%	90%	90%	91%
Overhead $(1-(k/n))$	0	0.5	0.6875	0.8125	0.8906
FRR	0.12	0.11	0.1	0.1	0.09
FAR	0.0012	0.0011	0.001	0.001	0.0009

created at enrollment. It is also noteworthy that the FAR does not increase with the error correction applied on the P-Hash vectors.

Our experimental results show that the P-Hash from a given iris image is computed in 0.105 seconds on average. The SVM model with 400 training instances was built in 8 seconds on average (once the suitable values for C and γ had been identified) and a given testing instance was classified in 0.013 seconds on average. Please note that the results related to the accuracy of classification mostly depend on the particular feature extraction algorithm used in the feature extraction phase of the proposed protocol. In our future work, we will explore other feature extraction mechanisms to further increase the accuracy of classifying biometric images.

5   Security Analysis

In analyzing the security of our approach, we identify the security and privacy related properties of the proposed protocol and related techniques. We also identify potential attacks against the proposed identity management protocol and show that the proposed protocol resists such attacks by preserving the desirable properties that the attackers try to compromise.

All three privacy sensitive elements related to the user's biometric identity (i.e: the biometric image, the P-Hash, and the generated BID) which are used in the intermediate steps of the enrollment and authentication phases of the protocol are discarded after the IDT is generated, and are not stored anywhere or transmitted to other parties. This ensures confidentiality of the user's biometric image, the P-Hash, and the BID which possess the uniqueness feature of the user's biometric identity. Since the three secrets used for creating the BID, the Pedersen commitment, and the meta-data used for error correction of the P-Hash are derived from a password provided by the user, and thus do not need to be stored anywhere as explained in Section 2.6, confidentiality of those secrets is assured as long as the password is kept secret by the user. The token verification process also assures the confidentiality of the secrets because of the use of the ZKPK protocol. The proposed protocol is also secure against replay attacks by external parties because each time a new challenge and new random values y and s are chosen during the proof of knowledge. The reason why we do not use distance matching as the biometric authentication mechanism coupled with P-Hash as mentioned in Section 2.1, is to protect the P-Hash of the user's biometric from being exposed to the service provider at authentication. However, as mentioned in Section 3.1.3, an external attacker or a malicious service provider can impersonate the user through a man-in-the middle (MITM) type of attack on the zero knowledge proof of identity commitments which is known as Mafia Fraud attack or Chess Grand Masters' Problem [13]. While a MITM attack carried out by an external attacker can be avoided with the proper use of secure communication channels such as SSL, preventing such attacks by only using such secure communication channels is not possible when the attacks are carried out by malicious service providers. In order to prevent such an attack by a malicious service provider, the unique identity (e.g., a registered name) of the service provider with which the user actually intends to interact is explicitly bound to the IDT itself. Users can request the IDP to do this binding in step 1 of Protocol 2a (section 3.2). In order to prevent the IDP from learning which service providers the users interact with, the users can create a commitment of the name of the service provider and request the IDP to bind that commitment to the IDT, instead of the actual name of the service provider. An example of a simple and efficient commitment scheme which can be used for this purpose is PRNG(name of SP | time stamp) where PRNG denotes a secure pseudo random generator. The time stamp is used to make the multiple commitments created with the name of the same service provider different. At authentication, when the user opens this commitment and proves the committed value, the service provider can confirm that it is not a MITM impersonation attempt carried out by another malicious service provider and that the genuine user actually intends to communicate with it.

The SVM is also a sensitive source of information since it encodes the labels of all the classes in the trained SVM which becomes part of the BID of a user. We have taken two steps to prevent attacks based on the SVM model. The first is to store the SVM in encrypted form in the hardware based TEE which can only be accessed by the authentication client application. The second is to randomly change the class labels in the base SVM model to obtain a customized SVM model for each user. Such step guarantees that an attacker, who gets hold of one SVM model, would not be able to figure out the possible class labels related to the BIDs of all the other users registered in the identity management system. Our approach for customizing the base SVM model for each user also enhances the revocability of the IDT. If a compromise happens, the user is able to cancel the already registered IDT for his/her biometrics and register a new IDT created with a new BID obtained from a new customized SVM model, or with a new secret or with new values for both. Any party which gets hold of the IDT, which is the only information exposed related to the user's biometric identity in this protocol, cannot successfully authenticate without being able to provide both the biometric and the password used to derive the secrets. The IDT thus provides ownership assurance of the biometric identity of the user which prevents identity theft and impersonation. The service providers also have assurance about the validity of the IDT by verifying the digital signature of the IDP on the IDT.

Therefore, we can observe that our approach and the proposed protocol preserves the confidentiality of sensitive information related with users' biometrics and the secrets used to generate the IDT and assures ownership of the biometric identity, and revocability and validity of the identity tokens. It also protects users' privacy against honest but curious (semi-honest) IDPs by not involving the IDP in the transactions between the user and the service provider, while being secure against adversaries which steal users' devices, eavesdroppers in the network and even the malicious service providers.

6   Related Work

A privacy preserving user centric identity management system has been previously proposed by Paci et al. in [9] to enable multi-factor identity verification, which is closely related to our work. The main difference is that our work supports biometrics-based authentication, whereas such previous work only supports non-biometric identifiers. Our approach of using SVM classification is closely related with the work by Bhargav-Spantzel et al. [3]. Our approach uses the P-Hash of users' biometrics as input to the SVM classifier and improves the accuracy in classifying biometric samples with respect to such previous work. The high accuracy classification results shown in [3] are due to fact that the same set of biometric images were used in both training and testing phases.

Another improvement in our approach is that we customize the trained SVM model for each user, which has several advantages compared to the use of one global SVM model proposed in [3]. In addition the BID generation approach proposed in [3] makes use of multiple class labels and expects the probability estimates of prediction confidences across multiple class labels to be repeatable in the output of the SVM classification, which does not happen practically based on the observation of our experiments. Instead, we use the single class output of the SVM classification and concatenate it with a sufficiently large key (S_1) to make the BID resistant against brute force attacks.

The error correction mechanism that we have used in the extended protocol to improve the repeatability of the created biometric identity is based on the work by Kande et al. [6]. We make use of only the first phase of their approach for reducing errors between two biometric samples of the same user (i.e: genuine errors). In contrast to their approach that uses Hamming distance based comparison to identify impostor errors between two biometric samples, which has certain drawbacks such as having to reveal the biometric feature vector to the verifier at authentication time, our approach uses SVM based classification which avoids such drawbacks. Another difference is that we do not store the key used in the error correction algorithms whereas the approach by Kande et al. requires to store the hashed version of the key which is generated during the encoding process to be used in the decoding process.

7   Conclusions and Future Work

In this paper, we have presented a novel and secure approach for user-centric biometrics-based authentication which preserves user's privacy. Since a real world authentication system needs higher accuracy, in our future work we will explore other feature extraction mechanisms which would help in further improving the repeatability of the BID while preserving its uniqueness. We plan to carry out further experiments to measure the performance of the proposed protocol in terms of computational time, resource consumption, and communication overhead in other types of user devices such as mobile phones. We also plan to extend this work by generalizing the proposed improvements.

References

1. IdentityX | World-Class Mobile Biometric Authentication, http://www.identityx.com
2. UBIRIS, http://iris.di.ubi.pt/
3. Bhargav-Spantzel, A., Squicciarini, A.C., Bertino, E., Kong, X., Zhang, W.: Biometrics-based identifiers for digital identity management. In: IDtrust 2010 Conference Proceedings. ACM (April 2010)
4. California State University, East Bay: Coding theory - hadamard codes, http://www.mcs.csueastbay.edu/~malek/TeX/Hadamard.pdf
5. Chang, C.C., Lin, C.J.: LIBSVM: A library for support vector machines. ACM Transactions on Intelligent Systems and Technology 2, 27:1–27:27 (2011), software available at http://www.csie.ntu.edu.tw/~cjlin/libsvm
6. Kande, S., Dorizzi, B.: Cancelable iris biometrics and using error correcting codes to reduce variability in biometric data. In: Computer Vision and Pattern Recognition. IEEE (April 2009)
7. Klinger, E., Starkweather, D.: phash.org: Home of pHash, the open source perceptual hash library (2008-2010), http://www.phash.org/
8. Kostiainen, K., Ekberg, J., Asokan, N., Rantala, A.: On-board credentials with open provisioning. In: Proceedings of ASIACCS 2009 (2009)
9. Paci, F., Bertino, E., Kerr, S., Lint, A., Squicciarini, A.C., Woo, J.: VeryIDX - A digital identity management system for pervasive computing environments. In: Brinkschulte, U., Givargis, T., Russo, S. (eds.) SEUS 2008. LNCS, vol. 5287, pp. 268–279. Springer, Heidelberg (2008)
10. Pedersen, T.P.: Non-interactive and information-theoretic secure verifiable secret sharing. In: Feigenbaum, J. (ed.) CRYPTO 1991. LNCS, vol. 576, pp. 129–140. Springer, Heidelberg (1992)
11. Proença, H.: The UBIRIS.v2: A database of visible wavelength images captured on-the-move and at-a-distance. IEEE Trans. PAMI 32(8), 1529–1535 (2010)
12. Proença, H., Alexandre, L.A.: UBIRIS: A noisy iris image database. In: Roli, F., Vitulano, S. (eds.) ICIAP 2005. LNCS, vol. 3617, pp. 970–977. Springer, Heidelberg (2005)
13. Schneier, B.: Applied Cryptography: Protocols, Algorithms, and Source Code in C, 2nd edn. Wiley (1996)
14. Zauner, C.: Implementation and Benchmarking of Perceptual Image Hash Functions. Master's thesis, Upper Austria University of Applied Sciences, Hagenberg Campus (2010)

A Dynamic Matching Secret Handshake Scheme without Random Oracles*

Yamin Wen[1] and Zheng Gong[2,3],**

[1] School of Mathematics and Statistics
Guangdong University of Finance & Economics
Guangzhou 510320, P.R. China
yamin.wen@gmail.com
[2] School of Computer Science
South China Normal University
Guangzhou 510631, P.R. China
cis.gong@gmail.com
[3] Shanghai Key Laboratory of Integrate Administration Technologies
for Information Security, Shanghai 200240, China
cis.gong@gmail.com

Abstract. Secret handshake schemes allow mutually anonymous authentication between members of organizations. In this paper, a new unlinkable secret handshake scheme with dynamic matching is proposed (which is named USH-DM). Considering the existence of multiple different groups, the implementation of USH-DM achieves dynamic matching between members among completely different groups. In particular, USH-DM enhances the privacy of group members, which enables the transcripts of group members to remain unlinkable and untraceable. Without using the random oracle, USH-DM is proved secure by assuming the intractability of the decisional bilinear Diffie-Hellman and subgroup decision problems.

Keywords: Anonymity, Secret handshakes, Unlinkability, Dynamic matching.

1 Introduction

With the amazing development of online applications via open communication networks, privacy-preserving techniques are increasingly significant for the future growth of web services. Privacy-preserving authentication plays an indispensable role among the whole privacy concerns. A promising cryptosystem,

---

* This work is supported by the Natural Science Foundation of China (No.61300204, 61100201), the Natural Science Foundation of Guangdong (No.S2012040006711), the Foundation for Distinguished Young Teachers in Higher Education of Guangdong (Yq2013051) and the Project of Science and Technology New Star of Guangzhou Pearl Rivel (2014J2200006).
** The corresponding author.

M.H. Au et al. (Eds.): NSS 2014, LNCS 8792, pp. 409–420, 2014.

which is named *secret handshake*, was first introduced by Balfanz *et al.* [2] for mutually anonymous authentication. Roughly speaking, secret handshakes require that one user will only discover his/her affiliation to the other user if they belong to the same organization. Thus participants only recognize that they are members of the same organization, without leaking their true identities in this organization. As suggested in [1,2], secret handshakes have many interesting applications. A typical example is that members of FBI secretly authenticate each other. The prover will reveal his affiliation (FBI) if and only if the verifier holds the same one, and vice versa. Moreover, a practical secret handshake scheme can also be used in networking protocols, such as the devices with legitimate credentials can be mutually authenticated for sharing secret keys. For instance, Li and Ephremides [12] proposed that secret handshakes are available for realizing the anonymous routing protocol in *ad hoc* networks.

To match up the security requirements of real-life applications, many extensions of secret handshakes have been proposed. One of the extensions is to include roles, so that users can authenticate with the members who hold specific roles in the same group [2]. Furthermore, Ateniese *et al.* [1] proposed the dynamic matching model which allows users to make more flexible authentication policies. The new model aims to allow secret handshakes between members from sister organizations instead of the same organization. For instance, an online game operator administers a distributed social networks on two cities. The two cities can be considered as sister groups and named as "City-A" and "City-B". Each registered user can designate his favorite attributes that his partner must satisfy, such as the city and the grade. And then users from the two cities can execute a successful secret handshake only if their attributes are matching. In other words, users from City-A can play with other users from City-B, without restricting to the same city.

The secret handshake scheme proposed by Ateniese *et al.* in [1] can realize above application well. However, Ateniese *et al.*'s scheme only realizes limited dynamic matching. Since the different sister groups are created and distinguished by group name in Ateniese *et al.*'s scheme, the different groups still share the same group public/private keys which are actually managed by an upper operator. And hence, the limited dynamic matching model still relies on a single Group Authority (GA) for different groups. In real-life applications, users may expect to authenticate with other partners from different groups with the assumption of multiple self-governed group authorities. In such a setting, more dynamic matching is possible. One of the most appealing applications would be the authentication between members from different Secret Interest Groups(SIGs) in online social networks. SIGs are self-managed groups which have independent Group Authorities (GAs). Two registered users (e.g., Alice and Bob) from different SIGs can secretly authenticate with each other if their polices can be matched. Therefore, it is necessary to search for a practical secret handshake scheme which can achieve the real dynamic matching in multiple-groups environment.

Related Works. After Balfanz *et al.*'s initial work [2], many secret handshake schemes have been proposed from different cryptographic primitives, such as pairing [2], CA-oblivious encryption [6] and ElGamal [27]. According to the life-time of credentials, the rich literature can be sorted as the following two types.

- **Secret handshakes with one-time pseudonyms.** The pioneering pub-lication is derived from Balfanz *et al.* [2] based on pairing. It uses one-time pseudonyms to ensure that the instances of the secret handshake protocol, which were performed by the same parties, cannot be linked. Subsequently, Castelluccia *et al.* [6] proposed a new secret handshake scheme using a novel tool so-called *CA-oblivious public-key encryption*. Since any Obliv-ious Signature Based Envelope (OSBE) scheme can easily be converted to a secret handshake scheme [13], Zhou *et al.* [27] constructed an improved scheme by using of ElGamal and DSA signature. These schemes are slightly more efficient than Balfanz *et al.*'s original scheme, but still does not satisfy unlinkability unless members use one-time pseudonyms. However, one-time pseudonyms based schemes require more storage and computation cost ow-ing to the single-use of pseudonyms for achieving unlinkability in practice. Since Group Authority (GA) has all secret information of group users, GA can impersonate or frame one user with malicious behaviors. Accordingly, the unlinkability against GA can unlikely be achieved by using one-time pseudonyms.

- **Unlinkable secret handshakes with reusable credentials.** Xu and Yung [25] first offers scheme which achieves unlinkability with reusable creden-tials in a weaker way. By using the blinding technique, Huang and Cao proposed a novel and efficient unlinkable secret handshake scheme [8] based on Balfanz *et al.*'s scheme [2]. Subsequently, Su [18] pointed out a successful impersonation attack on Huang and Cao's proposal [8]. And hence Gu and Xue[7] proposed an improved efficient secret handshake scheme with unlinkability by amending Huang and Cao's proposal [8]. Wen *et al.*[22] also presented a new unlinkable secret handshake scheme with reusable credentials under the random oracle. Based on the construction of identity-based encryption [20], Ateniese *et al.* [1] proposed the first efficient unlinkable secret handshake scheme without ran-dom oracles. However, there only needs selecting a name for the group when creating a new group in their scheme. Different groups are distinguished just through each name, while all groups share a pair of group keys in the whole secret handshake system. From the AddMember algorithm, we can see that the scheme treats a set of members with identical attributes as an entity instead of different individual. It is essentially a group key agreement scheme between different sub-group members in a large group environment and thus limits the popularization of secret handshakes. Due to the less efficiency of Ateniese *et al.*'s scheme [1], Zhao *et al.* [26] constructed an efficient unlinkable secret hand-shake protocol without random oracles. But Zhao *et al.*'s proposal [26] still can-not carry out dynamic matching in multiple-groups environment. Therefore, it is meaningful to realize a new unlinkable secret handshake scheme with dy-namic matching without random oracles, which can be adapted to more prac-tical applications.

Subsequently, Jarecki *et al.* [9] proposed an unlinkable secret handshake scheme with revocation by using central key management (broadcast encryption). But it strongly assumes that all groups have the same numbers of group users and revoked users. Also the group public key will increase linearly with the numbers of group users, which is impractical in large-scale applications (e.g., online social network). Based on Ateniese *et al.*'s scheme [1], Sorniotti and Molva [14,16] proposed revocable secret handshake schemes. Their proposals provide the revocation checking of the participants who have initiatively left their groups during handshakes. Nevertheless, they are still unable to trace and revoke malicious group members for complete unlinkability and untraceability. Moreover, their proposals still have the same weakness of Ateniese *et al.*'s scheme [1].

Our Contributions. A new construction of unlinkable secret handshake scheme with dynamic matching without random oracles, which is named USH-DM, is presented in this paper. Our new proposal USH-DM aims to fix the weakness of Ateniese *et al.*'s scheme. The enhancements of USH-DM are three-fold. Firstly, we apply a new technique of full domain subgroup hiding to realize a practical secret handshake scheme, which enables USH-DM can be applied to the real multiple-groups environment. Secondly, the authentication policies can be flexible for matching more complicated attributes based on different groups. USH-DM also achieves efficient and unlinkable with reusable credentials. Finally, USH-DM is provably secure without random oracles by assuming the intractability of Decisional Bilinear Diffie-Hellman and Subgroup Decision problems.

Organization. The remainder of this paper is organized as follows. In Section 2, we recall the preliminaries related to our work, including the definitions and security properties of secret handshake schemes. In Section 3, a new unlinkable secret handshake scheme with dynamic matching named USH-DM is described. Section 4 gives the security and performance analyses of our proposal. Section 5 concludes the paper.

2   Preliminaries

In this section, we recall the notions and definitions of bilinear pairings of composite order and complexity assumptions, which will be used in later sections. The definition and security requirements of secret handshakes are also briefly reviewed.

2.1   Bilinear Pairings of Composite Order

Composite order bilinear pairings were first introduced in [4], which will be used in our proposal. We first review some general notions about bilinear groups and pairings. Most of cryptosystems based on pairings are based on bilinear groups with prime order for simplicity. In our case, we define $\mathbb{G}$ is a (multiplicative) cyclic group of composite order N, where $N = pq$ is the product of two different primes p and q. Let g is a generator of $\mathbb{G}$. A one-way map $e : \mathbb{G} \times \mathbb{G} \to \mathbb{G}_T$ is a bilinear pairing if the following conditions hold.

- **Bilinear:** For all $g \in \mathbb{G}$, s.t., g is a generator of $\mathbb{G}$, and $a, b \in \mathbb{Z}_N$, $e(g^a, g^b) = e(g, g)^{ab}$.
- **Non-degeneracy:** $e(g, g) \neq 1$, i.e., if g generates $\mathbb{G}$, then $e(g, g)$ generates $\mathbb{G}_T$ with order N.
- **Computability:** There exists an efficient algorithm for computing $e(., .)$.

2.2 Complexity Assumptions

Definition 1. (Decisional Bilinear Diffie-Hellman (DBDH) Problem [20]) *Let* $\mathbb{G}, \mathbb{G}_T$ *be cyclic groups of prime order* q *along with a bilinear map* $e : \mathbb{G} \times \mathbb{G} \to \mathbb{G}_T$, *and let* $g \in \mathbb{G}$ *be generator of* $\mathbb{G}$. *The challenger flips a fair binary coin* β *and outputs the tuple* $(g, A = g^a, B = g^b, C = g^c, Z = e(g, g)^{abc})$ *when* $\beta = 1$. *Otherwise, the challenger outputs the tuple* $(g, A = g^a, B = g^b, C = g^c, Z = e(g, g)^d)$ *where* $d \leftarrow_R \mathbb{Z}_p^*$. *The DBDH problem is to output a guess* β' *of* β.

DBDH Assumption: We say that the (t, ϵ)-DBDH assumption holds if there exists no algorithm can solve the DBDH problem with a non-negligible advantage ϵ in a polynomial time bound t. In other words, for $g \in \mathbb{G}$ and $a, b, c, d \leftarrow_R \mathbb{Z}_p^*$, distinguish between tuples of the form $(g, g^a, g^b, g^c, e(g, g)^{abc})$ and $(g, g^a, g^b, g^c, e(g, g)^d)$ is infeasible.

Definition 2. (Subgroup Decision (SD) Problem [4,21]) *Given a tuple* $(p, q, \mathbb{G}, \mathbb{G}_T, e)$, *in which* p *and* q *are independent secure primes,* $\mathbb{G}$ *and* $\mathbb{G}_T$ *are two cyclic groups of order* $N = pq$ *with efficiently computable group operations and* $e : \mathbb{G} \times \mathbb{G} \to \mathbb{G}_T$ *is a bilinear map. Let* $\mathbb{G}_q \subset \mathbb{G}$ *be the* q-*order subgroup of* $\mathbb{G}$. *Given an element* x *which is selected randomly either from* $\mathbb{G}$ *or from* $\mathbb{G}_q$, *the subgroup decision problem is to distinguish whether* x *is in* $\mathbb{G}_q$.

The Subgroup Decision Assumption: Let the success probability of solving the subgroup decision problem is defined as $Adv_{sd} = \frac{1}{2} + \varepsilon$, we say that the subgroup decision assumption holds if ε is negligible.

2.3 Secret Handshakes: Definition and Security Requirements

A secret handshake scheme (denoted by SHS) operates in an environment which consists of a set of groups managed by a set of group authorities, and a set of users $U_1, \cdots, U_n$ registered into some groups. Based on the definitions in [1,2], an unlinkable SHS without traceability and revocation consists of the following probabilistic polynomial-time algorithms:

- SHS.Setup: The Setup algorithm selects high-enough security parameter κ to generate the public parameters **params** common to all subsequently generated groups.

- SHS.CreateGroup: CreateGroup is a key generation algorithm executed by GA to establish a group G. It inputs **params**, and outputs a pair of group public key gpk_G and group secret key gsk_G.
- SHS.AddMember: AddMember is a two-party protocol run by GA and a user. GA plays a role of the administrator for the group, which issues credential for a legitimate member of the group. After verifying the user's real identity(U), GA outputs the user's group credential $cred_U$ using GA's group keys (gpk_G, gsk_G). Thus, the user becomes a valid member of the group after the protocol.
- SHS.Handshake: Handshake is a two-party authenticate protocol executed by two anonymous users (A, B), who may belong to different groups. This protocol inputs the anonymous users' secrets ($cred_A$, $cred_B$) and public parameters. The output of the protocol for each member is either "1" or "0" depending on whether the authentication policies of participants are matched. If A's target requirements including group and properties are matched by B and vice versa, A and B will share a common session key K for subsequent secure communication and the protocol outputs "1". Otherwise, the output is "0".

A secret handshake scheme must satisfy the basic security requirements: *Completeness, Impersonator Resistance, Detector Resistance* and *Unlinkability*. The formal definition can be referred to [23,11]

Completeness: The SHS protocol will succeed with overwhelming probability, if the interactive participants satisfy the authentication policy of the counterparty.

Impersonator Resistance: An adversary who attempts to impersonate a legitimate user of one group cannot succeed with a non-negligible probability. In other words, any adversary not satisfying the authentication policies cannot accomplish a successful secret handshake.

Detector Resistance: An adversary will not succeed with non-negligible probability when he activates an SHS.Handshake with one honest member in order to determine whether he satisfies the authentication policies or not.

Unlinkability: This requirement implies that any adversary cannot find any relation between two instances of the Handshake algorithm, which involved with the same honest members.

3   A New Unlinkable Secret Handshake Scheme with Dynamic Matching

Developed from the idea of secret handshake [1], a new unlinkable secret handshake scheme (USH-DM) which supports dynamic matching in multiple-groups environment is designed as follows.

- Setup: Given a security parameter κ, the algorithm runs $Setup(1^\kappa) \rightarrow$ **params**. The public parameters **params** $= (N, \mathbb{G}, \mathbb{G}_T, e : \mathbb{G} \times \mathbb{G} \rightarrow \mathbb{G}_T, g, u, h, H_1, v_0, \cdots, v_n, F)$, which are shared by all participants in the scheme. Here g is a generator of a group $\mathbb{G}$ of composite order $N = pq$, where p and q are random primes. Let $\mathbb{G}_p$ and $\mathbb{G}_q$ be the cyclic subgroups of $\mathbb{G}$ with respective order p and q. The algorithm picks a generator h of $\mathbb{G}_q$. Other generators of $\mathbb{G}$ $u, v_0, \cdots, v_n$ are selected randomly from $\mathbb{G}$. In addition, $H_1 : \{0,1\}^* \to \mathbb{Z}_N^*$ is a cryptographic hash function. F is a function which represents attribute. Suppose that one attribute P is represented by n-bits string $(\mu_1, \mu_2, \cdots, \mu_n)$, $F(P)$ is denoted by $v_0 \prod_{i=1}^{i=n} v_i^{\mu_i}$.

- CreateGroup: The GA chooses $t \leftarrow_R \mathbb{Z}_N^*$, and generates $T = g^t$. GA outputs its group secret key $gsk = t$ and group public key $gpk = T$.
- AddMember: If a user U with property P wants to join the group, GA issues attribute credential for the user U. GA randomly selects $s \leftarrow_R \mathbb{Z}_N^*$, and computes attribute credential $cred_{U,P} = (C_{U1}, C_{U2}) = (u^t \cdot F(P)^s, g^{-s})$. The user verifies that the credential is valid by testing $e(C_{U1}, g) \cdot e(F(P), C_{U2}) \stackrel{?}{=} e(u, gpk)$.
- Handshake: Supposing A and B are two parties who want to execute a secret handshake protocol to authenticate each other without leaking their privacy. Participant A runs the protocol with $cred_{A,P_A}$ and (tpk_A, P_{AT}) which are the target group public key and target property (i.e., authentication policy) of the participant A, and participant B runs it with $cred_{B,P_B}$ and (tpk_B, P_{BT}) which are the target group public key and target property (i.e., authentication policy) of the participant B. For example, A who is a lawyer of insurance company wants to handshake with a professor (P_{AT}) of higher university (tpk_A), and simultaneously B who is a professor of higher university wants to handshake with a lawyer (P_{BT}) of insurance company (tpk_B). The protocol proceeds as follows:

1. $A \to B : \{\sigma_{A1}, \sigma_{A2}, \pi_A\}$
   (a) A chooses $t_{A1}, t_{A2}, r_A \leftarrow \mathbb{Z}_N^*$.
   (b) A computes

$$\sigma_{A1} = C_{A1} \cdot h^{t_{A1}} \cdot u^{r_A},$$

$$\sigma_{A2} = C_{A2} \cdot h^{t_{A2}},$$

$$\pi_A = g^{-t_{A1}} \cdot F(P_A)^{-t_{A2}}.$$

Finally, A sends σ_{A1}, σ_{A2} and π_A to B.

2. $B \to A : \{\sigma_{B1}, \sigma_{B2}, \pi_B, V_B\}$
   (a) B chooses $t_{B1}, t_{B2}, r_B \leftarrow \mathbb{Z}_N^*$.
   (b) B computes

$$\sigma_{B1} = C_{B1} \cdot h^{t_{B1}} \cdot u^{r_B},$$

$$\sigma_{B2} = C_{B2} \cdot h^{t_{B2}},$$

$$\pi_B = g^{-t_{B1}} \cdot F(P_B)^{-t_{B2}}.$$

   (c) B will compute k'_A according to tpk_B and P_{BT}

$$k'_A = \frac{e(\sigma_{A1}, g) \cdot e(F(P_{BT}), \sigma_{A2}) \cdot e(h, \pi_A)}{e(u, tpk_B)}.$$

(d) B generates the following verification value V_B such that

$$V_B = H_1((k'_A)^{r_B}||e(u,g)^{r_B}||0).$$

Finally, B sends both $\sigma_{B1}, \sigma_{B2}, \pi_B$ and V_B to A.

3. $A \to B : \{V_A\}$

(a) A also computes k'_B according to tpk_A and P_{AT}

$$k'_B = \frac{e(\sigma_{B1},g) \cdot e(F(P_{AT}),\sigma_{B2}) \cdot e(h,\pi_B)}{e(u,tpk_A)}.$$

(b) A verifies the V_B with the equation $V_B \overset{?}{=} H_1((k'_B)^{r_A}||k'_B||0)$. If the above equation holds, A will output "1" and send $V_A = H_1((k'_B)^{r_A}|| e(u,g)^{r_A}||1)$ to B. Else A outputs "0" and also responds a random value $V_A \leftarrow_R \mathbb{Z}_N^*$ to B.

(c) B verifies V_A with the following equation $V_A \overset{?}{=} H_1((k'_A)^{r_B}||k'_A||1)$. B outputs "1" only if the above equation holds, else B outputs "0".

Completeness. If the authentication policy of A and B are matching, it implies that $tpk_A = gpk_B, P_{AT} = P_B$ and $tpk_B = gpk_A, P_{BT} = P_A$. Namely, both A and B can recover the original message $k'_A = e(u,g)^{r_A}$ and $k'_B = e(u,g)^{r_B}$. The completeness of USH-DM can be verified as follows.

$$\begin{aligned}
k'_A &= \frac{e(\sigma_{A1},g) \cdot e(F(P_{BT}),\sigma_{A2}) \cdot e(h,\pi_A)}{e(u,tpk_B)} \\
&= \frac{e(\sigma_{A1},g) \cdot e(F(P_A),\sigma_{A2}) \cdot e(h,\pi_A)}{e(u,gpk_A)} \\
&= \frac{e(C_{A1},g) \cdot e(h^{t_{A1}},g) \cdot e(u^{r_A},g) \cdot e(F(P_A),C_{A2}) \cdot e(F(P_A),h^{t_{A2}}) \cdot e(h,g^{-t_{A1}}F(P_A)^{-t_{A2}})}{e(u,gpk_A)} \\
&= \frac{e(C_{A1},g) \cdot e(u^{r_A},g) \cdot e(F(P_A),C_{A2})}{e(u,g^{t_A})} \\
&= \frac{e(u^{t_A} \cdot F(P_A)^s,g) \cdot e(F(P_A),g^{-s}) \cdot e(u^{r_A},g)}{e(u,g^{t_A})} \\
&= \frac{e(u^{t_A},g) \cdot e(u^{r_A},g)}{e(u,g^{t_A})} \\
&= e(u,g)^{r_A}.
\end{aligned}$$

Simultaneously, A can get $k'_B = e(u,g)^{r_B}$ by similar method and verify the corresponding responses V_B as follows.

$$\begin{aligned}
V_B &= H_1((k'_A)^{r_B}||e(u,g)^{r_B}||0) = H_2((e(u,g)^{r_A})^{r_B}||e(u,g)^{r_B}||0) \qquad (1)\\
&= H_2(e(u,g)^{r_B})^{r_A}||e(u,g)^{r_B}||0) = H_1((k'_B)^{r_A}||k'_B||0).
\end{aligned}$$

By using the above method, B can check the corresponding response V_A. Hence A and B complete a successful secret handshake protocol. A session key $K = H_1(e(u,g)^{r_A \cdot r_B})$ is agreed between A and B for the following two-party communications, without leaking their affiliations.

4   Security and Performance Analysis

Now we provide the security results on the new construction USH-DM with respect to the impersonator resistance, detector resistance and unlinkability. Due to the limitation of the length, the proofs of the theorems are described in brief and the details can be referred to the full version.

4.1   Security

Theorem 1. USH-DM *is a secure unlinkable secret handshake scheme with dynamic matching under the decisional BDH and SD assumption.*

Proof (Sketch). We show that USH-DM satisfies the security requirements of secret handshakes in brief. Since the completeness has been analyzed in the above section, the proofs of impersonator resistance, detector resistance and unlinkability are described as follows.

- **Impersonator Resistance(IR).** If an adversary $\mathcal{A}$ breaks the IR property with a non-negligible probability ϵ, one can use $\mathcal{A}$ to derive a simulator $\mathcal{B}$ that solves an instance of the decisional BDH problem with a non-negligible probability related to ϵ. $\mathcal{B}$ is given an challenge of the decisional BDH problem such that $(g, A = g^a, B = g^b, C = g^c, Z)$ and is asked to output a guess β' of β that determine whether Z is equal to $e(g, g)^{abc}$ or $e(g, g)^d, d \leftarrow_R \mathbb{Z}_p$.
- **Detector Resistance(DR).** Assuming $\mathcal{A}$ breaks the DR property with a non-negligible probability, $\mathcal{A}$ has to distinguish a handshake instance with a true group member from an instance with a simulator SIM. During the handshake in our proposed scheme, we notice that the group member (e.g., A) sends only the blinded credential proof $(\sigma_{A1}, \sigma_{A2}, \pi_A)$ for authentication, which can provide the privacy of his identity. Since the transcript of a participant during the handshake seems to be random, $\mathcal{A}$ cannot determine whether it was generated by a true group member or a simulator.
- **Unlinkability.** Assuming $\mathcal{A}$ breaks the unlinkability property with a non-negligible probability $\frac{1}{2} + \epsilon$, $\mathcal{A}$ has to distinguish whether two handshake instances are related to the same participant or not. The implementation of attackers against unlinkability is similar to the parallel executions of two attack instances against Detector Resistance. Thus, the proof of unlinkability can be described by a similar way as in the proof of Detector Resistance. And hence the detailed proof is not provided here for brief.

$\square$

4.2   Performance Analysis

Here the performance of USH-DM will be analyzed by considering its computation costs. In the literatures, most of secret handshake schemes are provably secure under the random oracle. Only a few secret handshake schemes are implemented without random oracles, which are basically derived from the scheme

Table 1. A comparison of related secret handshake schemes

	Balfanz et al. [2]	Ateniese et al.[1]	USH-DM
Setup	0	$(2n+3)T_e$	0
CreateGroup	T_e	T_e	T_e
AddMember	T_e	$2T_e$	$2T_e$
Handshake	$4T_p$	$6T_p+6T_e$	$8T_p+8T_e$
Traceability	Yes	No	No
Dynamic Matching	No	Yes(Limited in a large group)	Yes
Rounds	3	2	3
One-time credentials	Need	Not Need	Not Need
Underlying Assumption	BDH	SXDH and BDH	DBDH and SD
Random Oracles	with	without	without

proposed by Ateniese et al [1]. For clarity, we describe the performance comparison among some representative schemes selected from the existing literatures. According to the related experiments' findings, one pairing operation and modular exponentiation are the most time-consuming computations in the cryptography schemes. Hence, we focus on giving the computation costs about the pairing and modular exponentiation operations. By using Barreto's ECC Pairing Library [5], we calculate the computational costs of the pairing and the modular exponential operations with respect to the schemes in our comparison. T_p denotes time for one bilinear pairing operation in the elliptic curve groups which costs about 12.23ms. T_e denotes time for one modular exponential operation which costs about 2.42ms. The experiments are based on Intel Pentium-4 2.8GHz with 512MB RAM. For clarity, the computational costs are considered with respect to the different phases of secret handshake schemes, which are described in Table 1.

From Table 1, we can see that Balfanz et al.'s scheme [2] achieve traceability and unlinkability using one-time credentials. But the scheme is proven secure in the random oracle model. For the Ateniese et al's scheme [1], since it distinguishes different groups through group identities which are all assumed to be n-bits strings, $2n+3$ modular exponentiations need to be computed in the Setup phase and every group must know and maintain $n+2$ modular exponentiations as the private values to issue group credentials in the CreateGroup phase. Towards the proposed scheme USH-DM, different groups are self-governed which have respective group public and private keys without needing the group identities for distinction. And hence the computation costs of USH-DM are reduced in both of the Setup and CreateGroup phases. By issuing attribute credentials, USH-DM also achieves the dynamic matching for flexible authentication policies about designated groups and concrete attributes. Specially, the advantage of our proposed scheme is that its applications can be extended to the more practical multiple-groups environment. In addition, we note that the Ateniese et al's scheme [1] also needs three rounds in order to implement a complete secret handshake protocol instead of only realizing a secret key agreement. Thus the corresponding computational costs are increased. Therefore, Ateniese *et al*'s scheme [1] can only be applied to the handshakes between departments from the same group instead of individual members from different groups.

5   Conclusion

In this paper, we have proposed a new unlinkable secret handshake scheme supports dynamic matching policy. Our new proposal extends the functionality of Ateniese *et al*'s scheme, which can be applied to the multiple-groups environment where each group is really different and independent. Combining the technique of full-domain subgroup hiding with attribute-base encryption, our new scheme not only achieves the strong unlinkability against GA, but also more flexible authentication policy including affiliation and attributes. The formal security reduction of our proposal is proven in the standard model by assuming the intractability of the decisional bilinear Diffie-Hellman and subgroup decision problems. An interesting future work is to find more practical secret handshake schemes from other public key cryptosystems, such as Lattice and Multivariate PKC.

References

1. Ateniese, G., Blanton, M., Kirsch, J.: Secret handshakes with dynamic and fuzzy matching. In: Network and Distributed System Security Symposium, NDSS, pp. 159–177 (2007)
2. Balfanz, D., Durfee, G., Shankar, N., Smetters, D., Staddon, J., Wong, H.: Secret handshakes from pairing-based key agreements. In: IEEE Symposium on Security and Privacy, pp. 180–196 (2003)
3. Boneh, D., Franklin, M.: Identity-based encryption from the weil pairing. In: Kilian, J. (ed.) CRYPTO 2001. LNCS, vol. 2139, pp. 213–229. Springer, Heidelberg (2001)
4. Boneh, D., Goh, E.-J., Nissim, K.: Evaluating 2-DNF formulas on ciphertexts. In: Kilian, J. (ed.) TCC 2005. LNCS, vol. 3378, pp. 325–341. Springer, Heidelberg (2005)
5. Barreto, P.: The η_T approach to the Tate pairing, and supporting (supersingular) elliptic curve arithmetic in characteristic 3, http://www.larc.usp.br/~pbarreto/Pairings.GPL.zip
6. Castelluccia, C., Jarecki, S., Tsudik, G.: Secret handshakes from CA-oblivious encryption. In: Lee, P.J. (ed.) ASIACRYPT 2004. LNCS, vol. 3329, pp. 293–307. Springer, Heidelberg (2004)
7. Gu, J., Xue, Z.: An improved efficient secret handshakes scheme with unlinkability. IEEE Communications Letters 15(2), 486–490 (2011)
8. Huang, H., Cao, Z.: A novel and efficient unlinkable secret handshake scheme. IEEE Communications Letters 13(5), 363–365 (2009)
9. Jarecki, S., Liu, X.: Unlinkable secret handshakes and key-private group key management schemes. In: Katz, J., Yung, M. (eds.) ACNS 2007. LNCS, vol. 4521, pp. 270–287. Springer, Heidelberg (2007)
10. Jarecki, S., Liu, X.: Private mutual authentication and conditional oblivious transfer. In: Halevi, S. (ed.) CRYPTO 2009. LNCS, vol. 5677, pp. 90–107. Springer, Heidelberg (2009)

11. Kawai, Y., Yoneyama, K., Ohta, K.: Secret handshake: strong anonymity definition and construction. In: Bao, F., Li, H., Wang, G. (eds.) ISPEC 2009. LNCS, vol. 5451, pp. 219–229. Springer, Heidelberg (2009)

12. Li, S., Ephremides, A.: Anonymous routing: a cross-layer coupling between application and network layer. In: Conference on Information Science and Systems, CISS, pp. 783–788 (2006)

13. Nasserian, S., Tsudik, G.: Revisiting oblivious signature-based envelopes. In: Di Crescenzo, G., Rubin, A. (eds.) FC 2006. LNCS, vol. 4107, pp. 221–235. Springer, Heidelberg (2006)

14. Sorniotti, A., Molva, R.: Secret handshakes with revocation support. In: Lee, D., Hong, S. (eds.) ICISC 2009. LNCS, vol. 5984, pp. 274–299. Springer, Heidelberg (2010)

15. Sorniotti, A., Molva, R.: Secret interest groups (SIGs) in social networks with an implementation on Facebook. In: SAC 2010, pp. 621–628. ACM Press (2010)

16. Sorniotti, A., Molva, R.: Federated secret handshakes with support for revocation. In: Soriano, M., Qing, S., López, J. (eds.) ICICS 2010. LNCS, vol. 6476, pp. 218–234. Springer, Heidelberg (2010)

17. Sorniotti, A., Molva, R.: A provably secure secret handshake with dynamic controlled matching. Computers & Security 29(5), 619–627 (2010)

18. Su, R.: On the security of a novel and efficient unlinkable secret handshakes scheme. IEEE Communications Letters 13(9), 712–713 (2009)

19. Vergnaud, D.: RSA-based secret handshakes. In: Ytrehus, Ø. (ed.) WCC 2005. LNCS, vol. 3969, pp. 252–274. Springer, Heidelberg (2006)

20. Waters, B.: Efficient identity-based encryption without random oracles. In: Cramer, R. (ed.) EUROCRYPT 2005. LNCS, vol. 3494, pp. 114–127. Springer, Heidelberg (2005)

21. Boyen, X., Waters, B.: Full-domain subgroup hiding and constant-size group signatures. In: Okamoto, T., Wang, X. (eds.) PKC 2007. LNCS, vol. 4450, pp. 1–15. Springer, Heidelberg (2007)

22. Wen, Y., Zhang, F., Xu, L.: Unlinkable secret handshakes from message recovery signature. Chinese Journal of Electronics 19(4), 705–709 (2010)

23. Wen, Y., Zhang, F.: A new revocable secret handshake scheme with backward unlinkability. In: Camenisch, J., Lambrinoudakis, C. (eds.) EuroPKI 2010. LNCS, vol. 6711, pp. 17–30. Springer, Heidelberg (2011)

24. Zhang, F., Chen, X., Susilo, W., Mu, Y.: A new signature scheme without random oracles from bilinear pairings. In: Nguyên, P.Q. (ed.) VIETCRYPT 2006. LNCS, vol. 4341, pp. 67–80. Springer, Heidelberg (2006)

25. Xu, S., Yung, M.: K-anonymous secret handshakes with reusable without random oracles from bilinear pairings. In: ACM CCS 2004, pp. 158–167. ACM (2004)

26. Zhao, G., Tan, C., Ren, Y., Fang, L.: An efficient unlinkable secret handshake protocol without ROM. In: IEEE International Conference on WCNIS 2010, pp. 486–490 (2010)

27. Zhou, L., Susilo, W., Mu, Y.: Three-round secret handshakes based on ElGamal and DSA. In: Chen, K., Deng, R., Lai, X., Zhou, J. (eds.) ISPEC 2006. LNCS, vol. 3903, pp. 332–342. Springer, Heidelberg (2006)

Formal Analysis of DAA-Related APIs
in TPM 2.0

Li Xi and Dengguo Feng

Trusted Computing and Information Assurance Laboratory
Institute of Software, Chinese Academy of Sciences
{xili,feng}@tca.iscas.ac.cn

Abstract. Direct Anonymous Attestation (DAA) is a signature scheme that provides a balance between user privacy and authentication in a reasonable way. Various DAA schemes are now supported by the latest TPM 2.0 specification. We propose a general symbolic model for DAA schemes and formalize DAA-related APIs in TPM 2.0 specification in applied pi calculus. We present new symbolic definitions of user-controlled traceability and non-frameability. Then we propose a novel property of DAA called forward anonymity. The application of our definitions is demonstrated by analyzing the implementation of an ECC-based DAA protocol using APIs proposed by the TPM 2.0 specification. Our analysis finds a weakness in an API which leads to attack against forward anonymity. We propose modifications to the API and verify our properties for the modified API.

1 Introduction

Direct Anonymous Attestation (DAA) is a special group signature scheme that enables remote authentication of a trusted platform while preserving the platform's privacy. There are three types of entities in a DAA protocol: an issuer, signers (trusted platforms), verifiers (usually service providers). A signer gains a credential associate with its DAA secret key from the issuer without revealing the key. Then he can sign arbitrary message and prove that the signature is indeed generated a valid TPM without leaking the signer's identity. While the identity of signer can never be revealed, DAA provides a way for the verifier to link different signatures signed by same signer with the signer's consent. Signatures signed under corrupted DAA secret keys can also be identified. A RSA-based DAA is proposed by Brickell et al. [1]. This RSA-based DAA is adopted by TCG and included in TPM 1.2 specification [2]. After that several ECC-based DAA [3–7] are proposed to achieve better performance and shorter signature length. Some of them are now supported by the TPM 2.0 specification [8]. Several APIs are defined in TPM 2.0 specification to support these DAA schemes [9].

Many researchers have worked on security analysis of DAA. In the computational model, Brickell et al. [1] and Chen et al. [10] introduce security definitions based on security models for multiparty computation. Brickell et al. [7] and Chen [6] propose security definitions based on interactive games . In the symbolic

M.H. Au et al. (Eds.): NSS 2014, LNCS 8792, pp. 421–434, 2014.

model, Backes et al.[11] analyze authenticity and anonymity of the RSA-based DAA using applied pi calculus. However, they do not propose a general framework for DAA and their formalization is tightly coupled with the RSA-based DAA, so it is not clear if their method could be used for analyzing ECC-based DAA. Moreover they consider a setting where the host and TPM are both honest: "TPM" in their model actually corresponds to trusted platforms. However, we expect that the adversary can not break authenticity even the host part of a trusted platform is corrupted. Ben Smyth [12] analyze user-controlled anonymity of an ECC-based ECC using symmetric pairings.

Proofs of complex security protocols such as DAA are known to be error-prone and hard to make for humans [13]. Hence formal methods with automated reasoning are promising techniques to analyze complex protocols such as DAA. While all former symbolic analyses of DAA focus on protocol prototypes, there may be a gap between protocol prototype and the implementation, for example, APIs in TPM 2.0 use a different method to issue credentials. It is important to analyze the security of DAA protocols under APIs proposed by the TPM 2.0 specification which is closer to implementation. During past few years, several vulnerabilities in the TPM API designs have been found, which highlight the importance of formal analysis of the API commands specifications. Chen et al. [14] discover a TPM impersonation attack in the case of sharing authdata between users are allowed. Delaune et al. [15] analyze authentication-related API commands and rediscover some known attacks and some new variations on them.

1.1   Contribution

We propose a general symbolic model for DAA schemes and formalize DAA-related APIs in TPM 2.0 specification in applied pi calculus. We formalize user-controlled traceability and non-frameability using correspondence. To the best of our knowledge, this is the first symbolic definition of these properties under formalization of APIs in TPM 2.0 specification.

Then we propose a novel property of DAA schemes called forward anonymity. This property assures that even if the host of a trusted platform is corrupted, the anonymity of DAA signatures signed by the platform previously will not be broken. We propose a security definition of forward anonymity based on interactive games. We also present a symbolic definition which is suitable for automated reasoning using ProVerif [16].

The application of the definitions is demonstrated by analyzing the implementation of an ECC-based DAA protocol under TPM 2.0 specification using our techniques. Our analysis shows that this DAA protocol satisfies user-controlled traceability and non-frameability. Our analysis finds a weakness in an API which leads to an attack against forward anonymity. We propose modifications to the API and verify our property for the modified API using proverif.

1.2   Paper Outline

The section 2 briefly reviews the applied pi calculus. Section 3 explains how we model DAA schemes and DAA-related APIs in TPM 2.0 specification. Section 4 presents novel formalizations of several important properties of DAA. In section 5, we analyze and fix the implementation of an ECC-based DAA under TPM 2.0 using our formal model. We conclude and discuss future work in section 6.

2   Applied Pi Calculus

We briefly recall the syntax and operational semantics of the applied pi calculus; more details can be found in [17, 18].

The applied pi calculus is a language for describing and analyzing security protocols. The calculus assumes an infinite set of names, an infinite set of variables, and a signature σ consisting of a finite set of function symbols each with an associated arity.Terms are built by applying function symbol to names,variables and other terms.To model equalities we use an equational theory E which defines a relation $=_E$.

Processes are defined as follows. $P|Q$: parallel; $!P$: replication; $\nu\, n.P$: name restriction; if $M = N$ then P else Q: conditional; $c(M).P$: message input; $\bar{c}\langle M\rangle.P$: message output; M/x: active substitution. $P(M_1, ..., M_n)$ means that process P takes $M_1, ..., M_n$ as arguments.

Biprocess is a pair of processes that have the same structure and differ only by the terms they contain.For a biprocess P containing terms like $\texttt{choice}[t_1 t_2], \texttt{fst}(P)$ is obtained by replacing $\texttt{choice}[t_1 t_2]$ with t_1 and $\texttt{snd}(P)$ is obtained by replacing $\texttt{choice}[t_1 t_2]$ with t_2.

An evaluation context is a context (a process with a hole) whose hole is not under a replication, a conditional, an input, or an output. A context C[ ] closes A when C[A] is closed.

The execution of a process without contact with its environment is captured by internal reduction $\rightarrow$:

Comm : $\bar{c}\langle x\rangle.P|c(x).Q \rightarrow P|Q$

Then : if $N = N$ then P else $Q \rightarrow P$

Else : if $L = N$ then P else $Q \rightarrow Q$ for ground terms L, M where $L \neq_E N$

We write $\rightarrow^*$ for the reflexive and transitive closure of $\rightarrow$.

Now we introduce notions of correspondence and equivalence which will be used in our security definition. Details about automated verification of correspondence and equivalence can be found in [17, 19, 20].

Definition 1 (Basic correspondence property). *A basic correspondence property is a formula of the form:event($\bar{f}\langle M\rangle$) $\rightsquigarrow$ event($\bar{g}\langle N\rangle$).*

The formula in the definition means if an event $\bar{f}\langle M\rangle$ must have been executed then event $\bar{g}\langle N\rangle$ must has been executed previously.Basic correspondence can be extended using conjunctions $\wedge$ and disjunctions $\vee$:$event(e_0) \rightsquigarrow event(e_1) \wedge$ $event(e_2)$ means if e_0 has been executed then e_1 and e_2 must have been executed previously; $event(e_0) \rightsquigarrow event(e_1) \vee event(e_2)$ means if e_0 has been executed then e_1 or e_2 must have been executed previously.You can also use equalities and inequalities after $\rightsquigarrow$,for example $\bar{f}\langle x \rangle \rightsquigarrow \bar{g}\langle y \rangle \wedge x = f(y)$ means if $\bar{f}\langle x \rangle$ has been executed then event $\bar{g}\langle y \rangle$ has been previously executed and $x = f(y)$.

We write $P \Downarrow c$ if $P \rightarrow^* C[\bar{c}\langle M \rangle .A]$ for some term M,channel c,process P and evaluation context $C[\_]$ that does not bind c.

Definition 2. *Observational equivalence* ($\approx$) *is the largest symmetric relation* $\mathcal{R}$ *between closed extended processes with the same domain such that* $A \mathcal{R} B$ *implies:*

1. *if* $P \Downarrow m$ *then* $Q \Downarrow m$;
2. *if* $P \rightarrow P'$ *then there exits* Q' *such that* $Q \rightarrow^* Q'$ *and* $P' \mathcal{R} Q'$;
3. $C[P] \mathcal{R} C[Q]$ *for all closing evaluation contexts* $C[\,]$.

We call a biprocess P satisfies observational equivalence if $\mathtt{fst}(p) \approx \mathtt{snd}(p)$

3   Formalizing DAA and DAA-related APIs in TPM 2.0

3.1   Formalizing DAA Protocols

We define a DAA process as an unbounded number of trusted platforms and verifiers together with one issuer that are running in parallel. A trusted platform obtains a credential corresponds to its DAA secret key from the issuer, then he can generate signatures to convince a verifier that it has a valid credential without revealing its identity.

The trusted platform (TP) consists of two parts: a trusted platform module (TPM) and a host. The host can utilize trusted computing functions provided by the TPM via a predefined set of commands (APIs). An interesting point of DAA is that by choosing different basenames, we can get two kinds of signatures: anonymous ones and pseudonymous ones. The anonymous signatures can not be linked to any other signatures while pseudonymous one can be linked to signatures signed under the same secret key and basename. To describe this, we divide verifiers into two kinds: anonymous ones called VerifierA (VA) and pseudonymous ones called VerifierP (VP). In the case of VerifierA, the basename $= \perp$ and the corresponding signatures are anonymous. In the case of VerifierP, the basename is chosen by the verifier and the corresponding signatures are pseudonymous. The whole DAA protocol is modeled by the process defined below.

DAA	$= \nu \, \tilde{n}. \, \nu \, \text{isk. let } ipk = \text{pub(isk) in} \quad !I(\text{isk}) \, |!VP(ipk)|!VA(ipk)$
	$|!TP(ipk, c_T)|MF(c_T)$
$MF(c_T)$	$= !(c_{pub}(x_{id}).\text{let } eps = \text{seed}(x_{id})\text{in} \qquad \text{let } esk = \text{ek}(eps) \text{ in}$
	$\text{let } epk = \text{pubkey}(esk) \text{ in} \qquad \text{let } ekcert = \text{ekcert}(epk) \text{ in}$
	$\overline{c_T}\langle eps, ekcert \rangle)$
$TP(ipk, c_T) =$	$\nu \, \tilde{m}. \, \text{TPM}(c_T)|\text{Host}$
$TPM(c_T)$	$= c_T(eps, ekcert). \text{ let } esk = \text{ek}(eps) \text{ in let } epk = \text{pubkey}(skt) \text{ in}$
	$\overline{c_{pub}}\langle epk, ekcert \rangle.\text{TPMAPI}(eps)$

The restrict names $\tilde{n}$ represent the secrets (e.g., secret values and restricted channels) shared between entities. For emphasis, we separately list the secret key of issuer isk. The issuer I takes isk as input and verifiers VA and VP use public key of the issuer ipk to verify signatures. Trusted platforms TP share a restrict channel c_T with the manufacturer MF. This restrict channel c_T is used by the manufacturer to inject secret information into TPM, such as the Endorsement Primary Seed (eps).

As TPM 2.0 supports various asymmetric algorithms such as ECC and RSA, there will be various Endorsement Keys for one TPM. It may be impractical for manufacturer to generate all EKs and store them in TPM due to the limited NV memory in TPM. So in TPM 2.0, the manufacturer creates an Endorsement Primary Seed (eps) for each TPM, then generates various EKs using eps and creates the certificate correspond to each EK. Only eps will be injected into a TPM and when various EKs are needed, the TPM can generate them by itself using eps.

The manufacturer is modeled by process MF. Getting input x_{id} from public channel C_{pub} corresponds to manufacturing a new TPM with a new id x_{id}. MF then generates eps and creates EK pair (esk, epk) and the corresponding EK certificate $ekcert$, then he outputs eps and $ekcert$ to a TPM through a restricted channel c_T. Notice here function seed and ekcert are *private* so that adversary can not use seed to produce eps from x_{id} or use ekcert to create certificates.

The restrict name $\tilde{m}$ in process TP represents the restricted channel between TPM and host. Process TPM receives eps and $ekcert$ from the manufacturer through restricted channel c_T, then it generates the EK pair (esk, epk) using eps and outputs the public key epk and the credential $ekcert$ to the host. We make a simplification here: the TPM only creates one EK pair. Then the TPM waits for calls from host by providing APIs to the host.

3.2 Formalizing DAA-related APIs in TPM 2.0 Specification

We do not formalize authorization data when formalizing APIs. While the user may need authorization data such as passwords to call a certain command with real TPMs, there is no authorization data in our formalization. We can view this simplification as adversary can obtain whatever authorization data he needs. It is direct to see that if a security property is proved even with over-approximation of adversarys ability, then we may conclude this property holds.

Generating DAA Secret Key. We can use two TPM 2.0 APIs to generate the DAA secret key: TPM2_Create() and TPM2_CreatePrimary(). The TPM 2.0 specification [8] recommends TPM2_CreatePrimary() to be used to generate DAA secret key thus the DAA secret key will always be the same no matter how many times the credentialing process is performed. This can prevent a rogue user from rejoining a community from which it has been barred. So we assume TPM2_CreatePrimary() is used to generate the DAA secret key. The analysis of TPM2_Create() is basically the same except that TPM2_Create() creates a random key while TPM2_CreatePrimary() creates a fixed key using a secret seed persistently stored in TPM. The formalization of TPM2_CreatePrimary() is as follows:

$$
\begin{aligned}
\text{TPM2\_CreatePrimary}() \quad = \quad & \text{let } tsk = \mathbf{prf}((eps, ipk)) \text{ in} \\
& \text{let } ipkbase = \mathbf{getparam}(ipk) \text{ in} \\
& \text{let } tpk = \mathbf{commit}(ipkbase, tsk) \text{ in} \\
& \overline{c_{pub}}\langle tpk \rangle.
\end{aligned}
$$

The API TPM2_CreatePrimary() uses primary seed eps and public parameters from issuer to generate the DAA secret key tsk. DAA public key is a commitment of tsk: $tpk = \mathbf{com}(ipkbase, tsk) = ipkbase^{tsk}$, where $ipkbase$ is a group member.

Obtaining DAA Credential. Recall that the TPM has an asymmetric endorsement key epk and the corresponding certificate $ekcert$. The owner of the TPM will provide, to the issuer, the public part tpk of a TPM key tsk for which a credential is desired along with $ekcert$. The issuer will verify the $ekcert$ and tpk to determine if he should issue a credential for tpk. If so, the issuer will issue a credential $cred$ for tpk, then he will generates a fresh symmetric encryption key k, then encrypts the tuple (tpk, k) using epk to get $enc_{epk}(tpk, k)$ and encrypts the credential $cred$ using k to get $(cred)_k$. The the issuer sends $enc_{epk}(tpk, k)$ and $(cred)_k$ to the platform. After receiving the encrypted credential and wrapped key, the owner will call API TPM2_ActivateCredential() using $enc_{epk}(tpk, k)$ as input. The TPM will first use the corresponding endorsement secret key esk to decrypt $enc_{epk}(tpk, k)$ and check if tpk *is loaded in the TPM*, if so, TPM will output k. Note that if tpk is not resident on the TPM, then the host can not get k thus can not decrypt $(cred)_k$.

The formalization of TPM2_ActivateCredential() is as follows. The TPM decrypts $eblob$ to get (pk, k) and checks if pk is loaded in TPM, i.e., is the same as the public key of tsk. If so, TPM outputs the symmetric key k.

$$
\begin{aligned}
\text{TPM2\_ActivateCredential}() \quad = \quad & c_{ac}(eblob). \\
& \text{let } (pk, k) = adec(esk, eblob) \text{ in} \\
& \text{if } pk = \mathbf{commit}(ipkbase, tsk) \text{ then} \\
& \overline{c'_{ac}}\langle k \rangle.
\end{aligned}
$$

DAA Signing. After a credential is obtained, the owner can sign an arbitrary number of times using APIs TPM2_Commit() and TPM2_Sign(). Combing the two APIs, the owner can obtain a modified Schnorr signature which can also be regarded as a proof of knowledge of equality of discrete logarithms [9].

We introduce the modified schnorr signature first. Given a group member S and a string b, TPM2_Commit generates a random number r, calculates $C_1 = S^r, C_2 = \mathtt{h}(b)^r, K = \mathtt{h}(b)^{tsk}$ where $\mathtt{h}$ is a hash function and tsk is the DAA secret key, and output C_1, C_2, K to the host. Host calculates a challenge $c = \mathtt{hash}(m, C_1, C_2)$ where m is the message to be signed, then calls TPM2_Sign, which generates a modified Schnorr signature $s = r + c \cdot tsk$. The modified Schnorr signature (s, c) is actually $PK\{(sk) : \mathtt{h}(b)^{tsk} = K \wedge S^{tsk} = W\}$ where $W = S^{tsk}$ is stored in the host.

TPM2_Commit() is used to generate the ticket $(B = \mathtt{h}(b), K)$ and two random commitment C_1, C_2 used in the modified schnorr signature; TPM2_Sign() uses the same random number r used in TPM2_Commit() to produce the final signature: $s = r + c \cdot tsk$. The formalizations of TPM2_Commit() and TPM2_Sign() are as follows:

$$
\begin{aligned}
\text{TPM2\_Commit()} \quad &= \quad c_c(S, b).\ \nu\ r.\ \text{if } S \neq \mathtt{none} \\
&\qquad \text{then} \quad \overline{c_c'}\langle \mathtt{commit}(S, r), \mathtt{commit}(\mathtt{h}(b), r), \mathtt{commit}(\mathtt{h}(b), tsk)\rangle \\
&\qquad \text{else} \quad \overline{c_c'}\langle \mathtt{commit}(\mathtt{h}(b), r), \mathtt{commit}(\mathtt{h}(b), tsk)\rangle \\
\text{TPM2\_Sign()} \quad &= \quad c_s(c).\ \overline{c_s'}\langle \mathtt{schnorrsig}(c, r, tsk)\rangle
\end{aligned}
$$

The whole TPM is formalized as follows:

$$
\begin{aligned}
\text{TPM}(c_T) \quad &= \quad c_T(eps, ekcert).\ \text{let } esk = \mathtt{ek}(eps) \text{ in} \quad \text{let } epk = \mathtt{pubkey}(esk) \text{ in} \\
&\qquad \overline{c_{pub}}\langle epk, ekcert\rangle. \\
&\qquad !(\text{TPM2\_CreatePrimary()}. \\
&\qquad\quad !(\text{TPM2\_ActivateCredential()}\ |\ !\text{TPM2\_Commit().TPM2\_Sign()}\ )\ )
\end{aligned}
$$

Briefly speaking, the TPM receives the primary seed eps the the certificate $ekcert$ from the manufacture through c_T, then utilizes eps to generate endorsement secret key esk and output epk and $ekcert$ to the host. After the TPM generates the DAA secret key tsk using TPM2_CreatePrimary(), it can join many times using TPM2_ActivateCredential(), and sign unlimited times using TPM2_Commit() and TPM2_Sign(). In process TPM, we use the form $P.Q$ mainly for the sake of simplicity, in which P and Q are processes. $P.Q$ is a *unconventional form*, for example, let $P = \overline{C}\langle M\rangle$, then $P.Q = \overline{C}\langle M\rangle.Q$, this case corresponds to TPM2_CreatePrimary().Q. If $P = $ 'if c then P_1 else P_2', then $P.Q = $ 'if c then $\{P_1.Q\}$ else $\{P_2.Q\}$', this case corresponds to TPM2_Commit().TPM2_Sign().

4   Security Definitions

This section devises novel formalizations in the applied pi calculus for several important security properties of DAA schemes. We start by defining user-controlled traceability and non-frameability using correspondence which is suitable for automatic reasoning. Then we propose a novel property of DAA called forward anonymity. We propose a security definition of forward anonymity based on interactive games. A symbolic definition based on observational equivalence which is suitable for automated reasoning is also presented.

4.1   User-Controlled Traceability

An interesting feature of DAA is to provide differing degrees of privacy. While DAA signatures can be totally anonymous, a pseudonymous signature can be linked to another signature by using a specific basename. So DAA schemes should satisfy user-controlled traceability which includes the following two aspects:

- Unforgeability: This property actually is authenticity. It means if a signature is accepted by a verifier, it must be signed by a honest TPM.
- User-controlled linkability: An adversary finds it hard to create two valid signatures under the same secret key and basename while the output of the algorithm Link shows the two signatures are unlinked.

In this scenario, the adversary can corrupt *all the hosts* of trusted platform and communicate with TPM directly, he can also corrupt TPMs adaptively, but the DAA secret keys of the corrupted TPMs will be added to a rogue list. The verifier would use a algorithm RogTag to find out if the signature is signed under corrupted DAA secret keys. Given these abilities, the adversary should not break unforgeability and user-controlled linkability. It means the following two points:

- If a tuple (msg, bsn, sig) is verified, where msg is a message, bsn is the basename, sig is the signature, then it will contain a output from a honest TPM by calling TPM2_Sign() OR it is signed under a rogue tsk and there exist a algorithm RogTag which outputs $\text{RogTag}(sig, tsk) = \text{True}$. AND
- There exist a algorithm link that for any valid signature sig' signed under the same identity and the same basename bsn, $bsn \neq \perp$, the output of $\text{link}(sig, sig') = 1(\text{linked})$.

We use two tricks in formalizing user-controlled traceability in applied pi calculus for automated reasoning. First, unforgeability means that if for each tsk in the rogue list, $\text{RogTag}(sig, tsk) = \text{False}$ (sig is not signed under any corrupted key) and $\text{Verif}(sig) = 1$ (valid signature), then sig must be signed by an honest TPM. However we can not maintain an unlimited rogue list in Proverif [16]. So instead, we will try to prove an equivalent proposition: if $\text{Verif}(sig) = 1$, then sig is signed by an honest TPM OR it is signed under a compromised key tsk and $\text{RogTag}(sig, tsk) = \text{True}$. Notice compromising a secret key tsk can be represented by an event LeakTPM(tsk), thus we can formalize unforgeability without formalizing an unlimited rogue list.

Second, it seems not direct to formalize linkability between any two signatures using correspondence which can be automatically verified by ProVerif. In DAA, a signature signed by a trusted platform contains a ticket $t = (B, K)$, where $K = \text{Com}(B, k) = B^{tsk}$, tsk is the DAA secret key of the trusted platform, $B = \text{hash}(basename)$ if $basename \neq \perp$. This ticket is used for linking and rogue tagging. Given two signatures, if the two tickets in signatures are the same, then these two signatures are linked. When rogue tagging, the verifier calculates $\text{Com}(B, k_i)$ for each k_i in the rogue list, then compares it to the ticket in the signature. If they are equal, then the signature is tagged rogue. So we can prove the existence of the algorithm link by proving a stronger property. We prove there exits a deterministic function Com and a valid signature always contains a commitment=$\text{Com}(basename, tsk)$, where tsk is the secret key that the signature is signed under.

Using the above two tricks, the user-controlled traceability can be modeled using correspondence. First we introduce the events we will use in our formal definition and the definitions of RogTag and link.

- event TPM2_Sign(w, tsk). Process TPM2_Sign will execute this event just before it outputs to the host, i.e., executes $\overline{c_s'}\langle\text{schnorrsig}(digest, r, tsk)\rangle$. Here w is the output of TPM2_Sign and tsk is the TPM's DAA secret key.
- event DAAVERIF(m, bsn, sig). Process verifier, i.e., VA and VP, will execute this event after it verifies a tuple (m, bsn, sig), where m is the message, bsn is the basename and sig is the signature, i.e., VA and VP are annotated as : If $\text{Verif}(m, bsn, sig) = 1$ then event DAAVERIF(m, bsn, sig).
- event LeakTPM(tsk). This event will be executed by process TPM described below just before the process TPM output its DAA secret key tsk to an adversary. It means if a DAA secret key tsk is compromised, then event LeakTPM(tsk) will be executed.

Now we introduce the process Game1 which models user-controlled traceability. The only difference of the process TPM in Game1 from the process TPM in section 3 is here we give adversary the ability to *compromise TPMs adaptively*. After the DAA secret key tsk is created by TPM2_CreatePrimary(), tsk can be compromised by the adversary. Before tsk is revealed to adversary, event LeakTPM(tsk) would be executed.

$$
\begin{aligned}
\text{Game1} \quad &= \quad \nu\, \tilde{n}.\ \nu\ \text{isk. let } ipk = \text{pub(isk) in} \quad !I(\text{isk}) \,|!VP(ipk)|!VA(ipk) \\
&\qquad\qquad\qquad\qquad\qquad\qquad\qquad\qquad\quad |!\text{TPM}(c_T)|\text{MF}(c_T) \\
\text{TPM}(c_T) \quad &= \quad c_T(eps, ekcre).\ \text{let } skt = \text{ek}(eps) \text{ in let } pkt = \text{pubkey}(skt) \text{ in} \\
&\qquad \overline{c_{pub}}\langle pkt, ekcre\rangle. \\
&\qquad !\text{TPM2\_CreatePrimary}(). \\
&\qquad (!\text{TPM2\_ActivateCredential}() \\
&\qquad |c_{pub}(x_{Tag}).\text{if } x_{Tag} = \text{Rogue then event LeakTPM}(tsk).\overline{c_{pub}}\langle tsk\rangle \\
&\qquad |!\text{TPM2\_Commit}().\text{TPM2\_Sign}()\ )
\end{aligned}
$$

Definition 3 (User-controlled traceability). *Given processes* $\langle I, TPM, VA, VP\rangle$, *user-controlled traceability is satisfied if there exist deterministic functions* com *and* RogTag, *and the process Game1 satisfies the following correspondence:*
$$event(\text{DAAVERIF}(m, bsn, \sigma)) \rightsquigarrow (event(\text{TPM2\_Sign}(\text{part}_2(\sigma), tsk)) \wedge \text{part}_1(\sigma) =$$
$$\text{Com}(bsn, tsk)) \vee (event(\text{LeakTPM}(k)) \wedge \text{RogTag}(m, bsn, \sigma, k) = \text{True}).$$
$\text{part}_1(\sigma)$ *returns the ticket in* σ *and* $\text{part}_2(\sigma)$ *returns the part of* σ *which is produce by* TPM2_Sign.

$$event(\text{DAAVERIF}(m, bsn, \sigma)) \rightsquigarrow (event(\text{TPM2\_Sign}(\text{part}_2(\sigma), tsk))$$
$$\vee (event(\text{LeakTPM}(k)) \wedge \text{RogTag}(m, bsn, \sigma, k) = \text{True}).$$
implies unforgeability; $\text{part}_1(\sigma) = \text{Com}(bsn, tsk))$ means a valid signature always contains a ticket used for linking, thus implying user-controlled linkability.

4.2 Non-frameability

We say a DAA protocol satisfies non-frameability if for a valid signature sig which is not tagged as rogue, if sig can be linked to another valid signature sig' signed by TPM id, then sig must contain a response from the same TPM with identity id.

We utilize the same trick in formalizing user-controlled traceability to formalize non-frameability. To avoid formalizing an unlimited rogue list, we prove an equivalent proposition: for each signature sig which satisfies $\mathtt{Verif}(m, bsn, sig) = 1$ (valid), if sig can be linked to another valid signature sig' signed by TPM id, then sig is generated by TPM id using the API $\mathtt{TPM2\_Sign}$ OR, the DAA secret key tsk of TPM id is corrupted and there exists a algorithm $\mathtt{RogTag}$ which satisfies $\mathtt{RogTag}(m, bsn, sig, tsk) = \mathtt{True}$.

We introduce the event we will use in our formal definition.

- event $\mathtt{ChalVerif}(m, bsn, sig, tsk)$. This event will be executed if an adversary produces a signature sig which can be linked to signatures signed by the platform whose identity $= id$. m is the message, bsn is the basename, sig is the signature on bsn and M, and tsk is the DAA secret key of the TPM whose identity $= id$.

Now we introduce the game process modelling non-frameability.

$$
\begin{aligned}
\mathrm{Game2} \;=\; & \nu\,\tilde{n}.\ \nu\ \mathtt{isk}.\ \mathrm{let}\ ipk = \mathtt{pub}(\mathtt{isk})\ \mathrm{in} \\
& !\mathrm{VP}(ipk, c_V)|!\mathrm{VA}(ipk, c_V)|!\mathrm{TPM}(c_T)|\mathrm{MF}(c_T)|\overline{c_{pub}}\langle\mathtt{isk}\rangle\ |\mathrm{Challenge} \\
\mathrm{Challenge} \;=\; & c_{pub}(id).c_V\,(tag, msg, bsn, sig). \\
& \mathrm{if}\ tag = \mathtt{True}\ \mathrm{then} \\
& \quad \mathrm{if}\ \mathtt{part}_1(sig) = \mathtt{Com}(bsn, \mathtt{prf}(\mathtt{seed}(id), \mathtt{ipk}))\ \mathrm{then} \\
& \qquad \mathrm{event}\ \mathtt{ChalVerif}(msg, bsn, sig, \mathtt{prf}(\mathtt{seed}(id), \mathtt{ipk}))
\end{aligned}
$$

If a tuple (msg, bsn, sig) is verified by a verifier, the verifier will output a tag $\mathtt{True}$ together with the tuple over private channel c_V. After receiving a identity id through c_{pub} from the adversary and a valid tuple msg, bsn, sig through c_V, the process Challenge checks if the signature sig can be linked to id by checking if sig contains a ticket equal to the ticket produced by TPM whose identity $= id$ (the third line of process Challenge). If sig can be linked to TPM id, then event $\mathtt{ChalVerif}$ will be executed.

Definition 4 (Non-frameability). *Given processes $\langle TPM, VA, VP \rangle$, then non-frameability is satisfied if there exist deterministic functions $\mathtt{Com}$ and $\mathtt{RogTag}$, and the process Game2 satisfies the following correspondence:*
$$
event(\mathtt{ChanlVerif}(m, bsn, \sigma, tsk)) \rightsquigarrow event(\mathtt{TPM2\_Sign}(\mathtt{part}_2(\sigma), tsk)) \vee
$$
$$
(event(\mathtt{LeakTPM}(tsk)) \wedge \mathtt{RogTag}(m, bsn, \sigma, tsk) = \mathtt{True}).
$$

The above definition means if $event(\mathtt{ChanlVerif}(m, bsn, \sigma, tsk))$ is executed, i.e., if a DAA signature σ can be linked to a TPM whose DAA secret key is tsk, then σ must be signed using the API $\mathtt{TPM2\_Sign}$ of this TPM, OR the key tsk has been corrupted and the algorithm $\mathtt{RogTag}$ can find out.

4.3   Forward Anonymity

All the previous definitions and analyses of anonymity of DAA consider a setting that the host and TPM are both honest. However, we find a DAA protocol which is proved to be secure under former definitions of anonymity may not be able to resist the following attack: the whole platform is honest when signing a signature, after the signature is signed, the adversary wants to find out whether this signature is signed by the platform, so he corrupts the host and gains information stored in the host and the ability to directly communicate with the TPM. With these capabilities, the adversary may be able to find out if the signature was signed by the platform before.

We propose forward anonymity. Informally, the notion of forward anonymity requires that the following property holds in the DAA scheme: even after an adversary compromised the host of a trusted platform, he can not find out whether a previous signed anonymous DAA signature (with basename $=\perp$) is signed by this trusted platform as long as the TPM is not corrupted. Notice that generally we can not expect a pseudonymous signature to remain anonymous after the host is compromised, because the adversary with ability to communicate with TPM can always generate a new signature using the same basename as the pseudonymous signature. Thus using function link, the adversary can decide if this pseudonymous signature is generate by the platform.

The notion of forward anonymity is defined via a game played by a challenger $\mathcal{C}$ and an adversary $\mathcal{A}$ as follows,

Initial: $\mathcal{C}$ runs Setup and gives the resulting isk to $\mathcal{A}$. Then $\mathcal{C}$ generates two identities id_1 and id_2 and outputs public parameters and the two identities on a public channel.

Phase 1: The adversary makes the following requests to $\mathcal{C}$: $\mathcal{A}$ submits a TPMs identity id along with the name of the API he wants to use, for example, TPM2_CreatePrimary(), and the data used in calling the API of his choice to $\mathcal{C}$, who acts as the TPM with identity id and responds with the output of the API. Of course, we assume the adversary always follows the order of APIs, for example TPM2_Sign() can be called only after TPM2_Commit() was called.

Challenge:$\mathcal{A}$ submits a message m and a nonce n_V of his choice to $\mathcal{C}$. $\mathcal{C}$ produces two anonymous signatures, i.e. using basename $= \perp$, as platforms with identity id_1 and id_2 using m and n_V, then output signatures to the adversary.

Phase 2: The adversary can do what he can in phase 1.

Result: The protocol satisfies forward anonymity if the adversary $\mathcal{A}$ cannot distinguish between the two signatures outputted during the challenge.

Our definition of forward anonymity can be modelled by the biprocess Game3 presented below using observational equivalence. The biprocess Challenge outputs two anonymous signatures (i.e., with basename $=$ none) signed by trusted platforms whose identities are id_1 and id_2 using the nonce n_V and the message m. The subprocess TPM in Game3 models the API oracle in the above game-based definition. Thus if the biprocess Game3 satisfies observational equivalence, then the adversary can not distinguish the two anonymous signatures even given the API oracle, which means the forward anonymity holds.

$$
\begin{aligned}
\text{Game3} \;=\; & \nu\,\tilde{n}.\;\nu\,\text{isk. let}\; ipk = \text{pub}(\text{isk})\;\text{in}\\
& !\text{TPM}(c_T)|\text{MF}(c_T)|\overline{c_{pub}}\langle\text{isk}\rangle\;|\text{Challenge}|\overline{c_{pub}}\langle id_1, id_2\rangle\\
\text{Challenge} \;=\; & c_{pub}(n_V, m).\nu\;r.\\
& \text{let}\; id = \text{choice}[id_1, id_2]\;\text{in} \quad \text{let}\; eps = \text{seed}(x_{id})\,\text{in}\\
& \text{let}\; tsk = \text{prf}(eps, ipk)\;\text{in} \quad \text{let}\; cred = \text{cred}(isk, tsk, r)\;\text{in}\\
& \text{TPMAPI}(eps)|\text{HostSign}(cred, n_V, \text{none}, m)
\end{aligned}
$$

Definition 5 (Forward anonymity). *Given a pair of processes $\langle TPM, Host\rangle$, forward anonymity is satisfied if the biprocess Game3 satisfies observational equivalence.*

5   Case Study: An ECC-Based DAA Using Asymmetric Pairing

Based on our previous security definitions, we analyzed an ECC-based DAA supported by TPM 2.0 specification using ProVerif. Details of this ECC-based DAA can be found in [5]. Our general framework is suitable for analyzing other ECC-based DAA protocols supported by TPM 2.0 specification.

5.1   Primitives and Protocol Model in Applied pi Calculus

Due to the page limit, the model will be given in the full version.

5.2   Security Analysis

After we modeled the ECC-base DAA in applied pi calculus, we use proverif to analyze the protocol.

User-controlled traceability and non-frameability: ProVerif is able to analyze traceability and non-frameability automatically. The ECC-based DAA satisfies *user-controlled traceability* and *unframeability* according to our definition, i.e. the correspondences are verified by ProVerif.

Forward anonymity: ProVerif find an attack against *forward anonymity*. We now explain the attack in detail. In DAA protocol, credential is stored in host and DAA secret key is stored inside TPM. Host uses credential and TPM to produce signatures. As is stated above, a DAA signature contains a randomized credential $credr = (R, S, T, W)$ which is also a valid CL credential for the DAA secret key k, i.e. $W = S^k$. So given a challenge signature which contains a randomized credential $credr = (R, S, T, W)$ and two TPMs whose DAA keys are respectively k_1 and k_2, the adversary can act as host using $credr$ and two TPMs to produce two signatures. For each TPM with secret key k_i, $i = 1$ or 2, the adversary first generates a basename bsn and calls API TPM2_Commit(S, bsn) to get

$(C_1, C_2, K_i = h(bsn)^{k_i})$, then calls TPM2_Sign($h(C_1, C_2)$) to generate the modified Schnorr signatures, i.e., the proof of knowledge of equality $\sigma_i = PK\{(k_i) : B^{k_i} = K_i \wedge S^{k_i} = W_i\}$, where $B = h(bsn)$, $W_i = S^{k_i}$. Note here W_i is not known by the adversary. As σ_i can only be verified using two tuples (B, K_i) and (S, W_i), the adversary can utilize (B, K_i) and (S, W) to verify σ_i, only one signature can be verified, i.e., $W = W_1$ or W_2. So the adversary can judge which TPM signed this signature.

Fix the DAA protocol and API to satisfy forward anonymity: The original CL credential get from issuer is a tuple (C, D, E, F), when signing, the host will generate a random number l, calculate a random credential $(R, S, T, W) = (C^l, D^l, E^l, F^l)$, calls TPM2_Commit($S, bsn$) and then TPM2_Sign to get a modified Schnorr signature. The attack ProVerif found is due to that TPM can not distinguish the original credential (C, D, E, F) between randomized credential (R, S, T, W). There is *no restriction* of the first parameter S of TPM2_Commit(S, bsn). To revise this API, we stored D inside TPM after the credential (C, D, E, F) is obtained from the issuer. The original API TPM2_Commit(S, bsn) is now revised to TPM2_Commit$_R$(l, bsn). When TPM2_Commit$_R$(l, bsn) is called, TPM generate a random number r, calculates $C_1 = D^{lr}, C_2 = h(b)^r, K = h(b)^k$ where k is the DAA secret key, and output C_1, C_2, K to the host. Notice now D^l is equal to the input S in the original API TPM2_Commit(S, bsn).

Now given a signature contains a random credential (R', S', T', W'), the adversary can not calculate the number l' which satisfies $D^{l'} = S'$, so element $S = D^l$ calculate inside TPM can not be equal to S'. So the attack found by proverif would not work: both signatures are invalid. To verify our improvement, we formalized our revised API and DAA schemes in applied pi calculus and proverif is able to prove our revised scheme satisfies forward anonymity.

6   Conclusion

We formalize DAA-related APIs in TPM 2.0 specification and present novel symbolic definitions of user-controlled traceability and non-frameability. Then we propose a new property of DAA called forward anonymity. We analyze the implementation of a DAA scheme using APIs in TPM2.0 and find a weakness in a API which leads to an attack against forward anonymity, then we propose a security fix and verify our fix using ProVerif. Our future work includes analyzing the computational soundness of our analysis and formalizing more APIs in TPM 2.0 using applied pi calculus.

References

1. Brickell, E., Camenisch, J., Chen, L.: Direct anonymous attestation. In: Proceedings of the 11th ACM Conference on Computer and Communications Security, pp. 132–145. ACM (2004)
2. Trusted Computing Group: TCG TPM specification 1.2 (2003), https://www.trustedcomputinggroup.org

3. Brickell, E., Chen, L., Li, J.: A new direct anonymous attestation scheme from bilinear maps. In: Lipp, P., Sadeghi, A.-R., Koch, K.-M. (eds.) TRUST 2008. LNCS, vol. 4968, pp. 166–178. Springer, Heidelberg (2008)

4. Chen, X., Feng, D.: Direct anonymous attestation for next generation tpm. Journal of Computers 3(12), 43–50 (2008)

5. Chen, L., Page, D., Smart, N.P.: On the design and implementation of an efficient DAA scheme. In: Gollmann, D., Lanet, J.-L., Iguchi-Cartigny, J. (eds.) CARDIS 2010. LNCS, vol. 6035, pp. 223–237. Springer, Heidelberg (2010)

6. Chen, L.: A DAA scheme requiring less TPM resources. In: Bao, F., Yung, M., Lin, D., Jing, J. (eds.) Inscrypt 2009. LNCS, vol. 6151, pp. 350–365. Springer, Heidelberg (2010)

7. Brickell, E., Chen, L., Li, J.: Simplified security notions of direct anonymous attestation and a concrete scheme from pairings. International Journal of Information Security 8(5), 315–330 (2009)

8. Trusted Computing Group: TCG TPM specification 2.0 (2012), https://www.trustedcomputinggroup.org

9. Chen, L., Li, J.: Flexible and scalable digital signatures in TPM 2.0. In: Proceedings of the 2013 ACM SIGSAC Conference on Computer & Communications Security, pp. 37–48. ACM (2013)

10. Chen, L., Morrissey, P., Smart, N.P.: On proofs of security for DAA schemes. In: Baek, J., Bao, F., Chen, K., Lai, X. (eds.) ProvSec 2008. LNCS, vol. 5324, pp. 156–175. Springer, Heidelberg (2008)

11. Backes, Maffei, M., Unruh, D.: Zero-knowledge in the applied pi-calculus and automated verification of the direct anonymous attestation protocol. In: 29th IEEE Symposium on Security and Privacy, pp. 202–215. IEEE Computer Society (2008)

12. Smyth, B., Ryan, M., Chen, L.: Formal analysis of anonymity in ECC-based direct anonymous attestation schemes. In: Barthe, G., Datta, A., Etalle, S. (eds.) FAST 2011. LNCS, vol. 7140, pp. 245–262. Springer, Heidelberg (2012)

13. Chen, L., Morrissey, P., Smart, N.: DAA: Fixing the pairing based protocols. Technical report, Cryptology ePrint Archive, Report 2009/198 (2009)

14. Chen, L., Ryan, M.: Attack, solution and verification for shared authorisation data in TCG TPM. In: Degano, P., Guttman, J.D. (eds.) FAST 2009. LNCS, vol. 5983, pp. 201–216. Springer, Heidelberg (2010)

15. Delaune, S., Kremer, S., Ryan, M.D., Steel, G.: A formal analysis of authentication in the TPM. In: Degano, P., Etalle, S., Guttman, J. (eds.) FAST 2010. LNCS, vol. 6561, pp. 111–125. Springer, Heidelberg (2011)

16. Blanchet, B.: An efficient cryptographic protocol verifier based on prolog rules. In: CSFW 2001: Proceedings of the 14th IEEE Computer Security Foundations Workshop, pp. 82–96. IEEE Computer Society (2001)

17. Abadi, M., Fournet, C.: Mobile values, new names, and secure communication. ACM SIGPLAN Notices 36, 104–115 (2001)

18. Ryan, M., Smyth, B.: Formal Models and Techniques for Analyzing Security Protocols, ch. 6. IOS Press (2010)

19. Blanchet, B., Abadi, M., Fournet, C.: Automated verification of selected equivalences for security protocols. In: Proceedings of the 20th Annual IEEE Symposium on Logic in Computer Science, LICS 2005, pp. 331–340. IEEE (2005)

20. Blanchet, B.: Automatic verification of correspondences for security protocols. Journal of Computer Security 17(4), 363–434 (2009)

21. Camenisch, J., Lysyanskaya, A.: Signature schemes and anonymous credentials from bilinear maps. In: Franklin, M. (ed.) CRYPTO 2004. LNCS, vol. 3152, pp. 56–72. Springer, Heidelberg (2004)

eCK Secure Single Round ID-Based Authenticated Key Exchange Protocols with Master Perfect Forward Secrecy

Tapas Pandit[1], Rana Barua[1], and Somanath Tripathy[2]

[1] Indian Statistical Institute, Kolkata, India
[2] Indian Institute of Technology, Patna, India

Abstract. Recently, extended Canetti-Krawczyk (eCK) model for Authenticated Key Exchange (AKE) protocol, proposed by LaMacchia, Lauter and Mityagin, is considered to be one of the stronger security models that covers many attacks on existing models. Unfortunately, it does not capture the very sensitive security barricades, the *Perfect Forward Secrecy* (PFS) and the *Master Perfect Forward Secrecy* (MPFS) in ID-based setting. An ID-based AKE protocol with PFS (resp. MPFS) ensures that the revealing of *static keys* of the parties (resp. the *master secret key* of the private key generator), must not compromise even a single bit of the session keys of the past sessions between the parties. In the current status, to the best of our knowledge, there is no ID-based eCK secure single round AKE protocol with either PFS or MPFS. Proposed here, are the ID-based eCK secure single round AKE protocols with PFS and MPFS in the random oracle model. Towards achieving this goal, we also construct ID-based eCK secure single round AKE protocols, one without Master Forward Secrecy (MFS) and the remaining one with MFS, almost at the same computational cost as the existing efficient ID-based eCK Secure Single Round AKE protocols. All of our protocols are secure under the Gap Bilinear Diffie-Hellman (GBDH) problem.

Keywords: Authenticated Key Exchange, ID-based cryptography, eCK-secure, perfect forward secrecy.

1 Introduction

Authenticated key exchange is a cryptographic primitive that plays an important role in secure communication and networks. Key establishment (KE) is a mechanism through which two or more parties can establish a common key called session key, which they can use for secure communication. If two parties U_i and U_j establish a common session key and no other parties learn the established session key, then the KE protocol is called an *authenticated key exchange protocol.*

Peer-to-peer key exchange mechanism introduced by Diffie and Hellman in [3], suffers from the man-in-the-middle attack because of lack of user authentication.

M.H. Au et al. (Eds.): NSS 2014, LNCS 8792, pp. 435–447, 2014.

Most common solution to address this issue is to combine key agreement protocol and certificate based digital signature to achieve authenticated key agreement. But the weakness of the certificate based key agreement protocol is to keep all the desired certificates in a secure place, namely, with the certificate authority. In 1984, Shamir [7] proposed an alternative idea of ID-based primitives, where the public key is the identity. The corresponding private key is generated by a trusted third party designated as private key generator ($\mathcal{PKG}$). Thus, the identity-based cryptosystems [15,21] simplify the process of key management.

At present, many identity-based key agreement protocols using pairings have been proposed [5,8,13,14,16,12,11,10,17,18]. Meanwhile, a few have been proposed [4,9,17,18] that are claimed to be eCK Secure.

The important security features not covered by the eCK model, are the Perfect Forward Secrecy and the Master Perfect Forward Secrecy. An AKE protocol with PFS [20,22], ensures that the revealing of static keys of parties by the adversary who is actively involved to choose the message (unlike weak PFS), can not compromise the session keys of the past sessions, between the parties. That is, the adversary is allowed to reveal the static keys of the parties but after the completion of the test session by the parties. Likewise, an ID-based AKE with MPFS protects the session keys of the past sessions even after exposure of the master secret key to the adversary. Similarly, the adversary is actively involved to choose the message of its own choice (unlike MFS). In both these cases, the adversary is not permitted to query the ephemeral keys for the test session and it's matching session.

Cas Cremers et al. [22] pointed out that using some authentication mechanism, e.g., signature scheme, one round eCK secure AKE protocol with PFS may be possible. Using the observation of LaMacchia et al. in [6], Huang et al. in [20] stated that the generic signature scheme is not adequate for one round eCK secure AKE protocol with PFS. In fact, an adversary against one round AKE protocol using randomized signature scheme may learn the static key if the adversary reveals these random coins and impersonates the honest party. So, this emphasize that the signature scheme must be deterministic for this purpose. Another required strong point is that the static key of AKE protocol should commute with static key of the hired signature scheme. All these discussions were made in the PKI setting.

However, managing one round eCK security with either PFS or MPFS is harder in the ID-based setting since static keys of the parties are connected via the master secret key. To the best our knowledge, till date, there is no ID-based eCK secure single round AKE protocol with either PFS or MPFS. Therefore, an eCK secure single round AKE protocol with either PFS or MPFS in the ID-based setting, is always welcome as the first existing scheme.

1.1 Our Contribution

In this paper, we propose eCK secure ID-based single round AKE protocols, Π_2 with PFS and Π_4, Π_5, Π_6 with MPFS from GBDH problem. Towards achieving this goal, we also construct eCK secure ID-based single round AKE protocols,

Π_1 without MFS and Π_3 with MFS, at almost the same computational cost as compared to the existing efficient eCK secure ID-based AKE protocols (for details comparison, see table 1). We show that all these AKE protocols are secure under GBDH problem. The main challenging task is to define the ephemeral public key(s) and pre-session key components (i.e., the part to be hashed to compute the final session key), so that the hard problem can be solved by these pre-session key components if a PPT adversary breaks this protocol.

Let Q_A and Q_B be respectively the public keys[1] of Alice (with identity ID_A) and Bob (with identity ID_B). Let $\mathcal{SK}_A$ and $\mathcal{SK}_B$ denote the static key of Alice and Bob respectively and let s be the $\mathcal{MSK}$. Also let $g_2 := e(Q_A, Q_B)$. In all of our schemes, we use one of the pre-session key components to be $\kappa := g_2^{s(\eta_A + \eta_B)}$. Another component, $\sigma := g_2^{s\eta_A\eta_B}$ is used along with κ as a pre-session key part in protocols Π_1, Π_2 and Π_3. These components κ and σ together will help to prove the security from GBDH problem. We analyze here, only a case, where the adversary $\mathcal{A}$ is not given $\mathcal{SK}_A$ and $\mathcal{SK}_B$. Similarly, other cases are handled using either κ or σ. Let the parameters, Q, aQ, bQ, sQ of GBDH problem be given to the simulator $\mathcal{S}$ and it's task is to compute $e(Q_A, Q_B)^{sab}$. $\mathcal{S}$ sets public keys as $Q_A := aQ$ and $Q_B := bQ$. Let the ephemeral public key be $\alpha_A := \eta_A Q_A$ (for Π_3, an additional ephemeral public key is $\beta_A := \eta_A P$) and $\alpha_B := \eta_B Q_B$ (similarly, for Π_3, it is $\beta_B := \eta_B P$) respectively for ID_A and ID_B. $\mathcal{S}$ is not aware about the ephemeral key η_B. Since, final hash H to output the session key is used as random oracle and $\mathcal{A}$ succeeds the test session, $\mathcal{A}$ must query with the tuple $(\kappa = g_2^{s(\eta_A + \eta_B)}, \sigma = g_2^{s\eta_A\eta_B}, ...)$ to the hash H. $\mathcal{S}$ first computes $g_2^{s\eta_B} := \sigma^{1/\eta_A}$. Then, it computes $g_2^{s\eta_A} := \kappa/g_2^{s\eta_B}$. Hence, the solution of the given GBDH problem is obtained as $g_2^s := (g_2^{s\eta_A})^{1/\eta_A}$. From the distribution of the pre-session key components, it is immediate that the revealing of master secret key $\mathcal{MSK} := s$ implies trivially breaking the system. Therefore, to protect the master forward secrecy, we add an additional ephemeral public key $\beta_A := \eta_A P$ and an additional pre-session key component $\tau := \eta_A \eta_B P$.

The protocol Π_2 carries one additional feature, viz, the perfect forward secrecy which ensures that even after the revealing of $\mathcal{SK}_A$ and $\mathcal{SK}_B$, the security of the past sessions can not be compromised. Basically, we assure that the ephemeral keys η_A and η_B could not be known to $\mathcal{A}$ and to accomplish this, a *peer authentication mechanism* is involved in the protocol. In peer authentication mechanism, Alice creates the peer authentication tag γ_A using the static key $\mathcal{SK}_A$, Bob's public key Q_B, ephemeral key η_A, ID_A and ID_B and it can only be verified by Bob's static $\mathcal{SK}_B$. Therefore, $\mathcal{A}$ can not create the peer authentication tag $\gamma_A := H_2(g_2^{s\eta_A}, g_2^s, ID_A, ID_B)$ as he is unaware of $\mathcal{SK}_A$ and $\mathcal{SK}_B$ before the completion of test session.

The protocols Π_4, Π_5, Π_6 have the pre-session key components κ and τ. The outgoing message from Alice, $Comm_A$ consists of $\alpha_A := \eta_A Q_A$, $\beta := \eta_A P$ and a peer authentication tag $\gamma_A := H_2(g_2^{s\eta_A}, g_2^s, *, ID_A, ID_B)$. If the protocol

---

[1] For ease of exposition, we slightly abuse the conventional meaning of public key, i.e., the public key stands for the hash value of an identity, though in ID-based setting, identity ID plays the role of public key.

is Π_4, then the '*' is $f_A^{s\eta_A} := e(sP, Q_A)^{\eta_A}$, else it is blank. These protocols provide an extra security barrier, viz, the master perfect forward secrecy which allows $\mathcal{A}$ to learn $\mathcal{MSK}$ but still, the security of the past sessions must not be compromised. Similarly as above, $\mathcal{A}$ can not create the peer authentication tag $\gamma_A := H_2(g_2^{s\eta_A}, g_2^s, *, ID_A, ID_B)$ as he is unaware of $\mathcal{MSK} := s$ before the completion of test session.

Table 1. Efficiency Comparison

Protocol	Pre-Comp	Post-Comp	eCK	MFS	PFS	MPFS	Assump
$Chow - Choo_1$ [11]	–	1P+3SM+2A	X	X	X	X	BDH
$Chow - Choo_2$ [11]	–	1P+5SM+2A	X	✓	X	X	MBDH
$Huang - Cao$ [4]	–	2P+3SM+4A	✓	✓	X	X	BDH
$Fujioka\ et\ al.$[17,18]	IP	1P+3SM+2A	✓	✓	X	X	GBDH
$Our\ Scheme\ \Pi_1$	1P	1P+1SM+2E	✓	X	X	X	GBDH
$Our\ Scheme\ \Pi_2$	1P	1P+1SM+2E	✓	X	✓	X	GBDH
$Our\ Scheme\ \Pi_3$	1P	1P+3SM+2E	✓	✓	X	X	GBDH
$Our\ Scheme\ \Pi_4$	2P	2P+3SM+2E+1$\mathcal{O}$	✓	✓	✓	✓	GBDH
$Our\ Scheme\ \Pi_5$	1P	2P+3SM+1E+1$\mathcal{O}$	✓	✓	✓	✓	GBDH
$Our\ Scheme\ \Pi_6$	1P	3P+3SM+1E	✓	✓	✓	✓	GBDH

In table 1, we show the efficiency comparison of our protocols with others. We use some notations to explain the computational cost: P for bilinear pairing, SM for scalar multiplication on $\mathbb{G}$, A for addition of two points of the bilinear group $\mathbb{G}$, E for exponentiation in $\mathbb{G}_T$ and $\mathcal{O}$ stands for decisional bilinear Diffie-Hellman test. Pre-Comp stands for the pre-computation i.e., the computations before choosing the ephemeral key (i.e., independent of ephemeral key). Post-Comp denotes the rest of the computations. Assump stands for assumption. Note that in PFS and MPFS, the adversary is actively involved, whereas, in wPFS and MFS, it is passive.

1.2 Related Work

Chow et al.[11] proposed two efficient ID-based AKE protocols based on their challenge response signature technique. They claimed that their protocol supports SessionKeyReveal queries in all cases and EphemeralKeyReveal queries in almost all cases, except for the sessions owned by the peer of the test session. Therefore, their schemes neither support the CK model nor the eCK model, as in both model, the adversary is allowed to make the EphemeralKeyReveal for all session except for test session and it's matching session.

Huang et al. [4] first proposed an ID-based AKE protocol using pairing which is provably secure in the eCK model (that includes MFS) under the BDH assumption. The main non-trivial task in simulation of the eCK model is to consistently answer the SessionKeyReveal queries, final hash oracle queries and EphemeralSecretReveal queries without knowing the static key (long term secret key). They used a technique called the TRAPDOOR Test to handle the above queries rather than using the Gap-CDH assumption.

A. Fujioka et al. [17] proposed eCK secure ID-Based AKE protocol with MFS from the GBDH problem. Performance wise, it is almost the same as [4] except, in [4], 4 addition operations are involved and the static key consists of 2 group elements, whereas in [17], 2 addition operations are involved and the static key consists of single group element. Later, A. Fujioka et al. in [18] extend this result using asymmetric pairing.

Ni et al.[9] constructed a provably eCK secure ID-based AKE protocol based on the same technique as Huang et al. However, they claimed that by using pre-computation ahead of time (or off-line computation), the session key computation time can be reduced. But the total computation cost is very high (it requires six pairing computations).

1.3   Organization

This paper is organized as follows. For better readable, we provide a brief background eCK security model in Section 2. The proposed ID-based AKE protocols and their security are discussed in Section 3. Finally, we conclude the work in Section 4.

2   Preliminaries

Notation For a set X, $x \xleftarrow{R} X$ denotes that x is randomly picked from X according to the distribution R. Likewise, $x \xleftarrow{U} X$ indicates x is uniformly selected from X. *poly* stands for polynomial.

For details of bilinear pairing and GBDH problem, refer to [19].

2.1   Security Model

The Canetti-Krawczyk [2] security model (CK-model) for AKE gives the power to the adversary to reveal the session state information except the test session and its matching session. In the extended-CK (eCK) [6] security model (defined in PKI-setting), the adversary is given full power on revealing both static and ephemeral keys without trivially breaking the session. The eCK model captures many security barricades that are not included by any single model, viz, weak perfect forward security (wPFS), key-compromise impersonation (KCI) attack, leakage of ephemeral keys attack etc. However, Cas Cremers first showed in [23] that CK model and eCK model are formally and practically incomparable. To achieve this result, they provide for each model some attacks on the protocols from the literature that are not captured by the other models. Huang et al. [4] first, formalize the eCK model in ID-Based setting, where it includes an additional attack, viz, master forward secrecy. Here, we separate out the MFS part from the eCK model due to Huang et al. [4] and we handle it separately, i.e., our eCK model is inspired by the original eCK model of [6].

Let $\mathcal{U} = \{U_i : i = 1, \cdots, n\}$ be the set of parties with each party U_i having an identity ID_i being a probabilistic polynomial-time (PPT) Turing machine. The protocol may run between any two of these parties. Each party may execute a polynomial number of protocol instances (sessions) in parallel with other parties. For each party U_i, there exists a public key Q_i that can be derived from its identity ID_i using hash function H_1. Let $Comm_i$ and $Comm_j$ be the outgoing messages, consist of ephemeral public key(s) and/or authentication tag from U_i and U_j respectively.

Let Π_{ij}^t be a completed session run between the parties U_i and U_j. Let sid stand for session identifier. It is defined as $sid := (Comm_i, Comm_j, ID_i, ID_j)$, where $Comm_i$ and $Comm_j$ are defined as earlier, ID_i is the owner of the session, ID_j is peer. A session Π_{ji}^t is said to be a matching session of Π_{ij}^t if Π_{ji}^t is completed and has sid of the form $(Comm_j, Comm_i, ID_j, ID_i)$.

The adversary $\mathcal{A}$ modelled here, is a PPT Turing machine which has full control on the communication network over which protocol messages can be altered, injected or eavesdropped at any time. The security of a protocol Π is defined as an adaptive game between the parties U_i and the adversary $\mathcal{A}$. This game executes in two phases. In the first phase to capture possible leakage of private information, the adversary is provided with the capability of asking the following additional oracle queries in any order.

EphemeralSecretReveal(Π_{ij}^t): $\mathcal{A}$ is provided the ephemeral secret key used in session Π_{ij}^t. This could be possible if the session-specific secret information is stored in insecure memory, or if the random number generator of the party be guessed.

SessionKeyReveal(Π_{ij}^t): $\mathcal{A}$ is given the session key for Π_{ij}^t, provided that the session holds a session key.

Long-termSecretReveal(U_i): $\mathcal{A}$ obtains the long term secret key of U_i.

EstablishParty(U_i): The adversary $\mathcal{A}$ can register ID_i on behalf of the party U_i. In this case, $\mathcal{A}$ obtains the long term secret key of U_i.

Send(Π_{ij}^t, m): The adversary's ability of controlling the communication network is modelled by the *Send* query. Here, the adversary sends a message m to party U_i in the tth session Π_{ij}^t on behalf of party U_j and gets responses from U_i according to the protocol specification.

The adversary begins the second phase of the game by choosing a fresh session Π_{ij}^t and issuing a $Test(\Pi_{ij}^t)$ query, where the fresh session and test query are defined as follows:

Definition 1. *(Fresh session) A session Π_{ij}^t executed by an honest party U_i with another party U_j is said to be fresh if none of the following conditions hold:*

1. *U_j is engaged in session Π_{ji}^t matching to Π_{ij}^t and the adversary $\mathcal{A}$ reveals the session key of Π_{ij}^t or Π_{ji}^t.*
2. *U_j is engaged in session Π_{ji}^t matching to Π_{ij}^t and $\mathcal{A}$ issues either both the Long-term secret key of U_i and the ephemeral secret of Π_{ij}^t, or both the Long-term secret key of U_j and the ephemeral secret of Π_{ji}^t.*

3. No session matching to Π_{ij}^t exists and the adversary $\mathcal{A}$ reveals either the Long-term secret key of U_j or both the static keys of U_i and the ephemeral secret of Π_{ij}^t.

Definition 2. *(Test Π_{ij}^t Query:). Pick $b \xleftarrow{U} \{0,1\}$. If $b = 0$, then set $\mathcal{SN} \longleftarrow SessionKeyReveal(\Pi_{ij}^t)$ else $\mathcal{SN} \xleftarrow{U} \{0,1\}^\mu$ and $\mathcal{SN}$ is returned to $\mathcal{A}$. Only one query of this form is allowed for the adversary. Of course, after the $Test(\Pi_{ij}^t)$ query has been issued, the adversary can continue querying provided that the test session Π_{ij}^t is fresh. $\mathcal{A}$ outputs his guess b' in the test session. Thus the adversary's advantage in winning the game is defined as*

$$Adv_{\mathcal{A}}^{\Pi}(\lambda) = |Pr[b' = b] - 1/2|$$

Definition 3. *(eCK Security). An authenticated key exchange protocol is said to be secure (in the eCK model) if matching sessions compute the same session keys and for any PPT adversary $\mathcal{A}$ the advantage in winning the above game is negligible.*

Definition 4. *(Master Forward Secrecy). An authenticated key exchange protocol is said to be secure with MFS if the definition 3 still holds even after the adversary is allowed to learn the master secret key[2].*

Definition 5. *(Perfect Forward Secrecy). An authenticated key exchange protocol is said to be secure with PFS if the definition 3 still holds even when the adversary is allowed to learn the static keys of the owner and peer but after the completion of the test session.*

Definition 6. *(Master Perfect Forward Secrecy). An authenticated key exchange protocol is said to be secure with MPFS if the definition 3 still holds even when the adversary is allowed to learn the master secret key but after the completion of the test session.*

3 Identity-Based Single Round Authenticated Key Exchange Protocol

Proposed below, are eCK secure ID-based AKE protocols with different additional features, viz, Π_1 without MFS, Π_2 with PFS, Π_3 with MFS and Π_4, Π_5, Π_6 with Master PFS. Although, the protocols Π_4, Π_5, Π_6 achieve the same security, but they have different computational cost analysis as given in table 1. The security of all these protocols rely on the GBDH problem. All the protocols proposed here, are based on the structure of Chow et al. [11].

---

[2] In definition 4, $\mathcal{A}$ is passive in the test session, otherwise $\mathcal{A}$ itself chooses an ephemeral key of the test session and trivially computes the session key.

3.1 eCK Secure ID-Based AKE Protocol without MFS (Π_1)

Described here, is our basic ID-based eCK secure AKE protocol without MFS from GBDH problem. This has almost the same computational efficiency as the existing protocols. A tabular representation of the protocol Π_1 is given in table 2.

Setup(1^λ): Let $\mathbb{G}$ be a bilinear group of prime order q, and let P be a generator of $\mathbb{G}$. In addition, let $e : \mathbb{G} \times \mathbb{G} \to \mathbb{G}_T$ denote the bilinear map. Assume that DBDH problem for $(\mathbb{G}, \mathbb{G}_T, e, q)$ is efficiently solvable. A security parameter, λ, will determine the size of the groups. Let $H_1 : \{0,1\}^\star \to \mathbb{G}$ and $H : \{0,1\}^\star \to \{0,1\}^\mu$, where $\mu = poly(\lambda)$, be hash functions. The $\mathcal{PKG}$ chooses $s \xleftarrow{U} \mathbb{Z}_q$ as $\mathcal{MSK}$. Then, it declares the public parameters as $\mathcal{PP} := \{\mathbb{G}, \mathbb{G}_T, e, P, sP, H, H_1\}$

KeyGen($\mathcal{PP}, \mathcal{MSK}, ID_A$): It first, computes the public key of the party ID_A as $Q_A := H_1(ID_A)$. Then, it sets the long term secret key of the party ID_A as $\mathcal{SK}_A = sQ_A$.

KeyAgreement: The following is the description of a single round ID-based key exchange protocol between two parties with identities ID_A and ID_B.

Table 2. Our eCK secure ID-Based AKE Protocol without MFS (Π_1)

ID_A	ID_B
$Q_A := H_1(ID_A), \mathcal{SK}_A := sQ_A$	$Q_B := H_1(ID_B), \mathcal{SK}_B := sQ_B$
Pre-Comp: $g_2^s := e(\mathcal{SK}_A, Q_B)$	Pre-Comp: $g_2^s := e(\mathcal{SK}_B, Q_A)$
$\eta_A \xleftarrow{U} \mathbb{Z}_q, \ \alpha_A := \eta_A Q_A$	$\eta_B \xleftarrow{U} \mathbb{Z}_q, \ \alpha_B := \eta_B Q_B$
$Comm_A := (\alpha_A) - - - - - - - - - - - - - - - >$	
$< - - - - - - - - - - - - - - - -Comm_B := (\alpha_B)$	
$g_2^{s\eta_B} := e(\mathcal{SK}_A, \alpha_B)$	$g_2^{s\eta_A} := e(\mathcal{SK}_B, \alpha_A)$
$\kappa_{AB} := (g_2^s)^{\eta_A}.g_2^{s\eta_B}, \ \sigma_{AB} := (g_2^{s\eta_B})^{\eta_A}$	$\kappa_{BA} := g_2^{s\eta_A}.(g_2^s)^{\eta_B}, \ \sigma_{BA} := (g_2^{s\eta_A})^{\eta_B}$
$\mathcal{SN}_{AB} := H(\kappa_{AB}, \sigma_{AB}, P, sP, sid)$	$\mathcal{SN}_{BA} := H(\kappa_{BA}, \sigma_{BA}, P, sP, sid)$
$sid := (Comm_A, Comm_B, ID_A, ID_B)$	

Pre-Computation : Let $g_2 := e(Q_A, Q_B)$. The parties ID_A and ID_B respectively compute $g_2^s := e(\mathcal{SK}_A, Q_B)$ and $g_2^s := e(\mathcal{SK}_B, Q_A)$. (This is independent of ephemeral key)

Post-Computation : The party ID_A picks an ephemeral key $\eta_A \xleftarrow{U} \mathbb{Z}_q$ and sends the ephemeral public key $\alpha_A := \eta_A Q_A$ to ID_B. Similarly, the party ID_B sends the ephemeral public key $\alpha_B := \eta_B Q_B$ to ID_A. Upon receiving the message $Comm_B = \alpha_B$ from ID_B, the party ID_A computes the pre-session key components as $g_2^{s\eta_A} := (g_2^s)^{\eta_A}$, $g_2^{s\eta_B} := e(\mathcal{SK}_A, \alpha_B)$, $\kappa_{AB} := g_2^{s\eta_A}.g_2^{s\eta_B} = g_2^{s(\eta_A + \eta_B)}$, $\sigma_{AB} := (g_2^{s\eta_B})^{\eta_A} = g_2^{s\eta_A\eta_B}$. Finally, ID_A computes the session key as $\mathcal{SN}_{AB} := H(\kappa_{AB}, \sigma_{AB}, P, sP, sid)$, where the session identifier sid is given by $(Comm_A, Comm_B, ID_A, ID_B)$. Similarly, Upon receiving $Comm_A = \alpha_A$ from ID_A, the party ID_B computes the pre-session key components as $g_2^{s\eta_B} := (g_2^s)^{\eta_B}$, $g_2^{s\eta_A} := e(\mathcal{SK}_B, \alpha_A)$, $\kappa_{BA} := g_2^{s\eta_A}.g_2^{s\eta_B} =$

$g_2^{s(\eta_A+\eta_B)}$, $\sigma_{BA} := (g_2^{s\eta_A})^{\eta_B} = g_2^{s\eta_A\eta_B}$ and the session key is computed as $\mathcal{SN}_{BA} := H(\kappa_{BA}, \sigma_{BA}, P, sP, sid)$.

Theorem 1. *If the* GBDH *assumption holds for* $(\mathbb{G}, \mathbb{G}_T, e, q)$ *and* H, H_1 *are random oracles, then the proposed Protocol* (Π_1) *is eCK secure.*

See footnote [3].

Table 3. Our eCK secure ID-Based AKE Protocol with PFS (Π_2)

ID_A	ID_B
$Q_A := H_1(ID_A), \mathcal{SK}_A := sQ_A$	$Q_B := H_1(ID_B), \mathcal{SK}_B := sQ_B$
Pre-Comp: $g_2^s := e(\mathcal{SK}_A, Q_B)$	Pre-Comp: $g_2^s := e(\mathcal{SK}_B, Q_A)$
$\eta_A \xleftarrow{U} \mathbb{Z}_q, \ \alpha_A := \eta_A Q_A$	$\eta_B \xleftarrow{U} \mathbb{Z}_q, \ \alpha_B := \eta_B Q_B$
$\gamma_A := H_2((g_2^s)^{\eta_A}, g_2^s, ID_A, ID_B)$	$\gamma_B := H_2((g_2^s)^{\eta_B}, g_2^s, ID_B, ID_A)$
$Comm_A := (\alpha_A, \gamma_A) - - - - - - - - - - - - - ->$	
	$< - - - - - - - - - - - - - -Comm_B := (\alpha_B, \gamma_B)$
$g_2^{s\eta_B} := e(\mathcal{SK}_A, \alpha_B)$	$g_2^{s\eta_A} := e(\mathcal{SK}_B, \alpha_A)$
It checks $\gamma_B \overset{?}{=} H_2(g_2^{s\eta_B}, g_2^s, ID_B, ID_A)$	It checks $\gamma_A \overset{?}{=} H_2(g_2^{s\eta_A}, g_2^s, ID_A, ID_B)$
If it is false, then aborts	If it is false, then aborts
$\kappa_{AB} := g_2^{s\eta_A} . g_2^{s\eta_B}, \ \sigma_{AB} := (g_2^{s\eta_B})^{\eta_A}$	$\kappa_{BA} := g_2^{s\eta_A} . g_2^{s\eta_B}, \ \sigma_{BA} := (g_2^{s\eta_A})^{\eta_B}$
$\mathcal{SN}_{AB} := H(\kappa_{AB}, \sigma_{AB}, P, sP, sid)$	$\mathcal{SN}_{BA} := H(\kappa_{BA}, \sigma_{BA}, P, sP, sid)$
$sid := (Comm_A, Comm_B, ID_A, ID_B)$	

3.2   eCK Secure ID-Based AKE Protocol with PFS (Π_2)

In this section, we present an ID-based eCK secure AKE protocol with PFS. The extra feature, PFS allows the adversary to learn the static key $\mathcal{SK}_A$ and $\mathcal{SK}_B$ with similar kind of security guarantee but after the completion of test session. Here, the adversary may actively involve to choose the message of its own choice. The computational efficiency of this protocol is almost the same as existing efficient eCK secure AKE protocol.

Setup(1^λ): This is almost similar to protocol Π_1, except there is an additional hash $H_2 : \{0,1\}^* \to \{0,1\}^\mu$ in $\mathcal{PP}$.

KeyAgreement and Pre-Computation: Same as protocol Π_1.

Post-Computation: Similar to protocol Π_1, except ID_A (resp. ID_B) additionally computes an authentication tag γ_A (resp. γ_B) and upon receiving $Comm_B$ (resp. $Comm_A$) from ID_B (resp. ID_A), it checks the tag γ_B (resp. γ_A). For details, refer to table 3.

Theorem 2. *If the* GBDH *assumption holds for* $(\mathbb{G}, \mathbb{G}_T, e, q)$ *and* H, H_1, H_2 *are random oracles, then the proposed Protocol* (Π_2) *is eCK secure with PFS.*

---

[3] Due to page limitation, the proof of theorem 1, 2, 3 and 4 will be found in the full version.

3.3   eCK Secure ID-Based AKE Protocol with MFS (Π_3)

We describe here, an ID-based eCK secure AKE protocol with MFS from GBDH problem. Note that we separate out the MFS part from the definition of eCK security. This protocol achieves the same computational cost in $\mathbb{G}$ as compared to the existing most efficient eCK secure AKE protocol in random oracle model.
Setup, KeyAgreement and Pre-Computation : Same as protocol Π_1
Post-Computation: Almost similar to protocol Π_1, except there will be an additional component $\beta_A := \eta_A P$ (resp. $\beta_B := \eta_B P$) in $Comm_A$ (resp. $Comm_B$). For details, see the table 4.

Table 4. Our eCK secure ID-Based AKE Protocol with MFS (Π_3)

ID_A	ID_B
$Q_A := H_1(ID_A), \mathcal{SK}_A := sQ_A$	$Q_B := H_1(ID_B), \mathcal{SK}_B := sQ_B$
Pre-Comp: $g_2^s := e(\mathcal{SK}_A, Q_B)$	Pre-Comp: $g_2^s := e(\mathcal{SK}_B, Q_A)$
$\eta_A \xleftarrow{U} \mathbb{Z}_q, \; \alpha_A := \eta_A Q_A, \; \beta := \eta_A P$	$\eta_B \xleftarrow{U} \mathbb{Z}_q, \; \alpha_B := \eta_B Q_B, \; \beta_B := \eta_B P$

$$Comm_A := (\alpha_A, \beta_A) - - - - - - - - - - - - - ->$$
$$< - - - - - - - - - - - - - - - Comm_B := (\alpha_B, \beta_B)$$

$g_2^{s\eta_B} := e(\mathcal{SK}_A, \alpha_B)$	$g_2^{s\eta_A} := e(\mathcal{SK}_B, \alpha_A)$
$\kappa_{AB} := (g_2^s)^{\eta_A} \cdot g_2^{s\eta_B}, \; \sigma_{AB} := (g_2^{s\eta_B})^{\eta_A}$	$\kappa_{BA} := g_2^{s\eta_A} \cdot (g_2^s)^{\eta_B}, \; \sigma_{BA} := (g_2^{s\eta_A})^{\eta_B}$
$\tau_{AB} := \eta_A \beta_B$	$\tau_{BA} := \eta_B \beta_A$
$\mathcal{SN}_{AB} := H(\kappa_{AB}, \sigma_{AB}, \tau_{AB}, P, sP, sid)$	$\mathcal{SN}_{BA} := H(\kappa_{BA}, \sigma_{BA}, \tau_{BA}, P, sP, sid)$

$$sid := (Comm_A, Comm_B, ID_A, ID_B)$$

Theorem 3. *If the* GBDH *assumption holds for* $(\mathbb{G}, \mathbb{G}_T, e, q)$, CDH *assumption holds for* $(\mathbb{G}, q)$ *and* H, H_1 *are random oracles, then the proposed Protocol* (Π_3) *is eCK secure with MFS.*

3.4   eCK Secure ID-Based AKE Protocol with MPFS (Π_4)

Presented here, is an ID-based eCK secure AKE protocol with Master PFS. The Master PFS guarantees the security of past session of AKE protocol, even after exposure of $\mathcal{MSK}$ to the adversary, i.e., the adversary may know the master secret key $\mathcal{MSK}$ but after the completion of test session. In this case, the adversary is forbidden to query the ephemeral keys of either side of the test session. For details, refer to table 6.
Setup and KeyAgreement: Same as protocol Π_2.
Pre-Computation: Let $g_2 := e(Q_A, Q_B)$. The parties ID_A and ID_B compute $g_2^s := e(\mathcal{SK}_A, Q_B), f_A^s := e(Q_A, sP)$ and $g_2^s := e(\mathcal{SK}_B, Q_A), f_B^s := e(Q_B, sP)$ respectively. (This is independent of ephemeral key)
Post-Computation: Due to space restriction, we leave the details.

Theorem 4. *If the* GBDH *assumption holds for* $(\mathbb{G}, \mathbb{G}_T, e, q)$, CDH *assumption holds for* $(\mathbb{G}, q)$ *and* H, H_1, H_2 *are random oracles, then the proposed Protocol* (Π_4) *is eCK secure with Master FPS.*

Table 5. Our eCK secure ID-Based AKE Protocol with MPFS (Π_4)

ID_A	ID_B
$Q_A := H_1(ID_A), \mathcal{SK}_A := sQ_A$	$Q_B := H_1(ID_B), \mathcal{SK}_B := sQ_B$
Pre-Comp: $g_2^s := e(\mathcal{SK}_A, Q_B)$	Pre-Comp: $g_2^s := e(\mathcal{SK}_B, Q_A)$
Pre-Comp: $f_A^s := e(Q_A, sP)$	Pre-Comp: $f_B^s := e(Q_B, sP)$
$\eta_A \xleftarrow{U} \mathbb{Z}_q, \ \alpha_A := \eta_A Q_A, \ \beta_A := \eta_A P$	$\eta_B \xleftarrow{U} \mathbb{Z}_q, \ \alpha_B := \eta_B Q_B, \ \beta_B := \eta_B P$
$\gamma_A := H_2((g_2^s)^{\eta_A}, g_2^s, (f_A^s)^{\eta_A}, ID_A, ID_B)$	$\gamma_B := H_2((g_2^s)^{\eta_B}, g_2^s, (f_B^s)^{\eta_B}, ID_B, ID_A)$
$Comm_A := (\alpha_A, \beta_A, \gamma_A)$ -- -- -- -- -- -- -- -- >	
	< -- -- -- -- -- -- -- -- -- -- $Comm_B := (\alpha_B, \beta_B, \gamma_B)$
$g_2^{s\eta_B} := e(\mathcal{SK}_A, \alpha_B), \ f_B^{s\eta_B} := e(\alpha_B, sP)$	$g_2^{s\eta_A} := e(\mathcal{SK}_B, \alpha_A), \ f_A^{s\eta_A} := e(\alpha_A, sP)$
ID_A checks two relations below	ID_B checks two relations below
$DBDH(P, sP, \beta_B = \eta_B P, Q_B, f_B^{s\eta_B}) \overset{?}{=} 1$	$DBDH(P, sP, \beta_A = \eta_A P, Q_A, f_A^{s\eta_A}) \overset{?}{=} 1$
$\gamma_B \overset{?}{=} H_2(g_2^{s\eta_B}, g_2^s, f_B^{s\eta_B}, ID_B, ID_A)$	$\gamma_A \overset{?}{=} H_2(g_2^{s\eta_A}, g_2^s, f_A^{s\eta_A}, ID_A, ID_B)$
If at least one of them is false,	If at least one of them is false,
then it aborts else proceeds	then it aborts else proceeds
$\kappa_{AB} := g_2^{s\eta_A} \cdot g_2^{s\eta_B}, \ \tau := \eta_A \beta_B$	$\kappa_{BA} := g_2^{s\eta_A} \cdot g_2^{s\eta_B}, \ \tau_{BA} := \eta_B \beta_A$
$\mathcal{SN}_{AB} := H(\kappa_{AB}, \tau_{AB}, P, sP, sid)$	$\mathcal{SN}_{BA} := H(\kappa_{BA}, \tau_{BA}, P, sP, sid)$
$sid := (Comm_A, Comm_B, ID_A, ID_B)$	

3.5 eCK Secure ID-Based AKE Protocol with MPFS (Π_5)

In this section, we propose an ID-based eCK secure AKE protocol with MPFS which requires less pairing computations than previous eCK secure protocol with MPFS (Π_4).
Setup, KeyAgreement and Pre-Computation: Same as protocol Π_2.
Post-Computation: For details refer to table 6.

Theorem 5. *If the* GBDH *assumption holds for* $(\mathbb{G}, \mathbb{G}_T, e, q)$, CDH *assumption holds for* $(\mathbb{G}, q)$ *and* H, H_1, H_2 *are random oracles, then the proposed Protocol* (Π_5) *is eCK secure with Master FPS.*

Proof. The proof is similar to that of theorem 4.

3.6 eCK Secure ID-Based AKE Protocol with MPFS (Π_6)

This is similar to protocol Π_5, except the oracle test $DBDH(P, sP, \eta_B P, Q_B, f_B^{s\eta_B}) \overset{?}{=} 1$ is replaced by $e(\alpha_B, P) \overset{?}{=} e(\beta_B, Q_B)$. Due to space limitation, we omit details.

Table 6. Our eCK secure ID-Based AKE Protocol with MPFS (Π_5)

ID_A	ID_B
$Q_A := H_1(ID_A), \mathcal{SK}_A := sQ_A$	$Q_B := H_1(ID_B), \mathcal{SK}_B := sQ_B$
Pre-Comp: $g_2^s := e(\mathcal{SK}_A, Q_B)$	Pre-Comp: $g_2^s := e(\mathcal{SK}_B, Q_A)$
$\eta_A \xleftarrow{U} \mathbb{Z}_q,\ \alpha_A := \eta_A Q_A,\ \beta_A := \eta_A P$	$\eta_B \xleftarrow{U} \mathbb{Z}_q,\ \alpha_B := \eta_B Q_B,\ \beta_B := \eta_B P$
$\gamma_A := H_2((g_2^s)^{\eta_A}, g_2^s, ID_A, ID_B)$	$\gamma_B := H_2((g_2^s)^{\eta_B}, g_2^s, ID_B, ID_A)$

$$Comm_A := (\alpha_A, \beta_A, \gamma_A) ------------->$$
$$<---------------Comm_B := (\alpha_B, \beta_B, \gamma_B)$$

$g_2^{s\eta_B} := e(\mathcal{SK}_A, \alpha_B),\ f_B^{s\eta_B} := e(\alpha_B, sP)$	$g_2^{s\eta_A} := e(\mathcal{SK}_B, \alpha_A),\ f_A^{s\eta_A} := e(\alpha_A, sP)$
ID_A checks two relations below	ID_B checks two relations below
$DBDH(P, sP, \eta_B P, Q_B, f_B^{s\eta_B}) \stackrel{?}{=} 1$	$DBDH(P, sP, \eta_A P, Q_A, f_A^{s\eta_A}) \stackrel{?}{=} 1$
$\gamma_B \stackrel{?}{=} H_2(g_2^{s\eta_B}, g_2^s, ID_B, ID_A)$	$\gamma_A \stackrel{?}{=} H_2(g_2^{s\eta_A}, g_2^s, ID_A, ID_B)$
If at least one of them is false,	If at least one of them is false,
then it aborts else proceeds	then it aborts else proceeds
$\kappa_{AB} := g_2^{s\eta_A} \cdot g_2^{s\eta_B},\ \tau_{AB} := \eta_A \beta_B$	$\kappa_{BA} := g_2^{s\eta_A} \cdot g_2^{s\eta_B},\ \tau_{BA} := \eta_B \beta_A$
$\mathcal{SN}_{AB} := H(\kappa_{AB}, \tau_{AB}, P, sP, sid)$	$\mathcal{SN}_{BA} := H(\kappa_{BA}, \tau_{BA}, P, sP, sid)$

$$sid := (Comm_A, Comm_B, ID_A, ID_B)$$

4 Conclusion

We have proposed here, single round eCK secure AKE protocols with PFS and MPFS in the ID-based setting from **GBDH** problem as the first existing schemes. To have these protocols, we applied the *peer authentication mechanism*, where Bob can verify Alice's message by only his static key. Due to this mechanism, our schemes seem to be efficient.

References

1. Bellare, M., Canetti, R., Krawczyk, H.: A modular approach to the design and analysis of authentication and key exchange protocols. In: ACM Symposium on Theory of Computing, pp. 419–428 (1998)
2. Canetti, R., Krawczyk, H.: Universally Composable Notions of Key Exchange and Secure Channels. In: Knudsen, L.R. (ed.) EUROCRYPT 2002. LNCS, vol. 2332, pp. 337–351. Springer, Heidelberg (2002)
3. Diffie, W., Hellman, M.E.: New directions in cryptography. IEEE Trans. Inform. Theory 22(6), 644–654 (1976)
4. Huang, H., Cao, Z.: An ID-based Authenticated Key Exchange Protocol Based on Bilinear Diffie-Hellman Problem. Cryptology ePrint Archive, Report 2008/224 (2008)
5. Joux, A.: A one round protocol for tripartite Diffie-Hellman. In: Bosma, W. (ed.) ANTS 2000. LNCS, vol. 1838, pp. 385–394. Springer, Heidelberg (2000)
6. LaMacchia, B., Lauter, K., Mityagin, A.: Stronger security of authenticated key exchange. In: Susilo, W., Liu, J.K., Mu, Y. (eds.) ProvSec 2007. LNCS, vol. 4784, pp. 1–16. Springer, Heidelberg (2007)

7. Shamir, A.: Identity-based cryptosystems and signature schemes. In: Blakely, G.R., Chaum, D. (eds.) CRYPTO 1984. LNCS, vol. 196, pp. 47–53. Springer, Heidelberg (1985)
8. Smart, N.P.: Identity-based authenticated key agreement protocol based on Weil pairing. Electronics Lett. 38(13), 630–632 (2002)
9. Ni, L., Chen, G., Li, J., Hao, Y.: Strongly secure identity-based authenticated key agreement protocols. Comput. Electr. Eng. 37(2), 205–217 (2011)
10. Wang, S., Cao, Z., Choo, K.R., Wang, L.: An improved identity-based key agreement protocol and its security proof. Inf. Sci. 179(3), 307–318 (2009)
11. Chow, S.S.M., Choo, K.-K.R.: Strongly-secure identity-based key agreement and anonymous extension. In: Garay, J.A., Lenstra, A.K., Mambo, M., Peralta, R. (eds.) ISC 2007. LNCS, vol. 4779, pp. 203–220. Springer, Heidelberg (2007)
12. Chen, L., Cheng, Z., Smart, N.P.: Identity-based key agreement protocols from pairings. Int. J. Info. Secur. 6(4), 213–241 (2007)
13. McCullagh, N., Barreto, P.S.L.M.: A new two-party identity-based authenticated key agreement. In: Menezes, A. (ed.) CT-RSA 2005. LNCS, vol. 3376, pp. 262–274. Springer, Heidelberg (2005)
14. Chen, L., Kudla, C.: Identity based authenticated key agreement protocols from pairings. In: Proceedings of the 16th IEEE Computer Security Foundations Workshop, pp. 219–233. IEEE Computer Society Press (2003)
15. Boneh, D., Franklin, M.: Identity-based encryption from the weil pairing. In: Kilian, J. (ed.) CRYPTO 2001. LNCS, vol. 2139, pp. 213–229. Springer, Heidelberg (2001)
16. Wang, Y.: Efficient identity-based and authenticated key agreement protocol. Cryptology ePrint archive, report 2005/108, http://eprint.iacr.org/2005/108
17. Fujioka, A., Suzuki, K., Ustaoğlu, B.: Ephemeral Key Leakage Resilient and Efficient ID-AKEs That Can Share Identities, Private and Master Keys. In: Joye, M., Miyaji, A., Otsuka, A. (eds.) Pairing 2010. LNCS, vol. 6487, pp. 187–205. Springer, Heidelberg (2010)
18. Fujioka, A., Hoshino, F., Kobayashi, T., Suzuki, K., Ustaoglu, B., Yoneyama, K.: id-eCK Secure ID-Based Authenticated Key Exchange on Symmetric and Asymmetric Pairing. IEICE Transactions on Fundamentals of Electronics, Communications and Computer Sciences E96-A(6), 1139–1155
19. Libert, B., Quisquater, J.J.: Identity based undeniable signatures. In: Okamoto, T. (ed.) CT-RSA 2004. LNCS, vol. 2964, pp. 112–125. Springer, Heidelberg (2004)
20. Huang, H.: Strongly Secure One Round Authenticated Key Exchange Protocol with Perfect Forward Security. In: Boyen, X., Chen, X. (eds.) ProvSec 2011. LNCS, vol. 6980, pp. 389–397. Springer, Heidelberg (2011)
21. Sakai, R., Ohgishi, K., Kasahara, M.: Cryptosystems based on pairing. In: Symposium on Cryptography and Information Security, Okinawa, Japan (2000)
22. Cremers, C., Feltz, M.: One-round Strongly Secure Key Exchange with Perfect Forward Secrecy and Deniability. Cryptology ePrint Archive, Report 2011/300 (2011)
23. Cremers, C.: Examining Indistinguishability-Based Security Models for Key Exchange Protocols: The case of CK, CK-HMQV, and eCK. In: Proceedings of the ASIACCS, pp. 80–91 (2011)

Efficient Sub-/Inter-Group Key Distribution
for *ad hoc* Networks

Bo Qin[1], Linxiao Wang[1], Yujue Wang[3,4], Qianhong Wu[2,3], Wenchang Shi[1],
and Bin Liang[1]

[1] School of Information, Renmin University of China, Beijing, China
{bo.qin,wenchang,liangb}@ruc.edu.cn,lxwangruc@163.com
[2] School of Electronic and Information Engineering
Beihang University, Beijing, China
qianhong.wu@buaa.edu.cn
[3] Key Laboratory of Aerospace Information Security and Trusted Computing
Ministry of Education, School of Computer, Wuhan University, Wuhan, China
[4] Department of Computer Science
City University of Hong Kong, Hong Kong S.A.R., China
wyujue2-c@my.cityu.edu.hk

Abstract. People need to communicate each other in many emerging
networks, i.e., in *ad hoc* networks. To ensure the security for group
communication, group key management as a fundamental cryptographic
primitive has been proposed. Although many proposals with regard to
group key managemet have been introduced, they cannot be efficiently
applied to realize secure subgroup and intergroup communications. In
this paper, we propose two group key distribution schemes providing
efficient solutions to these two problems. Our protocols do not require
interaction between users. Storage and computation analyses show that
our proposals are secure and efficient, compared with existing schemes.
Based on those basic schemes, we further present extensions for multipartite groups, by which the efficiency is greatly improved in this scenario.

Keywords: Group key distribution, *ad hoc* networks, Secure group communication, Access control polynomial.

1   Introduction

With the development of communication technologies and distributed computation, there is an increasing demand of group communication so that people
can communicate each other. Group communication brings new security concerns over the transmitted information among many participants. Among these
concerns, a major one is to achieve confidentiality in the sense that only the intended users can understand the messages transmitted among the group. Group
key distribution is fundamental cryptographic primitive for such applications.

As a special application scenario, in *ad hoc* networks, group key distribution
mechanism should provide some more robust and flexible functionalities. Since

M.H. Au et al. (Eds.): NSS 2014, LNCS 8792, pp. 448–461, 2014.
© Springer International Publishing Switzerland 2014

every node is mobile and keeps in touch with other nodes in dynamic mode, *ad hoc* network is self-organizing and without fixed infrastructures. Due to its self-organizing property, *ad hoc* network is very useful in disaster rescuing and battle field, *et al.* However, it is also challenging to guarantee secure communications in *ad hoc* networks as the involved nodes are generally with limited computational/storage capability, instable open communication, and the nodes may dynamically leave and join the system.

To address the problem regarding key distribution for *ad hoc* network, Zou, Dai and Bertino [31] proposed a group key distribution scheme based on the Access Control Polynomial (ACP). When distributing the private keys to the group members, a trusted center server constructs a polynomial by using the hash values of those private keys, and publishes the corresponding coefficients. In such a way, each involved participant can obtain the session key by re-evaluating the function with those polynomial coefficients at the point of her hash value, while any other participant not in the group can get no information useful.

The Zou-Dai-Bertino scheme [31] supports group communication in the dynamic environment. The involved members can dynamically leaving the system. Their scheme can resist various threats including external and internal attacks. However, there are still several issues with regard to group key distribution have not been well addressed in *ad hoc* setting. Specifically, their scheme cannot efficiently support secure subgroup communication or session key update. Also, it cannot support secure intergroup communication.

1.1   Our Contributions

We focus on subgroup key distribution and inter-group key distribution. Our contributions including the following aspects.

Our starting point is the Zou-Dai-Bertino group key distribution protocol [31]. The original Zou-Dai-Bertino protocol does not support secure subgroup or inter-group communication. We first extend the Zou-Dai-Bertino protocol with subgroup communication. For an initial group of n users, the dealer publishes $n + 1$ polynomials and assigns each member with a secret value. In this way, not only all the members in the initial group, but also those in every sub-group can share a distinct secret session key without interactions with other ones; all the users excluded from the intended subgroup cannot get any useful information about the subgroup secret key, even if these excluded users collude together. This feature enables our subgroup protocol especially suitable to the situations in which the participants are with limited computation capacities and bounded communication channels, i.e., they are difficult to update the keys due to heavily computations and highly interactions.

We next extend our extend our basic protocol with secure intergroup communication. To this end, we incorporate the elegant asymmetric group key agreement idea introduced by Wu *et al.* [22]. Specifically, $n + 1$ extra public keys are computed and published by the key dealer. Due to the aggregatability of the public keys and the polynomials, the users in different initial groups can exchange secret messages with the ElGamal's public-key crypto-system. This provides an efficient way to allow the participants in different groups to communicate with each other.

Finally, we further extend the above two schemes for multipartite groups. The entire initial group is logically divided into disjoint subgroups and each subgroup joins or leaves the system in an united way. Then the above basic protocols are applied to each of these subgroups. In this way, the protocol establishment communication and computation overheads are reduced. Analyses show that, compared with the existing schemes, our schemes are more efficient in terms of communication, computation and storage costs.

1.2   Related Work

Group key management is fundamental to secure group communications and has been extensively investigated. Most group key management schemes fall into two categories. One is referred to as group key agreement/exchange, by which the group members jointly establish a confidential broadcast channel among them. The other is referred to as group key distribution (or broadcast encryption or conference key distribution in different references), in which a trusted dealer is employed to help the group members to establish a confidential broadcast channel among the members.

The *group key agreement* protocols allow a group of users to negotiate a common secret key via open insecure networks. Then, a confidential intragroup broadcast channel can be established without relying on any trusted key server. The earlier efforts for group key agreement protocols [4,19] were made to establish the group key among a *static* group of users. The subsequent efforts have been made to *dynamic* group key agreement [18] in which members can join and leave. Logical key hierarchy has been proposed and improved to achieve better efficiency for the member joining and leaving the system [11,13,16]. It has been shown [17] that, in the worst case for a group with n members, logical key hierarchy requires $O(\log n)$ rounds of interactions to support its member's dynamic behavior. In this sense, the protocol proposed by Yu, Sun and Liu [25] is optimal for member changes in a key tree structure. Then, a protocol [6] without employing a tree-like key structure is presented by Dutta and Barua, which achieves constant rounds of interactions for member dynamics.

Recently, a new *asymmetric group key agreement* paradigm has been proposed. In traditional group key agreement, whenever a user wants to securely communicate with a group, she or he has to first join the group and run a group key agreement which usually requires multiple rounds of interactions. To address these limitations, Wu *et al.* [22] introduced the new notion of asymmetric group key agreement and realized the first one-round protocol. In their proposal, instead of a common secret encryption key, a common public encryption key is negotiated while each member holds a different decryption key. The original asymmetric group key agreement is secure against passive attacks. Subsequent efforts [26–30] have been made to ensure asymmetric group key agreement secure against active attacks in public-key infrastructure, identity-based and certificateless cryptosystem settings. More recently, Wu *et al.* [23,24] further extended asymmetric group key agreement so that the sender is allowed to exclude the receivers on demand. The proposal [24] allows runtime revocation of any subgroup of members without any extra interactions among the members. In contrast, the proposal in [23] requires one-round interactions among the neighboring members of the revoked users but enjoys more efficient system setup.

There are also two types of *group key distribution* systems. The first is the symmetric group key distribution in which a trusted key dealer generates the secret keys to potential users. Only the key dealer can send confidential messages to the members and only the intended members can read the encrypted messages. Member addition/deletion is not allowed in the early protocol [10]. Broadcast encryption usually involves group key distribution mechanism to allow the sender to runtime choose the intended receiver subset. This notion was first formalized by Fiat and Naor [7]. The tree-like key structures [9, 20] have been proposed to improve efficiency in symmetric-key broadcast encryption schemes, while the work [5] is also efficient without using any key tree structure.

In the asymmetric setting, Naor and Pinkas [14] formalized the public-key broadcast encryption model and realized the first scheme. Their scheme can resist collision attacks up to a threshold of revoked users. Boneh *et al.* [3] proposed a fully collusion-resistant public-key broadcast encryption scheme built from bilinear parings. Their scheme has $O(\sqrt{n})$ complexity in key size, ciphertext size and computation cost. A recent scheme [15] further reduces the size of the key and the ciphertexts. An up-to-date scheme [8] strengthens the security concept of public-key broadcast encryption schemes while keeping the same $O(\sqrt{N})$ complexity as [3]. The key management for the encryption in Differential Access Control, i.e., broadcast encryption, are considerer by [1, 2, 12, 21]. Furthermore, Zou, Dai and Bertino [31] proposed a scheme based on the innovative concept of Access Control Polynomial for trusted collaborative computing.

2   Preliminaries

2.1   Review of Zou-Dai-Bertino Scheme

We first briefly review the key management mechanism which is proposed by Zou, Dai and Bertino [31]. In which, an innovative construction of an Access Control Polynomial is introduced to distribute the group keys. Particularly, their scheme is efficient when deployed in the highly dynamic environments, i.e., where the users are allowed to dynamically join and leave.

Suppose q be a large prime and $H : \{0,1\}^* \rightarrow F_q$ be a collision-resistant hash function. There is a trusted Dealer who deals with key agreement and distribution for the group members $\mathcal{U} = \{U_1, \cdots, U_n\}$. Each user $U_i \in \mathcal{U}$ has been given a private key x_i which is distributed by the Dealer in advance. For any given session key $k \in F_q$ for group communication, it cannot be distributed directly to the group members. Otherwise, once one member loses the key, it may threaten the communication of the whole group. In addition, the transmission may be tapped by some other person. Thus, the Dealer constructs a polynomial over $F_q[x]$ as follows:

$$f(x) = (x - H(x_1, z))(x - H(x_2, z)) \cdots (x - H(x_n, z)) + k,$$

where $z \in_R F_q$ is a random integer. Then, rewrite the polynomial $f(x)$ as follows

$$f(x) = a_n x^n + \cdots + a_1 x + a_0.$$

The Dealer broadcasts the vector $(a_0, a_1, \cdots, a_n)$ and the random integer z to the group members.

In this way, each member U_i in the group can use her private key x_i, the random integer z and the hash function H to compute the session key as $k = f(H(x_i, z))$ without making any interactions with others. Furthermore, when some member leaving or joining into the group, the Dealer constructs a new polynomial by using the new members' private keys:

$$\begin{aligned} f'(x) &= (x - H(x_1, z')) \cdots (x - H(x_{n+1}, z')) + k' \\ &= a'_{n+1} x^{n+1} + \cdots + a'_1 x + a'_0, \end{aligned}$$

and broadcasts the new vector $(a'_0, \cdots, a'_{n+1})$ and the random integer z'.

It is easy to see that, the hash function H can improve the security of the scheme. Even if an attacker obtains a $H(x_i, z)$, he cannot get the private key x_i.

2.2   Problem Statements

Zou, Dai and Bertino's scheme [31] is efficient when implemented in the dynamic scenario. However, it still shows some weaknesses when applies to some real world scenarios, i.e., in a disaster relief situation as follows.

First, the membership of the group is fixed before setting off. For ensure the secure communication among the group members, there exists a trusted center server (i.e., the Dealer) to select and distribute the keys. Every group member receives a private key x_i and a random integer z, and computes the session key k. Then later on, in the wild, members may leave the group for different reasons and the facility may get lost, which means that the group session key should be updated. Thus, the members should request the Dealer for redistributing a new session key. However, in the wild, the Dealer may be unavailable, and thus it is impossible to update the session key by the Dealer.

Second, consider the situation that all the subsets of the group need secure communication. If distributing a distinct session key for each subgroup, then there are in total $2^n - n - 1 \ (= C_n^n + C_n^{n-1} + C_n^{n-2} + \cdots + C_n^2)$ keys should be distributed before the staffs setting off. By using Zou, Dai and Bertino's scheme [31], it means that there would be $2^n - n - 1$ polynomial coefficient vectors and random values should be published. Obviously, the complexity of secure subgroup communication is very high.

Third, there would be several teams, which managed by the same Dealer, jointly participate in the disaster relief. For ensuring successful cooperations among teams, secure intergroup communication is required. In this situation, every external people who wants to contact a group should request the Dealer for distributing a new polynomial, thus, not only the efficiency would degrade, but also even worse that the Dealer maybe unavailable.

To well address those problems, we propose two efficient group key distribution schemes in the upcoming section.

3   Our Basic Schemes

3.1   Subgroup Key Distribution

By using only $n + 1$ random polynomials, our subgroup key distribution scheme can provide a way to distribute the session keys for all the subgroups.

Suppose q be a large prime and $H : \{0,1\}^* \to F_q$ be a collision-resistent hash function. There is a trusted Dealer who deals with key agreement and distribution for the group members $\mathcal{U} = \{U_1, \cdots, U_n\}$. Each user $U_i \in \mathcal{U}$ has been given a private key x_i which is distributed by the Dealer in advance. We also assume that the group member would leave the group separately, and would not make any cooperations once they are left.

- The Dealer selects $n + 1$ polynomials and $n + 1$ random integers as follows, of which $f_0(x)$ contains all the members' private keys $\{x_i : 1 \leq i \leq n\}$, while $f_i(x)$ excludes the member U_i's private key x_i. Specifically, k_0 is chosen as the session key for the whole group.

$$f_0(x) = \prod_{i=1}^{n} (x - H(x_i, z_0)) + k_0$$

$$f_i(x) = \prod_{j=1, j \neq i}^{n} (x - H(x_j, z_i)) + k_i \text{ for every } 1 \leq i \leq n$$

- The Dealer rewrites all the polynomials and publishes all the corresponding coefficient vectors $\{(a_{i,0}, \cdots, a_{i,n}) : 0 \leq i \leq n\}$ and the random integers $\{z_i : 0 \leq i \leq n\}$ to group members.
- For secure communication with regard to the whole group, each member U_i can recover the session key by computing $k_0 = f_0(H(x_i, z_0))$ without interacting with others.
- For secure communication with regard to some subgroup $S \subset \mathcal{U}$, each member $U_i \in S$ first computes the polynomial

$$f_S(x) = \sum_{U_j \in \overline{S}} f_j(x),$$

where $\overline{S} = \mathcal{U} \setminus S$. Then, calculates the session key as

$$k_S = f_S(x_i) = \sum_{U_j \in \overline{S}} k_j.$$

Thus, the session key for secure subgroup S communication is also recovered without any interaction with others.

Theorem 1. *The above proposed subgroup key distribution scheme is correct.*

Proof. Since the session key k_0 for the whole group is recovered in the same way as that in Zou, Dai and Bertino's scheme [31], we then focus on the correctness for recovering the session key for a subgroup.

As we know, the polynomial $f_0(x)$ contains all the members' private keys $\{x_i : 1 \le i \le n\}$, while $f_i(x)$ does not include x_i. Thus, the group member U_i cannot obtain the random value k_i. For a subgroup $S \subset \mathcal{U}$, each member $U_i \in S$ can compute every $k_j = f_j(H(x_i, z_j))$ where $U_j \notin S$. Thus, we have

$$k_S = f_S(x_i) = \sum_{U_j \in \overline{S}} f_j(H(x_i, z_j)) = \sum_{U_j \in \overline{S}} k_j.$$

For each member $U_i \in \overline{S}$, she can only obtain

$$k_i' = f_i(H(x_i, z_i)) + \sum_{U_j \in \overline{S} \setminus \{U_i\}} f_j(H(x_i, z_j)) = f_i(H(x_i, z_i)) + \sum_{U_j \in \overline{S} \setminus \{U_i\}} k_j.$$

Since $f_i(H(x_i, z_i)) \ne k_i$, each member $U_i \in \overline{S}$ gets a different random value k_i'.   □

It is easy to see that our first scheme provides a solution to the former two problems that discussed in Section 2.2. To put it simply, the Dealer selects $n + 1$ polynomials and publishes $n + 1$ vectors and random integers among the group. Thus, when some member is leaving or some subgroup would like to communicate internally, the new session key can be computed locally by adding the corresponding function evaluations, i.e., they can be calculated without contacting the Dealer and any help from other members.

3.2   Intergroup Key Distribution

Regarding the third problem that discussed in Section 2.2, we present an intergroup key distribution scheme. We assume that the Dealer is responsible for key distribution for many groups. On the high level, the ElGamal asymmetric cryptographic scheme is used to ensure the confidentiality when external staffs (in some other group) communicating with the group members. That is, by publishing one public key for each group, the external staffs can use the ElGamal encryption scheme to securely communicate with the internal members. In this way, the efficiency is greatly improved when compared with Zou, Dai and Bertino's original scheme [31].

The Dealer randomly picks a large prime q such that $q - 1$ has a large prime factor, then chooses a primitive root g. The following description is based on the subgroup key distribution scheme.

- For each random value k_i ($0 \le i \le n$) that chosen in the subgroup key distribution scheme, the Dealer computes $y_i = g^{k_i} \bmod q$. The Dealer publishes $\{q, g, y_0, \cdots, y_n\}$ as the public key, by which the external staffs (in other groups) can securely communicate with the group members.

- When some external staff wants to send a message M $(0 \leq M \leq q-1)$ to all the group members, he picks a random integer $r \in_R [0, q-1]$ and computes

$$R = y_0{}^r \bmod q, \quad C_1 = g^r \bmod q \text{ and } C_2 = RM \bmod q.$$

At last, the external staff sends the ciphertext (C_1, C_2) to the group members. When received the ciphertext (C_1, C_2), the group members can compute

$$R = C_1{}^{k_0} \bmod q \text{ and } M = C_2 R^{-1} \bmod q,$$

then get the message M.

- When some external staff wants to send a message M $(0 \leq M \leq q-1)$ to some subgroup $S \subset \mathcal{U}$, he picks a random integer $r \in_R [0, q-1]$ and computes

$$R = \left(\prod_{U_j \in \overline{S}} y_j \right)^r \bmod q, \quad C_1 = g^r \bmod q \text{ and } C_2 = RM \bmod q.$$

At last, the external staff sends the ciphertext (C_1, C_2) to the group members. When received the ciphertext (C_1, C_2), each group member in S can compute

$$R = C_1{}^{k_S} \bmod q \text{ and } M = C_2 R^{-1} \bmod q,$$

then get the message M.

Theorem 2. *The above proposed intergroup key distribution scheme is correct.*

Proof. The correctness with regard to the secure communication between the external staffs and all the group members is straightforward. We then focus on the correctness when some external staff communicating with a subgroup.
Since

$$R = \left(\prod_{U_j \in \overline{S}} y_j \right)^r \bmod q = \left(g^{\sum_{U_j \in \overline{S}} k_j} \right)^r \bmod q = g^{r k_S} \bmod q = C_1{}^{k_S} \bmod q,$$

thus $M = C_2 R^{-1} \bmod q$ follows.   □

3.3   Security Analysis

We now analyze the security of our basic scheme. Since all the polynomials are independent, we can discuss the security for just one of them. On one hand, we consider the key space and the brute-force attacks. For any random integer $k \in_R [0, q-1]$, by the brute-force attacks, the attacker can guess either the session key k directly or the users' private keys x_i, or $H(x_i, z)$, so that he can compute the session key from one of them. For a group with n members, there is one k and n pairs of x_i and $H(x_i, z)$, i.e., the guessing space is $2n + 1$, and the guess probability to hit k is $(2n + 1)/q$. It is easy to see, the more members in the polynomial, the higher the probability of the success of the brute-force attacks. But for a fixed group, we can select a large prime q randomly, in this way, the brute-force attacks will be impossible.

On the other hand, we consider the internal attacks. Regarding the subgroup key distribution scheme, if some group member wants to participant in a communication that does not include him, then he should guess a private key of some others or the session key directly. As we discussed, he can only succeed with negligible probability. Furthermore, even though the attacker obtains some $H(x_i, z)$, he cannot get the private key x_i due to one-way property of hash function H.

From those analyses, we can conclude that our schemes are secure against both external and internal attacks.

3.4   Complexity Analysis and Comparison

In this section, we briefly analyze the storage complexity and the computation complexity of our subgroup key distribution scheme, and compare them with that of [31] as shown in Table 1.

Consider a group consists of n members and every subgroup can make secure communication. For our subgroup key distribution scheme, the Dealer constructs $n + 1$ random polynomials. Thus, each group member stores his own private key and $n + 1$ coefficient vectors and $n + 1$ z_i-es, i.e., the storage complexity in both sides of the Dealer and the member is $O(n^2)$. While in the scheme of [31], there are $2^n - n - 1$ polynomials in total, and the storage complexity is $O(2^n n^2)$. Our scheme consumes much less storage spaces.

We then consider the computation complexity. In the Dealer side, for constructing each polynomial, he should compute n or $n - 1$ hash evaluations which are independent from other parts, and $n - 1$ or $n - 2$ multiplications over F_q. In detail, they take $O(nH)$ and $O(n^2)$ computation costs, respectively, i.e., the total computation complexity of one polynomial is $O(n^2)$. In total, the Dealer's computation complexity of $n + 1$ polynomials is $O(n^3)$, while it should be $O(n^2 2^n)$ in [31].

For the computation complexity for the group members, the main time-consuming computations in both our scheme and that of [31] are $H(x_i, z) \bmod q$, $H(x_i, z)^2 \bmod q, \cdots, H(x_i, z)^n \bmod q$. Then the total computation complexity of our scheme is $O(n^2)$, while it is $O(n)$ in [31].

4   Extensions for Multipartite Groups

It is easy to see that, if the group consists of too many members, then both our basic schemes and that of [31] are not efficient enough. Thus, we proceed to consider a case with regard to multipartite groups, i.e., the whole group can be logically divided into little disjoint subgroups, that is, $\mathcal{U} = \mathcal{U}_1 \cup \cdots \cup \mathcal{U}_t$ and $\mathcal{U}_i \cap \mathcal{U}_j = \varnothing$ if $i \neq j$ and $i, j \in [1, t]$, and each subgroup would join or leave the system unitedly. Instead of generating a random polynomial for each participant,

Table 1. Comparison of Storage and Computation Complexities

Schemes		Storage Complexity	Computation Complexity
[31]	Dealer	$O(2^n n^2)$	$O(2^n n^2)$
	Users	$O(2^n n^2)$	$O(n)$
Ours	Dealer	$O(n^2)$	$O(n^3)$
	Users	$O(n^2)$	$O(n^2)$

the Dealer only generates a polynomial for each of such subgroup. In this way, the storage spaces, the computation costs and the communication overheads can be significantly reduced.

4.1   Subgroup Key Distribution for Multipartite Groups

Suppose q be a large prime and $H : \{0,1\}^* \to F_q$ be a collision-resistant hash function. There is a trusted Dealer who deals with key agreement and distribution for the group members $\mathcal{U} = \{U_1, \cdots, U_n\}$. Each subgroup $\mathcal{U}_i$ has been given a private key u_i which is shared by its members and distributed by the Dealer in advance. We also assume that the subgroup $\mathcal{U}_i$ would leave the group separately and unitedly, and would not make any cooperations once they are left.

- The Dealer selects $t+1$ polynomials and $t+1$ random integers as follows, of which $f_0(x)$ contains all the subgroups' private keys $\{u_i : 1 \le i \le t\}$, while $f_i(x)$ excludes the subgroup $\mathcal{U}_i$'s private key u_i. Specifically, k_0 is chosen as the session key for the whole group $\mathcal{U}$.

$$f_0(x) = \prod_{i=1}^{t} (x - H(u_i, z_0)) + k_0$$

$$f_i(x) = \prod_{j=1, j \ne i}^{t} (x - H(u_j, z_i)) + k_i \text{ for every } 1 \le i \le t$$

- The Dealer rewrites all the polynomials and publishes all the corresponding coefficient vectors $\{(a_{i,0}, \cdots, a_{i,t}) : 0 \le i \le t\}$ and the random integers $\{z_i : 0 \le i \le t\}$ to group members.
- For secure communication with regard to the whole group, each member $U_j \in \mathcal{U}_i$ can recover the session key by computing $k_0 = f_0(H(u_i, z_0))$ without interacting with others.
- For secure communication between many subgroups $\mathcal{S} \subset \{\mathcal{U}_1, \cdots, \mathcal{U}_t\}$, each member $U_i \in \mathcal{S}$ first computes the polynomial

$$f_\mathcal{S}(x) = \sum_{\mathcal{U}_j \in \overline{\mathcal{S}}} f_j(x),$$

where $\overline{\mathcal{S}} = \{\mathcal{U}_1, \cdots, \mathcal{U}_t\} \setminus \mathcal{S}$. Then, calculates the session key as

$$k_\mathcal{S} = f_\mathcal{S}(u_i) = \sum_{\mathcal{U}_j \in \overline{\mathcal{S}}} k_j.$$

Thus, the session key for secure communication between many subgroups is also recovered without any interaction with others.

Theorem 3. *The above proposed subgroup key distribution scheme for multipartite groups is correct.*

The proof is omitted due to its similarity to that of Theorem 1.

4.2 Intergroup Key Distribution for Multipartite Groups

The Dealer randomly picks a large prime q such that $q-1$ has a large prime factor, then chooses a primitive root g. The following description is based on the subgroup key distribution scheme for multipartite groups.

- For each random value k_i $(0 \leq i \leq t)$ that chosen in the subgroup key distribution scheme, the Dealer compute $y_i = g^{k_i} \bmod q$. The Dealer publishes $\{q, g, y_0, \cdots, y_t\}$ as the public key, by which the external staffs (in other groups) can securely communicate with the group members.
- When some external staff wants to send a message M $(0 \leq M \leq q-1)$ to all the group members, he picks a random integer $r \in_R [0, q-1]$ and computes

$$R = y_0{}^r \bmod q, \quad C_1 = g^r \bmod q \text{ and } C_2 = RM \bmod q.$$

At last, the external staff sends the ciphertext (C_1, C_2) to the group members. When received the ciphertext (C_1, C_2), the group members can compute

$$R = C_1{}^{k_0} \bmod q \text{ and } M = C_2 R^{-1} \bmod q,$$

then get the message M.

- When some external staff wants to send a message M $(0 \leq M \leq q-1)$ to many subgroups $S \subset \{\mathcal{U}_1, \cdots, \mathcal{U}_t\}$, he picks a random integer $r \in_R [0, q-1]$ and computes

$$R = \left(\prod_{\mathcal{U}_j \in \overline{S}} y_j \right)^r \bmod q, \quad C_1 = g^r \bmod q \text{ and } C_2 = RM \bmod q.$$

At last, the external staff sends the ciphertext (C_1, C_2) to the group members. When received the ciphertext (C_1, C_2), each group member in S can compute

$$R = C_1{}^{ks} \bmod q \text{ and } M = C_2 R^{-1} \bmod q,$$

then get the message M.

Theorem 4. *The above proposed intergroup key distribution scheme for multipartite group is correct.*

The proof is omitted due to its similarity to that of Theorem 2.

4.3   Discussions

As analyzed in Section 3.4, the storage and computation complexities of our extended subgroup key distribution scheme for multipartite groups are only dependent upon the subgroup number t. Thus, compared with our basic scheme, the storage complexity is reduced from $O(n^2)$ to $O(t^2)$ in both sides of the Dealer and users. Besides, the computation complexity for the Dealer is reduced from $O(n^3)$ to $O(t^3)$, and for the user side, it is from $O(n^2)$ to $O(t^2)$. Since t can be much less than n, the efficiency is greatly improved in our extensions.

For example, suppose there is a group $\mathcal{U}$ with 1000 participants. Implemented by our basic scheme, the Dealer will generate 1001 polynomials with degree 1000 or 999. However, if the group $\mathcal{U}$ can be logically partitioned into 100 subgroups such that each subgroup consists of 10 members, then only generate 101 polynomials with degree 100 or 99 should be generated and published.

5   Conclusion

We proposed two efficient group key distribution schemes which can be applied to the *ad hoc* networks. The first one extends the regular functionality of existing group key distribution, which also distributes a secret session key for each subgroup, thus, everyone in a subgroup can share a session key independently. Therefore, the whole scheme not only satisfies the requirement of efficiency and security for the group key distribution, but also can guarantee the security of communication among subgroups and the security of the communication under the circumstance that the members of the group may leave at any time but the Dealer is unavailable again. Thus, it is very suitable for some relatively separate networks which have limited computing capacity and cannot communicate with the outside world. The second one is designed based on the ElGamal asymmetric key scheme, which allows members in the group to communicate with external people securely. Thus, when secure communication should be carried out with external people, the second extended scheme can be used, which only incurs several additional public values. In addition, those schemes are further extended to support key distribution for multipartite groups. By computation and storage complexities analyses, our schemes are more efficient than the existing scheme.

Note that as most existing schemes, in our schemes, the functionality of allowing the new members to join the system is not as efficient as supporting dynamic leaving, thus, we leave it as an open problem on how to improve those efficiency.

Acknowledgments and Disclaimer. We appreciate the anonymous reviewers for their valuable suggestions. Dr. Bo Qin is the corresponding author. This paper was supported by the Natural Science Foundation of China through projects 61370190, 61173154, 61003214, 60970116, 61272501, 61321064 and 61202465, the National Key Basic Research Program (973 program) under project 2012CB315905, the Beijing Natural Science Foundation under projects 4132056 and 4122041, the Shanghai NSF under Grant No. 12ZR1443500, the Shanghai

Chen Guang Program (12CG24), the Science and Technology Commission of Shanghai Municipality under grant 13JC1403500, the Fundamental Research Funds for the Central Universities, and the Research Funds(No. 14XNLF02) of Renmin University of China, the Open Research Fund of The Academy of Satellite Application and the Open Research Fund of Beijing Key Laboratory of Trusted Computing.

References

1. Abdalla, M., Shavitt, Y., Wool, A.: Key management for restricted multicast using broadcast encryption. IEEE/ACM Transactions on Networking 8(4), 443–454 (2000)
2. Blundo, C., Mattos, L.A.F., Stinson, D.R.: Generalized Beimel-Chor schemes for broadcast encryption and interactive key distribution. Theoretical Computer Science 200(1-2), 313–334 (1998)
3. Boneh, D., Gentry, C., Waters, B.: Collusion Resistant Broadcast Encryption with Short Ciphertexts and Private Keys. In: Shoup, V. (ed.) CRYPTO 2005. LNCS, vol. 3621, pp. 258–275. Springer, Heidelberg (2005)
4. Burmester, M., Desmedt, Y.: A Secure and Efficient Conference Key Distribution System. In: De Santis, A. (ed.) EUROCRYPT 1994. LNCS, vol. 950, pp. 275–286. Springer, Heidelberg (1995)
5. Cheon, J.H., Jho, N.S., Kim, M.H., Yoo, E.S.: Skipping, Cascade, and Combined Chain Schemes for Broadcast Encryption. IEEE Transactions on Information Theory 54(11), 5155–5171 (2008)
6. Dutta, R., Barua, R.: Provably Secure Constant Round Contributory Group Key Agreement in Dynamic Setting. IEEE Transactions on Information Theory 54(5), 2007–2025 (2008)
7. Fiat, A., Naor, M.: Broadcast encryption. In: Stinson, D.R. (ed.) CRYPTO 1993. LNCS, vol. 773, pp. 480–491. Springer, Heidelberg (1994)
8. Gentry, C., Waters, B.: Adaptive Security in Broadcast Encryption Systems (with Short Ciphertexts). In: Joux, A. (ed.) EUROCRYPT 2009. LNCS, vol. 5479, pp. 171–188. Springer, Heidelberg (2009)
9. Halevy, D., Shamir, A.: The LSD Broadcast Encryption Scheme. In: Yung, M. (ed.) CRYPTO 2002. LNCS, vol. 2442, pp. 47–60. Springer, Heidelberg (2002)
10. Ingemarsson, I., Tang, D., Wong, C.K.: A conference key distribution system. IEEE Transactions on Information Theory 28(5), 714–720 (1982)
11. Kim, Y., Perrig, A., Tsudik, G.: Tree-based Group Key Agreement. ACM Trans. Inf. Syst. Secur. 7(1), 60–96 (2004)
12. Kogan, N., Shavitt, Y., Wool, A.: A Practical Revocation Scheme for Broadcast Encryption Using Smartcards. ACM Transactions on Information and System Security (TISSEC) 9(3), 325–351 (2006)
13. Mao, Y., Sun, Y., Wu, M., Liu, K.J.R.: JET: Dynamic Join-exit-tree Amortization and Scheduling for Contributory Key Management. IEEE/ACM Trans. Netw. 14(5), 1128–1140 (2006)
14. Naor, M., Pinkas, B.: Efficient Trace and Revoke Schemes. In: Frankel, Y. (ed.) FC 2000. LNCS, vol. 1962, pp. 1–20. Springer, Heidelberg (2001)
15. Park, J.H., Kim, H.J., Sung, M.H., Lee, D.H.: Public Key Broadcast Encryption Schemes With Shorter Transmissions. IEEE Transactions on Broadcasting 54(3), 401–411 (2008)

16. Sherman, A.T., McGrew, D.A.: Key Establishment in Large Dynamic Groups Using One-way Function Trees. IEEE Transactions on Software Engineering 29(5), 444–458 (2003)
17. Snoeyink, J., Suri, S., Varghese, G.: A lower bound for multicast key distribution. In: INFOCOM 2001, vol. 1, pp. 422–431. IEEE (2001)
18. Steiner, M., Tsudik, G., Waidner, M.: Key Agreement in Dynamic Peer Groups. IEEE Transactions on Parallel and Distributed Systems 11(8), 769–780 (2000)
19. Waldvogel, M., Caronni, G., Sun, D., Weiler, N., Plattner, B.: The VersaKey Framework: Versatile Group Key Management. IEEE Journal on Selected Areas in Communications 17(9), 1614–1631 (1999)
20. Wong, C.K., Gouda, M., Lam, S.S.: Secure group communications using key graphs. IEEE/ACM Transactions on Networking 8(1), 16–30 (2000)
21. Wool, A.: Key Management for Encrypted Broadcast. ACM Transactions on Information and System Security (TISSEC) 3(2), 107–134 (2000)
22. Wu, Q., Mu, Y., Susilo, W., Qin, B., Domingo-Ferrer, J.: Asymmetric Group Key Agreement. In: Joux, A. (ed.) EUROCRYPT 2009. LNCS, vol. 5479, pp. 153–170. Springer, Heidelberg (2009)
23. Wu, Q., Qin, B., Zhang, L., Domingo-Ferrer, J., Manjón, J.A.: Fast transmission to remote cooperative groups: A new key management paradigm. IEEE/ACM Transactions on Networking 21(2), 621–633 (2013)
24. Wu, Q., Qin, B., Zhang, L., Domingo-Ferrer, J., Farràs, O.: Bridging Broadcast Encryption and Group Key Agreement. In: Lee, D.H., Wang, X. (eds.) ASIACRYPT 2011. LNCS, vol. 7073, pp. 143–160. Springer, Heidelberg (2011)
25. Yu, W., Sun, Y., Liu, K.: Optimizing Rekeying Cost for Contributory Group Key Agreement Schemes. IEEE Transactions on Dependable and Secure Computing 4(3), 228–242 (2007)
26. Zhang, L., Wu, Q., Qin, B.: Authenticated Asymmetric Group Key Agreement Protocol and Its Application. In: 2010 IEEE International Conference on Communications (ICC), pp. 1–5 (2010)
27. Zhang, L., Wu, Q., Qin, B., Deng, H., Liu, J., Shi, W.: Provably Secure Certificateless Authenticated Asymmetric Group Key Agreement. In: Huang, X., Zhou, J. (eds.) ISPEC 2014. LNCS, vol. 8434, pp. 496–510. Springer, Heidelberg (2014)
28. Zhang, L., Wu, Q., Qin, B., Domingo-Ferrer, J.: Identity-Based Authenticated Asymmetric Group Key Agreement Protocol. In: Thai, M.T., Sahni, S. (eds.) COCOON 2010. LNCS, vol. 6196, pp. 510–519. Springer, Heidelberg (2010)
29. Zhang, L., Wu, Q., Qin, B., Domingo-Ferrer, J.: Provably secure one-round identity-based authenticated asymmetric group key agreement protocol. Information Sciences 181(19), 4318–4329 (2011)
30. Zhang, L., Wu, Q., Qin, B., Domingo-Ferrer, J., González-Nicolás, Ú.: Asymmetric group key agreement protocol for open networks and its application to broadcast encryption. Computer Networks 55(15), 3246–3255 (2011)
31. Zou, X., Dai, Y.S., Bertino, E.: A Practical and Flexible Key Management Mechanism for Trusted Collaborative Computing. In: The 27th Conference on Computer Communications, INFOCOM 2008, pp. 1211–1219. IEEE (2008)

A Novel Hybrid Key Revocation Scheme
for Wireless Sensor Networks

Mengmeng Ge[1] and Kim-Kwang Raymond Choo[2]

[1] University of Bristol, Woodland Road, Bristol, UK
gemengmeng.2011@my.bristol.ac.uk
[2] University of South Australia, GPO Box 2471, Adelaide, Australia
Raymond.Choo@unisa.edu.au

Abstract. As sensor nodes are deployed in an open and hostile environment, they are vulnerable to various attacks. It is of critical importance to be able to revoke compromised nodes in order to ensure the confidentiality of data traversing in the network. In this work, we propose a novel key revocation scheme which is a hybrid of centralized and distributed methods. The design of our scheme is based on Chan et al. (2005) but eliminates the requirement of prior knowledge. It mainly consists of a voting procedure among nodes and a global revocation by the base station. We also modify existing distributed revocation properties in Chan et al. (2005)'s protocol and extend them to key revocation properties of any hybrid schemes based on the voting process.

Keywords: wireless sensor networks, key revocation, secret sharing.

1 Introduction

Due to constrained computational resources and the fully distributed nature of wireless sensor networks, ensuring the security of wireless sensor networks is a constant challenge for both researchers and network designers [13,14]. One particular challenge is key management in wireless sensor networks. Unlike traditional wired networks, public key cryptography and trusted sever methods are not suitable because of the high computational overhead and the lack of a trusted infrastructure. Key pre-distribution schemes are generally regarded as the most effective key management schemes and have been extensively studied in the literature. However, several open problems remain, especially in the area of key revocation. Despite the importance of key revocation protocols, they receive much less attention than key distribution or establishment protocols (see [1,4,5]). Sensor nodes deployed in an open and hostile environment can be compromised by an adversary, and it is critical that sensor networks should have the ability to revoke secret keys of compromised nodes as quickly as possible to prevent the adversary taking control of the network.

Generally speaking, existing revocation schemes can be categorized into three classes (based on the involvement of central authority and sensor nodes), namely: centralized, distributed and hybrid. The centralized key revocation requires a

M.H. Au et al. (Eds.): NSS 2014, LNCS 8792, pp. 462–475, 2014.
© Springer International Publishing Switzerland 2014

central authority to detect and revoke compromised nodes. The risk is a single point of failure. The distributed method involves node collaboration in the revocation process. This improves reaction time but results in a more complex network design. In hybrid schemes, centralized and distributed methods are combined to increase revocation efficiency and accuracy. This is the basis of our proposed scheme in this paper. Hybrid scheme requires node co-operation on the voting procedure. Using the distributed method in our proposed scheme results in improved response time in the neighborhood and the centralized method realizes complete revocation in the entire network.

It should be noted that there are two known issues in several previously published distributed revocation schemes, such as the work presented by Chan et al. [2] and Chao et al. [3]. Firstly, each node is required to pre-load votes against all participants. Then the network topology needs to be known or broadcast to all participants before the deployment. However, this is not always possible for many applications. Secondly, only participants of the compromised node are notified of the revocation, and other nodes in the network will not be aware of the revocation. If a path-key between two nodes is established through a compromised node, packets through that node can be eavesdropped or even selectively dropped. More concerning, the revoked node can be re-inserted in other parts of the network via a colluding node [21]. In this paper, we modify Chan et al.'s [2] protocol in order to address the two above-mentioned issues. Our scheme uses autonomous generation and distribution of secret shares by sensor nodes to eliminate prior knowledge constraint, and a base station is used to realize complete revocation in the network. We demonstrate that our modified scheme is more efficient than Chan et al.'s protocol [2] in terms of space requirement, computational complexity and communication load.

The rest of the paper is organized as follows. In the next two sections, we describe several published revocation protocols for wireless sensor networks and the background materials. Our proposed revocation scheme, its security and performance are discussed in sections 4, 5 and 6 respectively. The last section concludes the paper.

2 Related Work

The centralized key revocation scheme was first presented by Eschenauer and Gligor [10]. In their scheme, the controller node broadcasts a revocation message in the network. To encrypt the message, it also unicasts a unique signature key to each node. Wang et al. [11] subsequently proposed another centralized scheme which uses session key distribution to update keys, thus excluding compromised nodes from the network. It is more efficient than the method of Eschenauer and Gligor since it only needs a single broadcast. In order to enhance the security of Wang et al.'s scheme, dynamic sessions were introduced by Park et al. [12]. The base station distributes a new session key when a compromised node is detected, thus minimizing any potential damages due to the compromised node.

Unfortunately, existing centralized revocation schemes may face the single point of failure. In order to avoid this problem and improve reaction time, Chan et al. presented the first distributed revocation scheme in [15] and extended it in [2]. They designed a voting procedure to revoke a compromised node and provided a precise definition of distributed revocation properties. Then Chao et al. [3] described a novel distributed revocation scheme based on Chan et al.'s scheme. They used Blom's matrix concepts [18] to achieve better performance in terms of space requirement, computational complexity and communication load. Their scheme also satisfies five distributed revocation properties.

Sanchez and Baldus [20] presented a hybrid revocation scheme for mobile sensor networks which are a subset of wireless sensor networks. They used local key revocation in a mobile sensor network, and global key revocation and replacement between other mobile sensor networks. Since their underlying key pre-distribution schemes are pool-based, the update of the key pool is also required to avoid key pool depletion. Jiang et al. [16] proposed yet another hybrid revocation scheme based on the key establishment in [6]. For intra-cluster, nodes vote against the compromised node and the cluster head broadcasts a revocation message when revocation is verified. For inter-cluster, if a cluster head is compromised, keys stored in the head are updated. This scheme has faster reaction time, less space storage and communication overhead. Chattopadhyay and Turuk [9] described an improved hybrid scheme based on Chan et al.'s scheme [2]. By utilizing hexagonal regions in the construction of the network model, they designed a voting process based on trivariate polynomials and introduced the concept of monitor nodes. This scheme eliminates the simplifying assumption of prior knowledge in Chan et al.'s scheme and also increases the security resilience.

3   Background

3.1   Definitions and Assumptions

The definition of terms used in our scheme is as follows:

1. Neighborhood refers to the communication range of a node.
2. Voting members are nodes that establish pairwise keys with another node, and the former is known as the voting members of the latter node.
3. Local voting members are nodes that establish a direct-keyed link with another node, and all local voting members are in the neighborhood of the latter node.
4. Local broadcast refers to the broadcast in the neighborhood of one node. Each local broadcast takes no more than Δl time to fully propagate in the entire neighborhood.

Generally, the revocation process is performed based on the following assumptions.

- *Assumption 1*: Nodes are immobile.
- *Assumption 2*: Similar to an intrusion detection system, the detection system has low rates of false positive and false negative. Therefore, if a compromised node is discovered by a neighboring node, it can also be discovered by other nodes in the same neighborhood.

- *Assumption 3*: Broadcast authentication schemes, such as μTESLA scheme in [8], should be utilized to ensure the security of broadcast messages from the base station.
- *Assumption 4*: The underlying key pre-distribution scheme is the random-pairwise key scheme presented by Chan et al. [2], any hybrid scheme of random key pre-distribution and λ-secure key establishment schemes, such as Liu and Ning [17] or any key pre-distribution scheme that provides deterministic node-to-node authentication.
- *Assumption 5*: The base station distributes a secret key to each sensor node, which is used to authenticate communications between the node and the base station.
- *Assumption 6*: The functionality to defense against Sybil attacks already exists in the revocation scheme, such as [19].
- *Assumption 7*: If the degree of a node is less than the number d_{min}, it will be discovered and centrally revoked by the base station [2].
- *Assumption 8*: The revocation process in our proposed scheme is conducted among m non-compromised nodes.

Table 1 describes the notations used in our scheme.

Table 1. Notations used in the scheme

Notation	Description
n	Number of sensor nodes in the network.
m	Number of nodes that can establish pairwise keys with one node.
t	Threshold number of votes against a compromised node.
Δl	Maximum time for a local broadcast to fully disseminate.
Δn	Maximum time for a network-wide broadcast to fully disseminate $(\Delta n > \Delta l)$.
Δs	Duration of a single revocation session in which the node is in an active state $(\Delta s > 2\Delta l)$.
Δr	Maximum time for a single revocation procedure, from the cast of the first vote to the complete revocation of the node from the network.
Δi	Maximum time for any node to send a message to the base station.
Δp	Maximum time for any node to restart path-key establishment with another node.
d_{max}	Maximum number of nodes that can establish a direct-keyed link with one node $(d_{max} \ll m)$.
d_{min}	Minimum number of a node's degree at which a node with a lower d_{min} is revoked by the base station $(d_{min} > t)$.
$H(x)$	Cryptographic hash of a value x.
$E_k(M)$	Message encrypted by key k using authenticated-encryption mode.

3.2   The Adversarial Model

We now describe the five properties of the adversarial model.

- *Property 1*: The adversary is able to select and capture a small number of nodes in the network.
- *Property 2*: When a node is compromised by an adversary, all data stored on this node is revealed to the adversary.
- *Property 3*: Compromised nodes have the ability to drop packets selectively and collude with each other by exchanging information.
- *Property 4*: The adversary will not be able to delay or jam neighborhood-wide or network-wide communications where both source and destination nodes are not compromised, since there is a sufficient number of legitimate nodes to forward packets.
- *Property 5*: Random node captures do not influence the connectivity of the whole network.

4   Proposed Revocation Scheme

Our proposed scheme has four phases, namely: initialization, connection establishment, process of session revocation, and completion of revocation.

4.1   Initialization

We assume the base station assigns a randomly chosen and unique ID for each node i before deployment, denoted as ID_i. Each ID has the same size len_{id}. There are two ways to distribute information required by the key revocation. For the off-line initialization, our scheme pre-loads some secrets for each node. Based on Shamir's threshold algorithm [7], the base station generates a $(t-1)$-degree polynomial for each node. Therefore each node i owns a secret S_i.

$$f(x) = S_i + a_1 x + a_1 x^2 + ... + a_{t-1} x^{t-1} \qquad (1)$$

Each node stores its unique polynomial (see Equation (1)) and $Hash(S_i)$ in their memory. Each node i is also assigned a mask, $Mask_i$, to be used with other nodes to encrypt and/or decrypt the vote against it. This results in a relatively small memory consumption in sensor nodes, but it does not incur any communication overhead. For the online initialization, the base station needs to unicast the polynomial, hashed secret and mask to each node, which will significantly increase the communication load particularly when the number of sensor nodes in the network increases. Thus, we decide to adopt the off-line initialization phase in our scheme.

4.2   Connection Establishment

After the key establishment phase, we assume that each node stores two lists of keys indexed by the node's ID. For each node i, these two lists include information about the partner nodes (i.e. nodes that share a pairwise key with node i). The first list is a local link list, which records information about nodes that have established a one-hop encrypted link with the node i. The pair in node i's local link list is denoted as $< ID_j, K_{ij} >$. The second (and final) list is a path-key list. If node i shares a path-key with node j, it records a list of $< ID_j, K_{ij}, ID_{N_1}, ID_{N_2}, ..., ID_{N_k} >$ where $ID_{N_1}, ID_{N_2}, ..., ID_{N_k}$ denote the IDs of intermediate nodes. Each node has the ability to check the record of the path-key list to determine whether a compromised node is an intermediary. We also assume that each node has a revocation list, which is empty initially. When a node is compromised, other nodes will add this node's information to the list to prevent re-insertion.

For the connection establishment, if two nodes share pairwise keys after the key establishment phase, they are voting members for each other. Our proposed scheme has an additional vote generation phase (compared to Chan et al.'s scheme). For each node i, it computes m secret shares for the m voting members. Here we assume the generated shares have the same size of secret S_i, denoted as len_s. The IDs of the voting members are used as inputs in the unique polynomial, which outputs S_{ij} for each member j. Node i then sends $S_{ij}, Mask_i$ and $Hash(S_i)$ (which are encrypted by its pairwise key with node j and unicast) to all members in the network. Upon receiving node i's message, node j decrypts the message with the correct pairwise key and stores the secret share, hash value and mask in its memory, presented as $< ID_i, S_{ij}, Mask_i, Hash(S_i) >$. As a result, each node only has the ability to vote against partner nodes (i.e. nodes that it has established pairwise keys with). If a node repeatedly refuses to send masks and secret shares to other nodes, it will be regarded as a malicious node since it wants the number of votes against it lower than the threshold t. Consequently, other nodes will drop links with this particular node after several (failed) attempts. Therefore, the malicious node with a low degree will be discovered and revoked by the base station [2].

4.3   Process of Session Revocation

In the process of session revocation, each node has two states. For node i, it maintains a waiting state at the beginning of the current session s. When it detects a compromised node a or receives the first vote against node a, it changes its state to active and immediately starts the timer for the session revocation. The duration of the timer is predetermined. At the same time, node i broadcasts the vote against the compromised node while continuing to receive, verify and record the votes until the time expires. Upon expiry, the node i terminates the current session and goes into the waiting state of the next session $s + 1$.

Figure 1 outlines the procedure of a session revocation.

We now present the voting procedure. When the node i discovers the malicious behavior of node a, it encrypts the ID, ID_i, and secret share given by a, S_{ai},

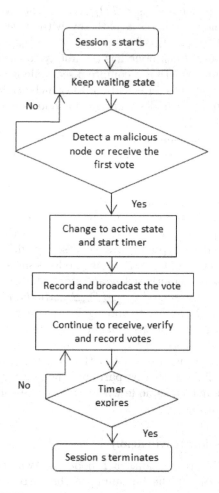

Fig. 1. The process of session revocation

under $Mask_a$ and broadcasts this message. It broadcasts the vote in both the current and next sessions, which ensures the vote cast near the expiry time of the current session will be fully disseminated to local voting members and counted by them in the next session. When a node j receives a vote, it decrypts the message by using the correct mask. It then stores the pair of ID_i and S_{ai}, and re-broadcasts the message. If a node receives the message but cannot decrypt it, it drops it. To avoid Denial of Service (DoS) attacks, only voting members re-broadcast the vote.

4.4   Completion of Revocation

When the timer of node i expires, each voting member terminates the current session and calculates the number of stored shares. If the number reaches threshold t, it can compute the secret S_a by using at least t pairs of IDs and corresponding shares. Then the node compares the hash value of the result with $Hash(S_a)$ in its memory. If they are not equal, the node clears all the pairs it has received. If they are equal, the revocation is verified. It cuts off links with node a by clearing the pair of node ID and key in its local link list, and adds this information to a revocation list. Then it broadcasts S_a encrypted by $Mask_a$. At the same time, it informs the base station of the revocation information and encrypts S_a using the secret key shared with the base station, prior to clearing all session-related information. Figure 2 outlines the process of revocation completion for a local voting member.

Once the message is received by non-local voting members, the message will be decrypted and the hash of S_a will be compared against $Hash(S_a)$ stored in the memory of the non-local voting members. If the verification returns true (i.e. both values are equal), the non-local voting members will remove the associated pairwise key with a in their path-key lists and store the pair of node a and path-key in the revocation list. They will also re-broadcast this revocation message. Otherwise, they will ignore this message.

Once the base station receives the revocation messages, it will compute $Hash(S_a)$ and compare it against the stored value. If both values are equal, the base station will broadcast the revocation message of node a in the network, and consequently, all non-voting members will be notified of the revocation. The non-voting members will then add a's information in the revocation list, as well as checking their path-key list to determine whether node a is an intermediary. If a is found to be an intermediary, the path-key establishment phase will commence with the node in the path-key record.

5   Security Analysis

In this section, we evaluate the revocation scheme against schemes in [2] and [3] based on distributed revocation properties proposed in [2]. As the properties are designed to analyze distributed revocation schemes (rather than hybrid schemes), we make a slight modification of the bounded time in Chan et al.'s

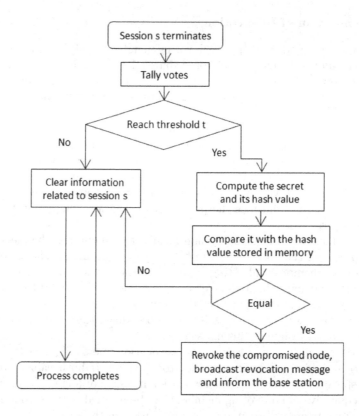

Fig. 2. The process of revocation completion

property 4 [2]. The below (modified) revocation properties can also be used to evaluate revocation schemes based on the voting procedure.

Property 1 (Completeness). If a compromised node is detected by t or more non-compromised neighboring nodes, then it is revoked from the entire network permanently (i.e. its subsequent re-insertion into another part of the network is not possible).

Proof. We assume that node a is captured by an adversary and node i is the first voting member of a to cast the vote in current session s. There are two scenarios which we need to consider. In general, we suppose the first vote is cast at time t_0 and node i's timer expires at time t_3.

In the first scenario, we also assume that at least $t - 1$ local voting members cast their votes before a time t_1. If $t_3 - t_1$ suffices for a maximum local broadcast time Δl, each of these members can propagate their votes to every local member based on assumption 4 of the adversarial model (see section 3.2). Then each local voting member can receive at least t votes against a in current session.

In the second scenario, we assume that $t - 2$ local voting members have cast their votes and another local voting member casts its vote at a time t_2. If $t_3 - t_2$ is less than Δl, node i may not receive the vote before its timer expires. Then less than t members can receive all t votes. However, in the proposed scheme, each node casts its vote in both the current session and the next session. At time t_3, node i starts the timer for session $s + 1$ and casts its vote. Other $t - 1$ voting members will also cast their votes immediately at their expiry time. We suppose all $t - 1$ voting members start the next session and cast their votes before time t_4. Since $\Delta s > 2\Delta l$, $t_4 - t_3$ is less than Δl. Therefore, when node i's timer for session $s + 1$ expires at time t_5, node i has sufficient time to receive all other $t - 1$ votes for $t_5 - t_4 > \Delta l$.

In both above scenarios, any node receiving at least t votes against a has the ability to compute the secret, verify it and revoke node a if the revocation is verified. Then they broadcast the revocation message to other voting members and inform the base station, and the latter will broadcast the revocation message to non-voting members in the network. In accordance with assumption 4 of the adversarial model, all broadcast can be received in bounded time. Therefore, all nodes in the network are notified of the revocation. Since each node records the information of the compromised node in a revocation list, node a cannot be re-inserted in other parts of the network and is removed permanently.

Property 2 (Soundness). If a node is revoked from the network, then at least t nodes must have agreed on its revocation.

Proof. To revoke a compromised node a, at least t pairs of node IDs and secret shares need to be tallied to calculate the secret S_a. Based on the property of Shamir's threshold scheme, any $t - 1$ or fewer shares cannot decide the exact value of the secret. Hence, the revocation does not take place.

Property 3 (Bounded Time Revocation Completion). Revocation decision and execution occur within a bounded time period (let this bound be Δr) from the time of sending the first revocation vote.

Proof. When the first vote is broadcast by node i, this node immediately starts the timer for the current revocation session. Then the maximum duration of the vote broadcast in the neighboring area is Δl. So the total time from the broadcast of the first vote until the expiry of all voting members' timers is equal to $(\Delta l + \Delta s)$. Since local voting members need to inform the base station of the revocation when the revocation is verified, the time takes at most Δb. According to assumption 4 of the adversarial model, the time required by the base station to fully disseminate revocation messages to the entire network is at most Δn. If the compromised node is another node's intermediary (as indicated in the path-key record), the particular node will need to restart the path-key establishment with the node in the path-key record. This takes at most Δp. Therefore, the bounded time Δr is at most $(\Delta l + \Delta s + \Delta b + \Delta n + \Delta p)$.

Property 4 (Unitary Revocation). Revocations of nodes are unitary (all-or-nothing). Specifically, if a node is revoked in one part of the network, then it will be revoked in the entire network within a bounded time (let this bound be Δd). If it is not revoked in one part of the network, then it will not be revoked in any part of the network in the time prior to the last Δd time period.

Proof. If a node is revoked in one part of the network, local voting members in that part can calculate the correct secret and then re-broadcast it in the neighborhood. Non-local members can verify the received revocation message. At the same time, local voting members also send the secret to the base station which takes Δb. Therefore, the time for the revocation broadcast sent by the base station to reach the entire network is at most Δn. Some nodes may need to restart the path-key establishment if the compromised node is an intermediary in the path of linking multi-hop nodes. Thus, all nodes in other parts of the network will be notified of the revocation and revoke the node within $(\Delta b + \Delta n + \Delta p)$.

For the converse statement, if a node is revoked in any part of the network before the last $(\Delta b + \Delta n + \Delta p)$ time period, it must be revoked from one part of the network. From the above proof, it easily follows that if a node is revoked in one part of the network, it will be revoked from the entire network and, therefore, it will be revoked in any specific part of the network.

Property 5 (Revocation Attack Resistance). If c nodes are compromised, then they can only revoke at most αc other nodes where α is a constant and $\alpha \ll \frac{m}{t}$.

Proof. If c nodes are compromised, they can get at most $c * d_{max}$ decrypted votes. Since nodes are static, at most $\frac{c * d_{max}}{t}$ non-compromised nodes are revoked. If $\alpha = \frac{d_{max}}{t}$, then $\alpha \ll \frac{m}{t}$ for $d_{max} \ll m$.

Schemes presented by Chan et al. [2] and Chao et al. [3] claim to satisfy the five distributed revocation properties. However, non-voting members are not aware of the revocation, thus violating the completeness property. In our scheme, the base station informs every sensor node of the revocation information. With the combination of the revocation list and intermediary checking, the compromised node will not be able to eavesdrop or re-join the network.

6   Performance Analysis

We now analyze the performance of our proposed scheme in three aspects, including its space requirement, communication overhead and computational complexity – see Table 2.

In our proposed scheme, in terms of

- storage space, each node is preloaded a polynomial. After the key establishment and connection establishment phases, the node stores pairwise key lists, secret shares, masks and hash values of its m voting members. In each revocation session, nodes also store t votes temporarily. So each node requires a storage space of $O(m \cdot t)$. Since the threshold value is a small constant compared with m, the storage requirement equals $O(m)$.
- communication overhead, nodes exchange masks, secret shares and hash values with their voting members in the connection establishment for vote verification. Thus the communication overhead associated with vote verification equals $O(m)$. In the voting process, each vote includes a pair of node ID and secret share. The communication overhead occurred is $O(1)$.
- vote generation, calculation and verification, each node needs to produce m secret shares based on its preloaded $(t-1)$-degree polynomial in the connection establishment process. So the complexity equals $O(m \cdot t)$. In vote calculation, each voting member receiving at least t votes is required to work out a $(t-1)$-degree polynomial to get the secret, which generates a computational complexity of $O(t \cdot t)$. During verification, each voting member operates hash function on the secret and compares it against a value stored in memory. Thus the complexity is only $O(1)$.

Table 2. Comparative summary of key revocation schemes

	[2]	[3]	Proposed Scheme
Space requirement	$O(s_{total} \cdot m \cdot \log m)$	$O(s_{total} \cdot m)$	$O(m)$
Communication overhead per vote broadcast	$O(\log m)$	$O(1)$	$O(1)$
Communication overhead per vote verification	$O(m)$	$O(m)$	$O(m)$
Computational complexity per vote generation	0	0	$O(m \cdot t)$
Computational complexity per vote calculation	$O(t \cdot t)$	$O(t \cdot t)$	$O(t \cdot t)$
Computational complexity per vote verification	$O(\log m)$	$O(1)$	$O(1)$

It is clear that our proposed scheme is more efficient than Chan et al.'s scheme [2] in terms of space requirement, computational complexity and communication load. As our scheme has less space storage requirement than Chao et al.'s scheme, it would be a more suitable candidate to be deployed on resource constrained devices. Moreover, as both Chan et al. and Chao et al.'s schemes require prior knowledge of deployment, they are impractical for deployment in many real-world applications. Our scheme avoids the limitation of vote pre-distribution by introducing a vote generation step in the connection establishment phase.

7   Conclusion

Key revocation protocols are an important component in ensuring the security of communications in wireless sensor networks. Research on effective and low cost revocation protocols will ensure the security of the entire network when nodes are compromised by a malicious adversary, as well as making efficient use of sensors' power in resource constrained environment.

We proposed a novel key revocation scheme, which eliminates the limitation of requiring prior knowledge before deployment. Our scheme satisfies the five essential security properties and achieves better performance in terms of space requirement, computational complexity and communication overhead.

Future research will include extending our research to distributed or hybrid revocation schemes for key-pool based pre-distribution protocols. Since key-pool based schemes lack node-to-node authentication and revoking many keys may deplete the key pool, it is a challenge to design accurate and efficient revocation protocols. Thus, it is not surprising that there are few, if any, published work on this topic.

References

1. Boyd, C., Mathuria, A.: Protocols for Authentication and Key Establishment. Information Security and Cryptography. Springer (2003)
2. Chan, H., Gligor, V.D., Perrig, A., Muralidharan, G.: On the Distribution and Revocation of Cryptographic Keys in Sensor Networks. IEEE Transactions on Dependable and Secure Computing 2(3), 233–247 (2005)
3. Chao, C.H., Yang, C.F., Lin, P.T., Li, J.S.: Novel Distributed Key Revocation Scheme for Wireless Sensor Networks. Security and Communication Networks 6(10), 1271–1280 (2013)
4. Choo, K.K.R.: Secure Key Establishment. Advances in Information Security, vol. 41. Springer (2009)
5. Choo, K.K.R., Boyd, C., Hitchcock, Y.: The Importance of Proofs of Security for Key Establishment Protocols: Formal Analysis of Jan-Chen, Yang-Shen-Shieh, Kim-Huh-Hwang-Lee, Lin-Sun-Hwang, and Yeh-Sun Protocols. Computer Communications 29(15), 2788–2797 (2006)
6. Jiang, Y., Shi, H.: A key Pre-distribution Scheme for Wireless Sensor Networks Using Hexagonal Deployment Knowledge. Chinese Journal of Electronics 17(3), 520–525 (2008)
7. Shamir, A.: How to share a secret. Commun. ACM 22(11), 612–613 (1979)
8. Liu, D., Ning, P.: Multi-level μTESLA: Broadcast authentication for distributed sensor networks. Trans. on Embedded Computing Sys. 3(4), 800–836 (2004)

9. Chattopadhyay, S., Turuk, A.K.: A Scheme for Key Revocation in Wireless Sensor Networks. International Journal on Advanced Computer Engineering and Communication Technology 1(2), 16–20 (2012)

10. Eschenauer, L., Gligor, V.D.: A Key-Management Scheme for Distributed Sensor Networks. In: ACM Conference on Computer and Communication Security, pp. 41–47 (2002)

11. Wang, Y., Ramamurthy, B., Zou, X.: KeyRev: An Efficient Key Revocation Scheme for Wireless Sensor Networks. In: International Conference on Communications, pp. 1260–1265 (2007)

12. Park, C.H., Zhang, Y.Y., Kim, I.T., Park, M.S.: DLS: Dynamic Level Session Key Revocation Protocol for Wireless Sensor Networks. In: 2010 International Conference Information Science and Applications (ICISA), pp. 1–8 (2010)

13. Zeng, P., Cao, Z., Choo, K.K.R., Wang, S.: Security Weakness in a Dynamic Program Update Protocol for Wireless Sensor Networks. IEEE Communications Letters 13(6), 426–428 (2009)

14. Zeng, P., Cao, Z., Choo, K.K.R., Sun, D.: On the Security of an Enhanced Novel Access Control Protocol for Wireless Sensor Networks. IEEE Transactions on Consumer Electronics 56(2), 566–569 (2010)

15. Chan, H., Perrig, A., Song, D.: Random Key Predistribution Schemes for Sensor Networks. In: IEEE Symposium on Security and Privacy, pp. 197–213 (2013)

16. Jiang, Y., Zhang, R.N., Du, X.J.: A New Efficient Random Key Revocation Protocol for Wireless Sensor Networks. In: 14th International Conference on Parallel and Distributed Computing, Applications and Technologies, PDCAT 2013 (2013)

17. Liu, D., Ning, P.: Establishing Pairwise Keys in Distributed Sensor Networks. In: ACM Conference on Computer and Communication Security, pp. 52–61 (2003)

18. Blom, R.: An optimal Class of Symmetric Key Generation Systems. In: Beth, T., Cot, N., Ingemarsson, I. (eds.) EUROCRYPT 1984. LNCS, vol. 209, pp. 335–338. Springer, Heidelberg (1985)

19. Newsome, J., Shi, E., Song, D., Perrig, A.: The Sybil Attack in Sensor Networks: Analysis and Defenses. In: Third International Workshop on Information Processing in Sensor Networks, IPSN (2004)

20. Sánchez, D.S., Baldus, H.: Key Management for Mobile Sensor Networks. In: Burmester, M., Yasinsac, A. (eds.) MADNES 2005. LNCS, vol. 4074, pp. 14–26. Springer, Heidelberg (2006)

21. Moore, T., Clulow, J.: Secure Path-Key Revocation for Symmetric Key Predistribution Schemes in Sensor Networks. In: Venter, H., Eloff, M., Labuschagne, L., Eloff, J., von Solms, R. (eds.) New Approaches for Security, Privacy and Trust in Complex Environments. IFIP, vol. 232, pp. 157–168. Springer, Boston (2007)

Rational Secure Two-party Computation in Social Cloud

Yilei Wang[1,2], Zhe Liu[3,*], Tao Li[1], and Qiuliang Xu[2,**]

[1] Ludong University,
School of Information and Electrical Engineering,
Middle of Hongqi Road 186, Yantai 264025, Shandong, P.R. China
wang_yilei2000@163.com, litao_888@sina.com
[2] Shandong University,
School of Computer Science and Technology,
Shunhua Road 1500, Jinan 250101, Shandong, P.R. China
wang_yilei2000@163.com, xql@sdu.edu.cn
[3] University of Luxembourg,
Laboratory of Algorithmics, Cryptology and Security,
6, rue Richard Coudenhove-Kalergi, L–1359 Luxembourg
zhe.liu@uni.lu

Abstract. Rational parties in secure two-party computation (STPC) are willing to maximize their utilities. However, they have no incentives to cooperate in STPC under correctness and exclusivity assumptions since cooperation will bring them inferior utilities. Consequently, both parties will not participate in STPC. Therefore, new methods must be introduced to make parties cooperate such that they can complete this computation task. In this paper, we redefine utility considering the notion of reputation derived from social cloud to promote cooperation. In social cloud, parties form their reputation when they interact with others. Parties will get a higher utility if they have a higher cooperative reputation. Therefore they have incentives to cooperate. The computation of reputation is completed in the social cloud, which reduce the computation work for parties. Furthermore, we prove that given proper parameters in rational STPC, it is possible to construct an efficient computation protocol, where only one exchanging round in the second stage of the hybrid protocol.

Keywords: Game theory, Social cloud, Reputation.

1   Introduction

STPC means that two distributed and distrustful parties want to compute a functionality using their respective inputs. The computation should be secure in the presence of some attacks, which are considered as corrupted by an external adversary. Traditionally, there are three kinds of adversaries (1) semi-honest adversary properly who follows the protocol except to keep a record of all its intermediate computations; (2) malicious adversary who may arbitrarily deviate from the specified program of a two-party protocol; (3) covert adversary who may arbitrarily deviate from the protocol specification in an

---

* Co-first author.
** Corresponding author.

M.H. Au et al. (Eds.): NSS 2014, LNCS 8792, pp. 476–483, 2014.
© Springer International Publishing Switzerland 2014

attempt to cheat, but do not wish to be "caught" doing so. Recently the notion of rational adversary is put forward to reason why parties have incentives to deviate from the protocol. Rational parties are a bit like covert adversaries while the latter ones have incentives to cheat without considering their utility. Since parties will inevitably have some profit motives in realities, rational parties can better characterize the incentives for parties in many commercial, political, and social settings.

Social cloud is one of such social settings, where parties therein dynamically share resources utilizing relationships established among members in a social network. In fact, parties especially the ones in commercial, political, and social settings can not get off a network, such as a social network. Social network is becoming an everyday part of many people's lives as evidenced by the large user communities. For example, Facebook has over 400 million active users. Individual users in social network have finite capacity and limited capability. However, many users may have surplus capacity or capability to share with others. A social cloud leverages preexisting trust relationships between users to mutually share in the social network. Each user accumulates his reputation according to the trust relationships. Furthermore, the reputation may affect the way others interact with him. For example, users incline to share his resource with users who have good reputation other than users with bad reputation. Motivated by this, we conclude that if reputation derived in the social cloud is considered into the utility definition, then rational parties in STPC have sufficient incentives to cooperate with the other party. Therefore, we fill the gap between social cloud and rational STPC such that rational parties participate in the protocol by utilizing the reputation derived from social cloud.

1.1 Related Works

Marks originally defines the social cloud towards the view of social networks [16] by means of OpenSocial [18]. Pezzi [19] presents a social cloud to develop self-organizing and resilient communities without giving any architectural details. Chard et al. [5] form a dynamic social cloud to leverage trust relationships among users. MyExperiment [20] for biologists and nanoHub [11] for the nanoscience community are such two examples to coordinate research communities. Social cloud is different from P2P network [6,13,14,21] in that the former is based on the encoded relationships. However social cloud follows a group-based cloud model rather than the completely decentralized model in P2P network. Social cloud can be also used to support scientific collaboration, such as SEIT@Home [12] and Folding@Home [3] etc. Chard and Caton [5] also consider how to measure social compliance utilizing reputation in social cloud.

In rational STPC scenario, the main task is to find an equilibrium such that parties have incentives to cooperate. Wang et al. [22] bridge social network and rational STPC without consider the cloud scenario. They also add reputation into the utility definition to boost cooperation [23]. S.J.Ong et al. [17] present a secret sharing scheme with an honest minority and a rational majority. Lysyanskaya and Triandopoulos [15] discuss rational secure multi-party computation in the presence of rational parties and malicious adversaries in universal composable (UC) model [4]. Very recently, Garay et al. [7] discuss the incentives in rational cryptographic protocols and model them as a two-party game between an protocol designer and external attacker. They did a good job of explaining the attacker's incentives considering costly corruption. In this paper, we take different step in the same direction and explain the incentives considering the effect of reputation.

1.2 Motivations and Contributions

As mentioned above, the main task of rational STPC is to encourage both rational parties to cooperate with each other. Besides, we also try to decrease the round complexity in the second stage for the sake of efficiency. The decisions for rational parties whether cooperate or not depend on their utilities. In previous works, the utility is defined similar to prisoner's dilemma (PD). However, it is well known that in one shot PD game, cooperation is not dominated strategy for both parties. New methods are expected to promote cooperation between them. In social cloud, parties form reputation when they repeatedly interact with each other and they are willing to cooperate with those who have high reputation. If reputation is introduced into rational STPC, then parties have incentives to cooperate with each other instead of non-cooperation. Motivated by this, we add reputation as an important part in utility. We also reconstruct the hybrid protocol in the presence of rational parties with new utility definition.

The basic frame of our protocol is similar to [1,10], which consists of two stages. The first stage is an ideal one, where a trusted party receives the inputs of both parties, computes specific functionality using the inputs, generates multiple shares of the functionality for each round at the second stage and finally assigns the shares to parties respectively. The trusted party chooses a right round such that parties can not obtain enough shares to retrieve the output before this round and both parties will retrieve the output after this round. Note that the probability that parties successfully guess the right round is small. Parties hoping to get the output of the functionality have to enter the second stage of the hybrid protocol. The second stage is a process for exchanging shares. Here cooperation means that parties are willing to send shares and fink means the opposite way. Mutual cooperation denotes that both parties send their shares to his opponent and finally successfully exchanging their shares. Consequently, parties may retrieve the result of the function using their shares. Previously, constant rounds in the second stage of the protocols are needed to achieve desirable secure property like fairness. The seminal part of this paper lies in that rational parties utilize reputation derived from social cloud such that there only need one round for parties to exchange shares. The reason is that cooperation is the only way to increase their utility. Otherwise they will get an inferior utility.

2   New Utility Based on Social Cloud Settings

The interactions between two rational parties in one round of rational STPC are presented in Fig. 1. In realities, people incline to cooperate with others who have good reputation. The new definition of utility consists of three assumptions. Equation (1)-(3) give the expression of each assumption respectively. Let $R^b_{-b}(t)^O \in (-1, 1)$ denote the reputation of P_b received from the social cloud with the outcome $O \in A$ in the tth round. Let $\tau_b(o) = R^b_{-b}(t)^o - R^b_{-b}(t-1)^o$ denote the increment of reputation. In other words, parties gain positive reputation if they cooperate and negative reputation if they fink.

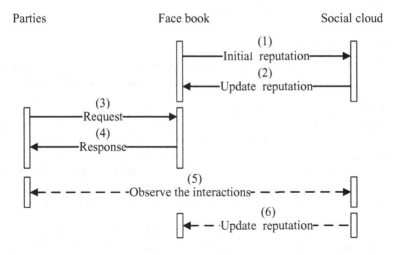

Fig. 1. The interactions of rational STPC based on social cloud

$$Greediness : \frac{|\tau_b(o)|}{\tau_b(o)}. \tag{1}$$

$$Selfishness : \delta_b(o). \tag{2}$$

$$Exclusivity : \frac{1}{num(o) + 1}. \tag{3}$$

Considering the above factors of each assumption, the extended utility definition under new assumptions is:

$$u_b(O) = \rho_1 \cdot \frac{|\tau_b(O)|}{\tau_b(O)} + \rho_2 \cdot \delta_b(O) + \frac{\rho_3}{num(O) + 1}. \tag{4}$$

For two rational parties, the new utilities with the outcomes are defined as follows:

1. (C, C): $(\tau_b > 0, \delta_b = 1, num(O) = 2)$ then $NU^+ = u_b^{(C,C)}(O) = \rho_1 + \rho_2 + \frac{\rho_3}{3}$.
2. (C, F): $(\tau_b > 0, \delta_b = 0, num(O) = 1)$ then $NU = u_b^{(C,F)}(O) = \rho_1 + \frac{\rho_3}{2}$.
3. (F, C): $(\tau_b < 0, \delta_b = 1, num(O) = 1)$ then $NU^- = u_b^{(F,C)}(O) = -\rho_1 + \rho_2 + \frac{\rho_3}{2}$.
4. (F, F): $(\tau_b < 0, \delta_b = 0, num(O) = 0)$ then $NU^{--} = u_b^{(F,F)}(O) = -\rho_1 + \rho_3$.

We can not confirm the Nash equilibrium only from this matrix since the relationships among the factors are not confirmed. There are various possible results according to different relationships of the factors. In the next section, we will analyze how to set proper factors to achieve desirable results.

3   The Model of Rational STPC

3.1   Execution in the Ideal World

The rational STPC in the ideal world is presented with the assumption that there exists a third trusted party (TTP). It's natural to complete the computation in the deal world.

1. **Initial phase:** TTP knows the utility matrix.
2. **Input phase:** Each party P_b (P_{-b}) sends his value x_b (x_{-b}) to TTP. In this phase x_b (x_{-b}) is restricted to a special symbol $\perp$ and x_b (x_{-b}) for rational parties.
3. **Computation phase:** If one of x_b and x_{-b} sufficing $x_b = \perp$ or $x_{-b} = \perp$, TTP sends $\perp$ to both parties and the protocol ends. Otherwise, the TTP computes $f(x_b, x_{-b})$.
4. **Output phase:** Rational parties output the value received from the TTP.

In the ideal world, the protocol is secure since there is an ideal TTP. That is, the TTP will guarantee privacy since parties can not get any information from the output received from TTP. Correctness is guaranteed by TTP since it is trusted and will correctly compute the function. Fairness is also achieved in the ideal world since TTP will assign same outputs to both parties. Consequently, if we construct a real protocol which can perfect simulate the ideal world, then the real protocol can achieve same security properties as in the ideal world.

3.2   Execution in the Real World

The rational STPC proposed in this paper is a hybrid protocol $\Pi^{ShareGen}$, which consists of two stages as mentioned in the first section. The first stage is the functionality *ShareGen* and the second stage is a real share-exchange protocol. (In both stages, the authentication messages are generated and verified by parties, but for simplicity, we omit these two processes.) The first stage is the same to [10], we will re-describe it for completeness.

The second stage is a protocol Π which is made up by four phases: initial phase, exchange phase, cheat phase and output phase. The protocol Π is much like the actual protocol in [2]. In this paper, we use secret sharing schemes as building blocks and achieve informational security in the presence of rational covert adversaries (ref.[8] section 7.6).

The first stage functionality *ShareGen*:

1. **Inputs:** *ShareGen* takes as input values x_b from $P_b, b \in \{1, 2\}$. If either input is of no vail, then *ShareGen* returns $\perp$ to parties.
2. **Computation:** Compute $f(x_b, x_{-b})$ and choose random shares s_b and s_{-b} such that $s_b \oplus s_{-b} = f(x_b, x_{-b})$.
3. **Outputs:** Send s_{-b} to P_b, and s_b to P_{-b}.

The second stage protocol Π:

1. **Initial phase**: Parties run the functionality *ShareGen* using their inputs. P_b receives s_{-b} and P_{-b} receives s_b.

2. **Utility computation phase**: Before parties decide to exchange their shares with each other, they first request the Facebook for his opponent' trust or reputation according to whether they are neighbors. Then they compute their utility.
3. **Exchange phase:** Parties exchange their shares according to the utility.
4. **Reputation updating phase**: The social cloud observes the action of both parties, updates their reputation according to their behaviors, and sends the trust or reputations back to Face book for future use.
5. **Output phase:** At the end of the protocol, each party determines his outputs.

In traditional rational STPC protocols, it's impossible for two rational parties to complete the computation in only one round. However, in this paper, it makes the impossible possible by using the trust and reputation in the social cloud. In section 3, the proof of when parties have incentives to cooperate is not discussed since it depends on the relationship of the three factors. Here we will prove that, given proper parameters, it is possible for two rational parties to exchange their shares within one round in the second stage of the protocol.

Lemma 1. *Given $4\rho_1 > 2\rho_2 > \rho_3 > 0$, (C, C) is a strict Nash equilibrium for rational parties.*

In the following, the main task is to prove the security of the protocol in the hybrid protocol. Note that the protocol consists of two stages and the first stage is an ideal one. As to the security of the hybrid world, we should use the proposition in [9].

Proposition 1. *Let ρ be a protocol that securely computes $\mathcal{G}$ with abort, and let π be a protocol that securely computes $\mathcal{F}$ with complete fairness in the $\mathcal{G}$-hybrid model (where $\mathcal{G}$ is computed according to the ideal world with abort). Then protocol π^ρ securely computes $\mathcal{F}$ with complete fairness.*

Canetti [4] proved that a real world secure-with-abort protocol for *ShareGen* in an ideal world existed if there are enhanced trapdoor permutations. Then applying Proposition 1, a real world protocol is secure if there are enhanced trapdoor permutations.

Theorem 1. *If the protocol ρ realizes the ideal functionality* ShareGen *when enhanced trapdoor permutations exist, then $\Pi^{ShareGen}$ securely computes function f.*

Proof. (Sketch) For simplicity, we only consider static corruptions and analyze the hybrid protocol $\pi^{ShareGen}$ where exists a trusted party computing $ShareGen$. To prove the security in the real world, we also need to apply Proposition 1 and the conclusion of [4]. Note that, we assume that the social cloud is also secure and the reputation derived from it is correct.

P_b **is corrupted.** The construction of an ideal simulator $\mathcal{S}$ given black-box access to a real adversary $\mathcal{A}$ corrupting P_b is described as follows.

1. $\mathcal{S}$ invokes $\mathcal{A}$ on the input x_b, the auxiliary input z and the security parameter k.
2. $\mathcal{S}$ computes $ShareGen$ using the input x'_b received from $\mathcal{A}$.
   (a) If $x'_b \notin X$, then $\mathcal{S}$ returns $\bot$ to $\mathcal{A}$ as its output from the computation $ShareGen$. $\mathcal{S}$ uniformly chooses $\bar{x}$ from X and sends it to the trusted party computing f, outputs whatever $\mathcal{A}$ outputs, and halts.

(b) If $x'_b \in X$, then $\mathcal{S}$ randomly chooses s_{-b} and then gives them to $\mathcal{A}$ as the output of $ShareGen$.

3. If $\mathcal{A}$ send *aborts* when computing $shareGen$, then $\mathcal{S}$ sends $\bar{x}_b$ to the trusted party computing f, outputs whatever $\mathcal{A}$ outputs, and halts. Otherwise, $\mathcal{S}$ proceeds as below.

4. If $\mathcal{S}$ has not halted yet, at the current round it output whatever $\mathcal{A}$ outputs and halts.

The construction of an ideal simulator when P_{-b} is corrupted is similar to the above. Therefore it's obvious that the distributions of the ideal simulator are computationally equal to these of the hybrid world. Consequently, we have that for every non-uniform, polynomial-time adversary $\mathcal{A}$, there exists a non-uniform, probabilistic polynomial-time adversary $\mathcal{S}$ corrupting the same party as $\mathcal{A}$ such that the protocol in the real world can simulate an ideal one.

4   Conclusions

This paper considers the affect of trust and reputation on parties' utility based on social cloud settings. We add reputation as a new part of the utility and consequently propose a rational STPC utilizing the new utility. Two rational parties belong to a social network and the value of reputation is not only affected by the interactions with the other party in rational STPC but also is affected by the interaction with other parties in the social network. Therefore, the reputation is local value for one party. This is different from previous works, where only consider the reputation between two parties in rational STPC. Towards the view of the previous works, reputation there is in fact the notion of trust in this paper. Therefore, we consider a more general setting for both parties.

Acknowledgements. This work was supported by the Natural Science Foundation of China under Grant No. 61173139, Natural Science Foundation of Shandong Province under Grant No. ZR2011FZ005 and Doctoral Fund of Ministry of Education of China under Grant No. 20110131110027.

References

1. Asharov, G., Canetti, R., Hazay, C.: Towards a game theoretic view of secure computation. In: Paterson, K.G. (ed.) EUROCRYPT 2011. LNCS, vol. 6632, pp. 426–445. Springer, Heidelberg (2011)
2. Aumann, Y., Lindell, Y.: Security against covert adversaries: Efficient protocols for realistic adversaries. Journal of Cryptology 23(2), 281–343 (2010)
3. Beberg, A., Ensign, D., Jayachandran, G., Khaliq, S., Pande, V.: Folding@home: Lessons from eight years of volunteer distributed computing. In: Parallel Distributed Processing (IPDPS 2009), pp. 1–8. IEEE (2009)
4. Canetti, R.: Security and composition of multiparty cryptographic protocols. Journal of Cryptology 13(1), 143–202 (2000)
5. Chard, K., Caton, S.: Social cloud computing: A vision for socially motivated resource sharing. IEEE Transactions on Services Computing 5(4), 551–563 (2012)

6. Cox, L., Noble, B.: Samsara: Honor among thieves in peer-to-peer storage. SIGOPS Operating Systems Rev. 37, 120–132 (2003)

7. Garay, J., Katz, J., Maurer, U., Tackmann, B., Zikas, V.: Rational protocol design: Cryptography against incentive-driven adversaries. In: 2013 IEEE 54th Annual Symposium on Foundations of Computer Science (FOCS), pp. 648–657. IEEE (2013)

8. Goldreich, O.: Foundations of Cryptography, vol. 2. Cambridge University Press (2004)

9. Gordon, S.: On fairness in secure computation. Ph.D. thesis, University of Maryland (2010)

10. Groce, A., Katz, J.: Fair computation with rational players. In: Pointcheval, D., Johansson, T. (eds.) EUROCRYPT 2012. LNCS, vol. 7237, pp. 81–98. Springer, Heidelberg (2012)

11. Klimeck, G., McLennan, M., Brophy, S.P., Adams III, G.B., Lundstrom, M.S.: nanohub.org: Advancing education and research in nanotechnology. Computing in Science and Engineering 10, 17–23 (2008)

12. Korpela, E., Werthimer, D., Anderson, D., Cobb, J., Leboisky, M.: Seti@home-massively distributed computing for seti. Computing in Science Engineering 3(1), 78–83 (2001)

13. Lakshman, A., Malik, P.: Cassandra: Structured storage system on a p2p network. In: 28th ACM Symp. Principles of Distributed Computing (PODC 2009), p. 5. ACM, New York (2009)

14. Lakshman, A., Malik, P.: Cassandra: a decentralized structured storage system. ACM SIGOPS Operating Systems Review 44(2), 35–40 (2010)

15. Lysyanskaya, A., Triandopoulos, N.: Rationality and adversarial behavior in multi-party computation. In: Dwork, C. (ed.) CRYPTO 2006. LNCS, vol. 4117, pp. 180–197. Springer, Heidelberg (2006)

16. Marks, K.: Future of web apis: The social cloud, future of Web Apps (2008)

17. Ong, S.J., Parkes, D.C., Rosen, A., Vadhan, S.: Fairness with an honest minority and a rational majority. In: Reingold, O. (ed.) TCC 2009. LNCS, vol. 5444, pp. 36–53. Springer, Heidelberg (2009)

18. OpenSocial and Gadgets Specification Group: Opensocial specification v0.9 (2009),
    http://www.opensocial.org/Technical-Resources/
    opensocial-spec-v09/OpenSocial-Specification.html

19. Pezzi, R.: Information technology tools for a transition economy (2009),
    http://www.socialcloud.net/papers/ITtools.pdf

20. Roure, D.D., Goble, C., Stevens, R.: The design and realisation of the myexperiment virtual research environment for social sharing of workflows. Future Generation Computer Systems 25(5), 561–567 (2012)

21. Rowstron, A., Druschel, P.: Storage management and caching in past, a large-scale, persistent peer-to-peer storage utility. SIGOPS Operating Systems Rev. 35, 188–201 (2001)

22. Wang, Y., Liu, Z., Wang, H., Xu, Q.: Social rational secure multi-party computation. Concurrency and Computation: Practice and Experience 26(5), 1067–1083 (2014)

23. Wang, Y., Liu, Z., Xu, Q.: New rational parties relying on reputation. Security and Communication Networks 7, 1128–1137 (2014)

How to Evaluate Trust Using MMT[*]

Khalifa Toumi[1], Wissam Mallouli[2], Edgardo Montes de Oca[2],
César Andrés[1], and Ana Cavalli[1]

[1] IT/ TELECOM & Management SudParis, EVRY, F-91011
{Khalifa.Toumi,César Andrés,Ana.Cavalli}@it-sudparis.eu
[2] Montimage, 39 rue Bobillot, 75013 Paris, France
{wissam.mallouli,edgardo.montesdeoca}@montimage.com

Abstract. Trust evaluation is becoming a more and more active and critical area mainly for guaranteeing secure interoperation between communicating systems. One of the basic parameters used to evaluate the trust in a remote entity (user or system) is the previous experience, i.e. the interactions already performed between the truster and the trustee. However the monitoring of the trustee behavior and the analysis of the collected data and events are not an easy task. First of all, we need to define relevant patterns that describe the desired behaviors to be monitored and check them using a dedicated tool.

Within this paper, we extended an open source tool (MMT) to monitor users' behavior and define behavior patterns using temporal properties. We also design some evaluation strategies and illustrate the whole approach by the application to a real case study related to a collaborative programming project.

Keywords: Trust, Multi-Organization Environment, User experience, Monitoring and events correlation.

1 Introduction

Collaboration between public/private organizations like companies, universities, banks and hospitals spread more and more rapidly and usually shapes according to different partnership strategies in a Multi-Organization Environement (MOE). This has many advantages such as: (1) the ability to use remote and professional resources, services and knowledge, (2) the reducing of intervention duration and (3) the gain of experts skills and experience.

MOE is a paradigm that contains at least two organizations: an O-grantor and/or an O-grantee. The O-grantor is the participant that offers resources. These resources are acceded by users of another organization called the O-grantee. The resource sharing task is based on some restriction rules that constitute an *interoperability security policy*, and it allows to control the access to these resources.

---

[*] The research work presented in this paper is supported by the European project Inter-Trust.

M.H. Au et al. (Eds.): NSS 2014, LNCS 8792, pp. 484–492, 2014.

Many works in the literature [2,4,7] focus on the trust and security challenges in distributed environment. In order to define a *trust level*, there are several different criteria that should be analyzed and evaluated. One of the most important criteria is the previous experience of a trustee.

"Experience is the teacher of all things." (Julius Caesar)

Different approaches have been proposed to evaluate this criteria based on the assessment of the historical interactions with the trustee. However, different challenges are still open. For instance, some assumptions related to the trustee behavior monitoring are considered in several works. Besides, no work proposes a detailed discussion *"How to monitor the trustee behavior?"* [2,5,7,6]. They generally assume that the monitoring is possible and that the different parameters (related to the trustee experience) are available as input which is not the case in real case studies. In order to target this issue, we propose in this paper:

- *A methodology to assess different interactions between at least two entities.*
- *An extension of a monitoring tool called MMT for the evaluation of a behavior based on the trust needs.*

Our approach is an extension of our previous work [7,6] to implement a prototype solution for trust evaluation framework. To reach this objective, we have adapted the MMT monitoring tool that allows to a real-time visibility of network traffic. Indeed, the paper approach consists of the following steps: (1) a new plug-in called 'trust-plug' is developed to analyze the interaction traces and to extract the different attributes that are relevant or can have an impact on the trust; (2)The formalism allowing the specification of MMT properties (denoting trust patterns) is extended, (3)MMT tool is also extended by adding periodical trace checking and a trust level notification has been also developed.

The rest of the paper is structured as follows. In Section 2, we define the trust parameters in MOE. Section 3 shows how to evaluate the satisfactory function and the possible strategies to evaluate a trustee. Afterwards, a case study is detailed in Section 4 in order to demonstrate the efficiency of the proposed approach. Finally, Section 5 concludes the paper and presents ideas for future work.

2   Trust Definition

Currently, there are several definitions of the concept of trust in the literature. We will use an adaptation of the one presented in [1]: Trust is not an objective property of an entity but a subjective degree of belief about an organization or a user. In this context, the trust is a relationship between a **truster** and a **trustee** related to a **situation** at a given **time**.

Definition 1. The truster is any organization that offers an access to a specific resource. Any *O-grantor* in MOE will be a truster.   □

Definition 2. The trustee can be an organization or a user that needs a service.
□

Definition 3. A situation is composed by an **activity** and a **view**. An activity is an action to be performed and a view is a set of objects that may be accessed by the user.
□

Definition 4. The time in MOE will be represented by intervals.
□

Definition 5. The degree of belief, also known as *the trust value* is used to measure the belief between two entities (the **truster** and the **trustee**). Its value allows us to determine if we can trust or not the trustee (related to a **situation** and a **time**).
□

In order to define the `belief` function in this framework we were based on the experience parameter.

Definition 6. Experience learning aims to establish wisdom on making decision. It is based on the evaluation of the previous interactions between the **trustee** and the **truster** related to a specific **situation** at a **period of time**.
□

There are considered two types of experiences.

- The experience of the trustee organization that takes into consideration the previous *behaviors* of all users of this organization,
- and the direct experience where only the previous *behaviors* between this user and the truster are considered.

The evaluations of these parameters depend on a satisfactory function that is used in order to evaluate an interaction. We assume that any interaction can be valuated as a *satisfactory* or *unsatisfactory* behavior.

If the valuation is unsatisfactory then it is considered as a *bad behavior*, that is, it will decrease the experience evaluation of the trustee. On the contrary, if the valuation is satisfactory it will increase the experience evaluation. We note that the output of this function is a value in [-1,1] assigned to the interaction. In this paper we present an approach of how to evaluate this function denoted `sat`.

Evaluation of the User Experience

For any $u \in$ `Subjects`, $s \in$ `Situations`, $\hat{T}_i \in \mathcal{I}_{\mathbb{R}_+}$,

we define the experience evaluation function with respect to org_A as:

$$\text{eX}_1(u, \text{org}_A, \hat{T}_n, s, l) = \frac{\sum_{i=0}^{n} \frac{\sum_{b \in l_i} sat(b)}{|l_i|}}{n}$$

where l_i contains the set of behaviors u that were performed before and during $\hat{T}_i$ related to the situation s and sat(b) is the function that will evaluate a behavior b. This function will be more detailed in Section 3.

Evaluation of the Organization Experience

For any $\text{org}_B \in \text{Organizations}$, $s \in \text{Situations}$, $\hat{T}_i \in \mathcal{I}_{\mathbf{R}_+}$, and for any not empty log l, we define the experience evaluation function of an organization org_B with respect to org_A as:

$$\text{eX}_2(\text{org}_B, \text{org}_A, \hat{T}_n, s, l) = \frac{\sum_{u \in \text{employee}(\text{org}_B, \text{org}_A)} \text{eX}_1(u, \text{org}_A, \hat{T}_n, s, l)}{|\text{employee}(\text{org}_B, \text{org}_A)|}$$

where $\text{employee}(\text{org}_B, \text{org}_A)$ are the set of employees of org_B that have collaborated with org_A.

3   Satisfactory Evaluation

In this section, we propose a satisfactory evaluation method that aims to assess a behavior b in MOE. This assessment associates a value between [-1,1] to this behavior, it will be denoted $\text{Sat}(b)$. If $\text{Sat}(b) \in [0, 1]$ then this means that the previous behavior does not respect some requirements and it is considered as a bad one that have to decrease the experience evaluation of the user. Otherwise b is considered as a good behavior that will increase the experience evaluation of the user.

3.1   Evaluation of the Satisfactory Function

Regarding the definition of satisfactory function, in this section we will present how to apply the definition and how to evaluate it. We will introduce it using the example presented in Figure 1.

As it is shown in Figure 1, for each *situation* we will have a list of *rules* that can be a security property to respect or an attack to detect. These *rules* will be written based on an extension of MMT language. Any *interaction* of a user will belong to one situation.

To evaluate it, we have:

1. To select the list of rules related to a fixed situation. In the running example, in Figure 1, we consider that the interaction of the user is related to S2.
2. To apply these rules as inputs of MMT tool. Then, it automatically computes which rules are respected, which rules are disrespected, and which are the different violations during the interaction.

In this proposal, **the influence of the different properties are not the same.** As it is shown in Figure 2, we provide three partitions of the different properties (high , medium and low) in order to differ between the list of properties. We will say that *in the case of a "security property", a high (resp. medium) security rule is more important than a medium (resp. low) rule.*

Based on the MMT tool and our new plug-in "Trust-plug", that analyzes the trace for trust proposals we are allowed to check that:

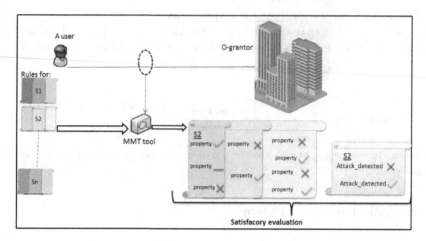

Fig. 1. Evaluation of an interaction

- If the rule is respected, then a value +1 is assigned to it.
- If the rule is not respected, then a value −1 is assigned to it.
- If we cannot have a decision about this rule during the interaction, then a value 0 is assigned to it.

Evaluation1: Based on the assigned values, we define the satisfactory function for a situation s as:

$$\begin{cases} -1 & if\ an\ attack\ is\ detected \\ \frac{e(H_s)+e(M_s)/2+e(L_s)/4}{SIZE} & otherwise \end{cases}$$

where H_s, M_s and L_s are the set of high, medium and low security properties defined for a situation s, $SIZE$ is the total number of rules for this situation, and e is a function that takes as inputs a set of properties and give as output the sum of their verdict.

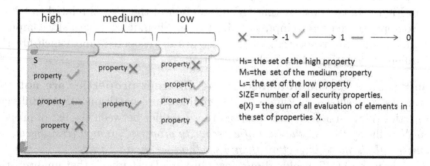

Fig. 2. Properties partition

4   Case Study

In this section we will present a case study, where we can show the usability of our solution.

4.1   Scenario

We will consider the following MOE scenario:

- Four organizations are participating in the same development of a project.
- The first organization org_A has a server where several virtual machines are offered.
- These are the considered **activities**: configure, modify, execute, test, and manage.
- The organization org_A also offers the following **views**: source_code, application, testing_script, OS_System and resources.
- In this scenario four different **external** roles are defined: engineer, researcher, tester, and project manager.

4.2   Specification of the Interoperability Security Policy

The first phase is the specification and the deployment of an interoperability security policy. This policy is the result of a negotiation process between the O-grantor and the O-grantee. An example of how to do it is detailed in [3]. We show on the following a part of the org_A interoperability security policy.

- R1: An engineer is permitted to manage OS_System.
- R2: A researcher is prohibited to manage resources.
- R3: An engineer is permitted to modify a source_code.
- R4: An engineer is permitted to execute an application.
- This rules are only applied for the **external** engineers and researchers that does not belong to org_A.

Related to this rule we have this trust policy:

- R1 is activated only if the trust evaluation of the user is more than 0.4 **and** the trust evaluation of the organization is more than 0.
- R2 is activated only if the trust evaluation of the user is less than 0 **or** (if the trust evaluation of the organization is between -0.3 and 0.2 **and** the trust evaluation of the user is between 0 and 0.4)
- R3 is activated only if the trust evaluation of the user is more than 0.5 **and** the trust evaluation of the organization is more than 0.7.
- R4 is activated only if the trust evaluation of the user is more than 0.5.

4.3 Trust Properties Definition

The second step is to define a list of properties and threats that permits to evaluate the different interaction with org$_A$. For each situation, we have to write a list of properties.

Example 1. Figure 3 shows the trust properties for the situation s_1 manage⊳OS_System. The Figure 4 shows how to write the the property p1 in our new extension of the MMT language. We add firstly a new parameter 'partition' for the tag <property> in order to precise the importance of the rule. Moreover, as it is shown in Figure 4, a trust plug-in is developed that has to analyze the xml trace and to extract several elements as the **external** role of the user, its organization and the type of the request. □

Security properties

❖ p1: Any interaction should not stay more than one half of a day. (medium)

❖ p2: The user cannot ignore 5 warning messages in the same session. (low)

Attacks

• t1: The same unauthorized action requested more than 3 times within a delay of 100 units of time is considered as a threat.
• t2: Different unauthorized actions requested more than 5 time within a delay of 100 units of time are considered as a threat.

Fig. 3. Trust properties for manage⊳OS_System

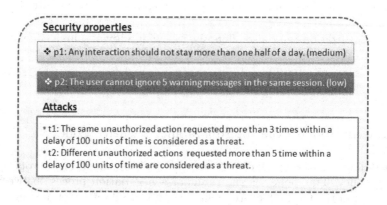

Fig. 4. A security property for the situation manage OS_System

Therefore, the satisfactory function of any interaction related to the situation manage⊳OS_System will be:

$$\begin{cases} -1 & \text{if } t1 \text{ or } t2 \text{ are detected} \\ \dfrac{e(\varnothing) + \frac{e(\{p1\})}{2} + e(\{p2\})/4}{4} & \text{otherwise} \end{cases}$$

Security rules summary results (period 4)

Id	Description	High	medium	low	✔	✖
p1	SECURITY RULE: Any interaction should not stay more than one half of a day		medium		1	0
p2	SECURITY RULE The user cannot ignore 5 warning messages in the same session		low		1	1

Attack summary results (period 4)

Id	Description	⚠	✔
t1	ATTACK: Unauthorized action requested more than 3 times within a delay of 100 units of time	0	0
t2	ATTACK: Different unauthorized actions requested more than 5 time within a delay of 100 units of time	0	0

Satisfactory evaluation (period 4)

Req_Id	user	Organization	Situation	TimeStamp	Sat
2117	a1	OrgA	manage OS_System	2013-06-04 16:34 12.000000	0.25

Fig. 5. Result file from MMT

4.4   Executing MMT with the Previous Rules

After each period, MMT provides a result file as it is shown in Figure 5. This
file contains three tables:

- The first one cites the different properties, how many times that are respected
  or disrespected, the partition of the property.
- The second table is about the detected attacks.
- Finally, the last one provides a table that show the interaction (request
  identity, the user, the organization, the situation and the timestamps) with
  its assigned satisfactory evaluation.

Based on these results, the trust level of the user and the organization org_A
will be updated in the configuration file.   These results with the trust and
the security policies will permit to give a response response for any request.
For example, a request that will be received during the period 5 to manage
OS_System will be accepted since:

- A permission rule (R1) is provided for this user (see subsection 4.2).
- R1 is activated since the trust evaluation of the user is equal to 0.5 more
  than 0.4 and the trust evaluation of the organization is equal to 0.1 more
  than 0.

This approach offers to an access control system to take into consideration the
new interactions between the trustee and the truster. This permits to react by
giving new permissions to unauthorized employee, to refuse an access for an
authorized user in the previous period and to have a dynamic policy based on
the analysis of the requester behaviors.

5   Conclusions and Future Work

In this paper, we present a methodology that permits to evaluate an interaction between a trustee and a truster. An extension of the monitoring tool MMT is proposed. Moreover, the basic function 'satisfactory evaluation' that permits to assess an interaction is well detailed. Finally, the different steps of how to do with a case study is presented.

As future work, we are planning to use our approach in other distributed system as the VANET networks and e-Voting system for the European project Inter-Trust and we aim also to integrate a new parameter 'reputation': its definition, evaluation and its spread between the different entities will be our interest on the future.

References

1. Abdul-Rahman, A., Hailes, S.: Supporting trust in virtual communities. In: 33rd Annual Hawaii International Conference on System Sciences, HICSS 2000, vol. 11 (January 2000)
2. Chakraborty, S., Ray, I.: TrustBAC: integrating trust relationships into the RBAC model for access control in open systems. In: ACM Symposium on Access Control Models and Technologies, SACMAT 2006, pp. 49–58. ACM (2006)
3. Cuppens, F., Cuppens-Boulahia, N., Coma, C.: O2O: Virtual private organizations to manage security policy interoperability. In: Bagchi, A., Atluri, V. (eds.) ICISS 2006. LNCS, vol. 4332, pp. 101–115. Springer, Heidelberg (2006)
4. Abi Haidar, D., Cuppens-Boulahia, N., Cuppens, F., Debar, H.: XeNA: an access negotiation framework using XACML. Annals of Telecommunications 64(1-2), 155–169 (2009)
5. Ray, I., Ray, I., Chakraborty, S.: An interoperable context sensitive model of trust. Journal of Intelligent Information Systems 32(1), 75–104 (2009)
6. Toumi, K., Andrés, C., Cavalli, A.: TRUST-orBAC: A trust access control model in multi-organization environments. In: Venkatakrishnan, V., Goswami, D. (eds.) ICISS 2012. LNCS, vol. 7671, pp. 89–103. Springer, Heidelberg (2012)
7. Toumi, K., Andres, C., Cavalli, A., EL Maarabani, M.: A vector based model approach for defining trust in multi-organization environments. In: International Conference on Risks and Security of Internet and Systems, CRISIS 2012. IEEE Computer Society Press (2012)

A Proposed Approach to Compound File Fragment Identification

Khoa Nguyen, Dat Tran, Wanli Ma, and Dharmendra Sharma

Faculty of Education, Science, Technology and Mathematics,
University of Canberra, ACT, Australia
Khoa.Nguyen@canberra.edu.au

Abstract. One of the biggest challenges in file fragment classification is the low classification rate of compound files known as high entropy files that contain different types of data, such as images and compressed text. It is seen that current methods for file fragment classification may not work for classifying these compound files. In this paper we propose a novel approach based on detecting deflate-encoded data in compound file fragments then decompress that data before applying a machine learning technique for classification. We apply our proposed method to classify Adobe portable document format (PDF) file type. Experiments showed high classification rate for the proposed method.

Keywords: Digital forensics, file type classification, compound file fragment classification.

1 Introduction

File fragment classification is defined as "the process of mapping a sample chunk of data, such as a disk block, to a specific type of data encoding" [1]. This topic has attracted research efforts over the last few decades. Current approaches apply the same classification framework to all file types [1-3]. This framework can solve the classification problem for some particular file types such as text, csv or some special structures of data stream such as mp3 and jpeg. However, it becomes inefficient and insufficient for classifying other file types which have high entropy values or compound files that normally contain different data types, compressed data portions (with different compression algorithms), metadata or images. Microsoft Office including Word, Excel and PowerPoint, and Adobe portable document format (PDF) are typical examples of these compound files [4, 5].

PDF is one of the file types seen in most of datasets for file type classification [6] because PDF is a popular file format and more importantly, the file type classification rate for PDF is very low, less than 30% as reported in [7, 8]. A higher classification rate is found in [9, 10], however only a few file types were investigated. Roussev and Garfinkel [3] claimed that previous approaches to compound file fragment classification became irrelevant because they treated compound files as unified data files and hence a PDF file fragment may be incorrectly classified as a JPEG file fragment if a JPEG image is embedded in that PDF file.

M.H. Au et al. (Eds.): NSS 2014, LNCS 8792, pp. 493–500, 2014.
© Springer International Publishing Switzerland 2014

Recently, several approaches have been proposed to detect compressed data portion among high entropy data fragments [1] or to distinguish compression from encryption data fragments [2]. These approaches can be applied to detecting specific data types in the content of compound files.

In this paper, we propose a new approach based on deflate data detection to classify deflate-encoded file fragments from a PDF file. Firstly, a deflate data excerpt is detected from a file fragment, then this data excerpt is decompressed to retrieve the underlying data known as inflate data. Secondly, due to the fact that the majority of deflate data portions of PDF files are PDF text compression, features including byte frequency distribution and bigram are extracted and Support Vector Machine (SVM) is used to efficiently recognize these inflate data fragments. SVM is chosen because it is efficient in classifying data fragments of low entropy file types such as text or html [8, 10].

The rest of paper is organized as follows. Section 2 presents some related studies in detecting file fragments, especially high entropy file fragments. Section 3 introduces our proposed approach. Section 4 presents our experiments and results. Finally, Section 5 includes conclusion and future work.

2   Related Work

Classifying PDF file fragments has attracted attentions from researchers for over a decade. However this classification is still a challenge since current classification methods performed on large and public data sets provide very low classification rates. High classification rates are only observed in experiments performed on small and private data sets [7, 8].

Li et al [9] investigated characteristics of file headers in a data set of five file types, namely EXE, GIF, JPG, PDF and DOC. They used k-means clustering to classify file types. They revealed that the highest accuracy would be nearly 100% if only the first 20 bytes in each file were analyzed but it would drop to 77% if the whole files were used. The drawback of their approach is that file headers always exist in files to be classified, which could not be applied to file fragment classification where most of file fragments come from the body of files.

Calhoun and Coles [11] applied linear discriminant analysis to classify file fragments of only four types (JPG, BMP, GIF, and PDF). Although this approach achieved good results, it is not convinced researchers because of the limitation of file types. In addition, Axelsson [7] made use of k nearest neighbors technique with normalized compression distance (NCD) as metric to classify file fragments from 28 different file types including PDF. The file fragments were obtained from the publicly available Govdocs1 corpus [12]. The author performed 10 trials and had classification rates for values k from 1 to 10. This approach only worked well for low entropy files such as EPS, CSV and TXT. Conversely, two worst cases were observed on compressed GZ and PNG files, because NCD had very small effect on these data types. His method only achieved 10.7% for the case of PDF file fragments.

Fitzgerald et al [8] applied SVM technique to classify file fragments from 24 different file types. They used features obtained from natural language processing. The classification rate for PDF file fragments of their method is better than Axelsson's method but still low – only 29.2%. Moreover, their confusion matrix shows that PDF file fragments were misclassified as GZ and PNG file fragments with the misclassification rate of 22.9% and 15.8%, respectively.

In [1], Roussev and Quates proposed an empirical approach that can be used to detect the deflate-encoded data in some popular file formats including Microsoft Office (DOCX, XLSX, and PPTX), PNG and EXE/DLL files. They analyzed a huge number of Microsoft Office files and realized that most of those files embed image files which are JPG, PNG, GIF and TIFF. Consequently, previous classification methods were not able to apply to those file types. Therefore, they proposed a new method that only be used to detect the deflate-encoded data in file fragments. They also recommended that the file fragment size should be 18 KB in order to achieve a nearly perfect classification rate of deflate-encoded data. However, the PDF file type was not included in their work, even though deflate compressed data are the major part of PDF content [3].

3   Proposed Approach

3.1   PDF File Analysis

A PDF file contains a number of autonomous objects to encode text and images. In addition, fonts, font program, layout, formatting and other information are also embedded to display the content of PDF on screen. Consider a data set of 85GB consisting of 131,000 PDF files downloaded from [3] with details presented in Table 1 below. The first column indicates the encoding method for those objects. Other columns present the total number of embedded objects, average size, total size and the fraction of total amount of data.

Table 1. Structural composition of PDF files [3]

Encoding	Count	Average Size (KB)	Total (MB)	Contribution
Deflate	10,406,780	4.11	41,730	49.1%
Image (jpeg/jpeg2000)	853,321	25.88	21,570	25.4%
BM Image (fax/JBIG2)	756,532	12.82	9,470	11.2%
PDF-Characteristic			8,236	9.7%
Application/XML/Form	520,220	3.18	1,614	1.9%
ASCII85/ASCIIHex	205,421	4.51	905	1.1%
Fonts	10,005	1.14	11	0.0%
Other	412,570	2.23	899	1.1%

It can be seen in Table 1 that deflate-encoded data is the largest part in PDF files. Deflate-encoded data portions contain text or font software programs.

3.2   Proposed Model

Current approaches treated all data types in PDF files in the same way. However, it is seen that those approaches do not work well for compound file fragments. Therefore, in order to increase the classification rate for PDF file fragments, we propose a model consisting of two phases – deflate encoded detection phase and PDF data fragment classification phase, as seen in Figure 2 below.

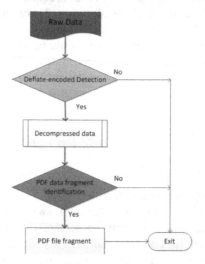

Fig. 1. The proposed model

- **Deflate-encoded data detection**: In this first phase, we detect then extract deflate-encoded data portions in a PDF file fragment using the approach in [1]. A deflate-encoded data fragment consists of a sequence of compressed blocks, each of which includes header, Huffman tables and compressed data. The header consists of 3 bits; the first bit shows whether this block is the last block in the sequence; the next two bits indicate how data is coded: 00 – raw data (uncompressed), 01 – compressed with static Huffman codes, or 10 – compressed with dynamic Huffman codes. Huffman tables depict the Huffman codes used in specific blocks. Compressed data is a stream of variable-length Huffman codes that represent the content of the block. To detect compressed data, we determine the header of a block by searching for 3 consecutive bits which have the form of a deflate header then try to decompress the data. If the first 3 bits do not have the form of a deflate header then we will shift left one bit and repeat the search. The process is presented in Figure 2 below.

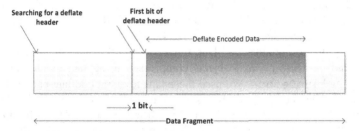

Fig. 2. The process of deflate-encoded data detection

When a deflate-encoded data portion is detected, it will then be decompressed and the obtained underlying data known as inflate data will be used as the input data for classification in the second phase.

- **PDF data fragment classification:** Compression algorithms that make the statistical properties of data cannot be used to classify the file type of a data fragment [3]. This is the reason why current approaches using statistical properties as feature vectors have low classification rates [8, 11]. In our proposed model, the underlying data to be classified is not compressed and have different characteristics from other deflate-encoded file types such as PNG and MS Office. A machine learning technique is now used to recognize whether an inflate data excerpt belongs to a PDF file fragment. A file fragment is classified as PDF file type if its inflate data is classified as an excerpt of the PDF underlying data.

```
0.0716 Tw
[(and 14% of the shorelines of the lax)12.4(gex northern Channel)]TJ
T*
0.0005 Tc
-0.0445 Tw
(Islands of San Miguel, Santa Rosa, and Santa Cruz, respec-)Tj
T*
0.0004 Tc
-0.0162 Tw
(tively \(Dugan et al. 1998a\).)Tj
```

Fig. 3. An example of PDF inflate data fragment

It is seen that text is the major part of a PDF document that is compressed by the deflate algorithm [3]. According to [6], text from a PDF document has a specific structure that is different from structure of text from Microsoft Office files. Furthermore, since SVM is a very efficient tool to recognize text data [8, 10, 11], SVM is deployed in the second phase of our proposed model.

4   Experiments and Results

Our data set consists of files from deflate-encoded file types which are PDF, PNG and MS Office (DOCX, XLSX and PPTX). We used 14827 PDF files from the Govdocs1 corpus [12] with total size of 16.3GB and over 7000 files for each file type DOCX, XLSX, and PPTX of MS Office with the total size of 24GB. PNG files were from the Govdocs1 corpus and other sources from the Internet.

According to [6], embedded data objects in PDF files are stored between obj.<< and .endobj., and objects compressed using the deflate algorithm are marked by /FlateDecode. We used these tags to extract deflate-encoded data. The total number of deflate-encoded objects extracted from those PDF files is 458988. We also extracted deflate-encoded data from MS Office and PNG files using the method in [1]. Finally the *zsniff* tool was used to decompress all of these deflate-encoded data.

The obtained decompressed data (i.e., inflate data) including fonts, font programs and text were then used to extract 256 features which are byte frequency distribution (BFD) values and form a 256-dimensional feature vector. We also applied bigram count method to these 256 features to form a (256x256) matrix of bigram where the value of element (i, j) in the matrix was the frequency of two consecutive bytes i and j in a data fragment. In our approach, each data fragment was represented by a bigram matrix, then this matrix was converted into a vector with 65536 elements (256x256 = 65536) regarded as a feature vector for that data fragment. In summary, every inflate data fragment in our data set was converted to a BFD feature vector (256 dimensions) and a bigram count feature vector (65536 dimensions). In order to evaluate our proposed method, we also applied these two feature extraction methods to the compressed data (deflate data) for comparison.

Finally we created 6 data sets as follows: 1) Inflate data set including text only and using BFD features, 2) Inflate data set including text only and using Bigram features, 3) Inflate data set including fonts, font programs and text and using BFD features, 4) Inflate data set including fonts, font programs and text and using BFD features. 5) Deflate data set using BFD features, and 6) Deflate data set using Bigram features.

For each of these 6 data sets, we randomly selected 40000 PDF data fragments and selected 40000 data fragments from the other file types to form a training set (30000 from PDF and 30000 from the others) and a test set (the remaining 10000 from PDF and 10000 from the others).

These 6 training sets were used to train binary SVM in linear kernel mode. The linear kernel was the most effective one as reported in [8, 13] for BFD-based file fragment classification. Following the recommendation in [14], feature vectors were scaled to decrease training time and improve the classification performance. In addition, the binary SVM was used to distinguish PDF data from the others (DOCX, XLSX, PPTX and PNG). The trained SVMs would be used to classify file fragments in the 6 test sets. All results are presented in Figure 4.

We can see in Figure 4 that the classification accuracy for the baseline deflate data set using BFD or bigram is very low, just 53.9%. This result is similar to the result in [7,8] and shows that classifying high entropy file fragments is still a challenge [1-3,7,8,13].

For the full inflate data set (including fonts, font programs and text) obtained from our method, we achieved the classification rates of 90.858% and 90.376% for BFD and bigram, respectively. There is not much difference between using BFD and bigram features. However, the bigram features require more computational time and resources.

For the inflate data set (including text only) obtained from our method, we achieved the classification rates of 99.98% and 99.95% for BFD and bigram, respectively.

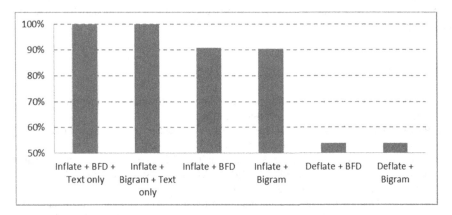

Fig. 4. PDF data fragment classification results. Note the Inflate data set in Inflate + BFD and Inflate + Bigram include fonts, font programs and text.

For the image part in PDF files (refer to Table 1 for more details), the JPG data fragments from PDF files can be recognized using RoC feature [1, 3, 15], the recognition rate is up to 98%. This very high result is achieved because of the special structure of JPG files. The 0xFFxx is used as a marker in the body of JPG files. Particularly, the value 0xFF is used to indicate the beginning of all metadata tags, and the value 0x00 is placed after every 0xFF byte in the body of the file. This creates high appearances of the pattern 0xFF00 which has a very high RoC.

We also performed more experiments on different sizes of file fragments to discover what size is best for file type classification. Our experiments showed that the highest classification rate of 89.93% will be achieved for file fragments whose block sizes are equal or greater than 18 KB. This result is similar to that reported in [1].

5   Conclusion and Future Work

File fragment classification is a very important task in digital forensics. Although many research efforts have been done, some problems still remain. Compound file fragment classification is one of those problems. Normally, compound files contain data encoded by different methods, in order to correctly classify the compound file fragments, specialized approach must be proposed.

The largest portion of a PDF file is deflate-encoded data and file fragments obtained from a PDF file are high entropy ones. Current approaches cannot provide high classification rate for high entropy file fragments [2, 3, 13]. This challenge motivates us to propose a new approach where deflate encoded data need to be decompressed to get the underlying data fragments in their own formats such as text object format in PDF files. We have showed in our experiments that the proposed approach can provide high classification rates for PDF files.

For the future work, other data encoding methods such as CCITFax-encoded and JBIG2-encoded bi-tonal images, ASCII85/ASCIIHex will be investigated. We strongly believe that other specialized approaches would be proposed for those data encoding methods.

References

1. Roussev, V., Quates, C.: File fragment encoding classification—An empirical approach. Digital Investigation 10(suppl.), S69–S77 (2013)
2. Penrose, P., Macfarlane, R., Buchanan, W.J.: Approaches to the classification of high entropy file fragments. Digital Investigation 10, 372–384 (2013)
3. Roussev, V., Garfinkel, S.L.: File Fragment Classification-The Case for Specialized Approaches. In: Fourth International IEEE Workshop on Systematic Approaches to Digital Forensic Engineering. SADFE 2009, pp. 3–14 (2009)
4. Rentz, D.: OpenOffice.org's documentation of the microsoft compound document (2007), http://sc.openoffice.org/compdocfileformat.pdf (The Spreadsheet Project, http://OpenOffice.org)
5. Park, B., Park, J., Lee, S.: Data concealment and detection in Microsoft Office 2007 files. Digital Investigation 5, 104–114 (2009)
6. Meehan, J., Rose, T.S.C.C.: PDF Reference. Adobe Portable Document Format, Version, 1, 1 (2001)
7. Axelsson, S.: The Normalised Compression Distance as a file fragment classifier. Digital Investigation 7(suppl.), S24–S31 (2010)
8. Fitzgerald, S., Mathews, G., Morris, C., Zhulyn, O.: Using NLP techniques for file fragment classification. Digital Investigation 9(suppl.), S44–S49 (2012)
9. Wei-Jen, L., Ke, W., Stolfo, S.J., Herzog, B.: Fileprints: identifying file types by n-gram analysis. In: Proceedings from the Sixth Annual IEEE SMC Information Assurance Workshop, IAW 2005, pp. 64–71 (2005)
10. Sportiello, L., Zanero, S.: File Block Classification by Support Vector Machine. In: 2011 Sixth International Conference on Availability, Reliability and Security (ARES), pp. 307–312 (2011)
11. Calhoun, W.C., Coles, D.: Predicting the types of file fragments. Digital Investigation 5(suppl.), S14–S20 (2008)
12. Garfinkel, S., Farrell, P., Roussev, V., Dinolt, G.: Bringing science to digital forensics with standardized forensic corpora. Digital Investigation 6(suppl.), S2–S11 (2009)
13. Li, Q., Ong, A., Suganthan, P., Thing, V.: A novel support vector machine approach to high entropy data fragment classification. In: Proceedings of the South African Information Security Multi-Conference, SAISMC 2010 (2010)
14. Chang, C.-C., Lin, C.-J.: LIBSVM: a library for support vector machines. ACM Transactions on Intelligent Systems and Technology (TIST) 2, 27 (2011)
15. Karresand, M., Shahmehri, N.: File Type Identification of Data Fragments by Their Binary Structure. In: 2006 IEEE Information Assurance Workshop, pp. 140–147 (2006)

Geo-Social-RBAC: A Location-Based Socially Aware Access Control Framework

Nathalie Baracaldo, Balaji Palanisamy, and James Joshi

University of Pittsburgh, School of Information Sciences, USA
{nab62,bpalan,jjoshi}@pitt.edu

Abstract. The ubiquity of low-cost GPS-enabled mobile devices and the proliferation of online social networks have enabled the collection of rich geo-social information that includes the whereabouts of the users and their social connections. This information can be used to provide a rich set of access control policies that ensure that resources are utilized securely. Existing literature focuses on providing access control systems that control the access solely based on either the location of the users or their social connections. In this paper, we argue that a number of real-world applications demand an access control model that effectively captures both the geographic as well as the social dimensions of the users in a given location. We propose, Geo-social-RBAC, a new role based access control model that allows the inclusion of geo-social constraints as part of the access control policy. Our model, besides capturing the locations of a user requesting access and her social connections, includes geo-social cardinality constraints that dictate how many people related by a particular social relation need to be present in the required locations at the time of an access. The model also allows specification of geo-social and location trace constraints that may be used to dictate if an access needs to be granted or denied.

1 Introduction

The ubiquity of low-cost GPS-enabled mobile devices and the proliferation of online social networks allow the collection of rich geo-social information that includes the whereabouts of the users and their social connections. A number of real-world applications demand an access control (AC) model that effectively captures both the geographic as well as the social dimensions of the users in a given location. It is often possible to use this information to help restrict access to a particular set of resources given the location and social context of a user. For instance, consider a hospital where a doctor can access a patient's record if and only if the doctor is the patient's primary physician and the patient is located in the waiting room outside the doctor's office. Similarly, we may want to protect the privacy of patients by ensuring that in case a third person enters a room that is not part of the medical personnel and is not the patient's spouse, the health record should be automatically closed to avoid leaking patient's information.

In addition to geo-locations, location traces also offer interesting potential in the context of geo-social AC. In these cases, the whereabouts of a user and the people she has recently met influence how trusted the person is and the AC decision itself.

M.H. Au et al. (Eds.): NSS 2014, LNCS 8792, pp. 501–509, 2014.
© Springer International Publishing Switzerland 2014

For instance, a trace-based geo-social AC policy may ensure that if a doctor was in a contagious unit, he cannot enter the new born unit unless he goes to a sanitizing facility first. It is also possible in some cases to bootstrap the trust of a user to access a resource based on the people that accompany him and the places where they have been together in the recent past. For instance, in a fast-food restaurant, a user who has just bought something should be allowed to access other areas of the restaurant such as restrooms and if she also has her kids with her, she should be allowed to use the kids' play area.

While there are many potential benefits of a geo-social AC model, unfortunately current literature does not provide a solution that allows the specification of such policies which include both geo-social as well as location traces with geo-social cardinality constraints. Most of the existing models support the specification of policies that depend on user location or other contextual factors such as time, type of device used to access the system and the type of connection used to access resources [3,5,16,6,11]. Given that many organizations use role based access control systems (RBAC) [7] to control their resources [12], several existing works have extended this model to include the location context [3,5,16,11].

In this paper, we propose a fine-grained geo-social AC model, Geo-social-RBAC, that allows the inclusion of geo-social constraints as part of the AC policy. Concretely, in this paper we make the following *contributions*:

1. To the best of our knowledge, the proposed Geo-social-RBAC model is the first role based AC model that allows the inclusion of geo-social constraints as part of the AC policy.
2. Our model, besides capturing the locations of a user requesting access and her social connections, supports geo-social cardinality constraints that dictate how many people related by a particular social relation need to be present in the required locations at the time of an access. The model also allows specification of fine-grained geo-social and location trace constraints that may be used to dictate if an access needs to be granted or denied based on the historical whereabouts of users.

The remainder of this paper is organized as follows. In Section 2, we discuss the requirements of the system and present an overview of the proposed model. In Section 3, we present the components that we use as part of the system to model the location and social relations and then introduce the proposed Geo-Social RBAC. In Section 4, we present the related work and we conclude our paper in Section 5.

2 Motivation and Requirements

In this section we motivate the need for the proposed Geo-social RBAC model and present the requirements that guide the design of our geo-social AC framework. We begin by discussing the types of policies that are unique to the proposed AC model that are not supported by existing systems. Current AC models do not have the capabilities to support policies that contain geo-social traces and constraints. In this work, we focus on a RBAC [7] based geo-social model because of RBAC's well-documented advantages [12] and wide adoption. In RBAC, users and permissions are assigned to roles. In order to acquire the permissions associated with a role, a user needs to be previously assigned to it and needs to activate it in a session. RBAC does not support location constraints and as a result, several extensions have been proposed to include location constraints [3,5,16,11].

We broadly classify the existing RBAC literature into two categories namely RBAC extensions that support location based decisions [3,5,16,11] such as Geo-RBAC [3] and LoT-RBAC [5] and models that extend RBAC with proximity constraints that include other user's proximity as part of the AC policies such as Prox-RBAC [10,9]. In Table 1, we compare existing approaches based on the following types of constraints:

1. *Pure location constraints:* these constraints only take the location of the user into account, e.g., to access a confidential file, a user may need to be in a specific room.
2. *Geo-social constraints:* these constraints consider both the location and the social dimensions of the users in the policies. We further classify this type of constraints as follows. *(i) Geo-social graph-based constraints* which are based on the social graph structure, e.g., to enter into a room a person needs to be in company of at least two friends that work there and are present. *(ii) Geo-social tag-based constraints* which capture the type of relationships between the users in the social graphs in addition to the location and social constraints. For example, a child can only access a pay-to-view movie if he is in presence of his parent or a nanny.
3. *Trace-based constraints:* These constraints are based on user's trajectory and whether the user has been in contact with a particular set of individuals. We distinguish between two types of constraints. *(i) Location trace-based constraints:* which capture the past location traces of a user as part of the AC policies. For instance, consider a silicon chip manufacture company where even a minimum amount of dust may ruin an entire production batch. If an operator has been in known dusty rooms of the factory, he cannot enter the sterile chip production room unless he has previously passed through the cleaning room. This is a location trace policy as the previous whereabouts of the user determine whether he would be able to obtain the requested access. *(ii) Geo-social trace-based constraints:* which capture both the location history and the social dimensions of the users. For example, in a company, if a visitor has entered into the rooms used for induction of new employees accompanied by an administrator, he can also access the welcome package files and the internal directory web pages.

As shown in Table 1, existing models do not support many geo-social constraints that the proposed Geo-Social-RBAC incorporates. We further consider the following requirements for our model. The proposed AC framework should allow backward compatibility with RBAC based systems and should effectively support pure location, geo-social and trace-based constraints. The model should allow policies for different spatial granularity, e.g., it should be possible to specify if someone needs to be in a point in the space, at a door, on a room or in a floor of a building, in a city, among others.

2.1 Overview of the Proposed Geo-Social RBAC Framework

In Geo-social-RBAC, the context of users is defined by the following information: the position of the user and his previous whereabouts, the proximity of the user to other users and the user's social relations with these individuals. The system consists of *users*,

Table 1. Comparison of types of policies supported by RBAC based systems

Policy	RBAC extended with location [3,5,16,11]	RBAC extended with proximity [10,9]	Our Approach: Geo-Social-RBAC
Pure location constraints	Yes	Yes	Yes
Geo-social graph-based constraints	No	Yes	Yes
Geo-social tag-based constraints	No	No	Yes
Location-trace-based constraints	No	No	Yes
Geo-social-trace-based constraints	No	No	Yes

geo-social roles, *permissions* and *trace-based* and *geo-social-cardinality constraints*. In our model, users are assigned to geo-social roles and geo-social roles are assigned permissions. To acquire permissions of a geo-social role, users need to be assigned to it and activate it in a session. Geo-social roles can only be activated by a user when his contextual constraints allow it. Hence, a user can only activate a geo-social role when the current location, his previous whereabouts, his proximity to other users and their social relations satisfy the associated activation constraints.

3   Geo-Social-RBAC

In this section we present the details of the proposed Geo-Social-RBAC.

3.1   Social Relations

Modeling social relations is of key importance when specifying policies in a Geo-Social context. For this purpose and without loss of generality, we consider a single social graph that captures the various social relationships among the users. Here, we note that we could also use multiple social graphs services to obtain relevant social information. Let $\mathcal{G} = \langle V, E \rangle$ be a directed and asymmetric *Social Graph*, where V is a set of vertices and E a set of edges that represent users and their relationships, respectively. We also assume that there is a set of *tags* W used to annotate social relations. For each $e_{(i,j)} \in E$ there is a set that contains one or more tags $W_{(i,j)} \subseteq W$ that denote the type of relation between users i and j. A tag represents a specific type of social relation between two users such as a manager-employee relationship. This asymmetry between relations is necessary to ensure that some policies of interest can be specified. For example, suppose $W_{(i,j)} = \{$nanny, school_mate$\}$ which shows that user i is the nanny and school mate of user j, while $W_{(j,i)} = \{$school_mate$\}$. This allows us to later specify policies of the type "a child cannot access a web page if he is not in presence of his parent or a nanny".

Often, social relations have an inherent hierarchical structure. To represent such partial order, tags in W are organized in a lattice L_W. For instance, L_W may show that tags *teacher* and *parent* are greater than tag *student* while *teacher* and *parent* do not have any clear ordered relation, as it is the case when a child request to watch a movie.

We use the functions presented in Table 2 to extract relevant information from social graph $\mathcal{G}$. Policies in geo-social-RBAC include relations between a particular user and other users in the social graph. A valid social relation predicate $\mathcal{S}$ is formed by the functions previously listed and allows verification of the existence of a particular(s) social relation(s) or to verify if a social relation has certain properties.

Table 2. Functions to extract relevant information from social graph $\mathcal{G}$

Function	Meaning
$getSocialRelation : V \times V \to 2^W$	Returns the tags of a given social relation, e.g., $GetSocialRelation(v_i \in V, v_j \in V) = W_{(i,j)}$.
$getSocialDistance : V \times V \to \{\mathbb{N} \cup \infty\}$	Returns the minimum number of edges between the specified vertices, e.g., for a direct social relation returns 1, for a friend-of-friend relation returns 2 and for two unconnected nodes ∞.
$superior : V \times V \to \{t, f\}$	Returns true if the first vertice, v_i, is *superior* to the second vertice, v_j given their tags $W_{(i,j)}$ and lattice L_W.
$commonNeighbors : V \times V \to \{t, f\}$	Given vertices v_i and v_j returns true if they have neihbors in common, otherwise returns false.
$kClique : 2^V \to \{t, f\}$	Returns true if the given vertices form a clique, otherwise returns false.

3.2 Geo Location and Location Traces

To model users location and their location traces in the proposed Geo-Social RBAC, we make use of the Open GeoSpatial consortium geometric model [1]. In this model, elements in a space called *geometries* are modelled as *points*, *polygons* and *lines*. Geometries of interest are given names and are called *features*, and are defined as a tuple $\langle type, name \rangle$ where $type \in \{point, line, polygon\}$ represents the geometry type and $name$ represent the name of feature f, respectively, e.g., a polygon that represents an office may be named office-501. The set of all features of the system is denoted as $\mathcal{F}$.

Additionally, it is necessary to establish a reference space that we denote as $\mathcal{M}$ that provides the limits of the system of interest. Let $\mathcal{L}$ be a set of functions to validate the location of users that take as input the location of the user and identify if the location is as expected with respect to a particular place. $\mathcal{L}$ contains operations such as *overlap*, *touch*, *cross*, *in*, *contains*, *equal*, and *disjoint* [1] and may also contain more refined proximity functions as the ones presented in [9]. These functions serve to measure the proximity between a coordinate and a particular location and may be used to establish how far away a user is from others. While $location(u)$ provides coordinates, a function $\ell \in \mathcal{L}$ verifies logical information with respect to a feature f, e.g., function ℓ takes the current location of user u, $location(u)$, and a feature and validates if a user is standing at a particular door. Hence, a tuple $\langle f, \ell \rangle$ defines a spatial scope of interest.

Traces: The proposed Geo-Social RBAC also considers the location and geo-social traces that users generate as they move around $\mathcal{M}$. A *location trace* of a user u shows the places that he has visited. Concretely, during a period $[t_s, t_e]$ starting at t_s and ending at t_e, his *location trace* $\wp l_{(u,t_s,t_e)}$ is defined as a list $\langle \langle p_1, t_s \rangle, ..., \langle p_i, t_j \rangle, ... \langle p_n, t_e \rangle \rangle$ where tuple $\langle p_i, t_j \rangle$ shows that the user was at the location point p_i at time instance t_j.

Similarly, his *geo-social trace* $\wp g_{(u,t_s,t_e)}$ besides showing his whereabouts through time, also shows who he has frequented. We define his geo-social trace $\wp g_{(u,t_s,t_e)}$ as a list of tuples $\langle \langle p_1, U'_1, t_s \rangle, ... \langle p_n, U'_n, t_e \rangle \rangle$. Each item in the list besides containing p_i and t_j also includes $U'_i \subseteq U$ which is the set of users in proximity as per function $\ell \in \mathcal{L}$ of user u at time t_j. If at time instance t_j the system has no record of the whereabouts of user u, $p_i = \bot$.

To be able to specify trace-based policies, we define a *trace constraint* $\mathcal{Q}$ which consolidates both geo-social and location constraints in a single construction. A *trace clause* is a location constraint $c = \langle \alpha, \top \rangle$ or a geo-social constraint $g = \langle \beta, \top \rangle$ that need to be fulfilled within a period of time T. More concretely, α is defined by a tuple of the form $\langle f \in \mathcal{F}, \ell \in \mathcal{L} \rangle$ and β by a tuple $\langle f \in \mathcal{F}, \ell \in \mathcal{L}, s \in \mathcal{S} \rangle$. A location constraint is fulfilled by user u if his location trace $\wp l_{(u,t_s,t_e)}$, for $\mathsf{T} = [t_s, t_e]$, contains locations that satisfy α. Similarly, a geo-social constraint is fulfilled if $\wp g_{(u,t_s,t_e)}$ satisfies β. Considering these definitions, $\mathcal{Q}$ is defined by the following grammar[1]: $C ::= C \wedge C \mid C \vee C \mid c \mid g$.

The previous construction allows the specification of policies where the whereabouts and the type of people that the user meets are relevant for making AC decisions. We use function *completeTrace* which takes as input a trace constraint $\mathcal{Q}$, a user u and determines if u has completed the trace by evaluating each trace clause q in $\mathcal{Q}$ and integrating the results. If the trace constraint is empty, *completeTrace* returns true.

3.3 Geo-Social Cardinality Constraints

Geo-social cardinality constraints are key to specify whether the locations of a user's social relations should interfere with the access decisions. A geo-social cardinality clause is a tuple $c = \langle f, \ell, n, \mathcal{S} \rangle$ where $f \in \mathcal{F}$ is the feature where at least n social connections that comply with social predicate $\mathcal{S}$ need to be located at according to the proximity function $\ell \in \mathcal{L}$. Based on c, grammar: $C ::= C \wedge C \mid C \vee C \mid T$ and $T ::= c \mid \epsilon$, defines a *geo-social cardinality constraint* C. We use function *peopleAt*(u, C), which takes a user u and a cardinality constraint C, to evaluate if the constraint is satisfied or not. When a cardinality constraint is empty (ϵ), *peopleAt*(u, C) returns true.

3.4 Geo-Social-RBAC

With the key building blocks of our model introduced in the previous subsections, we now present the proposed geo-social aware AC model. We first introduce Core-Geo-Social-RBAC and then extend it to include role hierarchy.

Core-Geo-Social-RBAC is defined as a tuple $\langle U, R_{\mathcal{GS}}, A, O, P \rangle$. The model consists of a set of geo-social roles $R_{\mathcal{GS}}$, a set of users U, a set of actions A a set of objects O and a set of permissions defined as $P = A \times O$. Users are assigned to geo-social roles and geo-social roles are assigned permissions. We use function *authorized*$(u \in U)$ to obtain the set of roles that u is authorized for.

Definition 1. *A geo-social role $r \in R_{\mathcal{GS}}$ is defined as a tuple $\langle SC, C, \mathcal{Q} \rangle$ where*

- *SC is a set that represents the spatial-scope of a role (places where the role can be activated). The set contains tuples of the form $\langle f \in \mathcal{F}, \ell \in \mathcal{L} \rangle$. When $SC = \bot$ the role does not have a spatial scope is specified.*
- *C is a geo-social cardinality constraint.*
- *$\mathcal{Q}$ is a trace constraint.*

In our model, a geo-social role without any constraint is equivalent to a standard role. Additionally, a geo-social role can be in one of two states *enabled*, or *disable*.

Definition 2. *A geo-social role $r = \langle SC, C, \mathcal{Q} \rangle \in R$ is said to be* enabled *for user u if all the following conditions are fulfilled: $r \in$ authorized$(u) \wedge$ peopleAt$(u, C) \wedge$ completeTrace$(\mathcal{Q}, u) \wedge \exists \langle f, \ell \rangle \in SC : \ell(location(u), f) \vee SC = \emptyset$. Otherwise r is disabled.*

---

[1] For simplicity grammars omit the parenthesis to avoid distracting readers from the main issues.

Table 3. Examples of policies that can be expressed in Geo-Social-RBAC

Pure location constraint policy: A *researcher* should be in the laboratory (fourth floor) in order to access any general files. Let r_1 be a researcher's geo-social role, with location scope $SC = \langle floor4, in \rangle$.
Geo-social cardinality constraint(for your eyes only): A *senior-researcher* can access a confidential vaccine compound formula only if he is in the confidential room by himself. Let r_2 be a senior-researcher's geo-social role, with location scope $SC = \langle ConfidentialRoom, in \rangle$ and a geo-social cardinality constraint $C = \langle ConfidentialRoom, in, 0, \epsilon \rangle$.
Geo-social cardinality constraint (tag): An *assistant* in the research lab can only see files with private medical information of subjects if he is in the 4th floor and there are three researchers or senior-researchers (superiors) in the general research unit. Let r_3 be a senior-researcher's geo-social role, with location scope $SC = \langle floor4, in \rangle$, an a geo-social cardinality constraint $C = \langle GeneralResearchRoom, in, 3, superior(u,x) \rangle$.
Trace constraint: A nurse needs to go to check all patients in their rooms in the last 2 hours before she can sign her electronically the round-sheet. Here, role nurse r_5 is associated with $Q = (\langle room_1, in \rangle \wedge \ldots \wedge \langle room_n, in \rangle, 2hours)$ and with permission sign electronically the round-sheet.

Henceforth, we refer to *geo-social roles* as *roles*. In the previous definition, a role r is enabled for a user u if u is assigned to r, she is in the required location and the geo-social cardinality and trace constraints are fulfilled. A user u can *activate* role r if it is enabled. When u activates r he can obtain all its privileges.

To show the expressiveness of our model, we present some examples in Table 3 that shows how our model can be used in a variety of scenarios.

Finally, we discuss Geo-Social-RBAC with Role Hierarchy. Role hierarchy [13] is a feature used by some RBAC systems in which roles are organized in a partial order. We define a Geo-Social-RBAC system as a tuple $\langle U, R_{GS}, A, O, P, R_H \rangle$ that in addition to the components in the core-Geo-social RBAC, also incorporates the geo-social role hierarchy R_H. The semantics of R_H are defined as follows.

Definition 3. *Let $r_i, r_j \in R_{GS}$ be two geo-social roles. r_i is said to be* senior *of r_j, written as $r_i \geq r_j$. If a user u assigned to r_i can activate r_j as long as r_j is enabled.*

In Geo-Social RBAC, a user that activates r_i does not automatically inherit the permissions of its junior roles unless those junior roles can be activated. A user that needs to acquire the permissions of a junior role would need to activate it in a session. We note that this design has several advantages. First, it ensures that all specified constraints are enforced in the system preventing and resolving policy conflicts that result when r_i and r_j are not simultaneously enabled. Also, it enforces the least privilege principle and automatically reduces the risk exposure of granting access [2].

We next discuss some related work for our Geo-social RBAC model.

4   Related Work

Several works have extended RBAC to include the context of the user such as the location and temporal constraints as part of the AC decision [3,5,16,6,11]. Unfortunately, these works do not allow the specification of geo-social constraints or location traces constraints as part of the policies. Some literature [15,8] have proposed to include social relations constraints as part of the AC model. TMAC [15] is a model to establish policies that require team cooperation. Fong present ReRAC [8] where decisions are based on the relationship between the resource owner and the access requester. Carminati *et al.* [4] propose an AC model where policies are expressed based on user-user and user-resource relationships. In contrast, our model considers both geographical and social dimensions of the users for making access decisions. In [14], AC decisions are made based on the location of the resource owner, the resource requester and possibly other co-located individuals. Unlike our model, their model assumes that individuals own the resources and it is not based on RBAC, making it less suitable for company settings. Also, it does not consider location trace constraints as captured by our model.

Few works have explored the inclusion of geo-social context as part of AC systems [10,9]. Prox-RBAC model [10] extends the Geo-RBAC model to include proximity of other individuals as part of the policy in indoor environments. Yet, Prox-RBAC does not allow the specification of geo-social constraints based on social graphs; in Prox-RBAC valid proximity constraints are based on the type of role of other individuals in proximity of the access requester hold. Gupta *et. al* [9] extended Prox-RBAC by providing formal definitions to determine the proximity between locations, users, attributes and time, each of which is referred to as a realm. However, their work does not allow the specification of the type of policies presented in this paper. More specifically, *(i)* the model presented in [9] does not allow the specification of trace-based constraints that is well captured in our geo-social-RBAC model, *(ii)* unlike our model, the model in [9] does not allow the specification of latices specify partial orders between social relations and *(iii)* finally, the AC model presented in [9] does not include hybrid realm policies while our geo-social-RBAC approach does. To the best of our knowledge, the proposed Geo-Social-RBAC is the first research effort dedicated to providing a comprehensive role-based AC model that effectively captures both social and as spatial dimensions of the users considering both geo-cardinality and location-trace constraints.

5   Conclusions

In this paper, we presented a new access control model that includes geo-social factors of the users as part of the access control decision process. The proposed model allows organizations to specify their policy considering the geographic and social contexts of the access requester users as well as that of the users located near them. We have introduced the concepts of location and geo-location traces, that allow the specification of policies based on the whereabouts of users not only during the access control decision, but during a longer period of time such as their recent past. Our model is compatible with RBAC systems and we believe that it helps mitigate information exfiltration threats and helps better control how users access resources. As part of future work, we are working on devising new techniques to efficiently enforce our policy model.

References

1. Opengis simple features specification for sql, tech. report ogc 99-049. Technical report, OpenGIS Consortium (1999)
2. Baracaldo, N., Joshi, J.: An adaptive risk management and access control framework to mitigate insider threats. Computers & Security 39, 237–254 (2013)
3. Bertino, E., Catania, B., Damiani, M.L., Perlasca, P.: Geo-rbac: a spatially aware rbac. In: Proceedings of the Tenth ACM Symposium on Access Control Models and Technologies, pp. 29–37. ACM (2005)
4. Carminati, B., Ferrari, E., Heatherly, R., Kantarcioglu, M., Thuraisingham, B.: A semantic web based framework for social network access control. In: Proc. of the 14th SACMAT, pp. 177–186. ACM (2009)

5. Chandran, S.M., Joshi, J.B.D.: *LoT-RBAC*: A location and time-based RBAC model. In: Ngu, A.H.H., Kitsuregawa, M., Neuhold, E.J., Chung, J.-Y., Sheng, Q.Z. (eds.) WISE 2005. LNCS, vol. 3806, pp. 361–375. Springer, Heidelberg (2005)

6. Covington, M.J., Long, W., Srinivasan, S., Dev, A.K., Ahamad, M., Abowd, G.D.: Securing context-aware applications using environment roles. In: Proc. of the 6th SACMAT, pp. 10–20. ACM (2001)

7. Ferraiolo, D.F., Sandhu, R., Gavrila, S., Kuhn, D.R., Chandramouli, R.: Proposed nist standard for role-based access control. ACM Trans. Inf. Syst. Secur. 4, 224–274 (2001)

8. Fong, P.W.: Relationship-based access control: protection model and policy language. In: Proc. of the First ACM Conference on Data and Application Security and Privacy, pp. 191–202. ACM (2011)

9. Gupta, A., Kirkpatrick, M.S., Bertino, E.: A formal proximity model for rbac systems. Computers & Security (2013)

10. Kirkpatrick, M.S., Damiani, M.L., Bertino, E.: Prox-rbac: a proximity-based spatially aware rbac. In: Proc. of the 19th ACM SIGSPATIAL Int. Conf. on Advances in Geographic Information Systems (2011)

11. Ray, I., Kumar, M., Yu, L.: LRBAC: A location-aware role-based access control model. In: Bagchi, A., Atluri, V. (eds.) ICISS 2006. LNCS, vol. 4332, pp. 147–161. Springer, Heidelberg (2006)

12. Osborn, Q.M.S., Sandhu, R.: Configuring role-based access control to enforce mandatory and discretionary access control policies. In: ACM Transaction on Information and System Security (2000)

13. Sandhu, R.: Role activation hierarchies. In: Proceedings of 3rd ACM Workshop on Role-Based Access Control (1998)

14. Tarameshloo, E., Fong, P.: Access control models for geo-social computing systems. In: SACMAT (2014)

15. Thomas, R.K.: Team-based access control (tmac): a primitive for applying role-based access controls in collaborative environments. In: Proc. of the 2nd ACM Workshop on Role-Based Access Control (1997)

16. Toahchoodee, M., Ray, I., McConnell, R.M.: Using graph theory to represent a spatio-temporal role-based access control model. Int. Journal of Next-Generation Computing (2010)

A New Approach to Executable File Fragment Detection in Network Forensics

Khoa Nguyen, Dat Tran, Wanli Ma, and Dharmendra Sharma

Faculty of Education, Science, Technology and Mathematics
University of Canberra, ACT 2601, Australia
Khoa.Nguyen@canberra.edu.au

Abstract. Network forensics known as an extended phase of network security plays an essential role in dealing with cybercrime. The performance of a network forensics system heavily depends on the network attack detection solutions. Two main types of network attacks are network level and application level. Current research methods have improved the detection rate but this is still a challenge. We propose a Shannon entropy approach to this study to identify executable file content for anomaly-based network attack detection in network forensics systems. Experimental results show that the proposed approach provides high detection rate.

Keywords: Network forensics, executable data detection, machine learning.

1   Introduction

Malicious data detection is the main purpose of network security and network forensic solution. Meanwhile, network security solutions are used to detect malicious behaviors in the real time network traffic, network forensics solutions are used to deal with post-mortem investigation of harmful activities. In the other words, network forensics process mainly on stored network packets. However, interception of all network packets is impossible in fast connection technologies such as fiber optic networks. Therefore, good mechanisms must be exploited in order to separate the benign and malicious network data packets [1]. Obviously, only malicious data are stored for further analysis and benign data will be bypassed by network forensics appliances. Malicious data are the first signal of network attacks, and they normally contain executable data such as Trojan, spyware and virus [1, 2]. Therefore, recognizing the executable data from network traffic plays an important role in network forensics.

Executable file type detection has been a difficult task for researchers. The biggest obstacle is low detection rate or high false positive which degrades dramatically the performance of network forensics systems. Therefore, many research works have been done in order to increase the detection rate [1, 3, 4], but this is still a challenge.

In this paper, we propose a new approach based on Shannon entropy [5] and support vector machine (SVM) [6] using byte frequency distribution (BFD) and rate of change (RoC) [7] to generate feature vectors that can effectively and efficiently detect data in executable files. Shannon entropy is one of effective tools used to

M.H. Au et al. (Eds.): NSS 2014, LNCS 8792, pp. 510–517, 2014.
© Springer International Publishing Switzerland 2014

identify the file type of a data fragment [8, 9]. Shannon entropy is very useful to separate low and high entropy data [9]. By calculating entropy for each segment of executable files, the results show that only small amount of data segments in executable files has low or high entropy values. The reason for this fact is due to the particular format of executable file format [10] which contains some specific sections such as .text and .data section in Windows operating systems. Therefore, we use entropy technique to cluster data fragments in the first phase of executable file content detection process. In addition, it is demonstrated that solutions to executable file type detection based on BFD attain good results [1, 3, 8]. However, in the cases of low and high data fragments, only BFD is not enough to provide high detection rate for executables because BFD does not consider the rate of byte value change in the data fragments, whereas RoC takes byte value change into consideration, because it measures the difference of two consecutive bytes in the data fragment. Therefore, the combination of BFD and RoC will provide better results for low and high executable data fragments.

The rest of paper is organized as follows. Section 2 presents related studies in detecting executables in network traffic and file fragments. Section 3 introduces our approach. Section 4 presents our experiments and results. Finally, Section 5 includes conclusion and future work.

2   Related Work

Network forensics is used to deal with post-mortem investigation of the attack. It evolves monitoring network data flow and recognizing abnormal activities in the traffic and identifying those activities that indicate attacks [11]. The critical goal of network forensics is to provide sufficient evidences to bring network criminals to be successfully prosecuted. A generic process model of network forensics is proposed by Pilli et al [2] as seen in Fig. 1 below. In this model, the detection phase plays a very important role during the whole process. It decides mainly the performance of a network forensics, the more accuracy that detection phase brings the better performance that system can achieve.

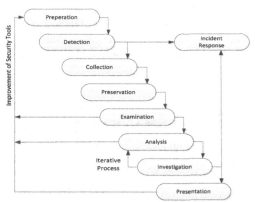

Fig. 1. Generic process model for network forensics

Network forensics consists of identifying attacks and reconstructing evidences in the network environment. Malicious behaviors in the network traffic are the signals of network attacks. Two typical methods are used to detect attacks, namely misuse and anomaly detections [1]. The misuse methods cannot be used to detect zero-day attacks because those methods are based on pre-defined attack signatures. However, zero-day attacks include a new kind or new varieties of existing attacks that do not have any patterns until at least their first launches. Zero-day attacks can only be detected by using anomaly detection methods. Moreover, one of the main sources of malicious data in the network traffic is in executables [1, 2]. Therefore, executable file type detection is an essential factor in network forensics systems.

File type identification of data fragments have been attracted many researchers for over a decade [8, 9, 12-14]. McDaniel and Heydari [12] used some statistical properties to detect the type file types consisting of Byte Frequency Analysis (BFA), Byte Frequency Cross-correlation (BFC) and File Header/Trailer (FHT). The FHT provided the highest accuracy rate 100% for executable files, because each file type has a very distinguishable header format. However, the FHT feature cannot be used in general cases because a huge number of data fragments come from the middle of files which do not have FHT information. Wei-Jen et al [15] also used the FHT to detect file type of files. Their findings revealed that the accuracy dropped to 77% for the case of executable files when the whole data in a file was examined. In addition, Karresand and Shahmehri [7] made use of centroid techniques combined with Byte Frequency Distribution (BFD) and Rate of Change (RoC) as feature vectors to detect file types. They achieved detection rate of 77% for executable file fragments, however, the false positive rate was up to 70%. In another work, Sprotiello [8] used SVM to classify file fragments of nine file types including executable type. They also used a number of feature vectors such as BFD and entropy. They revealed that the highest recognition rate for executable file fragments was 89%. However, this recognition rate is still low for network attack detection comparing with other works [3].

BFD was used to build a standard profile in order to detect executables in network traffic by Like et al [3]. BFD was computed from benign executable files to build the standard profile in the training phase. In the detection phase depicted in Fig. 2 below, the authors buffered ten consecutive incoming network packets, and then BFD was generated from buffered data and compared to standard profile by using Manhattan distance between two BFD values. They revealed that the detection rate achieved 95%. However, their data set was limited only within five file types: EXE, JPG, GIF, PDF and DOC.

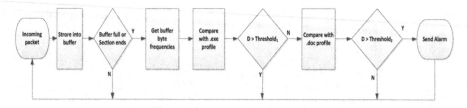

Fig. 2. Detection Phase of Like's method [3]

Although many works have been contributed, the executable file type detection methods still have drawbacks or shortcomings such as low detection rate or high false positive rate. Therefore, we propose a new approach to solving those problems.

3   Proposed Approach

Although solutions based on BFD, SVM, and entropy have been applied to identify executable file fragments [3, 8, 13, 16-18], no solution clustered data fragments into different groups based on their entropies before detecting executable data fragments among these groups. This is supplemented by the statement that it is more difficult to identify the file type of high entropy data fragments [19, 20]. Moreover, the change of data within one fragment can be observed in more details when we apply sliding window entropy technique. Therefore, we propose an approach that can cluster data fragments into three groups according to their entropy values and build three different models using SVM to detect executable file contents depending on the entropies of data fragments.

3.1   Shannon Entropy

Shannon entropy is very well-known, which is used to measure the uncertainty of the data [5]. The value of Shannon entropy is computed as follows

$$H(A) = -\sum_{i=1}^{n} p_i log_b(p_i) \qquad (1)$$

By examining the content of data fragments using the Shannon entropy technique, our findings is that a large number of executable file fragments (from executable files in Windows operating systems) have entropy values different from other files. Particularly, entropy of executable file fragments located mainly in the value range from 4 to 6.5, a small number of fragments have entropy less than 4, and a tiny number of fragments have entropy greater than 6.5, whereas a large number of data fragments of other file types have entropy either greater than 6.5 or less than 4.

3.2   Feature Extraction for SVM

It is demonstrated that SVM using BFD feature is a good solution for file type identification [13, 15, 18]. In addition, BFD has been used in detecting executable hidden file content in network traffic [3]. Therefore, BFD is an essential factor to build feature vectors for SVM in our work. BFD is computed by counting the frequencies of byte value (from 0 to 255) in a data fragment. However, the results in [8] show that only BFD feature does not provide the highest accuracy in executable file fragment identification. Therefore, we also use another feature named Rate of Change (RoC) in combination with BFD. RoC is defined as the absolute value of the difference between two consecutive byte values in a data fragment [7]. In addition, Sportiello et al. [8] used RoC as its nature form. Assuming that b_i and b_{i+1} are two consecutive bytes in a data fragment with corresponding values v_i and v_{i+1}, their difference is calculated as $d_i = v_i - v_{i+1}$, this difference can be a signed or unsigned value.

3.3   Proposed Model

According to the analysis in Section A (sliding window entropy), executable file data can be classified into three groups: low, medium, and high entropy. Therefore, three models should be built in order to detect executable file content corresponding to low, medium and high entropy data in network flow. The diagram of detection model is presented in Fig. 3 below.

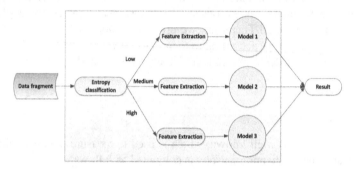

Fig. 3. Diagram of executable data detection

- **Training Phase**

Data fragments in the data set are put into three groups depending on their sliding window entropies. Model 1 is created from SVM using low entropy data set. Suitable feature vector extracted from medium entropy fragments used for SVM to build Model 2. Model 3 is created as the same way with Model 1 but based on high entropy data fragments.

- **Detection Phase**

In the detection phase, a data fragment from network traffic will be classified as a low, medium or high entropy data fragment. Depending on the entropy value, the corresponding feature vector will be extracted from the data fragment then fed into one of three models (Model 1, 2, or 3) in order to identify whether this data fragment contains executable file content.

4   Experiments

In this section, we present the results of our experiments. We describe the experiment setup and compare the results to previous works.

4.1   Data set

The data set contains 166MB of 23 non-executable file types downloaded from the Govdos1 [21] data corpora at the website http://digitalcorpora.org, and 49MB of executable files in Windows operating systems. Govdos1 is the most popular data corpora for digital forensics in file fragment classification. As a consequence, the total number of different file types in the datasets is 24 consisting of HTML, variety of image formats (BMP, GIF, JPEG), and other popular format such as PDF, TXT, RTF, as well as Microsoft office files (DOC, XLS, PPT). Files from this data set are split into data fragments with size of 1024 bytes. Data fragments are clustered into three groups (low, medium, or high entropy) based on their entropy values.

4.2   Experimental Results

- **Scenario 1**

In the first work of our experiment, we put all data fragments in the data set together and used BFDs as feature vector for SVM. SVM was used to classify data fragments with two labels which are executable and non-executable. Data fragments of 23 non-executable file types were labeled as non-executable. There were 1000 data fragments for each file type; thus, the number of fragments for non-executables is 23000. On the other hand, we selected randomly 23000 fragments from executables labeled as executable. As a sequence, the total number of executable file fragments in our experiment is 46000. SVM was used in 10-fold cross validation test. Moreover, in order to eliminate the over-fitting problem in SVM, we used the same 46000 data fragments to build a model, then we set up a test set which was completely different from the training set and used SVM to recognize and compared the result with the results of 10-fold cross validation. We repeated this experiment ten times with ten different training and testing data sets. The average detection rate was 93.80%. The highest deviation from one single test to the average detection rate is 0.06%. Furthermore, the false positive rate was 4.2%.

In the next experiment, we repeated the above experiment and used BFD and RoC combination (BFD-RoC) as features. Our experiment showed that BFD-RoC provided the same detection rate as BFD. Therefore, RoC did not contribute any improvement in the case of all data fragments treated equally in one group.

- **Scenario 2**

In this work, we classified data fragments into low, medium, and high entropy groups. The executable data set contains 48537 data fragments including 6948 low entropy fragments, 40,308 medium entropy fragments and 1281 high entropy fragments, which are 14.31%, 83.05% and 2.64% of the data set, respectively. For each of these groups, we used SVM in both BFD and BFD-RoC cases. The results of our experiments are presented in Table 1 below.

From the results in Table 1 we see that BFD-RoC works better in the case of low and high entropy data fragment. On the contrary, BFD works better in the case of medium entropy. In addition, data fragments belong to medium entropy group contribute the main part of executable data, over 80%. Moreover, in the feature extraction stage, calculating BFD only is much faster than calculating BFD-RoC. This means the performance of the system will boost when BFD is used as feature vector in the case of medium entropy data fragment.

Table 1. Accuracy rate for BFD and BFD-RoC

Entropy	Accuracy for BFD (%)	Accuracy for BFD-RoC (%)
Low	94.88	95.55
Medium	98.88	97.42
High	97.83	97.84

On the other hand, we computed the average detection rate and false positive from the confusion matrices reported by SVM. The average detection rate for the best case (BFD for medium entropy, BFD-RoC for low and high entropy) is 97.42% and the false positive rate is 0.66%. These results are significantly better than those in Scenario 1 which are 93.80% for accuracy and 4.2% for false positive rate.

5   Conclusion and Future Work

Network forensics plays an important role nowadays. It is an extensive phase of network security. There are many phases in a network forensics process. Each phase plays an important different role to each other. Network forensics not only helps to trace back the source of an attack but also makes the attack more cost, because attackers have to spend more time and cost in order to avoid network forensics.

The performance of network forensics depends much on the attack detection. High average detection rate and low false positive rate are two crucial factors. False positive prediction of attack leads to time and cost consuming. Our proposed approach has provided both high detection and low false positive rates.

In our proposed approach, a data fragment was identified as one of low, medium, or high entropy fragment before it was fed into classifiers. If the data fragment has low or high entropy then BFD-RoC will be computed to obtain a feature vector. On the other hand, if the data fragment has medium entropy then BFD will be used instead. Our experiments showed that the proposed approach outperforms the previous approaches with 97.42% for detection rate and 0.66% for false positive rate.

In future work, more data sets including network attacks will be used to test our proposed model. Moreover, other format of executables such as ELF on Linux will be the target for our research.

References

1. Perdisci, R., Ariu, D., Fogla, P., Giacinto, G., Lee, W.: McPAD: A multiple classifier system for accurate payload-based anomaly detection. Computer Networks 53, 864–881 (2009)
2. Pilli, E.S., Joshi, R.C., Niyogi, R.: Network forensic frameworks: Survey and research challenges. Digital Investigation 7, 14–27 (2010)
3. Like, Z., White, G.B.: An Approach to Detect Executable Content for Anomaly Based Network Intrusion Detection. In: IEEE International Parallel and Distributed Processing Symposium, IPDPS 2007, pp. 1–8 (2007)
4. Christodorescu, M., Jha, S.: Static analysis of executables to detect malicious patterns. DTIC Document (2006)
5. Shannon, C.E., Weaver, W.: The mathematical theory of communication, vol. 19, p. 1. University of Illinois Press, Urbana (1949)
6. Chang, C.-C., Lin, C.-J.: LIBSVM: a library for support vector machines. ACM Transactions on Intelligent Systems and Technology (TIST) 2, 27 (2011)
7. Karresand, M., Shahmehri, N.: File Type Identification of Data Fragments by Their Binary Structure. In: 2006 IEEE Information Assurance Workshop, pp. 140–147 (2006)
8. Sportiello, L., Zanero, S.: File Block Classification by Support Vector Machine. In: 2011 Sixth Int. Conf. on Availability, Reliability and Security (ARES), pp. 307–312 (2011)
9. Veenman, C.J.: Statistical Disk Cluster Classification for File Carving. In: Third Int. Symposium on Information Assurance and Security, IAS 2007, pp. 393–398 (2007)
10. Pietrek, M.: Inside Windows-An In-Depth Look into the Win32 Portable Executable File Format, Part 2. MSDN magazine, 87–100 (2002)
11. Yasinsac, A., Manzano, Y.: Policies to enhance computer and network forensics. In: Proc. of the IEEE Workshop on Information Assurance and Security, pp. 289–295 (2001)
12. McDaniel, M., Heydari, M.H.: Content based file type detection algorithms. In: Proc. of the 36th Annual Hawaii International Conference on System Sciences, p. 10 (2003)
13. Fitzgerald, S., Mathews, G., Morris, C., Zhulyn, O.: Using NLP techniques for file fragment classification. Digital Investigation 9(suppl.), S44–S49 (2012)
14. Axelsson, S.: The Normalised Compression Distance as a file fragment classifier. Digital Investigation 7(suppl.), S24–S31 (2010)
15. Wei-Jen, L., Ke, W., Stolfo, S.J., Herzog, B.: Fileprints: identifying file types by n-gram analysis. In: Proceedings from the Sixth Annual IEEE SMC Information Assurance Workshop, IAW 2005, pp. 64–71 (2005)
16. Shannon, M.: Forensic relative strength scoring: ASCII and entropy scoring. International Journal of Digital Evidence 2, 151–169 (2004)
17. Hall, G.A.: Sliding window measurement for file type identification (2006)
18. Amirani, M.C., Toorani, M., Mihandoost, S.: Feature-based Type Identification of File Fragments. Security and Communication Networks 6, 115–128 (2013)
19. Roussev, V., Garfinkel, S.L.: File Fragment Classification-The Case for Specialized Approaches. In: Fourth International IEEE Workshop on Systematic Approaches to Digital Forensic Engineering, SADFE 2009, pp. 3–14 (2009)
20. Roussev, V., Quates, C.: File fragment encoding classification—An empirical approach. Digital Investigation 10(suppl.), S69–S77 (2013)
21. Garfinkel, S., Farrell, P., Roussev, V., Dinolt, G.: Bringing science to digital forensics with standardized forensic corpora. Digital Investigation 6, S2–S11 (2009)

Tighter Security Bound of MIBS Block Cipher against Differential Attack

Xiaoshuang Ma[1,2], Lei Hu[1,2], Siwei Sun[1,2], Kexin Qiao[1,2], and Jinyong Shan[1,2]

[1] State Key Laboratory of Information Security, Institute of Information Engineering,
Chinese Academy of Sciences, Beijing 100093, China
[2] Data Assurance and Communication Security Research Center,
Institute of Information Engineering,
Chinese Academy of Sciences, Beijing 100093, China
{xshma13,hu,swsun,kxqiao13,jyshan12}@is.ac.cn

Abstract. Automatically calculating a lower bound of the number of differentially active S-boxes by mixed-integer linear programming (MILP) is a technique proposed by Mouha *et al.* in 2011 and it can significantly reduce the time spent on security evaluation of a cipher and decrease the possibility of human errors in cryptanalysis. In this paper, we apply the MILP method to analyze the security of MIBS, a lightweight block cipher proposed by Izadi *et al.* in 2009. By adding more constraints in the MILP problem, we get tighter lower bounds on the numbers of differentially active S-boxes in MIBS. We show that for MIBS, 18 rounds of iterations are sufficient to resist against single-key differential attack, and 39 rounds are secure against related-key differential cryptanalysis.

Keywords: MIBS block cipher, Differential attack, Active S-box, Mixed-Integer Linear Programming.

1 Introduction

Differential cryptanalysis was first proposed by Biham and Shamir in [3] and is one of the most powerful attacks on block ciphers. Differential cryptanalysis analyzes differential propagation patterns of a cipher to discover its non-random behaviors, and uses these behaviors to build a distinguisher or recover the key. Since the effectivity of differential attack heavily depends on an upper bound of the probabilities of differential propagation patterns which can be found by an attacker and the probability of a differential propagation pattern is characterized in terms of the number of active S-boxes involved, a practical approach to evaluate the security of a block cipher against differential attack is to determine the minimum number of active S-boxes under the differential propagation model.

In [11], Mouha *et al.* proposed an automatic method based on Mixed-Integer Linear Programming (MILP) for counting the minimum number of active S-boxes for some word-oriented symmetric-key ciphers, and used it to analyze the stream cipher Enocoro-128v2 [16].One significant advantage of the MILP based technique is that it can be applied to a wide variety of symmetric-key cipher

M.H. Au et al. (Eds.): NSS 2014, LNCS 8792, pp. 518–525, 2014.

constructions, which is composed of a combination of S-box operation, linear permutation layers and/or exclusive-or (XOR) operations, and less programming effort is needed with this technique compared with previous works which focus on automatically calculating a lower bound of the number of active S-boxes [6,4,5,9,13].

However, Mouha *et al.* 's method can not be applied directly to bit-oriented block ciphers. Sun *et al.* [14] extended this method applicable to symmetric-key ciphers involving bit-oriented operations by introducing new representations for XOR differences to describe bit/word level differences simultaneously and by taking the collaborative diffusion effect of S-boxes and bitwise permutations into account. In [15], Sun *et al.* gave a bound on the probability of the best related-key differential characteristic of the full-round LBlock block cipher by adding constraints of conditional differential propagation and constraints selected from the H-Representation of the convex hull of all differential patterns of the S-boxes. Very recently, Qiao *et al.* [10] refined the constraints about the XOR operation to avoid invalid characteristics due to a wider feasible region caused by inaccurate constraints of XOR operation, and achieved a tighter security bound of FOX.

In this paper, we apply the MILP based methods presented in [11,14,15] to MIBS [8], which is a lightweight 32-round lightweight block cipher. We get tighter lower bounds on the numbers of differentially active S-boxes for 2- to 7-round MIBS against both single-key and related-key differential attack. We prove that the 18-round MIBS is sufficiently secure against single-key differential attack, and for related-key differential attack we give an estimation of the security of the cipher against related-key differential attack and show the 39-round MIBS can resist against related-key differential cryptanalysis.

Organization of the Paper. In Section 2, we introduce the MIBS block cipher. In Section 3 we briefly describe the existing MILP techniques, and then we apply these methods to MIBS and present the results in Section 4. Finally we conclude the paper in Section 5.

2   The MIBS Block Cipher

2.1   Description of MIBS

In this section, we recall the design of MIBS and we refer the reader to [8] for more detailed description.

The MIBS block cipher, proposed by Izadi *et al.* [8] in 2009, is a lightweight 64-bit block cipher suitable for resource-constrained devices. MIBS is a Feistel cipher with 32 rounds of iterations and the block length is 64-bit, while two key lengths of 64-bit and 80-bit are supported.

The round function of MIBS is demonstrated in Fig. 1. It transforms the input block of the i-th round, $(L_{i-1}, R_{i-1}) \in \{0,1\}^{32} \times \{0,1\}^{32}$, to the output block $(R_{i-1} \oplus F(K_i, L_{i-1}), L_{i-1})$. The F-function of MIBS has an SPN structure which consists of four stages: an xor layer with a round subkey, a non-linear substitution layer of 4×4-bit S-boxes, a linear mixing layer with branch number 5, and a

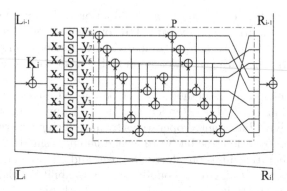

Fig. 1. The round function of MIBS

nibble-wise linear permutation. The operations in MIBS are all nibble-wise. The key schedule of MIBS is adapted from the key schedule of the PRESENT block cipher.

2.2 Known Cryptanalysis on MIBS

The designers of MIBS analyzed the security of MIBS against various attacks including linear cryptanalysis, differential cryptanalysis, algebraic attack and related key attack [8]. They showed MIBS is secure against differential and linear cryptanalysis.

In 2010, Bay *et al.* [1] presented multiple linear attack, linear attack, differential attack, and impossible-differential cryptanalysis on MIBS, which can attack the 17-round, 18-round, 14-round and 12-round MIBS, respectively.

3   MILP Based Methods

In [11], Mouha *et al.* presented a method based on MILP for counting the minimum number of active S-boxes for some word-oriented symmetric-key ciphers. Sun *et al.* extended Mouha *et al.* 's framework to be suitable for bit-level symmetric-key ciphers by imposing constraints describing S-box layers and adding constraints for conditional propagation and constraints selected from the H-Representation of the convex hull of all the differential pattern of the S-boxes [14,15]. In the following description, the difference's value is denoted "1" if the difference is nonzero and "0" otherwise, for bit-level symmetric-key cipher.

Suppose a bit-oriented block cipher is composed of the following three operations:

1) XOR operation $\oplus$: $\mathbb{F}_2^\omega \times \mathbb{F}_2^\omega \to \mathbb{F}_2^\omega$;
2) S-box substitution $\mathcal{S}$: $\mathbb{F}_2^\omega \to \mathbb{F}_2^\omega$; and
3) Bit permutation P: $\mathbb{F}_{2^\omega}^m \to \mathbb{F}_{2^\omega}^m$

where m is the word size, ω is the input and output bit length of the S-box.

Constraints Induced by the XOR Operation. Let $x_{in_1}, x_{in_2}, \cdots, x_{in_l} \in \mathbb{F}_2$ be the input differences of the combination of $l-1$ XOR operations, and $x_{out} \in$

$\mathbb{F}_2^\omega$ be the corresponding output difference. Then the following inequalities give the bit-oriented constraints of the XOR operation:

$$\begin{cases} x_{in_1} + x_{in_2} + \cdots + x_{in_l} - x_{out} - 2d_\oplus = 0, \\ d_\oplus \geq 0, \\ d_\oplus \leq \lfloor l/2 \rfloor, \end{cases} \quad (1)$$

where $d_\oplus$ is a dummy variable taking values in integers.

Constraints Induced by the S-box Operation. Introduce a new binary variable A_t to represent the S-box, where the value of A_t is 0 iff all input bit differences are 0 and $A_t = 1$ as long as there is at least one non-zero input bit difference. Suppose $(x_{in_0}, x_{in_1}, \cdots, x_{in_{\omega-1}})$ and $(x_{out_0}, x_{out_1}, \cdots, x_{out_{\omega-1}})$ are the input and output bit-level differences of an S-box marked by A_t. Then the following equations give the constraints of the value of A_t:

$$\begin{cases} A_t - x_{in_i} \geq 0, i \in \{0, 1, \cdots, \omega - 1\}, \\ x_{in_0} + x_{in_1} + \cdots + x_{in_{\omega-1}} - A_t \geq 0. \end{cases} \quad (2)$$

H-Reptesentation of the Convex Hull. The convex hull of a set X of discrete points in the Euclidean space is the smallest convex set that contains X. Let the convex hull of a specific $\omega \times \omega$ S-box be the convex hull $\mathcal{V}_S \subseteq \mathbb{R}^{2\omega}$ of all possible differential patterns of the S-box. Now we can describe the convex hull as the common solutions of a set of finitely many linear equations and inequalities as follows:

$$\begin{cases} \alpha_{0,0}x_{in_0} + \cdots + \alpha_{0,\omega-1}x_{in_{\omega-1}} + \alpha_{0,\omega}x_{out_0} + \cdots + \alpha_{0,2\omega-1}x_{out_{\omega-1}} + \alpha_{0,n} \geq 0, \\ \qquad \cdots \\ \beta_{0,0}x_{in_0} + \cdots + \beta_{0,\omega-1}x_{in_{\omega-1}} + \beta_{0,\omega}x_{out_0} + \cdots + \beta_{0,2\omega-1}x_{out_{\omega-1}} + \beta_{0,n} = 0, \\ \qquad \cdots \end{cases}$$

$$\quad (3)$$

In computational geometry, a number of algorithms are known for computing the convex hull for a finite set of points. However, there are a considerable number of equations and inequalities in the H-Representation of a convex hull. It is impractical to add all of them to an MILP problem for counting the number of active S-boxes. Sun *et al.* [14,15] proposed a greedy algorithm to select constraints from the H-Representation of the convex hull of all the differential pattern computed for the S-box. Moreover, these equations give the constraints that nonzero input difference must result in nonzero output difference and vice versa.

Further details on the word-level and bit-level MILP method for calculating the number of active S-boxes can be found in [11] and [14,15] respectively.

4 Application to the MIBS Block Cipher

In this section, we apply the MILP based methods presented in previous section to the lightweight block cipher MIBS, in both single-key and related-key models respectively.

4.1   Results on MIBS in the Single-key Model

We develop a C++ program to generate the MILP instances for MIBS in the "lp" format [7]. For single-key differential attack on MIBS, the objective function of the MILP problem is the sum of all variables representing the S-boxes, with the constraint that there is at least one active S-box to avoid the trivial case that all variables are zero. Then we call the Gurobi 5. 6 optimizer [12] to solve the MILP instances. By default we run Gurobi 5. 6 on a PC using 4 threads with Intel(R) Core(TM) Quad CPU (3. 40GHz, 8. 00GB RAM, Windows 7).

Table 1. Results for MIBS in the single-key model

Rounds	Nibble-wise			Bit-oriented			
	# Var.	# Con.	# Active S-boxes	# Var.	# Con.	# Active S-boxes	Time(s)
2	96	201	1	432	1073	1	0.02
3	152	305	2	664	1609	2	0.24
4	208	409	6	896	2145	6	34.42
5	264	513	8	1128	2681	9	753.24
6	320	617	9	1360	3217	11	10776.15
7	376	721	11	1592	3753	-	-

The lower bounds of the number of active S-boxes for a round-reduced MIBS in the single-key model are presented in Table 1.

However, some of the feasible solutions of the MILP model got from the Gurobi optimizer turn out to be invalid differential paths. For instance, one of the differential path of 6-round MIBS satisfies the above constraints is shown in Fig. 2. According to the difference distribution table of the MIBS S-box shown in [1], the S-boxes marked by slash notation are invalid differential propagation pattern for MIBS S-boxes. To avoid this situation, we apply a method proposed by Sun et al. [15] in 2013. By adding constraints selected from the H-Representation of the convex hull of all the differential pattern of the MIBS S-boxes, we have tightened the feasible region of the MILP model.

According to the greedy algorithm described in [15], we pick 27 inequalities out of the whole 378 constraints of the convex hull of MIBS S-box, which are shown in Appendix A . The results obtained with the inequalities selected from the H-Representation of the convex hull are summarized in Table 2.

In [9] Kanda et al. showed the minimum number $D^{(4r)}$ of active S-boxes in differential attack for a $(4r)$-round Feistel ciphers with SPN round function satisfies $D^{(4r)} \geq r \times B_d + \lfloor r/2 \rfloor$, where $B_d = 5$ is the differential branch number of the linear transformation for MIBS. Moreover, it is clearly shown in the difference distribution table of the MIBS S-box in [1] that the maximum differential probability for any differential propagation across this S-box is 2^{-2}. So, the designers claims that a lower bound of the number of active S-boxes with respect to differential cryptanalysis on the fully 32-round MIBS is $D^{(32)} \geq 8 \times 5 + \lfloor 8/2 \rfloor = 44$.

From Tables 1 and 2, we have learnt that the 5-round and 6-round MIBS in single-key model has at least 9, and 11 active S-boxes respectively. From the

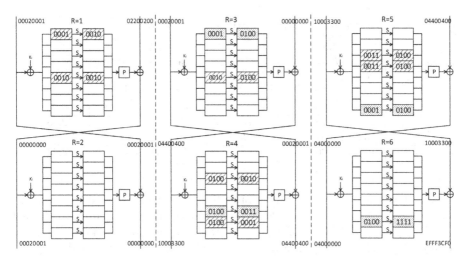

Fig. 2. The feasible solution of the 6-round MIBS MILP model got from the Gurobi optimizer. The blank boxes denote the zero differences, the boxes marked by dot notation denote the valid differences, and those with slash notation denote the invalid differences according to the difference distribution table in [1].

result the number of active S-boxes of fully 32-round MIBS is lower bounded by $4 \times 9 + 2 \times 11 = 58$, which is tighter than 44 given by the designers. Therefore, the upper bound of the maximum differential probability of the full-round MIBS is $(2^{-2})^{58} = 2^{-116}$, which is much lower than the probability of success of the brute force attack. We can conclude that the full-round MIBS is resistant to single-key differential attack. Since a lower bound of the active S-boxes of the 18-round MIBS is $3 \times 11 = 33 > 32$, it is clearly that for MIBS, 18 rounds of iterations are sufficient to resist against single-key differential attack.

4.2   Results on MIBS in the Related-key Model

Related-key attack [2] is a type of cryptanalysis which uses some weakness of the key schedule. In this section, we apply the MILP based methods to MIBS in related-key model.

For related-key differential attack, we add an extra constraint to ensure that there is a difference between the related-keys. Let $(k_1, k_2, \cdots, k_n)$ be the bit difference of the related subkeys, we require a constraint that $k_1 + k_2 + \cdots + k_n \geq 1$.

We denote the 64-bit user key version of MIBS as MIBS-64. The results obtained for a round-reduced MIBS-64 in the related-key model are presented in Table 2. In particular, we have proved that there are at least 7 active S-boxes in the best related-key differential characteristic for any consecutive 8-rounds of MIBS-64. Therefore, the probability of the best related-key differential characteristic of the 32-round MIBS-64 is $((2^{-2})^7)^4 = 2^{-56}$. This is slightly larger than the probability of success for an exhaustive search attack. Since the probability of the best related-key differential characteristic for 7-round MIBS-64

Table 2. Results for MIBS-64 with convex hull

Rounds	single-key model				related-key model			
	# Var.	# Con.	# A-S	Time(s)	# Var.	# Con.	# A-S	Time(s)
2	432	1505	1	0. 05	570	1893	0	0.03
3	664	2257	2	0. 20	839	2839	0	0.03
4	896	3009	6	91. 07	1108	3785	0	0.08
5	1128	3761	9	7601. 49	1377	4731	1	12.58
6	1360	4513	11	262080.50	1646	5677	3	31.61
7	1592	5265	-	-	1915	6623	5	4843.43

is upper bounded by $(2^{-2})^5$, the probability of the best related-key differential characteristic for the $39 (= 8 \times 4 + 7)$-round MIBS-64 is upper bounded by $((2^{-2})^7)^4 \times (2^{-2})^5 = 2^{-66}$. Thus, we prove that for MIBS-64, 39 rounds of iterations are sufficient to resist differential attack in related-key model.

5   Conclusion

In this paper, we have applied Mohua *et al.* 's and Sun *et al.* 's methods to the 32-round block cipher MIBS and obtained tighter upper bounds on the probability of best differential characteristics of MIBS in both the single-key and related-key differential attacks. We have shown that 18 rounds of iterations of MIBS are sufficient to resist against single-key differential attack and 39 rounds of iterations are sufficient to resist against related-key differential cryptanalysis for MIBS with 64-bit keys. Our work is expected to be applicable to other block ciphers with more complex diffusion layers.

Acknowledgements. The authors would like to thank anonymous reviewers for their helpful comments and suggestions. The work of this paper was supported by the National Key Basic Research Program of China (2013CB834203), the National Natural Science Foundation of China (Grant 61070172), the Strategic Priority Research Program of Chinese Academy of Sciences under Grant XDA06010702, and the State Key Laboratory of Information Security, Chinese Academy of Sciences.

References

1. Bay, A., Nakahara Jr., J., Vaudenay, S.: Cryptanalysis of reduced-round MIBS block cipher. In: Heng, S.-H., Wright, R.N., Goi, B.-M. (eds.) CANS 2010. LNCS, vol. 6467, pp. 1–19. Springer, Heidelberg (2010)
2. Biham, E.: New types of cryptanalytic attacks using related keys. Journal of Cryptology 7(4), 229–246 (1994)

3. Biham, E., Shamir, A.: Differential cryptanalysis of DES-like cryptosystems. Journal of Cryptology 4(1), 3–72 (1991)
4. Bogdanov, A.: Analysis and Design of Block Cipher Constructions. Ruhr University Bochum (2010)
5. Bogdanov, A.: On unbalanced Feistel networks with contracting MDS diffusion. Designs, Codes and Cryptography 59(1-3), 35–58 (2011)
6. Daemen, J., Rijmen, V.: The wide trail design strategy. In: Honary, B. (ed.) Cryptography and Coding 2001. LNCS, vol. 2260, pp. 222–238. Springer, Heidelberg (2001)
7. IBMsoftware-group: User-manual cplex 12 (2011), http://www-01.ibm.com
8. Izadi, M., Sadeghiyan, B., Sadeghian, S.S., Khanooki, H.A.: MIBS: A new lightweight block cipher. In: Garay, J.A., Miyaji, A., Otsuka, A. (eds.) CANS 2009. LNCS, vol. 5888, pp. 334–348. Springer, Heidelberg (2009)
9. Kanda, M.: Practical security evaluation against differential and linear cryptanalyses for Feistel ciphers with SPN round function. In: Stinson, D.R., Tavares, S. (eds.) SAC 2000. LNCS, vol. 2012, pp. 324–338. Springer, Heidelberg (2001)
10. Kexin, Q., Lei, H., Siwei, S., Xiaoshuang, M.: Improved MILP Modeling for Automatic Security Evaluation and Application to FOX (2014)
11. Mouha, N., Wang, Q., Gu, D., Preneel, B.: Differential and linear cryptanalysis using Mixed-Integer linear programming. In: Wu, C.-K., Yung, M., Lin, D. (eds.) Inscrypt 2011. LNCS, vol. 7537, pp. 57–76. Springer, Heidelberg (2012)
12. Optimization-Gurobi: Gurobi optimizer reference manual (2012), http://www.gurobi.com
13. Shibutani, K.: On the diffusion of generalized Feistel structures regarding differential and linear cryptanalysis. In: Biryukov, A., Gong, G., Stinson, D.R. (eds.) SAC 2010. LNCS, vol. 6544, pp. 211–228. Springer, Heidelberg (2011)
14. Sun, S., Hu, L., Song, L., Xie, Y., Wang, P.: Automatic security evaluation of block ciphers with S-bP structures against related-key differential attacks. In: Inscrypt 2013 (2013)
15. Sun, S., Hu, L., Wang, P.: Automatic security evaluation for bit-oriented block ciphers in related-key model: Application to PRESENT-80, LBlock and others. Cryptology ePrint Archive (2013), http://eprint.iacr.org/2013/676
16. Watanabe, D., Okamoto, K., Kaneko, T.: A hardware-oriented light weight pseudorandom number generator enocoro-128v2. In: The Symposium on Cryptography and Information Security, pp. 3D1–3 (2010)

A   The Convex Hull of the MIBS S-box

According to the greedy algorithm in [15], we pick 27 inequalities out of the whole 378 constraints of the convex hull of the MIBS S-box, which are given below. For instance, the vector $(-3, -3, 1, -2, 1, -2, 1, 2, 7)$ denotes the inequality

$$-3x_{in_0} - 3x_{in_1} + x_{in_2} - 2x_{in_3} + x_{out_0} - 2x_{out_1} + x_{out_2} - 2x_{out_3} + 7 \geq 0,$$

where $(x_{in_0}, \cdots, x_{in_3})$ and $(x_{out_0}, \cdots, x_{out_3})$ are the input and output bit-level differences of the MIBS S-box. According to the greedy algorithm in [15], we pick 27 inequalities out of the whole 378 constraints, which are marked by $*$.

(-3,-3, 1,-2, 1,-2, 1, 2, 7)	(-2,-1,-2, 1, 2, 2,-1, 1, 4)	(-2, 1,-3,-1,-1,-3,-2,-2,11)	(-2, 1,-1, 2,-2, 1,-1,-1, 5)
(-2, 1, 1,-1,-1,-1,-1, 2, 4)	(-2, 2, 4, 1, 3, 1,-3,-3, 4)	(-1,-4, 3, 2,-1,-3, 4, 2, 5)	(-1,-2,-4, 4,-4, 2, 1,-3,10)
(-1,-1,-1,-1, 3, 3, 3, 3, 0)	(-1,-1, 1,-1,-1, 0,-1,-1, 5)	(-1, 0, 0,-1,-1,-1, 1, 1, 3)	(-1, 2,-1,-1,-1, 1, 2,-2, 4)
(-1, 2,-1, 1, 2,-2, 1,-1, 3)	(-1, 2, 2,-2, 1, 0,-2, 1, 3)	(0,-1, 0,-1, 1,-1,-1, 1, 3)	(0,-1, 1,-1, 1,-1, 1,-1, 3)
(1,-2,-2,-1, 1,-2,-2, 0, 7)	(1,-2,-2, 2, 1, 1,-1,-2, 5)	(1,-1,-2,-2,-1,-1,-1,-1, 7)	(1,-1, 2, 1,-1, 1,-2, 1, 2)
(1, 1,-2,-1,-2,-1,-2, 1, 6)	(1, 2, 1, 2,-2, 1, 1, 1, 0)	(1, 3,-2,-3, 1, 3, 2,-1, 3)	(2,-3, 1, 1, 3, 2, 2, 1, 0)
(2, 1,-2, 2, 3,-1, 1, 2, 0)	(3,-2, 1,-2,-3, 3,-1, 1, 5)	(5, 4, 4, 3,-1,-2, 1,-2, 0)	

A New Multivariate Based Threshold Ring Signature Scheme

Jingwan Zhang and Yiming Zhao

Software School, Fudan University, Shanghai, China
{12212010026,zhym}@fudan.edu.cn

Abstract. In CRYPTO 2011, Sakumoto et al. presented a 3-pass identification protocol whose security is solely based on the MQ problem. This identification protocol was extended to a threshold ring signature scheme by Petzoldt et al. via Fiat-Shamir transformation in AAECC 2013. In this paper, we present a multivariate based Γ-protocol based on Sakumoto et al.'s work, and extend it to a threshold ring signature scheme by applying Γ-transformation (TIFS 2013). Compared with Petzoldt et al.'s work, our scheme reduces signature length and rounds by 21% and 29% respectively to achieve 80-bit security. What's more, our scheme has higher level provable security, enjoys much better performance on power limited devices, and can be flexible deployed in interactive protocols. To the best of our knowledge, it is the first application of Γ-transformation in post-quantum cryptography.

Keywords: Multivariate cryptography, Post quantum, Identification protocol, Γ-transformation, Threshold ring scheme.

1 Introduction

The MQ (short for multivariate quadratic) problem, which is to solve a set of multivariate quadratic polynomials over a finite field, is a popular topic in post-quantum cryptography. It has been proved to be a NP-Complete problem [4] and no known polynomial time quantum algorithm can solve it [8]. However, the security of most existing multivariate schemes are not only based on MQ problem but also another problem called Isomorphism of Polynomials (IP for short) problem [3], whose security is not as strong as initially thought. To put it simply, the IP problem is to recover affine transformations from the trapdoor of a multivariate polynomials system.

Related Work. In 2011, Sakumoto et al. [7] presented a 3-pass identification protocol whose security is solely based on the conjectured intractability of the MQ problem. Petzoldt et al. [6] extended this protocol to a threshold ring signature scheme by applying Fiat-Shamir transformation [2]. The signature length of Petzoldt et al.'s scheme is independent of the number of real signers and linear in the number of group members, and it's at least twice shorter than lattice-based [1] and code-based[5] threshold ring signature schemes, despite more rounds are needed to achieve the same level security. In 2013, Yao and Zhao [9] proposed

M.H. Au et al. (Eds.): NSS 2014, LNCS 8792, pp. 526–533, 2014.
© Springer International Publishing Switzerland 2014

a new transformation approach called Γ-transformation. Compared with Fiat-Shamir transformation, Γ-transformation keeps all its advantages, has higher level provable security and overcomes several major disadvantages such as inflexible deployment in interactive protocols and public/private storage limitation.

Our Contributions. In this paper, we present a multivariate based Γ-protocol, and extend it to a threshold ring signature scheme by applying Γ-transformation. Our (threshold ring) Γ-protocol is a zero knowledge argument of knowledge with cheating probability $2/3$ whose security is solely based on the intractability of MQ problem, and our threshold ring signature scheme is strongly existential unforgeable under concurrent interactive attack.

As to efficiency, the signature length of our scheme is independent of the number of real signers and linear in the number of group members. Compared with [6], our scheme reduces the cheating probability from $3/4$ to $2/3$. To achieve $80(100)$-bit security, our scheme has $21(25)\%$ shorter signature and needs $29(33)\%$ less rounds, while the public/private key size are the same.

Our scheme also enjoys the benefits of Γ-transformation over Fiat-Shamir transformation, such as flexible deployment in interactive protocols, better performance on power limited devices. To the best of our knowledge, our work is the first application of Γ-transformation in post-quantum cryptography.

2   Multivariate Based Γ-Protocol

MQ Problem. Denote by $MQ(n, m, \mathbb{F}_q)$ a set of multivariate quadratic polynomials $F(x) = (p_1(x), \ldots, p_m(x))$, in which

$$p_l(x) = \sum_{i=1}^{n} \sum_{j=i}^{n} p_{i,j}^{(l)} x_i x_j + \sum_{i=1}^{n} p_i^{(l)} x_i + p_0^{(l)}$$

where $x = (x_1, \ldots, x_n)$ and $p_{i,j}^{(l)}, p_i^{(l)}, p_0^{(l)} \in \mathbb{F}_q$ for $l = 1, \ldots, m$. Given a $F \in MQ(n, m, \mathbb{F}_q)$, find a vector $x = (x_1, \ldots, x_n)$ such that $F(x) = 0$ is called the MQ problem. It has been proved to be NP-Complete [4].

In this section, we extend the 3-pass identification protocol in [7] to a multivariate based Γ-protocol (refer to Figure 1). The private input of the Prover is $s \in_R \mathbb{F}^n$ satisfying $v = F(s)$, where $F \in MQ(n, m, \mathbb{F}_q)$ is a system parameter. (F, v) serve as the public key.

Theorem 1. *The Identification protocol in Figure 1 is a Γ-protocol for MQ problem under the e-condition that $R_e(d, e, d', e') = 1$ iff $d = d'$ and $e \neq e'$.*

Proof. According to the definition of Γ-protocol [9], we need to show that our protocol satisfies following properties.

- *Completeness.* If P, V follow the protocol, the verifier always accepts.
- *Perfect SHVZK.* With the knowledge of public key v, a random d and an arbitrary challenge Ch, the PPT simulator S works as follows: it first selects the response $Rsp = (r_i, t_j, \hat{e}_k)$ uniformly at random, in which $i, j, k \in \{0, 1\}$ are determined by Ch, then it picks a random $r_{i \oplus 1}$ from $\mathbb{F}^n$ uniformly. $a = (c_0, c_1, c_2)$ can be computed from $(d, r_i, r_{i \oplus 1}, t_j, \hat{e}_k)$, and S outputs

Prover's input: $((F, v), s)$		Verifier's input: (F, v)
Pick $r_0, t_0 \in_R \mathbb{F}^n, e_0 \in_R \mathbb{F}^m$		
$r_1 = s - r_0, t_1 = r_0 - t_0$		
$e_1 = F(r_0) - e_0$		
$c_0 = Com(r_1, G(t_0, r_1) + e_0)$		
$c_1 = Com(t_0, e_0)$	$(c_0, c_1, c_2),$	
$c_2 = Com(t_1, e_1)$	$\xrightarrow{d \in_R \mathcal{D}}$	
		Choose $Ch \in_R \{0, 1, 2\}$
If $Ch = 0, Rsp = (r_0, t_1, \hat{e}_1)$	$\xleftarrow{Ch}$	
If $Ch = 1, Rsp = (r_1, t_1, \hat{e}_1)$		
If $Ch = 2, Rsp = (r_1, t_0, \hat{e}_0)$	$\xrightarrow{Rsp}$	If $Ch = 0, check$
$(\hat{e}_0 = e_0 \oplus d, \hat{e}_1 = e_1 \oplus d)$		$c_1 \overset{?}{=} Com(r_0 - t_1, F(r_0) - \hat{e}_1 \oplus d)$
		$c_2 \overset{?}{=} Com(t_1, \hat{e}_1 \oplus d)$
		If $Ch = 1, check$
		$c_0 \overset{?}{=} Com(r_1, v - F(r_1) - G(t_1, r_1) - \hat{e}_1 \oplus d)$
		$c_2 \overset{?}{=} Com(t_1, \hat{e}_1 \oplus d)$
		If $Ch = 2, check$
		$c_0 \overset{?}{=} Com(r_1, G(t_0, r_1) + \hat{e}_0 \oplus d)$
		$c_1 \overset{?}{=} Com(t_0, \hat{e}_0 \oplus d)$

Fig. 1. Multivariate based Γ-protocol

(a, d, Ch, Rsp) as the simulated transcript. It's obvious that the transcript will be accepted and $s = r_0 + r_1$ is distributed uniformly over $\mathbb{F}^n$.

– *Knowledge-extraction w.r.t. e-condition.* Given two transcripts (a, d, Ch, Rsp) and (a, d', Ch', Rsp'), where $d = d'$ and $Ch \neq Ch'$. If either Ch or Ch' is 0, r_0 and r_1 can be derived from Rsp and Rsp', then we can get $s = r_0 + r_1$. If neither Ch nor Ch' is 0, t_0, t_1 and r_1 can be derived from Rsp and Rsp', then we can get $s = r_1 + t_0 + t_1$.

Theorem 2. *The Identification protocol in Figure 1 is a zero knowledge argument of knowledge, with a cheating probability of 2/3, if the commitment scheme Com is statistically hiding and computationally binding.*

Proof. The proof can be deduced from Theorem 2 and 3 of [7] directly.

3   Multivariate Based Threshold Ring Γ-Protocol

In a (t, N)-threshold ring identification protocol, at least t out of a larger group of N members are required to prove that they really know their secret keys. For the sake of simplicity, we just take the case of exactly t provers as example.

However, not each of the t provers interacts with the verifier directly. Instead, a leader is randomly selected before the interaction, he gathers the other provers' commitments and computes commitments for non-provers and himself, then sends the master commitment to the verifier. After receiving challenge from the verifier, the leader sends the challenge to the other $t-1$ provers. At last, the leader computes the master response and sends it to the verifier. Besides checking the correctness of the master response, the verifier also validates whether the number of real provers is at least t.

To enable the leader to compute commitments for non-provers without knowing their real secret keys, we require that the public key for every member in the group to be 0. By doing so, the leader can take 0 as each non-prover's secret key ($MQ(0) = 0$) when computing commitments for them.

Denote U as the set of N members and P the set of t provers, our protocol works as follows.

1. Each prover $P_i \in P$ chooses $r_0^{(i)}, t_0^{(i)} \in \mathbb{F}^n, e_0^{(i)} \in \mathbb{F}^m$, then sends the commitment values $c_0^{(i)} = Com(r_1^{(i)}, G_i(t_0^{(i)}, r_1^{(i)}) + e_0^{(i)})$, $c_1^{(i)} = Com(t_0^{(i)}, e_0^{(i)})$, $c_2^{(i)} = Com(t_1^{(i)}, e_1^{(i)})$, $c_3^{(i)} = Com(r_0^{(i)})$, $c_4^{(i)} = Com(r_1^{(i)})$ to the leader, where $r_1^{(i)} = s_i - r_0^{(i)}, t_1^{(i)} = r_0^{(i)} - t_0^{(i)}, e_1^{(i)} = F_i(r_0^{(i)}) - e_0^{(i)}$.
2. The leader computes $c_0^{(i)}, c_1^{(i)}, c_2^{(i)}, c_3^{(i)}, c_4^{(i)}$ for the non-provers, chooses a permutation $\Sigma \in_R U_N$ which re-arrange the N members to meet the source hiding property and $d \in_R \mathcal{D}$, and computes the master commitments $C_0 = Com(c_0^{(1)}, ..., c_0^{(N)})$, $C_1 = Com(\Sigma, c_1^{(1)}, ..., c_1^{(N)})$, $C_2 = Com(c_2^{(1)}, ..., c_2^{(N)})$, $C_3 = Com(\Sigma(c_3^{(1)}, ..., c_3^{(N)}))$, $C_4 = Com(\Sigma(c_4^{(1)}, ..., c_4^{(N)}))$. Then sends $C_0, C_1, C_2, C_3, C_4, d$ to the verifier.
3. The verifier chooses the challenge $Ch \in_R \{0, 1, 2\}$ and sends it to the leader. Then the leader sends Ch, d to the other provers.
4. The $t-1$ provers send their responses Rsp_i to the leader respectively.
   If $Ch = 0, Rsp_i = (r_0^{(i)}, t_1^{(i)}, e_1^{(i)} \oplus d)$
   If $Ch = 1, Rsp_i = (r_1^{(i)}, t_1^{(i)}, e_1^{(i)} \oplus d)$
   If $Ch = 2, Rsp_i = (r_1^{(i)}, t_0^{(i)}, e_0^{(i)} \oplus d)$
5. The leader computes Rsp_i for the non-provers and himself, computes the master response RSP and sends it to the verifier.
   If $Ch = 0, RSP = (\Sigma, Rsp_1, ..., Rsp_N)$
   If $Ch = 1, RSP = (Rsp_1, ..., Rsp_N)$
   If $Ch = 2, RSP = (\Sigma, Rsp_1, ..., Rsp_N, \Sigma(c_3^{(1)}, ..., c_3^{(N)}))$
6. The verifier checks the correctness of the commitments.
   If $Ch = 0$, he parses RSP into $\Sigma, r_0^{(i)}, t_1^{(i)}, \hat{e}_1^{(i)}$. For each $i = 1, ..., N$, he computes $\tilde{c}_1^{(i)} = Com(r_0^{(i)} - t_1^{(i)}, F_i(r_0^{(i)}) - \hat{e}_1^{(i)} \oplus d)$, $\tilde{c}_2^{(i)} = Com(t_1^{(i)}, \hat{e}_1^{(i)} \oplus d)$ and $\tilde{c}_3^{(i)} = Com(r_0^{(i)})$. Then checks $C_1 \stackrel{?}{=} Com(\Sigma, \tilde{c}_1^{(1)}, ..., \tilde{c}_1^{(N)})$, $C_2 \stackrel{?}{=} Com(\tilde{c}_2^{(1)}, ..., \tilde{c}_2^{(N)})$ and $C_3 \stackrel{?}{=} Com(\Sigma(\tilde{c}_3^{(1)}, ..., \tilde{c}_3^{(N)}))$.

   If $Ch = 1$, he parses RSP into $r_1^{(i)}, t_1^{(i)}, \hat{e}_1^{(i)}$. For each $i = 1, ..., N$, he computes $\tilde{c}_0^{(i)} = Com(r_1^{(i)}, -F_i(r_1^{(i)}) - G_i(t_1^{(i)}, r_1^{(i)}) - \hat{e}_1^{(i)} \oplus d)$ and $\tilde{c}_2^{(i)} = Com(t_1^{(i)}, \hat{e}_1^{(i)} \oplus d)$. Then checks $C_0 \stackrel{?}{=} Com(\tilde{c}_0^{(1)}, ..., \tilde{c}_0^{(N)})$, $C_2 \stackrel{?}{=} Com(\tilde{c}_2^{(1)}, ..., \tilde{c}_2^{(N)})$.

   If $Ch = 2$, he parses RSP into $\Sigma, r_1^{(i)}, t_0^{(i)}, \hat{e}_0^{(i)}, \Sigma(c_3^{(1)}, ..., c_3^{(N)})$. For $i = 1, ..., N$, he computes $\tilde{c}_0^{(i)} = Com(r_1^{(i)}, G_i(t_0^{(i)}, r_1^{(i)}) + \hat{e}_0^{(i)} \oplus d)$, $\tilde{c}_1^{(i)} = Com(t_0^{(i)}, \hat{e}_0^{(i)} \oplus$

d) and $\tilde{c}_4^{(i)} = Com(r_1^{(i)})$. Then checks $C_0 \stackrel{?}{=} Com(\tilde{c}_0^{(1)}, ..., \tilde{c}_0^{(N)})$, $C_1 \stackrel{?}{=} Com(\Sigma, \tilde{c}_1^{(1)}, ..., \tilde{c}_1^{(N)})$, $C_4 \stackrel{?}{=} Com(\Sigma(\tilde{c}_4^{(1)}, ..., \tilde{c}_4^{(N)}))$ and if there are at least t indices $i \in \{1, ..., N\}$ with $c_3^{(\Sigma(i))} \neq \tilde{c}_4^{(\Sigma(i))}$.

4 Multivariate Based Threshold Ring Signature Scheme

In this part, we construct a threshold ring signature scheme by applying Γ-transformation on our threshold ring Γ-protocol. As our threshold ring Γ-protocol has a cheating probability of $2/3$, we need to run our scheme number of rounds to guarantee the security, here we denote by $\#rounds$ the number of rounds to be executed, and our scheme works as below.

1. The leader gathers commitments of the other signers and generates commitments for non-signers and himself, then computes the master commitments
$$COM = (COM^{(1)}, ..., COM^{(\#rounds)})$$
in which $COM^{(i)} = (C_0^{(i)}, ..., C_4^{(i)})$ for round i.
2. The leader computes $d = (f(COM^{(1)}), ..., f(COM^{(\#rounds)}))$ and the master challenge $CH = h(m)^{(1)-(\#rounds)}$, where f is modelled as random oracle and $h : \{0,1\}^* \to \{00, 01, 10\}^{(\#rounds)})$ is a hash function, then sends d, CH to his co-signers. We require that the leader should publish $f(d)$ to the verifier before receiving the message to be signed. Notice that we use $f(d)$ instead of d here to reduce the signature length and the verifier checks the correctness of $f(d)$, not d in the step 5.
3. The leader gathers responses from the other signers and generates responses for non-signers and himself, then computes the master responses $RSP = (RSP^{(1)}, ..., RSP^{(\#rounds)})$. For round i,

If $CH^{(i)} = 0$, $RSP^{(i)} = \left(\Sigma, Rsp_1, ..., Rsp_N, C_0, C_4\right)^{(i)}$.

If $CH^{(i)} = 1$, $RSP^{(i)} = \left(Rsp_1, ..., Rsp_N, C_1, C_3, C_4\right)^{(i)}$.

If $CH^{(i)} = 2$, $RSP^{(i)} = \left(\Sigma, Rsp_1, ..., Rsp_N, \Sigma(c_3^{(1)}, ..., c_3^{(N)}), C_2\right)^{(i)}$.

4. The leader sends the final signature $\sigma = (f(d)\|RSP)$ to the verifier (actually only RSP is sent as $f(d)$ is already sent in Step 2).
5. The verifier parses σ into $f(d), RSP^{(1)}, ..., RSP^{(\#rounds)}$, and computes the master challenge CH. For each round $i \in \{1, ..., \#rounds\}$, the verifier parses $RSP^{(i)}$ to get each user's response, then computes the master commitments
$$\widetilde{COM}^{(i)} = (\tilde{C}_0^{(i)}, \tilde{C}_1^{(i)}, \tilde{C}_2^{(i)}, \tilde{C}_3^{(i)}, \tilde{C}_4^{(i)}) \quad \text{and} \quad \tilde{d}^{(i)} = f(\widetilde{COM}^{(i)})$$
At last the verifier checks $f(d) \stackrel{?}{=} f(\tilde{d}^{(1)}, ..., \tilde{d}^{(\#rounds)})$.

According to the property of Γ-transformation, our threshold ring signature scheme is strongly existential unforgeable under concurrent interactive attack.

5   Security Analysis

In this section, firstly we want to show that our threshold ring Γ-protocol is a zero knowledge argument of knowledge with cheating probability $2/3$, which can be proved by three properties: Completeness, Soundness and Zero Knowledge. Then we show that our threshold ring signature scheme is unconditionally source hiding. The Completeness is straight forward as the verifier will always accept a correct interaction from the prover.

Theorem 3 (Soundness). *An attacker who is able to pass r rounds of our protocol without detection with probability $> (2/3)^r$, can either break the binding property of the commitment scheme or extract t vectors $s_{i_1}, \ldots, s_{i_t} \in \mathbb{F}^n \backslash \{0\}$ satisfying $F_{i_j}(s_{i_j}) = 0$, where $i_1, \ldots, i_t$ are t indices from $\{1, 2, \ldots, N\}$.*

Proof. Assume that an attacker is able to pass r rounds of the threshold ring identification scheme with probability $> (2/3)^r$, he must be able to answer all three challenges in at least one round correctly. Denote $\tilde{c}_k^{(i,j)}$ as the value of $\tilde{c}_k$ the verifier computes for user i and challenge j. Due to the binding property of the commitment scheme we can get that

$$\tilde{c}_0^{(1,1)} = \tilde{c}_0^{(1,2)}, \ldots, \tilde{c}_0^{(N,1)} = \tilde{c}_0^{(N,2)} \tag{1a}$$

$$\Sigma^{(0)} = \Sigma^{(2)}, \tilde{c}_1^{(1,0)} = \tilde{c}_1^{(1,2)}, \ldots, \tilde{c}_1^{(N,0)} = \tilde{c}_1^{(N,2)} \tag{1b}$$

$$\tilde{c}_2^{(1,0)} = \tilde{c}_2^{(1,1)}, \ldots, \tilde{c}_2^{(N,0)} = \tilde{c}_2^{(N,1)} \tag{1c}$$

Again due to the binding property of the commitment scheme, (1a),(1b),(1c) can deduce following equations, $\forall i = 1, \ldots, N$

$$(\tilde{r}_1^{(i,1)}, -F_i(\tilde{r}_1^{(i,1)}) - G_i(\tilde{t}_1^{(i,1)}, \tilde{r}_1^{(i,1)}) - \tilde{e}_1^{(i,1)})) = (\tilde{r}_1^{(i,2)}, G_i(\tilde{t}_0^{(i,2)}, \tilde{r}_1^{(i,2)}) + \tilde{e}_0^{(i,2)}) \tag{2a}$$

$$(\tilde{r}_0^{(i,0)} - \tilde{t}_0^{(i,0)}, F_i(\tilde{r}_0^{(i,0)}) - \tilde{e}_1^{(i,0)}) = (\tilde{t}_0^{(i,2)}, \tilde{e}_0^{(i,2)}) \tag{2b}$$

$$(\tilde{t}_1^{(i,0)}, \tilde{e}_1^{(i,0)}) = (\tilde{t}_1^{(i,1)}, \tilde{e}_1^{(i,1)}) \tag{2c}$$

Then we can get $\tilde{s}_i = \tilde{r}_0^{(i,0)} + \tilde{r}_1^{(i,2)}$. Otherwise, if any one of (2a),(2b),(2c) doesn't hold, the binding property of Com is broken.

Next we show that at least t of the solutions are not 0.

To pass $Ch = 2$, there must be at least t indices $i_1, \ldots, i_t$ satisfying that $\tilde{c}_3^{(\Sigma^{(2)}(i_j),2)} \neq \tilde{c}_4^{(\Sigma^{(2)}(i_j),2)}$. As $\Sigma^{(0)} = \Sigma^{(2)} =: \Sigma$, there is $\tilde{c}_3^{(\Sigma(i_j),0)} \neq \tilde{c}_4^{(\Sigma(i_j),2)}, \forall j = 1, \ldots, t$, which is equivalent to $\tilde{r}_0^{(\Sigma(i_j),0)} \neq \tilde{r}_1^{(\Sigma(i_j),2)}, \forall j = 1, \ldots, t$.

Till now, the attacker has found t vectors $\tilde{s}_{\Sigma(i_j)} = \tilde{r}_0^{(\Sigma(i_j),0)} + \tilde{r}_1^{(\Sigma(i_j),2)} \in \mathbb{F}^n \backslash \{0\}$ satisfying $F_{\Sigma(i_j)}(\tilde{s}_{\Sigma(i_j)}) = 0, \forall j = 1, ..., t$.

Theorem 4 (Zero-Knowledge). *The threshold ring Γ-protocol is statistically zero knowledge if the commitment scheme Com is statistically hiding.*

Proof. Let S be a simulator of the leader who doesn't know the private keys of the group, and show that S can pass the scheme with probability $2/3$.

S chooses a value $Ch^* \in_R \{0,1,2\}$ as a prediction, of the challenge value that the verifier will *not* choose. For the group of N users, S chooses $\tilde{s}_i \in_R \mathbb{F}^n$ with at least t of the secret keys $\tilde{s}_i \neq 0$, and chooses $\tilde{r}_0^{(i)}, \tilde{t}_0^{(i)} \in_R \mathbb{F}^n$, $\tilde{e}_0^{(i)} \in_R \mathbb{F}^m$. Then computes $\tilde{r}_1^{(i)} = \tilde{s}_i - \tilde{r}_0^{(i)}$ and $\tilde{t}_1^{(i)} = \tilde{r}_0^{(i)} - \tilde{t}_0^{(i)}$. If $Ch^* = 0$, it computes $\tilde{e}_1^{(i)} = -F_i(\tilde{s}_i) + F_i(\tilde{r}_0^{(i)}) - \tilde{e}_0^{(i)}$, otherwise $\tilde{e}_1^{(i)} = F_i(\tilde{r}_0^{(i)}) - \tilde{e}_0^{(i)}$. If $Ch^* = 2$, it computes $\tilde{c}_0^{(i)} = Com(\tilde{r}_1^{(i)}, -F_i(\tilde{r}_1^{(i)}) - G_i(\tilde{t}_1^{(i)}, \tilde{r}_1^{(i)}) - \tilde{e}_1^{(i)})$, otherwise $\tilde{c}_0^{(i)} = Com(\tilde{r}_1^{(i)}, G_i(\tilde{t}_0^{(i)}, \tilde{r}_1^{(i)}) + \tilde{e}_0^{(i)})$. S computes the other four commitments $\tilde{c}_1^{(i)}, \tilde{c}_2^{(i)}, \tilde{c}_3^{(i)}, \tilde{c}_4^{(i)}$ for each user, then uniformly at random chooses a permutation Σ and a value $\tilde{d}$ from $\mathcal{D}$ to construct the master commitments.

Till now, S finishes Step 1 and Step 2 of the threshold ring identification protocol, the other steps are remained the same, then waits for the challenge from the verifier. If $Ch^* \neq Ch$, the response from S will be accepted.

Theorem 5. *The threshold ring signature scheme is unconditionally source hiding.*

Proof. For all challenge values 0, 1 and 2, the response of both signers and non-signers are completely indistinguishable, since r_0, t_0, e_0 are chosen uniformly at random and therefore the responses are random too. As to the verification for challenge value 2, actual signers and non-signers are mixed by a random permutation Σ, the verifier is not able to identify the actual signers although he knows which users (after permutation) have non-zero secret.

6 Efficiency

Table 1 compares our threshold ring signature scheme with Petzoldt et al.'s scheme [6], lattice-based [1] and code-based [5] threshold ring signature schemes. And we use the same parameters as [6] for our scheme, i.e. $\mathbb{F} = GF(2)$, $(m,n) = (80,80)$ for 80-bit security and $(m,n) = (100,100)$ for 100-bit security.

Table 1. Comparison of threshold ring signature schemes for $(N,t) = (100,50)$

Security	Scheme	TRSS-C [5]	TRSS-L [1]	TRSS-M [6]	Our scheme
2^{80}	rounds	140	80	193	137
	public key	1.5 MB	7.8 MB	3.5 MB	3.1 MB
	private key	700 bit	1280 bit	80 bit	80 bit
	signature length	1.4 MB	14.8 MB	0.62 MB	0.49 MB
2^{100}	rounds	190	100	256	171
	public key	2.2 MB	17.0 MB	6.8 MB	6.0 MB
	private key	850 bit	1728 bit	100 bit	100 bit
	signature length	2.4 MB	26.7 MB	1.03 MB	0.77 MB

Compared with [6], our scheme has 29% reduction in round number and 21% reduction in signature length for 80-bit security, 33% reduction in round number and 25% reduction in signature length for 100-bit security. Compared with[1] and [5], our private key and signature are pretty small, especially compared with [1].

7   Conclusion

In this paper, we present a Γ-protocol whose security is solely based on MQ problem, and extend it to a threshold ring signature scheme by applying Γ-transformation. Our threshold ring signature scheme offers higher level provable security and better efficiency compared with [6], and enjoys the benefits of Γ-transformation such as flexible deployment in interactive protocols and better performance on power limited devices.

References

1. Cayrel, P.-L., Lindner, R., Rückert, M., Silva, R.: A lattice-based threshold ring signature scheme. In: Abdalla, M., Barreto, P.S.L.M. (eds.) LATINCRYPT 2010. LNCS, vol. 6212, pp. 255–272. Springer, Heidelberg (2010)
2. Fiat, A., Shamir, A.: How to prove yourself: Practical solutions to identification and signature problems. In: Odlyzko, A.M. (ed.) CRYPTO 1986. LNCS, vol. 263, pp. 186–194. Springer, Heidelberg (1987)
3. Fouque, P.-A., Macario-Rat, G., Stern, J.: Key recovery on hidden monomial multivariate schemes. In: Smart, N.P. (ed.) EUROCRYPT 2008. LNCS, vol. 4965, pp. 19–30. Springer, Heidelberg (2008)
4. Garey, M., Johnson, D.: Computers and Intractability: A Guide to the Theory of NP-Completeness. Freeman, San Francisco (1979)
5. Melchor, C.A., Cayrel, P.-L., Gaborit, P., Laguillaumie, F.: A new efficient threshold ring signature scheme based on coding theory. IEEE Transactions on Information Theory 57, 4833–4842 (2011)
6. Petzoldt, A., Bulygin, S., Buchmann, J.: A multivariate based threshold ring signature scheme. Applicable Algebra in Engineering, Communication and Computing 24, 255–275 (2013)
7. Sakumoto, K., Shirai, T., Hiwatari, H.: Public-key identification schemes based on multivariate quadratic polynomials. In: Rogaway, P. (ed.) CRYPTO 2011. LNCS, vol. 6841, pp. 706–723. Springer, Heidelberg (2011)
8. Shor, P.W.: Polynomial-time algorithms for prime factorization and discrete logarithms on a quantum computer. SIAM Journal on Computing 26, 1484–1509 (1997)
9. Yao, A.C., Zhao, Y.: Online/offline signatures for low-power devices. IEEE Transactions on Information Forensics and Security 8, 283–294 (2013)

Capturing Android Malware Behaviour Using System Flow Graph

Radoniaina Andriatsimandefitra and Valérie Viet Triem Tong

CIDRE Research Group,
SUPELEC
Avenue de la Boulaie, 35510 Cesson-Sévigné, France
`firstname.lastname@supelec.fr`

Abstract. This article uses a new data structure namely System Flow Graph (SFG) that offers a compact representation of information dissemination induced by an execution of an application to characterize malicious application behavior and lead some experiments on 4 malware families DroidKungFu1, DroidKungFu2, jSMSHider, BadNews. We show how SFG are relevant to exhibit malware behavior.

1 Introduction

Android is an operating system dedicated to mobile devices. Due to its widespread adoption and the sensitive nature of data such devices may contain, Android became the target of malicious applications. As pointed out in different studies [1, 2], Android security mechanism is not efficient enough to perfectly protect users and sensitive data on their device from malware. Security groups have thus worked on security extensions for Android to improve its security level.

Monitoring applications to detect misbehaviours appears to us as a promising idea but we also believe that the analysis should not be restricted to the application itself but to its impact, direct or not, on the entire system. Indeed, traditional approaches limit themselves to the application itself and its direct interaction with its environment [3–6]. By doing so, some useful information about the action of the application may remain unnoticed. For instance, monitoring only a running sample of DroidKungFu1[7] and its child processes on Android, does not allow to observe that once it drops one of its payload in `/system/app`, the content of the payload is automatically used by two main system processes and propagated to other files in the system.

To overcome this shortcoming of traditional profiles, we choose to monitor information flows caused by an application in the whole system. Therefore we propose to define an application profile as a representation of how the application disseminates its data in the whole system and how these pieces of data are processed by the other applications. For that purpose, we use a data structure previously introduced in [8]. This data structure, called System Flow Graph (SFG), represents how an application disseminates its own pieces of data in an operating system during an execution. In this article we present how this structure helps to understand and classify malware.

M.H. Au et al. (Eds.): NSS 2014, LNCS 8792, pp. 534–541, 2014.

As stated in [9], malware authors are used to repackage applications with their malicious code and submit these repackaged applications on distribution platforms to infect users. These repackaged applications represent 86% of the malware samples in Android genome project according to the same source. As a malware author infects different applications with the same malicious code, these applications share a common behaviour and consequently we claim that they should share a common sub-SFG. This will be able to cope even with code that is obfuscated or ciphered. In the following we present related works in application analysis and tainting techniques for malware detection (section 2). Then, we present the underlying model of the information flow monitor we choose to use and a compact format to describe information flows (section 3). We then explain how a SFG is used to build a malware signature based on its behavior (section 4) and experiment our proposition (section 5).

2   Related Works

Tainting consists in marking pieces of information to monitor how they are disseminated in a program or in a system. They have been used to analyse how applications access sensitive data and how they process it. In [10], Yin et al. proposed to monitor information flow at hardware level to detect if suspicious applications accessed sensitive data and how they processed it. In subsequent work [11], Yin et al. used a similar approach and presented DroidScope, an Android analysis environment. Like Panorama, DroidScope monitors information flow at hardware level and aimed at detecting if a monitored application accesses to data considered as sensitive, when it is the case the application is considered as malicious. Tainting techniques have also been used on real devices to identify Android applications that leak confidential data. In [1], Enck et al. present TaintDroid, a modified version of Android that monitors information flow at application level. They selected pieces of sensitive data (e.g: IMEI and location data) that should be considered as confidential and monitored how they spread thanks to tainting techniques. When an application accesses a piece of tainted data, TaintDroid considers that the piece of data is flowing and propagates the corresponding taint to the destination container. In TaintDroid, destination containers that can be tainted are Java application variables, IPC messages and files. TaintDroid raises an alert whenever a piece of tainted data leaves the device. Their study showed that more than a third of thirty popular applications are responsible of sensitive data leakage to remote entities. If TaintDroid detects information leaks, it does not however give enough information to diagnose how the leaks happened. Furthermore, it only monitors information flow at Java application level: information flows involving native applications are not detected by TaintDroid because they do not run inside the Dalvik virtual machine which has been modified to monitor information flow.

As tainting techniques permit to understand how pieces of sensitive data are used, they give a better insight about the intent of an application compared to its use of functions. We therefore claim that such techniques are a better candidate to classify and detect pieces of malware. Unlike the approach used in DroidScope, Panorama and TaintDroid in which their authors focus on information they consider as sensitive, we think that the classification and detection should first be focused on the pieces of data owned by the application under analysis. To classify malware samples and detect their execution, we mark their origin container, `apk` file on Android and monitor how its content is disseminated in the system. From this dissemination profile, we regroup samples that propagate their own data in the same way and use this profile to detect execution of samples from the same malware family.

3   Capturing External Behaviours of Applications

In this work, we use Blare[1] [12], an intrusion detection system, to monitor information flows at system level. Blare is aware of information flows occurring between files, processes and sockets. Blare implementation relies on the Linux Security Module framework [13] that introduces hooks in the kernel to intercept syscalls. Blare uses these hooks to intercept syscalls that induce information flow between system objects and maintains tags on these objects. In particular, Blare maintains a tag called *itag* on each container of information at system level. This tag permits to know if a container has been contaminated by a marked piece of data. Besides intercepting syscalls, Blare also performs a finer monitoring of information flows occurring through the binder driver on Android. When Blare observes an interaction between system objects, it computes the corresponding information flow and performs the appropriate tag update. For example, when a process P reads a file F, it performs a `read` syscall. Blare intercepts this syscall and deduces that information flows from F to P. It then updates the tag associated to P to take into account its new content. If the file is later read by an other process then this process will have an *itag* indicating that its content has also been contaminated. In general, Blare updates the value of the *itag* attached to an object each time it considers that the content of this object has been changed. In this work, we use Blare to keep under surveillance a newly installed application that we do not trust. We assign a unique identifier i to information originating from the application and monitor how the pieces of information identified with i are disseminated in the whole system. Technically speaking this is done by assigning $\{i\}$ as the *itag* value of the `apk` file of the application we want to monitor. The `apk` file is the archive containing all the code and resources of Android applications. As we only focus on information from the application that we do not trust, there is no other identifier used in the system and the only possible values of *itag* are therefore $\varnothing$ and $\{i\}$. During an execution, if container c has an *itag* value equal to $\varnothing$, it means that c has not been contaminated by the marked application. Otherwise it means that the content of c may have been contaminated by the application. Each time Blare observes an information flow involving a content associated to an non-null *itag*, it adds an entry in its log to describe the observed flow. Each log entry describes the source container of

---

[1] `http://blare-ids.org/`

the flow, its destination and the information identifiers associated to the pieces of information that are propagating. It also contains a timestamp corresponding to the moment at which the flow was observed. Source and destination are described by their type, their name and their system identifier.

A log produced by Blare when monitoring an application exactly depicts how pieces of data owned by this application are disseminated within the system. However, the longer the monitoring of an application lasts, the bigger its log size grows. Some of the log entries may be repeated: for instance when a process reads a huge file it will repeat several times the same read syscall. We then propose in a data structure named System Flow Graph to compact the representation of a Blare log. A System Flow Graph (SFG) [8] describes how pieces of information are disseminated within the system during one execution. A SFG is a graph representation of a Blare log without information loss. A SFG has a more compact form. It is thus more readable than a log. Formally, a SFG is a labelled directed graph $G = (V, E)$. Each node $v \in V$ represents a container of information and each edge $e \in E$ from a node v_1 to a node v_2 an information flow from v_1 to v_2. Each node has three attributes: its system id, its name and its type (process, file or sockets). These three attributes are respectively denoted $v.id$, $v.name$ and $v.type$. An edge has two attributes identified as $e.flow$ and $e.timestamp$. $e.flow$ is a collection of information identifiers involved in the flow corresponding to e. The attribute $e.timestamp$ is a list of timestamps at which Blare observed the flow corresponding to e. SFG construction relies on the Blare log. We have a tool that transforms a log into an SFG.

4   System Flow Graph as Behaviour-Based Signatures

As malware authors are used to repackage original applications with their malicious code, applications infected with the same malicious code exhibit a common behaviour. Their corresponding SFGs therefore share a common sub-SFG that represents this common behaviour. We propose to use this common sub-SFG as a malware signature and explain below how to compute it.

A SFG describes how a piece of data disseminates in the whole system. In this study we propose to monitor how data originating from an application archive (apk file) is processed and thus how an application contaminates the operating system. To obtain the corresponding SFG we mark the apk file of the application right after it is installed on the device. Once the archive marked, the application is launched and monitored by Blare.

In the following we present a core algorithm used to classify a set of SFG into different subsets where each subset share a common sub-SFG that is the signature of the subset. The main algorithm is a classifier computing a fixed-point on the call of the function named one-step-classification on a classification list. A classification list is a list that associates a signature with all the SFGs that include this signature. A signature is a sub-SFG that appears at least in two SFGs given in input. This way, if the SFG list given as input contains at least two samples of the same malware family, our algorithm will output a signature.

More precisely, the main algorithm takes as input a list $[g_1, \ldots, g_n]$ of SFG and white a *white list* of SFG. First it stores in a variable named assoc a classification list initially set to $[(g_1, [g_1]), \ldots, (g_n, [g_n])]$. The main part is then a loop that computes a fix point of one-step-classification(assoc, white). The function one-step-classification is described in algorithm 1. In short, it computes the biggest common part of a list of SFGs deprived of all part that also appear in SFGs of benign applications characterized by the SFG list white.

When a fixed point is finally reached, the main algorithm will output a classification list of the form $[(s_0, [g_{0_1}, \ldots, g_{0_i}]), \ldots, (s_m, [g_{m_1}, \ldots, g_{m_k}])]$ where $s_0, s_1 \ldots s_m$ are the resulting signatures and $[g_{l_1}, \ldots, g_{l_i}]$ is the list of SFGs from the input that includes the signature s_l.

Algorithm 1. One-step-classification function

Input:
assoc a SFG classification list
white a list of trusted SFG
Output: a SFG classification list, one step further
begin

    $new\_assoc \leftarrow []$;
    forall the $g_1 \in$ keys($assoc$) **do**
        forall the $g_2 \in$ keys($assoc$) **do**
            v $\leftarrow$ [value($assoc, g_1$)] ;
            s $\leftarrow$ clean ($g_1 \cap g_2$,white) ;
            if $s \neq \varnothing$
            then
                forall the $g \in$ keys($assoc$) **do**
                    if s *is included in* g **then**
                        v $\leftarrow$ v @value ($assoc, g$)
            $new\_assoc \leftarrow$ add($new\_assoc, (s, v)$);

    return new_assoc;

---

5   Computing SFG Signatures

To evaluate our algorithm, we propose to extract SFG-signatures from the SFG of 19 malware samples: 5 samples of BadNews [14], 7 samples of Droid-KungFu1 [7], 3 samples of DroidKungFu2 [15] and 4 samples of jSMSHider [16].

BadNews is a malware of which samples are disguised as legitimate applications. Based on a manual analysis of these samples, we know that they are clients of a Command and Control (C&C) server from which they receive commands to execute. The different commands they can receive are to download and to install Android applications, to display news notifications (web-page to visit, software update etc) on the device, to install icons which links to an url or a down-loaded Android application and to change the address of the C&C server. During the period of our experiment, the C&C server only sent the news command to advertise two infected-application updates: Doodle Jump and Adobe flash. DroidKungFu1 and DroidKungFu2 are malware families that attempt to gain root privileges on the device and stealthily dump malicious applications on the device when root privileges are gained. Like DroidKungFu families, jSMSHider also exploits a vulnerability to install applications on the device. According to Zhou et al. [9], samples of DroidKungFu1, DroidKungFu2 and jSMSHider are repacked applications to which a malicious code was added.

Analysis Environment. To dynamically analyze applications and produce Blare log, we used a Samsung Nexus S device running the version of Android Ice Cream Sandwich from the Android Open Source Project. We used a kernel to which Blare was added. In user-space we added Blare related tools to set tag values, a standalone version of a toolbox named busybox and an application named Super User to get notifications when applications use the su command. No additional applications or components were added or modified.

Application Analysis. We wanted to observe how an application disseminates its data within the system. We therefore installed the application and marked its apk file before its first execution. The apk file contains the resources and the code of the application when it arrives on the device.

Sample Execution and Monitoring. The malicious code is not always automatically executed when the application is launched. We therefore introduced events in the system to trigger the malicious behaviour of some malware samples to shorten the duration of the application analysis. For some samples of DroidKungFu1 and DroidKungFu2, the associated value of a key named start in a file named sstimestamp.xml must be set to a small value (e.g 1). For BadNews, the malicious code is executed once a component of the application named MainService receives an intent that asks him to start running. In order to launch the application malicious code, the intent must come with an extra boolean value set to true. We manually craft this intent and send it to the application during the analysis of the samples of BadNews. In addition to introducing these key-events, we also use the application as a normal user.

SFG Signature Computation. Once we obtained the logs resulting from the analysis of 19 samples, we built the corresponding 19 SFGs. We then gave these SFGs to a program that implements the classification algorithm. The program returned a classification of 4 groups. 17 out of the 19 samples are exactly classified as in their origin database. The two remaining are samples of DroidKungFu1 that were classified as belonging to the same group as the samples of DroidKungFu2. This is due to the fact that these two samples exhibit the same behaviour as samples of DroidKungFu2 and also produce the same information flows. This is thus not an error of our algorithm. The SFG-signatures associated to each class describe the malicious behaviour of the code introduced in repackaged applications. We present in figure 1 the signature computed for BadNews. It

describes the download, a part of the installation and execution of two applications (`doodle.jump.apk` and `adobe.flash.apk`). We can see from the figure
that the browser sends data to a server : `213.x.x.x`. We intentionally replaced a
part of the IP addresses with the letter `x` to avoid revealing the original address.
This address correspond to a remote server from which malicious applications
are downloaded.

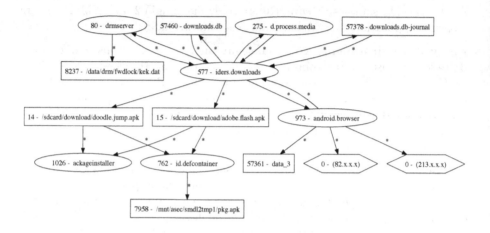

Fig. 1. SFG signature of BadNews

6   Conclusion

We made a proposition to classify Android malware in this work. First, we proposed to use a data structure named System Flow Graph (SFG) as a profile of
an application. It describes in a compact and human readable way how a particular execution is responsible of information dissemination within the operating
system and can be constructed from the log of an information flow monitor.

Second, we proposed to use SFGs to characterize malware samples. The main
idea behind the approach is that when applications are infected by the same
piece of malware, it should be possible to exhibit a similar sub-SFG in their
respective SFGs. Following this idea we have proposed a classification algorithm
that regroups SFGs according to the maximal sub-SFG(s) they have in common.
We have applied the proposed algorithm to compute the signature of pieces of
malware discovered during the last two years. Our algorithm has successfully
extracted a signature for each malware family from which we picked samples
for our experiment and each signature only matches the samples of the malware
family to which they belong. In future work, we plan to use these signatures in
a new form of malware detection engine.

References

1. Enck, W., Gilbert, P., Gon Chun, B., Cox, L.P., Jung, J., McDaniel, P., Sheth, A.N.: Taintdroid: An information-flow tracking system for realtime privacy monitoring on smartphones. In: Proc. of the USENIX Symposium on Operating Systems Design and Implementation, OSDI (2010)
2. Vidas, T., Votipka, D., Christin, N.: All your droid are belong to us: a survey of current android attacks. In: Proceedings of the 5th USENIX Conference on Offensive Technologies, p. 10. USENIX Association, Berkeley (2011)
3. Rieck, K., Trinius, P., Willems, C., Holz, T.: Automatic analysis of malware behavior using machine learning. J. Comput. Secur. 19(4), 639–668 (2011)
4. Rieck, K., Holz, T., Willems, C., Düssel, P., Laskov, P.: Learning and classification of malware behavior. In: Zamboni, D. (ed.) DIMVA 2008. LNCS, vol. 5137, pp. 108–125. Springer, Heidelberg (2008)
5. Bayer, U., Comparetti, P.M., Hlauschek, C., Kruegel, C., Kirda, E.: Scalable, behavior-based malware clustering. In: Proceedings of the 16th Annual Network and Distributed System Security Symposium, NDSS 2009 (January 2009)
6. Lanzi, A., Balzarotti, D., Kruegel, C., Christodorescu, M., Kirda, E.: Accessminer: using system-centric models for malware protection. In: Proceedings of the 17th ACM Conference on Computer and Communications Security, CCS 2010. ACM (2010)
7. Jiang, X.: Security alert: New sophisticated android malware droidkungfu found in alternative Chinese app markets,
   http://www.csc.ncsu.edu/faculty/jiang/DroidKungFu.html
8. Andriatsimandefitra, R., Viet Triem Tong, V., Mé, L.: Diagnosing intrusions in android operating system using system flow graph. In: Workshop Interdisciplinaire sur la Sécurité Globale (2013)
9. Zhou, Y., Jiang, X.: Dissecting android malware: Characterization and evolution. In: Proceedings of the 2012 IEEE Symposium on Security and Privacy, SP 2012, pp. 95–109. IEEE Computer Society, Washington, DC (2012)
10. Yin, H., Song, D., Egele, M., Kruegel, C., Kirda, E.: Panorama: capturing system-wide information flow for malware detection and analysis. In: Proceedings of the 14th ACM Conference on Computer and Communications Security, CCS 2007 (2007)
11. Yan, L.K., Yin, H.: Droidscope: Seamlessly reconstructing os and dalvik semantic views for dynamic android malware analysis. In: Proceedings of the 21st USENIX Security Symposium (August 2012)
12. Viet Triem Tong, V., Clark, A., Mé, L.: Specifying and enforcing a fine-grained information flow policy: Model and experiments. Journal of Wireless Mobile Networks, s, Ubiquitous Computing and Dependable Applications (2010)
13. Wright, C., Cowan, C., Smalley, S., Morris, J., Kroah-Hartman, G.: Linux security module framework. In: OLS 2002 Proceedings (2002)
14. Rogers, M.: The bearer of badnews, https://blog.lookout.com/blog/2013/04/19/the-bearer-of-badnews-malware-google-play/
15. Jiang, X.: Security alert: New droidkungfu variants found in alternative Chinese android markets, http://www.csc.ncsu.edu/faculty/jiang/DroidKungFu2/
16. Strazzere, T.: 2011 security alert: Malware found targeting custom roms, jsmshider (June 15, 2011), https://blog.lookout.com/blog/2011/06/15/security-alert-malware-found-targeting-custom-roms-jsmshider/

Evaluating Host-Based Anomaly Detection Systems: Application of the Frequency-Based Algorithms to ADFA-LD

Miao Xie[1], Jiankun Hu[1], Xinghuo Yu[2], and Elizabeth Chang[1]

[1] UNSW Canberra, Canberra, ACT 2612, Australia
[2] RMIT University, Melbourne, VIC 3001, Australia

Abstract. ADFA Linux data set (ADFA-LD) is released recently for substituting the existing benchmark data sets in the area of host-based anomaly detection which have lost most of their relevance to modern computer systems. ADFA-LD is composed of thousands of system call traces collected from a contemporary Linux local server, with six types of up-to-date cyber attack involved. Previously, we have conducted a preliminary analysis of ADFA-LD, and shown that the frequency-based algorithms can be realised at a cheaper computational cost in contrast with the short sequence-based algorithms, while achieving an acceptable performance. In this paper, we further exploit the potential of the frequency-based algorithms, in attempts to reduce the dimension of the frequency vectors and identify the optimal distance functions. Two typical frequency-based algorithms, i.e., k-nearest neighbour (kNN) and k-means clustering (kMC), are applied to validate the effectiveness and efficiency.

Keywords: host-based intrusion detection system (HIDS), Unix system call.

1 Introduction

In the area of host-based anomaly detection [1], most of the existing benchmark data sets, such as UMN [2] and DARPA [3] intrusion detection data sets, are compiled a decade ago and have failed to reflect the characteristics of modern computer systems. To fill this gap, ADFA-LD [10] [11] is released recently, which is generated from a Linux local server configured to represent a contemporary computer system. This server provides a range of services such as file sharing, database, remote access and web server, with the operating system of fully patched Ubuntu 11.04 (Linux kernel 2.6.38). The FTP, SSH and MySQL 14.14 are enabled with their default ports. Apache 2.2.17 and PHP 5.3.5 are installed for web-based services. In addition, TikiWiki 8.1 is installed as a web-based collaborative tool. During a given sampling period, the system calls invoked by each specific process is collected from this server in the form of a trace and, for simplicity, the index of the system call is recorded rather than its name. 833 and 4373 normal traces are captured respectively for the purposes of training and

M.H. Au et al. (Eds.): NSS 2014, LNCS 8792, pp. 542–549, 2014.

validation, during which no attacks occur against the host and a variety of legitimate applications are operated as usual. Subsequently, six types of cyber attack [10], i.e., **Hydra-FTP, Hydra-SSH, Adduser, Java-Meterpreter, Meterpreter** and **Webshell**, are launched in turn, each of which generates $8 \sim 20$ attack traces. Table 1 summarises the composition of ADFA-LD, in according with type, number and label.

Table 1. Composition of ADFA-LD

Training	Validation	Hydra-FTP	Hydra-SSH	Adduser	Java-Meterpreter	Meterpreter	Webshell
833	4373	162	148	91	125	75	118
normal	normal	attack	attack	attack	attack	attack	attack

There are two common categories of technique to detect intrusions/anomalies using system call traces: short sequence-based and frequency-based [6]. Short sequence-based techniques tend to mine patterns from subsequences of system call traces and a decision is often made through a comparison to the model of the normal patterns [4] [5] [7] [8] [9] [11]. Although this category of techniques are able to generate an accurate normal profile, the learning procedures are extremely time-consuming. Frequency-based techniques, on the contrary, are much cheaper in terms of computation, since they reorganise the system call traces into equal-sized vectors based on the concept of 'frequency' and deal only with the resulting frequency vectors [12] [13] [14]. However, their accuracies in modelling a normal profile may be deteriorated due to the loss of positional information.

Previously, we have conducted a preliminary analysis of ADFA-LD and shown that most of the intrusions/anomalies presented in ADFA-LD can be identified by the frequency-based kNN algorithms [15]. In this paper, we intend to further exploit the potential of the frequency-based algorithms against ADFA-LD. First, it attempts to map the original $n-$dimensional space of frequency vectors into a lower $p-$dimensional space by using principal component analysis (PCA). Second, various distance functions are attempted separately to validate their effectiveness. In different settings, two typical frequency-based algorithms, i.e., kNN and kMC, are tested respectively. Detection accuracy (ACC) and false positive rate (FPR) are employed as the performance metrics, which are given in the form of RoC curve.

The rest of this paper is organised as follows. Section 2 introduces how to reduce the dimension of the frequency vectors and the distance functions. Section 3 details the kNN and kMC algorithms and presents their performances obtained from ADFA-LD and, finally, section 4 summarises this paper.

2   Model, Dimension Reduction and Distance Functions

In this section, we define the model by which, as previously mentioned, the system call traces can be transformed into equal-sized frequency vectors. Then, we discuss how to reduce the dimension of the frequency vectors, as well as various distance functions which will be used for measuring the similarity between two frequency vectors.

A system call trace is a discrete sequence, with a variant length and the elements ranging from 1 to n (the maximal index of a system call). The indexes of the system calls and n are determined by the operating system; for example, Linux kernel 2.6.38 provides a total of 325 system calls [16] such that $n = 325$. Let s denote a system call trace, $|s|$ its length and f_i the number of occurrence of the system call indexed by i, where $i = 1, 2, \cdots, n$. The element of the frequency vector can be defined as

$$\bar{f}_i = \frac{f_i}{|s|}.$$

Although the system call traces can be transformed into shorter and equal-sized frequency vectors according to the above model, while operating these n dimensional vectors, the computational cost is still considerable. As most of the frequency vectors are sparse, intuitively, the dimension can be largely reduced and a comparable performance can be achieved as long as most of the variance is retained. Let m denote the total number of the training system call traces. The training data set, say $\mathbf{T}$, can be organised in the form of a $m \times n$ matrix by which we can reduce the dimension using PCA [17] [18]. If the sample covariance matrix of $\mathbf{T}$ is denoted by Q, using eigen decomposition, Q can be factorised as $Q = W\Lambda W'$ where $\Lambda = diag(\lambda_1, \lambda_2, \cdots, \lambda_n)$ is a diagonal matrix with respect to the descending eigenvalues $\lambda_1 \geq \lambda_2 \geq \cdots \geq \lambda_n$ and W is the $n \times n$ orthogonal matrix that contains the eigenvectors, i.e., $W = [w_1\ w_2\ \cdots\ w_n]$. By specifying r, $0 < r < 1$, it can obtain a subset of the eigenvectors from W, i.e., $\check{W} = [w_1\ w_2\ \cdots\ w_p]$ where $p < n$ and

$$r \leq \sum_{i=1}^{p} \lambda_i.$$

For any frequency vector s, the dimension can be reduced according to

$$\bar{s} = s\check{W}.$$

Let $\mathbf{V}$ and $\mathbf{A}$ denote the validation and attack data sets respectively. After the dimension is reduced, the training, validation and attack data sets are denoted by $\bar{\mathbf{T}}$, $\bar{\mathbf{V}}$ and $\bar{\mathbf{A}}$ respectively, where $\bar{\mathbf{T}} = \mathbf{T}\check{W}$, $\bar{\mathbf{V}} = \mathbf{V}\check{W}$ and $\bar{\mathbf{A}} = \mathbf{A}\check{W}$.

Let $\bar{Q}$ and $\bar{\Lambda}$ denote the sample covariance matrix of $\bar{\mathbf{T}}$ and the diagonal matrix obtained from the eigen decomposition of $\bar{Q}$ respectively. Given any two p dimensional frequency vectors, denoted by x and y for short, some distance functions are defined for measuring their similarity, as shown in Table 2.

3   The Frequency-Based Algorithms

Application of the frequency-based algorithms to ADFA-LD is presented in this section. We specify $r = 0.8$, which indicates that 80% variance of the raw data

Table 2. Distance functions

Distance/Metric	$distance(x,y)$	Distance/Metric	$distance(x,y)$
Euclidean	$(x-y)(x-y)'$	Minkowski	$\left\{\sum_{i=1}^{p}|x_i-y_i|^q\right\}^{\frac{1}{q}}$
Standardised Euclidean	$(x-y)\bar{\Lambda}^{-1}(x-y)'$	Cosine	$1-\dfrac{xy}{(xx')^{\frac{1}{2}}(yy')^{\frac{1}{2}}}$
Mahalanobis	$(x-y)\bar{Q}^{-1}(x-y)'$	Correlation	$1-\dfrac{1}{n}\dfrac{(x-\mu_x)(y-\mu_y)'}{\sigma_x\sigma_y}$

is retained; as such, $p = 9$. By testing a range of each parameter, the ACC and FPR of each algorithm against each type of attack are given in the form of a RoC curve. In particular, ACC is the number of successfully detected abnormal traces (attack involved) dividing by the total number of abnormal traces and FPR is the number of normal traces which are identified as abnormal dividing by the length of the validation data set.

3.1   kNN

kNN is the most widely used algorithm in the area of anomaly detection [18] [19] [20] [21]. Based on the kNN algorithm, we detect a system call trace by searching its p dimensional frequency vector's k nearest neighbours within a radius of d from $\bar{\mathbf{T}}$ in terms of a certain distance function. That is, for any $y \in \bar{\mathbf{V}} \cup \bar{\mathbf{A}}$ and all $x \in \bar{\mathbf{T}}$, if

$$\#\left(distance(x,y) \leq d\right) \geq k,$$

y is normal; otherwise abnormal.

Table 3. Parameters of kNN

Distance/Metric	d	step width	Distance/Metric	d	step width
Euclidean	$[0.01, 0.1]$	0.01	Minkowski $q=2$	$[0.1, 1]$	0.1
Standardised Euclidean	$[1, 10]$	1	Minkowski $q=3$	$[0.05, 0.5]$	0.05
Mahalanobis	$[0.5, 5]$	0.5	Cosine	$[0.05, 0.5]$	0.05

There are two parameters d and k to be specified in the algorithm, where d varies according to the distance function adopted and $\frac{k}{m}$ indicates a small probability. We fix $k = 20$ empirically, i.e., the small probability is equal to 0.024, and test a range of d for each distance function separately. The parameters are summarised in Table 3, with the results shown in Figure 1.

3.2   kMC

kMC algorithm is originated from signal processing [22] and has been widely used for the problems of anomaly detection [23] [24]. It aims to partition the given observations into k clusters in which each observation belongs to the cluster in terms of the nearest mean. Then, an observation is detectable according to its distances to the clusters.

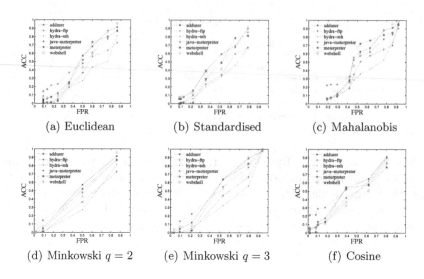

(a) Euclidean   (b) Standardised   (c) Mahalanobis

(d) Minkowski $q = 2$ (e) Minkowski $q = 3$ (f) Cosine

Fig. 1. The results from kNN

Given the observations $\{x_1, x_2, \cdots, x_m\}$, i.e., the set of the p dimensional training frequency vectors ($\bar{\mathbf{T}}$), the kMC algorithm partitions the observations into k clusters $\mathbf{C} = \{C_1, C_2, \cdots, C_k\}$ by minimising

$$\arg\min_{\mathbf{C}} \sum_{i=1}^{k} \sum_{x_j \in C_i} \| x_j - c_i \|$$

where c_i is the centre of C_i. Although solving the problem is computationally difficult, there are a number of efficient heuristic algorithms which are usually similar to the idea of the expectation-maximisation (EM) algorithm. For example, Lloyd's algorithm [25] is able to reach the local optimum by an iterative process which, in particular, alternates between two steps: assignment and update. In an assignment step, each observation is assigned to the cluster whose mean yields the least within-cluster sum of squares and, in an update step, the centres of the observations in the new clusters are calculated.

Table 4. Parameters of kMC

Distance/Metric	τ	step width	Distance/Metric	τ	step width
Euclidean	$[0.005, 0.15]$	0.005	Cosine	$[0.025, 0.5]$	0.025
Minkowski metric $q = 1$	$[0.15, 0.9]$	0.05	Correlation	$[0.025, 0.5]$	0.025

When $\{c_1, c_2, \cdots, c_k\}$ are ready, the frequency vector of a system call trace, say y, $y \in \bar{\mathbf{V}} \cup \bar{\mathbf{A}}$, can be detected through the following inequation,

$$\min_{i=1,2,\cdots,k} distance(c_i, y) \leq d.$$

If this inequation is true, the system call trace is identified as normal; otherwise abnormal. There are also two parameters k and d to be specified in the KMC algorithm. k is related to the distribution of the given observations and, by manually adjusting, it is fixed to 5. d is not easy to empirically specify as it varies according to the distance function. As a result, we employ the maximum of the within-cluster distances obtained from $\bar{T}$ as a scale d^*, and test d by multiplying a range of coefficient τ and this scale, i.e., $d = \tau d^*$. All the parameters are given in Table 4 and the results are shown in Figure 2.

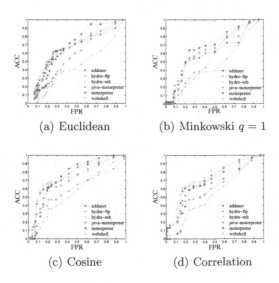

(a) Euclidean   (b) Minkowski $q = 1$

(c) Cosine   (d) Correlation

Fig. 2. The results from kMC

3.3   Evaluation

In this subsection, we evaluate the results according to three aspects: (1) the performances of the two frequency-based algorithms against ADFA-LD, (2) the performances against each type of attack, and (3) the correlation between the performances and the distance functions.

The kNN algorithm fails to effectively detect the attacks with the low dimensional frequency vectors no matter what distance function is used and its performance is much worse than that of the original frequency vectors. However, the kMC algorithm is able to achieve an ACC of higher than 60% with a FPR of lower than 20% for most types of attack. In addition, the kMC algorithm is much more efficient than the kNN algorithm in terms of computation, as each time of detection requires only computing the distances to the k centres. Thus, it can conclude that the kMC algorithm outperforms the kNN algorithm when the dimension of the frequency vector is reduced.

As far as the performances against each type of attack, **Java-Meterpreter** is the easiest type to detect using both the algorithms. **Hydra-FTP** and **Hydra-SSH**, on the contrary, can not be effectively addressed by the frequency-based algorithms for which, basically, an ACC of 50% will incur an FPR of 50%. This result indicates that a frequency-based algorithm is not versatile against any type of attack.

Finally, we look at how the performance is relating to the distance function. The result from cosine distance is the best which, in particular, achieves an ACC of 60% with a FPR of around 10% except for **Hydra-FTP** and **Hydra-SSH**, when the kMC algorithm is employed. Correlation distance is the second choice, by which the performance is comparable with that of cosine distance. Although Euclidean and Mahalanobis distances are most commonly used distance metrics, their performances, in this case, are not impressive. In short, distance function is not a crucial factor to performance.

4   Conclusion

In this paper, following the preliminary analysis, we applied two typical frequency-based algorithms to ADFA-LD. After transforming the system call traces into the frequency vectors, in order to further reduce the computational cost, we attempted to reduce the dimension of the frequency vectors using PCA, and the subsequent analysis was conducted in a lower dimensional space. The results shown that the kNN algorithm is ineffective against the attacks, and the kMC algorithm can detect most types of attack effectively. In the future, we will continue to study the characteristics of ADFA-LD and attempt to design more efficient and effective algorithms for detecting the attacks.

References

1. Stavroulakis, P., Stamp, M.: Handbook of information and communication security. Springer (2010)
2. http://www.cs.unm.edu/~immsec/systemcalls.htm
3. http://www.ll.mit.edu/mission/communications/cyber/CSTcorpora/ideval/data/
4. Forrest, S., Hofmeyr, S., Somayaji, A., Longstaff, T.A.: A sense of self for Unix processes. In: Proceedings of the 1996 IEEE Symposium on Security and Privacy, pp. 120–128 (1996)
5. Kosoresow, A.P., Hofmeyer, S.A.: Intrusion detection via system call traces. IEEE Software 14, 35–42 (1997)
6. Forrest, S., Hofmeyr, S., Somayaji, A.: The Evolution of System-Call Monitoring. In: Annual Computer Security Applications Conference, ACSAC 2008, pp. 418–430 (2008)
7. Eskin, E., Wenke, L., Stolfo, S.J.: Modeling system calls for intrusion detection with dynamic window sizes. In: Proceedings of the DARPA Information Survivability Conference Exposition II, DISCEX 2001, pp. 165–175 (2001)
8. Hoang, X.D., Hu, J.: An efficient hidden Markov model training scheme for anomaly intrusion detection of server applications based on system calls. In: Proceedings of the 12th IEEE International Conference on Networks (ICON 2004), pp. 470–474 (2004)

9. Hoang, X.D., Hu, J., Bertok, P.: A program-based anomaly intrusion detection scheme using multiple detection engines and fuzzy inference. Journal of Network and Computer Applications 32, 1219–1228 (2009)

10. Creech, G., Hu, J.: Generation of a new IDS test dataset: Time to retire the KDD collection. In: 2013 IEEE Wireless Communications and Networking Conference (WCNC), pp. 4487–4492 (2013)

11. Creech, G., Hu, J.: A Semantic Approach to Host-Based Intrusion Detection Systems Using Contiguous and Discontiguous System Call Patterns. IEEE Transactions on Computers 63, 807–819 (2014)

12. Liao, Y., Vemuri, V.R.: Use of K-nearest neighbor classifier for intrusion detection. Computers & Security 21, 439–448 (2002)

13. Chen, W.-H., Hsu, S.-H., Shen, H.-P.: Application of SVM and ANN for intrusion detection. Computers & Operations Research 32, 2617–2634 (2005)

14. Sharma, A., Pujari, A.K., Paliwal, K.K.: Intrusion detection using text processing techniques with a kernel based similarity measure. Computers & Security 26, 488–495 (2007)

15. Xie, M., Hu, J.: Evaluating host-based anomaly detection systems: A preliminary analysis of ADFA-LD. In: 2013 6th International Congress on Image and Signal Processing (CISP), pp. 1711–1716 (2013)

16. http://osinside.net/syscall/system_call_table.htm

17. Jolliffe, I.: Principal component analysis. Wiley Online Library (2005)

18. Xie, M., Han, S., Tian, B.: Highly Efficient Distance-Based Anomaly Detection through Univariate with PCA in Wireless Sensor Networks. In: 2011 IEEE 10th International Conference on Trust, Security and Privacy in Computing and Communications (TrustCom), pp. 564–571 (2011)

19. Xie, M., Hu, J., Tian, B.: Histogram-Based Online Anomaly Detection in Hierarchical Wireless Sensor Networks. In: 2012 IEEE 11th International Conference on Trust, Security and Privacy in Computing and Communications (TrustCom), pp. 751–759 (2012)

20. Xie, M., Hu, J., Han, S., Chen, H.-H.: Scalable Hypergrid k-NN-Based Online Anomaly Detection in Wireless Sensor Networks. IEEE Transactions on Parallel and Distributed Systems 24, 1661–1670 (2013)

21. Hu, J., Gingrich, D., Sentosa, A.: A k-Nearest Neighbor Approach for User Authentication through Biometric Keystroke Dynamics. In: IEEE International Conference on Communications, ICC 2008, pp. 1556–1560 (2008)

22. Hartigan, J.A., Wong, M.A.: Algorithm AS 136: A k-means clustering algorithm. Applied Statistics, 100–108 (1979)

23. Mahmood, A.N., Hu, J., Tari, Z., Leckie, C.: Critical infrastructure protection: Resource efficient sampling to improve detection of less frequent patterns in network traffic. Journal of Network and Computer Applications 33, 491–502 (2010)

24. Xi, K., Tang, Y., Hu, J.: Correlation keystroke verification scheme for user access control in cloud computing environment. The Computer Journal 54, 1632–1644 (2011)

25. Lloyd, S.: Least squares quantization in PCM. IEEE Transactions on Information Theory 28, 129–137 (1982)

A New Public Key Encryption with Equality Test

Kaibin Huang[1], Raylin Tso[1], Yu-Chi Chen[2], Wangyu Li[1], and Hung-Min Sun[3]

[1] Department of Computer Science, National Chengchi University, Taipei, Taiwan
kyle@iis.sinica.edu.tw, raylin@nccu.edu.tw, 9716015@gmail.com
[2] Institute of Information Science, Academia Sinica
wycchen@ieee.org
[3] Department of Computer Science, National Tsing Hua University, Hsinchu, Taiwan
hmsun@cs.nthu.edu.tw

Abstract. We proposed a new public key encryption scheme with equality test (PKEET), which stands for a public key encryption scheme with comparable ciphertext. The equivalence among ciphertext under PKEET schemes can be verified without decryption. In some PKEET algorithms like Tang's AoN-PKEET, which is called authorization-based PKEET, the equality test functionality is restricted to some authorized users: only users who own authorities are able to perform equality test functions. For the best of our knowledge, the authorities of all existing authorization-based PKEET schemes are valid for all ciphertext encrypted under the same public key. Accurately, we propose a CBA-PKEET scheme following Tang's AoN-PKEET scheme, which means a PKEET scheme with ciphertext-binded authorities (CBA). Each ciphertext-binded authority is valid for a specific ciphertext, rather than all ciphertext encrypted under the same public key. Then, we compare the features and efficiency between our CBA-PKEET and some existing authorization-based PKEET schemes. Finally, the security of CBA-PKEET is proved in the random oracle model based on the some hard problems.

Keywords: ciphertext-binded authority, equality test, public key encryption.

1 Introduction

In CT-RSA 2010, Yang et al. [12] proposed his public key encryption scheme with equality test (PKEET). PKEET [5][9][10][11][12] schemes provide the functionality that the equivalence among ciphertext can be verified without decryption. For any two ciphertext, say $\mathcal{E}_{pk_1}(m_1)$ and $\mathcal{E}_{pk_2}(m_2)$, encrypted under different public keys, the equality testing algorithm only indicates the equivalence result 1 for identical or 0 for different, other information about plaintext m_1 and m_2 will not be leaked. Through this technique, some privacy preserving services could be achieved. For example, the financial service providers only know the bill is correct or not, but they don't know the amount or detail about the transaction.

M.H. Au et al. (Eds.): NSS 2014, LNCS 8792, pp. 550–557, 2014.

Following Yang et al.'s work, Tang proposed his all-or-nothing PKEET scheme (AoN-PKEET [11]) in 2012. The authority concept is adopted in Tang's work. Only authorized proxies or users are able to perform equality test functions. By the way, the authority is permanently valid; that is: once someone gets Alice's authority, all ciphertext encrypted under Alice's public key becomes comparable.

Motivation: considering a situation that Alice only authorizes a specific ciphertext to Bob, not all of Alice's ciphertext, is it possible? For example, the dentists are only permitted to know those medical records about teeth, not heart, nor bonds. For the best of our knowledge, there is no existing PKEET algorithm which provides a ciphertext-binded authority (CBA) for equality test purpose, which the authority is valid only for one ciphertext, not all ciphertext encrypted under the same public key.

Our Contribution: first, we construct a PKEET scheme with ciphertext-binded authorities (CBA-PKEET). Then, the features and efficiency between Tang's works and our CBA-PKEET scheme are compared and shown in tables. Finally, following Tang's definition, there are type-I adversaries who can acquire all authorities and type-II adversaries who can not acquire any authority. By Tang's classification, we prove that our CBA-PKEET scheme is one-way secure against type-I adversaries and IND-CCA2 secure against type-II adversaries based on decisional Diffie-Hellman problem.

Paper Organization: after the abstract and introduction, we first discuss some preliminaries and in the next section. Tang's AoN-PKEET scheme is introduced in section 3. Next, we follow Tang's AoN-PKEET scheme, define model and introduce our CBA-PKEET scheme in section 4. The comparison between CBA-PKEET scheme and previous PKEET schemes are also shown in form of tables. The security proof is omitted due to the page limit, which will be shown in the full version paper. Finally, we provide a brief conclusion in the last section.

2   Preliminaries and Related Works

In this section, there are some preliminaries discussed before the PKEET issues. We first define some symbols and operations which will be frequently used in the later computations.

2.1   Operation Definition

1. Let $||$ be the concatenation symbol; $\oplus$ stands for the XOR operation; $\perp$ represents for null; $\cong$ is "approximately equal"; $\Rightarrow$ means "imply"; $e \in_R \mathbb{G}$ denotes that e is an element randomly selected from the group $\mathbb{G}$.
2. We define two substring operations, for any given string s:
   - $LSB_{\mathcal{L}}[s]$ returns the least significant $\mathcal{L}$-bit segment.
   - $MSB_{\mathcal{L}}[s]$ returns the most significant $\mathcal{L}$-bit segment.
3. $\Pr[H] = 2^{-range(H)}$. Let H be a one-way cryptographic hash function. $\Pr[H]$ stands for the probability that given any input h, find the corresponding hash value $h' = H(h)$ without querying hash oracle in the random oracle model.

4. For any exponential operations in the multiplicative group, e.x. $g^x \pmod{p}$, in Tang's scheme [11] and our CBA-PKEET scheme, we omit all $\pmod{p}$ expressions for clear. That is, $g^x \pmod{p}$ will be abbreviated as g^x in the following paragraphs and sections.

Second, for security proof, the related hard problem in cryptography is introduced here.

2.2 CDH and DDH Problems

CDH denotes computational Diffie-Hellman problem. Given a secure parameter k, a multiplicative cyclic group $\mathbb{G}$, a prime order $q = q(k) = order(\mathbb{G})$, a prime modular p, a generator $g \in \mathbb{G}$ and two elements $g^\alpha, g^\beta \in \mathbb{G}$ ($\alpha, \beta \in_R \mathbb{Z}_q^*$); CDH problem is defined to find the element $g^{\alpha\beta} \in \mathbb{G}$. Generally, CDH is a hard problem in cryptography; the probability of breaking CDH problem is described as:

$$\Pr[g^{\alpha\beta} \leftarrow Adv(k, \mathbb{G}, q, p, g, g^\alpha, g^\beta)] \leq negl(k)$$

Besides those parameters in CDH problem, adversaries of DDH problem are given one more parameter g^γ. DDH problem can be described as: given $(k, \mathbb{G}, q, p, g, g^\alpha, g^\beta, g^\gamma)$; decide whether $g^\gamma = g^{\alpha\beta}$ or not. For clear, we define a boolean value $b \in \{0, 1\}$: $b = 1 \iff g^\gamma = g^{\alpha\beta}$; $b = 0$ otherwise. Although DDH problem is trivially weaker than CDH problem, it is also considered hard in the cryptography; the probability of breaking DDH problem is described as:

$$\Pr \begin{bmatrix} b \in_R \{0, 1\}; e \leftarrow_R \mathbb{G}; g^\gamma \leftarrow_b \{e, g^{\alpha\beta}\}; \\ b' \leftarrow Adv(k, \mathbb{G}, q, p, g, g^\alpha, g^\beta, g^\gamma) \end{bmatrix} : b' = b \end{bmatrix} \leq \frac{1}{2} + negl(k)$$

2.3 Properties of PKEET Schemes

Formalized by Yang et al., they propose that a PKEET scheme $\Pi = \{\mathcal{G}, \mathcal{E}, \mathcal{D}, \mathcal{C}\}$ has ciphertext comparability with error ϵ for some function $\epsilon(\cdot)$ if there exists an efficiently computable deterministic function $\mathcal{C}(\cdot, \cdot)$ such that for every secure parameter $k \in \mathbb{N}$, we have

Definition 1. *Perfect consistency:* $\forall m \in MgSp(1^k)$,

$$\Pr \begin{bmatrix} (sk_1, pk_1) \leftarrow \mathcal{G}(1^k); (sk_2, pk_2) \leftarrow \mathcal{G}(1^k); \\ c_1 \leftarrow \mathcal{E}_{pk_1}(m); c_2 \leftarrow \mathcal{E}_{pk_2}(m) \end{bmatrix} : \mathcal{C}(c_1, c_2) = 1 \end{bmatrix} = 1$$

Definition 2. *Soundness:* $\forall m_1, m_2 \in MgSp(1^k)$, for every polynomial-time adversary Adv,

$$\Pr \begin{bmatrix} (c_1, c_2, sk_1, sk_2) \leftarrow Adv; & m_1, m_2 \neq \perp \\ m_1 \leftarrow \mathcal{D}_{sk_1}(c_1); & : \wedge m_1 \neq m_2 \\ m_2 \leftarrow \mathcal{D}_{sk_2}(c_2) & \wedge \mathcal{C}(c_1, c_2) = 1 \end{bmatrix} = \epsilon(k) \in negl(k)$$

3   Tang's AoN-PKEET

Following Yang et al.'s PKEET scheme, Tang proposes his all-or-nothing public key encryption scheme with equality test, which is AoN-PKEET. The key point of Tang's AoN-PKEET is that:

$$c = (\mathcal{E}_{pk}(m), \mathcal{E}_{pk'}(H(m)))$$

The former one is used for decryption and the latter one is used for equality testing.

Parameters: let $\mathbb{G}$ be a multiplicative group of prime order q; g stands for a generator of $\mathbb{G}$; k is a secure parameter; H_1, H_2 and H_3 are three cryptographic hash functions: $H_1 : \{0,1\}^* \rightarrow \{0,1\}^{M+l}$, $H_2 : \{0,1\}^* \rightarrow \mathbb{Z}_q$ and $H_3 : \{0,1\}^* \rightarrow \{0,1\}^k$. Here M denotes the bit length of messages in $\mathbb{G}$, and l is the bit length of q.

- $\mathcal{G}(1^k)$: select $x, y \in_R \mathbb{Z}_q$ as the private keys, and compute g^x and g^y as the public keys.
- $\mathcal{E}_{pk}(m)$: let c be the encrypted message, $c = (c^{(1)}, c^{(2)}, c^{(3)}, c^{(4)}, c^{(5)})$ composed of 5 parts:

$$u, v \in_R \mathbb{Z}_q, c^{(1)} = g^u, c^{(2)} = g^v, c^{(3)} = H_1(g^{ux}) \oplus (m||u),$$

$$c^{(4)} = g^{H_2(g^{vy})+m}, c^{(5)} = H_3(c^{(1)}||c^{(2)}||c^{(3)}||c^{(4)}||m||u)$$

- $\mathcal{D}_{sk}(c)$: first calculate $m'||u' \leftarrow c^{(3)} \oplus H_1((c^{(1)})^x)$ and then check both $c^{(1)} \overset{?}{=} g^{u'}$ and $c^{(5)} \overset{?}{=} H_3(c^{(1)}||c^{(2)}||c^{(3)}||c^{(4)}||m'||u')$. Return the plaintext m in case that both of these two equations are tenable.

If some trusted type-I users request to perform the equality test computation on c, the authority will be generated as:

- $\mathcal{A}_{sk} = y$.

Otherwise, $\mathcal{A}_{sk} = \perp$.

Let U_1 and U_2 be two users; $\mathcal{E}_{pk_1}(m_1)$ and $\mathcal{E}_{pk_2}(m_2)$ stand for two ciphertext encrypted under pk_1 and pk_2 respectively. Anyone owns y_1 and y_2 can run the comparison algorithm $\mathcal{C}$ to test the equivalence between c_1 and c_2.

- $\mathcal{C}(c_1, c_2, y_1, y_2)$: the algorithm returns 1 or 0 by computing

$$c_1^{(4)} \cdot g^{-H_2((c_1^{(2)})^{y_1})} \overset{?}{=} c_2^{(4)} \cdot g^{-H_2((c_2^{(2)})^{y_2})}$$

If the equation is tenable, it returns 1 as identical; otherwise, it returns 0 which means distinct.

Since $c^{(1)} = g^u$, $(c^{(1)})^x = g^{ux}$, the decryption is intuitive so that we do not infer it step by step. In the comparison phase $\mathcal{C}(c_1, c_2, y_1, y_2)$:

$$c_1^{(4)} \cdot g^{-H_2((c_1^{(2)})^{y_1})} = g^{H_2((c_1^{(2)})^{y_1})+m_1} \cdot g^{-H_2((c_1^{(2)})^{y_1})} = g^{m_1}$$

Similarly, $c_2 = g^{m_2}$. By definition of the multiplicative group $\mathbb{G}$, the comparison returns 1 if and only if $m_1 = m_2$. The perfect consistency holds. On the other hand, by definition $m_1 \neq m_2$ if and only if $\mathcal{C}(c_1, c_2) = 0$. Obliviously, $m_1 \neq m_2 \iff g^{m_1} \neq g^{m_2}$. The perfect soundness holds.

4   CBA-PKEET

We propose the model of CBA-PKEET before introducing the scheme.

Definition 3. *Model of CBA-PKEET schemes*

- *Key generation, $(sk, pk) \leftarrow \mathcal{G}(1^k)$: a polynomial time key generation algorithm which takes a secure parameter k as input and then generates a secret and pubic key pair (sk, pk) of the PKEET scheme.*
- *Encryption, $c \leftarrow \mathcal{E}_{pk}(m)$: a probabilistic encryption algorithm which encrypts a message m under the public key pk, and then returns the ciphertext $c = \mathcal{E}_{pk}(m)$ in a polynomial time.*
- *Decryption, $m \leftarrow \mathcal{D}_{sk}(c)$: a deterministic decryption algorithm which returns the plaintext $m = \mathcal{D}_{sk}(c)$ in a polynomial time.*
- *Authentication, $\mathcal{A}_{sk}(c)$: if an authorized user requests the authority which makes the ciphertext c comparable, the authentication algorithm takes the private key sk into computation and output the ciphertext-binded authority $\mathcal{A}_{sk}(c)$. Otherwise, it returns $\perp$.*
- *Comparison, $1/0 \leftarrow \mathcal{C}(c_1, c_2, \mathcal{A}_{sk_1}(c_1), \mathcal{A}_{sk_2}(c_2))$: let $c_1 = \mathcal{E}_{pk_1}(m_1)$ and $c_2 = \mathcal{E}_{pk_2}(m_2)$ denote two different ciphertext encrypted under two different public keys. Anyone owns authorities $\mathcal{A}_{sk_1}(c_1)$ and $\mathcal{A}_{sk_2}(c_2)$ can perform the comparison algorithm $\mathcal{C}$, which returns the equivalence between m_1 and m_2 without decryption in a polynomial time. 1 stands for identical; 0 means distinct.*

Remark 1. *The comparison of CBA-PKEET is different from the comparison of Tang's AoN-PKEET. While replacing another ciphertext $c'_1 = \mathcal{E}_{pk_1}(m')$ to c_1 and keeping the authority $\mathcal{A}_{sk_1}(c_1)$ (even c_1 and c'_1 are encrypted under the same public key pk_1), the comparison algorithm $\mathcal{C}(c'_1, c_2, \mathcal{A}_{sk_1}(c_1), \mathcal{A}_{sk_2}(c_2))$ does not work in CBA-PKEET.*

4.1   Our Scheme

Based on Tang's works, we take advantage of Fujisaki-Okamoto translation [7] to construct our CBA-PKEET scheme. Before introducing that, we have to introduce the concept of our scheme for ease of understanding.

$$c = \mathcal{E}_{pk}(m) = c_m || c_{H(m)}$$

The previous part of ciphertext denotes the encrypted message c_m, and the latter part $c_{H(m)}$ represents for the encrypted hash value of m for equality test purpose.

There are some public parameters (G, g, p, q, l, k) and three collision resistant one-way hash functions: H_1, H_2 and H_3, which are defined as:

G is a multiplicative cyclic group with prime order q and modular p.
The bit length of q is l, $l \cong k$.
Each element in G is k-bit long.
g is a generator in G.
Set the message space to G.
k stands for a secure parameter.
$H_1 : \{0,1\}^{2k+l} \to \mathbb{Z}_q^*$; $H_2 : G \to \{0,1\}^{2k+l}$; $H_3 : \{0,1\}^* \to \{0,1\}^k$.

- $\mathcal{G}(1^k)$: select $x \in_R \mathbb{Z}_q^*$, keep it as a secret key and publish the public key $y = g^x$.
- $\mathcal{E}_{pk}(m)$: to encrypt a message m into the ciphertext c, we first randomly pick $r \in_R \mathbb{Z}_q^*$, and then compute $c = (c^{(1)}, c^{(2)})$ following:

$$u = H_1(m||r||H_3(m)), c^{(1)} = g^u, c^{(2)} = H_2(y^u) \oplus (m||r||H_3(m))$$

- $\mathcal{D}_{sk}(c)$: once receiving the ciphertext c, the owner of secret key x is able to decrypt it by the following algorithm:
  1. Compute $(m'||r'||R) \leftarrow c^{(2)} \oplus H_2((c^{(1)})^x)$, $u' = H_1(m'||r'||R)$.
  2. Check if $c^{(1)} \stackrel{?}{=} g^{u'}$ and $R \stackrel{?}{=} H_3(m')$? If both two equations are tenable, then $m' = m$, the decryption algorithm returns the plaintext m; otherwise, it returns $\perp$ and terminates.
- $\mathcal{A}_{sk}(c)$: once a trusted party sends an authentication request with respect to the ciphertext c to the owner of secret key sk. He or she follows step 1 and 2 in the decryption phase. If $c^{(1)} \stackrel{?}{=} g^{u'}$ and $R = H_3(m')$, then he or she returns the ciphertext-binded authority

$$\mathcal{A}_{sk}(c) = LSB_k[H_2((c^{(1)})^x)]$$

Otherwise, $\perp$ will be returned.
- $\mathcal{C}(c_1, c_2, \mathcal{A}_{sk_1}(c_1), \mathcal{A}_{sk_2}(c_2))$: let c_1 and c_2 be two ciphertext which are encrypted under different public keys pk_1 and pk_2 respectively. Anyone can perform the comparison algorithm after getting two authorities $\mathcal{A}_{sk_1}(c_1)$ and $\mathcal{A}_{sk_2}(c_2)$. The comparison algorithm is shown as the following equation:

$$LSB_k[c_1^{(2)}] \oplus \mathcal{A}_{sk_1}(c_1) \stackrel{?}{=} LSB_k[c_2^{(2)}] \oplus \mathcal{A}_{sk_2}(c_2)$$

If this equation is tenable, then those two plaintext m_1 and m_2, which relates to the ciphertext c_1 and c_2, are identical; otherwise, they are distinct. The inference of the comparison is provided below. Let $u_1 = H_1(m_1||r||H_3(m_1))$,

$$
\begin{aligned}
& LSB_k[c_1^{(2)}] \oplus \mathcal{A}_{sk_1}(c_1) \\
=& LSB_k[H_2(y_1^{u_1}) \oplus (m_1||r_1||H_3(m_1))] \oplus \mathcal{A}_{sk_1}(c_1) \\
=& LSB_k[H_2(g^{u_1 x_1}) \oplus (m_1||r_1||H_3(m_1))] \oplus LSB_k[H_2(g^{u_1 x_1})] \\
=& LSB_k[H_2(g^{u_1 x_1})] \oplus LSB_k[m_1||r_1||H_3(m_1)] \oplus LSB_k[H_2(g^{u_1 x_1})] \\
=& LSB_k[m_1||r_1||H_3(m_1)] = H_3(m_1)
\end{aligned}
$$

Table 1. Efficiency comparison

	$\mathcal{G}$	$\mathcal{E}$	$\mathcal{D}$	$\mathcal{A}$	$\mathcal{C}$	Equality test($2\mathcal{A} + \mathcal{C}$)
PKEET[12]	1 exp	3 exp	3 exp	N/A	2 pairing	2 pairing
PCE[5]	1 exp	4 exp	2 pairing	N/A	4 pairing	4 pairing
AoN-PKEET[11]	2 exp	5 exp	2 exp	0	4 exp	4 exp
FG-PKEET[10]	2 exp	4 exp	2 exp	3 exp	4 pairing	4 pairing
CBA-PKEET	1 exp	2 exp	2 exp	1 exp	2 xor	2 exp

Similarly, $LSB_k[c_2^{(2)}] \oplus \mathcal{A}_{sk_2}(c_2) = H_3(m_2)$. The comparison becomes:

$$LSB_k[c_1^{(2)}] \oplus \mathcal{A}_{sk_1}(c_1) = H_3(m_1) \stackrel{?}{=} H_3(m_2) = LSB_k[c_2^{(2)}] \oplus \mathcal{A}_{sk_2}(c_2)$$

The perfect consistency obliviously holds. On the other hand, if $m_1 \neq m_2$, by definition, the probability that $\mathcal{C}(c_1, c_2, \mathcal{A}_{sk_1}(c_1), \mathcal{A}_{sk_2}(c_2)) = 1$ can be estimated by

$$\Pr \begin{bmatrix} (sk_1, pk_1) \leftarrow \mathcal{G}(1^k); (sk_2, pk_2) \leftarrow \mathcal{G}(1^k); \\ m_1 \neq m_2; c_1 \leftarrow \mathcal{E}_{pk_1}(m_1); c_2 \leftarrow \mathcal{E}_{pk_2}(m_2) : \mathcal{C}(c_1, c_2, w_1, w_2) = 1 \\ w_1 \leftarrow \mathcal{A}_{sk_1}(c_1); w_2 \leftarrow \mathcal{A}_{sk_2}(c_2) \end{bmatrix} = \Pr[H_3]$$

Because $\Pr[H_3] \in negl(k)$, the soundness holds for secure parameter k.

Efficiency comparison: let xor, exp and $pairing$ be the time cost of XOR, exponential and pairing computations respectively.

$$xor << exp < pairing \cong 8\ exp$$

We take Yang et al.'s [12], Tang's [10] and [11] and Canard et al.'s [5] into comparison, and show the efficiency comparison on the $\{\mathcal{G}, \mathcal{E}, \mathcal{D}, \mathcal{A}, \mathcal{C}\}$ model in table 1. The whole process of private equality test needs two times of authorization and one time of comparison.[1] Obliviously, the CBA-PKEET scheme works much more efficiently than those previous works.

Remark 2. *Security proof*
Due to the page limit, the security proof is omitted, which will be shown in the full version of this paper.

5   Conclusion

We notice that PKEET with ciphertext-binded authorities is useful especially in finance fields. But so far, there is not a CBA-PKEET scheme existed. Following

---

[1] Since the authorities in Tang's works [10][11], are valid for all ciphertext encrypted under the same public key, the equality test algorithm only costs the comparison time $\mathcal{C}$, not $2\mathcal{A} + \mathcal{C}$.

Tang's AoN-PKEET scheme, we propose the first CBA-PKEET scheme. It works much more efficiently than previous authorization-based PKEET schemes do. Then, we prove our CBA-PKEET scheme in the random oracle model based on Diffie-Hellman hard problems. Due to the page limit, the proof is omitted here, and it will appear in the full version of this paper.

Acknowledgment. Raylin Tso would like to thank the National Science Council, Taiwan, R.O.C. for supporting this research under Grant No. NSC 101-2628-E-004-001-MY2. Hung-Min Sun would like to thank the National Science Council, Taiwan, R.O.C. for supporting this research under Grant No. NSC 100-2628-E-007-018-MY3.

References

1. Agrawal, S., Boneh, D., Boyen, X.: Efficient lattice (H)IBE in the standard model. In: Gilbert, H. (ed.) EUROCRYPT 2010. LNCS, vol. 6110, pp. 553–572. Springer, Heidelberg (2010)
2. Bellare, M., Desai, A., Pointcheval, D., Rogaway, P.: Relations among notions of security for public-key encryption schemes. In: Krawczyk, H. (ed.) CRYPTO 1998. LNCS, vol. 1462, pp. 26–45. Springer, Heidelberg (1998)
3. Bellare, M., Rogaway, P.: Random oracles are practical: A paradigm for designing efficient protocols. In: ACM Conference on Computer and Communications Security, pp. 62–73 (1993)
4. Bellare, M., Rogaway, P.: Optimal asymmetric encryption. In: De Santis, A. (ed.) EUROCRYPT 1994. LNCS, vol. 950, pp. 92–111. Springer, Heidelberg (1995)
5. Canard, S., Fuchsbauer, G., Gouget, A., Laguillaumie, F.: Plaintext-checkable encryption. In: Dunkelman, O. (ed.) CT-RSA 2012. LNCS, vol. 7178, pp. 332–348. Springer, Heidelberg (2012)
6. Canetti, R., Halevi, S., Katz, J.: A forward-secure public-key encryption scheme. J. Cryptology 20(3), 265–294 (2007)
7. Fujisaki, E., Okamoto, T.: How to enhance the security of public-key encryption at minimum cost. In: Imai, H., Zheng, Y. (eds.) PKC 1999. LNCS, vol. 1560, pp. 53–68. Springer, Heidelberg (1999)
8. Goldwasser, S., Micali, S.: Probabilistic encryption. J. Comput. Syst. Sci. 28(2), 270–299 (1984)
9. Lipmaa, H.: Verifiable homomorphic oblivious transfer and private equality test. In: Laih, C.-S. (ed.) ASIACRYPT 2003. LNCS, vol. 2894, pp. 416–433. Springer, Heidelberg (2003)
10. Tang, Q.: Public key encryption schemes supporting equality test with authorisation of different granularity. IJACT 2(4), 304–321 (2012)
11. Tang, Q.: Public key encryption supporting plaintext equality test and user-specified authorization. Security and Communication Networks 5(12), 1351–1362 (2012)
12. Yang, G., Tan, C.H., Huang, Q., Wong, D.S.: Probabilistic public key encryption with equality test. In: Pieprzyk, J. (ed.) CT-RSA 2010. LNCS, vol. 5985, pp. 119–131. Springer, Heidelberg (2010)

A Probabilistic Algebraic Attack on the Grain Family of Stream Ciphers

Pratish Datta, Dibyendu Roy, and Sourav Mukhopadhyay

Department of Mathematics,
Indian Institute of Technology Kharagpur,
Kharagpur-721302, India
{pratishdatta,dibyendu.roy,sourav}@maths.iitkgp.ernet.in

Abstract. In 2005, Hell, Johansson and Meier submitted a stream cipher proposal named Grain v1 to the estream call for stream cipher proposals and it also became one estream finalists in the hardware category. The output function of Grain v1 connects its 160 bits internal state divided equally between an LFSR and an NFSR, using a non-linear filter function in a complex way. Over the last years many cryptanalyst identified several weaknesses in Grain v1. As a result in 2011 the inventors modified Grain v1 and published a new version of Grain named Grain-128a which has a similar structure as Grain v1 but with a 256 bits internal state with an optional authentication is the latest version of Grain family resisting all known attacks on Grain v1. However both these ciphers are quite resistant against the classical algebraic attack due to the rapid growth of the degree of the key-stream equations in subsequent clockings caused by the NFSR. This paper presents a probabilistic algebraic attack on both these Grain versions. The basic idea of our attack is to develop separate probabilistic equations for the LFSR and the NFSR bits from each key-stream equations. Surprisingly it turns out that in case of Grain-128a our proposed equations hold with all most sure probability, which makes the sure retrieval of the LFSR bits. We also outline a technique to reduce the growth of degree of the equations involving the NFSR bits for Grain v1. Further we highlight that the concept of probabilistic algebraic attack as proposed in this paper can be considered as a generic attack strategy against any stream cipher having similar structure of the output function as in case of the Grain family.

Keywords: Boolean Function, Grain v1, Grain-128a, Algebraic Attack, Probabilistic Algebraic Attack.

1 Introduction

Grain v1 [12] is one of the finalist in the hardware category of the estream project. This cipher is based on an 80 bits LFSR, an 80 bits NFSR and a non-linear filter function. This stream cipher was introduced by Hell, Johansson and Meier [12] in 2005. The key-stream generation function combines some particular state bits of the LFSR as well as the NFSR using the non-linear Boolean function in a complex way. Detail specification of this cipher is described in Section 2.

M.H. Au et al. (Eds.): NSS 2014, LNCS 8792, pp. 558–565, 2014.
© Springer International Publishing Switzerland 2014

Grain-128a [2] is the latest modified version of Grain family. This cipher is based on an 128 bits LFSR , an 128 bits NFSR and a non-linear filter function and two different modes of operations: with or without authentication. This cipher is proposed by Agren, Hell, Johansson and Meier in 2011. Design specification of this cipher is described in [2].

Algebraic attack, introduced by N.T. Courtois and W. Meier [6], is a well studied cryptanalytic technique against stream ciphers. The basic principle of this attack is to express the relation between some internal state (may be the secret key itself) and some known key-stream bits (may not be consecutive) as a large system of multivariate polynomial equations and attempt to solve this system in order to retrieve that secret internal state subsequently. There are some existing algorithm e.g. re-linearization, XL algorithm [5] and Gröbner bases [14], [10], [11] etc. for solving systems of multivariate polynomial equations. However, the efficiency of these algorithms strongly depends on the algebraic degree of the equations. The detail of the attack model is described in [6].

However, this classical version of algebraic attack is well suited for combiner or filter models purely based on LFSR, this method cannot be applied directly to stream ciphers involving NFSR such as Grain v1 [12] or Grain-128a [2]. This is due to the non-linear feedback function and presence of bits from NFSR bits in non-linear filter function, the degree of the generated equations increases quite rapidly in successive clockings.

In 2005, An Braeken and Bart Preneel [4] introduced one type of probabilistic variant of algebraic attack for LFSR based stream ciphers combined with non-linear Boolean function. Their method involves finding probabilistic equations of certain low degree by determining approximate low degree annihilators of the combiner or filter function or its boolean complement with high probability. But this method is again unsuitable for Grain family due to the structure of its output function.

In many papers in the literature they have given different types of attack on Grain v1 [1], [13] [15], [3]. The only paper concerning the algebraic attack on Grain v1 is by Mehreen Afzal and Ashraf Masood [1]. But in [1], the author described algebraic attack on Grain v1 based on computer simulations. But there is no proper explanation of the results obtained. In case of Grain-128a, however, no such attempt has yet been made.

In this paper we attempt to develop a probabilistic algebraic attack on Grain family. The basic idea of our attack is to generate two simultaneous probabilistic equations, one involving only LFSR bits and the other only NFSR bits, from each output equations. Then we can construct two separate probabilistic systems corresponding to LFSR and NFSR bits respectively. Now the classical algebraic attack strategy can be applied on the LFSR part. For the NFSR part of Grain v1 we show that by knowing half of the NFSR state bits provides sufficient number of low degree equations which may helpful for algebraic attack. In this connection we would also like to mention that, though the basic process of generation of the probabilistic equations in both the cases is the same, for Grain-128a we obtain overwhelming probability (close to 1) of the generated equations which makes our attack more effective for this case. We also show that the probability of obtaining the correct internal state of LFSR part for Grain family following our strategy. Our approach in this paper can be viewed as a general attack strategy against stream cipher having similar structure of the output function as in case of the Grain family. To the best of our knowledge, this type of probabilistic approach in algebraic attack has not been attempted in the literature previously. The details of our attack is described from Section 4. The full version of this paper is available in [9].

2   Design Specification of Grain v1 Stream Cipher

Grain v1 [12] stream cipher is based on one 80 bits LFSR, one 80 bits NFSR and one non-linear filter function of 5 variables. The initial LFSR's bits are denoted by s_i, $i = 0, 1, \ldots, 79$ and the initial NFSR's bits are denoted by b_i, $i = 0, 1, \ldots, 79$. The non-linear filter function is denoted by $h(x)$. The detail design specification of Grain v1 is given in [12]. These contents of LFSR and NFSR are the current states of the registers. From these states 5 variables are taken as the input for the non-linear function $h(x)$. This $h(x)$ is a non-linear function of 5 variables of non-linearity 12. Among 5 inputs in $h(x)$ 4 are coming from LFSR and one input is coming from NFSR. $h(x) = x_1 + x_4 + x_0x_3 + x_2x_3 + x_3x_4 + x_0x_1x_2 + x_0x_2x_3 + x_0x_2x_4 + x_1x_2x_4 + x_2x_3x_4$, where the variable x_4 is coming from NFSR and the other variables x_0, x_1, x_2, x_3 are coming from the LFSR, where x_0, x_1, x_2, x_3 correspond to s_{i+3}, s_{i+25}, s_{i+46}, s_{i+64} and the variable x_4 corresponds to b_{i+63}. The expression of the key stream bit is $z_i = \sum_{k \in A} b_{i+k} + h(s_{i+3}, s_{i+25}, s_{i+46}, s_{i+64}, b_{i+63})$ where $A = \{1, 2, 4, 10, 31, 43, 56\}$. The $h(x)$ can be rewritten as $h(x) = x_4 \cdot u(x_0, x_1, x_2, x_3) + v(x_0, x_1, x_2, x_3)$, where $u(x_0, x_1, x_2, x_3) = 1 + x_3 + x_0x_2 + x_1x_2 + x_2x_3$ and $v(x_0, x_1, x_2, x_3) = x_1 + x_0x_3 + x_2x_3 + x_0x_1x_2 + x_0x_2x_3$ [3].

The latest version of Grain family is Grain-128a [2]. The detail of the cipher is given in [2].

3   Existence of Low Degree Multiple of Non-Linear Feedback Function of Grain v1

In this section we will show the existence of low degree multiple of non-linear feedback function of Grain v1. The degree of the non-linear feedback function is 6 . Now if we multiply b_{i+80} by $b'_{i+28} \cdot b'_{i+60}$ we will get,
$b_{i+80} \cdot (b'_{i+28} \cdot b'_{i+60}) = b'_{i+28} \cdot b'_{i+60}[s_i + b_{i+62} + b_{i+52} + b_{i+45} + b_{i+37} + b_{i+33} + b_{i+21} + b_{i+14} + b_{i+9} + b_i + b_{i+37}b_{i+33} + b_{i+15}b_{i+9}]$.

So, if we multiply b_{i+80} by $b'_{i+28} \cdot b'_{i+60}$ then we are getting $b_{i+80} \cdot (b'_{i+28} \cdot b'_{i+60})$ as a multiplication of two low degree Boolean functions of degree 2. Using this technique we can reduce the degree of the equations of the key-stream bits.

4   Probabilistic Algebraic Attack on Grain v1

In this section we will introduce a new probabilistic algebraic attack on the stream cipher Grain v1. The key-stream expression of the Grain v1 stream cipher has two components, one is a linear combination of the NFSR bits and the other is the output of the non-linear filter function. Precisely, $z_i = A_i + b_{i+63}u(\cdot) + v(\cdot)$, where $A_i = \sum_{k \in A} b_{i+k}$ where $A = \{1, 2, 4, 10, 31, 43, 56\}$. Now for $z_i = 0$ we are getting $A_i + (b_{i+63}u(\cdot) + v(\cdot)) = 0$, similarly for $z_i = 1$ we will get $1 + A_i + (b_{i+63}u(\cdot) + v(\cdot)) = 0$. First we consider the equation for $z_i = 0$, i.e. $A_i + (b_{i+63}u(\cdot) + v(\cdot)) = 0$. Now multiply this equation by $u'(\cdot) = 1 + u(\cdot)$. After this multiplication we get $u'(\cdot)A_i + u'(\cdot)v(\cdot) = 0$. This equation is of the form $X_i + Y_i = 0$ where $X_i = u'(\cdot)A_i$ and $Y_i = u'(\cdot)v(\cdot)$ (exactly in the same way we can construct similar type of equation for $z_i = 1$ with $X_i = (1 + A_i)u'(\cdot)$, $Y_i = u'(\cdot)v(\cdot)$).

We will discuss the case for $z_i = 0$, the discussion will be similar for $z_i = 1$. Now for $z_i = 0$ we are getting $X_i + Y_i = 0$. From this equation we can easily tell that there are only two possible cases for X_i, Y_i either (i) $X_i = 0, Y_i = 0$ or (ii) $X_i = 1, Y_i = 1$. Let $p = Pr[X_i = 0, Y_i = 0]$ and $q = Pr[X_i = 1, Y_i = 1]$. Now obviously we will choose the case corresponding to the higher one between p and q in order to increase our success probability. In fact we will prove shortly that $p > q$ and similarly for $z_i = 1$.

Thus in this way, for each clocking we get two probabilistic equations with certain probability. Now consider the equations corresponding to Y_i's. These equations will be of the form $u'(\cdot)v(\cdot) = Y_i$, where $Y_i \in \mathbb{F}_2$. This is a probabilistic system of equations involving only LFSR bits, which we can solve using the classical algebraic attack technique to obtain probabilistic values of the LFSR state bits. The low degree multiple of these equations, as described in [6] can be useful in this respect.

After solving the previous system involving the LFSR state bits we will put all LFSR bits values to the original equations of z_i. Then the form of these equations will be $z_i = \sum_{k \in A} b_{i+k} + b_{i+63} \cdot u(\cdot) + v(\cdot)$ where $u(\cdot)$ and $v(\cdot)$ are known as all bits of the LFSR state are now known, only NFSR bits are now unknown variables in these equations. The procedure for reducing the growth of degree of the NFSR bit equation is described in [9].

Now we will calculate $p = Pr[X_i = 0, Y_i = 0]$. Firstly we note that here we assume that the probability of each of the initial state variables being 0 or 1 after the key initialization phase is $\frac{1}{2}$. Moreover as clearly mentioned in [12] the NFSR feedback function is balanced, so $Pr[\sum_{k \in A} b_{i+k} = 0 \ or \ 1]$ is $\frac{1}{2}$. Also the functions $u'(\cdot)$ and $v(\cdot)$ both are balanced Boolean functions, but $Y_i = u'(\cdot)v(\cdot)$ is not balanced in fact $Pr[Y_i = 0]$ is $\frac{3}{4}$. Now,
$p = Pr[X_i = 0, Y_i = 0] = Pr[X_i = 0|Y_i = 0] \cdot Pr[Y_i = 0] = \frac{3}{4} \cdot Pr[X_i = 0|Y_i = 0]$
Now we need to find $Pr[X_i = 0|Y_i = 0]$. It can be shown that $Pr[X_i = 0|Y_i = 0] = \frac{5}{6}$. So the required probability will be $p = Pr[X_i = 0, Y_i = 0] = \frac{5}{8}$. The details of the calculation is available in [9].

Thus we see that for $z_i = 0$; $X_i = 0, Y_i = 0$ has the higher probability of occurrence. A similar study can be done for $z_i = 1$. Now due to the independence of the equations corresponding to different clockings, the probability of the total system of equations will be obtained by multiplying all the probabilities corresponding to all the clockings considered.

Now we have to solve the system of equations involving LFSR bits only. From the above discussion we are getting $Y_i = 0$ for $z_i = 0$ with high probability. Now $Y_i = 0$ implies $u'(\cdot)v(\cdot) = 0$. This $u'(\cdot)v(\cdot)$ is a function of degree 3. By the theorem in [6] we can surely tell that $u'(\cdot)v(\cdot)$ has low degree multiple such that the degree of the resulting function becomes at most 2. So finally we have a probabilistic system of equations of degree at most 2 involving only LFSR bits as unknowns. This system can be solved by using any existing polynomial system solving algorithms [5], [14], [10], [11]. After solving this system we will get the probabilistic LFSR state bits.

Time Complexity for Solving This System: The complexity of Gauss reduction for this system will be $\frac{7 \cdot T^{log_2 7}}{64} \approx 2^{30}$ CPU clocks which is less than exhaustive search, where $T = \binom{80}{2} = 3160$. The calculation is described in [9].

5   Some Observations on the Degree of the Equations Involving NFSR Bits of Grain v1

In this section we will discuss some observations on the NFSR bits' equations. In the Section 4 we have discussed how to tackle the LFSR bits equations using classical algebraic attack technique. However due to the non-linear feedback function, the degree of the equations involving the NFSR bits does not remain fixed, rather it increases quite rapidly. In this section we will try to control this rapid increase in the degree of the equations and will finally show that if we know half of the NFSR bits, then we obtain sufficient number of equations of quite low degree (at most degree 4) which is feasible to solve by the existing algorithms.

The equation involving the NFSR bits are of the form $\sum_{k \in A} b_{i+k} + b_{i+63}u(\cdot) + v(\cdot) = 0$ where $A = \{1, 2, 4, 10, 31, 43, 56\}$. Note that unless $i + 63 = 80$ i.e. $i = 17$ no equation of above form will involve any of the bits that are derived from the non-linear feedback. Thus we will obtain 17 linear equations involving the NFSR bits. Now consider the following strategy: for all derived bits present in the output equation, we will multiply the equation by appropriate variables in view of reducing the degree of the equation. But it has been observed that the degree of the 80-th equation still becomes strictly greater than 33. Next we are going to present a new strategy to find low degree equations.

Consider the scenario when half of the NFSR bits are known. In the following we assume that all the bits in the odd positions are known. The argument will be similar for even position bits also. Note that now we have only 40 unknown bits and therefore now we will require much less number of equations, closed to 40. Now as we have mentioned earlier in this case also we have 24 linear equations over the NFSR bits. Now look at the non-linear feedback equation. The distribution of odd and even position bits in the terms of degree ≥ 3 is given in [9]. It has been observed that when all the odd bits are known and the expression of a derived bit in terms of the NFSR feedback function does not contain any other previously derived bit, the degree of the expression is 2 if it is an even bit and 4 if it is an odd bit. Note that in the non-linear feedback equation, the highest variable present within the non-linear terms is b_{i+63}, next b_{i+60} and next is b_{i+52}. Thus the first 17 derived bits will not have any previously derived bits among the non-linear terms in their expression, the next 3 has only one derived bit and the next 8 has only two. Now as noted earlier after the first 17 linear equations, the next 7 equations have derived bits in only one position namely b_{i+63} and the next 13 in two positions namely b_{i+63} and b_{i+56} and the next 12 equations in three positions namely b_{i+63}, b_{i+56} and b_{i+43}. So from the above discussion it is clear that following the first 17 linear equations we will get 7 equations which will be of degree 2 and degree 4 alternatively, the next 12 equations are of degree 2 or 4 and the next equation is of degree at most 6 and next 8 equations are of degree at most 8. Thus upto this point we have obtained an over defined system of 45 equations in 40 unknown variables of which 17 linear, 19 quadratic or bi-quadratic one equation is of degree 6 and 8 equations of degree 8. We observe that the degree of the equations involving NFSR bits is not increasing so fast after using 40 known values of states, which may be helpful for algebraic attack on the NFSR part.

6   Probabilistic Algebraic Attack on the LFSR Part of Grain-128a

In this section we will discuss the probabilistic algebraic attack on the LFSR part of Grain-128a [2]. The expression of the key-stream bits of Grain-128a [2] has two parts one is the linear combinations of some NFSR bits and one LFSR bit other one is the output of the non-linear function $h(\cdot)$. Precisely $z_i = A_i + h(\cdot)$ (when $IV_0 = 0$, similar study can be done for $IV_0 = 1$), where $A_i = \sum_{k \in A} b_{i+k} + s_{i+93}$ where $A = \{2, 15, 36, 45, 64, 73, 89\}$. For $z_i = 0$ we are getting $A_i + h(\cdot) = 0$, similarly for $z_i = 1$ we will get $1 + A_i + h(\cdot) = 0$. We will discuss the case for $z_i = 0$ when $IV_0 = 0$, similar study can be done for other cases as degree of the LFSR part remains same for all cases. For the operation with authentication we will consider the initial internal state of the cipher to be the one of the clocking when the authentication register has also been initialized. So for $z_i = 0$ we are getting $A_i + x_0 x_1 + x_2 x_3 + x_4 x_5 + x_6 x_7 + x_0 x_4 x_8 = 0$. Where $x_0, x_1, \ldots, x_8$ correspond to $b_{i+12}, s_{i+8}, s_{i+13}, s_{i+20}, b_{i+95}, s_{i+42}, s_{i+60}, s_{i+79}$ and s_{i+94} respectively. Now multiply the equation by $x_1' \cdot x_5' \cdot x_8'$ then we will get $x_1' \cdot x_5' \cdot x_8' \cdot [x_2 \cdot x_3 + x_6 \cdot x_7] + x_1' \cdot x_5' \cdot x_8' \cdot A_i = 0$. Let $u_1(x) = x_1' \cdot x_5' \cdot x_8'$ and $u_2(x) = x_2 \cdot x_3 + x_6 \cdot x_7$. i.e. we are getting $u_1(\cdot) \cdot u_2(\cdot) + u_1(\cdot) \cdot A_i = 0$, where $u_1(\cdot), u_2(\cdot)$ are two functions involving only LFSR bits $s_{i+8}, s_{i+13}, s_{i+20}, s_{i+42}, s_{i+60}, s_{i+79}$ and s_{i+94} respectively.

Let's take $X_i = u_1(\cdot) \cdot u_2(\cdot)$ and $Y_i = u_1(\cdot) \cdot A_i$. i.e. for $z_i = 0$ implies $X_i + Y_i = 0$. From this equation we can easily tell that there are only two possible cases for X_i, Y_i, either (i) $X_i = 0, Y_i = 0$ or (ii) $X_i = 1, Y_i = 1$. Let $p = Pr[X_i = 0, Y_i = 0]$ and $q = Pr[X_i = 1, Y_i = 1]$. Now we will choose the case where probability will be high. In fact we will prove that $p > q$ and similarly for other cases ($IV_0 = 1$, $z_i = 1$). Indeed this probability p is quite overwhelming. Thus in this way we get probabilistic system of equations $X_i = u_1(\cdot) \cdot u_2(\cdot)$ and $Y_i = u(\cdot) \cdot A_i$ where $X_i, Y_i \in \{0,1\}$. Now $X_i = u_1(\cdot) \cdot u_2(\cdot)$ is an equation involving only LFSR bits only. In this way we can construct a probabilistic system of equations with high probability involving only LFSR bits, which we can solve by using any existing algorithm in literatures [5], [14], [10], [11] to obtain the LFSR bits with high probability.

Now we will find the probability $p = Pr[X_i = 0, Y_i = 0]$. Firstly we will assume that the probability of each of the initial state variables being 0 or 1 after key initialization is $\frac{1}{2}$. Moreover as clearly mentioned in [2] that the NFSR feedback function is balanced, so $Pr[\sum_{k \in A} b_{i+k} + s_{i+93} = 0 \ or \ 1]$ is $\frac{1}{2}$. From the truth table of $u_1(\cdot)$ and $u_2(\cdot)$ it has been observed that $Pr[X_i = 0] = \frac{61}{64}$. Now, $p = Pr[X_i =, Y_i = 0] = Pr[X_i = 0] \cdot Pr[Y_i = 0 | X_i = 0] = \frac{61}{64} \cdot Pr[Y_i = 0 | X_i = 0]$. Now, we need to calculate $Pr[Y_i = 0 | X_i = 0]$. It can be shown that $Pr[Y_i = 0 | X_i = 0] = \frac{117}{122}$. So the required probability is $= \frac{61}{64} \times \frac{117}{122} = 0.914$, which is quite overwhelming. The detail calculation is given in [9].

Hence we see that for $z_i = 0$; $X_i = 0, Y_i = 0$ has the higher probability of occurrence. Now we will choose $X_i = 0$ for $z_i = 0$ to construct a probabilistic system of equations (similarly for $z_i = 1$) involving LFSR bits only, then by using classical algebraic attack technique described in [6] we can get the probabilistic LFSR bits after key initialization step of Grain-128a.

Time Complexity for Solving the System Involving LFSR Bits Only: The complexity of Gauss reduction for this system will be $\approx 2^{63}$ CPU clocks which is less than exhaustive search. The calculation is described in [9].

Note: The solution obtain from it will have probability $\geq \left(\frac{1}{2} + p\right)^k$ of matching with the exact solution, where k is the number of equations to be solved. The calculation is described in [9].

7   Conclusion

In this paper we have described a feasible probabilistic algebraic attack on the LFSR part of the Grain family of stream ciphers. Note that Grain v1 and Grain-128a has been designed so as to restrict the classical form of algebraic attack on stream ciphers. This is mainly because of the fact that due to the presence of the NFSR bits in the output function, the degree of the algebraic equations increases rapidly in state of remaining fixed as was the case for classical algebraic attacks on simple LFSR based stream cipher. Our approach in this paper has two significant features. Firstly by our method we are able to separate out the equations involving the LFSR and the NFSR bits for Grain v1 and Grain-128a. Then we are able to recover whole LFSR state of Grain v1 and Grain-128a with significant probabilities (surprisingly quite higher in case of Grain-128a). Secondly our approach may be considered as a generic version of probabilistic algebraic attack on stream cipher with similar structure of the output function as in case of Grain family.

References

1. Afzal, M., Masood, A.: Algebraic cryptanalysis of a nlfsr based stream cipher. In: 3rd International Conference on Information and Communication Technologies: From Theory to Applications, ICTTA 2008, pp. 1–6. IEEE (2008)
2. Ågren, M., Hell, M., Johansson, T., Meier, W.: A new version of grain-128 with authentication. In: Symmetric Key Encryption Workshop (2011)
3. Banik, S., Maitra, S., Sarkar, S.: A differential fault attack on the grain family of stream ciphers. In: Prouff, E., Schaumont, P. (eds.) CHES 2012. LNCS, vol. 7428, pp. 122–139. Springer, Heidelberg (2012)
4. Braeken, A., Preneel, B.: Probabilistic algebraic attacks. In: Smart, N.P. (ed.) Cryptography and Coding 2005. LNCS, vol. 3796, pp. 290–303. Springer, Heidelberg (2005)
5. Courtois, N., Klimov, A., Patarin, J., Shamir, A.: Efficient algorithms for solving overdefined systems of multivariate polynomial equations. In: Preneel, B. (ed.) EUROCRYPT 2000. LNCS, vol. 1807, pp. 392–407. Springer, Heidelberg (2000)
6. Courtois, N., Meier, W.: Algebraic attacks on stream ciphers with linear feedback. In: Biham, E. (ed.) EUROCRYPT 2003. LNCS, vol. 2656, pp. 345–359. Springer, Heidelberg (2003)
7. Crama, Y., Hammer, P.L.: Boolean models and methods in mathematics, computer science, and engineering (2010)
8. Cusick, T.W., Stănică, P.: Cryptographic Boolean functions and applications. Academic Press (2009)
9. Datta, P., Roy, D., Mukhopadhyay, S.: A probabilistic algebraic attack on the grain family of stream cipher. Cryptology ePrint Archive, Report 2014/510 (2014), http://eprint.iacr.org/2014/510.pdf
10. Faugére, J.C.: A new efficient algorithm for computing Gröbner bases (F4). Journal of Pure and Applied Algebra 139(1-3), 61–88 (1999), http://www-salsa.lip6.fr/~jcf/Papers/F99a.pdf
11. Faugére, J.C.: A new efficient algorithm for computing Gröbner bases without reduction to zero (F5). In: Proceedings of the 2002 International Symposium on Symbolic and Algebraic Computation, ISSAC 2002, pp. 75–83. ACM, New York (2002), http://www-salsa.lip6.fr/~jcf/Papers/F02a.pdf
12. Hell, M., Johansson, T., Meier, W.: Grain: a stream cipher for constrained environments. International Journal of Wireless and Mobile Computing 2(1), 86–93 (2007)
13. Karmakar, S., Roy Chowdhury, D.: Fault analysis of grain-128 by targeting NFSR. In: Nitaj, A., Pointcheval, D. (eds.) AFRICACRYPT 2011. LNCS, vol. 6737, pp. 298–315. Springer, Heidelberg (2011)
14. Segers, A.: Algebraic attacks from a Gröbner basis perspective. Master's Thesis (2004)
15. Zhang, H., Wang, X.: Cryptanalysis of stream cipher grain family. IACR E-print Archive, Report 109 (2009)

Multi-domain Direct Anonymous Attestation Scheme from Pairings

Li Yang[1,*], Jianfeng Ma[1], Wei Wang[2], and Chunjie Cao[2]

[1] School of Computer Science and Technology, Xidian University, Xi'an, China
{yangli,jfma}@xidian.edu.cn
[2] Science and Technology on Communication Information Security Control Laboratory,
Jiaxing, China
{wwlofgy,caochunjie}@gmail.com

Abstract. In trusted computing, a Trusted Platform Module(TPM) is used to enhance the security of the platform. When the TPM proofs his identity to a remote verifier, the Direct Anonymous Attestation (DAA) method is adopted by the Trusted Computing Group(TCG) to provide anonymous authentication. But the original DAA scheme in TCG specifications can only work well in a single domain, which can not be used in multi domains directly. It is necessary to improve the single domain DAA to be available in multi domains. In this paper, we proposed a multi-domain DAA scheme, which is based on proxy signature and a pairings based DAA method. The proxy signature is used to delegate the trusted relationship and domain authentication, while the pairings based DAA method is used for the computation platform authentication when a trusted platform accessing another domain. Then the DAA authentication protocol is also designed. Finally, the analysis on the protocol are given, the results show that the proposed scheme is secure and effective.

1 Introduction

The main idea of trusted computing is building a hardware-based security chip into the platforms, which is called a Trusted Platform Module(TPM)[1]. Nowadays, millions of personal computing equipments such as notebooks have been shipped with TPMs. TPM is the base for measuring and validating the trusted attribution for the platform. It can provide security functions as encryption and protected storage. However, according to TCG specifications, the real identity of the TPM can not be uncovered when he proves to a remote verifier. Furthermore, the verifier can not be allowed to deduce the real identity of the TPM even he knows about past attestation messages.

The Direct Anonymous Attestation(DAA) method is proposed by Brickell, Camenisch and Chen[2] to this aim. Then it is adopted by TCG as his specification. After the first DAA scheme has been proposed, DAA has made a lot of attention. Many researchers have worked on designing different DAA schemes [3–6]. But these previous DAA schemes are designed to the single trusted domain. They are unavailable for

* This work is supported by the National Natural Science Foundation of China (No.U1135002, No.61202390, No.61202389, No.61173135, No.61100230, No.61100233), and the Natural Science Basic Research Plan in Shaanxi Province of China (No.2012JM8025).

M.H. Au et al. (Eds.): NSS 2014, LNCS 8792, pp. 566–573, 2014.

multi-domain directly. Because different TPM manufactures set their DAA Issuers and form independent trusted domains. The participants in different trusted domains trust their own DAA Issuers. However, in some cases when the verifier and the platform may be in different trusted domains. As in mobile networks, users are usually roaming from the home network to a visiting network, then the home network and visiting networks make a multi-domain network environment. The users may trust certain DAA Issuer which is designated by different TPM manufactures.

For this aim, some multi-domain DAA scheme are presented based the original DAA scheme. In [7], the authors designed a multi-domain DAA scheme by introducing additional two kinds of certificates and it is low efficiency. In [8], a DAA protocol in multi-domain is proposed. They set certificate issuers outside of the trusted domain for issuing the DAA certificate in the scheme. In [9], Sun et al present a strict inter-domain anonymity attestation scheme. They introduce a new trusted party Trusted Auditor (TA) to prove the trustworthiness between different domains. But these two schemes are unreasonnal on setting a TPM to use his unique secret value for applying different DAA certificates. In [10], Chen et al. proposed a lightweight multi-domain direct anonymous attestation scheme based on pairings. They use a CA system to assure the authenticity of Issuers and Verifiers in different DAA domains. In addition, there are two DAA-Join operations in the scheme, which cost the additional computation both on the TPM and DAA issuers. It makes the scheme more complex for certification management and difficult in implementation.

In this paper, we propose a new multi-domain direct anonymous attestation (mDAA) scheme based on proxy signature and pairings. We use a pairings based proxy signature to delegate the domain signature authority to gain authentication among multi domains. Then we extend a simplified direct anonymous attestation scheme from pairs for the platform with TPM when access another trusted domain and verified by its verifier. We designed the mDAA authentication protocol under our multi-domain system model. The analysis results show that our mDAA protocol not only acheives security but also lies in the unforgeability and anonymity. The scheme is effective and suitable for multi-domain DAA authentication.

2 System Model

We describe the system model of mDAA in our paper as below. For simplicity, we set two different trusted domains Trusted Domain A (TD_A) and Trusted Domain B (TD_B) in the model. The DAA Issuer acts as the trusted domain managers in their own domain. Then the TD_A is managed by DAA Issuer A (IS_A), which is also the DAA certificate issuer in TD_A. The DAA Issuer B (IS_B) is not only the trusted domain manager in TD_B, but also the DAA certificate issuer. Trusted Platform A (TP_A) is composed by a host $Host_A$ and a TPM TPM_A. While $Host_B$ and TPM_B constitute the trusted computing platform in TDB as TP_B. There are two verifiers as Verifier A (V_A) and Verifier B (V_B) locate in TD_A and TD_B, respectively. TD_A and TD_B are connected by backbone networks or Internet.

According to the system model shown in Fig.1, based on the paring based DAA scheme[6] and the proxy signature[11], we design the multi-domain DAA (mDAA) in our paper. Our method is inspired by the proxy signature, which is the delegation of the power to sign messages. The delegation relationship in our system is between the domain manager (the DAA Issuer) and the trusted platform. The DAA issuer works as the original signer while the trusted platform is the proxy signer. And the mDAA scheme includes three stages: mDAA system setup, mDAA join, mDAA sign and verify.

3   Multi-domain DAA Protocol

The mDAA scheme based on a simple and pairings based DAA method[6], which only supports single domain trusted authentication. By using the proxy signature between the platform and Issuer server, then adding DAA signature on domain information, we extend it to be available in multi trusted domains. As described above, our mDAA scheme includes three steps: mDAA system setup, mDAA join, mDAA sign and verify.

3.1   mDAA System Setup

The system parameters are generated by the domain management server, the DAA Issuer IS. The definition and the value range of these parameters are same as in[6] and [11].

(1)IS generates the trusted domain system parameters: The domain parameters is $D\_par = \{G_{d1}, G_{d2}, e_d, q_d, P, H_{d1}, H_{d2}\}$. Where G_{d1} is a cyclic additive group generated by P with order q_d and $P \in G_{d1}$. G_{d2} is a cyclic multiplicative group of the same order q_d. e_d is a bilinear pairing as a map: $e_d : G_{d1} \times G_{d1} \rightarrow G_{d2}$. Two cryptographic hash functions are defined as: $H_{d1} : \{0, 1\}^* \rightarrow Z_{q_d}$, and $H_{d2} : \{0, 1\}^* \rightarrow G_{d1}$

As the domain management server, IS also generates the public key of the domain system. IS chooses a random number $s_{td} \in Z_{q_{d1}}$, computes $PK_{ts} = s_{td}P$. So, the public key is $PK_{ts} = (PK_{ts}, S_{ts})$.

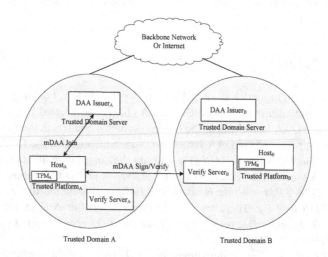

Fig. 1. System Model

(2)IS generates the DAA certificate parameters: As the DAA issuer IS should generate the DAA certification parameters for the TPM in the trusted computing platform. All DAA certificate parameters generated by IS are $IS\_par = \{q_i, G_{i1}, G_{i2}, g_{i1}, g_{i2}, e_i, H_{i1}, H_{i2}, l_q, l_H, l_\Phi\}$, where $G_{i1} =< g_{i1} >, G_{i2} =< g_{i2} >, e_i : G_{i1} \times G_{i1} \to G_{i2}, q_i$ is a big prime number.

IS chooses x, y as $x \leftarrow^R Z_{q_i}, y \leftarrow^R Z_{q_i}$, and computes its DAA group public key as $X := g_{i1}^x, Y := g_{i1}^y$. Here we define $H_{i1}(.), H_{i2}(.)$ as $H_{i1} : \{0,1\}^* \to \{0,1\}^{l_H}, H_{i2} : \{0,1\}^* \to G_{i2}$. So the Issuer's DAA group public key is $ipk := (q_i, g_{i1}, G_{i1}, g_{i2}, G_{i2}, e_i, X, Y)$, the Issuer's private key is $isk := (x, y)$. The ipk will be published.

3.2 mDAA Join

The mDAA Join process also includes two sub-steps: DS-Join and IS-Join. With a DS-Join, TP may join his home domain and gets his domain proxy signature key. While with an IS-Join, TP will join the home DAA issuer group and gets his DAA certificate.

(1)DS-Join: A trusted platform joins his home trusted domain which is managed by the domain management server.

Firstly, a trusted platform should join the trusted domain and get its domain proxy key from the domain manager server. TP chooses a random number $s_{tp} \in Z_{q_d}^*$ as its domain secret key, and computes its domain public key as $PK_{tp} = s_{tp}P$. So the domain key pair of TP is (PK_{tp}, s_{tp}).

After received the a request for the domain certificate from TP. The domain manager IS makes a domain certificate $CW = \{ID_{DS}, ID_{TP}, PV, RA, Other\}$ which will include the domain identity, TP identity, period of validity, range of application and other useful information.

IS computes $S_{tp} = s_{tp}H_{d2}(CW)$ then sends (S_{tp}, CW) to TP. Upon received it, TP checks if $e_d(S_{ts}, P) \stackrel{?}{=} e_d(H_{d2}(CW), PK_{ts})$. If correctness, TP then computes $S_{tp} = S_{ts} + s_{tp}H_{d2}(CW)$. Then the domain certificate of TP is $DM_{Cert} = (PK_{tp}, CW)$.

(2)IS-Join: A trusted platform joins a DAA issuer group after got its domain certificate. The IS-Join process in our scheme is similar to which is in [6].

At first, we suppose that IS has already a long-term public key as K_I. TPM computes $f := H_{i1}(DAASeed\|K_I) \bmod q_i, F := g_{i1}^f$ we can add some trusted domain information here. The $DAASeed$ is unique secret random number created by TPM, which will never be disclosed by TPM itself. Issuer has a single K_I value, and with different K_I each TPM can have multiple values for f.

TPM chooses $r_f \leftarrow^R Z_{q_i}, T := g_{i1}^{r_f}$, sends T, F to Host. IS chooses a random string $n_i \in \{0,1\}^{l_H}$, sends it to Host. Then Host computes $c_h := H_{i1}(q_i\|g_{i1}\|g_{i2}\|X\|Y\|F\|T\|n_i)$, and sends it to TPM. After received c_h, TPM chooses $n_T \in \{0,1\}^{l_\Phi}$; computes $c := H_{i1}(c_h\|n_T), s_f := r_f + cf \bmod q_i$. TPM sets its private key as $tsk := f$, then sends (F, c, s_f, n_t) to Issuer by Host.

Upon receipt of the message IS checks it in TPM rogue list by F. computes $T' := g_{i1}^{s_f}F^{-c}$. It can be done in rogue check phase, which will be discussed later. IS checks $c \stackrel{?}{=} H_{i1}(H_{i1}(q_i\|g_{i1}\|g_{i2}\|X\|Y\|F\|T'\|n_i\|n_t)$, if correctness, then chooses $r \leftarrow^R Z_{q_i}$, and computes $a := g_{i1}^r, b := a^y, c := A^x F^{rxy}$, where (a, b, c) are the CL-LRSW signature on f. IS sends $cre = (a, b, c)$ to TPM as its DAA credential.

Then once required, TPM computes $d = b^f$, and sends it back to Host. Host should check whether $e_i(Y, a) = e_i(g_{i1}, b), e_i(g_{i1}, d) = e_i(F, b), e_i(x, ad) = e_i(g_{i1}, c)$ are all satisfied. After DS-Join and IS-Join process, TP obtains its domain certificate and DAA certificate. Then they can be used together to sign message and make the remote attestation to a verifier.

3.3   mDAA Sign

Host computes $B := H_{G_{i2}}(1 \| bsn_v)$, where bsn_v is the basename associated with the Verifier. Then Host sends B to TPM. After received, TPM checks B as $B \overset{?}{\in} G_{i2}$, then computes $K := B^f$ and sends K to the Host. Host chooses $r, r' \overset{R}{\leftarrow} Z_q$, $a' := a^{r'}, b' := b^{r'}, c' := c^{r' r^{-1}}, v_x := e(X, a'), v_{xy} := e(X, b'), v_s := e(g_1, C')$, then sends v_{xy} to TPM.

TPM and Host make proxy signature and DAA signature together as below. We suppose that m is the message to be signed by TPM and Host. TPM checks $v_{xy} \overset{?}{\in} G_{d2}$ then make signature as $SPK\{(r, f) : v_s^r = v_x v_{xy}^f \wedge K = B^f\}(n_v, n_T, m)$. Where SPK means a signature proof of knowledge[12]. Host computes $r_p = e_d(P, P)^{k_p}, k_p \in_R Z_{q_d}{}^*$, $C_p = H_{d1}(m \| r_p), U_p = c_p S_{tp} + k_p P$, then lets $M = (m, C_p, U_p, CW), c_M = H_{i1}(M)$. Host sends $r_r \in Z_{q_i}, T_{1t} := v_s^r, c_H := H_{i1}(q_i \| g_{i1} \| g_{i2} \| X \| Y \| a' \| b' \| c' \| v_x \| v_{xy} \| v_s \| B \| K \| PK_{ts} \| PK_{tp} \| c_M \| n_v)$, sends it to TPM.

TPM chooses a random number $r_f \overset{R}{\leftarrow} Z_{qi}$ and a nonce $n_T \in \{0, 1\}^{l_\phi}$, computes $T_1 := T_{1t} v_{xy}^{-rf}, T_2 := B^{rf}, c_d := H_{i1}(c_H \| T_1 \| T_2 \| M \| n_T), s_f := r_f + c \cdot f mod q_i$. And TPM sends to Host c_d, s_f, n_T. Host computes $s_r := r_r + c \cdot r \bmod q_i$, makes DAA signature as $\sigma = (B, K, a', b', c', c_d, s_r, s_f)$, and sends (σ, M, n_T) to the Verifier.

The result is a signature proof of knowledge on proxy signature of m as described above. Which will then be directly checked by a verifier for the purpose of domain authentication and TPM identity authentication.

3.4   mDAA Verify

Using public keys of DAA Issuer which has been known before verification by secure channel or backbone network. The verifier can check the validation of the TP's signature.

Firstly, the Verifier checks if $K \overset{?}{\neq} B^{f_i}$ and to confirm that f_i is not in the Rouge List. The Rouge List stores the key pairs of TPMs which are no longer legal or have already been broken by adversaries. Then checks whether $e_i(a', Y) \overset{?}{=} e_i(g_{i1}, b'), K \overset{?}{\in} G_{i2}$, then computes $v'_x := e_i(x, a'), v'_{xy} := e_i(x, b'), v'_s := e_i(g_1, c'), T_1' := v_s'^{s_r} v_{xy}'^{-s_f} v_x'^{-c_d}, T_2' := B^{s_f} K^{-c_d}, c'_M = H_{i1}(M)$. Then he verifies $c_d \overset{?}{=} H_{i1}(H_{i1}(q_i \| g_{i1} \| g_{i2} \| X \| Y \| a' \| b' \| c' \| v'_x \| v'_{xy} \| v'_s \| B \| K \| PK_{ts} \| PK_{tp} \| c'_M \| n_v) \| T_1' \| T_2' \| M \| n_T)$, checks $C_p \overset{?}{=} H_{d1}(m \| e_d(U_p, P) e_d(H_{d2}(CW), PK_{ts} + PK_{tp})^{-C_p})$. If and only if above two equations are all satisfied. The verifier shall accept that the TP comes from a correct domain and has a legal platform identity.

If a platform is cracked. Then its public key should be published on Rogue List(RL), it can easily be accessed by Issuers and Verifiers. The RL stored on some servers on internet managed by a trusted party. In our scheme in mDAA verify process, the verifier checks whether $K \stackrel{?}{\neq} B^{f_i}$ then makes a judgement contrasting with the rouge list. When a new faked TPM key pair found, then the verifier or IS should inform the trusted third party to update the Rogue List.

4 Security Analysis

The security of domain authentication depends on the security of the proxy signature [11], while security of the platform authentication depends on DBDH and LRSW assumption[13]. Because the System Setup and mDAA Join process work in a closed single domain, their security can be easily guaranteed. Then we mainly focus on the security of the mDAA Sign and Verify protocol. For simplicity, we assume that the Host and TPM as a whole party, they should not cheat each other.

(1) Security of Domain Authentication

In mDAA scheme, the platform can make a proxy signature to present his domain identity. The verifier in domain B can distinguish TP_A's proxy signatures from a normal signature by using the domain manager's public key. Then from the proxy signature, the verifier can be convinced of the domain manager's original agreement on the signed message. As TP_A is a legal member in TD_A, he can represent the domain manager to generate a correct proxy signature. By the validation of the proxy signature V_B will confirm that TP_A comes from domain TD_A. Furthermore, our mDAA sign operation and verification of mDAA signature are also designed on the CL-signature[14] as the DAA scheme[6]. From the specification of the mDAA signature, we can see it is security and the authentication on TPM's identity is correctness.

(2) Forgery-resistance

In trusted domain TD_A, the TP_A's proxy secret key is S_{tp}, and the proxy public key is $PK_{tp} + PK_{ts}$. Then as a designated proxy signer, TP_A can create a valid proxy signature for the domain manager IS_A, the original signer. Even if the original signer IS_A or the other third parties in the domain, who are not designated as a proxy signer, then they can not create valid proxy signature. So the adversaries can not forge TP_A's domain certificate too. While showing his domain certification, TP_A signs on a warrant CW. And due to using the warrant, it satisfies the forgery-resistance. The adversary can not get the S_{ts} of the domain manager IS_A. Even if the S_{tp} of the proxy signer TP_A be got, the adversary still cannot forge the proxy signature due to the security of BLS signature[15] on which the proxy signature is based. When makes a DAA signature on a message, the secret value f will be required. But f only knows by TPM_A, any other entities even $Host_A$ of TP_A can not get it. Then no adversaries can forge a valid TPM's DAA signature without the secret value.

(3) Anonymity

The anonymity of the mDAA scheme includes anonymous and untraceability on the platform identity. When TP_A shows his DAA certification to the verifier, the signature and verification operation are same as in [6], except the mDAA sign on the domain information. And the security of the mDAA relies on the DBDH assumption and the LRSW assumption. If the adversary breaks anonymity of the scheme, then in this way, the adversary may construct a simulator which has the ability to find a instance of the DBDH problem. But it is obviously there is no polynomial time algorithm to solve the

DBDH problem[13]. So mDAA scheme is anonymous. Meanwhile, the mDAA scheme is untraceable under the LRSW assumption. Suppose there is an adversary which succeeds with anon-negligible probability to break traceability of the scheme, then TP_A is traceable to the adversary. Which means the adversary can construct a polynomial time algorithm to solve the LRSW problem. So the mDAA scheme is untrabeability too.

5 Efficiency Analysis

We compares the efficiency of signing and verification algorithms of our scheme with other related schemes[7, 10]. We did not compare the efficiency of the join protocol because the join protocol is executed much less frequently than the sign and verification. As in[5], we let $G_i (i = 1, 2, T)$ denote the cost of an exponentiation in the group $\mathbb{G}_i$, and G_i^m denote the cost of a multiexponentiation of m values in the group G_i. We let P denote the cost of a pairing computation. For simplicity, we set G_i and G_d as same size and let G_N denote the cost of an exponentiation modulo N, and G_N^m denote the cost of a multiexponentiation of m values modulo N.

Table 1. Computation Comparison

Scheme	Host	TPM	Verifier
[7]	$2G_N + 4G_N^3 + 2G_N^4 + 1G_N^5 + 1G_N^9 + 1P$	$G_N^3 + G_\Gamma$	$2G_N^3 + 6P$
[10]	$16G_1 + 1G_1^2$	$1G_1^2$	$4G_1 + 2G_1^3$
Ours	$3G_1 + 2G_T + 3P$	$4G_T$	$1G_T + 1G_T^2 + 1G_T^3 + 5P$

From Table 1, we can see that the computation cost of TPM in our scheme is lower than the compared schemes. For Host, much complex exponents computation are needed, the computation costs in scheme[7] is more than ours. While compared with scheme[10], there are some pairing computations added to the Host in our scheme, but we avoid complex exponents computation as G_1^2. These pairing computations will be carried out by Host rather than TPM. Since Host is more powerful than TPM, the overall performance of the system will be unaffected.

For verifier, the computation costs are less than in scheme[7], while a little more than which in scheme[10]. Because the verifier are always servers or stations with high-performance computation and high-capacity storage. So the overall performance of the system will be unaffected too. Furthermore, the compared scheme requires additional public certificates such as $IssuePassport$ and $IssueVisa$ in scheme[7] and $Cert_{DAA-CA}$ and $Cert_{DAA-B}$ in scheme[10]. Then in general, our mDAA scheme is efficient.

6 Conclusion

In this paper, we proposed a scheme for multi trusted domains DAA which is based on proxy signature and a simple DAA method from pairings. Our scheme can provide both domain authentication and platform authentication. Trusted relationship is delegated among multi domains by the proxy signature. The DAA method is used for the platform authentication when he has been checked by the verifier in other domains. And the security analysis has shown that our mDAA protocol has the properties of security and anonymity. The scheme is efficient in computation cost when compared with some existing schemes.

References

1. Trusted Computing Group. TCG specification architecture overview (2007),
   http://www.trustedcomputinggroup.org
2. Brichell, E., Camenisch, J., Chen, L.: Direct anonymous attestation. In: Proc. of the 11th ACM Conf. on Computer and Communications Security, pp. 132–145. ACM, New York (2004)
3. Ge, H., Tate, S.R.: A direct anonymous attestation scheme for embedded devices. In: Okamoto, T., Wang, X. (eds.) PKC 2007. LNCS, vol. 4450, pp. 16–30. Springer, Heidelberg (2007)
4. Brickell, E., Chen, L., Li, J.: A new direct anonymous attestation scheme from bilinear maps. In: Lipp, P., Sadeghi, A.-R., Koch, K.-M. (eds.) TRUST 2008. LNCS, vol. 4968, pp. 166–178. Springer, Heidelberg (2008)
5. Chen, L., Morrissey, P., Nigel, P., Smart, N.P.: Pairings in trusted computing. In: Galbraith, S.D., Paterson, K.G. (eds.) Pairing 2008. LNCS, vol. 5209, pp. 1–17. Springer, Heidelberg (2008)
6. Brickell, E., Chen, L., Li, J.: Simplified security notions of direct anonymous attestation and a concrete scheme from pairings. Int. J. Information Security 8(5), 315–330 (2009)
7. Chen, X., Feng, D.: Direct anonymous attestation for next generation TPM. J. Computers 31(7), 1122–1129 (2008)
8. Yang, Y., Cao, L., Li, Z.: A Novel Direct Anonymous Attestation Protocol Based on Zero Knowledge Proof for Different Trusted Domains. China Communications 41(3), 54–61 (2010)
9. Sun, L., Chang, G., Sun, D.: A strict inter-domain anonymity attestation scheme. In: 2010 International Conference on Computer Design and Applications (ICCDA 2010), vol. 3, pp. 291–295. IEEE Press (2010)
10. Chen, L., Hu, A., Huang, J., Virkki, J.: A Lightweight Inter-domain Direct Anonymous Attestation Scheme for Machine-to-Machine Networks. In: Datta, A. (ed.) International Workshop on Cloud Computing and Information Security (CCIS 2013), pp. 545–550. Atlantis Press (2013)
11. Zhang, F., Safavi-Naini, R., Susilo, W.: An efficient signature scheme from bilinear pairings and its applications. In: Bao, F., Deng, R., Zhou, J. (eds.) PKC 2004. LNCS, vol. 2947, pp. 277–290. Springer, Heidelberg (2004)
12. Camenisch, J.L., Stadler, M.A.: Efficient group signature schemes for large groups. In: Kaliski Jr., B.S. (ed.) CRYPTO 1997. LNCS, vol. 1294, pp. 410–424. Springer, Heidelberg (1997)
13. Lysyanskaya, A., Rivest, R.L., Sahai, A., Wolf, S.: Pseudonym systems (Extended abstract). In: Heys, H.M., Adams, C.M. (eds.) SAC 1999. LNCS, vol. 1758, pp. 184–199. Springer, Heidelberg (2000)
14. Camenisch, J.L., Lysyanskaya, A.: Dynamic accumulators and application to efficient revocation of anonymous credentials. In: Yung, M. (ed.) CRYPTO 2002. LNCS, vol. 2442, pp. 61–76. Springer, Heidelberg (2002)
15. Boneh, D., Lynn, B., Shacham, H.: Short signatures from the Weil pairing. In: Boyd, C. (ed.) ASIACRYPT 2001. LNCS, vol. 2248, pp. 514–532. Springer, Heidelberg (2001)

Author Index